DEAR MISS MANNERS:
Who says there is a "right" way of doing things and a "wrong"?

GENTLE READER:
Miss Manners does. You want to make something of it?

ALL OVER THE NATION, REVIEWERS AND READERS HAVE MADE IT A BIG BESTSELLER!

"Opinionated, astringent, and hilarious...will leave you giggling dementedly among the dunes. The style is nicely poised between Fran Lebowitz and Queen Victoria, the material as varied as the etiquette of one-night stands and the proper response when a dinner guest arrives towing a brace of famished bodyguards...Good wicked fun, and helpful too."

—Cosmopolitan

"One big, fat indispensible volume [of] her very best advice...The book is as captivating as a novel, as gripping as a mystery and as wry as Woody Allen..."

—The Dallas Morning News

"Comprehensive...chatty...full of interesting, quirky observations about American manners and mores...what I appreciate most about Judith Martin is that she has legitimized her own bossiness.... Besides, Miss Manners is so delightful, even when trivial, that her correctness almost seems beside the point."

—The New York Times Book Review

Miss Manners'®
Guide to Excruciatingly
Correct Behavior

Judith Martin

Illustrated by Gloria Kamen

WARNER BOOKS

A Warner Communications Company

Miss Manners *is a registered trademark of United Feature Syndicate, Inc.*

Warner Books Edition

Text copyright © 1979, 1980, 1981, 1982 by United Feature Syndicate, Inc.
Illustrations copyright © 1982 by Gloria Kamen
All rights reserved.

This Warner Books edition is published by arrangement with Atheneum Publishers,
597 Fifth Avenue, New York, NY 10017.

Warner Books, Inc., 666 Fifth Avenue, New York, NY 10103

 A Warner Communications Company

Printed in the United States of America
First Warner Books Printing: September 1983
10 9 8 7 6

*Composition by American-Stratford Graphic Services, Inc.,
Brattleboro, Vermont
Designed by Mary Cregan*

Library of Congress Cataloging in Publication Data

Martin, Judith, 1938–
  Miss Manners' guide to excruciatingly correct
behavior.

  Reprint. Originally published: New York : Atheneum,
1982.
  Includes index.
  1. Etiquette. I. Title.
[BJ1853.M294 1983]   395   83-10271
ISBN 0-446-38632-4 (U.S.A.)
ISBN 0-446-38633-2 (Can.)

For Nicholas and Jacobina

Contents

3. *Basic Civilization*

4. *Rites de Passage*

5. *Marriage (for Beginners)*

6. *Work*

Illustrations

The Characters of This Book, Some Perfect, Others Awful

Preface

The chief characters of this book are Daffodil Louise Perfect and Jonathan Rhinehart Awful, 3d. You may recall that Daffy's and Rhino's wedding, with ten perfectly matched bridesmaids and coordinating groomsmen (Mrs. Perfect held auditions), was the social highlight of an otherwise boring decade.

The bride's wish that the wedding be "the happiest day of my life" came true. Each succeeding day was slightly less happy than the one before, and finally the amusing young Awfuls were divorced. Correctly combining her maiden and married surnames, the divorcée is known as Mrs. Perfect Awful.

Her parents are Mr. and Mrs. Geoffrey Lockwood Perfect (the former Clara Grace Proper). Mrs. Perfect's only adviser, confidante, and equal is Patience Perfect, the widow of Mr. Perfect's brother, Plue. As a widow, she is correctly known still as Mrs. Plue Perfect; she would rather die herself than use the title of Mrs. with her first name.

Daffodil's aunt, Primrose Jane, married the Reverend Cotton Pious. Their daughter, Poppy, is a clergywoman but, unlike her father, she has a doctorate of divinity degree; their son, who received his mother's family name as a given name, is a member of the United States Congress. The Honorable Perfect Pious has reason to hope that he may become a United States senator if he is acquitted, and perhaps an ambassador if he is not.

It is the feeling of the family that Daffodil's three children are unfortunately more Awful than Perfect. Alexandrina, who married Ian Fright nearly three years ago, is nearly four years behind in her thank-you letters. Her grandmother and Aunt Patience are pleased that she has developed what they call "a nice sense of family," although the term she used, calling herself a "roots buff," led them to believe that she also shares their interest in gardening. She wants to show her affiliation with both sides of her distinguished maternal family and has lately been calling herself Ms. Perfect-Awful-Fright, but it is cumbersome and she keeps changing her surname in the hope of a simpler solution.

The matter is getting crucial, because the Frights now have a baby, named for his maternal great-grandfather, who died of a heart attack at the christening when he discovered that, in perpetuating his name, they were spelling it Jeffrey.

The second daughter, Victorine, lives with her whatchamacallit, Christopher Wrong. Trying to introduce Mr. Wrong properly at family gatherings has ruined the blameless old age of her grandmother.

The third child, Gregory, lives with a young man called Lars Uhmm, whom his grandmother would be satisfied to introduce as Gregory's roommate or friend. But Gregory, true to the Perfect blood, insists on his and Lars' being correctly treated as a couple in every finicky detail.

The picturesque old cemetery in which the late Mr. Geoffrey Lockwood Perfect is buried has rumbled so violently of late that rumors arose of its being made into a subway station. The local historical preservation society had some ugly confrontations with city authorities until it was established that the commotion was merely the result of the amount of spinning Mr. Perfect does in his grave when he thinks of his descendants.

Jonathan Rhinehart Awful, 3d, is directly descended from Jonathan Rhinehart Awful through Jonathan Rhinehart Awful, Junior. He has a cousin named Jonathan Rhinehart Awful, 2d, who is not in the direct line of nomenclature. Shortly after Rhino married Daffodil, his grandfather died, whereupon everyone had to change numbers. His grandmother added "senior" to her name for the first time; his father dropped the "junior" and Rhino took it up. Daffodil, who had boxes of freshly engraved letter paper, informals, and cards in which she was designated as Mrs. 3d, was much affected by her grandfather-in-law's death. The cousin was also distraught, not being able to figure out his own promotion, and after a brief period of calling himself modestly 1½, he changed his name to Corky.

Rhino is the noodle of his family, never having made a go of his chosen career as a gentleman of leisure, but his sisters, Tracy, Stacey, and Lacy, are great successes.

Tracy is an orthopedic surgeon known professionally as Dr. Tracy Tremor, that being the surname of her first husband, an anesthetist who unfortunately got a dose of his own medicine, to whom she was married when she made her reputation. Socially, she prefers to use the name of her present husband, and they may be addressed at home as Dr. and Mrs. Brian Botchitt or as the Doctors Botchitt.

Their daughter, Erica, is a dentist and uses her title socially, and their son, Sean, uses the title of doctor incorrectly, because his is a scholastic degree.

Stacey married quite late, after she had already achieved the rank of vice admiral in the United States Navy, and finds it difficult to drop her maiden name completely at this stage in life. She married a general in the United States Army, whom she met at intermural war games. On official business, they are properly addressed as Vice Admiral Stacey Awful, United States Navy, and General Trevor Nuisance, United States Army, but socially they are General Nuisance and Mrs. Awful-Nuisance.

Lacy is, by profession, a superstar-celebrity, and changed her name for euphonic purposes. She is known both professionally and socially as Lacy Lawful. She has never married, but she has a daughter, Chastity, who shares her cousin Victorine's interest in family history. Chastity found, through diligent research, that the distinguished Awful ancestor whose courageous decision to migrate to America in a century that would admit his descendants to all the best genealogical organizations—he chose this as an alternative to being hanged—had changed his name upon arrival. In the old country, so to speak, the family had been widely known as Those Godawful People. Out of respect for history and family feeling, Chastity has restored her surname to its full dignity of Godawful.

Rhino married a second time. His wife, Kimberly, is considerably younger than he, and when he met her, on a nudist beach, he failed to notice that she had no last name. By the time she had her clothes on, it was too late, and the wedding invitations had to go out as ''Cindy and Tom request the honour of your presence . . .''

Old Mrs. Perfect tried to prevent her grandchildren from attending their father's remarriage, on the grounds that tradition forbade it and out of the certain knowledge that they would never be able to recover the values she had tried to instill in them. They went, anyway, citing modern custom, and she sadly feels that time has borne her out.

Her only slight comfort is that they are not as bad as the new litter of Awful children who resulted from this marriage, Lisa, Adam, Jason, and Kristen. By all reports, they are entirely innocent of manners of any kind.

It is for them that this book has been written.

Introduction

Some Thoughts on the Impulse Rude and the Mannerly Way of Life

"Assertiveness," "Looking out for number one," and other systems for the dissemination of rudeness are abhorrent to Miss Manners. That people should spend hours studying vile little books and then disciplining themselves so as best to add to the general unpleasantness in the world is shocking.

Why, they could be spending that time learning to behave like Miss Manners.

Miss Manners is unfailingly polite. When Miss Manners is treated badly, she responds courteously. This is known as Not Stooping, or Shaming Them, or Setting a Good Example. It generally works. In any case, Miss Manners believes that two wrongs make a blight.

Miss Manners also believes that, if one always does the right thing, one does not have to read nasty little books about how to deal with guilt. One never has any.

Nevertheless—and this is the interesting part—Miss Manners does not suffer from the indignities that "assertiveness" asserts it can correct. No one ever takes advantage of Miss Manners without her consent. (What happens when she consents is also interesting, but another story.)

It is true that Miss Manners occasionally says "Yes" when she means "No" and, on special occasions, "No" when she means "Yes." Some ambiguity is desirable in social relations, if only to keep us all paying attention. What Miss Manners usually says when pressed to do something she does not wish to, is

"Oh, I would *so* love to, but I can't possibly," or "How delightful—*do* let me call you when I see my way clear."

As for the rudeness of others, Miss Manners finds that is conquered by politeness. For example, a gentleman of Miss Manners' acquaintance dislikes being honked at by impatient drivers for not starting his automobile quickly enough when a traffic signal turns to green. Instead of honking back, however, he puts on his emergency brake, emerges from his car, presents himself to the honker in the vehicle behind, and inquires gently, "Did you summon me?"

It is not, however, that Miss Manners has never felt the Impulse Rude. You wouldn't trust a preacher who never experienced the temptations of sin, would you?

The rudeness of others arouses that bestial desire in Miss Manners: the hotel clerk who shrugs when you ask what "Guaranteed reservation" means if having one doesn't entitle you to a room; the waiter who snaps "Can't you see I'm busy?" when you want to get a check and leave, believing your business to be as important as his; the secretary who demands your name, puts you on hold, and then comes back minutes later and demands your name again; the taxi driver who asks your destination and then drives away while you are telling it.

How one longs to strike back. But if rudeness begets rudeness, which begets more rudeness, where will it all end? (And when did Miss Manners turn into a preacher? The verb "to beget" was never in her vocabulary before, surely.) There are now many believers in the art of getting back, and many books, classes, and discussions on techniques for doing so. Miss Manners often receives letters from people who assume that she is such a believer and can supply a method for "putting down" this person or that.

Alas. At the risk of sounding unbearably saintly, Miss Manners will not subscribe to such behavior. She does not allow rude people to spoil her life, but she does not seek satisfaction in spoiling theirs.

For one thing, they outnumber her. One can easily encounter a dozen provoking rudenesses on the way to work in the morning, and a matching set on the way home. A lunch hour spent shopping, or, for that matter, trying to buy lunch, can increase the total tenfold. For another thing, counterrudenesses are escalating, sometimes beyond rudeness itself into violence. Even the lexicon of rudeness one hears these days is explicitly violent, although the specific words are usually sexual. (Does anyone know why such a nice practice as sex should have to supply the words for uncontrolled hostility? Miss Manners needs that explained to her, because she has never understood. On second thought, she would prefer that it not be explained to her.)

What, then, does one do with one's justified anger? Miss Manners, who makes a distinction between people and things, will sometimes look the other way if you wish to take out your anger on objects, within the limits of legality. Yet that can be dangerous. A gentleman of Miss Manners' acquaintance who recently kicked a large inanimate object—a Buick—that had offended him, found a large animate object emerging from it to continue the fight.

Miss Manners' meager arsenal consists only of the withering look, the insistent and repeated request, the cold voice, the report up the chain of command, and the tilted nose. Also the ability to dismiss inferior behavior from her mind as coming from inferior people.

You will perhaps point out that she will never know the joy of delivering a well-deserved sock in the chops. True—but she will never inspire one, either.

On Helping Others

As if self-improvement weren't bad enough, we now have a world full of new, improved people who are ready to move on to improving others. This had better stop before there are no good people left, to say nothing of no decent social intercourse.

Miss Manners has been accosted by a variety of people who do missionary work under the pretense of friendship, generously spreading their newly acquired insights in the hope of making others as attractive as themselves. There are those who offer to explain to Miss Manners how to deal with her guilt. As you know, Miss Manners doesn't have any guilt. Others want to teach her to be free of her inhibitions. Miss Manners does have a few inhibitions, as it happens, but she needs them and is, if anything, hoping to develop a few more. People have even offered to help Miss Manners find God, Who Miss Manners hadn't known was lost.

The zeal of such people is so great that they will spare nothing, not even the feelings of those they want to save, in this quest to make others feel better. If you are skeptical about their solutions' working for you, they give you a patronizing smile and say, "That's the way I felt once." If you protest that you have no problems, they offer to help you with the problem of not being able to recognize your problem. If you admit that you are happy, they reply, "Ah, but perhaps you only think you are happy." What the difference is between being happy and thinking yourself happy Miss Manners has never been able to figure out.

It is unfortunate that one of her inhibitions, one of those to which she had better hold on if she wants to preserve her unsullied reputation for perfect politeness, is about saying, "That's none of your business."

On Correcting Others

It would be futile for Miss Manners to pretend to know nothing of the wicked joy of correcting others.

There is that pleasant bubble in the throat, a suppressed giggle at another person's ignorance; that flush of generosity accompanying the resolve to set the poor soul straight; that fever of human kindness when one proclaims, for the benefit of others, one's superior knowledge. Isn't that, after all, the great reward of the trade that Miss Manners practices? Can Miss Manners, whose vocation, whose calling, is correcting people for their own good, condemn the practice?

Certainly.

Miss Manners corrects only upon request. Then she does it from a distance, with no names attached, and no personal relationship, however distant, between the corrector and the correctee. She does not search out errors, like a policeman leaping out of a speed trap. When Miss Manners observes people behaving rudely, she never steps in to correct them. She behaves politely to them, and then goes home and snickers about them afterward. That is what the well-bred person does. The only way to enjoy the fun of catching people behaving disgustingly is to have children. One has to keep having them, however, because it is incorrect to correct grown people, even if you have grown them yourself. This is the mistake that many people make when they give helpful criticism to their children-in-law, who arrive on the scene already grown.

Miss Manners is constantly besieged by people who want to know the tactful manner of pointing out their friends' and relatives' inferiorities. These people, their loved ones report to Miss Manners, chew with their mouth open, mispronounce words, talk too loudly, crack their knuckles, spit, belch, and hum tunelessly to themselves. They have bad breath and runs in their stockings. They are too fat, dress badly, and do their hair all wrong.

How can those who love these people dearly, for reasons that are not clear, and who wish to help them, for reasons that unfortunately are clear, politely let them have it?

The answer is that they cannot, certainly not politely. There are times, in certain trusting relationships, when one can accomplish this impolitely. One can sometimes say, "Cracking your knuckles drives me up the wall and if you do it one more time I'll scream," or "Have a mint—there's something wrong with your breath," or "What's that thing on your left front tooth?" No reasonable person should take offense at these remarks. Because they are so frank, they do not seem to carry a history of repulsion long predating the offense. Also they deal with matters that are more or less easily correctable (although Miss Manners knows some determined knuckle crackers she suspects aren't half trying to stop), and which it is plausible to assume the offenders hadn't noticed.

What is unacceptable is to criticize things a person cannot easily remedy or may not want to. People who you think are too fat either disagree about what too fat is, are trying to do something about it, or are not trying to do something about it. In no case is it helpful for them to know that other people consider them too fat.

It is admittedly difficult to arrest the pleasure of correcting and advising long enough to ask oneself who will feel better after the correction is delivered—the person issuing it, or the one who gets it full in the face? But it is well worth the effort, not only for kindness' sake, but because it is a law of nature that he who corrects others will soon do something perfectly awful himself.

Even if it be proven that the mistakes of others come from gross ignorance or from maliciousness, it is not the place of anyone except God, their mothers, or Miss Manners to bring this to their attention. As dear Erasmus said, "It is part of the highest civility if, while never erring yourself, you ignore the errors of others."

Miss Manners prefers to believe that everyone means well, and that if anyone seems to be doing something wrong, it is probably not from intent but from forgetfulness, busyness, absence of mind, or illness. Miss Manners may be mistaken in this now and again, but she leads a happier life for believing it.

On Making Others Comfortable

At a great London banquet, dear Queen Victoria lifted her fingerbowl and drank all the water. She had to. Her guest of honor, the Shah of Persia, had done it first.

At a Washington embassy dinner party, the king of Morocco plunged his fingers into his teacup and wiped them on his napkin. He had to. His guest of honor, President Kennedy, had done it first.

Then there was the time that Mrs. Grover Cleveland attempted to engage a tongue-tied guest in conversation by seizing on the nearest thing at hand, an antique cup of thinnest china. "We're very pleased to have these; they're quite rare and we're using them for the first time today," she is supposed to have said.

"Really?" asked the distraught guest, picking up his cup and nervously crushing it in his hand.

"Oh, don't worry about it," said the hostess. "They're terribly fragile—see?" She smashed hers.

Mr. Grover Cleveland, on another social occasion, carefully added sugar and cream to his coffee, stirred it, and poured some into his saucer. Observing this, all his guests felt obliged to do the same. There they all were, pouring their coffee into their saucers, when the President leaned down and put his saucerful on the floor for his dog.

Miss Manners relates these alarming incidents to illustrate a great danger. It is not the peril of serving watery tea, engaging in diplomacy with Persians, permitting dogs in dining rooms, or other such grand scale hijinks. It is the terrible burden one assumes when attempting the practice of Making Others Feel Comfortable.

Miss Manners is sensitive to this because she often hears the great and subtle art of etiquette described as being "just a matter of making other people feel comfortable." As if etiquette weren't magnificently capable of being used to make others feel uncomfortable.

(All right. Miss Manners will give you an example, although you are spoiling her Queen Victoria mood: If you are rude to your ex-husband's new wife at your daughter's wedding, you will make her feel smug. Comfortable. If you are charming and polite, you will make her feel uncomfortable. Which do you want to do?)

On Class Consciousness

There are three social classes in America: upper middle class, middle class, and lower middle class. Miss Manners has never heard of an American's owning up to being in any other class. However, if there is one thing that all Americans agree upon, no matter what their background, it is that the middle class is despicable. The shame of having been born into it is sufficient excuse for a lifelong grudge against one's parents. This is not a happy state of affairs.

The problem, in Miss Manners' opinion, is that the classes have traditionally behaved badly—either oppressively or obsequiously—to those below or above them. Being in the middle, the middle class has the opportunity to do both. Being a democracy, we extend this opportunity to everyone.

One would think, therefore, that an entirely middle-class nation would stop despising people on the basis of middle classhood, or that everyone who could make or lose enough money would quickly scurry into one of the other classes. Let us explain this with a small story. Miss Manners' mother always told her to travel either first or third class, but never second, when crossing. (Not crossing class lines, silly: crossing the Atlantic Ocean, in the days when that was done properly, with bouillon at eleven on the promenade deck and tea at five in the salon.)

In first class, in those days, you had luxury; in third class, you had fun. This is the proper distribution of the world's blessings. In second class, you had neither. Naturally, then, someone invented the one-class ship, where the advantages of second class could be enjoyed by all, which is probably why we have those overanxious things called airplanes for crossings these days.

You see the problem. Here are Miss Manners' solutions: First, some people must volunteer to be in the upper class, and others must volunteer to be in the lower class. This is a democracy, so admission will be based solely on ability to pay. But, then, people must behave according to the class they have chosen. We will have no confusion with upper-class people wanting to be earthy, or loved for themselves alone, or lower-class people coveting status symbols. Nor will members of any class be allowed to be ashamed of their own class. We have a fine new example of pride in the enthusiasm, during the last few years, of Americans for their racial and ethnic origins. All Miss Manners is asking is that people who now own up proudly to their grandparents be willing to own up to their parents, as well.

The last rule is the most important of all. Miss Manners will not tolerate the classes' taunting one another in any way, not even at recess.

On Sunday Best

Put on your best clothes and come into the best parlor. If you are on your best behavior, you may have tea on the best china, and stir it with one of the best spoons.

Can you imagine anything worse?

The concept of Sunday Best, so popular in previous generations, has become distasteful to modern people who pride themselves on stylistic consistency. Those who do still distinguish the Best actually adhere just as much to one standard—by making provision for a Best Occasion that never arrives. Nevertheless, Miss

Manners, who is never afraid to take an unpopular stand when it is all for the best, would like to make a plea for the reinstitution of Sunday Best. The opposite of Best, in this instance, is not worst, but Ordinary Everyday.

In the heyday of Sunday Best, Sunday came regularly once a week. There was a sense, as in the stiff but—Miss Manners maintains—not unattractive parlor scene she has described, that one had at one's command more than one way of living. A version of this remains among those who observe Sunday Worst by slopping around the house on weekends in a manner markedly different from their weekday habits.

Most people nowadays fail to make any distinctions. They dress and act the same any day of the week, usually at the stylistically lowest common denominator. Among the genteel folk known to the people who worship informality as the *petite bourgeoisie*, there is a Best, but it is always yet to be. People who put slipcovers, doilies, plastic protectors, and cellophane on everything good that they own rarely live to see an occasion so good that all these covers are removed.

Miss Manners thinks that everyone should have two modes of living ever available, just as everyone should have a year-round residence and an opportunity to vacation elsewhere. Regular change is refreshing as well as exciting. If given the choice, she would prefer one to be Ordinary and the other Best, rather than one Ordinary and the other Worst.

Everyday dishes and fine china, good stainless steel and better silver, sensible clothes and fancy ones, and family manners, as opposed to company manners, seem to her excellent combinations. If no one is ever allowed into the living room for fear of spoiling the white upholstery, and the good china is never used so it won't break, and the party clothes are left in the closet so they won't get dirty—why, Miss Manners believes, that is worse than the absence of best altogether.

The only excuse for the luxury of maintaining two styles is their continual use. The times to be at one's best are Sundays; days when company is coming; opening nights at the opera; holidays, both traditional and spontaneous.

Miss Manners does understand that the old custom came to be synonymous with dreariness and deprivation of the imagination. She is therefore willing to allow an alteration for modern times. Wednesday Best.

On Modesty

Modern modesty is difficult to define, even for Miss Manners, who does that sort of thing so well. Is it, for instance, immodest to wear a bathing suit on a nude beach, thus calling attention to one's body?

Worse than immodesty of dress or undress, in Miss Manners' opinion, is the current immodest fashion of dressing up one's experience so that one appears to be more than one really is. The ideal of the well-bred person should be, as the German proverb has it, "To be more than you appear." This proverb antedates the invention of the Mercedes-Benz, paid for on installments.

The concept of appearing to be less than one is survives now only in the tattered blue jeans worn by the rich. Everyone else is busy trying to appear more sexy, rich, sophisticated, or youthful than he or she really is.

Magazines are full of suggestions to help one fool people about one's identity. The techniques are becoming complicated. It used to be thought that if a newly divorced middle-aged wage earner merely bought a sports car and an oversized bed, wore a turquoise-and-silver necklace and shoes decorated with horse bits, and, of course, unbuttoned his shirt to the waist, no one would ever know that he was not a twenty-one-year-old rock star.

Now he is also told to purge himself of some dated popular culture, recast other such information as vicariously learned pseudo-nostalgia, and memorize the current weeks' supply. (He is warned to load his kitchen cabinets with fish poachers and terrines in order to give the impression of being a fancier of good cooking.) The popularity of places where one's background is not checked, from discos to holiday clubs, is not surprising when there is such a passion for falsification.

Miss Manners questions whether image inflating leads to happiness. She is not recommending the shocking policy of face-value honesty, but merely calling attention to the pleasures of being discovered to be better than one has presented oneself to be. The cottage that turns out to be a palace, the ''Mr.'' or ''Ms.'' who turns out to have a doctorate, the gray-haired person whose face looks younger than that of a blonde of the same vintage, the struggling worker who turns out to have a trust fund—it is when these discoveries are made that the true joys of modesty are experienced.

Such things rarely happen in an age when people are continually confessing to being discriminating and demanding connoisseurs of life. It is getting so that Miss Manners' heart skips a beat if her dinner partner declares that he knows nothing whatever about vintages of wine.

On Embarrassment

While guilt is an emotion Miss Manners does without, having taken the simple precaution of always doing everything right the first time, embarrassment interests her. Miss Manners cannot be expected to experience embarrassment firsthand, but it is something for which she has a moderate amount of sympathy. The proper use of embarrassment is as a conscience of manners. As your conscience might trouble you if you do anything immoral, your sense of embarrassment should be activated if you do anything unmannerly. As conscience should come from within, so should embarrassment. Hot tingles and flushes are quite proper when they arise from your own sense of having violated your own standards, inadvertently or advertently, but Miss Manners hereby absolves everyone from feeling any embarrassment deliberately imposed by others.

The less scrupulous of those who sell funeral services try to embarrass people with the suggestion that anyone who cares about the recently deceased will ''spare no expense'' in the burial, an emotional non sequitur if ever there was one. The same tactic has been adopted by other professions. The whole posture of being what is termed, in the vernacular, "snooty" is cultivated by some headwaiters, real estate salespeople, boutique clerks, and others who hope to embarrass honest customers into spending more than they wish to spend.

This should be seen as a commercial ploy, not a challenge of manners. It is perfectly good manners to check over one's bill and ask for an explanation if it seems to be wrong; it is good manners to spend what one wishes to spend and not what one doesn't want to or cannot afford; and it is good manners to ask for what is coming to one if it does not seem to be forthcoming. What is dreadful manners is to attempt to embarrass anyone into spending money. That is a matter that ought to make those who practice it feel horribly guilty.

Then there are the people who keep trying to entice Miss Manners to play Gotcha! It is a nasty game, and Miss Manners wants nothing to do with it.

Gotcha! has a particularly sneaky opening move. The player sidles up to Miss Manners, or to a surrogate Miss Manners among his acquaintance, and says innocently, "Tell me, my dear Miss Manners, what do you think of such and such a behavior? Is that considered impolite? Would you even say it was rude?" There follows an example of the most horrendously bad behavior, with no possible ambiguity. Poor Miss Manners is forced to agree, and the questioner smiles quietly and says only, "I thought it might be, but I'm glad to have your opinion."

Miss Manners has now learned to recognize that sly smile and knows when she sees it that she has been trapped, once again, in a game of Gotcha! The game continues when the questioner goes running back to the wrongdoer, armed with the awesome authority of Miss Manners, and endeavors to carry out his true purpose, which was to make someone feel just terrible.

Therefore, the purpose of Gotcha! is to create unproductive discomfort in others. Miss Manners' unwitting aid in this unpleasant procedure is obtained fraudulently. The story told to Miss Manners always turns out to have been deliberately constructed so as to leave out all mitigating circumstances that might have swung the case to the other side.

Gotcha! creates gratuitous discomfort because it concerns itself with a situation that is already past. If the wedding was planned wrong, it is of no use now to tell the bride's parents. They are not going to do it all over again right.

Miss Manners hereby declares the entire game of Gotcha! to be rude.

Gentle Readers Wrestle with Philosophical Problems Arising from the Great Study of Manners

DEAR MISS MANNERS:

Who says there is a "right" way of doing things and a "wrong"?

GENTLE READER:

Miss Manners does. You want to make something of it?

On Manners and Morals

DEAR MISS MANNERS:

Can deceit find a home in good manners? To the unmarried couple living together, who were considering staying with (I hope only visiting) her parents, you advise the male, "Unpack your suitcase in whatever room they say. . . . If after bedtime you should stumble into the wrong room, that is your business."

You are simply saying that the rules of the house of the host may be violated after dark, when no one knows they are being violated. Do you really believe that this kind of thinking is good manners? It is to be hoped that you will rectify this sort of deceit in the future, so that your faithful readers may understand that the rules of the house visited are to be observed in the still of the night, as well as in the bright light of day.

12

GENTLE READER:

Miss Manners would do anything for a reader who writes ''it is to be hoped'' rather than ''hopefully,'' but please allow her to defend her distinction between manners and morals. Manners involve the appearance of things, rather than the total reality. Both may need regulating—Miss Manners is not prepared to argue whether this young couple is right to live together without marriage, or whether her parents are right about disapproving the arrangement—but hosts have no right to rule on the behavior of their house guests except as it directly affects them. (They can, of course, refuse to invite people of whose way of life they do not approve, but parents are understandably reluctant to go this far with their grown-up children.)

On Friendship

DEAR MISS MANNERS:

Now don't get me wrong—I am not a boor. I know perfectly well to keep my elbows off the table, I do not take my shoes off at formal gatherings, and I have never asked for a doggy bag at the Watergate. I seem to be suffering, however, from a case of severe social jealousy. The problem is that my best friend is a well-born, upper-class, blue-blooded gentlewoman. I am not talking about the kind of ostentatious display of manners of the *nouveau riche;* my friend has the real thing—authentic social *éclat.*

What it boils down to is this: she has Taste. Her makeup is flawlessly done with Princess Marcella Borghese; I slap a little Vaseline Intensive Care onto my face each morning and consider myself ready for the day. She turns heads when she wafts into a room; I raise eyebrows in the same room because I trip over furniture. She lifts her *coquilles St. Jacques* gracefully to her lips without spilling a drop; it is all I can do to get my coffee from table to mouth without pouring it on my lap. Several weeks ago we were in a restaurant and the waiter was so overcome by her that he spent three-quarters of an hour describing to my friend everything on the menu and left with her order, only to return a few minutes later to ask if, by any chance, I, also, wanted anything to eat.

My friend has background, sophistication, edification. She can name any piece of music within the first two bars: ''Why, it's Bruch's Swedish Dances for Piano with Four Hands, Opus 63,'' she says casually. My singular musical achievement was learning ''Für Elise'' by heart in high school.

Miss Manners, what I need to know is this: Can a friendship between an aristocrat and a *bourgeoise* possibly survive? Is there common ground somewhere between those who have presence and those who just take up space?

GENTLE READER:

Miss Manners urges you to continue this friendship, for the sake of common humanity. You are probably the only friend this poor lady has. Believe Miss Manners, it is not easy to be perfect these days. It is quite out of fashion and attracts the admiration of no one except garrulous waiters. Yet there are those of us who cannot help it, and we, too, have souls and crave simple affection from those more fortunate than ourselves.

It was not always thus. Until recent years, people strove for perfection, and the person who achieved it was universally admired and imitated. Once, it might have been a charity for a person such as your friend to overlook the awkwardnesses and anxieties of someone such as yourself and value you for your best qualities.

Now, however, it is our faults for which we are loved. Imperfect table manners are considered a sign of subscribing to the principles of democracy; ignorance of high culture to be an indication of spirituality; and blurting, rough speech to be a clue to perfect honesty.

Miss Manners hopes you will be grateful for what you have, and tolerant of the handicaps of your friend.

A Rule of Thumb

DEAR MISS MANNERS:

Do you have any guidelines that will help me to feel correct in all situations?

GENTLE READER:

Yes, two, both of which were given to her by her Uncle Henry when Miss Manners was a mere slip of a girl. They have served her well in all the vicissitudes of life ever since. They are:

1. Don't.
2. Be sure not to forget to.

Birth

Prebirth Manners for Parents and Others

Being considerate of one's own mother requires no particular instruction, because everyone does that instinctively. The exception is that children must be taught that mothers should be assumed to despise breakfast in bed unless they specifically state otherwise.

Knowing how to treat other people's mothers politely does not, however, come naturally. This is especially noticeable in the way that people treat pregnant women, possibly because pregnant women are especially noticeable. (A mother cannot be identified with as much certainty after pregnancy. There could be another reason for a woman's keeping a stuffed animal in her purse, or having a habit of saying, "Now, you stop that.") Even then, mistakes are possible. Miss Manners' first rule of respect for potential mothers is to allow them to make their announcements themselves. To inquire of a person whether she is pregnant is to ask for big trouble in this girdle-free era when so many people believe that frozen yogurt has practically no calories.

As a return courtesy, the prospective mother should time the announcement properly; that is to say, one week before they could tell without being told (two weeks for gossip-prone grandparents). Anything earlier only prolongs the period in which she will have to engage in inane chatter with everyone she meets. The excuse is that one waited to be sure everything was going well. The late announcement also puts some distance between the fact of the pregnancy and the imagination of its cause. A lady should take time to comb her hair before she announces her pregnancy.

Similarly, onlookers who know where babies come from should not stress this point when addressing pregnant women. Remarks about women's breasts, for example, are as vulgar at this time as at any other, and unsolicited appraisal of the fruitful body is no more adorable than other such critiques. Patting the pregnant stomach is in the same category as other bodily contact: except for the prospective father, who has reason to assume that his advances are acceptable, no one may be certain, without inquiring, that physical attentions are welcome.

Naturally, carrying a baby about under one's dress is an open invitation for advice from everyone. If a lady does not want others to tell her how to run her life, she should not be having a baby, because it is only a matter of a few years before that baby will consider this one of his or her chief duties.

There are certain subjects that should be avoided in conversation with pregnant women. Advice on whether and when to have a baby is of less practical value to pregnant women than their friends seem to suppose. Questions as to whether the deed was done on purpose insult the mother and father. Information on the problems of overpopulation insults the forthcoming child. The greatest nonquestion to ask prospective parents is whether they want a boy or girl—with the hope of using their answer against them later—or perhaps it is to ask the prospective siblings whether they want a brother, a sister, or neither. Stories of difficult labors or birth defects do not make appropriate conversation with pregnant women. What you may tell them is how lovely your children are, and how wisely you brought them up. You may also smile at them a great deal. That they just have to learn to take with good grace.

The Proper Response

DEAR MISS MANNERS:

When I was growing up, I was always taught that "Congratulations!" was the proper response upon learning that a woman was pregnant. Even if the mother-to-be was being forced by her family to marry the seventeen-year-old father, one was supposed to rejoice with her in the creation of a new life and utter disapproving remarks about modern morality well out of her hearing. What I need to know, Miss Manners, is has this rule of polite behavior changed?

I am twenty-nine and am more than five months pregnant. My husband and I are looking forward with joy and excitement to the birth of our first child. When casual acquaintances and colleagues at work learn of my condition, however, their typical response is to open their eyes wide and blink at me, saying "Oh!" or "Well!" After a few moments of awkward silence, I feel compelled to assure them that yes, it was wanted and, of course, planned. At this point, the startled listener has recovered enough to mumble, "Well, good!" still staring in confusion and embarrassment.

What is the correct response upon learning that a woman is expecting a child?

Have you any snappy comebacks which would serve to alert the other person(s) that the situation suits me fine and I don't wish to pursue its more personal aspects casually? I tried telling one woman that my husband and I were appalled by the high cost of meat and were growing our own, but this just prolonged the blinking stage.

GENTLE READER:

First, congratulations. Miss Manners is very happy for you. She is also puzzled to find that it is usually the same people who claim to have a special interest in sex who are most horrified by its natural consequence. Your friends are, no doubt, worried about the population increase and are unable to perceive that, by having a first child at twenty-nine, you have hardly littered the landscape.

Too bad for them. Miss Manners happens to believe that children are a joy (if you have no descendants, how do you expect to have the pleasure of being an ancestor?) but has no wish to force her views on others and is, in fact, reassured by the idea that people who don't want children often don't have them.

The best you can do at the moment is to alert people to the fact that you consider it a matter for congratulation by saying "I'm so thrilled" when you speak of your pregnancy. Soon you will be too busy to care.

DEAR MISS MANNERS:

What do you say to congratulate a friend on a pregnancy that you know was an unwanted accident? A friend of mine who has three small children had been planning to return to school as soon as her youngest was in school himself. Now she is pregnant again. When she told me about it, she did not look like the picture of a joyous young madonna, to say the least. Apparently she is not considering abortion, but I can tell that she is resentful. In fact, she kept saying to me, "We certainly didn't plan on this," and "I can't face doing diapers again," and things like that. Do I try to talk her into being more accepting, or do I commiserate with her, or what?

GENTLE READER:

Contrary to the credo of this society, Miss Manners firmly believes that there are certain honest, understandable, deeply felt emotions that ought never to be expressed by anyone. First among them is that one does not want a child one is going to have.

It is a sad fact of nature that such a statement, unlike other carelessly confided remarks, will never be forgotten. One day, someone who heard it will repeat it to the child, and it will poison whatever maternal devotion the reluctant mother may have lavished from that moment on. Any sensitive person can understand that it is possible for a good woman to feel negative or ambivalent about being pregnant.

The best thing to do when someone has spoken the unspeakable is to fail to hear it. The greatest kindness you can do your friend is to pretend that you do not understand, or even catch, her feelings. When the baby is born, treat it as a joyous event. By that time your friend's feelings may have come around to that view; if not, at least you will be expressing the sentiments of a brand-new friend, who will be badly in need of someone to share them.

Commanding Respect

DEAR MISS MANNERS:

Would you please advise me on the proper response to the hearty greeting of "Hi, mama!" or, worse, "Hi, big mama!" when the person being addressed is not the mother of the greeter, but is, in fact, pregnant. I have tried ignoring the speaker, but he/she normally just repeats the greeting—louder, in case being pregnant has affected my hearing. I have also tried responding, "Hello, sonny/daughter," but this appears to be too subtle for most. Do you think "Shut up, you stupid idiot" is too direct?

Another problem I have encountered since becoming pregnant is the violation of my privacy by people (practically strangers) who feel some compulsion to put their hand on my stomach, without asking, of course.

Do you have any ideas as to how to combat these serious breakdowns in civilized behavior?

GENTLE READER:

It is indeed unfortunate that certain conspicuous physical conditions, such as pregnancies and ski injuries, are perceived by many people as being a fitting subject for hilarity. The idea seems to be that people who have manifestly enjoyed themselves should then be obliged to provide fun for others. It is rude.

It is, however, difficult to discourage, without being even ruder. Perhaps when someone pats your tummy, you could double over in such a way as to suggest that the unwarranted blow has brought on premature labor; but it is a strong measure to take, even though it would undoubtedly cure that individual of the habit for life.

Miss Manners would suggest, instead, a patient, resigned, mirthless smile, indicating that you have been the subject of a transgression but are too weary and good-natured to react. You will find this expression extremely useful, when you are, in due course, the mother of a second grader.

The Baby's Gender

DEAR MISS MANNERS:

My sister has recently given birth to her fourth daughter. It's no secret that they were trying for a boy, and yet I know it hurts her when people keep mentioning this fact when they come to visit the new baby. I mean, she's not going to send it back, so what's the point?

GENTLE READER:

Indeed, but what was the point in her expressing her preferences beforehand? Unless there is a throne to be filled, the official position of prospective parents should always be that they don't care what sex the baby is. (The phrase "so long as it's healthy" is an optional extra.) However untrue this may be, there is nothing to be gained by stating first choice. Refusing to do so may discourage rude postnatal evaluations on the part of others. It will also deprive the baby of a lifetime of attributing her every discontentment to the idea that "I was supposed to be a boy."

Parents' Names

DEAR MISS MANNERS:

We are about to have our first child. I am fairly young, younger actually than my wife, and I think it would be appropriate for our child to call us by our first names. I had to call my father "Sir," and it didn't help the relationship any.

My wife has no strong objection to this, although she sometimes says she likes the thought of being somebody's "Mommy." We don't have to have matching titles, of course. She could be "Mommy" and I could be "Frank." But my in-laws have hit the ceiling. They maintain that it is bad taste for a child to call his father by his first name. I would appreciate your telling them that it is common enough these days to be considered proper.

GENTLE READER:

Indeed, a Mommy and Frank household is quite usual these days, but there is generally a Daddy and Jeannie household for the same child somewhere else. Be prepared for people not so much thinking that you are young, but that you arrived late on the scene.

First names for parents are in vogue from time to time, as people think they sound sporty. Miss Manners has no violent objection to this on the grounds of etiquette, although she can't for the life of her see why a grown person would want to seek the semblance of equality with an infant or an adolescent, or an unruly middle-aged child, for that matter.

Showers

Showering a Relative

DEAR MISS MANNERS:

My daughter-in-law is expecting her first child. I have a shower planned for her, because her only sister, her mother, and her best friend live in California. My son is an only child so I am not able to put a daughter's name on the invitations as so many of my relatives and friends have done in the past for showers, both bridal and baby. Will it be in bad taste if I put my name on the invitations? My husband feels we should do this if that's what we'd like to do. I feel a bit uncertain.

GENTLE READER:

Showers are tricky, and a lot of people get caught in them. The word "shower" is used here as in "to shower with presents," making this the only form of grown-up entertainment at which a present is mandatory. Therefore such an event is not properly given by any member of the guest of honor's immediate family—daughter, sister, mother, or mother-in-law. However, since your relatives and friends have been making mistakes about this right and left, Miss Manners suggests you do not worry about it and go ahead and give your party. If you want to be perfectly correct, call it a tea, not a shower, thus establishing that you wish to bring joy but not bounty into the family.

Second Showers

DEAR MISS MANNERS:

Does it really matter if a friend gives a baby shower for someone who is having her second child? Isn't a baby shower just a nice thing to do for a friend? I find it hard to believe there could be a rule saying only the first child receives a shower.

GENTLE READER:

So does Miss Manners, who was a second child. However, there is a rule. If you will be patient while Miss Manners explains the reason for the rule, Miss Manners will help you circumvent it.

A shower is held for the purpose of showering a novice (at marrying or mothering) with the equipment she did not need in her previous state (of spinsterhood or childlessness), but which is essential in the life she is about to enter. That is why Miss Manners and her friends at college always gave ''lingerie showers''; in those days, no nice girl needed pretty underwear before marriage. This is also why showers are not needed for women having their second, or eighth, babies. It is why members of the family are not supposed to give showers when they could just equip the honoree themselves and not ask her friends to do it.

However, it is a charming custom to entertain a lady who is about to do something again, even though she has a good idea of what it is all about. Miss Manners merely suggests you not call it a shower, and therefore get around the rule, while also leaving the question of presents vague so that the guest of honor is not trying the feelings of friends who attended earlier showers.

Sexist Showers

DEAR MISS MANNERS:

You seem intolerant—and justifiably so—of nonsense masquerading as correctness. But what about sexism and oppression disguised as polite tradition? I'm referring to wedding and baby showers. Do these traditions not have considerable sexist and oppressive components? Are they not designed to reinforce women who accept the roles society deems most acceptable for women, rewarding them with vacuum cleaners, kitchen utensils, and baby paraphernalia when they assume their rightful roles as wives and mothers?

Are you sympathetic to such thinking? How should a person with such views respond to an invitation to attend a shower? A simple ''No, thank you'' seems too unfriendly or, worse, cheap. A political discussion is probably counterproductive.

GENTLE READER:

Few of our social institutions can bear severe philosophical scrutiny. Neither can using an invitation to participate in other people's pleasures as an opportunity for dampening them with one's disapproval. It is not impolite simply to decline an invitation that goes against your principles, provided you do not explain that fact.

In the matter of showers, things are changing. Miss Manners can't help noticing that your signature indicates that you are a man, and pointing out that a few years ago you would not have been invited to showers. Presumably, the bridegroom or father will also be a guest of honor at such a shower, and your present should be given to both husband and wife. Vacuum cleaners and baby clothes are not, in themselves, sexist objects. They become so when it is presumed that only the woman should put them on the rug or the baby.

(For bridal showers, please see pp. 313–314.)

Announcements

Look what's in the mail today: printed joy, in red ink on a heavy white card. What could it be? We don't even know this person making the announcement:

> Nehemiah Torky–Van Hoft
> announces his arrival
> to his joyous parents
> Stephanie Torky and Dave Van Hoft . . .

Wait a minute; we do know dear Stephanie and Dave. It's a birth announcement, that's what it is. But why should the baby be announcing it to his parents? Surely they—oh. He's announcing that he's been born to them. No, no, these are married. We got an announcement ages ago from the Torkys saying they "took great joy in announcing" the wedding, so naturally everyone thought Stephanie must be pregnant or why would her parents be so uncontrollably joyous that she was married? It turned out she wasn't at all. In fact, she's been saying for years now that she saw no point in having a baby, until about a year ago, when she was telling us at a party that her "biological clock was ticking," and we were afraid to ask her what that meant in front of all those strangers, but it seemed to have something to do with her reproductive system, as she called it. So now she has a baby. Isn't that lovely?

No, not really. It's lovely, Miss Manners agrees, that people get married, and it's lovely that they have babies, but it isn't lovely that they put out mass mailings to announce how they feel about it. Of course they are joyous. No one assumes that they are doing this for reasons of state. But to suggest that they have some special corner on the market of happiness is to invite speculation that something is wrong.

It is natural that people newly experiencing some of life's greatest pleasures believe that no one else has ever been so in love, or that there was never a more perfect baby born to mortals. To let such a feeling show in one's face is to win the hearts of everyone. But to brag of it in print is naïve and mildly offensive.

Originality is not needed for momentous occasions. Each society develops its conventional forms for publicizing the major events of a lifetime, and it is more attractive to let one's happiness shine through the conventional wording than to put out flashy signs of a special claim to happiness.

How peculiar it is that the idea of being conventional has gotten such a bad name in our time. There is, after all, nothing so conventional as falling in love or producing a baby.

Formal Birth Announcements

DEAR MISS MANNERS:
Should birth announcements be sent or not? Even though our baby's due date is three months hence, we have begun to inquire about birth announcements. (We may not need them if you reply in the negative to the first question.) I have been informed that the proper announcement is as follows:

Baby Newborn Couple
Birth date
Mr. and Mrs. Happy New Couple

These are separate cards, joined with a pink or blue ribbon, whichever is appropriate. Unfortunately, the company that engraves these announcements takes four weeks. The only other company that does the new "pseudo engraving" cannot guarantee quality. We shall be moving within weeks of the baby's birth to a distant city. Secondly, engraving costs four times what the other costs. We could have a single sheet of paper pseudo-engraved with the words I previously wrote, and without the ribbon. A company could have them in approximately two weeks.

I realize that perhaps we shouldn't be having a baby if we have to ask how much birth announcements cost. However, being a young couple, money does enter into many of our decisions. Should we get as close to propriety as we can afford, or do nothing?
GENTLE READER:
Do go ahead and have the baby. Miss Manners is fond of babies, provided they don't leak on visitors, and to help you along in this venture will now save you a pile of money.

321 Primrose Path

Mr. and Mrs. Geoffrey Lockwood Perfect

We are delighted to announce the birth of our daughter, Daffodil Louise, on April first at Merciful God Hospital.

The announcement of a birth, written on a married couple's engraved message card. (The card, which can also be made with the woman's name only from the same plate, may be used for any informal note, invitation, reply to an informal invitation or message accompanying flowers or a present.) Any plain or marked writing paper is suitable for announcing a birth, but in that case it must be written in the form of a letter. (Most people include the baby's birth weight; Mrs. Perfect omitted it because she does not care to have the Perfects judged by the pound. However, on some cards she included such additional comments as "She has the Perfect expression already!" or "Do come and see us at home next week.")

Order no announcements. The engraved baby announcement you describe is, in Miss Manners' opinion, a silly misuse of formality. The rationale is that the tiny card with the baby's name, attached to the parents' card, is the little one's "card," in case it should decide to pay formal calls or send flowers to hostesses. This is not only pretentious and expensive, but impractical because, as you point out, it arrives so much later than the baby. A poor quality substitute for it would be even sillier.

Nor is Miss Manners fond of informal, fill-in announcements which strain to be cute and which include a line for the baby's weight to show whether you have produced something substantial. The solution is simple, gracious, and cheap. Take a box of pretty paper to the hospital with you, and a roll of stamps. It is an agreeable and restful occupation to write brief letters to your friends, informing them that you have a new baby and, in your case, that you will have a new address. Two lines are enough, and if you don't feel up to it, make the papa do it. The time involved is less than that for ordering or choosing cards. Now take that money you were to have given to the engravers and put it in a college fund for the baby.

Unannounced Births

DEAR MISS MANNERS:

I am sorely puzzled. This past season, four different couples I know all produced their firstborn children. During the pregnancies, I asked at various times how the mother was, etc. But in each case, once the baby was born, no one bothered to let me know about the actual birth, and whether they had a boy or girl. Have birth announcements vanished from our culture? Is it proper to ask: "Did Marilyn finally have the baby?" I feel a bit put out at the parents in question for not letting me know of their blessed event.

GENTLE READER:

What has vanished is the simple, guileless note telling people something they might like to know. Why bring children into a world where no one writes letters?

By birth "announcements" you probably mean the wee cards that come in two styles: cutesy and pseudo-formal. The reason some new parents don't send them is that they are afraid they would be interpreted as bids for presents.

The best way to find out is to tell an expectant father, "Please put me on your list of people to call when the baby is born." Telephoning is considered a new father's first duty. You take the risk of his assuming that you are awake when he is.

Otherwise, you can certainly ask, but do it kindly or you will some day ask with that "put-out" tone in your voice and be told, "The baby was stillborn." Miss Manners has her reasons for objecting to heavy sarcasm.

Presents

DEAR MISS MANNERS:

Is it still considered good taste to send birth announcements? I am expecting my second child in June. I did not receive announcements from many of my friends for their first child and very few for the second. Is an announcement considered a request for a present?

GENTLE READER:

Many people are needlessly troubled by the fear that they are inadvertently requesting presents simply by letting others know that they are managing to get from one milestone of life to another. No announcement, whether it is for a first or second child, first or second marriage, or first or second attempt to be graduated, requires the recipient to send a present (please see pp. 521–523).

Names

According to the law, you may change your name at will, provided you do not do so with the intention of escaping justice. According to Miss Manners, you may change your name at certain specified times, provided you are merciful in judging those who have allowed the changes to escape them.

The wise parent will bestow an adolescent nickname upon an infant and a grown-up name upon a child. The tenderest of babies will soon sprout hair in unlikely places, and the gangliest of teenagers will some day sprout some unlikely desire for dignity. It is well to stay ahead in the nomenclature.

But ultimately, each person is responsible for fashioning his or her own name. The first opportunity comes with entry into the educational system. Anyone allowing himself to be announced at roll call in nursery school by the nickname his parents fashioned from his own inability to pronounce his name in infancy will be marked for life.

Daffodil Louise Perfect made the mistake, at the age of fourteen months, of referring to herself as "Doopsie" instead of employing the personal pronoun. Although her blood relatives will continue to call her this until the day she dies, partly from fondness, partly from bad memory, and partly for the annoyance value, she had the sense to announce herself as Daffodil when she first went to school.

Two years later, another Daffodil showed up in her school as a transfer student, and Daffodil was told she had to be called Daffodil P., to distinguish her from Daffodil R. Our Daffodil did not like this one bit, but it opened to her a world of possibilities. At summer camp, she went for her middle name, and told everyone she was called Louise. That fall, she endeavored to get her old classmates to call her Lou, but, this not being a natural breaking point as was camp, it didn't work. So she waited until she moved from lower school to middle school, and successfully grafted her new choice, becoming Daffodil-Lou.

Tiring of this as soon as it had taken, she tried to continue the evolution, but was unable to budge her teachers or classmates. Fortunately, the school tired of her at this time, and at boarding school she was able to effect a complete break and persuade everyone that she should be called Samantha.

After a year at Miss Waffles' School, she was sent home to complete her education at Midtown Country Day School, where her uncle was a benefactor, and there she began to style herself D. Louise. At the next changing point, entry into college, she became known as D.L., until her engagement, when she resumed the full dignity of Daffodil Louise. In tender moments, her fiancé called her his Doopsie. When they were divorced, she became Daffy, to her new friends.

You see here the possible, as well as the impossible, times that changes may be made in given names. And that's even without changing last names, through marriage, divorce, hyphenation, and the desire to depart from, or return to, one's point of ethnic origin.

The general rule is that a change of location or legal status is always good for a fresh start, but that one cannot expect the same people to acknowledge more than one change each in given name and surname (and that many people will not be able to master even that). Grateful that her mother has made the transition from her infant nickname to her baptismal names and that her bridesmaids were able to memorize her married surname, Daffy accepts as a natural accompaniment to life's development that her chum from seventh grade still writes her as Daffy-Lou. It is only because of her own poor memory that she addresses this woman, now a federal judge, as Poo-Poo instead of Prudence.

There is nothing wrong with children playing with their names, provided that they clean up the mess when they are finished. Miss Manners even recommends that parents give their children the proper equipment—middle names, good combinations of initials, nicknames, names that have alternate spellings—to use when the children inevitably decide that they can no longer tolerate their childhood identities.

What Miss Manners objects to is grown-up people who continue to play with their names and then are insulted when their friends can't keep up with the changes. Changing names around always has been an American habit, but it's getting worse. Take, for example, a typical American family of four generations. The family's American history began with a man who Americanized his surname when he arrived and a woman whose last name reflects a misspelling by an immigration officer. In the next generation, there is a daughter who married three times, changing her name successively to the full name of each husband, preceded only by "Mrs."; and a son who is a movie star and was issued a completely new name when he signed a studio contract. After that, there is a daughter who has a hyphenated last name, consisting of her maiden name and her husband's last name. She is no longer married to him and has, in fact, married someone else, but she must retain that hyphenated name because she has made her professional reputation with it. Also in this generation is a son who has had an attack of ethnic nostalgia and changed his name to that of the family name in the old country. These people's children, the result of unions with various people who changed their names to X, Ben Moses, and Khrishna, are called Che, Noah, Vishnu, and Kunta Kinte. They are still young, but they are already plotting to change their names because they have found that all the other children in their respective homerooms are named Che, Noah, Vishnu, and Kunta Kinte.

Miss Manners has decided, for the sake of order, to put some limits on all this. Here are the new rules:

Up to the age of seventeen, children are allowed free play with their names. They are even allowed to change the names that end in *y* to *i* and vice versa, which of course they all do anyway.

Upon leaving high school, they must each pick a permanent first name. On beginning college or employment, they may tell everyone the new name, pretending they have always had it, but they are not allowed to chastise relations and childhood friends for using the old one.

When they either marry for the first time or settle on a first serious career, they must pick a permanent last name. It is wise not to associate these names with philosophies or spouses who are likely to prove fleeting, because this is the surname they must keep. Miss Manners suggests sticking to the original family surname—but in the female line. The basic family unit has now become the mother and children of whom she has been awarded custody, and it is simpler if they all have the same name and keep it, no matter who happens to join them later. The system of the matriarchal line worked fairly well in ancient societies, before women made the mistake of telling men that they had any connection with the production of children.

Moving Up

DEAR MISS MANNERS:
We were lucky enough to have, until last month, four generations of our family living: Grandpa, who was Curt Nicholson, Sr.; my husband who is Junior; our son, who is 3d; and his baby, who is 4th. Is it true that now that Grandpa is gone, everyone moves up a notch? This would distress me because I have lots of paper marked Mrs. Curt Nicholson, Jr., and if my husband becomes Senior, I would have to throw it away.

GENTLE READER:
Do not throw that paper away. Miss Manners congratulates you on already having your daughter-in-law's Christmas present.

Everyone does move up a notch. You and your husband are not Senior, but merely Mr. and Mrs. Curt Nicholson. Only a widow uses Senior, to distinguish herself from her daughter-in-law who, as the wife of the eldest living person of the name, does not use any suffix, as you and your husband should not now. Your son is now junior, and his son is now 3d.

DEAR MISS MANNERS:

Will you please settle two burning issues that recently arose in our family. The problems are as follows:

1. William Wellborn has a son, William Wellborn, Jr., who has a son William Wellborn, III. Young William, wishing to ensure his son's inheritance, names the first of his 2.3 children William Wellborn, IV. When William, Sr., passes on, how are the rest to be called? I believe the American custom is that the oldest living person of that name is William Wellborn, his son William, Jr., and so on. My interlocutor says that William, IV stays "William, IV," even if he is the oldest living person of that name. I believe that the system of continuing Roman numerals from generation to generation should be reserved for reigning monarchs and that ordinal numbers are reserved for marquesses and the like. Will you please settle this?

2. William Wellborn marries Miss Elizabeth Gotbucks. She is Mrs. William Wellborn, and, upon his untimely death, so remains. If she wises up and divorces him, she is Mrs. Gotbucks Wellborn until her remarriage. When, if ever, is she Mrs. Elizabeth Wellborn? This is a matter of curiosity, not politics.

GENTLE READER:

Politics always enters into problems of nomenclature, and being a reigning monarch does not ensure a neat succession of Roman numerals. Just when you think it is perfectly clear that you are William III, for example, everyone starts calling you William and Mary.

In the examples you give of the proper names for nonreigning Americans, you are absolutely correct. The oldest living William Wellborn is numberless, and one starts counting Junior, III, IV (or 3d, 4th, a form Miss Manners prefers), and so on from there. You are also correct in your intimation that no one is ever correctly styled "Mrs. Elizabeth Wellborn," come death, divorce, or famine.

However, let us now consider the politics of the matter. The above rules are correct. You know it and Miss Manners knows it. Popular opinion is often against us nevertheless, and the populace has a great deal to say about it, particularly when people are talking about their own names. Ask any reigning monarch whether it is safe to disregard public opinion.

Many men consider that the word indicating their place in the family line at birth is actually part of their full name; 4th gets used to being called 4th, and even if he is willing to become 3d when great-grandpa dies, his father doesn't know what to do about his dear old widowed grandma, who has all those cards engraved Mrs. Grandpa, only to be told that that title now belongs to her daughter-in-law, the former Mrs. Jr., who never uses cards anyway, and what a waste of good money that would be. Such people may refuse to change, and you must respect their wishes, even if they start producing Williams the 12th.

Then there are the people who want to change when no change is necessary, as in the case of a widow who has always used her husband's name. And then—things are never simple when you are dealing with popular opinion—there are the people who, for a variety of reasons, dislike a traditional form (such as Mrs. Gotbucks Wellborn for a divorcée) or a useful modern form (such as Ms. Elizabeth Wellborn for a woman of whatever marital status who wishes to use her own name—please see page 35). Such a person may insist on being addressed as Mrs. Elizabeth Wellborn, whether you and Miss Manners like it or not.

DEAR MISS MANNERS:

When a man is named after his grandfather, say, I was under the impression he was John Smith, 2d. Our minister is always written up as John Smith, II. Am I wrong in thinking Roman numerals are reserved for royalty?

GENTLE READER:

Yes, but not nearly so wrong as some royalty Miss Manners could name but won't, who think they can use the numeral I before they have been replaced by II. A king who is the first of his line to bear the given names of, say, Juan Smith (Miss Manners has disguised the name) should style himself King Juan Smith, not King Juan Smith I. Commoners are as entitled to use Roman numerals as Arabic, if they use them correctly.

DEAR MISS MANNERS:

My grandfather, Thomas, lost his first son, whom he named Thomas. He named my father George after his bachelor brother who died at thirty. I am also named George. Question: Is my son George, III, or is he legitimately George, IV?

GENTLE READER:

If your father is alive and calls himself George, II, your son is George, IV, God save him. (God save Miss Manners, too, who has a wastebasket full of sketches of your family tree.) However, people, short of kings, tend to get lopped off the tree when they die. Your father could therefore be George, Sr., which would make you Junior, and your son III. If your father is dead, then you are Senior, and your son is Junior. In any case, George IV was unquestionably legitimate, but the same unfortunately cannot be said of all of his children.

The Dual-Purpose Name

DEAR MISS MANNERS:

My husband and I are expecting our third, and last, baby in a few months. We plan to use a family name for the baby's middle name as we did with our first two children. We are torn, however, between the maiden name of my paternal grandmother—a surname that has died out in this generation—and a name in my mother-in-law's genealogy, on which she has devoted ten years of research collecting genealogical queries, answers, and data. We are considering using both, but would prefer hyphenating the two to produce one hyphenated middle name.

It is on this consideration that we post three questions: Would this hyphenation be acceptable? If so, is there a correct order or is it merely a matter of what is most pleasing to the ear? In using a hyphenated middle name, does one use only the first letter of the first name for an initial, does one use both initials separately, or does one use both initials, but hyphenated?

GENTLE READER:

Miss Manners wishes you would reconsider about making this your last baby. She knows that this may seem to you now to be a lot of trouble, but it would be far easier on her if you would give one of those names to your third child and the other to the fourth.

However, if you insist on resisting this simple solution, she will try to find another.

Yes, it is perfectly proper to hyphenate the two names. If the child wants to get married some day and hyphenate its surname with that of its spouse, the result will be a big mess—the monogrammed sheets in *their* daughter's trousseau will look like the front pages of newspapers—but that is a problem for the future.

In choosing the order for the names, pay careful attention not only to the sound, but to the initials. If three initials are used, the middle one would be the first one of the hyphenated middle name. The use of four initials is permissible, but it often leaves people with the impression that they are dealing with a government agency, rather than a person.

New Surnames

DEAR MISS MANNERS:

I received the strangest announcement I have ever seen from a young couple who are expecting a baby. Apparently, they have not known what last name to give the baby—who isn't born yet—so they made up a name, and everybody is taking it—Mama, Daddy, and Baby. Before, she used her name and he used his, but instead of hyphenating the names, as some liberated couples do, they are starting all over with a fresh name. The explanation is that it makes them "a family" all to have the same name, but they couldn't pick one of the existing ones because that would be favoring the man's family over the woman's, or something like that. I don't really understand. But I do know that it's crazy to call a grown-up man one name one day and a different one the next. What do you think of all these shenanigans? Have you ever heard of a grown-up voluntarily taking a new name unless it's to escape a criminal record?

GENTLE READER:

Why, yes. Until the last few years, every married woman in America did it. A mighty strange experience it is, too, for a grown-up to change last names, however voluntarily. Miss Manners cannot see that your friends have solved the problem, however, which is to identify families as belonging together. Their solution applies only to the nuclear family and they are going to feel left out when everybody is playing Roots.

In the Name of Civility

DEAR MISS MANNERS:

My husband and I have been married almost two years. For personal, as well as professional, reasons, I didn't change my name when we married. We now have a child whose last name is a combination of my last name and my husband's, hyphenated.

My problem: Neither of our families fully approves of these circumstances, and therefore call not only me, but also our son, by the wrong name. How can I tactfully tell them I don't want our child growing up not knowing his or his mother's correct name?

GENTLE READER:

The important thing is for your child to grow up knowing that, as we live in confusing and changing times, and probably always will, it behooves us all to be flexible and tolerant. Your families are admittedly being inflexible, but this gives you the opportunity of setting an example of tolerance. Your son will, no doubt, find out his name some time before he has to fill out his college entrance applications.

Uncertain Origins

DEAR MISS MANNERS:

My twenty-year-old niece lives out of state and is doing the usual twenty-year-old things, college and all that. Last week, I got a casual letter from her mother, and, just as a mention, word that the niece is giving birth soon and "Harvey" and niece are very happy.

I seem to have missed out on some in-between events, except I now understand that Harvey is a forty-year-old divorced father of some others. Niece and Harvey's marital status is left hanging, but later news told me that they had a boy, and used Harvey's middle name and last name in the baby's name. My problem: I want to send a gift. Just looking at baby clothes is a lot of fun. But how to address the package? I feel funny calling my niece Mrs. Harvey Whatever. Miss sounds dumb for a new mother. And Ms. doesn't fit the bill, either. Help!

GENTLE READER:

Indeed, "Ms." does exactly fit the bill, in Miss Manners' opinion, as it was designed to skip over the question of whether a woman is married, which is apparently what you mean when describing your niece's behavior as "the usual twenty-year-old things . . . and all that." However, if you don't like it, Miss Manners will not attempt to force it on you. Instead, she will give you special dispensation to address the present to the baby himself, since you have been supplied with his name. Ordinarily, Miss Manners finds this rather too cute, but something tells her that your niece is not a stickler for formalities.

Baptisms and Circumcisions

The Christening

The christening of newborn Christian babies is one of only two social events that most people have in a lifetime in which they can be both the undisputed center of attention and completely free from responsibility for either the arrangements or their own behavior. The other such event comes at the extreme other end of life.

The baby who is having a christening may cry and yell, turn purple in the face, or drop off to sleep in the middle of the festivities—actions we have all been tempted to perform at other social events, but mustn't—without being disgraced.

The burden of behaving well thus falls on the parents, the godparents, and the guests. What the parents must do, in addition to producing the baby, is to:

—Arrange with a clergyman the appropriate time and place for the ceremony. A church christening usually takes place during the church's off hours, although more churches now are including them in Sunday services. A home christening, if permitted, requires that a formal table be set up with a bowl, usually silver, to be used as a font.

—Send out informal invitations—that is, individual letters giving the time, place, and baby's name and a sentence of urging, such as ''We hope you will be

36

able to join us''; or the information may be written on the parents' card—to relatives and close friends. This is not an occasion for casual acquaintances.

—Give a small party afterwards, such as a luncheon or tea party. Caudle, a hot eggnog punch, and white cake iced with the baby's initials or other such fancies are traditional, but most people prefer champagne now to a heavy glug.

—Decorate the house in flowers and the baby in white. When the baby wears the traditional elongated christening dress, the whole thing takes on the charming look of a postscript to the wedding.

—Choose the godparents, two of the baby's sex and one of the opposite, from among their extremely close friends, whose general outlook on life they would not object to the baby's sharing.

The godparents' duties are to:

—Hold the baby at the christening.

—Present it with a present of some permanence, such as one of the many adorable silver objects of unknown utility on which names and the date can be engraved.

—Act as second-string parents to the child, providing moral and religious instruction, birthday and Christmas presents, and asylum when the child has had a teenaged quarrel with its parents.

The duties of guest are to:

—Put on dressy street clothes (no black for women) and attend the ceremony and party.

—Declare convincingly that the baby, though alternately dozing noisily and yelling itself purple, is perfectly beautiful.

Bris and Circumcision

DEAR MISS MANNERS:

Can you tell us about the ritual of circumcision if our baby is a boy? When my husband was born, it was just done at the hospital, but we would like some celebration. Also, what about if it's a girl? We are joining a local synagogue, but I don't want to start out by asking questions whose answers the rabbi would expect us to know, and I also want to know about the rules of etiquette for making this a social occasion that everyone will enjoy.

GENTLE READER:

Well, not everyone. The Berith Milah, or Bris, like all the great ceremonies of life, is designed to be enjoyed by everyone except the guest of honor.

The actual circumcision may, of course, be done at the hospital, but as traditionally it must be performed on the eighth day after birth and as maternity wards no longer encourage lengthy confinements, this is not a down-the-hall convenience. One can return to the hospital and have the reception there, or do both at home.

Miss Manners needn't tell you that this cannot be done for a girl. A daughter is formally named at services on the Sabbath after her birth, and you may give her a reception in the temple or at home afterward.

Since the baby will be your firstborn, a son may also have a Pidyon Haben ceremony, in which he is dedicated to the service of God and then redeemed by his parents. This, too, is followed by a reception.

It is customary for all of these receptions to be small. Only close friends and relatives are invited, and usually just wine and cake are served. This is to give your extended circle and the caterer time to prepare for the child's bar or bat mitzvah.

Age Requirement

DEAR MISS MANNERS:
What is the proper age for baptism?
GENTLE READER:
It varies, depending on a variety of factors. For example, have you just been born or were you born again?

The Office of Godparent

DEAR MISS MANNERS:
Please, could you tell me what the duties are of a godmother, so named at a child's christening? I have been one for thirty-five years and have been chided about neglecting my responsibilities. Is it too late to do anything? What should I have done?
GENTLE READER:
The responsibility of the godmother is to see to the spiritual upbringing of the child, so that the world is not full of adults who chide others about neglecting their duties.

The formal side of the job is to educate the child in the history, beliefs, and ceremonies of his or her religion. The informal side is to provide the child with a concerned older person who is certified as responsible by the child's parents but has the advantage of not being a parent. Both of these services can be of great benefit to thirty-five-year-olds as well as children.

Social Life Begins

The Proper Infant

Surely we are all agreed now that children cannot begin too young to learn manners. Miss Manners does not any longer expect an argument.

There used to be parents who believed that a child should be allowed to develop naturally, with no artificial standards of behavior imposed on his or her innocent instincts, but we have all had a gander at the results of that. A child who is able to express his true feelings without the restraints of convention is a menace to society, and Miss Manners trusts that no one will deliberately attempt to rear such a creature in the future.

That decided, when do we begin to torture the baby? The first formal social occasion in a person's life is generally the call that friends pay on him and his mother when they return from the hospital. Friends of the family customarily telephone as soon as they hear of the birth and ask when they may be permitted to visit, a request that should not be refused. Recent childbirth is no excuse for either participant to avoid social duties. (Miss Manners has heard of those who attempt to make an earlier social occasion out of the birth, recounting or even filming it for the benefit of those who could not attend, but considers this to be on a taste level with publicizing the conception.)

The round of visits to newly enlarged families can be charming if the baby understands the rules. Some allowances are made for error on account of the baby's youth and inexperience, but an ambitious baby will not count on excessive indulgence outside of the immediate family. New parents can be of great assistance in displaying the baby to his best advantage. This does not include pretending to speak or write for the baby. Parents should never issue birth announcements or write letters of thanks that pretend to be coming directly from the baby; they should write in their own names on his or her behalf. Speaking for someone else is a vile practice that the baby will resent increasingly over the years.

One thing parents can do is to schedule visiting so that the baby's less attractive functions can be accomplished privately. Hours may be suggested by parents so that the baby has a decent chance of freshening up between onslaughts.

Unlike other members of the family, the newborn baby is permitted to sleep while visitors are present, and even to have a meal without offering whatever he is enjoying to everyone else. But he must be made to understand his obligation to allow visitors to satisfy their curiosity as to his looks. For example, if he wishes to sleep on his stomach, he should turn his head toward the room so that he presents a three-quarter view of his face.

A child who is less than a month old is not expected to produce social smiles, but neither should he produce anything else with his mouth, such as food or excessive noise. He should expect to be passed around to visitors and should remember to bring some protective covering with him. Wetting or otherwise inconveniencing well-wishers is not a good way to begin a social career. He should never show a negative reaction to a compliment or a present. Crying in response to an innocent remark or shifting one's head when a new bonnet is placed there are both bad form. A baby who receives, say, a silver toothbrush with his initials on it, should never volunteer that he has one already or that he has no teeth.

Parents who think of these visits as occasions for encouraging their children to cater to the comforts of guests, rather than the other way around, will be getting their children off to a good beginning.

Entertaining New Parents

DEAR MISS MANNERS:
It seems that all my friends are having babies these days. How soon after the birth is it polite to ask them out? Should we allow them to bring the baby with them?

We don't have children, and are not sure we ever will, but we don't want to drift away from our friends who do. What adjustments should we make for them in our social lives?

GENTLE READER:
The chief kindness is to remember that your friends now have children and to try not to hold it against them. That is, you must appear to sympathize with both their admiration for their babies and their difficulties in parking them with responsible people so that they can get away from them.

Of course, you have paid a visit to each newborn and expressed your appreciation of its beauty; and of course, you will continue to include your friends in your usual social activities, giving them time to make arrangements for baby-sitters.

Allow Miss Manners to suggest some other social niceties:

Soon after the baby is born, before the mother is prepared to go out, you might invite the new parents to a dinner in their own home. You cook, you serve—on trays, if necessary—and you clean up. This can be counted as a baby present.

If you have several friends with new babies, you might give a party at which you provide a baby-sitter. Each couple brings its baby and turns it over to your sitter, in a part of your house as remote from the festivities as possible.

Schedule interruptable social events to which your friends may bring their babies. A relaxed Sunday teatime, for example, isn't marred if a parent has to get up at feeding or crying time, but a seated dinner is.

Beautiful Babies

DEAR MISS MANNERS:

You wrote about visiting newborn babies, but you didn't say what the visitor should say if the baby is a mess. I mean, really ugly. I have seen some terrible-looking babies, believe me. And there are the parents, standing there, waiting for me to say something. I heard someone suggest, "My, that *is* a baby!" but that's an old one, and I think the parents are on to it. Can you suggest something for people who don't want to lie and say the baby is beautiful?

GENTLE READER:

It is not a lie. All babies and all brides are beautiful by definition. That is a fact of nature.

Do Not Get Upset Yet

DEAR MISS MANNERS:

People keep asking me if my infant son does things "yet." "How come he doesn't sit up yet?" "Does he eat solids yet?" "Does he recognize you yet?" "He doesn't have much hair yet, does he?" Things like that. The implication seems to be that he is behind what he ought to be doing at his age, and I don't like it. Why should he have to conform to their timetables? Am I wrong to take offense?

GENTLE READER:

As it is difficult to ask a newborn baby if he has seen any good movies lately, one does what one can in the way of conversation. You are free to turn the conversation away from the baby. Miss Manners does not, however, recommend doing so by asking visitors, "Is your daughter married yet?" or "Have you found a new job yet?"

Adoption

DEAR MISS MANNERS:

We have recently adopted a beautiful baby boy, whose arrival we happily announced, and many of our friends have sent him nice presents. But most of them behave embarrassingly when they come to visit. Some of them say, "Who does he look like?" and then stop short when they remember he's adopted. Others ask who his "real" parents are or make remarks that suggest that it must be a deep mystery where he came from. As a matter of fact, we know who his natural parents are, but we don't want to talk about them, and we find the term "real" insulting. Why do people behave so strangely with an adopted baby?

GENTLE READER:

Actually, people behave strangely, in one way or another, about any new baby, because there is so little to say about a person of such limited experience. After "How long were you in labor?" and "I think he has your eyes," neither of which is really first-rate conversation, there isn't much left to say, which is why people are at a loss with an adopted baby. As the standard comments are not much less dumb than the ones you are getting, you might as well accept the verbal paucity of the situation and resolve not to be offended. Telling people pleasantly that there are things you refuse to discuss with them sets an excellent example for your baby.

Diapers

DEAR MISS MANNERS:

My mother-in-law and I had always been friends until my baby was born. It seems mom-in-law excels in giving advice, and though I appreciate some helpful hints, I'm up to my diaper pins in hers.

I admit that she slowly needles me into feeling totally inadequate. (I have a degree in child care.) Now, for the nitty-gritty. Is it proper to change one's baby in mixed company? I feel there is nothing vulgar about diapering; m-in-l swiftly disagrees. In fact, she goes as far as snatching my naked child away from me and rushing into an empty room to complete the diapering. Isn't this a bit perverted?

GENTLE READER:

Perverted is perhaps a little strong (presuming that what she does to the baby in the other room is to diaper it). It is a normal instinct for a new grandparent to needle a new mother, and just as normal an instinct for the new mother to have to defend herself.

On the actual issue, Miss Manners must side with your mother-in-law, unless the mixed company consists only of father and grandfather. You would be surprised at how uncute people who are not closely related to the baby think it is to watch a wet or soiled diaper being changed. This is especially true since most babies take the opportunity to hit the fresh diaper before it is even pinned.

In the larger problem, you are right. Degree or no, it is up to you to decide how to rear your baby. The usual way is to thank the grandmother for her advice but not follow it; but as this one seems to be a baby-snatcher, perhaps you had better explain gently that you must learn to do the best you can.

Public Nursing

DEAR MISS MANNERS:

What is your opinion of women who nurse their babies in public?

GENTLE READER:

Miss Manners is fully aware of what will follow her answer. Lactation apparently stimulates the flow of ink in the pen, and nursing mothers emit great cries about the naturalness and beauty of this function and therefore its appropriateness under any circumstances. These cries tend to be louder than the original cries of the babies. Nevertheless, Miss Manners is against the public nursing of babies (or anyone else). There seems to be a basic confusion here between what is natural and/or beautiful, and what is appropriate in public. The two often have very little to do with each other. When people carry on about their right to perform perfectly natural functions in public, Miss Manners suspects them of wanting to add interest to functions normally of interest only to the participants, by performing them in unnatural settings.

DEAR MISS MANNERS:

I believe your opinion of breastfeeding in public was a bit simplistic in that it failed to distinguish between nursing per se and exhibitionism, which a minority of nursing mothers practice while they feed their babies. It is hard to understand why you would oppose discreet public breastfeeding (it can easily be done so discreetly that the only obvious sign of it is the swallowing noise) any more than you would oppose bottlefeeding in public. I feel etiquette is rather poorly served by social pressure either to bottlefeed (known to be nutritionally and medically inferior to breastfeeding) or to remove oneself from society.

GENTLE READER:

Miss Manners knew, when she took up the subject of public breastfeeding, that she was going to end up accused of depriving hungry infants of warmth, love, and sustenance. This was not her intention. Nor does saying a thing is inappropriate in public constitute ''social pressure'' against its being performed at all; if so, the human race would have ended some time ago.

Exposing the female breast for any purpose other than getting a suntan on southern French beaches is considered an exhibition, which is not to say it should not be done when that is the intent. You are asking about mothers whose intent is only to feed their babies. In that case, Miss Manners' only objection about doing it discreetly is the fear that babies don't breathe well under ladies' sweaters.

Public Fusses

DEAR MISS MANNERS:
What can you do about people who make a fuss over your baby in a public place, such as a bus or the supermarket? People will lean into the baby's face, talk baby talk, and grab her hand. First of all, that's a good way for a baby to get a cold, and anyway, it seems to me the baby is entitled to as much privacy from people we don't know as I am. Nobody tries to get cute with me when I'm on a bus without the baby.

GENTLE READER:
In one sense, all babies are the property of the human race. In another sense, it is the parents, rather than the human race, who stay up with them at night when they have colds. If you accept restrained admiration gracefully, you may ward off close contact with the placid remark, "I hope it's not something catching that Baby has."

Baby Talk

DEAR MISS MANNERS:
Pamela and I have been best friends all our lives, and I hope always will be. We survived lots of squabbles when we were little kids, living two blocks from each other, and a big problem when she left college, where we shared a room, to marry a boy I didn't then like. Now he's a best friend of mine, too, and was the main one who helped me two years ago, when my father died. One problem I had at their house has now been solved—they used always to be urging me to get married, and if I brought a boyfriend there, they would go into this newlywed happiness act, holding hands, etc., to give the boy the idea, and I had to stop taking anyone there who might scare easily.

I say that's solved now, because I am getting married, and there's no reason that the four of us can't be best friends, as my fiancé likes them very much.

Now we have a new, similar problem. Pamela and Richie have a four-month-old baby. We have great times when they get a baby-sitter and we all go out together, but that's all there is to the friendship anymore. If I go over to the house during the day, Pamela is always too busy to talk to me, even if the baby is asleep. If I go there in the evening, with or without my fiancé, they make the baby the center of attention, and then they do a new act—about how wonderful it is to be parents and how we ought to have lots of babies. We're not even married yet, and anyway, I'm not sure I ever want to have children. Not if it dominates my life like it does theirs.

Are Pam and Richie always going to be one step ahead like that? Should we forget about them and find friends who share our interests now?

GENTLE READER:
1. Yes. 2. No.

Indeed, the great milestones of life, such as marriage and parenthood, are fascinating to those who are in them and less so to those who are not. It is interesting that Richie was of particular comfort to you during another, less attractive, such time; perhaps he had known what it was, before you did, to lose a parent, as he has known before you the joys of marriage and parenthood. This time difference will sometimes be an annoyance to you, and sometimes an advantage. Are we to have only temporary friends whose experiences happen, at the moment, to match ours? Miss Manners sometimes fears that we live in a society where friends, and even spouses, are supposed to be relevant, like college courses in the 1960s, or else discarded.

Her suggestion to you is to make a new friend—of that baby. If you do have children of your own, you will find the experience useful, and if you don't, you may be especially grateful some day to have a friend in a generation younger than your own. One should not wait to begin such a friendship until the child reaches whatever stage of development you now consider interesting. If you begin to enjoy that child now, either while the mother is there or, giving the mother a chance to get away, by yourself or just with you and your fiancé, you will enrich your friendship with her parents and probably develop a new lifelong friend.

Baby-sitters

DEAR MISS MANNERS:

I can handle my social life fine—the part when I'm out, that is. It's before I go out and after I come home that the etiquette problems occur. With the baby-sitter. I've had them ranging in age from twelve to eighty-two, and the problems range from the one I found asleep in our bed with a friend (and this wasn't one of the teenagers, either) to the one who rearranged everything in the kitchen cabinets. I've been told to provide special foods, transportation to and from their homes, and a new television set because ours doesn't get the educational channels. Over one thing or another, most of them have gone away mad, including two who were the children of friends of mine, or rather, ex-friends. Could you please tell me what the proper behavior is toward baby-sitters, not forgetting to include the correct thing to say when you come home and find comparative strangers making love in your bed.

GENTLE READER:

There is no use deciding what the correct thing would be to say under those circumstances, because you will undoubtedly say, anyway, "Hey—what are you doing?" This isn't even a sensible question, because it is perfectly obvious what they are doing, but it is always asked on such an occasion.

As for the rest of it, you can minimize the problems by spelling out beforehand what the working conditions are. Baby-sitters should not be expected to do housework, other than cleaning up after themselves, unless there is extra compensation, but they should not be able to use your house as a free motel, either. The employer is generally expected to provide transportation and some food; the employee to enjoy some mild amusement, such as watching television, after the children have been put to bed. You might spell out your resources and expectations when you provide the standard information, such as feeding and disciplining instructions, emergency numbers, your whereabouts, and the hour of your return. "I don't feel that this is a job that allows you to entertain others during working hours" is the way you phrase the rule about not messing up your sheets.

DEAR MISS MANNERS:

I am divorced with three small children, ages two through eight years. Here is my question: When I go out on dates, I am usually stuck with paying the baby-sitting bill. This can range anywhere from five dollars to as much as ten dollars for one evening. Is it proper for the man to offer to pay for the sitter? After all, I would not be out this money if it were not for going out on the date. All my dates are far more well off than I am financially. Having three children and being single, I am on a very fixed budget. Sometimes I have to turn down dates because I cannot afford to pay the sitter. Is it proper to let the person know you cannot go out with him unless he volunteers to pay for the baby-sitting? I have talked with a lot of other women in my same situation. Please let us know what is the best way to handle this problem.

GENTLE READER:

Please do not think Miss Manners unsympathetic to single mothers with financial problems. She must tell you that the sort of thinking that begins, "After all, I would not be out this money if it were not for . . ." can lead to no good.

You would also possibly not be out the money for the dress you wore; and you are missing any money you could be earning by working that evening. On the other hand, you have transferred your food and entertainment costs to someone else. Do you see how detestable that type of calculation is? However, Miss Manners wouldn't dream of leaving you the poorer for being proper. She has a suggestion. Get together with all those other women in the same plight, and take turns baby-sitting for one another free.

Basic

Civilization

Concerning Children

❧ MANNERS TOWARD CHILDREN

Parental Rudeness

A well-bred person always takes the side of the weak against the strong, but nevertheless Miss Manners has promised to say something on behalf of children against their parents.

Namely: Rudeness to children counts as rudeness. The fact that people are smaller and blood relatives does not mean that it is open season on insulting them. Besides, it teaches them the technique and thus leads to such tedious exchanges as "Don't you dare talk to Mommy like that," "But that's what you said to me," "That's different," "Why is it different?" and so on. What makes it different is that when children do it, parents call it "sassing," and when parents do it, parents call it "discipline."

Heaven knows that Miss Manners is not against the disciplining of children. We are all born charming, frank, and spontaneous and must be civilized before we are fit to participate in society. In a fit of exasperation, Miss Manners once demanded of a six-year-old person how it could be so childish and was forced to

49

admit the justice of its reply, "I'm a child." Admission of this state is a temporary excuse at best, and one that one's loved ones should help one to overcome. However, humiliation is neither a proper nor an effective method of disciplining children. Personal insults and public rebukes should be avoided.

It is one thing, for example, for a well-meaning parent in the sanctity of the home to deliver a mild reprimand: "You do that once more and I'll kill you." It is quite another thing if other people are present, or if the remark is personalized, as in, "Get it through your thick head that if you do that once more . . . ," etc. Miss Manners rules out the use of invective under any circumstances. The other problem—the question of going public—is more complex. Children invite public denouncement by their many social sins of omission and commission, and are stimulated to produce more if they think they are safe from criticism.

Therefore, Miss Manners considers it essential to child rearing that every parent develop a code that the children understand but outsiders do not. Anyone who has ever been married has had experience with such codes. One person at a social gathering smiles and lifts the eyebrows very slightly in the direction of his or her spouse. It is nothing that anyone else, including the hosts, cannot be allowed to see. Yet it clearly means, "I can't stand this anymore—let's get out of here." Similarly, a parent must develop a way of smiling at a child, perhaps with narrowed eyes, or a way of holding the child's wrist, which conveys to the child that he is storing up serious trouble. One also needs a way of staring brightly at the child that prompts him to search his mind for the phrase, such as "How do you do?" or "Thank you" or "I'm sorry I broke your lamp," that he has neglected to utter.

As an incentive, the child might be encouraged to develop a way of looking sadly at the parent that will remind the parent not to commit other rudenesses in public, such as answering questions that were asked of the child, or falsely citing the child's needs as a social excuse for not doing something the parent doesn't want to do.

Insults from Others

DEAR MISS MANNERS:

I would like to share with you some comments made to my tall and lovely thirteen-year-old daughter—comments made by well-bred, usually courteous adults:

Good grief! You're so tall for your age!

You've grown so much since I saw you three weeks ago!

How on earth does your family keep you in clothes!

Never do these adults consider their negative remarks about another's physical appearance to be the least bit rude. But how would these same individuals like to hear some of the following remarks about their physical appearance:

What's left of your hair is getting so gray!

You've gained so much weight since I saw you three weeks ago!

Why are your teeth so brown?
My, but you're flabby for your age!
Do you dye your hair?
Several facts need to be faced.

1. Kids are getting taller and healthier and more physically fit than previous generations. Thank goodness!

2. One's size is determined at the time of conception. There is, therefore, little that one can do about height.

3. Constantly hearing negative utterances about one's height can only make a child feel that there is something very wrong, in spite of parental assurances that tall is beautiful and normal. The end result will be self-consciousness, shyness, poor posture, and a negative self-concept. Please, if you've ever made negative remarks about a child's size—think about it. Say something positive to the child or buzz off!

GENTLE READER:

Indeed. Miss Manners hopes you will not for a moment accuse her of arguing with your principle—that personal remarks addressed to individuals of any age should be complimentary—if she quibbles with your examples.

The expressions of surprise that children grow taller, rather than smaller, are not stunning instances of observation and tact. Miss Manners does not see them as insults, either. It is generally agreed upon in society that aging is an excellent thing from birth to, say, thirty, but a terrible misfortune from then on. Miss Manners has never understood why this is. To watch individuals change with the years can be interesting, if predictable, but to regard it as either a miracle or a shame seems naïve and futile.

However, that is society's attitude, and Miss Manners is normally given to accepting conventions rather than fighting them. Given this assumption, comments on your daughter's growth should be taken as compliments. Miss Manners suspects you see in them an attitude that she hopes and believes has been discarded by society—that boys, but not girls, should be tall. Without arguing genetics with you, she endorses your policy of conveying a positive attitude to your daughter, and suggests that you extend this by teaching her to reply properly. Not, ''And I see you're getting to be a little stooped over as you get older,'' but ''Why, thank you very much.''

DEAR MISS MANNERS:

My child bites his nails. He is a sensitive child, and it hurts him very deeply when adults say to him, as they often do, ''Oh, I see you're a nail biter,'' or something like that. Why do people think they can say such personal things to children that they wouldn't dream of saying to grown-ups?

GENTLE READER:

Because children are smaller than they are. This is not a legitimate excuse, but it does explain the bullying techniques of many adults. You never hear such people making helpful critiques to fifteen-year-olds on the high school wrestling teams. You might teach your child to explain that his violin teacher (fencing master, typing instructor—whatever) requires that he keep his nails short.

Children Should Be . . .

The idea that children should be heard, as well as seen, has been abroad in the land for some time now, and just look at the place. Miss Manners believes that civilized society as we know it will come to an end on the day the present fourth graders are let loose upon the world.

If the wise adage needed amendment, it might be added that some children should never be seen, either. Most, however, merely need to be taught to listen. Miss Manners has noticed many well-meaning parents doing their children a disservice by encouraging them to express themselves, particularly when the adults are trying to talk. It would be more in the children's interest if they were encouraged to listen to adult conversation. They might pick up something they can use against their elders later.

The current school of child rearing is based on two mistaken notions: that children are naturally good, and that they are naturally creative. If children are naturally good, why do they teach themselves to walk by holding on to the edge of the dining room tablecloth? If they are naturally creative, why do they all draw alike?

Miss Manners is not, however, advocating switching to suppressing rudely the spontaneity of little children. It can be done politely. (Miss Manners is a non-allied power in the war of the generations and also attacks adults who are rude to children.)

Rather than zipping up their wee mouths, Miss Manners suggests that adults stun babbling children into silence by asking them nicely to explain what they mean. If they are being truly natural and creative, they have neglected to figure out this point. One hopes that the more promising ones may therefore be shocked enough by this question to rummage around in their minds, sort out the mess, and endeavor to express themselves with clarity and supporting evidence. This should not only make it possible for the adults to hear themselves think, but for the children to be forced to think. As a by-product, we may get some creative adults from these children. Haven't you noticed that all artistic people brag about having been suppressed as children?

Children at Table

DEAR MISS MANNERS:

My husband is a fanatic about table manners. Every evening he comes up with a new rule. This is very nerve-racking to my daughter and me.

Will you please give me a list of the absolute no-no's? I have tried to convince him that some of the strict rules have been relaxed. Our daughter is eight years old, and our son is five. They are expected to eat perfectly or the dinner becomes a fiasco. I say that nagging and disrupting what should be an enjoyable family time is bad manners. What do you say?

GENTLE READER:

Is the choice between family harmony and teaching the children table manners? If so, Miss Manners would like to be excused from your table.

There are two social purposes to family dinner: the regular exchange of news and ideas, and the opportunity to teach small children not to eat like pigs. These are by no means mutually exclusive. Mrs. Perfect, for example, merely has to maintain a patient and cheerful tone: "Cutlip, dear, do tell us about your class trip to the zoo. . . . Now, swallow what's in your mouth first, and then we'll all listen. . . . Daffodil, dear, take your fingers out of your plate. How did your social studies report go . . . . Mommy's going to tell you what she said to the traffic policeman. Just pick it up quietly, Cutlip, and say excuse me and take it into the kitchen and throw it away and then come back and finish your vegetables. . . . Don't interrupt, darling. It'll be your turn to talk in a minute. Sit up, please, and put your left hand in your lap. So the policeman came up and Mommy said, 'Wait a minute, officer' . . ." And so on. One can become quite proficient at this amiable patter; the trick is to omit the instructive parts when attending formal dinner parties outside of the house.

It would be a mistake for Miss Manners to provide you with a list of no-no's. It may never have occurred to your children to laugh with a mouthful of soup, for instance, or to discharge unappreciated salad ingredients into the napkin. Here, instead, are a few yes-yes's. Small children should be expected to wait until their mother begins eating; to use their forks, knives, and napkins as God meant them to be used; to refrain from mentioning their dislikes on the menu; to pretend to listen attentively when others are speaking; to ignore the toy potential of various food items; and not to leave the table without permission. Older children should be expected to have table manners as good as or better than their parents'.

Expectations are not always fulfilled, of course. What Miss Manners really means is that children should be repeatedly reminded to do these things in such a way as not to interfere with the opportunity for pleasant family conversation, but as to make basic table manners such a constant requirement that they become automatic before the children reach maturity. Then you and your husband can dine in peace.

Guest Children

DEAR MISS MANNERS:

I don't allow bad language in my house, and I believe my children have learned our standards enough not to say those words elsewhere either, although I know that most people do. Last night, my son's friend, who was having dinner with us, said a four-letter word at the table. It slipped very casually into the conversation, but I was stunned. Too stunned, I'm afraid, to say anything. And yet when I thought about it afterwards, I felt as if I had set a bad example to my children in permitting another child to do what I would not let them do. How should I have handled this?

GENTLE READER:

Exactly as you did: by looking stunned but saying nothing. It is one thing to teach children to behave better than the rest of the world, and quite another to teach them to teach the rest of the world. If you make their task that heavy, they are likely to abandon it.

The Children of Others

DEAR MISS MANNERS:

While attending a dinner with my husband's family, I was irritated by the obnoxious behavior of my husband's nieces and nephew, ages four to ten: running about, screaming, chasing each other, the youngest son repeatedly banging on the organ, etc. All the while, the parents did little to discourage the noise and activity, even encouraging their "creativity." Already somewhat uncomfortable, I was provoked to remark to my sister that I felt the children were far too wild, and that the parents just weren't raising them right.

Too late, I realized the father, my husband's brother-in-law, might possibly have overheard my comment. I'd like to apologize to him if he did overhear me, but in case he didn't, I don't want to imply that anything was wrong. Please, can you suggest a tactful way to handle this?

GENTLE READER:

Why is it that Miss Manners assumes you have no children of your own? If that is the case, you probably insulted your brother-in-law less than you fear. Childless people firmly believe that being brought up properly prevents children from making noise or running about. Parents, having been childless themselves, tend to remember that attitude with some humor. No doubt your in-laws are chuckling happily about the disillusionment in store for you if you have children of your own. One compliment about the children, unconnected with the previous insult, should remove any hurt.

But this is not to say that Miss Manners does not believe that children can be taught to behave themselves. It's just that behaving themselves is not the same thing as behaving like little adults for long periods of time.

At the Perfects' family dinner, the proper entertainment for children is not sitting around discussing whether Aunt Primrose is going dotty, or if Cousin Victorine is going to marry that creature who seems to be sharing her apartment. They are sent out to play, whether it is outdoors or in another room. With luck, that will tire them enough to keep them quiet at the dinner table.

If you really want to improve the behavior of these children, you, as their aunt, may arrange occasions to consort with them individually and impart some manners to them. You could invite one to your house and gently explain the "rules of the house" when she or he exhibits poor manners. Invite one out for a treat, such as lunch in a restaurant, and insist on proper behavior. The privilege of individual attention from an adult other than a parent should be enough to compensate for the expectation of manners.

However, you may not have that much interest in contributing to the education of these children—perhaps your deepest motivation is to keep them from knocking your drink into your lap while you are attending obligatory family dinners. In that case, grab an offending child by the arm and say, with a firm voice and hypocritical smile, "I think you'd better stop that—you might get hurt." It helps if you have a tight grip on the arm while saying this.

Unrelated Children

DEAR MISS MANNERS:

My neighborhood used to be nice, eleven years ago when we had an orchard, but when they tore it down to put up a housing development, well, that's when my troubles began. "Kids" with dirty mouths—I mean six-, eight-, and nine-year-olds and even thirteen-year-olds—are bothering me. They write bad things, throw walnuts, spray water over the fence, stone the house—well, I could go on and on. Everything is calm at the moment, but what am I to do if it starts again? I am in the middle, with no children of my own.

GENTLE READER:

Two approaches tend to become confused when one is dealing with unmannerly (and unrelated) children. One is protecting oneself, and the other is teaching them to behave. Both are difficult to accomplish, and it is unfortunate that many innocent people suffer from the rudenesses of children whose parents have neglected to teach them to behave.

You cannot assume the parental function of instructing strange children. As much as it may need doing, it simply cannot be done. If you want to take the trouble to make friends with these children to the point that they will want to please you, that is another matter. If, however, your desire is merely to protect yourself from annoyance, you must confine your complaints to recognizably punishable offenses and not small rudenesses, however unpleasant. Miss Manners would ignore rubbishy mail, for example, but report property damage to the police and let them explain the laws to the parents. If you can control the sticks and stones, that is, the words will never hurt you.

MANNERS FOR CHILDREN

What a pity it is that most children have become too hardened by life to be capable of imagining what it is like to be a grown-up. The wonder and the innocence with which parents regard the early years of schooling is something that children are simply unable to understand.

The harsh truth is that there is no more hostile and humiliating social environment than grades K through eight. There is no ambiguity in the insults; descending the scale of popularity is not like stepping on a down escalator but rather like stepping into an empty elevator shaft; and there is no escape, either, into new circles or old philosophy.

Yet parents, bless their hearts, see it as a rosy time of laughter and irresponsibility. That is why the most loving of them will pooh-pooh the announcement of a social stomachache—the child's equivalent of the social headache—or cut off a story of full-scale social warfare with, "Oh, I'm sure it'll all be forgotten by tomorrow and you'll be as good friends as ever." There is charm to this naïveté, and the thoughtful child will take care to preserve parental illusions. Let those dear people be, in their own happy world, and come and listen to some tough social truths from your own Miss Manners.

You have heard, perhaps, of such advantages as beauty, brains, wealth, or charm. Forget them. It may be accepted, in your class, that this person is "pretty" and that one "smart"; it may be known that one has a big allowance and another is always nice enough to share. In this age group, none of these characteristics has anything to do with popularity, and often they have nothing to do with the people who are supposed to have them.

The child who is thought good-looking is merely one (often a plain one) who is smart enough to make people think so. The one with a reputation for being smart is dumb enough to think that if he or she cultivates the teacher, class favor will result. Those who flash money or press their possessions on others are taken for suckers.

The only social skill worth having in this unpleasant milieu is the ability to appear indifferent to the opinions of others, neither seeking their love nor noticing their scorn. Those who can manage this will be rewarded with popularity, and those who seem anxious to possess popularity will be either slaves or outcasts, the toadies or the victims of those who have it. Popular children often behave badly because, as we know, power corrupts. But those who commit the sin of wanting to be popular usually behave scandalously, competing in their cruelties to one another for the favor of those above.

Miss Manners begs you, whatever your rank, not to indulge in the practice of taunting or maligning others. She would not dream of appealing to your moral sense with this plea, but advances it on strictly practical grounds. Excessive meanness, like excessive generosity, is correctly interpreted by children as anxiety to please, which they consider the greatest of social crimes. It is also a terrible gamble. The cards are shuffled every summer in this age group, with many people smartening up over the holidays through new experiences or having read Miss Manners. The person it was safe to taunt last year may be the ruling power this year.

Calm, cheerful, pleasant, unruffled indifference, no matter how severe the provocation, is your only hope of achieving popularity. Even if you fail, you will be loved later in life by those to whom you recount your brave attempts. Confessing to having been a bully is worth nothing in the tame adult world.

Caring for Grown-ups

A well-behaved grown-up is a credit and a joy to his or her child. It distresses Miss Manners to see so many children carelessly trampling on their grown-ups' tender feelings, when a little courtesy and attention would transform sullen and edgy adults into cheerful and cooperative parents.

The sensitive child will notice that grown-ups worry endlessly about the judgment of their peers and can be thrown into agonies of embarrassment by trivial transgressions of conventionality. It does not take much effort to cater to these little prejudices, and the returns, emotional and otherwise, are enormous.

Adults are full of secrets. They find it humiliating to have people know the most basic, and often the most obvious, facts about themselves. A child is expected to reveal his age and grade level whenever asked, and he is constantly asked. But adult society pretends to make a mystery of such things as age and income, and the polite child will respect this, no matter what he thinks of it. He will steadfastly claim ignorance of what birthday a parent just celebrated, what was paid for the house, and what was said at the dinner table discussion of who is getting ahead of whom at the office.

Loyalty also demands that the child suppress any knowledge of behavior that makes his parents look bad. Cute stories about their squabbles and their party behavior should not be repeated outside the family, no matter how amusing.

On the contrary, the child has an obligation to defend his family against any disparagement, no matter how justified he believes it to be. To know, better than anyone, how impossible your relatives are, and to be ready to kill the outsider who suggests such a thing, is the essence of family chivalry.

Respect must be shown to the grown-ups' peculiar ideas of what is proper and what improper in matters of dress and behavior. The intelligent child knows that such customs are not questions of right and wrong but of transitory group standards, and he is able to master more than one standard. To dress as your parents prefer when going out with them or appearing before their friends should entitle one to adopt the fashions of one's contemporaries when one is among them. Observing their social rituals, including pretending to be interested in their friends, is extremely important. The child who greets his parents' guests, engages in small talk with them, and excuses himself politely when he can bear no more of their silliness, has earned the right to have his own friends made appropriately welcome.

None of this is difficult to perform, although it requires some patience to make parents understand that courtesy is reciprocal. In the end, a parent who is continuously exposed to high standards of politeness and consideration cannot fail to be the better for it.

Important Interruptions

DEAR MISS MANNERS:
Should you tell your mother something if it is important when she is talking to company? I am six.
GENTLE READER:
Yes, you should (after saying "Excuse me").
Here are some of the things that are important to tell your mother, even though she is talking to company:
"Mommy, the kitchen is full of smoke."
"Daddy's calling from Tokyo."
"Kristen fell out of her crib and I can't put her back."
"There's a policeman at the door and he says he wants to talk to you."
"I was just reaching for my ball, and the goldfish bowl fell over."
Now, here are some things that are not important, so they can wait until your mother's company has gone home:
"Mommy, I'm tired of playing blocks. What do I do now?"
"The ice cream truck is coming down the street."
"Can I give Kristen the rest of my applesauce?"
"I can't find my crayons."
"When are we going to have lunch? I'm hungry."

The Child Who Came to Dinner

DEAR MISS MANNERS:
I got a friend. My mommy invited him to dinner one time. Now he comes for dinner every day. My mommy told me to let him eat because we don't want to hurt his feelings. How can we tell him not to come every day?
GENTLE READER:
Ask your mommy to call his mommy. She could say, "We have enjoyed having Adam to dinner this week, Mrs. Awful. We hope he can come again. Two weeks from Saturday would be the next time that is good for us—could he come then?"

Secrets

DEAR MISS MANNERS:
I told my closest friend a deep dark secret that I didn't want anyone else in the world to know, and she went around blabbing it to everyone. Don't you think that's disgusting and wrong? I don't feel I can trust anybody now.
GENTLE READER:
One can never learn to trust others until one has learned to trust oneself. Who blabbed first, you or she?

Privacy

DEAR MISS MANNERS:

Every time this situation comes up, I don't know what to do. I am fifteen years old and when my mother or father receives a package in the mail, for example, or when a package comes from a fish store or a package to my mother comes from my grandparents, I am very curious as to what is in the box. Should I hold back my curiosity and let them open their own mail, or go ahead and open it?

GENTLE READER:

You are setting yourself up for a loss of privacy. You will not always be fifteen. You will some day be old enough to receive interesting mail. Your parents will be very curious as to what is in it. Will you want them to hold back their curiosity and let you open your own mail, or do you want them to go ahead and open it, or even ask your permission to open it?

The proper attitude toward other people's mail, especially that of one's close relatives, is to pretend ignorance of its existence and to let the recipient speak of it, show it, share it, or not, as that person chooses. Believe Miss Manners that such a policy will be well worth your establishing. The package from the fish store probably only had fish in it, anyway.

A Civil Native Tongue

DEAR MISS MANNERS:

I have a good friend in high school who is from another country. She speaks English fluently. Another girl came up to us who is foreign and also speaks English, and they began talking in their language. I was left out in the cold. My mother says I should tell them to speak English. What should I say?

GENTLE READER:

Try asking them pleasantly, "What does that mean?" every time they say two words. This will double the amount of time it takes them to say anything, and may encourage them to realize that it would be simpler for them to speak English. If not, it will give you the opportunity to learn their language, so it will be time well spent.

The Double Insult

DEAR MISS MANNERS:

My father always criticizes me when my little sister does something wrong. I don't mean he blames me for what she has done, but he says things like "Why are you two always breaking things?" or "Children—stop that this instant." But I wasn't doing anything wrong! It's so unfair! Don't you think it's insulting to do that to a person who wasn't at fault?

GENTLE READER:

Yes, but it's an interesting category of insult, which may be taken as offhandedly as it is given. What your father is administering is known as the Double Insult. Technically, only one insult has been delivered—to you—because what your sister has received is a reprimand. The trick is to include in one's remark as many innocent people as possible. If your father were more advanced in this specialty, he might say, for instance, "You children are always so clumsy, just like your mother." Presuming that you and your mother were both minding your own business when the act that set him off was committed, he will have gotten two extra people for the price of one. Or he could say "like your mother's side of the family," which would, with four extra words, extend the insult to countless numbers of other people, depending on how many generations you consider this to include. Or he could say "your generation" instead of "you children," thus including people who aren't even related to him. As you see, it is a great art, and your father is practicing only a mild version of it.

Condescension

DEAR MISS MANNERS:

I am tired of being treated like a child. My father says it's because I am a child—I am twelve-and-a-half years old—but it still isn't fair. If I go into a store to buy something, nobody pays any attention to me, or if they do, it's to say, "Leave that alone," "Don't touch that," although I haven't done anything. My money is as good as anybody's, but because I am younger, they feel they can be mean to me. It happens to me at home, too. My mother's friend who comes over after dinner sometimes, who doesn't have any children of her own and doesn't know what's what, likes to say to me, "Shouldn't you be in bed by now, dear?" when she doesn't even know what my bedtime is supposed to be. Is there any way I can make these people stop?

GENTLE READER:

Growing up is the best revenge.

Being Kind to Creeps

DEAR MISS MANNERS:

The mother of a boy in my class is a friend of my mother's. This boy is also a creep and no one likes him. My mother wanted me to invite him to my birthday party, but I told her it would spoil everything, and she said it was my birthday, so I didn't have to, but I did have to be nice to him in some way. So I offered to show him my report card if he would show me his, but he ran away and told his mother I was mean to him and she told my mother. Now I'm in trouble. Do you believe me that I was being friendly, or do you think I was being mean, or what?

GENTLE READER:

Or what. Miss Manners hopes you are in sufficient trouble now so that you will not grow up to offer to compare paychecks with people you believe to be earning less than you.

(For the behavior of children in a divorce, please see pp. 569–571.)

❧ CHILDREN'S SOCIAL EVENTS

Birthday Parties

Of all the social rituals practiced in our civilization, the birthday party for young children is by far the most revolting. It must be endured, however, because it is a learning experience.

Miss Manners is, of course, referring to the lessons to be learned by parents who partake in such events. Children occasionally also learn something, such as how to control their rage and smile weakly after a parent has publicly inquired, "Did you say thank you?" but that skill is hardly worth the event. Certainly no child has learned from social exposure to produce an intelligent answer to the question "What does it feel like to be eight years old?" But, then, as Miss Manners has never heard an intelligent answer to the question "What does it feel like to be forty?" perhaps that fault is in the question.

It is the parents of the birthday child who learn most from the experience, sometimes such handy information as the replacement value of their property. The smart ones also learn quickly to find sites for parties other than their homes. (The behavior of children at a birthday party is not necessarily a result of their being badly brought up. Group dynamics nullify the results of discipline, and six well-behaved six-year-olds are the social equivalent of six hundred angry Bolsheviks.)

Parents learn social planning through these parties, which require both precision and flexibility in amounts never dreamed of by those who have mastered the giving of seated formal dinners for eighteen. The minimum time for which one can decently invite guests is two hours. Children do not engage in the activity of "chatting," the standard fill-in between chewing periods in adult entertainment. For that matter, they cannot be depended upon to consume time, or sometimes even food, at chewing time. A party of children under ten years of age will spend an average of twelve minutes at the luncheon table, including the time taken up by one child's explaining to the resident parent how exactly his allergies match the menu.

Parents also learn rehearsal techniques, as they instruct their children on that great social skill, faking pleasure, as it is applied to duplicate presents and wallflower guests. The parent then enjoys the sensations of a theatrical director who stands at the back of the auditorium on opening night, watching everything he has attempted to do go down the drain. A parent must also learn the restraint of a director, who usually controls himself from rushing onto the stage to correct everyone.

The most important lesson to be learned by the host parent is what it feels like to:

1. Look out the window with a child at the appointed time of arrival and not see anyone at all running up the steps with a package under the arm.

2. Look out the window, at the appointed time of departure, your living room full of chaos behind you, and not see any parents trudging up the steps.

If the parent learns to deliver and fetch his own children on time when they are attending another child's birthday party, it will have been a successful learning experience.

A Courteous Child

DEAR MISS MANNERS:

My little daughter was heartbroken about each child who couldn't attend her seventh birthday party. It seems to matter so much to them at that age. So we have worked out a system when she can't go to another child's party. She invites the child over some time within the week of the birthday and gives her a birthday present.

GENTLE READER:

That is charming. Miss Manners is always gratified to hear of the existence of another polite child in the world. There were so few at last count.

Saying Thank You

DEAR MISS MANNERS:

I am trying to teach my child, who is a precocious five-year-old, to be natural in company, but what do I do about getting him to be polite? The case in point is a birthday party at which I prompted him, when I picked him up, to tell his hostess that he had a nice time. I was mortified, because he said, "I didn't!" It later turned out that he had gotten into a quarrel at the table with the birthday child and another little boy, and a lot of tears were shed. Obviously, he didn't have "a nice time." Is there something else he could say, which is polite but not dishonest?

GENTLE READER:

"Thank you for inviting me." However, this is not going to solve your basic problem, which is that you have given the child an impossible task by asking him to express his true feelings and, at the same time, to be gentle with other people's feelings. Miss Manners would choose the latter. Teaching a child to "be natural" seems a silly endeavor, but teaching him to say a big booming "Thank you" will serve him forever.

Christmas Day

Dear Aunt Patience,
    Now I can hardly
wait for snow so I can
use your nice present!
Thank you very much.
    I hope you are
having a wonderful
Christmas, too, and are
getting lots of things
you need.

       Love,
       Daffodil

A letter from a child, thanking the giver of a present. Children may use almost any colorful or fanciful writing paper, and are therefore excellent recipients of the paper that adults sometimes buy on impulse or receive from others, which is too silly for them to use. Note the date on this letter.

Writing Thank You

DEAR MISS MANNERS:
What do you think of sending thank-you notes to hosts after a three-year-old's birthday party? It seems to me an exaggeration of a social convention, vulgar because it is inappropriate.
GENTLE READER:
Inappropriate, but not vulgar. The appropriate letter for a three-year-old's parents to write to people who have been his hosts at a party of small children is an apology.

Cakes with Candles

DEAR MISS MANNERS:
After a certain age, people prefer a token number of candles on their birthday cakes. What is that age?
GENTLE READER:
Sixteen. After that, there may be a good year or two left in which one's exhaling powers can keep up with the task, but it is best to stop piling on the kindling while one is still sure of being equal to the spark one has inspired. (These metaphors tend to run away with your Miss Manners, and if she seems to be advising you to trade passion for companionship in the mid-teens, please disregard.)

Spending the Night

Children dear, if you don't learn now the proper way to behave when you spend the night with a friend, how do you expect to have any fun when you grow up?

Staying overnight is the second most common major social activity among medium-sized children and therefore second among the opportunities they have to disgrace their own parents and disgust the parents of their friends. The first is the birthday party, as we have seen. The number of guests and the malleability of the food at a birthday party enable an enterprising child to develop, during its mere two-hour span, a level of hellishness that is impossible to achieve even during the eighteen-hour overnight visit.

Nevertheless, spending the night offers many occasions for big and small rudenesses, and the child who wishes to grow up popular, or in some cases who wishes to grow up at all, should be taught to avoid them. Knowing the proper manners for being a graceful overnight guest will serve a person in good stead, in fact in better and better stead, all his or her life.

The first rule is to bring the proper equipment, and to take it home with you when you leave. It is not at all cute, at any age, to expect to share a toothbrush or hairbrush with a friend, and small items can be tucked in pockets, knapsacks, or schoolbags when any possibility of an impromptu overnight visit exists. Children should inquire whether they should bring their own sleeping bags, if they have them. Leaving things behind, whether from the hope of being asked back or the failure to double-check the room, is a nuisance for hosts.

The guest must be friendly to everyone there, not just the person who invited him. That includes parents, siblings, and other guests. The child who doesn't look his friend's parents in the eye and talk to them will grow up to pretend a friend's roommate doesn't exist. In both cases, he will have induced reluctance to have him there again.

Make the time of departure specific, and depart on time. This may entail the child's nagging his own parents to be sure to pick him up when they are supposed to. Urging to stay longer should, in all ordinary cases, be ignored. Leave 'em crying for more is a principle best learned early in life.

By law, guests of any age enjoy doing and eating whatever their hosts want to do and to eat. Some wily people attempt to throw children off by asking them to say what they want to do or whether they like what is being served for dinner. The clever guest admits to no food dislikes, short of things that give him violent physical reactions—and those should be explained at the time of accepting the invitation—and will name a preferred activity only when given a multiple choice by the hosts. Instructions to leave the bed unmade are in the same category with invitations to forget about going home. Nobody is ever revolted by a guest's excessive neatness.

Thank everything that moves. Not only the host and his parents, but the sibling who may have given up his room, the maid who may have to do the sheets, and the goldfish who may have had to move his bowl to give you somewhere to put your hairbrush.

Common Courtesy for All Ages

♣ INTRODUCTIONS AND GREETINGS

Who outranks whom, and therefore who should be introduced to whom, is a matter that Miss Manners is particularly anxious to discuss.

No, that's not quite true. Introductions, these days, range from perfunctory to perfectly dreadful, but Miss Manners has almost learned to live with that. What made her anxious to bring up the subject was the necessity to prove that she knows how to handle "who" and "whom." As for introductions, the rules are simple. One introduces inferiors to their superiors. Thus, men are introduced to women, strangers to one's relatives, young people to old, and common people to exalted ones. There is clearly no problem in performing an introduction between your teenaged cousin who makes license plates and the dowager Duchess of Smelt-Hargrove.

Suppose, however, you have to rank an assistant curator of Japanese beetles and a mechanical engineer specializing in the rolltops of desks—especially if you are not certain what sex they are, let alone what vintage? One would have to quiz them so thoroughly that the introduction, when it was finally performed, would be an anticlimax. Fortunately, Miss Manners has an all-purpose formula for introductions. Let us begin with the classic introduction, and then Miss Manners will explain how to adapt this to baffling circumstances.

Rory Hoppity, who used to be married to your stepsister, has a new job with the snow lobby and has persuaded you to introduce him to your friend the First Lady, whom he has long admired for her unusual ability to reach the President. It is safe to assume that she outranks him.

"Mrs. Eagle," you say, "may I present Mr. Hoppity?" Politics being what they are, Mrs. Eagle restrains herself from replying, "No," and the introduction is complete. Now, suppose, you had said, "May I present Mr. Hoppity, Mrs. Eagle?" That's the same thing, isn't it? The name of the person addressed could really go on either end.

The fill-in words could also be "I have the honor to present" or "I would like to introduce you to," or "this is," or even "do you know," the last being a useful form in introducing apparent strangers when you can't remember if they were once married to each other. We don't always say all the fill-in words, though, do we, in this speedy age? A person who says "Ham on rye" to a waitress is understood to be saying, "I wonder if you would be so good as to ask the chef to prepare me a sandwich, using rye bread, perhaps moistening it a bit with mustard, with a filling of ham in it, please?"

Therefore, the introduction, "Mrs. Perfect, Mrs. Awful," has become common. Everyone understands that this is short for "Mrs. Perfect, may I present Mrs. Awful?" and knows you would never mean to say "This is Mrs. Perfect, Mrs. Awful."

So there you are: a foolproof introduction—unless, of course, you have forgotten the name of one of the people you are introducing. In that case, the form is, "May I present Ms. Tutu?" A person whose name you have forgotten always takes precedence over one whose name you remember.

A Gay Introduction

DEAR MISS MANNERS:

What am I supposed to say when I am introduced to a homosexual "couple"?

GENTLE READER:

"How do you do?" "How do you do?"

The Unspeakable Introduction

DEAR MISS MANNERS:

How do I introduce people who are living together but not married without embarrassing them or offending my other guests?

GENTLE READER:

What type of entertainment do you give, that everyone's sexual affiliations must be declared at the door? Introduce people by their names.

Introducing Servants

DEAR MISS MANNERS:

I have read that it is improper to introduce the maid to one's friends, even if the friends are staying overnight and need to know her name. I read that you perform a half-introduction, such as "Mary will look after your needs; Mary, Mr. Brown will be here two nights." I feel funny about this. I don't want to do the wrong thing in front of a friend, yet I don't want to embarrass my maid, either, or do anything that is undignified toward anyone.

GENTLE READER:

People who are lucky enough to have servants should realize how comparatively easy it is to find a good friend. Miss Manners' inclination, therefore, is to worry about the dignity of the employee before the dignity of the friend. Unless the employee is committed to the old-fashioned method you describe, Miss Manners would prefer that you perform a decent introduction, which includes providing everyone with a last name. "This is Mary Jewel; Mary, Mr. Brown will be occupying the Queen's Bedroom."

Introducing Children

DEAR MISS MANNERS:

I have taught my children to introduce their friends to me, but sometimes they forget. If a child is visiting here, should I, as the lady of the house, greet him first or expect him to greet me?

GENTLE READER:

As you have noticed how hard it is to train one's own child, Miss Manners is astonished that you are contemplating waiting for someone else's child to carry the social burden. She recommends your saying, "I'm Christopher's mother; you must be Scott," rather than waiting, perhaps forever, until your visitor says, "I'm Scott; you must be Christopher's mother."

Introducing Undesirable Relatives

DEAR MISS MANNERS:

My half-brother showed up in town with his dreadful mother, who used to be married to my father, and some equally awful cousins. How can I introduce my brother, whom I like very much, without seeming to be related to the rest of the crowd, whom I don't?

GENTLE READER:

"This is my brother, and some relatives of his, the Boors." The best you can hope for, in this case, is that people think your brother, rather than your father, married badly.

Introducing the Roof Principle

DEAR MISS MANNERS:
How should one conduct oneself in the presence of another whom one has known for an extended period in another place, yet never spoken to? Let me explain. While boarding a bus on my way home from work recently, I noticed on the same bus a fellow with whom I was graduated from law school last June. Although we attended many of the same classes for three years, we never spoke to one another (both being true gentlemen, it could not have been otherwise, since we were never properly introduced). Now that it appears that we will be riding the same bus home, it seems a bit silly to continue ignoring one another, particularly should we ever end up sharing the same seat. Could you arrange an introduction?

GENTLE READER:
Allow Miss Manners to introduce you to a principle: "The roof constitutes an introduction." This does not apply to every roof. It does not apply to a bus, for example, although it does apply to a ship. It does, however, apply to an academic institution. Therefore, it is as proper for you to say, "I believe we were in class together" as it would be, if you had been "properly introduced," to say, "I believe we met at the Wintergreens' last Christmas."

The Assisted Introduction

DEAR MISS MANNERS:
Suppose I'm talking to someone I'm supposed to know, but I can't remember his name. Another person joins us. Can I get them to tell each other their names?

GENTLE READER:
Certainly; who would be in a better position to know what they are? If you know the name of one of them, you can address the other with a firm statement, "This is Hollister Stranger," and then adjust your shoe, thus removing yourself from view and leaving the field clear for the unknown to complete the introduction. If you know neither name, it is wise to remove yourself from the scene entirely, after saying brightly, "I'm sure you two know each other!"

Elusive Memory

DEAR MISS MANNERS:
Is it so awful not to be able to remember people's names? I've tried all kinds of systems, and it never seems to work. I find that if I fake a person's name when

I don't know it, I get caught, but I'm afraid to admit right off that I don't know a name because people get insulted.
GENTLE READER:
We have a great deal of admiration in this country for people who have the ability to remember names. It is considered enough of a talent to qualify an otherwise undistinguished person for public office. If one votes for a candidate because he has remembered one's name from one minute of a campaign appearance to another, it is not reasonable to except such a feat from every private citizen. Miss Manners promises not to be offended if you ask her what her name was again.

Name Tags

DEAR MISS MANNERS:
Where is the correct place to pin a name tag? We use them at our club parties, and I hope you don't disapprove of this practice, because it's very useful. But it looks odd to see everyone bending over, reading one another's bosoms.
GENTLE READER:
Miss Manners disapproves of name tags only at strictly social functions, because she believes they make things too easy and thus take away the fun. When they are used, they should be placed at collar level, for the reason you mention, and they should be on the right-hand side of the wearer. This makes it possible for people to sneak a quick look halfway between the handshake and the face, and then to pretend to have remembered the other person's name.

Mistaken Identity

DEAR MISS MANNERS:
I have struggled unsuccessfully for years with the following problem:
Although I introduce myself to people as "Joanna" or "Jo," many of them immediately (or eventually) call me "JoAnne." Perhaps I would not mind this if my name were JoAnne, but it isn't, and I don't like it.
This is the dilemma: If I make a correction right away, my new acquaintance feels embarrassed and then hostile. But if I wait until we are better acquainted, the person has already formed a bad habit—and you know (not from personal experience, of course) how hard it is to break a bad habit, because practice makes perfect. And he or she will then be angry—"Why didn't you tell me that long ago?"
What would you suggest I do?
GENTLE READER:
Miss Manners very much admires your delicacy in worrying about the embarrassment suffered by people who address you by the wrong name. The next step would be to change your name to accommodate their errors. (Miss Manners was

actually advised to do this by her bank, which mistakenly issued her a card with her given names only, omitting her surname, and then recommended that she use it anyway, with that as her signature. Miss Manners thought this was rather cheeky of the bank, and egotistically insisted that the bank correct its error, rather than that she change her name.)

You need only smile indulgently and say, "It's Joanna with an *a* at the end—a lot of people find it confusing."

Entitled to a Title

DEAR MISS MANNERS:

Some years ago, an elder relative told me one should not announce oneself as Mr. Soandso, because "Mister" is a title and "one does not give a title to oneself."

Having been around for some time and traveled a lot, I have come to know a number of persons with titles of nobility, from the heir apparent of an ex-maharaja to American women who had married European title holders and who, after these men had shed or been shed by the women, went on calling themselves the Baroness von This or the Contessa di That forever. In the British Isles, I once had occasion to telephone Lord Suchandsuch; he answered simply, "Suchandsuch here!" Thus he followed my kinsman's system. But at a convention in England last year, a man in the elevator recognized me, stuck out his hand, and said, "Hello! My name's Lord Thusandso!" He did not obey my relative's rule.

Now, what is the drill on this, if, indeed, there is any rule for (a) "Mister" and (b) titles of nobility? Not that, as an American, I shall ever have a title of nobility; but it would be nice to know.

GENTLE READER:

Your kinsman is obviously one of nature's noblemen. Isn't it nicer to have Miss Manners say that than for him to have to announce it himself?

Why? Because a person who uses a title in reference to himself or herself, whether the title is grand duchess, doctor, maharaja, or even mister, seems suspiciously anxious to establish that he is entitled to that title. People naturally adore addressing others by fancy titles, but they grudge even the simplest to those who insist on them.

The correct British peer would no more dream of using his own title than he would of using his own umbrella, although he carries both and is proud of their age. Your Lord Thusandso probably has a new title and a new umbrella, too, which he enjoys opening in people's faces. Miss Manners has been trying for years to get people who have doctoral degrees to understand this principle of modesty, but they keep protesting that they earned their titles and want to show them off. They fail to understand the greater impact there is in being discovered to have a title that one has not bothered to show off.

People who have titles that are not officially recognized should be even more careful in doing this. Your Baroness von This and Contessa di That are badly in need of such a lesson. Never mind what happened to the baron or the conte— the German and Italian titles themselves have been legally abolished and are only used socially, by courtesy. The best way to ensure their use is by protesting, "Oh, no, we're just plain Hapsburgs now, like everyone else." Your ladies could try the now fashionable Proud American routine that goes, "Please, I can't bear to be called princess—why, I was born and bred in Grand Forks, North Dakota." Either of these approaches will have people on their knees; but an American woman who calls herself "contessa" is assumed to be in the boutique business.

This is true on down the line. The person who announces stiffly, "I'm Mr. Ipswitch" has undoubtedly given you his highest claim to dignity; but the one who says quietly, "My name is Isabel Bourbon," has left some room for grander assumptions.

The Doctors

DEAR MISS MANNERS:
I have several physician friends and when I introduce them and their wives at formal gatherings, the "Doctor and Mrs." title seems just fine. But I have a more troublesome set of friends—a couple in which she is a doctor and her husband is not. I introduced them as "Doctor and Mr." at our last dinner party and he winced as if his hiatal hernia were acting up. How can I properly introduce this couple without discriminating against my female friend or doing irreparable damage to her husband's ego?

GENTLE READER:
Miss Manners fails to understand why a female doctor is any more troublesome to society than male doctors naturally are, or why a man should be more abashed than a woman at being married to someone who takes money from the sick. You introduced him properly. Perhaps his hiatal hernia *was* acting up, in which case he should see a doctor.

DEAR MISS MANNERS:
I have a friend who married a medical doctor. She is also a doctor, and although she legally took his name, she continues to use her maiden name (with the title "Doctor") professionally. My question is: How does one introduce them in social situations?

GENTLE READER:
There are so many possibilities—and people are so unreasonably touchy if you guess the wrong one—that the safest thing is to ask them. Since you ask Miss Manners, however, she suggests that you address them jointly as "the Doctors Botchitt" and introduce each of them as "Dr. Botchitt." Traditionally, a married woman did not use a professional title socially, and so was "and Mrs. Brian Botchitt" socially, while being "Dr. Tracy Tremor" professionally. Miss Manners would now consider this a high-risk approach without the doctor's prior consent.

The Doctorates

DEAR MISS MANNERS:

I was introduced to a Dr. Soandso at a party and was embarrassed to have him him say, after I had discussed at length an interesting disease in my family, that he didn't know anything about medicine. I suppose he was a doctor of philosophy, but should he then call himself a doctor?

GENTLE READER:

What you have there is either an honest medical practitioner or an uncertain Ph.D. Only people of the medical profession correctly use the title of doctor socially. A really fastidious doctor of philosophy will not use it professionally, either, and schools and scholarly institutions where it is assumed that everyone has an advanced degree use "Mr.," "Mrs.," "Miss," or "Ms."

Many people feel strongly possessive about their scholarly titles, however, and it is Miss Manners' principle to allow them to call themselves what they want. She will only offer them a story: Miss Manners' own dear father, who would never allow himself to be addressed as doctor, used to say that a Ph.D. was like a nose—you don't make a fuss about having one because you assume that everyone does; it's only when you don't have one that it is conspicuous. For sheer snobbery, doesn't that beat insisting on being called doctor?

Honors and Underwear

DEAR MISS MANNERS:

I have recently received an honorary doctorate and am especially pleased about it as I have had no formal higher education, and so this is my first degree. However, it seems to be show-offy to use the title of "doctor" under these circumstances. Many of the doctors of philosophy I know don't even use theirs. Yet—what good does the title do me if nobody knows about it?

GENTLE READER:

You are in the position of a woman who has invested in silk underwear. She must derive her satisfaction from knowing that she has it on, and perhaps the knowledge of an intimate or two. To let everyone know cheapens the effect. However (to drop the underwear), you might look out for the chance to ally yourself with the doctors of philosophy who do not use the title by telling those who do, "I would never dream of calling myself 'doctor'—after all, I'm not a physician."

A Reverend Introduction

DEAR MISS MANNERS:

Is it true that I shouldn't introduce our pastor as "Reverend Jones"? Maybe I wasn't paying close attention at church, but it seems to me I've always heard it done that way.

GENTLE READER:

Maybe you weren't paying close attention at school. "Reverend" is an adjective. The correct introduction is, therefore, "*the* Reverend Cotton Pious."

Clergywomen

DEAR MISS MANNERS:

What is the correct way to address a Protestant clergywoman? What about when she is with her husband, who has no title?

GENTLE READER:

The form is the same as for a clergyman—the Reverend Angela Mather, or the Reverend Dr. Angela Mather, and Mr. Mather. Miss Manners is scandalized by those who believe that God is more interested in sex than service when contemplating those in His or Her ministry.

Introducing a Professor

DEAR MISS MANNERS:

A nephew of mine is a professor in one of the large colleges. When introducing him, do I say "Mr. Wells" or "Professor Wells"?

GENTLE READER:

The title of professor is used, in America, for exactly this case—when you want to show off your nephew, but he doesn't have a doctorate. In Europe, it is a higher title than "doctor." Personally, Miss Manners prefers "Mr." but, then, her nephew hasn't finished kindergarten.

The Ms. Mystery

Just because Miss Manners isn't Ms. Manners, don't think she is going to lend her good name (Manners) to all you silly people who carry on about what a dreadful innovation you think the title of "Ms." It happens to be a clever, useful invention, and as for all that whining about its not being pronounceable—well, "Mrs." doesn't have any vowels in it, either.

It is not as though anybody had gotten the hang of the old system. Miss Manners was constantly being appalled by the way women were being misaddressed, all these years, with the traditional titles of Miss and Mrs. The form "Mrs. Daffodil Awful" does not properly fit anyone—not a widow, not a divorcée, not a businesswoman.

The correct sequence is:

From birth, Daffodil Louise Perfect is styled "Miss," although her brother, Cutlip, is called "Master" rather than "Mr." until he is big enough to knock down anyone who tries it. However, the older sister of Miss Daffodil Louise Perfect is not addressed as Miss Viola Brentwood Perfect, but, because she is the ranking daughter, only as Miss Perfect.

When Daffodil marries Jonathan Rhinehart Awful, 3d (after breaking the engagement several times and driving everyone crazy, especially the lady at the department store bridal registry), she becomes Mrs. Jonathan Rhinehart Awful, 3d. When she then opens a yarn and Pakistani leathergoods boutique, there is no right way at all that she can be addressed in business correspondence. "Mrs. Daffodil Awful" would be incorrect, and "Mrs. Jonathan Awful" would be inappropriate. After Daffy and Rhino are divorced, she correctly combines her maiden surname with her ex-husband's, thus becoming Mrs. Perfect Awful. The strict old rule was that a divorced woman could continue to use her husband's full name if she was the innocent party in the divorce, but this no longer applies, as nobody is innocent anymore.

Had Daffy murdered Rhino instead, which she considered in order to simplify the property settlement, she would have remained Mrs. Jonathan Rhinehart Awful, 3d. The name of an undivorced woman is the same whether her husband ·is dead or alive, however much the old friends of broken-hearted widows enjoy taunting them by insisting that they cannot continue to use their husband's name as they did before bereavement.

Now do you feel a little more kindly inclined toward the use of "Ms."? Daffodil can correctly be styled Ms. from birth to death, without anyone's having to ask her where Rhino is (if you find out, several tradesmen would like to know) before knowing the correct form. Does "Ms." still seem so odd and difficult?

One note of caution. Women who prefer the old forms should not be bullied into giving them up. In this period of transition, it is courteous to address people in the fashion with which they feel comfortable. Miss Manners herself is still struggling, valiantly and democratically, to make the adjustment from being called Lady Manners in the old country.

Last Names First

DEAR MISS MANNERS:

Is it now considered appropriate for everyone to address everyone else by first names, without even asking permission? Is this no longer considered taking a liberty? In the past few months, my insurance salesman, a man who sold me a car part, and a man who sold me a pair of shoes have all considered it their privilege to address me by my first name. My name is on my credit cards, etc., and cannot be kept from the world. How do I inform people, particularly prospective employers, that I do not wish to be addressed in this manner, without appearing rude myself? I am not from a bygone age. I am twenty-six years old and appalled by this new rudeness, which passes for casualness or friendliness. Please help.

GENTLE READER:

The answer to your question is, Miss Manners regrets to say, that yes, indeed, it has become commonplace to use first names promiscuously. The answer to your plea for help, however, is that yes, we will fight this unfortunate practice together, with anyone else who cares to join this noble cause. Such usage is not only undignified, but makes a sham of the ideas of friendship and equality. There is no such thing as instant intimacy.

As you recognize, however, the ticklish part of the fight for good manners is to exhibit them oneself during battle. One cannot go around correcting others. However, one can go about driving others crazy in a perfectly polite fashion. One method of doing this is to keep saying, "No, no, I'm terribly sorry, you must have misunderstood—Geoffrey is my first name. My last name is Perfect." Another is to address the offenders by their last names, no matter how many times they urge you not to. If they tell you only a first name or say, "Call me Sam," then address that person as "Mr. Sam." Miss Manners is not guaranteeing that this will teach others respect, but it will pay back some of the irritation you have experienced and serve to alert them that something is wrong, even if they can't figure out what.

Friends of Different Ages

DEAR MISS MANNERS:
I have recently moved to a neighborhood peopled largely with retired couples and older widows. I am considerably younger than these neighbors, but they have been very helpful and kind to us. I want my children to call them "Mrs." or "Mr." but, in these days of informal manners, how should I address them? They have introduced themselves by first names and I want them to call me by my first name, but I'm not comfortable calling someone considerably older than myself by a first name. I now call them by their titles and most of them appear a little uncomfortable with this—but they haven't suggested otherwise. What do you suggest?
GENTLE READER:
Asking someone to use your first name is a gesture of warmth and friendship, but it cannot be made unless titles are used before the request. Continue to address them as you do, and if they get really uncomfortable, they will request you to do otherwise. If they want to stay uncomfortable, that's their lookout.

Friends of Different Generations

DEAR MISS MANNERS:
I am a thirty-year-old mother of two boys. Several teenagers in the neighborhood baby-sit for us. Many times they stop by to visit after school and ask advice on teenage problems. I'm alone a lot, and it's nice when someone drops over.

The problem is, some have stopped calling me "Mrs." and have switched to my first name. My husband doesn't like it. He became livid when I told one girl she could call me by my first name. I did this because she is close friends with the college boy next door (with whose family we are close) and I felt silly when he called me by my first name and she called me ''Mrs.'' when they were here together. Another girl just switched to my first name because she decided to. I didn't like it. I'm friends with her mother—what can I do? Basically, I think it's no big issue, but my husband thinks I'm being a jerk, that these teenagers won't respect me, that I'm ''older'' and should be more formal. Needless to say, no one calls him anything but ''Mr.'' They wouldn't dare!

GENTLE READER:

Miss Manners is having a most peculiar reaction to your letter. Most peculiar, indeed. In theory, she agrees with your husband. There is altogether too much blithe usage of first names—automatic assumptions of what ought to be the privilege of intimacy. The equality implied in the use of first names between generations does indicate a lack of respect for age or an attempt by an older person to seem younger.

However, in Miss Manners' heart, she knows you are right. There is no disrespect intended; that is evident from the fact that these teenagers seek your advice. It would be a slap in the face at this point to insist on making such a relationship more formal, as the informality is a general one these days, and your young friends have probably not been taught anything different. It is possible to say, ''I'm not quite comfortable with being called by my first name.'' But could you acknowledge that your husband and Miss Manners are correct in this matter, and then go on doing as you have been doing?

The Professor's Wife

DEAR MISS MANNERS:

I am about to marry a man who was once my professor. He still teaches, and I am now in the advanced stages of my graduate work. My problem is this: How do I address my former (and, in a few cases, current) professors when we meet at social functions? My husband will naturally be calling these people by their first names. Do I continue to show deference as a good graduate student should, until I am otherwise instructed? Or do I leap into the breach with utmost confidence and assume social equality? These professors have always called me by my first name, so their greetings to me will be no indication of what propriety requires.

My fiancé suggests I call anyone his age (early thirties; I myself am in my mid-twenties) or younger by his or her first name. Would following this rule of thumb be proper manners? I do wish to make as graceful an entrance as possible into my new social role.

GENTLE READER:

Socially, husband and wife assume the same rank, and it is the higher rank of the two. This applies to a professor's wife as much as it does to a prime minister's husband, and to use of first names as well as of titles. To address your husband's colleagues at parties as you do in your capacity of professional inferior would be wrong, as it would suggest that you were there as a graduate student, when in fact you are invited as the professor's wife. Besides, it would emphasize your youth as compared with the age of the other women there—as you well know. In class, Miss Manners hopes you both revert to titles and last names.

Establishing First Names

DEAR MISS MANNERS:

You have many times pointed out that it is presumptuous, rude, annoying, and everything else short of illegal to call people by their first names when you hardly know them. My question is, how do you properly get on a first-name basis with someone you are beginning to know well? Suppose you find youself with an acquaintance you have always addressed as "Mrs." at a social gathering where everyone else is on first-name basis? Or you want to indicate to an older person that you consider him a friend, rather than just an object of respect? Or you meet, for the first time, the spouse of someone whose first name you have been using? If you just plunge right in and use that person's first name, will Miss Manners write you off as a clod who doesn't know any better?

GENTLE READER:

Now, now. You don't know Miss Manners very well if you think she goes about applying the name of clod to people who are earnestly trying to get the nuances of behavior right. Therefore, you may continue to call her "Miss Manners."

One reason Miss Manners stresses waiting to address people by their first names is that the little ceremony involved is so charming. The woman who goes around announcing herself to strangers as "Hi, I'm Kimberly," will never have the pleasure of blushing and saying, "Oh, I do wish you would call me Kimberly, now that we're friends." In a heterosexual situation, so to speak, this is the privilege of the woman; among people of the same gender, it should be done by the elder.

Aunts Who Aren't

DEAR MISS MANNERS:

I have been visiting a household in which I am addressed by several small people as "Aunt Ann," a name I detest. It sounds like the beginning of a sneeze. However, my sister-in-law has instructed my nieces and nephews to use the title of aunt with my name, and my preference, that they simply call me by my first name, doesn't seem to make any difference. They have to check with her, and her word goes. She doesn't want to allow them to be too familiar with grown-ups, so I am stuck with this. Must I sacrifice my good name to their good manners?

GENTLE READER:

It is the essence of good manners to address people as they prefer to be addressed, which means adapting one's usage of titles, nicknames, and even surnames (as in the case, for example, of couples who have made themselves a hyphenated surname different from that of either family). Children should be taught to start with the most formal form appropriate (Mr. and Ms. or Mrs. to nonrelatives, Aunt to aunts), and then to accept modifications as offered by the person being addressed. It leaves them with an odd collection of usages, but the lesson that respect has to do with respecting the wishes of others.

✣ HANDSHAKES, KISSES, AND OTHER INTRODUCTORY GESTURES

DEAR MISS MANNERS:

If a woman offers you her hand in greeting, should you shake it only or should you grasp it, squeeze it gently, and at the same time pull her toward you and peck her on the cheek?

It would appear to me most appropriate to kiss a woman on the cheek, but if she offers you her lips instead, what should you do—kiss her on the lips or go round to a cheek?

Once you have kissed a woman as a greeting, are you expected to continue with the practice in all future greetings involving that person? If you don't, is that person likely to be offended?

GENTLE READER:

A gentleman must, in these circumstances, take what he is offered. If it is a hand, shake it. If it is a cheek, kiss it. If it is a pair of lips, kiss it. If it keeps reappearing, it must be rekissed.

Remember that we are talking about a formal, public gesture, and the fact that parts of the body and ways they are used may duplicate private expressions of emotion is irrelevant.

Just because gentlemen no longer have the exclusive right to initiate private kissing does not mean that they may now share in the ladies' privilege of initiating—or withholding—public kissing.

Shaky Handshakes

DEAR MISS MANNERS:

The event that has reddened my face every time I recall it happened months ago at a semiformal Christmas party. Please confirm, once and for all, if my action was so atrocious that I should become a hermit, due to apparently unforgivable etiquette.

My date and I were introduced to General and Mrs. General in this way: "General and Mrs. General, this is Mr. A . . ."—at which time I extended my hand—"and Miss B." General ignored my hand and turned to the lady with me. My open hand was left hanging in midair for what seemed like an eternity before it fell, shaky but unshaken, to my side. I have been confounded ever since.

Does a man not offer a handshake until after his female companion has been introduced and/or shaken the hand/s of the party to whom they are being introduced? Am I a bumbler or had I merely run into the city's most arrogant stick-in-the-mud? My habit has always been to extend my hand immediately upon my name's being pronounced.

GENTLE READER:

If Miss Manners sent you off to be a hermit, she would also have to send off the general and the person who did the introducing, which would make it much too crowded a hermitage. The proper introduction, with accompanying gestures, would have been: "Mrs. General, may I present Miss B . . . and Mr. A." Mrs. General then puts out her hand, first to Miss B, then to you—or doesn't, in which case there is no handshaking. The choice is hers. Then, it goes "Miss B, this is General Nuisance. General, this is Mr. A." Miss B decides whether to shake hands with General, and General decides whether to put a hand out to you, unless, of course, you are commander in chief of the armed forces and you outrank him. Then, you would outrank even the women and initiate those handshakes. The point is that the higher-ranking person—socially this means women before men, except in the case of presidents, kings, or popes, and the greater age and more exalted positions before the younger and less significant—either sticks out a hand or doesn't. The worst error is to pass by a hand that has been extended, however erroneously. Therefore, the general gets demoted, and you now outrank him. Congratulations.

DEAR MISS MANNERS:

It used to be my understanding that a woman could extend her hand to shake with a man, but that it was not good form to shake another woman's hand. However, in recent times, I have had women offer to shake hands with myself, a woman. Is this now considered good etiquette?

GENTLE READER:

It has always been proper for women to shake hands with each other. What was considered improper was for a man (or a younger woman) to offer his or her hand before the woman offered hers.

DEAR MISS MANNERS:

Please clear the air between a male friend and me. According to him, a man must never offer a firm handshake to a woman. I, on the other hand, believe one should always shake firmly, lest one be considered wishy-washy. What to do?

GENTLE READER:

How firmly are we talking about? Many ladies wear rings on their right hands, and many of these rings have stones in them. In the area between seeming wishy-washy and slicing off a lady's finger at the knuckle with her own diamond, Miss Manners would rather a gentleman erred toward the wishy-washy. However, it should not be difficult for a gentleman of ordinary digital and manual sensitivity to adjust his handshake in response to the strength of a lady's.

DEAR MISS MANNERS:

What is the proper way to shake hands when being introduced to someone who has accidentally lost his/her right hand? This situation occurs often enough to me in my work (sales and management) to risk embarrassing the less fortunate person. If he extends his right (artificial or stump), do you extend your right and shake his (a) artificial hand or (b) his right forearm or shoulder? Several people have the same question and none of us has found a satisfactory answer— "social graces" columnists have usually responded with "do whatever you think is right" or some such nonresponsive answer. I'd like to know what you think.

GENTLE READER:

Miss Manners is fully sensible of the fact that if everyone did whatever she or he thought was right, Miss Manners would be out of business. Please do not take it as nonresponsiveness, therefore, if she tells you that neither she nor you is the person who knows best what the amputee would feel most comfortable doing.

That individual—the one with the hand missing—must therefore take the lead in this common social situation. Some people extend a left hand, others extend the right arm or artificial device affixed to it. All you need to know is that you always shake hands with your right hand. What you shake is whatever is offered to you.

DEAR MISS MANNERS:

I don't know about artificial limbs, but for some time after I was shot in the neck in World War II, I had to shake hands left-handed. One day, someone extended his left hand to mine and this felt much more natural than the upside down right hands that everyone else had been giving me. Since then, whenever I have been offered a left-handed shake, I have shaken with my left hand. Several people have commented that this was more pleasant and natural for them, too. Will you modify your dictum that "you always shake hands with your right hand"?

GENTLE READER:

You are quite right, and Miss Manners never meant to suggest that right-handed shaking was something everyone must do, able or not. Offering the left hand is a thoughtful gesture to someone unable to shake with the right hand. The only problem is that some people are not quick-witted—or quick-handed—enough to make this adjustment. The disabled person therefore usually undertakes the courtesy of adjusting to the gesture.

Social Kissing

There is a great deal of kissing going on these days among people who do not especially like one another. Miss Manners is not referring to the popular teenage pastime of this description, but to what is known as social kissing, an activity common among consenting, if unenthusiastic, adults.

Why everyone is doing it when no one can agree on how it should be done is a question that could also be asked of more invigorating forms of bodily contact. The consequences of kissing improperly range from having one's cheek hanging jilted in midair, to getting one's lip neatly severed by a diamond ring. Miss Manners had better explain the use of the kiss as a tactile aid to the oral statement "Hello, again." Note the word "again." It is improper to kiss people upon meeting them for the first time, and this includes baby molesting on the part of political candidates.

In the act of greeting, with a social kiss, someone already known, the following surfaces may be employed:

Lips.

The right cheek only.

The right cheek, followed by the left cheek.

The hand.

This is a complete list of acceptable places for the social kiss. If you intend to use any other, Miss Manners requests that you and the object of your intentions step quickly behind the nearest curtain for the purposes. If you should unintentionally deliver the kiss on another area, such as the nose or the ear, it is just as bad. Good intentions count for nothing here.

Much of the confusion comes because each participant asssumes he or she is choosing the type of social kiss to be performed, and the two choices don't match.

Lip kissing and hand kissing in America must be heterosexual, regardless of private preferences. Lip kissing is ladies' choice: the woman presents her lips by tilting her face upward without moving it to either side, and the gentleman has no choice but to perform. Gentleman's choice is the hand kiss, although there must be some excuse of a continental background. Charter trips of twenty-one to forty-five days are not enough.

Cheek kissing, in this country, requires a minimum of one lady, but the partner may be either a lady or a gentleman. All cheek kisses begin with the presentation of the right cheek by the ranking lady. The recipient also presents the right cheek. The first presenter gets to choose whether they will actually kiss each other's cheeks, make a smack-smack noise in the air, or simply bump cheeks. That person should also decide whether to proceed with the European version, of repeating the adventure using left cheeks, or whether to call it a day. The partner's job is still to be alert in order to follow suit and not go after someone who doesn't mean it or walk away from someone who does.

Eye Contact

DEAR MISS MANNERS:

In the past couple of years, my relations to people are changing since I can no longer make eye contact with adults. My middle back muscles now prevent my straightening up. Here is my problem: the uncomfortable inability to look above a person's chest when I am speaking with a woman. The women in my office, I think, tend to shun me. Should I wear a button that apologizes for my

inability to look above their chest? or have some cards printed with that message?
GENTLE READER:
If you could, instead, rearrange your facial features to cultivate a look of
shyness that would explain your downcast stance, Miss Manners feels sure that
your popularity would soar.

DEAR MISS MANNERS:
Please bring the issue of eye contact into focus for me. I am a twenty-five-
year-old unmarried half-Oriental female. My entire life has been spent in the
Far East, where staring into the pupils of another is the height of impropriety
(or come-and-get-it-ness). I have, since coming here, been accused of avoiding
the issue, and now feel that my adjustment to the United States will never be
complete without some kind of "code of looks."
GENTLE READER:
What pretentious people call "body language" and make fortunes writing
paperback books about, Miss Manners considers merely details of etiquette that
vary from culture to culture. In a way, it is more important to learn these when
going from one society to another than it is to learn the more obvious forms, such
as table manners, because people often fail to realize that such behavior as eye
contact is learned, and they pounce on it as being psychologically revealing.
Miss Manners once had a similar problem, when she was a girl, back before
she became perfect. After a year's residency in South America, she found she
was standing closer to people when she conversed with them than is customary
in North America, and that her perfectly decent behavior was being interpreted
as flirtatious. The solution was merely to relearn the North American standard
for the proper distance between conversing acquaintances.
Miss Manners advises you to learn the American etiquette with regard to eye
contact for use here, rather than to endure the handicap of being misinterpreted
by people who are ignorant of foreign customs. In this country, it is considered
polite to look people in the eye when conversing with them. If you find this difficult, an alternative is to look away but maintain a smile, in which case your
behavior will be misinterpreted as charming demureness. That, at least, is better
than being considered shifty.

Speaking When Spoken To

DEAR MISS MANNERS:
Would you please give me the correct etiquette on speaking or greeting people
when entering a room of people, and when meeting on the street. Should the
person entering the room speak first? Should the youngest speak first, respecting
their elders? I have relatives in their late teens and also young adults (married)
who will never speak unless spoken to first. I was brought up differently.
GENTLE READER:
Even Queen Elizabeth has given up the rules about speaking first, and she was
brought up differently, too. Several years ago, when she visited America, she

greeted with regal silence anyone who presumed to speak to her before being spoken to; on her bicentennial tour, while she was not up to calling out "Howdy" to everyone, she at least returned all greetings. Miss Manners feels that it is always gracious to address another person civilly and to acknowledge civil addresses, and is pleased to see anyone master this ability, whatever her upbringing and however late in life.

Street Greetings

DEAR MISS MANNERS:

I hope you can settle an argument that has been going on for months. My boss says that when a man and woman enter a room at the same time, or when passing on the street, the woman should say hello first. Also, if a woman is with an escort and passes another man, who should say hello first? The man or the woman? I say it is proper etiquette for the man to say hello to the woman first. We are waiting for your answer.

GENTLE READER:

All right, but it's not going to end the argument. You are both right, or, looked at another way, both wrong. The European custom is that men greet women first, the American custom that women greet men first. As neither is much observed in either locality, you may choose the one you prefer.

Walking with Ladies

DEAR MISS MANNERS:

Can you do some research for me about old-fashioned manners or customs that few of us do today? I'm thinking of the men who always used to tip their hats in the presence of a lady, or when men always used to walk on the street side of the sidewalk. It's interesting to think about the traditions of just a few years ago.

GENTLE READER:

Gentlemen, to this very day, walk on the street side of the sidewalk, unless they are European gentlemen, in which case they walk to the lady's left. Miss Manners, who can bear the idea that styles of clothing change, but not that the small courtesies of life do, firmly believes that the only reason men do not tip their hats is the same as the reason they do longer smack one another across the face with their gloves when they are angry: They don't have the sartorial equipment.

Hat Tips

DEAR MISS MANNERS:

Does a gentleman's "tipping" his hat look too much like a military salute? Since I seldom see any male wearing a real hat, I'd almost forgotten this gesture.

I think it's been at least twenty years since this has meant grasping the hat brim and either lifting the hat an inch or two, or just grasping and releasing the brim.

GENTLE READER:

You have obviously not met a polite cowboy for twenty years. The rule is the same now as it always was: A gentleman removes his hat when speaking to a lady or sharing an elevator with one, and lifts his hat as a gesture to a stranger from whom he receives a courtesy or thanks for a courtesy of his. As you have noticed, however, it does require a hat and is therefore seldom performed. The military salute is much more energetic, but it also comes with PX privileges.

DEAR MISS MANNERS:

I have been trained to take off my hat upon entering an elevator, but in crowded office lifts, the space is insufficient to hold a doffed hat—save over the face (stifling) or under the chin (funereal). So the hat stays on. At the sight of it, however, attractive women of my age utter little humphs, purse their lips, avert their eyes. My face reddens. To halve these elevator contretemps, I no longer go out for lunch. I am brown-bagging (attaché-casing, actually). But the sandwich fare, though economical, is monotonous. Far more serious, this desk dining deprives me of any chance encounter with an attractive woman who might not instantly humph. If you will please proclaim lift-hats-off passé, I shall display your decree in my hatband. On the elevator, lids will flutter, lips part, humphs give way to susurrations. Soon, lunch counters will no longer be needed, I shall have a new friend who knows countless kinds of sandwiches, and every morning —as my attaché case and her ample handbag leave home to start the workday— we shall tip our hats to you.

GENTLE READER:

How can Miss Manners resist you? Three little words, you beg, and happiness will be yours. Yet she cannot bring herself to say them. Hold the hat in the space now occupied by the attaché case, which you will no longer need as a sandwich carrier because hordes of women, falling in love with the gallantry, will compete to take you out to lunch.

Arms and the Gentleman

DEAR MISS MANNERS:

When does a gentleman offer his arm to a lady as they are walking down the street together?

GENTLE READER:

Strictly speaking, only when he can be of practical assistance to her. That is, when the way is steep, dark, crowded, or puddle-y. However, it is rather a cozy juxtaposition, less compromising than walking hand in hand, and rather enjoyable for people who are fond of each other, so Miss Manners allows some leeway in interpreting what is of practical assistance. One wouldn't want a lady to feel unloved walking down the street, any more than one would want her to fall off the curb.

Sidestepping

DEAR MISS MANNERS:

I hope you will give me the answer to a problem that confronts me every now and then: Two people (a male and a female) walk toward each other on a sidewalk. As they pass each other, should each step to the right, even though the curbside is on the female's right, or should the male step to the curbside and the female to the inside, even though the inside is to the female's left? If two females pass each other, no problem—each steps to the right. I presume the same holds true for two males. It is so embarrassing to step to the right and have the other person step to the left at the same time—and then to have each reverse. This impromptu ''Turkey Trot'' can be repeated three or four times, with both parties apologizing profusely, until one or the other stands still and lets the other go by. If both were to stand still simultaneously, I can visualize the problem recurring, but this is unlikely. Once I ''danced'' with a dog. I didn't have time to notice whether it was male or female, but after three times going from side to side, it barked at me and passed me by stepping off the curbing. I wonder why I didn't think of stepping off the curbing before the dog did. Right or wrong, that dog made a fool of me. I'll very much appreciate your advice as to the accepted directions in which a male and female pedestrian should step when passing each other on the sidewalk.

GENTLE READER:

Miss Manners advises you not to get into a chess game with that dog, because the dog will win. The idea in chess, as in life, is to see what is coming before it arrives and plan ahead to avoid undesirable confrontations. The basic move is that everyone steps to the right on uncheckered sidewalks—ladies, gentlemen, dogs, knights, and bishops.

Saving Steps

DEAR MISS MANNERS:

My wife and I, along with another couple, recently attended a play. Being a gentleman, plus the fact that it was a cold December evening, I drove up to the front of the playhouse and left off my wife and the other couple (man and wife). As I drove about two blocks to the rather full parking lot, I noticed every other couple walking from their cars, some almost two and a half blocks away from the playhouse. Which is acceptable? To drop your wife off or have her accompany you to the parking lot? Also, does another couple in the car make any difference?

GENTLE READER:

Offering to save other people an inconvenience that you cannot yourself avoid is certainly polite. Your wife then has the choice of accepting that offer gratefully or saying, ''No, I'd rather stay with you.'' Which she chooses probably has more to do with her footgear than with her affections. The presence of another couple makes a difference only because some people tend to treat their families more gallantly when there are witnesses present.

✿ SAYING NO:
SILENCE AS A SOCIAL SKILL

Quick: What are the correct answers to the following questions?

1. "It was so nice of you to ask us for the weekend. We can't, but you know who would just love to? Rhino's first wife is getting married this summer, so she can't take the kids, and frankly Rhino and I have got to be alone now—I don't count Kristen; she's only two—if we're going to salvage anything. Anyway, his kids are big now, you'd be surprised, and they're dying to come down and spend some time there. They won't be any trouble because they'll bring their own sleeping bags and I told them they have to get summer jobs, and when they do, I'm sure they'll want to get their own place. They're great kids; you'll love them; and they think this is so great of you. OK?"

2. "My twins are in your son's class and we're asking all the mothers to help out. It's about the school dance. They need a strobe light and a new amplifier, and the school simply will not supply them, and we thought of asking the kids to pitch in but some of them are, you know, uh, well, scholarship students and it might not be fair to ask them, if you know what I mean. Anyway, we decided to have a raffle, and each mother just has to sell twenty tickets so it's not much work for anyone. You could sell them around your neighborhood in no time, or some people who can't be bothered are just buying them all themselves. OK?"

3. "Are you and Buckley free for dinner three weeks from Wednesday? Marvelous—we have some darling friends you'll just love. When they heard you were a tax lawyer, they were thrilled, because they have some kind of terrible tax situation they'd love to ask you about, and of course everyone is dying to meet Buckley. We're counting on his putting in a good word for us on this secret project we'll tell you all about at dinner. Is seven thirty all right?"

Notice that Miss Manners has asked for *correct* answers. She can hear all those answers that sprang to your minds, through inspiration, assertiveness training, or self-defense, and they are not *correct* answers. What is more, they are not answers that many people would say to friends or acquaintances. It's all very well to talk about the need for saying "No"; but the real need in the lives of civilized people is to say, "No, thank you."

Because of this lack, people who refuse to be rude—and bless them for that— find themselves answering either, "Well, we'd love to, but we think Noah might be getting appendicitis then and there's been an electrical fire in our family room and I find my time is so limited now that I have to keep reporting to my probation officer''; or, what is worse, they answer, ''Yes.''

The correct answers are simple. All they require, to be both gracious and effective, is that one close one's mouth after saying them and not continue talking. The correct answer to any of the initial questions is ''Oh, I'm so terribly sorry, I just can't.'' Got that? In most cases, that is enough. However, if anyone asks why not, the correct answer is ''Because I'm afraid it's just impossible.''

The sentences are not difficult to pronounce, but many people find the silence following them impossible to accomplish. They fill it by running off at the mouth with increasingly complicated and farfetched excuses until the only hope of wiping out all their dreadful lies is to turn themselves in and do what was asked of them. They would do well to practice shutting up. It is a social grace few can afford to be without. In the meantime, Miss Manners has an exercise for intermediate students. They may say, ''I have to check with my husband (wife, broker, boss, dog's baby-sitter, house plants)'' and then call back later and try again to give the correct answer.

No, Again

DEAR MISS MANNERS:

I agree with your theory about how to say ''No.'' But I have tried it, and I just can't stop after that one word ''No.'' It sounds curt. So to cover that, I go back into all that complicated talk, and get myself right back into the trouble I am trying to avoid. Help! Can't you give me a modified version of ''No'' that isn't so short?

GENTLE READER:

''Oh, dear, thank you so very much, I would simply love to if there were any way I were able, but it's absolutely impossible, and what a terrible shame that is because I would so have enjoyed to, and you were so very kind to have asked me.''

"No" for an Answer

DEAR MISS MANNERS:

I have a lifelong weight problem, and have finally, after years of doctors, crash diets, binges, pills, and everything else, gotten myself under control. I know, for instance, that I can't take ''just a little'' of certain kinds of food—one bit and I'd be off again. The trouble is that now that I'm finally decent looking, nobody believes that I really need to keep dieting, and I am always being pressed to ''Just have a taste'' of this or told ''I worked so hard making this—won't you even try it?'' Frankly, if it comes to a choice, I'd rather lose friends and pounds than keep both. But is there a way to say ''No'' and make people believe it and not keep urging you anyway?

GENTLE READER:

The way to say "No" is often. People who won't take "No, thank you" for an answer are rude, rather than, as they suppose, hospitable. Don't try to explain why—just keep repeating those three words pleasantly until they give up.

COMMON ANNOYANCES

Annoying the Disabled

It was the popular belief that etiquette is simply a matter of acting naturally that drove Miss Manners from her comfortable chaise longue into this business. Miss Manners does not want people to act naturally; she wants them to act civilly.

Nowhere is the difference more evident than in the uncivil way most people naturally treat the disabled. You turn a well-meaning, good-hearted, average, sensitive citizen loose on someone who is not as ablebodied as himself, and just watch the well-meaning, good-hearted insults fly.

Why do the Temporarily Ablebodied, as they have been called, behave so unpleasantly to others? Perhaps out of fear that such a fate could befall them, perhaps because the disabled have been segregated in the society. Miss Manners is not interested in hearing excuses. Miss Manners just wants you to learn how to behave properly.

Insults to the handicapped seem to be based on the absurd assumption that they are not full-functioning adults and therefore—like patients or children—must do as others think best for them.

That is why people cheerfully invade their privacy, address them with patronizingly false good cheer, and blithely overrule their expressed wishes.

A typically sympathetic person will think nothing of accosting another human being, if he or she is in a wheelchair, demanding to know what is "wrong." This is personal information which someone may or may not want to volunteer. As a disabled lady of Miss Manners' acquaintance put it, "You wouldn't go up to a person and ask, 'Hey, why are you so ugly?'" Nor should you lean close into the face of someone you hardly know with what she describes as "that gooey smile" with which the disabled are often presented.

Miss Manners fails to see why a person seated in a wheelchair should be approached differently from one seated in an ordinary chair—one leans at an acceptable distance or sits nearby, and does not clutch the arm of another's chair —or why the ordinary rules of conversation, as to taste or lack of it, should not apply.

Along with the presumption about lack of privacy there is an assumption about a lack of sexuality. Miss Manners has long since learned not to make such assumptions about anyone.

Another area of offensiveness is the matter of offering assistance. A polite person will offer assistance to anyone who seems in need of it, but the key word here is ''offer.'' Disabled people often find, to their peril, that assistance is given to them after they have declined it or contrary to their instructions on what assistance would be helpful.

If the disabled person has some aid, such as a cane or a Seeing Eye dog, it should be entirely under his or her control. Attempts to grab the cane arm or to pet a dog on duty are as helpful as playing with the controls of a car someone else is driving. If there is a companion accompanying the disabled individual, that assistant is not to be presumed to be a guardian. You address disabled people directly, instead of talking about them in the third person in their presence, and when you talk to a deaf person, you face him, not his interpreter.

Some leeway is allowed to children when they ask ''What is wrong with you?'' or ''How do you operate that thing?'' But this is only because everybody understands that children don't know any better than to act naturally.

DEAR MISS MANNERS:
A new family moved in next door to us with a daughter who is about the same age as my roommates (early twenties) and I. We want to be friendly, but don't know anything about how to be helpful to the blind, which she is. For instance, when I was introduced, I blurted out, ''You must come see us sometime,'' and then nearly died because I realized that, of course, she can't see.
GENTLE READER:
You may well be embarrassed. A woman in her twenties who does not know the difference between the literal and figurative use of a simple word like ''see'' ought to be ashamed of herself.

Blindness means that a person cannot see literally and nothing more. When dealing with the blind, therefore, one makes some adjustments relating to lack of vision, but no others. One does not, for example, change one's manner of speaking. Blind people use and understand the language like everyone else.

For some strange reason, people often assume that a blind person must have other disabilities, physical and mental. This is rude, as well as illogical. One does not shout at the blind, one does not ask their companions about them as if they did not understand, one does not touch them without permission, and one does not assume that they are lost or helpless as a matter of course.

One of the greatest handicaps the blind have to deal with is the number of people who will pounce on them while they are minding their own business and start pushing them around, literally as well as figuratively.

There are, however, things you can do if you want to be helpful to your neighbor (Do not expect Miss Manners to congratulate you on initiating the friendship; it is neither more nor less charming than welcoming any new neighbor, for the purpose of giving friendship the chance to develop or not as it will.)

Identify yourself when you see her. She may learn to recognize your voice, but ''Hi'' is a short sample to go by, guessing games are atrocious for all people under all circumstances, and a friendly wave is no help at all. You should also announce your departures, so that she is not left talking to you after you are gone. Do as you would in a telephone conversation.

Mention whatever you see that might be useful or amusing for her to know. "There's a plate of cucumber sandwiches on the table to your right," "Here comes Mrs. Awful heading straight for you, and does she look furious," "You dropped your napkin near your left foot," "Erica's pearls don't look real," "We've moved the piano across the room since you were here last," "The man who keeps bumping against you is General Nuisance, whose wife is over by the bar."

When she really does seem to need help, offer it orally: "Do you want to take my arm going down the stairs?" Miss Manners should not have to remind you it is always considered polite to take no for an answer.

If she asks for help, it is helpful to give it without unsolicited advice or editing. If you read a menu to her, read the whole menu, with prices, not what you think she might like; and if you read her mail to her, do not interpret it.

The basic rules of identification, offering specific information, and refraining from molestation also apply to blind strangers. "I'm waiting for the bus, too, and the T-7 is coming," is preferable to mugging a person silently to shove him on the bus; and "Stop! There's a pothole in front of you" is more useful than a general "Watch out!" which could apply literally, don't you see, to an escaped lion's coming down the street or figuratively to the idea that inflation is going to get us all.

With Good Intentions

DEAR MISS MANNERS:

All right, my day is now complete. I just got yelled at by a white-haired old lady in a wheelchair for trying to help her into the intersection when the light turned green. You know what she said? "F—— off, buddy." Nice? No doubt, I am a male chauvinist pig for trying to help her, and also a racist and an oppressor of the poor, handicapped, and elderly. I have learned my lesson about that. I promise never to try to be a gentleman again. But you know what else? *I am damn sick of people hating me for trying to be a nice guy. And I can't stand it any longer.* I am going to go out and punch the first sweet little old lady I see right in the mouth. What do you think of that? Hurrah for modern manners.

GENTLE READER:

There, there. Please try to calm yourself. Miss Manners doesn't hate you. Miss Manners knows you meant well. You just sob quietly on Miss Manners' shoulder for a minute, and when you feel up to it, she will explain to you what happened.

All right? Feel a little better now? The desire to help people is a noble one. But you must first make sure that they are in need of help. Surely the smallest Boy Scout has learned by now that it doesn't count as a good deed to help an old lady across the street if she doesn't want to cross the street—or if she doesn't want to be helped. You made an assumption that the old woman in the wheelchair must be in need of help; must be, in a word, helpless. But how do you suppose that she got to the intersection where you saw her? Did she fall out of a nursing home window, wheelchair and all?

No, you have to assume that she got there after having set out, knowing, as all rational beings do, the extent of her own capabilities. You also have to realize, when you think about it, that a wheelchair occupant is bound to know more about how to handle a wheelchair than you, as a passerby. Your assistance may have endangered not only her dignity, as a person entitled to be considered in control of herself unless she specifically asks for help, but it may also have endangered her safety.

Miss Manners dearly hopes you will not discontinue helping damsels in distress, and mensels, too, for that matter. Just make sure, before you do so, that they are in distress. Helping someone into distress, however courteously, is not a good deed.

Modern Necessities

A gentleman Miss Manners knows has no automobile, no telephone, and no television set. You notice that Miss Manners does not refer to this gentleman as a friend. He doesn't have any of those, either.

There is a connection among these lacks, and a beastly unfair one it is, too. If the gentleman had no money, some people might not hold it against him. (Others might, of course.) But that he can afford these blessings of civilization and doesn't want them is roundly resented by all. If truth be told, there are a few of these appliances still around his house. It is just that he is careful to keep them in nonworking order. The telephone never rings because he has taken care to conceal its number. The television set lives in hope that he will remember once, every four years, to turn it on and let it tell him who has been elected President of the United States. There was a car once, but it died and he has preferred to live in bereavement rather than try to meet a new one.

If more truth need be told, Miss Manners is as bewildered as he about why his friends, other than she herself, departed with the dry goods. She has noticed, however, that people who do not watch television are considered a threat to society. Perhaps it is because there was a wave of fashion, in the early days of television owning, to brag of not having a set, as if that were an intellectual achievement, like getting an advanced degree, only cheaper and less time consuming. People who confess now to not watching television are haughtily informed that there is "good" or "educational" television, as if it were the basest ingratitude not to watch that. It seems to Miss Manners that we have come to a peculiar pass when any pastime is considered so irresistible that people who don't want to participate need substantial excuses.

The lack of a readily available telephone line is considered even more of an affront. If the gentleman had taken a telephone-less cottage in Maine to escape from his friends and write a great novel, they all would have been sympathetic. That he should simply want to live in his own house without a bell to summon him from his dinner, thoughts, or slumber is apparently unthinkable.

Miss Manners thinks it was lovely of dear Mr. Bell to take all that trouble to invent the telephone for people who want to be in instant communication with the world, but wonders why everyone should have to agree to be so available. After all, dear Mr. Pony Express took trouble, too, to invent the mails, and they are still open to all. Miss Manners' friend would be perfectly happy to go to the trouble of opening his front door every morning and rummaging in his mailbox for news or invitations from his friends.

Even if he got any, he would lose the friends because he does not keep an automobile. Living in the center of a city, he uses its public transportation for most of his needs and rents an automobile when he wishes to travel. If he does neither and is invited to a dinner, say, far out in the suburbs, he is treated by automobile owners who do not want to share with all the warmth with which people regard public charges. Because most people believe that everyone has a duty to own a car, they are not gracious about offering rides to those who, choosing not to, do not seem to be holding up their end.

The poor gentleman. Miss Manners remembers when the basic equipment one needed to have friends was charm.

Not Partial to Pets

DEAR MISS MANNERS:
I hate it when animals jump on me, but other people's pets are always doing so. Dogs, particularly, are such sycophants that they always ignore the guests who are trying to pet them and throw themselves at animal haters, such as myself. I'm not flattered by this repulsive attention. I'm not above kicking a pesky pet, either, when the owner isn't looking, but what can I do to get rid of it when my host is looking right at me?

GENTLE READER:
The most tactful thing to do would be to announce an allergy. This is not strictly a lie if you define ''allergic'' loosely, the way sophisticated children have learned to do, as in, ''I think I'm allergic to vegetables.''

Dogs

DEAR MISS MANNERS:
This problem may be outside your bailiwick. It concerns the neighbors' dogs and the stretch of sidewalk and grassy parking that I am responsible for. When the dogs are out on their own, a well-aimed missile, the business end of the garden hose, or just a loud, threatening noise can usually discourage them. The dog walkers, when the dogs have them out on a leash, could probably be discouraged in the same fashion, but this doesn't seem quite—well, quite.

If the proper procedure is to speak to them, what is the proper thing to say? I hesitate to try speaking ad lib, because it makes me so doggone mad I don't know what I would end up saying. If they are so certain that using the area I mow, rake, and walk on for a canine latrine is so unobjectionable, why don't they do themselves a great big favor and train their dogs to use their own front lawn? Signs tacked on the trees saying "Please curb your dog" are not the answer. I have to get in and out of my car along that curb.

GENTLE READER:

If refraining from defecating on other people's property is not a matter of basic manners, Miss Manners would like to know what is. However, you seem to be dealing with two species who do not realize this, and while your method of notifying the unaccompanied dogs is working, Miss Manners agrees that turning a garden hose on a neighbor is not a good way of asking for his consideration. You must do so in words, and should do it as pleasantly and neutrally as possible, when you are first informing him of your feelings. "Please don't have your dog use my property," for example. If this is ignored, the problem is no longer one of correcting ignorance, and you may allow yourself to inject some of your feelings into your words.

Corrections

DEAR MISS MANNERS:

What does one do when the bearded gentleman you may be talking with at a cocktail party has a few crumbs of cake or quiche in his beard? Likewise, when a person you know, perhaps but slightly, has spinach stuck between his or her front teeth? Do we gently tell them, ignore it all, or, in the case of the beard, lean over and brush it off?

GENTLE READER:

You are talking about a problem of such complex delicacy that it requires exquisite tact to judge each individual instance. Miss Manners can see that you realize that there can be no one solution applicable to all such situations. You do not, for example, suggest leaning over and picking the spinach out of someone's front teeth.

Here are some guidelines for making a judgment:

1. Is this something that others are likely to notice?

2. Is this something that the victim is likely to realize after it's too late to do anything about it?

3. Is there a way of correcting the problem without seeming to take it seriously?

For example, one of the severest cases of That Sinking Feeling is brought on when one returns home, satisfied that one has been unusually witty and merry at a dinner party, and then sees, in the bathroom mirror, that one has spinach on the teeth. It does not take long to calculate when the spinach was consumed and for how long afterward one displayed one's triumphant smile. This is not a nice feeling. In the case of a crumby beard, one may possibly assume, especially if one has a quiche-colored beard, that no one else has noticed it.

Miss Manners would therefore point out the spinach but ignore the crumb, unless the crumb could not possibly have gone unnoticed—if it were an inch square, say, and covered with tomato sauce.

Now we get to how to do this. The correcter should seem to have some doubt, in order to convince the sufferer that the problem is of minimum noticeability. "Excuse me—I can't quite tell. Is there something on your tooth?" Or perhaps the brushing off of a crumb could be accomplished with a slightly flirtatious gesture. (You begin to see why delicate individual judgment is required.)

If you think your examples are difficult, what about the lady of Miss Manners' acquaintance who only realized *after* a tea at the State Department, in the days when pants were considered dressy, that her fly had been open all the time and nobody had told her? She still holds this against each and every woman at that tea.

DEAR MISS MANNERS:

Is it right to tell a woman that her slip is showing, or she has a run in her stocking? I figure she might want to know, but I don't want to be offensive. If I had a spot on my jacket, I would want her to tell me before I went in to see the boss, for instance, so I could fix it.

GENTLE READER:

Yes, but suppose you had a spot on your tie, which everyone knows is impossible to remove. First you would try to fix it, succeeding in making it worse, and then you would go in knowing that you were a Man with a Spot on His Tie. Consider, before you point out a problem, whether it is solvable (or, in the case of your spot, soluble) before mentioning it. The slip can probably be hiked up. The run cannot be undone.

DEAR MISS MANNERS:

Can you tell me a tactful way of letting a friend know that she is getting too fat?

GENTLE READER:

Can you tell Miss Manners a tactful reason for wanting to do so?

Sharing

DEAR MISS MANNERS:

When I play cards with three other women, the hostess usually serves luscious chocolates, which I cannot eat because I am diabetic. To appease my sweet tooth, I carry a couple of sugar-free goodies in my purse. Invariably, the others are curious about the candy, thinking they are calorie savers—of course, they are not. Nevertheless, I am always at a loss about my conduct. I don't want to be rude or seem selfish, yet it would necessitate bringing half a box in order to ensure having a piece for me. To date, the choices have been doing without, or munching one small patty with three sets of drooling eyes upon me. Any suggestions?

GENTLE READER:

When nursery schools became interested in the mistaken notion that children should be taught to express themselves freely, they began to neglect the purpose of preschool education, which was to teach the rule: If you haven't got enough cookies for everybody, don't bring any. Unfortunately, this rule also applies to people with doctors' excuses. Miss Manners suggests that you bring enough sugar-

free goodies for everyone at least once, in the hope that they will compare
unfavorably with the luscious variety and that therefore you will not again be
troubled by requests. Or that you stuff yourself with them before you arrive—or
during an otherwise explained absence from the card room—and pretend not to
be interested in any refreshment. Incidentally, your friends should be made
aware that drooling is properly done with the mouth, not the eyes.

Dropping Friends

DEAR MISS MANNERS:
I am attempting to cut off communication with a former friend of mine. I
would like to do so tactfully and politely. However, this person apparently has
not received the message that I no longer wish to associate with him. For example,
I never call him and do not even remember his phone number. However, he does
call me, though I did not give him my number. When he calls, and I happen to
be unlucky enough to answer the phone, I am polite, but do not attempt to
continue the conversation. Still, he calls. Miss Manners, what can I do?
GENTLE READER:
Of the two ways of dropping people who have been friends—With Cause, and
Without—With Cause is easier. It is too bad that your friend did not offend you
mortally, but probably unethical to pretend that he did so. Anyway, this one
would probably kill himself trying to explain. Better forget that angle. Miss
Manners is sorry she brought it up.
Saying no to friendship is like saying no to unwanted food, drink, or romantic
attention. You just have to keep saying it, firmly and politely, until people stop
pressing it on you. Try not to consider your ex-friend's behavior as an attempt
to drive you crazy with obtuse persistence; regard it as his polite wish to give
you the benefit of the doubt, in case you were neglecting him inadvertently.
Every time he calls, you must say, kindly, ''I'm so sorry, I can't talk now.''
After a few years, he is bound to get the idea.

Returning Empties

DEAR MISS MANNERS:
How does one graciously get one's containers back? Last fall, I asked my son's
new in-laws if they would like to try to save my plants over the winter, since
I had no place to keep them myself. They seemed delighted to do so. There were
several dozen plants, which were in new containers and good clay pots—even a
hanging basket, carefully planted. I had used all my pots for cuttings. Since
every plant died, I expected to get my pots back, so that I could plant them
this next spring. Well, the Mrs. had replanted the pots for her own use, and I
believe I created ''hard feelings'' along with a nasty comment when I went to
retrieve my pots. Am I wrong to expect people I share my culinary delights
with to return the containers also?

GENTLE READER:

Let Miss Manners put it this way: people presume a no-deposit/no-return policy, unless it is otherwise stated. It is not unreasonable for you to expect your containers back only if you have mentioned this hope. Something like "I can put those pots to other use if the plants don't survive" or "that's a favorite platter of mine—I'll pick it up next week, if that's all right" would cover you. Otherwise, it seems excessive to think of burglary in connection with items you have more or less graciously handed over to someone yourself.

Curbing Curiosity

DEAR MISS MANNERS:

Someone in our office collapsed suddenly, and a crew of paramedics had to be called. They gave him assistance right there and then took him to the hospital on a stretcher. We were all terribly concerned, and many of us stood around until he was taken away, only to be told later, by some co-workers, that it was awful of us to watch what was going on. This was not a stranger who had an accident on the street—this was someone we work with, and we were there because we wanted to see if he would be all right.

GENTLE READER:

Nevertheless, the same rule applies as at accidents. If you cannot fulfill the need for medical or practical assistance, help fill the need for privacy. The discipline required for studying medicine is nothing compared to that needed to stifle one's curiosity.

Speedy Shoppers

DEAR MISS MANNERS:

I like to shop quickly, usually on my lunch hour, when every minute counts. I know what I want (and what I don't want) and can flip through a rack of dresses or blouses very rapidly, picking out the ones I want to try on. Most shoppers, though, are abominably slow, and I often find myself standing and waiting behind some woman who is holding out one dress, staring at it, and blocking me from going on down the rack. Saying "Excuse me" doesn't usually budge these people. What else can I say?

GENTLE READER:

You could say "Coming through!" in a tone that means business, but it is the tone, rather than the words, that announces the determination, and this can be applied to saying "Excuse me." Why don't you look quickly at the dress the parked person is considering, in case you want it if she puts it back, and go around her? A skillful racer always takes into account the possibility of traffic breakdowns.

Disturbers of the Peace

DEAR MISS MANNERS:

Please write something about people who insist upon talking while in church. They are the bane of my existence. At the end of a harried week, I love to be quiet in some lovely church and prepare myself for the coming week. Yesterday, I went to the cathedral in the hopes of doing just that. A choir was to perform for an hour before the eleven o'clock service. For a while it was sheer heaven to hear the blending of those lovely voices. Then a woman tourist came and sat beside another woman. They struck up a conversation and for the next twenty-five minutes covered topics all the way from the interior of the cathedral to life on a farm!

I looked at them, I coughed, I twisted, I used ESP to no avail. Finally, I let out a sigh, saying under my breath, "Oh, me." The quiet woman on my other side said, "Isn't it awful?" Now, in retrospect, I know I should have said something—especially since they were too insensitive to get my various hints. This talking when one should be quiet happens everywhere these days—in theaters, libraries, churches, etc. Why is it?

GENTLE READER:

This is what comes of such evils as transistor radios, background music, and keeping the television set going during dinner and homework. Many people believe that constant noise is normal. These people are, perhaps, not responsible for themselves, as sound has melted their brains. However, this diatribe does not help your problem, any more than a diatribe on your part would contribute to the proper atmosphere in church. You could ask politely for silence, but, perhaps because she is small as well as polite, Miss Manners does not believe in direct confrontation with evildoers in public places, beyond the sort of coughing, twisting, and staring you have already tried. Aggression on the part of shushers is often ruder and noisier than the original crime. She suggests that you appeal to a higher authority. In a theater, this might be an usher; in a library, a librarian. In church, you might even appeal, out loud, to a Higher Authority. "O God, grant me the serenity of a peaceful place to worship, and the patience to bear with those who disturb it."

Applauding in Church

DEAR MISS MANNERS:

Your views on the propriety of applauding in church would be timely. It seems to me that whatever talent one displays in church—musical or oratorical —is offered up to the glory of God, not to solicit the admiration (true or feigned) of one's fellow sinners.

GENTLE READER:

Even when ecclesiastical oratory was more stirring than it usually is nowadays, it was never received with applause. If God wishes to applaud in church, He may, but it is inappropriate for anyone else to do so.

Traveling in Literary Circles

DEAR MISS MANNERS:

When I read the newspaper at the breakfast table, my wife, who has another section of the paper in front of her, starts reading the back of the section I am holding up. So do my children, who ordinarily wouldn't read anything. It's not just a family problem, either. People do it when I'm reading on the bus. I find it annoying to have people lurking behind me while I'm trying to read, shifting about if I happen to drop the paper down slightly to hold my coffee cup or whatever. If I then offer my section to my wife, she always says, "Oh, no, I don't want it, I was just looking at that one little thing that caught my eye." Do you consider it legitimate for people to read the backs of other people's papers?

GENTLE READER:

Within reason, yes. Miss Manners believes it is one's duty to contribute to an informed public. However, when they start asking you to turn the page, reason and duty end.

RELATIONS BETWEEN THE GENDERS

Taking Offense

Technically, there is no such thing as accidental rudeness. Try to remember this when you are stabbed with an umbrella, trodden on, given a dial tone after being told to "hold" on the telephone, greeted by a name that is not yours, stood up by a dinner guest, or sneezed upon. However, a true insult, Miss Manners believes, must be intentional. The insulter must understand what is expected, and do either something else or nothing at all.

Today, however, the insult threshold seems to have lowered below this standard. All sorts of people are running around sulking, pouting, acting huffy, or retaliating as the result of kindly meant actions.

This is most apparent in the relationships between gentlemen and ladies, partly because these are in a state of transition, open to misinterpretation, and also because everything always becomes more apparent when it's between gentlemen and ladies.

A gentleman holds the door open for a lady, and she sails through, insulted by the suggestion that she is too weak to manage the door herself. A lady gives her seat in the subway to a gentleman many years her senior, and he haughtily rejects it because it seems to suggest that the power of his manhood is past. A married woman is insulted by being considered socially as half a couple, so that she is not invited when her husband cannot or will not attend. An unmarried man is insulted by being invited socially without his live-in lover's being included.

Some women are insulted by being styled ''Ms.''; others by ''Mrs.'' or ''Miss.'' Couples are insulted by being addressed conventionally by those who do not know which name they have decided is to come first, or how they have used their mutual inheritance of surnames for themselves and their children.

All this has got to stop. There is little enough courtesy in the world, Miss Manners has observed; we cannot afford to go around rejecting what attempts to pass for it. In chaotic times, a consideration of motivation becomes important. Complete ignorance of prevailing manners is not much of an excuse, but perhaps it is a little—in unfortunate children whose parents brought them up to be ''free'' rather than polite. But ignorance of revisions in manners since one was reared, or of the custom-made preferences of individuals, is more of an excuse.

It is true that manners grow and change, as does language, but also true that traditional usage has a special sweetness to those who have long known it. What social reformers must realize is that there can be a gap between reason and habit. It is rude to subject tiny courtesies to philosophical scrutiny.

The polite thing to do has always been to address people as they wish to be addressed, to treat them in a way they think dignified. But it is equally important to accept and tolerate different standards of courtesy, not expecting everyone else to adapt to one's own preferences. Only then can we hope to restore the insult to its proper social function of expressing true distaste.

Being Ladylike

DEAR MISS MANNERS:

Those of us working for women's rights have been advised to take a ''ladylike'' approach. We tried emulating the behavior of our opposition, but this hardly seemed ladylike. Could you provide a precise definition of ''ladylike''?

GENTLE READER:

A lady is, above all, someone who is passionately concerned that others be treated with dignity, fairness, and justice. It has always been considered ladylike, for instance, to fight for these things on behalf of children, animals, and one's husband. The difficulty you are encountering on the subject is that many people do not consider it ladylike to fight that battle on one's own behalf. Therefore, if a woman truly wishes to be ladylike, she will fight for dignity, fairness, and justice, not for herself, but for all other women.

Improper Proposals

DEAR MISS MANNERS:

In these times of relaxed social mores, some of us who grew up with a fairly rigid definition of acceptable behavior are finding ourselves somewhat socially dysfunctional. I am a middle-aged divorcée who is afraid to accept dates for fear that my escort may offer an "improper suggestion" at the end of the evening. I would not care to accept an invitation for which payment was expected "later," and I do not wish to insult the extenders of invitations by suggesting in advance that they may have ulterior motives. I have, on a few occasions, accepted invitations with the understanding that we would go dutch, but some men find this offensive and others seem to think that such liberation is just a prelude to wild, amorous abandon. Have you any advice that will help me and my fellow anachronisms cope with the changing scene?

GENTLE READER:

That is what Miss Manners is here for. Let us first identify what it is in the current scene, as you say, that has actually changed. Surely there have always been gentlemen who have interpreted any behavior at all on the part of a lady, including screaming, "No, no!" as "a prelude to wild amorous abandon." In addition, the vulgar assumption that money spent on entertaining a lady is a short-term investment, collectible before the food has left her digestive tract, is of long standing.

The difference you observe is made by inflation. In the past, a gentleman might consider himself sufficiently rewarded by a smile or a press of the hand. The price of dinner and theater tickets having gone up, some gentlemen have come to expect a kiss at the doorstep or even, Miss Manners is told, something more. At the same time, there has been a deflation in language. A gentleman who might once have begged a lady to pity his lovesick heart is now apt to state somewhat more expressly what he expects her to do with what.

None of this should obscure the outrageousness of the ancient premise that a gentleman who spends money on a lady has legitimately purchased her favors. Such transactions are available commercially, Miss Manners is given to understand, but have no place in decent society. We all know that the only reason a true gentleman takes a lady out is for the pleasure of her society, and that the only reason a lady gives her favors is that she is overcome by uncontrollable passion. If the passion seizes her before she has asked him his last name, or if he hopes to implant such a passion by taking her to Paris for the weekend—well, that does not negate the principle.

What, then, should you do when a gentleman makes an "improper suggestion"?

You should decline it, of course. In these vulgar days, improper suggestions are made rather routinely, and extreme outrage is not appropriate unless the man (being no longer entitled to be called a gentleman) is so crude as to state that premise about the payment being due. As Miss Manners has indicated, most gentlemen mistakenly believe this premise, but only a cad would put it into words.

The important thing is that you must understand that you have incurred no such obligation. If you firmly believe this, and if the gentleman has made his improper suggestion with acceptable delicacy, you will be able to decline graciously, as you would if a hostess offered you her special dessert, of which she was enormously proud, but for which you had no desire.

The Upright Gentleman

Dear Miss Manners:
No etiquette book I've found has the answer to this one: When ladies and gentlemen are sitting at tables in a restaurant, or at a large party, and a lady has to leave the table to powder her nose, does her escort stand when she departs, and also stand when she returns? I say, of course. My husband says no. He says that if the escort stands, that will just call attention to the fact that the lady is leaving on a mission better imagined than described. What do you say? This story has been bandied about a bit in our circle, so that now when I get up from the table, every man stands with hand over heart, which is not funny.
Gentle Reader:
Please allow Miss Manners to take exception to two assumptions. First, there is nothing wrong with a lady's powdering her nose, which is one of only two possible reasons for her leaving the table. The other is to make an urgent telephone call. Both of these are, in fact, better described than imagined, but if gentlemen insist on imagining something else, they all can at least do so standing. Second, it is, too, funny.

Seating Ladies

Dear Miss Manners:
A waiter in a fancy restaurant tried to push my chair in for me, and nearly catapulted me into the sharp edge of the table. Not many men perform this service anymore, which is probably just as well for the hospitalization insurance rates, but what does a woman do if they attempt it?
Gentle Reader:
This is a confusion between the performance of a courtesy and the performance of a useful function, and Miss Manners is not surprised that the result of so basic a misunderstanding may be fractured kneecaps. The proper procedure for a man pushing in the chair of a woman has nothing whatever to do with moving her chair physically. It goes as follows: She approaches the chair. He puts a hand on the back of the chair. She sits on the chair. She scoots along toward the table, surreptitiously dragging the chair with her by means of her own hand, placed stealthily behind her knees to grip the front of the chair seat. The gentleman allows his hand to move along with the back of the chair as she scuttles toward the table. She then turns and gives him a half-smile to acknowledge her indebtedness for his contribution to her comfort.

Helping the Helpful Gentleman

DEAR MISS MANNERS:

I was brought up to believe that it was the man's place to hail a taxi, call the waiter, etc. I know these things are changing, but the men I know date from my own era, so that doesn't affect us. But I often find myself in a position where we will both lose from the man's inattention, when I could have saved the situation. For example, we are standing on a street corner, and I see an empty cab, but he doesn't until it is going past us. Or I spot the waiter, when we have been waiting twenty minutes for drinks, but since I can't call him, I can only tell my escort that I saw him—which doesn't help, because by the time I explain this, the waiter is gone. What can you suggest?

GENTLE READER:

You obviously have the wrong intonation when conveying this information. If you say to the gentleman, "There's a T-A-X-I!!!" or "I see our WAAAAAITER!!!!" you can accomplish what you wish without committing the sin of summoning help on your own.

Car Doors

DEAR MISS MANNERS:

What should an enlightened male do to help a (presumably also enlightened) female into his (or her) car? My boyfriend feels that it is demeaning to the woman when the man opens her door, waits around until she gets all tucked in (probably fuming impatiently), and then closes the door after her. At present, I notice he unlocks and opens my door for me, leaving me to close it for myself. I find this quite satisfactory and I agree that most women have no difficulty mustering the strength to close a car door. (We both feel that mothers and grandmothers should be treated in the traditional manner if they are accustomed to it.) My boyfriend wonders if not shutting the woman's car door after her would be frowned upon at a formal occasion. Also, could you say a few words about the liberated woman's role with regard to car doors? I always unlock and open my young man's door from the inside, after he is kind enough to unlock mine and help me in first, but I notice that some men are uncomfortable with this.

I also feel it is a gesture of respect to open a friend's door first if I am taking someone into my car, but I notice that most men are uncomfortable with this. It seems to me that women are let off too easily where manners are concerned. Equal rights demand equal courtesy from us. But rarely do I see another woman so much as reach across to unlock her escort's door from the inside—something that seems a basic courtesy. What is your opinion?

GENTLE READER:

Miss Manners has a puzzling time trying to decide why one courtesy is "demeaning" and another is a "gesture of respect," and therefore would like to forget the entire symbolic aspect of this ritual. Once we agree that the opening and shutting of car doors will not be a test of character or physical strength, we are left with two methods of accomplishing the opening: the traditional and the practical. If the traditional is performed, it should not be half done. The gentleman who has opened a door for a lady must also close it, preferably after waiting for her to pull her leg inside the car. It is also permissible for men and women to open doors for themselves and unlock them for each other. The difficulty comes only when the two methods are employed at the same time, as when the lady waits patiently inside the car because she is following the first method, while the gentleman, who is following the second, departs from the parking lot and enters, say, a restaurant, only noticing that something is wrong when the captain asks if he wants a table for one. The other consequence of mixed methods that you mention, the discomfort of some men when women attempt to be helpful and courteous to them, is very low down on Miss Manners' list of things to fret about.

In the Classroom

DEAR MISS MANNERS:

I can no longer get a mathematics section to teach without women midshipmen. In my twenty years at the Naval Academy, I have tried to keep correct form. Please tell me the feminine gender of "Sir, you have lost a minus sign," and the common gender of "I don't believe any of you gentlemen did any calculus last night."

GENTLE READER:

The first is "Madam, you have lost a minus sign," rather a swanky statement compared to the masculine form. As for the second, presumably you have rejected "ladies and gentlemen" on the grounds that it is too cumbersome or too much like the opening to an announcement that the star will not dance in tonight's performance. If this makes you uncomfortable, say, "I don't believe any of you did any calculus last night."

On One's Knees

DEAR MISS MANNERS:

Is there an etiquette rule concerning the crossing of knees? I ask because I must soon take oral comprehensives to qualify for my master's degree at a local university. During these interviews, appearances are important. Unfortunately, I recently skinned my right knee playing Frisbee, and I would like to cross my left leg over my right knee to hid the rather unattractive scab. Slacks are out of the question, since the event is considered semiformal, and I do not believe the board of examiners would appreciate it if I stood for the entire interview. (My skirt would be long enough to cover the scab if I were standing.) Can you offer me any guidance?

GENTLE READER:

Miss Manners will refrain from pointing out that your problem arises from the fact that you were out playing Frisbee when you should have been studying for your orals. Here is a quick course in knee crossing:

Neither gentlemen nor ladies properly cross their knees and the fact that this is universally done does not make it right. A gentleman's at-ease posture while seated is to place one ankle upon the opposite knee. A lady's is to cross her ankles. Take care that the examiners do not uncover other such areas of ignorance in you.

Discouraging Strangers

DEAR MISS MANNERS:

The last time I was in New York, I enjoyed everything about the city except being stared and whistled at by construction workers. I am not a prude, and any appreciative response to my physical charms ordinarily pleases me. But this is something else. I can't very well travel blocks and blocks out of my way to avoid such situations, nor do I wish to take to the veil, or take cabs. Within the bounds of propriety, then, what can I reply to a burly stranger who approaches me and announces, "Beautiful!" or "Very nice!" Even better, what, other than sprinting, can I do to dissuade him from approaching me at all?

GENTLE READER:

What, pray, did you contemplate saying that would convince these gentlemen of the construction business that you are an unapproachable lady? Miss Manners shudders to think. The idea you wish to convey is—is it not?—that no social intercourse, much less the personal remark of which the appraisal of one's body is an extreme form, is appropriate. Such arts as the frigid walk, the cut, and the shattering snub are, Miss Manners fears, lost in this age. These techniques from the past must be redeveloped, while another antique notion, that it is a compliment for a woman's looks to be noted before one has gotten to know her sweet character, must be dropped. Learn to walk with your nose in the air without falling off the curb.

Dueling

DEAR MISS MANNERS:

Even in the best of company and the most genteel of circumstances, it can happen that a man hideously insults one's wife. Given that dueling, alas, is outmoded, what is the best approach for the gentleman? Just how forceful can and should one become?

GENTLE READER:

Even in the heyday of the duel, there were gentlemen who preferred the cutting remark, or the cut direct of refusing to acknowledge the existence of a cad, to playing around with swords or pistols, which can be dangerous. Such cutting is still legal. Let Miss Manners give you a warning, however. A gentleman who attempts to defend his wife's honor without obtaining her full agreement to the idea that she has been hideously insulted will soon find that his life is no longer worth living.

❧ THE VIRTUOUS LIFE IN WICKED CITIES

Urban Neighbors

Good fences may or may not make good neighbors, but shared walls, particularly when the people living on different sides park their electronic equipment against them, do not. Miss Manners would therefore like to spell out some special rules of neighborliness, based on city living.

Urban neighborliness means that one has an obligation to notice disreputable characters who seem to be fooling around with a neighbor's house, and to report them. Urban neighborliness also means that one has an obligation not to notice disreputable characters whom one's neighbor has invited to his house for purposes of fooling around. A person who lives in the city should take in his neighbor's mail and newspaper when requested, so that the house whose tenant is absent will not seem deserted. A person who lives in the city should not take in the papers or magazines of those living in nearby apartments if the owners are merely late risers. Friendly gossip about the neighbors is as much a part of city as country living. It is not, however, friendly to pass on possibly damaging speculation about one's neighbors, particularly if interviewed about them by the Federal Bureau of Investigation.

Greater individuality is permitted in the city than in small towns or suburbs. Provided that your hours, your taste in music, and the color you paint your house suit the wishes of the person next door, there should be no conflicts. And if there are, an impartial arbitrator is no farther away than the corner squad car.

The Flowers Are Greener . . .

DEAR MISS MANNERS:

My neighbor's tree grows over the fence into my yard. I didn't mind, because last summer I could cut the blossoming branches—actually, I had to, to get them out of the way of my hammock. But I have also used them, instead of throwing them away. That is, I put some in vases in my house. My neighbor saw them there and got furious, claiming they were his flowers, not mine, and I had no right to keep them even if they grew over my property, in what he says is air that belongs to neither of us. We used to be fairly friendly, but if we don't settle this before next spring, there's going to be blood on the grass. I say the flowers are mine if they're on my side of the fence. What do you say?

GENTLE READER:

How high is the fence? For that matter, how big is your neighbor?

Overly Close Neighbors

DEAR MISS MANNERS:

Every spring and fall, when the evening weather is fine, we have a problem with our neighbors. We live in a first-floor apartment and all of our windows open immediately onto the backyards and patios of a group of individually owned town houses. Most of these town house types we never see or hear, but one family, the one whose patio is directly off our bedrooms, uses its patio continually in good weather. For four springs and autumns, we have had to shut ourselves up in our apartment or have these people hold their parties, discipline their children, and shush their barking dog virtually in our bedrooms. It is especially galling because they are very well off, we are not, and their attitude toward us has always been contemptuous and condescending. My complaints about parties have been met with, "Well, you see, we are getting together with old friends from Harvard, and I am sure that whatever momentary discomfort you feel is outweighed by our pleasure in seeing these wonderful old friends."

We'd like to move, but really can't afford to. I've thought of calling the police, but I can't say that, objectively speaking, they are so very noisy; it's just that they're in our laps when we want peace. We tried playing loud and horrible music, but there's a limit to how much Schoenberg I can listen to, and seemingly no limit on how much they can stand. We no longer care about maintaining any semblance of neighborliness; we just want them to hold it down. They are not stupid or evil people, just remarkably callous and thoughtless.

If you have no ideas, I'm afraid my husband is going to pour battery acid on their car.

GENTLE READER:

That is not a good idea. You would only be giving them the opportunity to sic the police or Schoenberg on you.

Please recognize that the villains here are not your neighbors, or even Harvard (unless you can trace the problem to the School of Design), but your architects, whoever they were. People should be able to entertain friends from the college of their choice and discipline their children and dogs in the free air without annoying their neighbors.

This is why Miss Manners recommends a semblance of neighborliness. Approach them again, preferably with other apartment dwellers who have been bothered by the noise. Miss Manners feels certain that they will sympathize if you explain to them how awkward it is for you to be the unwilling auditors of their family secrets and the indiscretions of their guests.

Disposable Problem

DEAR MISS MANNERS:

After large parties, I find my garbage cans filled to capacity. Is it acceptable to place my empty whiskey bottles in a less social neighbor's trash can?

GENTLE READER:

There are two possible problems here. First, your neighbor may suddenly take to drink and find that he has no room in his trash can for his own whiskey bottles. Second, he may be hit by sudden fame and find that the contents of his garbage can have become of interest to trashy publications or government departments, in which case the profiles of him they reconstruct as a result of your deposits will be misleading. Perhaps you could place your empty soda bottles in his trash can, thus leaving room in your trash can for your whiskey bottles. It would be a special nicety to ask his permission, if you are planning to do this on a grand scale—"Would you be so kind as to allow me to share your garbage can?"

An Elegant Address

DEAR MISS MANNERS:

Is it more elegant to spell out the number of your house, "Nine Hundred and Six," than to have it in numerals, as "906"? I see a lot of expensive new town houses with the numbers in words, and wonder if this is considered posher than the old way?

GENTLE READER:

Miss Manners has some moribund affection for the postal service, from the time that it employed her dear friend Anthony Trollope. Mr. Trollope saw to it that everyone had mail delivered in time to read at the breakfast table and things have gone from bad to worse since his death, but that is another matter. Miss Manners' point at the moment is that if Mr. Trollope had had to stand in front of houses trying to match such dreadful designations as "Eleven Aught Three" with respectable numbers written on letters by honest people, he would not have had time to write all those lovely novels.

Strangers on the Street

DEAR MISS MANNERS:

Please, sometime, offer some put-down for people who seek instant information from complete strangers who are going about their business and not bothering anyone. I seem to be the born victim of such people, who stop me on the street wanting to know the time (because I am wearing a highly unreliable watch) or when the shops open or, in the case of tourists (with cameras for identification as such), where one can get a good breakfast. This always seems a particularly stupid question to fire at an obvious resident (without a camera) who has to get up and make it herself. What's the best way to squash such people? They usually ask for directions when your arms are full of bundles so a blunt instrument isn't too practical.

GENTLE READER:

Miss Manners is not in the business of disseminating "put-downs" for the purpose of humiliating problem-ridden strangers. It seems to Miss Manners that even with a bad watch and full arms, the quickest way to dispense with the problem is to say "Sorry—I don't know." May you never be lost in a strange city where everyone else is busy minding her own business.

Sidewalk Pamphleteers

DEAR MISS MANNERS:

A lot of kids stand along the streets where I walk to work, handing things out. Usually it's religious pamphlets, but sometimes it is advertising of one kind or another, or political flyers. There I am, walking along, and someone shoves paper at me so that I have no choice but to be a litterbug or carry a bunch of literature with me through my whole walk until I get to a wastebasket. Can I just refuse to take it? It seems rude to turn one's head away from a church person, and I hate to hurt people's feelings. I've never done this sort of work myself, but I can imagine how awful it must be to have to stand on the street all day being rebuffed by strangers.

GENTLE READER:

If one takes a job, for spiritual or other reasons, which involves accosting strangers on street corners, one must accept the possibility of being rebuffed. The papers you mention are, regardless of their content, in the category of personally delivered junk mail and may be as properly refused as that which has been delivered by post.

Picketing

Although Miss Manners is a great believer in fresh air and acting out one's beliefs, she cannot say that she is happy to see so many people out picketing these days. The weekly sums that unions are able to allow to members who engage in this activity do not seem to Miss Manners to be commensurate with the strenuousness of the job and the working conditions on most sidewalks.

It is for this reason that Miss Manners would especially urge consideration to picketers on the part of the public, quite aside from the moral or social issues. Miss Manners also expects picketers to treat the public with courtesy. So does the law, for that matter.

The conventions of picketing allow the striking workers to make known their views through ritualistic marching in an orderly oval pattern, the carrying of signs, and distributing of leaflets. Miss Manners expects them to observe the amenities by not making their signs obscene or forcing leaflets on those who do not wish to take them.

Proper dress for picketers is either outdoor apparel appropriate to the weather, or the working clothes of the striking profession. Miss Manners was glad to see Washington striking musicians wearing white tie, and was even willing to waive for the occasion the general rule about not wearing evening dress during the day. In return, Miss Manners expects the public to remember the dignity of labor and not engage in undignified behavior toward its representatives. This means no shouting at them, no throwing of fruit or other objects, and no deliberate jostling. It also means that while one can decline to accept a leaflet, one may not take it and then visibly treat it with contempt, such as tearing it up or throwing it on the sidewalk. Ideological differences are no excuse for rudeness.

Passing Through

DEAR MISS MANNERS:
When one encounters a motorist waiting at a red light or stop sign whose automobile is occupying the pedestrian crosswalk, what should one do? I say that climbing onto and walking across the hood, or, if he is driving a small car, the roof, of his vehicle is always proper. My friend insists that this is correct only for small or two-door autos. In his view, when one encounters a four-door car blocking one's path, the proper action is to open the near-side door and walk through the vehicle, excusing oneself to any occupants of the rear seat. Which of us is correct?

GENTLE READER:
In your spirit of consideration to motorists, Miss Manners suggests that you extend the courtesies by knocking at the automobile window and asking the driver which method he or she would prefer. It is not polite to rush these things, which should last through two green lights.

Eating on the Street

DEAR MISS MANNERS:
Is it proper for one to eat while in the public right of way? Are fruits and vegetables fine, but not fried chicken? Of course I carry a napkin and do not litter with my leftovers, but what is really correct? Tomorrow's breakfast may depend on your response.

GENTLE READER:
Dessert is the only course that may be properly eaten while strolling on the sidewalk, and only certain desserts, at that. Apples, bananas, and pears are

acceptable; peaches and grapefruit are not. Ice cream cones and chocolate bars are fine, but pineapple upsidedown cake is out. You will notice that dessert means that no meats or vegetables are permitted, nor are the usual breakfast foods, such as pancakes with maple syrup or eggs once over lightly.

DEAR MISS MANNERS:

With the nice weather now, I enjoy eating my lunch in the park, bringing sandwiches, salads, chips, etc. Sometimes I don't quite finish the potato chips before it's time to go back to the office, so I nibble on them on my way back. If I'm still eating my chips when I get on the elevator at my office, must I share them, or do I keep them to myself? I don't want to be selfish, and I do want to do what is right.

GENTLE READER:

If Miss Manners told you to share with your co-workers, you would soon be worrying about strangers who had wandered into the elevator to visit other offices. If you agree to offer the chips to anyone with whom you engage in prolonged conversation, Miss Manners absolves you from sharing them with anyone else.

The Waiting Game

Many things in life are worth waiting for, but not all that long. Miss Manners would put a time limit on how long one should wait for salespeople to finish their conversations with each other before writing up one's order, or for a spouse who has departed with someone else to realize what a terrible mistake that was.

Nevertheless, waiting is now in a class with working as a popular pastime. A waitologist has estimated that the average adult spends one-tenth of his or her waking time waiting. There are waits for buses, banks, stores, theaters, gas stations, court cases, elevators, driver's licenses, and dentist appointments. One could easily pass one's life enduring just such basic waits. But there are also intermediary waits, such as waiting for the rain to stop, and advanced waits, such as waiting for your ship to come in. Some of these go in fashions. There was a time when all of America was waiting to be discovered by a movie talent scout in a drugstore, and now everyone is waiting for a television camera to come along and ask him to tell the world what he thinks.

It is the elementary and comparatively short-term wait with which Miss Manners is concerned at the moment. (If you want to hear about the others, you will just have to wait.) There are correct ways to wait and correct ways not to wait, as well as incorrect ways to wait and incorrect ways not to wait. For example, it is perfectly correct, although not many people realize it, to refuse to wait on the telephone. When Miss Manners is asked "Can you hold on for a minute?" she often replies, "No," and it is too bad that the person on the other end ties up his own line by putting her on hold anyway, because that person has not waited for Miss Manners' reply. One should also refuse to wait for inefficient or indefinite service. A restaurant should be able to tell you how long the wait will be, and a service person should not keep you waiting except to attend a previous customer.

It is rude to refuse to wait by announcing that one's needs take precedence over those of other waiting people. Miss Manners can think of no circumstances in which a person transacting the ordinary business of life can plead with legitimacy that it is more outrageous to expect him to wait than to expect it of others. "Let me go through, please—I'm in labor," perhaps, but what are you doing at the stockings sale then, anyway?

The only polite way to wait, if one must do so, is to bring one's own portable work or amusement. An unoccupied person waiting in line is by definition a potential raving maniac. A nice Jane Austen novel ready-to-go has preserved even the naturally tranquil spirits of Miss Manners. Using conversation as a means to pass the time is dangerous, in Miss Manners' opinion. Two people quietly discussing what a shame it is to have to wait are, by that same definition, a potential mob.

Parasols and Umbrellas

DEAR MISS MANNERS:

I have very delicate skin, and have never even tried to get a suntan, after dreadful childhood troubles with burns, and I now realize this is just as well, as I have been reading that sun can be damaging and drying to the skin. I am considering using a parasol this year. When does one carry a parasol and how?

GENTLE READER:

Anyone who can master the use of the umbrella can master the parasol, which is easier because it is not raining. That is, one keeps it close to the body when furled, and out of other people's faces when unfurled. One also takes care to do the furling and unfurling in an open space. The important thing to remember is that this instrument is not a weapon as is, for instance, the walking stick.

DEAR MISS MANNERS:

While walking through shopping crowds on a rainy Saturday afternoon and while maneuvering through rush-hour crowds at subway stops on drizzly mornings, I have narrowly missed being speared by many an out-of-control umbrella. I assume that common sense should prevail, but just what are the rules for opening, closing, carrying, and otherwise manipulating this potentially lethal accessory?

GENTLE READER:

Managing an umbrella is just like managing a parasol, only it is raining out.

DEAR MISS MANNERS:

I carry a big black umbrella, even if there's just a thirty percent chance of rain. May I ask a young lady who is a stranger to me to share its protection? This morning, I was waiting for a bus in comparative comfort, my umbrella protecting me from the downpour, and noticed an attractive young woman getting soaked. I have often seen her at my bus stop, although we have never spoken, and I don't even know her name. Could I have asked her to get under my umbrella without seeming insulting?

GENTLE READER:

Certainly. Consideration for those less fortunate than you is always proper, although it would be more convincing if you stopped babbling about how attractive she is. In order not to give Good Samaritanism a bad name, Miss Manners asks you to allow her two or three rainy days of unmolested protection before making your attack.

DEAR MISS MANNERS:

When two people are walking down the street together, sharing an umbrella, who should hold the umbrella? The man? Suppose it is the woman's umbrella?

GENTLE READER:

The taller of the two should hold the umbrella. This is not a matter of etiquette so much as it is having the sense to come in out of the rain.

❧ TRANSPORTATION

Driving

Machines do not have feelings. There is no use trying to tell Miss Manners how bad your answering machine feels when someone hangs up on it, or to engage her in a discussion of whether the automatic elevator is hurt if you keep pushing its button when it heard you the first time and is rushing up and down as fast as it can.

This is not to say that no inanimate objects have feelings—toys are loaded with feelings, for instance, and only a monster would break the heart of a rag doll—nor that property should not be treated with care. But if you are faithfully courteous to your fellow human beings, Miss Manners does not mind if you tell off your toaster or your computer terminal.

What she does mind is the way people crawl inside of machines and then start behaving rudely to others. You may kick your automobile, if it deserves it, but you may not park your own manners outside when you get into it. Miss Manners is amazed at the number of otherwise gentle souls who turn nasty when they are driving. And they all suffer from the wonderful, ostrichlike delusion that they cannot be identified because they are safely inside their cars.

It seems silly to her to have to say what good driving manners are. They are the same as the simplest, most obvious of nondriving manners, except that each person is surrounded by thousands of dollars in treacherous metal. You do not shove your way in front of others, and so you do not break into parking lot lines or force your way into crowded lanes. You do not occupy two seats in a bus, and so you do not allow your car to occupy more than the marked-off space of one parking place. You do not leave your things about in ways that block the progress of other people, and so you do not double park or cut off people's driveways. You do not shoplift, even if no one is looking, and so you do not break traffic laws, even if no one is looking. You do not breathe down the necks of people who don't walk as fast as you do, and so you do not tailgate slow cars. You do not yell at people, except in emergencies, and so you do not honk at people, except in emergencies. You don't scream insults at passing strangers—so you don't scream insults at passing strangers.

Why isn't all this obvious? Why does Miss Manners have to waste her time on such obvious decencies, instead of spending it on important matters, such as what to call the person your grown-up child lives with or how to keep the clam sauce on the spaghetti on the fork?

Probably it is because all the foolish anthropomorphizing that is done has led people to envy the capricious, aggressive, irresponsible lives led by machines, and tempted them to disguise themselves as machines and do likewise.

This Miss Manners cannot allow. For one thing, it sets a bad example to dishwashers and garbage disposals.

Standing for Equality

In one area alone, Miss Manners has noticed, women have achieved total equality. Even the most unenlightened of men are now allowing women to stand up on crowded buses while they, offering no argument at all, sit in comfort.

This is a complete triumph for equality because it is extended to all women. Elderly, disabled, and pregnant women are accorded the same standing privilege as their stronger sisters. Miss Manners is always pleased to see consideration for the rights of others, and trusts that this first step that men have taken will lead to their equally enthusiastic support of women's rights in other areas. Money, for example.

By way of encouragement, Miss Manners will take on the task of smoothing difficulties that arise when old systems are discarded and new ones have not yet taken their place. The bus situation is far from solved. Buses are now full of resentful faces and overactive elbows, because no system of precedence has been instituted to replace the old one based on gender.

Women who expect seats become indignant. Men who see women indignant because they expect seats become indignant. Young men look embarrassedly away from elderly women to whom they are not offering their seats. Elderly men look embarrassedly away from young women who offer them their seats. Seated people of both genders are discovering the real reason that it is undesirable to have women standing. It isn't because of any supposed weakness, but because of the strength a purse has when swinging on the arm of a standing woman, at the level of a seated person's head.

Recognizing that precedence by gender is disappearing and thoroughly disliking an approach based on every-man-for-himself and every-woman-for-herself, Miss Manners proposes precedence based on ability. It is the reverse of the present method, by which seats go to those most able to push their way into them. Standing room should be the reward going to those most able to stand comfortably.

It works simply. Any person who would obviously find it a hardship to stand because of advanced age, or extremely unadvanced age, for that matter; infirmity, or such temporary burdens as born or unborn babies, has first claim on a seat. After these people have been accommodated, the next opportunity goes to people who have burdens that are not acts of God but willfully incurred, such as groceries. (Miss Manners considers pregnancy an act of God and will not listen to your argument for putting it in this second category.) After that, the strong may seat themselves wherever they like. And now that you are seated, gentlemen, let us get on with that matter of money.

Dangerous Bags

DEAR MISS MANNERS:

There I'll be, sitting in a bus, maybe reading the paper, maybe just staring ahead, but not making any trouble for anyone, and some woman will hit me in the head with her shoulder bag. Those shoulder bags are a menace. They just swing right along, banging innocent people. What can I do to put such a woman in her place?

GENTLE READER:

No doubt you would consider putting her in your place, or what used to be known as giving a lady a seat, too drastic a measure. Miss Manners presumes that the swinging bag was not intended as a weapon, but that its owner is simply not aware of what is happening. To call it to her attention, you might offer courteously to hold her purse for her. That should send her scurrying to the other end of the bus, clutching it tightly.

Self-defense

DEAR MISS MANNERS:

What is the proper etiquette on a crowded bus? If some little old lady with a pointy umbrella hits me in the shins first, may I kick back?

GENTLE READER:

It is rare, nowadays, to have a deep-seated, well-motivated sensual urge that you are forbidden ever to gratify. However, Miss Manners must tell you that kicking little old ladies in the shins is one of them. Scream "Ow!" and stare at her with a frightened expression.

The Ever Useful Book

DEAR MISS MANNERS:

My question is on subway etiquette. I often meet a co-worker whom I do not like on the subway platform; we are heading for the same destination. May I say hello and go farther down the platform in order to read my book? Saying, on a sunny day, that I must run back to the office for my umbrella is losing its credibility.

GENTLE READER:

The instrument you require is in your hands, and it is not an umbrella. All travelers should carry books, whether they read or not, as weapons of defense against conversational assault. You need not move along the platform after you have greeted your colleague politely; merely move your nose downward toward your open book. If the person says anything more than a return hello, you pause, look up with a puzzled smile, and say slowly, "What?" as if awakening from a deep sleep. If the statement is repeated, you reply "Oh," with another vague smile, and then return to the book. Two or three rounds of whats and ohs should polish off even a determined talker.

Libraries in Transit

DEAR MISS MANNERS:

I start work fairly late—nine thirty in the morning—and by the time I get on the bus, it looks like a trash basket. The early commuters all read papers and then just leave them all over the place. I carry mine off the bus with me when I'm finished and throw it away. There are public trash baskets near practically every bus stop. Why can't people use them?

GENTLE READER:

Why can't people recycle their reading material? Miss Manners would like to see baskets placed at the doors of buses, in which riders may place their discarded magazines or papers or morning mail, and other riders may find something to read. At the least, Miss Manners hopes that you discard your paper neatly at the top of the public trash container, so that anyone who happens to be browsing inside will find it in legible condition.

Bus Chivalry

DEAR MISS MANNERS:

A young woman from my office who lives near me takes the same bus to work every day that I do. We have even occasionally paid each other's fares when one or the other of us doesn't have the exact change. Since we work at the same place, naturally we get off at the same stop. I want to be correct with her, but always letting her go first has been awkward. When we get on, does it depend on who pays the fares? How about getting off? She seems to stand back then, and one of these days we're going to miss our stop.

GENTLE READER:

A lady gets off a bus after the gentleman with her, although she boards the bus before. That way, if she can't make the steps in either direction, he will be there to catch her. (Don't blame Miss Manners for these rules; she doesn't make them up.) This order need not be violated if she pays both fares. She merely fixes the bus driver's attention with a half smile and nods toward the accompanying gentleman to indicate the financial relationship.

Subway Conventions

DEAR MISS MANNERS:

Is there a convention that subway exits and entrances should both be from the right? One usually sees only pushing and shoving. But even where people try to be courteous to each other, every time doors open to load and unload passengers, there's a jam-up.

GENTLE READER:

The American subway conventions have always consisted precisely of pushing and shoving. Those who practice it think of it as a challenging social form and pride themselves on adroit maneuvering during jam-ups. However, Miss Manners thinks you raise a valid point when you question whether more courteous subway riders should not develop their own conventions for the situation. In that case, yes, the sensible thing would be for those disembarking to precede those embarking.

Escalators

DEAR MISS MANNERS:

There is a very long escalator at my subway stop, and running down it often makes the difference for me in making or missing a train. In fact, there's a second, short escalator you have to take next, but as that is rarely working, everybody has to walk or run down it. My problem is that people standing on the working escalator are always in my way as I run down it, and get annoyed if I bump them, which I try not to do but can't always help. It seems to me there ought to be some rules of organization about escalators. I've been on them in other countries, where people who are not walking on them are instructed to stand to the right, leaving the left free for the walkers.

GENTLE READER:

That, of course, is an excellent system, and one that Miss Manners hopes will be adopted in this country as we catch up with the technological advances of more privileged nations. In the meantime, Miss Manners suggests you adopt skiers' precautions and call out ''On your left!'' as you come down behind them or, as the case may be, ''Out of control!''

Elevators

DEAR MISS MANNERS:

What is the proper way to enter an elevator, please? By the time all inside come out, the door is closing on those trying to enter. Why can't those inside come out on one side, so those going in can enter more easily? I ride elevators all day long for a delivery service, and some folks just won't give you room to get into it or hold the door. You should ride some with me—it would make you a drinking person.

GENTLE READER:

Thank you, but Miss Manners does not mix drinking with elevator travel because, for the reasons you describe, she considers it dangerous. While acknowledging your problem, she sees only additional problems in your solution, what with all the people inside pushing one another to get ready for their one-sided landings. The key courtesy here is door holding. If the person nearest the button panel keeps the doors open long enough for the exiting, followed by the entering, more people would travel on the same side of the doors as their limbs.

DEAR MISS MANNERS:

When the elevator stops at your floor, but you don't know whether it's going up or down, do you ask the people inside which direction it is going by saying the one you want, or the one you assume? Let me try again: Do you say ''Up'' if you want to go up, or if the elevator seems to be going up, even if you want to go down? You only get a second to ask the question, of course, because the doors shut right away, but I've had it happen that I say ''Down'' and the people inside say ''No, up,'' and close the doors when I really want to go up; and I've also had it happen the other way around.

GENTLE READER:

You should pronounce the direction that is your goal interrogatively. In a confusing world, we must all be able to state our own intentions, without taking on unbidden tasks such as second-guessing mechanical contrivances about their whimsical intentions.

DEAR MISS MANNERS:

Who should get out of an elevator first?

GENTLE READER:

The person nearest the doors. Provided, of course, it is his or her floor.

Table Manners

The Great Fork Dilemma

If Miss Manners hears any more contemptuous descriptions of etiquette as being a matter of "knowing which fork to use," she will run amok with a sharp weapon, and the people she attacks will all be left with four tiny holes in their throats as if they had been the victims of twin vampires.

Knowing or caring which fork to use is regularly cited as proof that one is narrowly fixed on a detail of life that is probably a deliberate booby trap set by the snobbish to catch the unsuspecting, and that therefore one has no time or heart left for the great spiritual values of life. The Great Fork Problem is used to ridicule the holy subject of etiquette, but the defenders of etiquette use it, too, when they claim that manners are "a matter of being considerate of others, not which fork to use." In either case, this is like declaring that as long as you truly have love for humanity, it is not important that you happened to put your left shoe on your right foot and your right shoe on your left foot.

Forks are not that difficult. It is possible that anyone who has learned to operate a computer, kitchen machine, or washer with delicate fabric cycles may also be capable of being trained to operate as many as three forks.

Why is this important? Because the person who has not mastered the fork is going to make a mess, miss the last course of dinner, or make the hostess get up

FORMAL PLACE SETTING. *The fork resting in the soup spoon is for oysters, which will be followed by soup. Then comes fish (use the outer fork and outer knife), then meat (the center fork and knife), then salad and cheese (the inner fork and knife). Above the soup spoon is a glass for sherry, to be drunk with the soup. The front center glass is for white wine (with the fish), and the glass at left is for red wine (with the meat). Behind that is the water goblet; to its right, the champagne glass (with dessert).*

from the table. Also, the forks may get tired some day of being bad-mouthed, and may cut off your food supply. Therefore, we will now take a minute to learn everything there is to know about Which Fork to Use.

Use the one farthest to the left.

That's it. That's all there is to know. Now run outside and cultivate the spirit until dinnertime. When you come in to dinner, you will find, typically (if you are dining with Miss Manners), that there are three forks to the left of your plate, three knives to the right, a soup spoon, and a teeny-weeny little forklet lying on the diagonal, resting its head in the bowl of the spoon. Now, what does this tell you? It tells you that you are not going to go to bed hungry; that's what it tells you.

The wee little fork is the oyster fork, which may not actually be farthest to the left, but is pointing left, to give you a hint. Use it to eat your oysters, dear. For the next course, you may relax from the fork question, and just eat your soup. With the spoon, dummy. The third course is a fish, which you will recognize immediately from the funny look in its eye. If you remember your lesson, you will reach for the fork farthest to the left, the outside fork, and guess what?

FORMAL DESSERT SERVICE. *Dessert equipment is a spoon, a fork, and a fingerbowl with doily, all on a plate. The guest moves the spoon to the right of the plate, the fork to the left and the finger bowl and doily to the left. The gentleman has done so, but the oblivious lady has left the footman to contemplate dumping the mousse on her lap.*

That is the fish fork! Then will come the meat, and the next fork you will discover will be . . . ? Show of hands, please. That is correct; the meat fork. Now we will eat salad, and the fork we will find will be . . . yes, it will be the salad fork.

This is presuming that the hosts set the table correctly and did not, for example, set out the forks in order of size rather than usage. Of course, if your hosts set things incorrectly they can hardly sneer at you for using the wrong fork. If they have to fetch you a fresh one because you ran out by following their system, it should teach them a lesson.

Naturally, the knives to the right of the plate will be moving right along at the same time. Miss Manners has not mentioned them because no one ever complains of not knowing which knife to use. They don't dare make nasty remarks about knives, because knives don't fool around.

There will now be a moment of panic in which you will become aware of the fact that you have no forks left, nor knives, nor spoons, and you haven't eaten your dessert. Have you done something wrong? Is it so wrong that you will be sent to bed without any dessert? No, indeed. All is well. The dessert plate is about to arrive. On it will be, of all things, a dessert fork and a dessert spoon. You will remove these, putting the spoon to the right of your dessert plate and the fork to the left, so you'll know just where they are when you need them.

That wasn't so hard now, was it?

A Reply

DEAR MISS MANNERS:

A dessert fork or spoon is *never* served on the dessert plate unless you are eating in a "hash house," or "greasy spoon" restaurant. I have worked in some of the finest restaurants and hotels in the country, in the dining room, and have been served dinner in elegant homes and have never seen silver served on the plate. That's as bad as a steak knife being shoved under your steak on a dinner plate at a fast-service steak house.

GENTLE READER:

If good manners were what is done in "some of the finest restaurants and hotels in the country," instead of what Miss Manners tells you, filled plates would be plopped in front of guests, sugar would be served in little packets with advertising on them, and conversation would be continually interrupted by such remarks as "Coffee now or later?"

Strict formal service does, indeed, mean that the dessert fork and (not or) the dessert spoon are brought on the dessert plate. Often the finger bowl is placed between them although there should really be a fruit course after the sweet dessert, in which case the finger bowl is brought in on the fruit plate, between the fruit fork and the fruit knife. Want to make something of it? If hash houses and greasy spoon restaurants wish to follow this correct procedure, so much the better for them. The rich have no monopoly on manners.

(For more complete instructions on formal service, please see pp. 498–499.)

(For a complete list of silver for formal service, please see pp. 376–377.)

The Wrong Fork

DEAR MISS MANNERS:

I was at a dinner party the other night where a lot of silver was spread out at each place, for many courses. I know you taught us which fork to use when, but I forgot. Kill me. My question concerns the next step after one uses the wrong fork. I realized, by looking at the hostess' place, that I would never come out even, and, in fact, I had to ask for something to eat the salad with. If I promise to go back and study fork order, would you consent to tell me what to do about mistakes?

GENTLE READER:

Miss Manners is a tolerant soul, but feels that you are concealing from her the extent of your mistake. If, for example, you ate the fish with the salad fork, why did you not have the fish fork left, with which to eat the salad? Miss Manners is always ready to receive back a sinner, but not those who steal the forks. However, she will let you in on the secret of correcting mistakes, if you promise not to tell anyone she said so. Lick clean the wrong fork you have just used and slip it back on the tablecloth while no one is looking.

American vs. European Eating

DEAR MISS MANNERS:

Could Miss Manners resolve a problem for a confused foreigner? I was brought up (as opposed to raised) to believe that it is correct to hold one's fork in one's left hand, tines pointing down, and one's knife in one's right. The fork is used to secure the particular square inch of food on which one has set one's sight, and the knife to sever it from its main body. The morsel of food thus attached, in single action, to the fork is conveyed by that utensil (tines still pointing down, of course) to the mouth. The knife remains poised for further use, at a suitably discreet angle and elevation, in the right hand. This procedure is repeated until all the food on one's plate (but not the gravy) has been eaten, or until the appetite is satiated, whichever happens sooner.

When I came to the United States over two years ago, I was broad-minded enough to realize that in America it is normal practice to transfer food from plate to mouth with the fork (tines up) in the right hand, but chauvinistic enough to suppose that actually it is more correct to do it in the manner described above. Now I am being asked by those of my friends who are concerned for my reputation in polite circles to believe that it is incorrect (a) to hold the fork with the tines pointing down; and (b) to have both knife and fork in hand at the same time. Am I to abandon all the tenets of English etiquette which I have held as true for so long?

GENTLE READER:

A simple answer to your question is that the left-handed eating technique you describe so well is the correct way to eat in Europe, and the fork-switching method is correct in the United States. However, there are several hidden issues here that complicate one's choice. If you will be patient, Miss Manners would like to address these more subtle matters.

Among reasons cited for using the "continental" method in the United States are the habits of childhood and loyalty to one's national origin, the desire to appear European, and the wish to eat as quickly and efficiently as possible. In your case, the first reason would be sufficient for you to stick to your original training. For Americans the second has to do with Western Europeans' being considered chic in America, while other countries are not, and their former citizens are usually therefore encouraged to become "Americanized" as thoroughly as possible. Miss Manners does not approve of native Americans changing their habits in order to appear fashionably foreign. Nor does she accept their excuse that the foreign method is more efficient. Efficiency in food service or consumption is not desirable.

Dissenting Opinion

Dear Miss Manners:

I am not asking for advice on manners. Instead, I am offering advice on how to advise others. You wrote about the use of various forks when eating in the presence of well-mannered people. How interesting! I have never thought that such things would be important to those who do not know how to use the knife and the fork in the first place—that is, to Americans.

The socially proper and internationally adopted handling of eating implements may date back to the days of the French and English courts. In those days, the manners of the nobility were imitated by the masses and since then have become an integral part of today's society, the American part not considered. In my service for the U.S. government since 1947, or almost thirty-two years, I spent seven years in foreign countries. Quite often, I had to participate in social occasions, and I was embarrassed at the way the Americans handled the eating implements, when even citizens of other countries here considered uncivilized could do much better than Americans, who have no manners to speak of. This abysmal ignorance of international etiquette must certainly contribute to the progressive deterioration of the American image in the eyes of the world. If no American diplomat, perhaps not even the President, knows how to handle the knife and the fork properly, then what should anyone think of the country that they represent?

According to the international rule of etiquette, the fork is always held in the left hand and the knife in the right. The fork may be put down temporarily for picking up a roll or some other tidbit, but the knife must stay glued to the right hand, except when the eating is temporarily interrupted, in which case the knife and fork should be left at an angle (not parallel). There are numerous such rules, some written, some not, of which the Americans have not the slightest conception. The most disgusting American habit is to cut the meat into small pieces and then put down the knife and proceed one-handedly with the right hand. Just like children, which just about reflects the overall mentality of the nation. As for myself, I would rather have no established manners than the manners by which this country now lives.

Gentle Reader:

Unlike you, Miss Manners is not easily embarrassed, but the thought of being represented abroad by an American exhibiting ignorance of his country and disrespect of the American people has succeeded in embarrassing her.

American table manners are, if anything, a more advanced form of civilized behavior than the European, because they are more complicated and further removed from the practical result, always a sign of refinement. One switches the fork from left hand to right each time a single piece of meat is cut, not after cutting all meat, an elaborate, time-consuming, and therefore impressive procedure. You do not impress Miss Manners by speaking of table etiquette at the French and English courts where, you will find from simple research, the use of the knife and fork are comparatively recent developments.

(For more information on American behavior abroad, please see pp. 660–664.)

Original Method

DEAR MISS MANNERS:

To me, the cut-and-shift American way of using a fork is silly and I find the tines-down English way to be inefficient.

I hold my fork mainly in my left hand when there is food to be cut or pushed onto the fork with my knife. The tines are up, and the handle rests on my ring finger and first knuckle, with two fingers and the thumb on top. I hold the fork the same way in my right hand for certain foods. On several occasions, remarks have been made about this alleged peculiarity of mine. I respond by making it clear I know the alternatives. You may say that people who make such remarks have more to learn about manners than what they assume I do not know. Would you, however, advise me to change a comfortable habit just to earn the good opinion not only of those who question me about it, but also of people with the decency to be quiet?

GENTLE READER:

You, sir, are an anarchist, and Miss Manners is frightened to have anything to do with you.

It is true that questioning the table manners of others is rude. But to overthrow the accepted conventions of society, on the flimsy grounds that you have found them silly, inefficient, and discomforting, is a dangerous step toward destroying civilization.

Dessert Service

DEAR MISS MANNERS:

I think it's ridiculous to put out both a fork and spoon just to eat dessert, as a number of people do for dinner parties, to show off their silver, I suppose. If it's a cake-type thing, all you need is a fork, and if it's a pudding-type thing, you just need the spoon.

GENTLE READER:

Miss Manners knows what type-thing you are: You are the type-thing that is more often discovering that you don't have enough equipment with which to eat. If there is no fish knife, you want to use a meat knife on the fish instead of making do with your fork, and if there is no salad knife, you think you have the right to use your butter knife on the lettuce. Be grateful for bounty. Besides, Miss Manners saw you sneaking cake crumbs into your mouth with a wet fingertip. Between the dessert fork, in the left hand, and the dessert spoon, in the right hand, you could have fed your greed gracefully.

DEAR MISS MANNERS:

At the dinner I was at the other night, there was a big oval spoon at the top of the plate (parallel to the edge of the table). It looked like a soup spoon, but there wasn't any soup served. Some people ate dessert with it, but there was a teaspoon on the coffee cup, so I used that.

GENTLE READER:

The big spoon is a tablespoon, helping with dessert under the assumed name of a dessert spoon. A dessert spoon, and not a teaspoon, is correctly used for eating dessert. The reason it may look like a soup spoon is that it may be a soup spoon. In that case, it would only work the soup shift on clear soups—there is another, round spoon for cream soups—and moonlight afterward on the dessert. If you want to know why, check the prices of silver flatware these days. Now, that teaspoon had no business attending the dinner party at all. It was taking an honest job away from a demitasse spoon. Miss Manners is going daft trying to explain all this, so would everyone pay attention and try to get it straight next time? (If you are still confused, please turn to pp. 376–377 for an exhaustive explanation of the employment of silver flatware.)

Pushing

DEAR MISS MANNERS:

We have an important question to ask you about "pushers"—the nondrug variety. When our four-year-old succumbs to our pleas to use eating utensils, he sometimes runs into the problem of needing something—other than his fingers—for pushing his food onto his fork. We've run into a family crisis: I was taught to use a small piece of bread as a pusher. My husband (although brought up at table with silver pushers that looked like little hoes—ugh!) insists it's more practical, proper, and less caloric to teach our son to use a knife. What would you push?

GENTLE READER:

Using the knife to push food onto the back of the fork is a European custom. Using bread to push food onto a fork is also a European custom. Both date from the time that Europe needed all the help it could get.

What do we Americans do? We have a marvelous time chasing the food merrily around the plate with a fork turned tines upward; or we use the fork to sneak up on the food unawares and scoop it up before it knows what hit it.

This is indeed a difficult motor skill, but lots of fun once you get the hang of it. Four-year-olds love learning to balance lots of little funny things, as you no doubt realize every time you try to pick up the marbles and Lincoln logs on the floor. Eventually, he should be able to master no-push eating. Nothing in life worth having, including plump garden peas, comes easily.

The Roll's Role

DEAR MISS MANNERS:

Our family has raised this question several times at the dinner table, and with several opinions. Is it good manners to hold food, such as bread or a dinner roll, in one's hand while using your fork in the other hand?

GENTLE READER:

This is not the proper role for a roll. However, they are often hired, free-lance, by forks in need of discreet assistance. If the fork cannot, for instance, capture those last three peas singlehandedly, it may engage the roll to take a quick swipe at the peas to make them surrender to the fork. This must be done without the apparent knowledge of the person attached to both fork and roll, who must assume an absent-minded expression. To hold two items of food in two hands with a purposeful expression makes one look greedy.

DEAR MISS MANNERS:

First, presuming there is no butter plate, do you place your roll on the cloth or the side of the plate? If there is no butter knife, do you use your own? Second, doesn't the vegetable go to the right and the dessert to the left? Some places differ.

GENTLE READER:

1. One does the best one can with the available materials. If there is no bread-and-butter plate, use the tablecloth for parking the roll, and the luncheon plate for parking the butter. Bread, or rolls, with butter are not correct at a formal dinner (please see p. 494). If the hosts serve bread and butter they should provide butter plates and knives. If there is no butter knife, use your own. If you don't have one, call it quits. An essential of good manners is knowing when to give up.

2. Side dishes for vegetables are used only in restaurants, and dessert is put on the table when another course occupies the center of each place only in bad restaurants. In household service, the vegetable is put on the same plate as the meat, smack in front of the person who is to eat it, and when that has been removed, the dessert is put there. If you demand to have a dozen little dishes in front of you, eat curry.

The Full Mouth

DEAR MISS MANNERS:

It seems that whenever I have just popped a bite of food into my mouth, I am asked the title of my master's thesis or my views on women's liberation—nothing, in short, that I can get out of with a simple nod of the head. What is the correct response in this situation? Must I force my questioner to wait until I've chewed and swallowed that bite? If it was almost completely chewed, can I stash that

last morsel in a spare cheek and answer—provided the answer is short? Any
choice seems rude, but as more and more business is conducted over meals, this is
becoming a real problem. When I am dining with someone I wish to impress,
my boss for instance, I take small bites just in case.

Gentle Reader:

In today's hectic world, one is often faced with the choice, at business lunches
or dinners, of losing the opportunity to make a statement or losing one's unfinished plate to an impatient waiter. Small bites and cheek stashing are, indeed,
two legitimate solutions. Another is to develop a facial expression that, without
opening the busy mouth, suggests that wonderful words are about to come out of
it, well worth the waiting. The eyes brighten, the lips smile knowingly, and a
hand is raised slightly. If you will practice this expression before a mirror, you
will find that you can develop it into something mesmerizing that will buy you
the time to swallow your food in silence.

Elbows

Dear Miss Manners:

My home economics teacher says that one must never place one's elbows on
the table. However, I have read that one elbow, in between courses, is all right.
Which is correct?

Gentle Reader:

For the purpose of answering examinations in your home economics class,
your teacher is correct. Catching on to this principle of education may be of
even greater importance to you now than learning correct current table manners,
vital as Miss Manners believes that is.

Elbows are banned during eating because of the awkward, cranelike motion
it gives to the hand on the other end of the elbow, trying to get down to table
level for food. Also it is a delightfully easy error to catch children in, whose
other errors may be more subtle.

When one is not actually eating, it is still a good rule to keep one's arms close
to the body, but a less formal posture, with one elbow parked close to the plate
during a pause in the meal, is no longer punishable by hanging.

Grace

Dear Miss Manners:

What is the procedure when one has the first bite of potato halfway to the
mouth and then discovers that everyone else is waiting for the host to say grace?
Do you proceed and pop it into the mouth, or lay the fork down at once? If the
former, does this invalidate the grace?

GENTLE READER:

God will forgive all sins, even gluttony, but to talk with your mouth full—even to say "Amen"—is unforgivable in this life. Therefore, Miss Manners considers it theologically safer to put down the fork, gracefully.

When to Begin

DEAR MISS MANNERS:

My husband, who is in all other respects a gentleman and a scholar, is extremely incorrect in one particular. When we give an occasional dinner party, he always sits down and serves himself and begins eating, sometimes even before the other guests have been alerted to the fact that dinner is ready. There is almost always enough food to go around, and it's not that good anyway, so I can't understand his behavior. I tell him the guests should be served (or allowed to serve themselves) first and then we should all begin eating together, but he says this is old-fashioned and silly, and it's every man for himself these days.

GENTLE READER:

Your husband's justification is the second worst explanation Miss Manners has ever heard for the rudeness of eating before one's guests. The worst was from a gentleman of Miss Manners' acquaintance who explained the fact that his wife had eaten her dessert in the kitchen before giving the guests theirs by saying, "She doesn't believe in delayed gratification."

If you can persuade your husband to reverse his barbaric practice, do so. If not, allow Miss Manners to suggest to you a better excuse. As he begins eating, say to your guests, "Wait a minute, please. Rhino always likes to make sure the seasoning is just right before he lets our guests have this dish." As your meals are "not that good anyway," this will be a convincing explanation.

While Waiting to Begin

DEAR MISS MANNERS:

In households where people still observe the custom of waiting for everyone to be served before anyone can start eating, thus making all the people who were served early eat their dinners cold, what are you supposed to do while waiting? Just pretend the food isn't there in front of you and sit with your hands folded, trying not to let your mouth water?

GENTLE READER:

Miss Manners senses a negative feeling from you about this custom, which was instituted on the principle that no one should be ready for seconds before everyone has had firsts. The violation of this principle leads to the uneven distribution of food in the world which, in turn, brings on famine, war, and other things too unpleasant to mention at the dinner table. While waiting for your hostess to signal the beginning, you may break open your potato, and even butter it. That is quite enough excitement before dinner.

Dear Miss Manners:

Is it considered bad manners to take a sip of your drink at dinner, before everyone has been served food?

Gentle Reader:

It is considered an act of survival.

Passing Directions

Dear Miss Manners:

Which way does one pass the food, to the right or the left?

Gentle Reader:

Food platters should travel left to right, as most people are right-handed and can serve themselves more easily with the right hand reaching over to the left side. If the majority at the table is left-handed, the food should travel from right to left. Guests have no responsibility for such decisions, as they will encounter a platter already marching along as whoever launched it has seen fit. If you try to reverse whatever pattern is underway, you will end up with the most dreadful traffic jam, to say nothing of gravy all over your lap.

Salad Servers

Dear Miss Manners:

I am always confused when confronted with salad servers. How does one handle the situation?

Gentle Reader:

By the handles, of course. Miss Manners assumes that you are talking about the salad spoon and fork accompanying bowls or plates of salad, from which one is supposed to serve oneself a portion. Using both fork and spoon in one hand, as opposed to taking one in each, is an impressive feat, but of more importance gymnastically than socially. A failure, when salad is involved, is apt to be a dramatic one. Occasionally one sees the fork and spoon joined together scissors-fashion, but that hardly seems of real service to those who have trouble with the one-handed operation, or fair to those who have mastered doing the one-handed trick. If you encounter them, pretend they are tongs; use only one hand.

Placing the Salad Bowl

Dear Miss Manners:

Where exactly does the salad bowl go?

Gentle Reader:

Directly under the salad. Where this combination is then placed on the table depends on whether the salad is being served by itself, in which case it takes center stage, or whether it is in a crescent-shaped plate, in which case it is served on the side. The left side.

Placing Used Silver

DEAR MISS MANNERS:

Yesterday, my fourteen-year-old daughter came home from school and we were discussing where to put your silverware after you finish eating. She says her teacher said it's wrong to place them on the dinner plate with knife, fork, and spoon neatly across the top of the plate, the knife blade turned in. My parents were bugs on manners and table setting, and I was brought up that way, so I've always told my children the same.

My daughter never did say what the teacher thought was proper. What do you do with the silverware—put it on the tablecloth and possibly stain it? I thought I'd ask you. Whatever—I will be gracious, even if corrected.

GENTLE READER:

Miss Manners hopes that the teacher will be equally gracious. Your method is essentially correct. That disclaimer, "essentially," is put in because Miss Manners wonders what the spoon is doing there. A spoon and fork may be used together for eating dessert, but the presence of the knife indicates that you are talking about a meat course and there is no business for the spoon's intruding, even if the meat was swimming in béarnaise sauce.

The knife blade should, as you say, be turned toward the eater, but there is a difference of opinion among those of us who care whether the fork prongs should be up or down. Some leeway is also permitted in the angle at which the fork and knife are to be placed—straight across the plate, or diagonally across, usually from eleven o'clock to five o'clock. Perhaps the teacher was confused by two positions associated with the unfinished meal. If one is pausing while eating, the fork and knife placed in a crossed position—the handle of the fork to the left and the handle of the knife to the right, with the two instruments crossed at the center plate—tells the waiter or footman or host that you have not finished. Another position, knife and fork at right angles to the table edge, but off to the right-hand side of the plate, is used when passing the plate to a host for seconds, as it leaves the central part of the plate bare to receive more food.

Whew. They teach these things in schools these days?

Napkins

DEAR MISS MANNERS:

Is there a rule of etiquette that covers when one should place a dinner napkin on the lap? Recently, a friend corrected me on this. He feels it is correct, when in a restaurant, or club, to unfold the napkin and place it across the lap the moment one sits down at table. I feel that when planning to spend some time

over cocktails before ordering, common sense rules that I place the napkin on my lap as the dinner is ordered—or better yet, when dinner is served.
GENTLE READER:
Common sense has nothing whatever to do with etiquette, but in this case, it happens to coincide with the hard-and-fast rule that one puts one's napkin on one's lap immediately upon sitting down at the dinner table, regardless of whether it is a cocktail or soup that one is first planning to spill onto one's lap.

"Serviettes"

DEAR MISS MANNERS:
When is a napkin a "serviette"?
GENTLE READER:
When it is trying to show off.

DEAR MISS MANNERS:
I must comment on your statement that a "napkin" is called a "serviette" only when the person is being snobbish. Actually, a napkin is rightly called a serviette in England, Australia, Canada—most English-speaking countries. They consider a "napkin" to be the sanitary type, or a baby's diaper, neither of which would be appropriate for a dinner table. I have no doubt that you will receive many corrections on this item.
GENTLE READER:
Indeed, you are right. About receiving "corrections," that is, not about the napkin. Most of the letters on the subject (but not all) were so courteous that the most gracious thing Miss Manners could do would be to admit to error. Unfortunately, this is not possible. Miss Manner refers you to "U and Non-U. An Essay in Sociological Linguistics" by Alan S. C. Ross, part of dear Nancy Mitford's *Noblesse Oblige: An Enquiry into the Identifiable Characteristics of the English Aristocracy.* Professor Ross (of Birmingham University in England) lists "serviette" as "non-U," or not upper class, and "napkin" as "U," or upper class, usage in England. He adds that the choice between these words is "perhaps the best known of all the linguistic class-indicators of English." This would sound very snobbish if it were not that, according to the thesis of his essay, fancy, snobbish-sounding words are non-U, while plain English ones are U.

Napkin Rings

DEAR MISS MANNERS:
What about napkin rings?
GENTLE READER:
Yes, what about them? Napkin rings are used only at the family dinner table but even there are a complicated subject, involving many levels of reasoning.

Miss Manners would like to explain the complexities before reaching a judgment. Let us start from the top:

1. The highest level of thinking about napkin rings is that they are horrible, because they presuppose that not everyone is issued a freshly laundered napkin at every meal.

2. Next, we have the school of thought that this is an imperfect world, and one ought to make the best of it by at least ensuring that one person does not have to suffer for the sins of another, as would happen if a fastidious person and a greasy one regularly ate together without benefit of napkin ring.

3. At the bottom of the social level, we have people who habitually use paper napkins. These people do not object to napkin rings, but are puzzled about what they are for.

Miss Manners finds herself in the unusual position of favoring the middle course. She feels that napkin rings promote social morality by forcing people to live with the consequences of their behavior.

A cloth napkin that is not to be reused before being laundered is left looking like a paper airplane—pointed at the top, and the sides both extended to form an elongated triangle. Actually it is always politely presumed that napkins are never reused, the only exception being the family dinner, at which each person folds his or her napkin and inserts it into the proper napkin ring. A houseguest may follow this procedure also. Not doing so suggests the presumption of fastidiousness on the part of one's hosts, but they will probably not appreciate this fine point.

As for paper napkins, whatever is left of them at the end of the meal should be left as neatly as possible at one's place. Miss Manners refuses to think about the possibility of their being refolded for possible reuse.

Paper Napkins

DEAR MISS MANNERS:

Why can't I use paper napkins—the heavy kind—at a dinner party? They look all right, do the job, and it's more practical to be able to throw them away instead of cleaning them, but some people are fussy about them.

GENTLE READER:

The identical claims were made, a few years ago, for paper underpants. How come you don't wear them?

Declining Food

You were brought up to believe that you must at least toy with food that you cannot stomach, as it were. As a guest in someone's house, you are served a dish you cannot eat. Perhaps you are allergic to it, perhaps it is against your religion or principles, or perhaps you just hate it.

What you do, to be polite, is to mess it up. Grabbing the top of your fork, to keep as much distance as possible between you and the despised goodie, you shove it from one end of the plate to another. Or you hide it under the nearest green leaf. If you are really adventurous, you might excuse yourself and drop it into the potted plant, the dog's mouth, or the toilet. Anything to avoid admitting that you haven't yum-yummed it right down.

If everyone followed these rules, Miss Manners would not be eating lobster salad for lunch today, and Miss Manners is excessively fond of lobster salad.

Young Mr. Cutlip Perfect, as Miss Manners' houseguest, was expected to jump out of his dining room chair with the thrill of it all when lobster was passed. Lobster is not often served in private households these days, what with the difficulties of taking out second mortgages. Indeed, he did try to look pleased, but there was a distinct difference between his valiant version of the look and the genuine versions that appeared elsewhere around the table. When Miss Manners called him on it, he admitted his true reaction to seeing what he considered a hostile-looking crustacean staring up at him.

Miss Manners would not have solicited this response under many circumstances, and Mr. Perfect was correct not to volunteer it until asked. If it had been a large dinner party, for example, Miss Manners would not have undertaken to deal with the problem, preferring to consider it that the hostess' responsibility ended with providing edible food and that any difficulties after that were the responsibility of the guest.

However, this was an informal gathering, and Miss Manners was pleased that the young gentleman had the sense to respond frankly to her question. There is a limit—directly related to the price per pound—to foods that should be messed up for the sake of manners. So Mr. Perfect got scrambled eggs, and Miss Manners gets lobster salad.

Second Helpings

DEAR MISS MANNERS:

My grandmother always said, "You must never ask anyone, 'Would you like a second cup of coffee?' or 'Will you have some more dessert?'" She said it should always be, "Would you like a cup of coffee?" or "Will you have some dessert?" no matter how many portions the person has had already. The other way, she said, only calls attention to the fact that the person is having a lot to eat or drink and is therefore impolite. Is this a general rule?

GENTLE READER:

It should be. There is something less than gracious about being urged, "Oh, come on, have a fifth slice of pie—you've hardly eaten anything." Consider this wisdom from dear Lewis Carroll's *Alice in Wonderland:* " 'I've had nothing yet,' Alice replied . . . 'so I can't take more.'

" 'You mean you can't take *less*,' said the Hatter: 'it's very easy to take *more* than nothing.' "

Crème de la Crème

DEAR MISS MANNERS:

A guest who asked for cream in his coffee took one taste of what I gave him and spluttered and splattered it all over, shouting, "That's not cream!" in an accusing voice. Well, technically, it wasn't cream, I suppose. None of us in the house uses cream, and we don't keep it on hand unless we're having a big party because it spoils so quickly. What we keep, usually, is skim milk, and that's what I gave him. (He was one of several neighbors who had dropped in to talk about taking action to get a stop sign put up at an intersection that is dangerous; we rounded up people Sunday morning, and I volunteered our house, but hadn't been expecting them earlier. Nobody else asked for cream.) I thought it was awful of this man to make a scene in front of everyone, but he obviously thought I was being awful. Which of us was wrong?

GENTLE READER:

Making a scene takes precedence, in rudeness, over untruth in packaging. "Will you take cream?" is rather a charming expression, and Miss Manners would certainly not pursue truth so far as to ask, "Will you take some artificial white powder?" One compromise is to ask, "Will you take milk?" without specifying "skim." Another is to ask, "Will you take cream?" hoping that no one will. Then, if someone should say yes, you can add quietly to that person, "I'm afraid, actually, all we have is skim milk. Will that do?" This, too, has a nice *Alice in Wonderland* quality, if done properly.

Picnic Table Manners

One reason that picnics are popular is that many people believe that the rules of table behavior do not apply to tables made out of moss or worse. So here comes Miss Manners, like a queen bee on a rare royal tour, anxious to spoil your pleasant little outing by telling you that they do, too.

It is true that some rules for eating outdoors are different from those that apply indoors. For example, it is permissible to execute extraneous wildlife found crawling across the picnic table, while any such creature making an appearance at a private, indoor dinner table must be ignored by the guests. At picnics, one may kill ants, but not complain of their presence. Accepting discomfort cheerfully is the basic rule of picnic behavior. If one is unalterably opposed to being bitten, sunburnt, and having sand mixed with one's food, one should not go picnicking. The exception is that a small child drowning in a creek may call out to the adults at the picnic table, even if it means interrupting their conversation.

Nevertheless, it is important not to introduce the discomforts of civilization into a picnic to compete with nature's own discomforts. Radios, plastic forks and knives, paper plates and napkins, and tin cans are among the abominations that one has no right to bring to the countryside. The well-supplied picnic basket must include implements with which food may be served and eaten in dignity, and no one can eat decently from a paper plate with a plastic fork, since when the side of the latter is applied to the center of the former, they both buckle, with disastrous results.

Food should be chosen that can be served at its proper temperature, and it should be repackaged so that it may be served with no commercial containers appearing on the table or grass. If food is cooked at the picnic area, no more allowances are made for the chef's ruining it than would be made at a dinner party indoors.

The differences between indoor and outdoor manners are:

One may never spill food accidentally indoors, but it is permissible to spill outdoors onto the grass, although not the blanket, tablecloth, or dog.

Children may be served first at picnics in the hope that they will then go play in the poison ivy.

One may perform such normally unacceptable acts as reaching across the table, reclining at one's place, and licking one's fingers, provided that they are done with grace.

Everyone gets to help clean up, this not being, as indoors, the sole privilege of the hosts.

There is no seating plan, so that people may sit where they wish, although it is customary to ask permission before putting one's head on someone else's lap.

❧ AT THE FAMILY TABLE

Dear Miss Manners:

Another big family dinner! I can't stand it, I can't stand it, I can't stand it! First of all, they'll all show up looking like slobs because "it's only family." The kids will be dirty before they get here, and it won't be ten minutes before they'll get a good fight going, and then the various grown-ups will start one by making remarks about how this child or that one was brought up (meaning they weren't). It's all right to insult people, you see, because families should be frank. I don't even want to think about the table manners. The children don't have any, and the grown-ups do but don't use them because "among family" it's fine to hunch over the table, talk with your mouth full, eat with your fingers, and discuss your digestion problems. Also, they'll turn on the television during dinner, and in the interests of "saving work," they'll offer to lick their dinner forks and use them for dessert, and ask for paper napkins. Believe it or not, these people—my relatives!—are not animals when they take clients out to dinner or see their friends. Just when they're with family. I keep hearing that "the family is dying" in America. Any chance of this happening before dinner today?

GENTLE READER:

Miss Manners has heard a great deal about the death of the family, but little about the death of the family dinner. In her opinion, the crimes are inseparable, as a murder-suicide.

Properly practiced, the family dinner is a pleasure that makes keeping the family together worthwhile. People who know only the company dinner table and the kitchen counter, with nothing in between, don't know what they're missing. Your family is among these unfortunates. If each household representing part of the greater family were to learn the ritual through daily practice, you might even be able to save the extended family, which sounds as if it is heading straight for extinction, probably today.

Here are the rules:

Family dinner is regularly scheduled every night of the week, and delays or absences must be registered in advance.

A reasonable attempt is made to make the table and the participants presentable. It's amazing what cloth napkins can do for the one and washcloths for the other.

Entertainment is live, not electronic. First, each person gets a turn to present his or her news of the day, and then general conversation is held. Television and telephone interruptions are not allowed, but bragging is, and even encouraged.

Good table manners are practiced, but they are good family table manners, as opposed to good company table manners. The chief difference is that chicken, spareribs, and other such messes may be picked up and thus enjoyed in a way they never satisfactorily are with knife and fork. Spoons may even be used for getting up all of special sauces—but only in the privacy of the family, with a strict pact never to tell outsiders. This delicate blend of politeness and piggishness is extremely pleasant. Neither eating out nor eating directly from stove top or refrigerator can compare with it. It even justifies keeping one's family alive.

Family Manners

DEAR MISS MANNERS:

Whenever we stay with my sister and brother-in-law in Florida and have chicken, we encounter this same situation. We all finish about the same time, but my sister insists upon going over each bone in the chicken breast and "sucking" it clean, whilst commenting how delicious it is. This takes a good ten minutes or more, as you know how many bones there are. Are we remiss in leaving? We were told we were rude in not sitting through this "drama."

GENTLE READER:

The one great rule of family dining is that it is permissible to pick up the chicken bones. As one may not do this, unless specifically invited to, at the tables of nonrelatives, and as it is one of life's great pleasures, we need this privilege as an incentive to keep families together. Granted that your sister somewhat overdoes it, she seems to be having a good time. It is not really polite to leave town while she is doing this. Nor is it polite for her to compliment her cooking. However, you may exercise another family intimacy by getting up and clearing the table under the pretense of being helpful. If you start with your own plate and make it to the kitchen before she protests, you will have conveyed the idea that the chicken course is over.

Dunking

DEAR MISS MANNERS:

At home, I am a "dunker." I love to dunk everything (doughnuts, cakes, etc.) in my tea or coffee. It's the way I enjoy my milk and cookies. However, when I am in a restaurant or visiting someone, I "hold back" because I feel it is considered bad manners. Is it?

GENTLE READER:

In admitting that it is, Miss Manners is tempted to add a word of consolation, indicating that she knows what fun you must be having at home and is sorry to keep you from transporting it beyond your door. On second thought, it occurs to her that you wouldn't have nearly as much pleasure from dunking your cookies in your milk at home if you weren't aware that it was naughty.

Going Too Far

DEAR MISS MANNERS:

The other night, my family and I were having a discussion. My father said that nowadays it was acceptable in a restaurant to pick up lamb chop bones with your fingers to get the last few bites of meat. We all disagreed with him and made a bet. Please answer this soon and settle the bet. I could sure use the money.

GENTLE READER:

It is yours. But when you take it, please express Miss Manners' warm sympathy to your father, whose principle of not wasting food Miss Manners finds thoroughly understandable. In fact, Miss Manners began her career among Victorian families who thought it a status symbol to waste food as the heroine of the admonition, "Leave something on your plate for Miss Manners." We no longer believe in this arrogant behavior and Miss Manners has found more dignified sources of nourishment. She does not like to see good food wasted; however, she cannot carry it so far as to recommend gnawing at lamb chop bones in public. Tell your father that outside of the privacy of the home, much can be accomplished in the way of digging, with a sharp and agile knife.

Alternate Methods of Eating

DEAR MISS MANNERS:

At the family table, where meals are usually served as one course and on one plate, which of the following approaches to eating a meal is considered more proper: (1) Partaking alternately of the different items at one's place, or (2) consuming each item in its entirety before proceeding to the next? Or are both ways equally correct?

GENTLE READER:

Miss Manners is tempted to turn tolerant now and say, "Oh, go ahead. Eat in the order you like. What does it matter?" But then she began to consider that you probably have children and that their future must be considered. So here is a more responsible answer:

In the American style of eating, fork in the right hand, it is improper to put more than one food on the fork for each trip it makes to the mouth. Surely you will grant that. Technically, then, there is nothing wrong with taking, say, a forkful of steak, sequestering it in the cheek, and then sending along a forkful of mashed potatoes to accompany it—provided, of course, that you do not open your mouth while it contains food. (In manners, as in less worthy causes, cheating and discretion must be inseparable.)

This is a variation on the principle of alternation, which is the conventional method and the one Miss Manners recommends you train your children to prefer even if it is too late for the adults. Why? Because the variations possible on the principle of eating all of one food, and then going on to another are even more fraught with danger, if you can imagine that.

Do you eat the food you like best first and the one you dislike most, last? Or do you start with the chore and save the treat? Both methods are practiced, but children always choose the first, because they have no real sense of future. If you allow them to do so, your life will be filled with conversations that go:

"Eat your eggplant, dear."

"I can't, I'm all full."

Is that the memory you wish them to take through life of the beloved ritual of the family dinner?

For choosers, Miss Manners recommends taking no more than three consecutive mouthfuls of one food before breaking it with one of a different food. This is a compromise, but so is life.

Food Rejects

DEAR MISS MANNERS:

My mother-in-law has awful table manners. Not only does she not use serving forks, but she eats with her fingers, saying the food tastes better, and spits out the "skins," or anything she feels too tough, in half-chewed wads onto her plate. We are going to visit her soon. Is there some polite way to tell her how unpleasant this is? She does not take criticism at all well.

GENTLE READER:

In the annals of crimes against etiquette, correcting one's elders and correcting others in their own house are more heinous than expectorating food onto one's plate. Miss Manners suggests you direct your critical feelings toward your children's table manners. Children have no choice about taking criticism. If it will enliven your visit, you may correct them at their grandmother's table for doing the same thing their grandmother is doing.

Fingers

DEAR MISS MANNERS:

I have acquaintances who seem to remember the teaching that crusts or other "pushers" to assist food onto a fork are taboo beyond the nursery table. Their solution is to use one or more fingers for the purpose, with fingers busy in their plates throughout a meal. This could be something that has developed from the proliferation of dips and fast foods, but I find it somewhat distressing to see. Would you please say whether I am just slow in moving with the times, or whether I may be permitted to shudder?

GENTLE READER:

Yech. Distressing it certainly must be, to see all your friends with their busy little fingers in their plates, but when they claim to be doing this in the sacred name of manners, bragging that they are not using bread for the purpose—well, that is truly disgusting.

Using bread to sop up sauces or help spear difficult foods is a middle-European custom of dubious class origins. The way to do it, if you must do it at all, is to put a small piece of bread on the dinner plate, spear it with the fork as if it were a food legitimately domiciled there, and then quickly mop up.

It is Miss Manners' belief that Americans with pure minds and bodies are perfectly capable of triumphing over any article of food without calling in assistance from the breadbasket. Sopping up sauces with bread should be confined to the nursery—"nursery," in this sense, meaning the family, of whatever age, at home enjoying garlic butter in privacy. Using the fingers should be confined to oblivion.

Rank at the Family Table

DEAR MISS MANNERS:

Could you elaborate on family etiquette regarding meals? Who serves? Who is served first? What is served first? Also, who is served second, etc., when the family is alone, and when the family has one or two guests?

GENTLE READER:

In a simple, family-style meal, consisting of perhaps six people—a grandparent, two parents, two children, and a guest—it is possible to combine four different ranking systems, so that everyone gets his just desserts, except, of course, children who don't deserve them.

The systems are blood, age, gender, and ability.

The privilege of serving dinner should go to the adult (age) in the family (blood) who is most likely to get the food divided and transferred from platter to plate without its lingering along the way on the tablecloth (ability). The first portion goes to the oldest (age) unrelated (blood) female (gender). Within the family, adult women are served by generation (first Grandmama, then Mama), and then adult men by generation (Grandpapa after Mama but before Papa). (As one of these people is likely to be doing the serving, that person is removed entirely from the order of precedence. Serving oneself last not only looks modest, but gives one a clean place in which to work.)

The youngest generation should be served last, by the same rules, beginning with unrelated females, and so on. However, many adults have noticed the advantage, in large family gatherings, of serving children first and then "excusing" them from the table. Ability is an important factor in children's ranking, as a person who lacks the ability to restrain his wailing when he sees food on the table but not in front of him is likely to find that he has rapidly passed the entire ranking system. There is an unfortunate moral in that.

Enlisting Help

DEAR MISS MANNERS:

It's not that I mind having the big family Christmas dinner at my house every year. I do a lot of work—we're about fifteen people, usually, not counting the babies—and look forward to having people enjoy the decorations and the food. But then every year, I end up in the kitchen while the grown-ups are watching television or playing Scrabble, and I'm also the one who has to deal with the children when they start fighting. How can I enlist some help coping with all this? Usually, they just help clear the table and then go off into the living room, thinking they've done enough.

GENTLE READER:

Do not let them have this feeling of accomplishment. Announce merrily, "Oh, let's leave things for a minute," and then go with them yourself, into the living room, for coffee. An hour later, as the postdinner stupor sets in, you can then say, with equal graciousness, "Well, I suppose we ought to get to those dishes," and accept the help offered. Someone who does not volunteer may then be told sweetly, "Will you look after the children for us while we clean up?"

Take-Out Food

DEAR MISS MANNERS:

What is the proper way to serve carry-out Chinese food or pizza? I don't want you to think that I don't know how to serve a proper meal that I cook myself, but what about impromptu gatherings, when you just send out for something? Should I try to pass it off as mine—which is difficult if everybody hears the doorbell ring when it's delivered—or should I just put it out the way it arrives?

GENTLE READER:

Many Americans are under the mistaken impression that small paper cartons with metal handles are correct serving dishes in China (or Taiwan), and that large flat cardboard boxes are in Italy. Transfer the carry-out food into your own serving dishes. This does not imply that you cooked it yourself. The cow gets credit for having produced the milk, even if it is put into a glass before serving.

Reading at Table

DEAR MISS MANNERS:

Would you please comment on the proper etiquette for reading at the dinner table? In particular, is it considered proper to prop a letter against the salt shaker or to lean the newspaper against a carton of cottage cheese, in order to free the hands for eating?

GENTLE READER:

Miss Manners was about to duck this question, on the grounds that it is never proper to read at the dinner table if anyone else is present and that what you do when you eat alone is between you and your God, and not a matter of etiquette. Then she came to the cottage cheese container. No decent person would put a food package—including ketchup bottles, milk cartons, or cereal boxes—on the table, even at home alone with the shades drawn.

❧ MANNERS FOR PARTICULAR FOODS

Artichokes

DEAR MISS MANNERS:

What is the most efficient way of eating artichokes?

GENTLE READER:

For those who want to eat efficiently, God made the banana, complete with its own color-coordinated carrying case. The artichoke is a miracle of sensuality, and one should try to prolong such treats, rather than dispatch them speedily. An important part of sensuality is contrast. First pull off a leaf with a cruel, quick flick of the wrist, dip it in the sauce, and then slowly and lovingly pull the leaf through the teeth, with the chin tilted heavenward and the eyes half closed in ecstasy. If the sauce drips, a long tongue, if you have one, may be sent down to get it. When the leaves are gone, the true subtlety of the artichoke reveals itself : a tender heart, covered with nasty bristles. To contrast with the fingering, there should be a sudden switch to cool formality. The fuzzy choke should be removed with dignified precision and a knife and fork, so that the heart may then be consumed in ceremonial pleasure.

Asparagus

DEAR MISS MANNERS :

The other night at the dinner table, my eight-year-old son started to eat his asparagus with his fingers. When I brought this to his attention, my wife informed me that it is considered good manners to eat this with the fingers. Good etiquette tells me you don't use the fingers for this vegetable. Your opinion please ?

GENTLE READER :

Miss Manners tells you that you do. Asparagus is, indeed, correctly eaten with the fingers, in a very old tradition of which few modern people seem aware. Those who do know can therefore have a marvelous time doing this in company or in restaurants and being reprimanded or at least stared at, only to have the disapproving people find out later that they were in the wrong. What Miss Manners wonders is how an eight-year-old boy found out about this ? Would he like to meet a refined Victorian lady ?

A Reply

DEAR MISS MANNERS :

I am afraid that I must take exception to your response to the reader who asked if it was proper to eat asparagus with your fingers. I have it on good authority that one's fingers should never be eaten with any other food. I suspect that you misunderstood the question.

GENTLE READER :

How right you are. But after the fingers convey the asparagus to the mouth, the fingers may then be eaten with whatever remains of the hollandaise sauce.

Bacon

DEAR MISS MANNERS:

When I am eating breakfast out, or when I'm staying at someone's house, how do I eat breakfast bacon—with the fingers or a fork?

GENTLE READER:

The correct way to eat bacon is with a fork. Limp, greasy bacon is easily eaten this way, but is not worth the eating. Crisp bacon is delicious, but impossible to eat correctly. Life is often like that, but it's a shame it has to be that way at breakfast time.

Bread and Butter

DEAR MISS MANNERS:

Why can't bread be buttered all at once instead of in the time-consuming method of breaking off small pieces, buttering each one, and then eating it before breaking off another piece?

GENTLE READER:

It is not for nothing that bread has earned itself the title of Staff of Life, as anyone will verify who has failed to catch a waiter's eye in a restaurant. Good bread deserves respect and must be eaten in the traditional fashion out of reverence. Poorly made bread is consumed only as a pastime by people whose meals are inadequate or late, and therefore should be eaten in as complicated a manner as possible to fill the time. Children who make little balls out of bread have the right motivation, although the wrong method.

DEAR MISS MANNERS:

My mother puts the butter on the table in a butter dish with its own little knife. She won't let us use that knife to put the butter on our potatoes or bread or vegetables. We have to put the butter onto our plates with that knife, and then switch to our own knives to put the butter on the food. This is a big waste of time. It would be easier just to butter whatever we want from the butter dish. Her method doesn't make any sense.

GENTLE READER:

It does if you think of it as a transportation system. The express train goes only on the main route, and all the little side trips from there are handled by smaller, local trains. It also keeps crumbs out of the butter.

Cake

DEAR MISS MANNERS:

How do you eat cake?

GENTLE READER:

So that you can have it, too. This is done by cutting a bite-sized piece with the end of the fork and lifting it up to the mouth in such a way that crumbs drift down and lodge themselves in the shirtfront. These may be furtively picked up and eaten later.

Candy

DEAR MISS MANNERS:

How do you take a piece of candy when a box is passed around? How can you tell which are the kind you like? Can you take more than one? Do you take the paper frill it comes in along with the candy, or just the piece of candy?

GENTLE READER:

Of course you know that "Take the one you touched" used to be the first rule of social behavior. Well, it still applies to candy. So does taking one at a time. As for the paper frill: Never leave behind evidence of how much you have taken.

DEAR MISS MANNERS:

When you advised a reader to throw away the paper frills that boxed candy comes in, you said, "Never leave behind evidence of how much you have taken." Clearly this means that I must kill the person sitting next to me if he saw me take a piece of candy. Tell me, Miss Manners, what is the proper way to kill another houseguest? Please rush your answer, as I plan to attend a party in the near future and I may want some candy while I am there.

GENTLE READER:

People are not "evidence"; they are "witnesses." Killing witnesses is a dreadful idea. Miss Manners hopes she has caught you in time.

Chips and Dips

DEAR MISS MANNERS:

Please be kind enough to give me the correct way of eating chips and dip. I was recently at a party and was very upset when quite a few of the guests repeatedly put the same chip they had taken a bite out of back into the dip. The bowl that contained the dip was for everyone. Was this proper?

GENTLE READER:

Your reading of the law—that one does not put food from one's mouth back into a communal dish—is correct. However, consider the circumstances of the defense. The path of chip to dip to mouth is a treacherous one. The chip may be broken into the dip. The dip may slide off the chip. A full chip, laden with dip, is apt to end up on the lip. Half a dip makes a safer trip.

Allow Miss Manners to propose one compromise, and one rhetorical question, as soon as she can stop babbling. The compromise: Suppose we require people to rotate their half-eaten chips, presenting a fresh edge for the refill? The question: How many germs can balance on the end of a potato chip, anyway?

Clams

DEAR MISS MANNERS:

What are long-necked clams, and how do you eat them?

GENTLE READER:

Long-necked clams are a comma-shaped creature of the sea that God invented for people who can't sop up enough garlic butter with snails. To eat them, you need the following equipment:

Bowl of long-necked clams

Bowl of nasty, gray, watery broth

Bowl of garlic butter

Washable tablecloth

Towel disguised as napkin

Bathtub (optional)

Grab the slippery little devil firmly by its neck and rip away its shells. Holding on to the base of the neck, pull back the tough outer skin covering the neck, stripping the thing naked. All of this has a hostile tinge, but now comes the caring part. Holding on to the edge of the neck, dip the clam, as if it were Achilles, into the broth for a wash. Then dip it again into the garlic butter. All of these activities are exciting in different ways, but the challenge is to get the clam into the mouth before all the butter is absorbed into the tablecloth. The fastidious clam eater will take a complete bath after each clam.

Corn on the Cob

DEAR MISS MANNERS:

The advent of the corn-on-the-cob season raises the disturbing question of nibbling etiquette. I have been dismayed at the lack of uniformity in nibbling styles. The two most commonly observed have been variously described, but I shall term them the ''piano'' and the ''rotary'' techniques. The former involves nibbling horizontally across the cob, reminiscent of one attempting to play all the octaves of the keyboard in a single stroke with one's teeth. The latter involves holding the teeth stationary, while rotating the cob in a fashion similar to honing a knife on a spinning stone. I would appreciate definite guidelines on the relative social acceptability of these, or other preferred techniques.

GENTLE READER:

Miss Manners is partial to the typewriter method, which involves a strict progress in orderly rows. It is a social error to say "Bing!" at the end of each line. However, she is willing to allow for such creativity as you describe, provided one does not leave odd kernels on the cob when one is finished. Odd kernels drive Miss Manners berserk.

DEAR MISS MANNERS:

What is the proper way to eat corn on the cob?

GENTLE READER:

Left to right.

Fake Food

DEAR MISS MANNERS:

What can one do about the increasingly common problem of fake food?

In a restaurant, it is easy. I simply ask the waiter or waitress to remove the nondairy creamer and bring me real milk for my coffee. Although I feel I am polite about my request, friends have said they find it embarrassing to be with me at this time. Do you feel I am incorrect?

At a private home, the situation is more difficult. A week ago, a friend asked if I would like strawberries and whipped cream. I enthusiastically accepted. However, when the dessert arrived, it turned out to be strawberries and canned whip, quite a different thing from what had been promised. I scraped the offending stuff off and ate the berries only, while receiving puzzled looks from my friend. My husband says I should have choked it down to be polite. Was I so obligated, having been trapped into accepting it?

Also, I am frequently offered butter for rolls, etc., and the so-called butter turns out to be margarine.

I can think of several reasons why people serve fake food—financial, medical, atrophied taste buds—but can think of no reasons why they could not admit what they are serving and let their guests decide if they want to accept or reject said foods. How should one deal with this problem politely?

GENTLE READER:

Miss Manners will uphold your right to truth in advertising if you promise to apply it to commercial transactions only, and not to social ones. She does not want you claiming fraud when your friends ask you to dinner to meet what they say are interesting people you will be crazy about.

In restaurants you are certainly allowed to insist upon getting what was on the menu. In people's houses, you accept what you are given, but you do not have to eat it. It is rude to point out to people that they have allowed their language to deteriorate and their words have spoiled.

Eclairs

DEAR MISS MANNERS:
How does one properly serve chocolate éclairs for a bridge party dessert?
GENTLE READER:
With enough equipment for people to eat them properly. Chocolate éclairs are too good to waste on clothes, upholstery, or bridge hands, however poor. Everyone should be issued a plate, fork, and napkin with the éclair, and probably also a more stable surface on which to cut it than a lap.

Fish

Fish think they're so smart. Just because they get to loll in the water all the time, while the rest of us have to get out when our lips turn blue or our two weeks' holiday runs out, they think they deserve special treatment in everything.

At the dinner table there are special rules for the eating of fish that friendly animals, such as veal and mutton, wouldn't dream of requiring. Take the matter of bone and pit removal. Miss Manners is always telling people the simple rule about removing undesirable material from the mouth: It goes out the way it came in. A bit of chicken bone that went in by fork goes out by fork; a grape seed that went in by hand goes out by hand. But that's not good enough for fish. Fish have to be the exception, and fish bones that go in by fish fork are nevertheless entitled to a return trip by hand. This unwillingness to go along with the crowd does not make fish popular. Some people won't eat them at all because they don't want anything to do with them, and others who, out of kind-heartedness, don't eat agreeable animals, don't mind eating fish, whom they think of as being cold. You might call someone a "cold fish," but you wouldn't call a different sort of person "a hot, passionate fish."

This may be the reason that fish is often served with the head still on. No one would have the gumption to dig into a turkey while its beady eye was staring up from the plate, but a fish head is not considered to have a reproachful expression, so many people are able to ignore it. They have enough troubles dealing with the body.

Characteristically, fish require special tools. The old-fashioned equipment was two forks, which were used to rake the fish meat as if it were gravel in a Japanese garden. In Victorian times, the fish fork and fish knife were invented. The knife blade has an interesting shape, as if someone had ironed an obelisk and bent it off to one side. Those who aspire to the British upper classes are advised (most recently by Debrett's in its republication of the U and Non-U concepts of Nancy Mitford and in *The English Gentleman*) not to use fish knives and forks in order to imply that one acquired one's family silver before the Victorian period. How-

THE PROPER DISSECTION OF A
FISH UNDER SOCIAL CONDITIONS.
*Anchor fish with fork and cut
along dotted line with fish knife
or a second fork. Pry flesh open
at C-B, and lift top section.
Eat, starting at A; then lift
B section and eat, from left to
right, or head to toe—no, tail.
Remove skeleton with knife and
eat underside. The fish may be
de-capitated before eating.
Squeeze lemon with right hand,
using left hand as umbrella to
protect dinner partner's eyes.*

ever, Americans do not have a severe problem with accepting the shocking modernity of the Victorian period. If an American lives in a Victorian house, he is not expected to complain of its newness.

The fish knife and fish fork should be enthusiastically adopted by brides, restaurants, and anyone else who expects fish in his life. By grabbing the fish fork firmly in the left hand and the fish knife in the right, pencil style, one arms oneself for a fair contest with any fish. Without them, the fish, using its tiny white bones as darts, is likely to win in the end.

Some people believe in decapitating the fish first and detailifying it, too; others preserve its form, placed across the plate, head to the left and tail to the right. To eat a whole fish that is facing to the right is disgusting and vulgar. The method of attack, which dear Evelyn Waugh called ichthyotomy, is to use the knife to slit the fish from gill to tail just above the middle of its side, where it keeps its backbone, before it has a chance to realize what is going on. If you then lift the fish meat off carefully, it should be bone-free. If not, see above method of bone removal. If the bone has gone too deep for that, see a doctor.

After that half has been eaten, the backbone may be removed so that the entire fish skeleton may be placed to the side of the rest of the food. Sometimes that doesn't work, however, so one waits until no one is looking and then flips the fish until it again presents a whole side, which is slit as the first side was.

If you can accomplish all this, you have the satisfaction of knowing that you have fought by the fish's own rules, and won. You may then proceed to the meat course, glowing with triumph.

Fruit

DEAR MISS MANNERS:
I am uncertain about the correct way to eat fruit, although I like nothing better. Does it depend on what the fruit is, or the circumstances under which it is served, or is it a matter of individual preference? I am referring to such questions as peeled vs. unpeeled, and hand vs. fork. More and more often, probably because of everybody's dieting, I see bowls of fruit used as centerpieces for dinner parties and then being passed as the dessert course.

GENTLE READER:
Fruit occupies the place in the food world that the ingenue does in society. That is, it is usually fresh (but occasionally stewed) and, although welcome anywhere for its charm and simplicity, it requires more complicated treatment when going about socially than it does when it is just hanging around the house.

Also, it is a mistake to treat individual members of this group in the same fashion, because some of the strongest-looking ones are frank and adaptable, while others look soft but have hearts of stone.

The least formal way to eat fruit is to pick it from a tree or fruitstand and pop it into your mouth with your hand. It is customary to secure the permission of the owner, and a good rinsing doesn't hurt, either.

The most formal method is to attack it with fruit knife and fork until it is halved, then quartered and, if you wish, skinned. As all this fierceness might be considered overkill with, say, a grape, small fruits are formally eaten by hand, with the pits quietly transferred from tongue to hand to plate.

Here are the details:

Apples
Informal: Grasp at ends, bite, and rotate.
Formal: Stab with fork, quarter and peel (optional); eat with fork.

Apricots
Informal: Same as apple, but with emergency napkin poised, and rotating from left to right, as well as back to front.
Formal: Halve, cut out pit, and eat with fork.

Bananas
Informal: Strip peel gradually, using bottom part as holder.
Formal: Strip peel entirely away, cut slices, and eat with fork. N.B.: Eating a banana with a knife and fork is almost as funny to spectators as slipping on a banana peel.

Berries
Informal: Grasp stem with hand and pull with hand while securing berry with teeth.
Formal: Use a spoon.

Cherries
Informal: Same as berries, then remove pit with hand.
Formal: Use a spoon, especially if the cherry is nestling in ice cream.

Grapes
Informal: Grape goes in by hand, and seed comes out by hand.
Formal: Cut cluster with grape scissors and then follow same procedure.

Oranges
Informal: Cut in quarters and hold by peel while slurping noisily. Better yet, squeeze into glass.
Formal: Peel and then cut, or cut and then peel, whichever is easier (both are nearly impossible), and eat sections with fork.

Peaches
Informal: Same as apricots, but with more absorbent napkin.
Formal: Cut in quarters around pit, peel, and eat with fork. Apologize to hostess for staining tablecloth.

Pears
Informal: Same as apples.
Formal: Fresh, same as apple; stewed, with dessert spoon and fork.

Pineapple
Informal: Same as formal. It is a mistake to hold an unpeeled pineapple in the hand and bite into it.
Formal: Quarter, cut from peel, slice and eat with fork. Wonder why hosts didn't perform this in pantry.

Watermelon
Informal: Same as pineapple, but flecking away seeds with knife.
Highly informal: Put face into watermelon and see who can spit the seeds farthest.

Grapefruit

DEAR MISS MANNERS:
    What is the best way to eat grapefruit?
GENTLE READER:
    Carefully, if at all. The grapefruit is a particularly vicious piece of work with a sour disposition, just lying in wait to give someone a good squirt in the eye. If the grapefruit sections have not been loosened with a grapefruit knife before serving, or if you are not armed with a pointed grapefruit spoon, give up. It will get you before you get it.

Ice

DEAR MISS MANNERS:

Now that the summer heat is upon us in full force, you simply must help us down here in Charlottesville by answering a rather perplexing question. Which is more proper, to eat ice with a spoon or with a fork? Please don't tell us that it is not to be done, because eating ice as an appetizer has become all the vogue here lately. I was under the impression that it was acceptable to eat ice with a spoon, until I was informed rather coldly during dinner that the correct way of transporting ice from one's water glass to one's mouth is by means of a fork. Miss Manners, will you tell us which mode of ice eating is preferred?

GENTLE READER:

Why would you think that Miss Manners would disapprove of eating ice? What else is so low in calories, violates nobody's special diet restrictions, and harms no one's budget? If ice is served in a water glass, one drinks the water first. Then one tilts the glass until the ice hits one's nose, which is very refreshing. The glass is then lowered with the ice at its edge, and the ice is allowed to enter the mouth.

By this method, neither spoon nor fork is necessary. If you feel you must fish ice out of a glass, however, do it with an iced tea spoon. The sight of a hand in a glass up to the wrist, trying to get an ordinary teaspoon at the bottom, is not pleasant and sometimes not easy to remove from the glass. Ice, particularly when it is melting, is not eaten with the fork.

It is not considered good manners to gnaw on ice sculpture that is used as a table decoration nor to break off parts, such as snapping the neck of an ice sculpture swan to munch the head.

Ice Cream

DEAR MISS MANNERS:

Is it proper to mush ice cream that is served in a bowl? I prefer to eat it soft.

GENTLE READER:

No, it isn't, but it does taste better that way, doesn't it? The proper method is to become vivaciously engaged in conversation as soon as the ice cream has been served, and then, when it has turned into a puddle on its own, to eat it.

Ice Cream Cones

DEAR MISS MANNERS:

Admittedly, it sounds silly to have to ask how to eat an ice cream cone. But I always end up with a mess dripping all over myself. Can it be that there is a right and a wrong way to eat ice cream cones?

GENTLE READER:

Much more than that, it is an art. Many parents mistakenly think that there is a natural instinct for the eating of ice cream cones, and then they make a dreadful fuss about the upholstery.

The problem is a seemingly insoluble one, namely that the cone is served empty with the scoop or scoops of ice cream on top of its fragile rim, but the eater is expected to place the frozen substance inside the cone during the course of his eating. It may be done, but it requires the ability to plan, manual and lingual dexterity, and a knowledge of physics and geometry.

First, lick the ice cream in a clockwise motion (counterclockwise for left-handed people), until the scoop is not wider than the rim of the cone. No over-lap is permitted. Then, placing the tip of the tongue in the center of the remaining scoop, push gently downward. This requires much skill because if you apply too much pressure, the cone will burst in your hand like a crystal goblet. After each such push, additional edge licking will be needed, as the pressure forces the scoop outward. With careful planning, you should be able to fill the cone at the same time that you are filling your stomach. The cone, once full, is nibbled clockwise down to the tip, which is put whole into the mouth. This sounds like a great deal of work, but once mastered, the ability will serve you well in other, more sophisticated areas of life, such as frozen yogurt cones.

Ice Cream Sodas

DEAR MISS MANNERS:

There are so few places where ice cream sodas are still made—I mean the kind where the syrup and ice cream and soda have to be mixed right there at the soda fountain, by hand—but I still love them. My question is how to eat the soda properly, when I get the chance, without spilling it all over the place. There is a certain amount of mixing that has to be done by the person who is eating it, and that's what I have the problem with.

GENTLE READER:

Miss Manners quite agrees with you about the value of the ice cream soda, which is one of the great gastronomical treats of the American cuisine. A true artistic creation goes by its own rules, some of which would be considered scan-dalous if practiced in connection with lesser achievements. This is the way you eat an ice cream soda:

First eat the cherry alone with the spoon. Next, remembering Archimedes' principle, eat the whipped cream with the spoon, without attempting to force it into the full glass. You then have a slight amount of space between the level of the drink and the rim of the glass, which is your working space. The spoon is then inserted into the glass and poked at the ice cream scoop. The first sip may be taken through the straw. It will not be a perfect blend of soda, ice cream, and syrup, but will serve as a prelude to the perfection that occurs when, through the efforts of the eater and the natural consequences of putting ice cream into soda water, full blending may take place. The great paradox here—

and fine art is full of ironic contradictions—is that the soda begins to disappear just as it reaches its perfect state. How like life itself. It is for this reason that Miss Manners has given the ice cream soda a unique privilege. And that is that the drinker may take three—he is entitled to no more than three—noisy slurps to get up those few last drops.

DEAR MISS MANNERS:

I know that you told us that a person eating an ice cream soda, which is an almost forgotten art, is allowed to take three slurps to get up the delicious drops at the bottom of the glass. I would like to know, however, if a soda is being shared, how many slurps is each person allowed? Is it three to a soda, or three to a person?

GENTLE READER:

More than etiquette is involved when two people are sharing an ice cream soda. This is, after all, the preteen version of trial marriage.

As it would be aesthetically offensive, as well as nutritionally unproductive, for six slurps to be taken from one soda, each person takes one slurp and the third is taken by the person who values that combination of syrup, melted ice cream, and soda more than the romance at the other end of the straw. Miss Manners advises the young that many love affairs eventually prove disappointing, but ice cream sodas will never let you down.

Junk Food

It is the opinion of many people who never attend formal dinner parties that to be obliged to eat under such circumstances is a dreadful ordeal. (Many people who do attend such events also consider them an ordeal, but that is a different matter; these people are referring to the conversation.) Actually, the formal dinner is one of the easiest ways there is of taking sustenance. What is impossible to eat, without covering yourself with embarrassment or worse, is junk food.

When a waiter appears at your left with a platter of carefully apportioned food, there is nothing to it. If you don't know what it is, you can ask him, and if you have trouble taking some, he apologizes. You are provided with a variety of sturdy tools with which to attack the food: large china plates, solid silver knives and forks, a huge damask napkin to protect you from your own mistakes. Should you select the wrong implement, a whispered word will bring you a replacement. In any case, such errors are less serious than popularly supposed. Most formal dinner tables are not patrolled by fork-enforcement officers, and unless you use three implements at a time, it is hard to come out short at the end. The dessert brings its own equipment with it, so you'll not be sent to bed without it no matter how badly you muddle the rest of the meal.

Contrast this with the traditional junk food procedure. Looking at your filled plate and asking the person who handed it to you "What is this supposed to be, anyway?" is not advised. What a plate it is. Any fool can sit at a mahogany table and eat breast of guinea hen; the challenge is to eat a chiliburger from a paper plate while standing up. If you break your plastic fork while eating in a fast food establishment you may, of course, request another fork. What you cannot do is find all the broken-off tines of the first fork because they have disappeared into the food. The refined eater of junk food consumes many slivers of white plastic.

Here is Miss Manners' list of really difficult-to-eat foods (oysters, artichokes, and frogs' legs not being among them) :

Hot Dogs

While the hot dog in a bun is finger food, this does not include using the finger to push the meat along so that it will come out evenly with the bun at the end. The way to eat a hot dog is to accept the fact that nothing—not the mustard, nor the relish, nor the meat—will come out even, so a wad of tasteless bun must be consumed at the end.

Fried Chicken

The fingers are of great use here, in prying off the huge globs of fried fat and placing them quietly on the side of the plate so that the chicken itself may be eaten.

Pizza

This may be lowered into the mouth by hand, small end of the triangle first, taking care that the strings of cheese also arrive in the mouth.

Sloppy Joe

The only way to eat this neatly is to eat the paper plate on which it is served; lifting the food out of it is a mistake.

Cheese Snacks

If a fingerbowl is not served with these, it is best to find a water fountain afterward for the same purpose. Do not shake hands with anyone directly after eating cheese snacks.

French Fries

A quick motion of the wrist, such as one uses to shake down a thermometer, will remove excess ketchup.

Lobster

DEAR MISS MANNERS:

Lobster bibs make people look silly. I hate them. I have actually been ignored, however, by waiters who fasten them around my neck, without asking, when I tell them I want to eat my lobster without one, taking my own chances about soiling my clothes. Do I have to order something else at a restaurant unless I am willing to wear their bib?

GENTLE READER:

The reason that God made the lobster delicious, messy, and expensive, all at once, was to reserve for humanity one treat that is better enjoyed in the privacy of the home. There is nothing better than boiled lobster with garlic butter, but you pay a restaurant a considerable markup for something that is simple to make at home, and, as it is impossible to eat neatly, you expose yourself to public ridicule. Eat your lobster at home, wearing washable clothes, and you will not need a bib.

Nuts

DEAR MISS MANNERS:

We often have friends dropping in, and also our family likes to snack while watching TV, so I generally have a bowl or two of nuts out in the family room. My husband and some of our friends are in the habit of messing around in the bowl until they find the kind of nuts they want, leaving the others. To me, such manners are selfish and disgusting. Why should handling food and not eating it be any nicer when it's mixed nuts than it is for candy or whatever? Doesn't this type of behavior make you think about the way a person was brought up?

GENTLE READER:

Actually, this type of behavior gives Miss Manners philosophical thoughts. It makes her think that life is a bowl of mixed nuts, and that the temptation to go for all the cashews is irresistible.

Parsley

DEAR MISS MANNERS:

Is it permissible to eat watercress or parsley that is used as decoration? Does one do so with the fork or the fingers?

GENTLE READER:

Miss Manners does not quite know how watercress and parsley, which are delicious, lost their full citizenship rights as vegetables and were put on a pedestal, or platter, to be treated as mere decoration. They would be far happier to be restored to their rights and eaten with the fork at dinner or the fingers from finger-food platters, than to continue to lead vain, empty lives.

Peas

DEAR MISS MANNERS:

I know that peas should not be eaten with a knife, but how do you eat them? I have trouble getting them on my fork. Should I mash them first?

GENTLE READER:

Peas are unique in that they are the only vegetable with a herd instinct. Thus it is easily possible to catch them when armed only with a fork if they are crowded together and feeling safe; but impossible by conventional means to catch one or two that have strayed from the herd and are therefore on their guard. Don't even try. You will only work yourself into a rage and end up with one or two peas dancing around the rim of your plate, laughing at you.

Pickles

DEAR MISS MANNERS:

I love eating pickles, but I'm afraid that eating them whole, as I often do, might not be considered proper. I know that it's all right to put pickle slices on hamburgers and sandwiches, but I am not sure if they should be eaten by themselves. Do you know of a correct way to eat them?

GENTLE READER:

Pickles should be eaten with relish. No—not that kind of relish; enjoyment. A large, slurpy pickle is eaten from the hand under informal circumstances, while the more dressed-up pickle, which is either small or sliced, may find its way to more formal meals, where it should be eaten by fork.

Pomegranates

DEAR MISS MANNERS:

Please settle a small dispute between friends. She says there is no polite way to eat pomegranates in public, and therefore they should not be served. I say that providing they have been completely peeled and the seeds separated, one can eat them, singly or in groups, and discard the pits via a spoon, on one's plate. Please don't answer that a squeezer would solve the problem by allowing you to have pomegranate juice.

GENTLE READER:

Why not? Why should you have all the fun? If you are eating pomegranates, it seems to Miss Manners that you are having about as much fun as a human being can stand. The pomegranate is nature's little tease, inviting you to guess which parts of it are edible and which are not. Some people throw out the seeds and are sorry afterwards, and some people eat the pulp and are sorry about that. The key skill here is knowing how to admit defeat gracefully, which is to deposit mistakes neatly in the spoon and then on the plate, as you describe. If you can do that without making a face, Miss Manners will permit you to eat pomegranates, singly or in groups.

Potatoes

DEAR MISS MANNERS:

I am extremely fond of baked potato, and the heck with the calories. I eat so many, the least I can do is to eat them correctly. But if you slice into the potato, you get a smooth surface and the butter slides right off it. Everybody knows that baked potato tastes best with the butter mashed right into it, but I can't find anyone who knows how to do this politely.

GENTLE READER:

Well, now you have. Baked potato is properly broken up with the fingers, from which we get the expression "a hot potato." (Considerate cooks cut an X on the top before serving, so that the heat escapes somewhat, but how many considerate cooks are there?) This gives an irregular surface. Then the butter is put on it—not with the knife, as you might expect, but with the fork. A flick of the wrist mashes some of the butter in and no one will be the wiser. You may do this one half at a time, eating from the shell, which you may steady with the left hand. Shell eaters may then cut up the shell with fork and knife.

Potato Chips

DEAR MISS MANNERS:

What is the proper way to eat potato chips?

GENTLE READER:

With a knife and fork. A fruit knife and an oyster fork, to be specific. For pity's sake, what is this world coming to? Miss Manners doesn't mind explaining the finer points of gracious living, but feels that anyone who doesn't have the sense to pick up a potato chip and stuff it into his mouth probably should not be running around loose on the streets.

Prunes and Pits

DEAR MISS MANNERS:

When eating stewed prunes, where is the proper place to put the pits? I am assuming that the whole prune is put into the mouth. Is the pit eased as unobtrusively as possible back onto the spoon and then put in—on—where?

GENTLE READER:

Stewed or not, you must take inedibles out the way you put them in. The rule is that if you put it into your mouth with your hand, you must take it out with your hand; if you put it in with the spoon—and let's hope that in the case of stewed prunes, that is what you did—it comes out onto the spoon. (The exception to this rule is fish bones. Fish never do anything like anybody else, which is probably what comes of breathing water. Please see page 148.) The skill here is to get the pit clean while it is still in your mouth, so that what comes out has no food attached to it. It is fun to watch the facial maneuvers of a person trying to do this. Now, where do you put the pit? On the plate under the dish in which the prunes were served.

Salt

DEAR MISS MANNERS:

You wouldn't think that something so common and ordinary as table salt would require training to use, but I find myself with several unresolved problems having to do with this seasoning.

1. What is the formal way to serve salt? I am thinking of where it should be put on the table, and in what. Also, how much—that is, how many guests to a salt shaker?

2. When someone asks me to pass the salt, it is often a reminder that I haven't yet salted my own food. May I do so before passing the salt?

3. If there is a salt and pepper set, do I pass both together, even if only the salt was requested?

GENTLE READER:

Common salt may be, but ordinary it is not, being truly a seasoning for all.

1. The really fastidious person will serve salt in tiny open dishes, with salt spoons, at a formal dinner, and not use a salt shaker. Almost no one except Miss Manners is that fastidious, however. Such salt cellars are placed between every two guests, or, if you want to go all out, one in front of each guest.

2. No, you may not. That is like using a friend's engagement announcement to notice how suitable a partner the betrothed would make for yourself.

3. Keep them together. Like many couples, one is sought after and the other generally ignored, but the polite person will treat them as a couple and invite them together.

Sandwiches

DEAR MISS MANNERS:

I like to have a club sandwich for lunch, but my mouth isn't big enough to get all the layers in at one bite. Should I try to eat it with a knife and fork?

GENTLE READER:

The club sandwich is typical of the club decision, usually thought of by a committee that tries to fit in everyone and ends up making a mess. You will never manage to pack all that stuff onto a fork. Save the fork for eating whatever has dropped out of the sandwich when it is eaten, as a civilized sandwich is intended to be eaten, with the hands.

DEAR MISS MANNERS:

When a multistory sandwich is served, such as a club sandwich, and it is held together with frilled toothpicks, what do you do with the toothpicks?

GENTLE READER:

You take them out of the sandwich. What did you think: you eat them?

Shish Kebab

DEAR MISS MANNERS:

When eating shish kebab, are the pieces of meat, onion, etc., left on the stick, or are they removed before eating, and if so, how?

GENTLE READER:

Are we talking about a vicious metal skewer, or about an oversized toothpick at a cocktail party? Miss Manners needs to know these things. There is no use coming in here and claiming you want help until you are ready to bare your very soul. The metal weapon served for a meal is held daintily by one end in the left hand, while the other hand (right), wielding a fork, slides the goodies off onto the rice. The wooden portable variety is eaten from, as ice cream is from a stick, with about the same lack of success in the areas of neatness and grace.

Shrimp

DEAR MISS MANNERS:

I have a recipe for broiled shrimp with garlic that doesn't say anything about peeling the shrimp before cooking. Can unpeeled shrimp be served at a luncheon? How do people peel them? Do I provide a dish for the peelings? How are you supposed to eat this dish?

GENTLE READER:

You are supposed to eat this dish while sitting in a Spanish café, sipping sherry. Peeling the shrimp is half the fun. You grab each shrimp by its wee little legs, tugging to pull them all off as an unpleasant child would pull the wings from a fly. You then dig the thin shell away from the shrimp and eat the shrimp. Then you find that the shrimp is so delicious that you attempt to catch a waiter's eye to reorder. In the forty-five minutes before the new order comes, your eyes and fingers gradually wander toward the shrimp shells, which smell of garlic. Surreptitiously, you slip a shell into your mouth. The shell tastes like fingernail parings, but the garlic is so good that you eat the remaining shells. You then crumple your napkin on top of your plate so the waiter won't look around to see what became of the shrimp shells.

As you can see, all of this is such an adventure that you could hardly conduct a decent luncheon party while it is going on. Miss Manners suggests you save this recipe for the privacy of your family.

Snails

DEAR MISS MANNERS:

What is the proper equipment necessary to eat snails? And then, how do you use it?

GENTLE READER:

Surely you mean to ask: What is the maximum equipment you can use to eat snails, and how can you make the biggest fuss and have the most fun doing it?

Snails, after all, may be prepared in many delicious ways and served in a sauce on a plate or on toast that is, in turn, on a plate. All you need then is a fork, and some dexterity in cutting the sodden toast with the edge of the fork.

To make the most of the dish theatrically and still have something slurpy to eat, you can buy snail plates, tongs, and forks, hide the snails in shells to give them a sporting chance, and then attack them with both hands and all this metal.

The snail plates are ceramic or metal, with indentations for the snail shells, in which are put the snails themselves, usually floating in garlic butter. The whole mess has probably been broiled as a unit, so slyly steadying your plate with your fingers, never proper, is in this case promptly and severely punished.

Snail tongs have a bowl that opens when you press the handle and closes around the snail shell, anchoring it. The fork is narrow, with two prongs that pierce the snail and drag it out of its lair. As the tongs are held in the left hand and the fork in the right, it is permissible to empty the shell of its sauce over the extracted snail.

Now comes the real conflict of the conscience. As you know, Miss Manners does not approve of sopping up sauces with bread. However, she approves of garlic butter. That is why you see her turning discreetly away from you at the table, and also why you hear her offering to clear the snail dishes from the table.

Soup

Do you have a kinder, more adaptable friend in the food world than soup? Who soothes you when you are ill? Who refuses to leave you when you are impoverished and stretches its resources to give you hearty sustenance and cheer? Who warms you in winter and cools you in summer? Yet who is also capable of doing honor to your richest table and impressing your most demanding guests?

Why, then, do people so mistreat this inestimable friend? They dump it unceremoniously into all the wrong containers, pay no attention to its modest preferences in spoons, tilt it from side to side until it is afraid of perishing in an oceanic storm, make frightful noises at it, and leave spoons pitched into it, like daggers in trusting hearts.

Soup does its loyal best, no matter what undignified conditions are imposed upon it. But soup knows the difference. Soup is sensitive. You don't catch steak hanging around when you're poor or sick, do you? Soup deserves to be treated well. If soup could talk—and it doesn't, because it feels there is quite enough unpleasant noise made in its immediate vicinity—here is what it would say:

Not all soups are alike, and if possible, we would like you to distinguish among us. Like you, we enjoy going differently to different occasions; what is appropriate at home with the family is not at a formal dinner. So don't just put us all in cereal bowls and attack us with teaspoons. We like soup spoons, which have large, oval bowls, although we are perfectly happy to lend these to desserts when we are finished with them. If you can manage it, we also like smaller, round-bowled spoons for soups served in cups.

Handled cups are what all jellied soups like, and cold soups prefer. We generally like cups at luncheon, with little matching plates underneath. At dress-up dinners, we prefer soup plates, which are wide, and have broad, flat rims for the same reason that you are required to have a concrete apron around a swimming pool. You can put the soup plate right on the place plate, if you like, or on an underliner. The only thing we really can't bear, even in the kitchen or on the sick-bed tray, is not having any plate at all beneath the soup plate or cup.

As for serving soup, we are really very accommodating about that, even for formal dinners. We could insist that soup be passed at the table, as every other food does, but passing a soup tureen on a platter is madness, we recognize, so we agree to the easier method of serving up in the kitchen and putting the soup plates on the table, already filled. We love tureens for family-style service, however.

We have become very modern about allowing you to tilt the soup plate gently away from you at the finish of the soup course, knowing what a shame it would be to force you to leave good soup uneaten. Handled soup cups we encourage you to pick up and drink from, while cautioning you that it is wiser to eat the fishballs, mushrooms, or noodles first with your spoon.

Now, about that spoon. Please hold it parallel to your mouth. It is the side of the spoon that should kiss the mouth, not the oval tip. The soup is gently and quietly poured from the soup spoon bowl, over its side, into the mouth. It is not inhaled. If you knew how often people do dreadful things to soup, kind, caring soup, you would weep. And even as the tears rolled from your cheeks, your faithful soup would expand in response.

DEAR MISS MANNERS:

Your column on soup was interesting, but left unanswered a question that has been a bone of contention in my family for some time.

Which side of the spoon should be dipped into the soup? I always thought the far side was supposed to be dipped in. Not the oval tip, and not the side nearest the user. Which side is right?

GENTLE READER:

Soup should always be kept flowing in the opposite direction from one's lap. The soup spoon should be filled from its far side and the soup then poured gently into the mouth with its near side.

DEAR MISS MANNERS:

Did I commit a faux pas? I served good New England clam chowder with oyster crackers; several of my guests were sniggering behind their Pouilly-Fume. Truly, I did hunt through the shops for clam crackers. Is my social life ruined?

GENTLE READER:

Yes. It is obvious that you will never have a satisfactory social life. Devote yourself to spreading Pouilly-Fume among the poor!

Spaghetti

DEAR MISS MANNERS:

How do you eat spaghetti with a spoon?

GENTLE READER:

Bite your tongue. This is not an eating instruction, but an old-fashioned reprimand to anyone who would even entertain such an outrageous idea as eating spaghetti with a spoon.

Actually, there simply is no easy, foolproof way to eat spaghetti, and that is just as well when you think of how gloriously fat we would all be if there were. The inevitable slippage of spaghetti from the fork back onto the plate is Nature's way of controlling human piggishness. A fork is the only utensil that may be used to eat spaghetti while anyone is looking. It must make do with whatever cooperation it may muster from the plate and the teeth. The fork is planted on the plate, and the spaghetti is then twirled around the tines of the fork. If you can manage to use the grated Parmesan cheese to add grit to the mixture for better control, so much the better. The twirled forkful is then presented to the mouth. If this were an ideal world, all the spaghetti strands would begin and end in the same place, so that the mouth could receive the entire forkful at once. However, we have all learned that compromises must often be made, and the fact is that one will often find a few long strands hanging down outside of the mouth.

As you may not spit these parts back onto the plate, what are you to do with them? Well, for heaven's sake. Why do you think God taught you to inhale?

DEAR MISS MANNERS:

Eating spaghetti is a two-handed exercise, and it does employ the use of a spoon. But consider first your proposed method, the fork perched like a flagpole on the plate, twirling the spaghetti around its base as though to drill a hole in the china. Ugh. Proper, perhaps, for a Roto-Rooter man. The correct way to eat spaghetti is with a fork and a soup spoon. The soup spoon is held in the right hand, the fork in the left. One cannot eat spaghetti properly without a soup spoon. Shame on you.

GENTLE READER:

That many people use spoons to assist forks in eating spaghetti, Miss Manners is well aware. That correct spaghetti eating, with fork only, is not easy, Miss Manners also knows. (Why Miss Manners is suddenly writing her sentences backwards, she does not know.) The most rewarding things in life require patience and diligence. In the civilized world, which includes the United States and Italy, it is incorrect to eat spaghetti with a spoon. The definition of "civilized" is a society that does not consider it correct to eat spaghetti with a spoon.

Steak

DEAR MISS MANNERS:
Would you please tell me, is it proper to put your steak sauce on the steak, or off to the side and dip your meat?
GENTLE READER:
If you are asking about *sauce béarnaise*, which is Miss Manners' idea of a steak sauce, the answer is to ladle it right onto the meat, where it will do the most good. If, however, you are talking about bottled steak sauce, you must allow Miss Manners to beg you, fervently, to have it decanted from the commercial bottle into something fit for the table before you even think about putting any on your steak. It, too, may then be ladled directly on the steak. The principle about putting things to one side is to avoid using a community utensil, such as the butter knife that travels with the butter—as opposed to your very own butter knife—on your individual portion. Ladles and even (Miss Manners is closing her eyes and pretending not to see this) bottles dribble onto your portion, rather than touch it.

Taffy

DEAR MISS MANNERS:
What is the correct way to eat saltwater taffy?
GENTLE READER:
With the mouth closed. Actually, that is the way to eat all food, but saltwater taffy is the only food capable of enforcing the rule.

Tomatoes

DEAR MISS MANNERS:
Will you please tell me the proper way to eat cherry tomatoes (large and small ones)? I like them very much, but don't eat them when eating out for fear of being embarrassed.
GENTLE READER:
The cherry tomato is a wonderful invention, producing, as it does, a satisfactorily explosive squish when bitten. This sensation must, however, be confined to the inside of the mouth, not shared with one's friends or one's tie or blouse. Small tomatoes should be chosen for one-bite consumption in a closed mouth. Large ones may be treated as ordinary tomatoes and sliced, which is not as much fun. Medium-sized ones are neither here nor there.

Social Intercourse

❦ CONVERSING
(RATHER THAN COMMUNICATING)

Let us make a special effort to learn to stop communicating with one another, so that we can have some conversation.

Miss Manners realizes that it is the national goal for everyone to communicate, and she appreciates what an effort that is. Especially the part about having to communicate the need for communication. It isn't very interesting, is it? Miss Manners' hope is that, having learned to communicate, people have now rid themselves of their emotional backlogs and are willing to return to talking like civilized people.

In communication, people express their true feelings and tell everything about themselves with complete honesty, holding back nothing except their last names. "Hi," a good communicator will open, "I'm Josh!" Or "I'm Heather!" And by the end of the soup course, you will know how this person feels about our environment, the role of women, an ex-spouse and/or recent ex-lover, joggers, Humphrey Bogart, people who are not afraid to show their feelings, people who are not afraid to be vulnerable, the materialistic society, the media, what people would eat if they knew what was good, and the rewards of working with people.

A true communicator will take the trouble to find out your name and to insert it into his recital often, the way creators of form letters are now able to do through the wonders of technology. A form question will appear now and again also, inviting the communicatee to fill in his or her taste preferences, but only if they conform to those stated. (Can you imagine trying to tell such a person that you don't like Humphrey Bogart movies, or have never seen any?) Because the communicator is telling all, many of these questions will be what used to be called nosy, and still should be. Such exchanges are achieved more efficiently by buttons, T-shirts, and bumper stickers. These are available ready-made to announce one's politics, preferences, and availability, so there is no need to devote time to them that could otherwise be pleasantly spent in conversation.

True conversation cannot be preprinted. One must bring ready-made ingredients, such as information, experience, anecdotes, and opinions, prepared to have them challenged and to contribute to a new group effort. That is what conversation is: developing and playing with ideas by juxtaposing the accumulated conclusions of two or more people and then improvising on them.

Conversation is not:

Gossip about oneself. The preliminary to conversation consists of asking and stating personal information, but that is only for the purpose of choosing a real topic. As soon as a common interest has been found, the quizzing should be stopped and the development of conversation begun.

Recitals. Conversation being an exchange, long stories, such as jokes or travelogues, cannot be included unless they are abbreviated and offered in illustration of the conversation's idea.

News. Startling bulletins may be effective in suggesting ideas, but the popular notion that being able to recite current political and cultural news accurately makes one a conversationalist is erroneous. The person who has actually read the book that everyone is supposed to be talking about is a menace unless everybody is really talking about it.

Advertisements. From the direct sales pitch to a play for the goodwill of influential people, the rule is that if it is designed to advance your career, it isn't conversation. The same is true of public service announcements, such as recommending one's therapist or one's diet.

Salon Conversation

In Miss Manners' set, the equivalent of "Let's put on a play in the barn!" is "Let's start a salon." The chances of these projects being followed through to become brilliant successes seem to be about the same. A salon, as Miss Manners understood it from dear Germaine de Staël whose house was such a joy to us all, is a regular gathering of compatible intellects. The people in whom these intelligences dwell needn't be entirely compatible. They must have a common body of knowledge and be able to use it with imagination and daring.

Miss Manners does not wish to denigrate the activities practiced at ordinary social gatherings. Eating, drinking, gossiping, flirting, and showing off are the staples of human intercourse, without which there would be little incentive to stir from one's own hearth from one season to the next. Nor does she suggest that these pleasantries be excluded from the well-run salon. But even food, much less sex, is not enough to keep the same people interested in encountering one another week after week in somebody's drawing room.

What is wanted is thought. Ideas that can be flirted with, masticated, gulped to giddiness, and batted about are the only fit attractions for a salon. That is why Miss Manners has come to despair of the salon's being revived in modern times. We live in an era when people want only what they expect. Intellectual stimulation, to most, means hearing themselves deliver lectures on matters they have already figured out to their satisfaction. Arguing is considered to be exchange of thought. People keep citing their own experience and feelings, not because they have fresh firsthand material to offer, but from lack of other sources of knowledge. Education and professional skills are so specialized that we have no common body of reference and can only exchange trade gossip with immediate colleagues. Social turnover is required because we keep repeating ourselves, rather than continuing to develop our ideas.

All this leaves us with nothing but small talk. A salon requires big talk. Miss Manners has heard of gatherings at which everyone agrees in advance to read the same book and to limit conversation to discussing it, but this seems to her a paltry substitute for the free exchange of ideas.

It is, however, a start toward amassing and using knowledge for pleasure, rather than for personal or professional advancement. We could all benefit, in her opinion, from shifting our attention from our own feelings to other people's thoughts. In the meantime, Miss Manners is going down to the barn to see what's playing.

Personal Questions

In a society that considers "How do you feel about your divorce?" to be a conventional conversation opener, what, Miss Manners wonders, is a personal question?

There is a bizarre notion that it is both charming and beneficial to force a person to yield, for general consumption, everything there is to know about himself. The interrogators are thus able, while indulging their base nosiness, to maintain a complacent air that is part compassionate glow and part scientific inquiry. Widespread as the practice is, Miss Manners knows that those questioned feel neither charmed nor benefited. They are always asking her for ways to "put down" their tormentors.

Now, you know that Miss Manners does not believe in snappy comebacks designed to make other people feel terrible, no matter how richly they deserve it. She believes that the way to answer any question that intrudes on one's privacy is, "I'd rather not talk about that, if you don't mind," or "I'm afraid that's too private for me to discuss.'' These may be accompanied by anything from a pleasant, regretful smile, suggesting that this policy will change when you know each other better, to a raised-eyebrow stare, suggesting that you had better not try that again.

The question remains, however, of what a personal question is. In certain groups, it is acceptable to ask one's age—say, 4 to 6X. In other groups, it is common to ask the price of a newly purchased house—say, $135,000 to $225,000.

Nevertheless, these are never general rules, and the fastidious person will refrain from ever inquiring about age or money. It's too tricky.

Let us assemble, then, a beginner's sampler of personal questions to be avoided in all beginning, and probably also intermediate, relationships:

Age: ''That was an awfully nice young man you brought over the other night, but tell me, isn't he a little young?''

Birth Control: ''Isn't this your third? Did you plan it that way?''

Children: ''Shouldn't he be talking by now?''

Divorce: ''And we thought you were the ideal couple. What went wrong?''

Energy: ''Don't you think you keep this house too hot?''

Food: ''I'm surprised to see you eating that. Didn't you tell me you were on a diet?''

Good Works: ''Our development officer has figured out what a person of your income level can afford to give. Would you like to hear what it is?''

Health: ''You didn't tell us what that test was you went into the hospital for. But let me just ask this: Was it benign?''

I: ''I think you ought to . . .''

Enough of this alphabet stuff. When you keep going with this sort of thing, you get to X, and then you have to try to make xylophones seem relevant. They aren't. It's permissible to ask a perfect stranger about his xylophone, or his zither.

The two big questions you must never ask and never answer are, according to Miss Manners' grandmother:

1. ''How old are you?''
2. ''How much money do you have (or make)?''

Miss Manners' grandmother was not, as you can imagine, the sort of lady who fooled around. Another of her maxims was ''Colored stones are vulgar,'' and so she gave away any family jewelry with rubies or sapphires, thus saving Miss Manners herself from the temptation of eventually falling into such vulgarity. All her descendants naturally bless her for this. The family was never rich, but we try to behave ourselves.

With such sensitivity, it is fortunate that Grandmother Manners did not live to hear of a whole world of other unanswerable questions that modern ladies are asked. But Miss Manners trusts that she will not be dishonoring the dear lady's memory by suggesting that it is, perhaps, time to halve the original list. It is as vulgar as ever to inquire into, or confess to, the state of personal finances. We do not judge people by the amount of money they have (do we?), and therefore any interest in such amounts is unseemly. But why should age be considered unmentionable?

As a matter of fact, it isn't always, and never has been. One could always ask people under twenty-one what their age was ("How did you know they were under twenty-one?" you may well ask), or men if they were successful and under the age of forty. The taboo really applied only to grown-up women and to both sexes between the ages of forty and seventy-five, when it became all right again.

In examining this pattern, Miss Manners detects an unpleasant suggestion that while being very young or very old is considered fetching, being fully grown-up is not, particularly for women. Our most usual form of flattery is to tell people that they look much younger than they are, such compliments often being supported in the most ludicrous fashion. How discouraging to think that the natural progress of life is downhill.

Miss Manners has found that age does bring change, but its chief movement seems to be in the direction of sense. She is therefore rebelling against Grand-mama's dictum and, when asked, discloses her age. (She does not ask others for theirs, in case they do not care to follow her lead.) However, she promises, faith-fully, not to run around dripping with rubies and sapphires.

Money

Miss Manners would welcome a fine old fight about religion, sex, or politics if you would only stop telling her how much you paid for your house, how much the other houses in the neighborhood are going for now, how much your silver is worth, how much it's costing you to insure it, how much it would cost you to replace it, and whether she knows what they are charging these days for a decent pair of shoes.

Miss Manners sympathizes with the motivation to discuss prices in these rapidly changing times. There are two real statements being made through all these statistics, and both of them are among the most satisfying communications one human being can make to another. They are:

1. My, I was clever.
2. My, things have changed for the worse since I was younger.

The first covers all statements about things the speaker has purchased that are now more expensive; the second, all things he didn't buy when the prices were lower than they are now. Therefore, no one is excluded from such conversations; they are, indeed, tempting. Would you like Miss Manners to tell you what her dear mother paid for the handmade silver tea service, now Miss Manners', which Mama bought in Mexico in 1948? No, you really wouldn't. Let us go back to considering discussions of money vulgar, to protect ourselves from the worse attribute, which is that they are boring.

Miss Manners will tell you, instead, how erratic the weather has become since she was a girl (My, things have changed for the worse), and how she is never-theless able to avoid ever catching cold (My, she is clever).

A Glossary of Social Terms

Whether it is a deficiency in abstract reasoning or of language skills, Miss Manners is not certain. But she does know that people who insist on taking social idiomatic expressions literally have a problem. Two problems, actually. The second one is being tiresome.

"Why did she ask me how I feel if she didn't want to hear about what I've been through?"

"I'm not going to address him as 'dear' or sign myself 'Yours truly' or 'Sincerely,' when he's certainly not dear to me and I'm not truly or sincerely or any other way his."

"They told me I could stay with them any time I'm in town, and when I wrote them about next weekend, they said they already had plans and didn't offer to cancel them."

Naturally patient and tolerant, not to say saintly, Miss Manners nonetheless grows testy with people who make such arguments. She cannot believe that they honestly don't understand what a conventional phrase is. She thinks they want to strip these remarks of their usefulness and then laugh at their nakedness. What a nasty urge that is.

However, it does occasionally happen that an expression of that sort can change its meaning somewhat, or that it could have more than one meaning, depending on how and by whom it is said. Here, therefore, is a short glossary of social idioms:

How do you do? How are you? Both of these mean *Hello.* The correct question, when you want to know how someone's digestion or divorce is getting along, is *Tell me, how have you really been?*

Call me. This can mean *Don't bother me now—let's discuss it on office time,* or *I would accept if you asked me out* or *I can't discuss this here* or *Don't go so fast.*

I'll call you. This has opposite meanings, and you have to judge by the delivery. One is *Let's start something* and the other is *Don't call me.*

Let's have lunch. Among social acquaintances, this means *If you ever have nothing to do on a day I have nothing to do, let's get together.* Among business acquaintances, it means *If you have something useful to say to me I'll listen.*

Let's have dinner. Among social acquaintances, it means *Let's advance this friendship.* Among business acquaintances, it means *Let's turn this into a friendship.*

Please stop by some time and see me. Said to someone who lives in the same area, it means *Call me if you'd like to visit me.* Genuine dropping in disappeared with the telephone, so if you want to encourage that, you have to say *I'm always home in the mornings. Don't bother to call; just drop by.*

Please come and stay with me. Said to someone from another area, this means *I would consider extending an invitation at your convenience if it coincides with my convenience.*

We must get together. Watch out here, because there are several similar expressions. This one means *I like you but I'm too busy now to take on more friendship.*

We really must see more of each other. One of the tricky ones, this actually means *I can't make the time to see you.*

We must do this more often. Another variation. This one is really *This was surprisingly enjoyable, but it's still going to happen infrequently.*

Yours truly, Yours sincerely. The first is business, the second distant social. Both mean *Well I guess that's all I've got to say so I'll close now.*

Is all that clear? Oh, one last thing. People who say *I only say what I really mean,* really mean *I am about to insult you.*

A Dangerous Game

DEAR MISS MANNERS:

A woman I met at a party asked me to guess her age. I thought she was about forty, even though she was wearing a satin disco dress and carrying a pocketbook shaped like a heart, and I said so. Well, it turns out she's thirty-three and is always being asked for proof that she's of legal drinking age, so I was supposed to guess that she was a teenager. I felt trapped by the whole thing. What should I have done?

GENTLE READER:

You were trapped, so you might as well have gone along with the silly game. Why didn't you demand to see her teeth before answering?

Discussing the Will

DEAR MISS MANNERS:

When my father passed away this spring, my mother had my and my sister's names put on a joint account card to her savings account. (She has a considerable amount of money.) Later, in a telephone conversation, she mentioned that she had done this rather than write a will. I wrote to her to say, if she wished to leave anything to me, didn't she think a will would offer more protection to my interests?

My fear was that my sister, who lives in California (as does my mother) where the accounts are all located, would withdraw everything before I even knew what happened.

My mother wrote, after a long delay, to tell me how heartbroken she was that all I cared about was her money. She further stated that there will be no will, that she's going to spend all her money so we girls will have nothing to fight over.

My husband says I should apologize for offending her. I feel that since I only asked her to put in writing whatever she wished, that I've done nothing to apologize for.

Tell me, Miss Manners, have I been an insensitive clod? You have a delicious way of telling the awful truth.

GENTLE READER:

Why, thank you. Here you have, in one sentence, charmed Miss Manners, a stranger not likely to leave you a considerable sum of money—so how did you manage to upset your own mother so thoroughly?

Miss Manners understands that you did not mean to do so. You ask if you have been insensitive and, by implication, whether your mother has been unduly sensitive. Without condemning either of you, Miss Manners would like to point out that you are looking at the situation from vastly different points of view.

The distinction is not one of sensitivity as opposed to insensitivity, or even sentimentality as opposed to practicality. It is simply the difference between contemplating the death of another person, however beloved, and contemplating one's own death.

We all cherish hopes of leaving legacies of sorrow tempered by wisdom. That is, one's heir should feel overcome with grief at the loss, but at the same time grateful to have had the privilege of benefiting from the loving guidance of the deceased.

No doubt you will express these sentiments at the funeral. But in your pre-funeral discussion, the only one your mother is likely to hear, the only legacy you are acknowledging is the one in the bank. To a survivor, this is naturally more conspicuous, shall we say, than a heritage of fond memories. But you have led your mother to believe that it is her sole legacy to you. What is more, you have denigrated her achievements as a mother by suggesting that she reared a potential thief and failed to inspire any family bonds likely to survive the settling of her estate.

This was not a good idea, as you have noticed. Of course you should soothe her feelings, even though your error was one of omission, rather than commission.

None of this is to be interpreted as Miss Manners' saying that any discussions of the transfer of property initiated by potential heirs is either rude or necessarily doomed. Indeed, there are often compelling reasons for holding them. Your mother's reluctance to face the necessity of settling her affairs is undoubtedly going to create trouble for you and your sister, whatever your and her motives.

Miss Manners' suggestion is that all discussions of legacies should involve mention of the emotional, as well as the cash, inheritance. "Mother, Justine and I are going to be in no state to deal sensibly with all that difficult financial stuff if you're taken from us. Please, just get a lawyer now to fix it up whatever way you think would be best." Or, more slyly, "Mother, I'm terribly worried about Justine. I sometimes feel that temptation is really bad for her; she can't handle it. Is there any way you can arrange things so that I can give her a little help and guidance?"

Occupations

Miss Manners has observed that when people meet one another they often say, "What do you do?" instead of "How do you do?" It is the grown-up version of that snappy opener at college mixers, "What are you majoring in?"

Miss Manners feels that there are worse ways to begin sizing up new people than by their occupations. Those who object to being "defined" by what they do for a living may well be asked exactly how they propose to "define" themselves in a simple sentence following a handshake. One may not have had complete freedom of choice about one's job, but it had to involve more choice than one has about one's birth or family, which is what other societies use to begin sizing people up. However, Miss Manners has been hearing from people who find this question offensive and want to know how to head it off or to cut it off with a smart, but uninformative, reply.

As it happens, these people are housewives and writers who work at home. Miss Manners considers both of these to be respectable occupations and doesn't think people who pursue them should feel touchy when questioned by people who work in offices, but they do. For instance, a person who works at home always complains that those who interrupt with visits or telephone calls or coffee invitations are indicating that they don't take one's work seriously. People who work in offices adore being interrupted.

Miss Manners feels that anyone doing honest work should be able to say so without apology. To those who insist on evading the question, she can offer three ways of answering, none of them involving fancying up one's job title to make it sound office-y. No "household technicians," please. At most, one can make the job one does seem more in demand. "I'm trying to finish up a book due two years ago" sounds better than "I'm trying to write a novel," except, of course, to one's publisher. It is better to interpret the question as meaning "What do you do when you have the choice?" There is nothing to stop one from replying, "I assist reluctant sky divers" or "I am a bird feeder" or whatever one prefers to do. However, if the motive is to achieve status with a questioner who smugly holds a glamorous position, one must switch the value system. Instead of accepting the idea that occupation is the basis of status, supply an answer in terms of money or social class. "I have to manage the family property" or "I'm cataloguing my library" are examples of honest answers that should do it.

Women's Work

Some people are quite rude to women they meet socially these days, asking them right off, "What do you do?" as if they wouldn't be worth talking to unless they had professional affiliations. Others are quite rude by not asking women what they do, as if to assume that they wouldn't be doing anything professionally. Social life is so much more interesting now than it was when there was only one way for a gentleman to insult a lady. Miss Manners herself has managed to alienate various gentlemen who have asked her, "Do you work?" or "Do you still work?" or "Do you work full time?" simply by replying to each, "Oh, yes; do you?" Gentlemen are so touchy.

Miss Manners, who ordinarily dislikes the cute opening remark, is therefore recommending indirect questioning, such as:

"Do you have any way of knowing what's going to happen to the dollar?" ("No, I'm a potter.")

"Are you a musician? You have a musician's hands." ("No, I'm a tax consultant. But I've always bitten my nails.")

"Haven't we met? I feel as if I know you." ("I feel as if I know you, too. I'm your ex-wife's therapist.")

As soon as you know the other person's occupation, you can choose a conversation topic that is entirely unrelated to it. One always asks a housewife who is really running the city government, and a corporation president which is the best of the new kitchen machines. That is what we call charm.

"Just a . . ."

DEAR MISS MANNERS:

I'm a secretary—not the cute, young kind, but a mature woman, married forty-four years, who spent twenty-five years as a housewife. I was always careful to avoid qualifying my title, as in "*just* a housewife." I'm equally careful to avoid saying "*just* a secretary."

However, it seems that either title demeans one socially. The other night, a young woman asked where I worked and was very impressed when I told her the name of the prestigious institution. She immediately wanted to know what I did there and when I said I was a secretary, you would have thought I had suddenly come down with a terminal disease. Even worse were her parting words, "Well, even though you're just a secertary, it must be an interesting place to work."

Miss Manners, I'm so tired of wearing this scarlet S. Can you suggest any way to avoid this situation?

GENTLE READER:

"Just a" is, indeed, an offensive qualifier, and the only sure way to avoid hearing it is to stay away from rude people. That is hardly possible in this world.

You know that Miss Manners does not allow her readers to answer rudeness with rudeness. But you might say, with polite pride, "Oh, no, you're mistaken. I started out as just-a-secretary, but now I'm a full secretary."

"Career Girls"

DEAR MISS MANNERS:

A well-dressed, middle-aged man sitting next to me in an airplane asked me if I was "a career girl." I know what this means, and I consider it an insult. It means am I some young chick busying herself by playing at working while waiting to get married—and maybe interested in some "fun" with the likes of him in the meantime. I have a "career," of course, if that means that I work for a living like everyone else—but you don't go around asking strangers if they have jobs. I just said "No" curtly and turned away from him, but I'm still mad. What should I have said?

GENTLE READER:

Miss Manners hesitates to assume evil intent in matters where differences of age may make significant semantic differences. You should merely have asked him, in turn, if he was a career boy.

Professional Hazards

DEAR MISS MANNERS:

As a member of a college English department, I share a distressing problem with many of my colleagues: Whenever we are introduced at social gatherings and our profession is indicated, we are greeted with at least one gleeful shout of "Oh, dear; I'm certainly going to have to watch the way I talk in front of you— you're an English teacher!" To a man (or woman), we cringe. Is there a correct response?

I have toyed with both "Yes, and as a specialist in the eighteenth-century novel, I intend to pounce on any error you may utter regarding that field, embarrassing you in front of all these people, because, as you have correctly assumed, I have no manners or tact whatsoever" and the more concise "Thank you, but I'm perfectly capable of forming a low opinion of you on completely different grounds." Neither, however, seems entirely satisfactory. You would oblige us all greatly by advising us of the proper etiquette for managing these situations.

GENTLE READER:

Thank you. You have hit on the one problem that drives Miss Manners bananas in her own life. People are always saying to her, "Oh, dear; I'm certainly going to have to watch the way I eat in front of you. . . ."

As you can imagine, Miss Manners does not care to solve the problem with rude remarks and cannot endorse the ones you suggest. Her own rejoinder is, "I'm not really a traffic policewoman—I don't hand out tickets at the dinner table," but she admits it is a weak one. If you can think of a better, she would be obliged to you. We all need to be reminded that every profession attracts its particular stupid remark, and that the correct thing to say when being told someone's profession, is simply, "Oh, how interesting."

"Any Babies?"

DEAR MISS MANNERS:

I react to questions about my daughter-in-law and son from people who ask, "Well, any babies?" or "Are you going to be a grandmother?" etc., by glaring at them and saying, "I don't ask them such questions." Certainly it is not my business, nor anyone else's, but even so, perhaps I have blown this up more than is necessary. Is there a polite response?

GENTLE READER:

One can hardly exaggerate the rudeness of inquiring into the contents of someone else's womb. Sooner or later, these people will get a burst of tears for an answer, from some couple unable to conceive a child. Miss Manners considers your answer, or a cool "I have no idea," civil enough, under the circumstances.

Short of producing those tears, the couple may answer when or why questions about babies ("When are you going to have children?" "Why don't you have children yet?" or "Why aren't you going to have children?") with a frosty look and a firm, "One never knows, does one?" Miss Manners does not approve of rude answers, even to rude questions, and rough but honest answers, such as "Why should we burden ourselves?" are as bad.

Do-you questions ("Do you have any children?") are legitimate and should be answered legitimately. (That is, one only has to admit to legitimate children.)

Boasting

"I apologize for boasting," says Nicholas Devize in *The Lady's Not for Burning* by dear Christopher Fry, "but once you know my qualities, I can drop back into a quite brilliant humility."

He says it in verse, but you do see his problem. Humility is easy, although Miss Manners much admires brilliant humility. The usual variety, with its claims about feeling awed and hoping to be worthy, is tiresome. But it is extremely difficult to make others acquainted with how very much one has to be humble about. No, that's not quite what Miss Manners meant to say. What is difficult is to establish gracefully that one has cause to be proud and haughty, before one can be contrastingly humble.

The ideal solution is to get others to broadcast one's achievements, so that the achiever has only to handle the humility. Only a few boastworthy matters can be counted on to attract such assistance. If you are elected President, you can generally get the networks to announce it for you. Enlisting your relatives for such a job is, however, tricky. Miss Manners has seen few family acts in which the boast ("Alexandrina has been chosen to play the Madonna in the Christmas pageant because she's the most popular girl in the school") is followed by a convincing amount of humility (''Oh, Mo—ther! Pul—*eeze!*''). Besides, the person who has the role of boaster then seems to be boasting on his or her own behalf for having amazing relatives. This sabotages the separation of the two functions.

The safest thing is to do it all oneself, but to blend the two parts. In artful boasting, one states all the information necessary to impress people, but keeps the facts decently clothed in the language of humility. Useful approaches include Disbelief, Fear, and Manic Elation. For some reason, these are considered to be more attractive human emotions than justifiable pride or self-satisfaction. Probably because they are not as much fun.

Here are some samples of each. The dots stand for the listener's predictable questions and responses. The best-prepared social speeches always allow for such interruptions.

Disbelief:

''My God, there must be some mistake. . . . My test scores—I can't believe it. . . . I know I couldn't have done that well—the number must have been copied wrong, because I know I messed up. . . . What did you get? . . . You see? There's a mistake. I know you had to do better than I because you know more. . . .''

Fear:

''Oh, oh, now I've had it. . . . Well, you see, I—uh, I got the promotion. . . . Yes, I'm going to be the superviser. . . . I know, but I'm not sure I can handle it. . . . I don't think they thought enough about how young I am and how little time I've been there. . . . Yes, I suppose so, but I'm terrified I can't handle it. . . .''

Manic Elation:

''I can't stand it! . . . It worked! It worked! . . . They bought my idea! They bought it! I'm going to be rich and famous! . . . Well, listen to what they're going to pay me! It's wild! You know what this could lead to? Let me tell you how they're going to promote it! . . . Isn't this the most fantastic thing you ever heard of? . . .''

Miss Manners doesn't claim that any of this dialogue is sparkling. But at least it doesn't inspire the dislike that bald boasts do. Plain statements, such as ''I just inherited a million dollars,'' or ''I got three proposals this year—from a congressman, a movie star, and a president of a bank'' do not arouse unmixed admiration.

Gossip

Gossip is now the national sport, having narrowly edged out the previous favorites, baseball and hanging around. But there does not seem to be any general agreement on the rules, let alone good sportsmanship. This is a serious problem. People who gossip unskillfully will find that they have succeeded only in getting themselves talked about, and nobody likes that. We all know that gossip does not consist of excited whispers about how well someone is behaving.

Therefore, we prefer to tell our own stories ourselves and let others furnish the subjects for gossip.

The astute will be able to figure out from this that gossiping is a dangerous sport. If the person it concerns is not going to like it, and if, by its very nature, it gets around and is likely to get back to that person—well, the only wise course is not to do it at all. This is equally true of extramarital sex, and the warning has about as much effect.

The question to ask oneself before indulging in gossip, then, is not so much "Is it true?" or "Is there any useful reason for repeating it?" (no, and no again), but "Is this likely to come around again and hit me in the face?" Yes, it is. But applying some discipline to the exercise will minimize the blow.

Let us consider the different types of gossip, with the safeguards that should be used for each.

1. Gossip about oneself. This is a peculiar form of gossip, as the gossiper does not call it that—he calls it a "confidence"—and does not understand that it becomes gossip the minute it has left his mouth. The only precaution one has against making one's confidences known is to keep them confidential. Promises extracted from the hearer mean nothing; if you haven't been able to resist telling, why should he? As dear Erasmus said in *"De Civilitate,"* "It is safe to admit nothing that might embarrass one if repeated."

2. Gossip one has heard firsthand from and about someone one knows. This is the receiving end of the first category and is considered quality gossip because it is presumed to come from an informed source. However, it is the worst gossip to repeat, as the subject can also trace the gossip source. Repeating it and asking one's listener not to do the same is ridiculous. Skip this category and move on to the next.

3. Gossip received secondhand about someone one knows. This is better than the first two, as you can pass it on along with the name of your source, who will then be blamed for blabbing. Gossip this far removed from original research also makes better stories, as the facts are flimsy enough to be bent into whatever shape you need to make the story illustrate a larger truth about human nature. Just make sure you're not telling it to someone who is in a position to know the information better than you do. In other words, find out first if your listener is the brother-in-law of the person you're gossiping about.

4. Gossip received secondhand about someone you don't know. This is celebrity gossip, and the best kind. It is highly unlikely to be true, as all celebrity gossip is made to fit a pattern of simple irony and assumes that people are always the opposite of what they seem, but it's a lot less likely than the other to get back to them and inspire them to get back at you.

Name Dropping

The well-bred person does not drop names carelessly on other people's clean tablecloths. The only permissible reasons are that one's social rank needs to be clarified, or to save another person from embarrassment. It is courteous for a close friend of a celebrity to reveal the friendship rather than allow a guest who is innocent of this information to insult the celebrity.

The rules of polite behavior must prevail, however. If anything, one should be particularly scrupulous when name dropping. An honest person does not drop a name he does not legitimately possess; a tasteful person is careful to drop less of it than he could. An intimate of the President could not make a more grievous error than to say, "Well, Ronnie told me . . ." Rather, he should say, "That's interesting—I hardly ever get in to see the President anymore, so I hadn't heard that." You will notice how understated this is. You will also notice the use of the dropped name's title, rather than a first name or a nickname.

(Miss Manners observed an excellent example of this at a state dinner President Kennedy gave early in his administration, if one may be permitted to drop an event. The less important people grabbed his arm and called him "Jack." The Attorney General, who as a sideline was the President's brother, greeted him by saying, "Good evening, Mr. President." You will notice, as well, how much more effective this is.)

Openers

DEAR MISS MANNERS:
What do you consider a good conversation opener?
GENTLE READER:
Almost anything except, "I've been on a wonderful journey of self-discovery lately, and I'd like to share it with you."

DEAR MISS MANNERS:
As a newly arrived young man in town, I now find I am substantially dependent upon my own devices to meet appropriate young women. Lacking a proper introduction in so many circumstances, I find that if I am going to have the chance to meet some attractive miss, I must initiate a conversation out of nowhere. I have read that the two grand modes of making conversation interesting are to enliven it by recitals calculated to affect and impress your hearer, and to intersperse it with anecdotes and smart things. Reputedly, Count Antoine Rivarol, who lived from 1757 to 1801, was a master in the latter mode. My question is, could you suggest an anecdote or some smart thing that could start the ball rolling, so to speak?
GENTLE READER:
Since 1801, the world has become overpopulated with Counts of No Account just brimming with smart openings and impressive anecdotes. Miss Manners therefore suggests you try something of startling, unconventional simplicity, such as "How do you do? May I get you a drink?"

Filling Social Openings

DEAR MISS MANNERS:

What suggestions can you offer to a "social klutz" who absolutely dreads going to parties and social events where I will meet new people? I get so uptight about saying the wrong thing that I usually do. I am fine around people who know me and I'm a fairly successful hostess, but am a terrible guest.

GENTLE READER:

Most people develop clever opening lines for such events. If you let them deliver these statements and say only, "How interesting—tell me about it," you will soon have a reputation as a charming person and a fascinating conversationalist.

Conversing with Children

DEAR MISS MANNERS:

My children hate it when adults say, "My, how you've grown!" or something like that. People do it all the time, of course, and I tell them they just have to expect it. Yet I find myself at a loss when confronted with other people's children. There is some kid, hiding behind his parents' legs, and I find myself saying things just as bad as what others say to my children. What should grown-ups say to children on such occasions?

GENTLE READER:

Nothing that would be considered rude if the child said it back. A child of Miss Manners' acquaintance who was brought along to an adult party and told, when he left, that he had "behaved like a perfect gentleman," replied to the host, "So did you." Miss Manners feels that the child came out ahead in this encounter. All basic social remarks are silly; the best one can do is to keep them from being patronizing, as well. "How do you like this weather?" and "Stock market killing you?" may not be brilliant, but they are better than "The last time I saw you, you were only so high."

Edgewise

DEAR MISS MANNERS:

I am basically a nonpushy, nonaggressive conversationalist. For a long time, I just called myself "a good listener." There are times, though, when I'd like the chance to talk myself. Yet so many people just talk right over me. Sometimes I'm halfway into a sentence or an idea when they burst in with their own. I have tried politeness, patience, and even, once, repeating a sentence over and over again (six times) till that person finally listened. Is there a polite way to deal with conversation hogs?

GENTLE READER:

Conversation, which is supposed to be a two-way street, is treated by many people as if it were a divided highway. They may acknowledge that traffic must go in both directions, but speed independently on their own way, expecting you to do the same on your side.

If you are, in fact, a practiced "good listener," you have not been traveling through life in silence. You have been asking questions, inserting relevant information, and providing commentary on what the chief talkers to whom you have been listening are saying. A good listener is not someone who has to be checked every now and then by the speaker to see if he or she is awake.

Presuming, therefore, that you have been doing some of the talking (and if you have not, you might begin by adapting your listening method), you need only to make the transition from supporting role to leading role. It is unfortunate that this (if Miss Manners may drop the new metaphor and go back to her original one, which was more clever) is often like trying to drive over a grassy highway divider.

The way to get across is to say something related, however vaguely, to what has been said before. While lulling the speaker into believing that you are responding as a listener, this tactic can be a shortcut to the main highway. (Getting back to that metaphor was not as easy as Miss Manners anticipated. She now feels lost and is considering staying right where she is until someone comes and finds her.) Once in the driver's seat (to go bravely and recklessly on), you should try to be a good talker. That is to say, you must allow proper interruptions that are in the tradition of good listening, and even encourage them by asking occasionally and perhaps superfluously, "Don't you think so?" or "What do you think?"

If people persist in trying to wrest the controls away from you, put up warning signs. "Just a minute—I haven't finished" is one; "But wait—I haven't told you the point yet" is another.

(All right. If everyone will now stop talking for a minute, perhaps we can find a volunteer to go and rescue a lady caught out there in the verbal traffic jam.)

Ad-Libbing

DEAR MISS MANNERS:

What is today's directory of protocol in (1) business, (2) social conversation? I am put into situations that require ad-libbing in strange groups and therefore do not have time to determine what is expected or proper for that particular group. My innate tendency is to keep quiet until I am able to find out, but too often that is impractical.

Is there somewhere a universal directory that I can rely on that will pull me through all sorts of situations?

GENTLE READER:

Life is a situation that requires ad-libbing in strange groups. The only certain rule is the one that you have already discovered—Keep your mouth shut and no will know you are a fool—but you have also already discovered its limitations. The universal directory is called experience, and it requires a lifetime of trial-and-error ad-libbing to perfect. Miss Manners suggests you get started.

Quotations

DEAR MISS MANNERS:

A gentleman's language should be easy and unstudied, marked by graceful carelessness that never oversteps the limits of propriety. Although there are a great many talkers, few know how to converse agreeably. The art is, in truth, the very soul of good breeding, which renders us agreeable to all with whom we associate. A friend of mine, by all measures well bred, has a verbal affectation that is annoying. He has a mania for Greek and Latin quotations. I believe this is particularly to be avoided. It is like pulling up stones from a tomb wherewith to kill the living. How can I let him know his pedantry is wearisome?

GENTLE READER:

A gentleman does not let another gentleman know that that gentleman's conversation is wearisome. However, there is nothing to prevent a gentleman from arming himself with Chinese or Sanskrit quotations with which to answer another gentleman's remarks.

Ancestors

DEAR MISS MANNERS:

I have a friend who talks all the time about his ancestors. He didn't used to, but now he's involved in what he calls a "history project" about his family, and we're never going to hear the end of it. It sounds to me like plain old bragging. Isn't this topic considered taboo among polite people?

GENTLE READER:

Among polite people descended from the upper classes, yes. But bragging about one's ancestors is quite fashionable now if one can claim to be descended from the lower classes. Many such claims are exaggerated, of course.

Divided Attention

DEAR MISS MANNERS:

Is it impolite to gaze about the room while someone is talking to you, or is it only a bad habit? Thank you for your undivided attention to this problem.

GENTLE READER:

You are welcome. The person who is—what were you saying? Please forgive Miss Manners; her attention was distracted for a moment by something more interesting going on up there in the tree.

Certainly, it is a bad habit. It means that one is searching about for someone better with whom to talk than one's present companion. It is, however, standard procedure at cocktail parties; but, then, cocktail parties are a bad habit too.

DEAR MISS MANNERS:

Shame on you! You wrote about people who look about the room while someone is talking to them; I do it too. The reason? Same as it's always been—I'm terribly shy.

GENTLE READER:

You seem to be getting over it.

Avoiding the Personal

DEAR MISS MANNERS:

Some months ago, I was mugged. I've spent weeks going around replacing everything in my purse, filling out forms, and so on. As if that isn't enough of a nuisance, everywhere I go, everyone—friends, credit department clerks, people at the office—asks me for details about what happened. Why do they do this? It was a nasty experience and I would like to forget it.

GENTLE READER:

Because they are dying to know if you were raped. Do not tell them.

Dreams

DEAR MISS MANNERS:

Is it polite to tell other people your dreams? A man in my office who is, I believe, in analysis, recites his in a loud voice the first thing every morning to whoever will listen, and all of us around the coffee machine can plainly hear every word. Sometimes they involve sexual fantasies about women at the office.

I reached the breaking point yesterday, when he made dirty remarks about a woman I am seeing regularly, and I was about to punch him in the nose, but she took me aside and said that wasn't fair, because they're only dreams, and discussing his dreams is an important part of his recovery. Frankly, it makes me wonder about her, in regard to him.

GENTLE READER:

It makes Miss Manners wonder about a society in which such privilege is given to illness, provided it is not identifiable physical illness. Would people feel equally tolerant about the spreading of cold germs or, for that matter, other regurgitation?

Interrupted Dreams

DEAR MISS MANNERS:

Last night, a friend was telling me her dream. The subject matter and her description of it were both personal and esoteric. We were interrupted by a friend of mine, a stranger to her, coming over. I interrupted her, saying that perhaps she should finish later.

When the visitor left, I suggested she finish her story. I felt she was slightly hurt—she changed the subject, and I heard no more about her dream. This must be a common occurrence. Did I act improperly? If so, what should I do in the future?

GENTLE READER:

Life is full of interrupted dreams. But Miss Manners doesn't know that it is all that common to have the dreamers pout about not being allowed to tell them to strangers. You behaved properly.

Shocking Society

It was a sad day when Miss Manners lost the capacity to be shocked. Such a delicious feeling it used to be—that tingle while one thought, "He doesn't really mean *that*" or "She *can't* have said what I thought she said." Nowadays, there is no doubt that that is what he meant, and that is what she intended. It certainly does take the fun out of conversation. Miss Manners is thinking of buying a jumbo-family-size box of detergent and washing out everyone's mouth with soap, so we can all start talking dirty afresh.

It is a common misconception that shocking conversation is that which reveals to the hearer ideas that were previously unknown. Not at all. There are only so many ideas in that area, and everyone over the age of eight knows what they are. To hear them uttered aloud—that used to be something. Papas who used vile expressions were understood to have been pushed beyond human endurance. Mamas given to such extremes had three-generation families quailing. Young gentlemen and young ladies who exclaimed "Damme" (with the "e" on it; that was important) were taken seriously; if they said worse, they were treated as dangerous madmen, a useful way to be regarded when you require quick action.

Now every babe in arms can reel off the whole vocabulary, and nobody pays them the slightest attention. There is nothing more infuriating, when you are furious, than to have people shrug off your severest expressions of displeasure. The fact is that through overuse of three or four words, we no longer have language that adequately describes such situations as being splashed with mud by an empty taxi that one has tried in vain to hail. On such occasions, Miss Manners has been driven to exclaiming, "My goodness gracious!" or "Upon my word!"

These are not nice, as she is the first to acknowledge, but desperate times call for desperate measures.

Improper Remarks

DEAR MISS MANNERS:
I have failed at the art of conversation and most desperately need your help! While my husband and I were sitting at dinner the other night with another married couple, the other man turned to me and, apropos of nothing in the conversation, declared that he was now ''safe.'' Naïve as always, I asked, ''What do you mean by 'safe'?'' ''A vasectomy,'' he proudly announced.

Nearly speechless, I frantically searched for the proper response, but a splutter and a giggle were all I came up with. Any suggestions?

GENTLE READER:
Ah, isn't it wonderful what passes for conversation these days? You can hardly sit down at dinner anymore without being told what everyone does with the parts of the body that cannot be seen above the table. Miss Manners is going to take to shocking perfect strangers by looking them deep in the eyes and saying, ''Beastly weather we've been having lately, don't you think?''

But she cannot improve on your response, which was perfectly proper—unless it would be by accompanying your splutter and giggle with the appropriate gesture of staring the man straight in the napkin.

DEAR MISS MANNERS:
What is your response to a lewd remark?

GENTLE READER:
People do not make lewd remarks to Miss Manners. If they did, her response would be a sweet smile, accompanied by a naïve but earnest request to explain exactly what the remark meant. The result would be that even if a person made a first lewd remark to Miss Manners, he would never make a second.

Tasteless Jokes

DEAR MISS MANNERS:
What do you do when someone makes a bigoted remark or tells a joke with a slur in it? These offend me—and not only when my own race is the target. Should I show that I am offended? Should I keep quiet—doesn't silence indicate some kind of endorsement? Are there any guidelines about how to behave in connection with such remarks or jokes?

GENTLE READER:
Certainly there are. There are guidelines for everyone, regardless of. . . . They are:

1. Bigoted jokes or expressions are properly used only by members of the group being slurred, addressed to other members of that group. A nonmember

would be well advised not to join in the fun. When an ethnic joke is told among nonmembers of the group, disapproval may be expressed by a stony face and a frosty smile.

2. If a nonmember slurs a group of which you are obviously a member, you may walk haughtily out of the room, or inquire menacingly, "Just what do you mean by that?" or otherwise indicate that you are insulted. Not enough women take advantage of this opportunity.

3. If a nonmember slurs a group without knowing you are a member or have some other close connection, you may convey this information ("Perhaps you don't know that my wife is black"). In this case, there is no need to emphasize it with angry behavior—the statement is more devastating if given in a simple, factual way.

4. The only effective recovery that the offender may offer is a counterclaim. "Oh, really? So am I. Hadn't you noticed?" If that is not even remotely possible, one must at least dredge up a second cousin; "best friends" won't do. Nor will the common mutter, "I was only kidding." Bolstering this remark with "Don't you people have any sense of humor?" only compounds the problem.

5. If you are running for political office or are contemplating ever running for political office, train yourself never to let any such words pass your lips. If you just can't resist, don't tell them on the press bus.

6. Dirty jokes in unmixed company—that is to say, jokes that depend on a shared belief in the inferiority of the other sex—aren't safe any longer, either. It's not only that someone present might be married to a person of the other sex, but nowadays you can never tell when people might care more for those with whom they live than those with whom they share public bathrooms.

7. Jokes that make fun of the teller's own wealth, ancient lineage, or prestigious school or neighborhood are successful only among those who share these handicaps.

8. Jokes about other people's proper names are never successful. For one thing, the people have all heard every possible one before. You will never manage to satirize anybody's name in a fashion he has not heard since nursery school, and Miss Manners isn't even going to tell you the name of the person who first told her that.

9. The only truly safe and proper subject for a joke is oneself. Many a person who thought this privilege extended to his or her spouse, parent, or child, has lived—but not very long—to find otherwise.

Responding

DEAR MISS MANNERS:

What is the correct response when someone makes a bad joke? I never know what to do! A friend told me that one should say "dung" and make a gesture with the right index finger extended upward. Is this proper? I know this sounds utterly crazy and I would feel so silly doing it, but I don't know what else to do.

GENTLE READER:

Your friend is making a bad joke and should be stared at with an expression somewhere between bland and puzzled until he or she wants to forget the whole thing.

Mispronunciations

DEAR MISS MANNERS:

Can you suggest a graceful way of calling a friend's attention to a word that has been egregiously mispronounced? I am thinking especially of a well-educated person with a reasonably good vocabulary at his or her command who makes this kind of gaffe in a conversational circle. I recall someone saying ''reticent'' as if it were ''re-tie-cent'' with the accent on the ''tie.'' Just recently a friend spoke of ''maniac-depressive.'' Trying to be objective, one would like to help a friend, to help avoid a repetition of the mistake, but at the same time one would not want to seem to be putting on airs.

GENTLE READER:

Nobody knows better than Miss Manners the joy of ''helping a friend'' by graciously indicating how much more one knows than he or she. For example, Miss Manners would adore pointing out that your ''someone saying 'reticent' '' ought to be ''someone's saying 'reticent,' '' but is reticent about doing so because of the unlikely chance you may then catch Miss Manners in a tiny error and the whole thing might never end, with each of us becoming increasingly bitter. At best, you may inquire of your friend, ''Oh, is that the way you pronounce that? I've always heard . . .'' However, you do this at your own risk.

Colorful Expressions

DEAR MISS MANNERS:

Help. I have a dear friend who, at the tender age of thirty-three, has turned into an old Jewish woman. The phrases ''Oy vay'' and ''God forbid you should'' have invaded her speech to the extent that I need a comeback—a quick retort— or something.

GENTLE READER:

The phrases you quote strike Miss Manners as being vivid and useful, if not eloquent, and Miss Manners is not so foolish as to attempt to top them.

Pointing

DEAR MISS MANNERS:

Many adolescents, not particularly known for their politeness, rudely declare, ''It's not polite to point,'' when someone points a finger at them for emphasis. It seems to me that in this case they learned only half the lesson. It is impolite for A, while speaking to B, to point to C, who is beyond the range of hearing but within the range of sight, and therefore doesn't know the reason for the pointing. But if A, while speaking to B, points a finger at B to stress an idea, such as "It's up to you!" or "The error was yours!" there is nothing impolite about such pointing. Am I not correct?

GENTLE READER:

Please remove your finger from Miss Manners' eye. Thank you.

The unpleasantness of being pointed at applies not only to strangers at a distance, but also, you will be surprised to hear, to close-by acquaintances shouting "The error is yours!" This is partly because of the words with which the gesture is associated, "Uncle Sam Wants You!" However, you are correct that the error of pointing out errors to one's elders is worse.

Giving Compliments

DEAR MISS MANNERS:

After attending a recital in which a friend had taken part, I was asked by the friend what I thought of his performance. What would be the proper response for a poor performance? Should one give a detailed criticism of the faults and merits, or simply a pat on the back, "very good," etc.? And for an exceedingly good one, is bubbling enthusiasm appropriate, or merely a standard compliment?

GENTLE READER:

Bubbling enthusiasm is alike appropriate for poor and exceedingly good performances, the idea being deliberately to confuse the performer about which one he gave. This is what friends are for. Music teachers and music critics exist for other purposes.

DEAR MISS MANNERS:

With reference to your reply to the individual who asked how to respond to a friend's inquiry about a poor musical performance, I would like to suggest that you might have advised the writer to state: "You played one (or more) of my favorite selections." One can say this without becoming directly involved in commenting on the quality of the performance. The better part of being a friend is to avoid, whenever possible, causing unhappiness. Of course, if one is pressed further for a specific comment on a performance, comments on those portions performed adequately could be made, such as, "Your interpretation was very good." In response to the question, "What did you think of my performance?" a friend can always say, "I appreciated your effort and enjoyed the selection."

GENTLE READER:

Miss Manners agrees that the object is not to cause unhappiness, or possibly even to cause happiness. Remind her, though, not to ask you if you think she looks all right. You might reply, "Well, I appreciate your effort."

DEAR MISS MANNERS:

What is the appropriate comment to make about a portrait of a person you do not wish to insult, if the portrait is dreadful? My friend paid a lot of money to get this atrocity painted and is very proud of it. I don't want to hurt his feelings, but I don't want him to quote me to mutual friends as approving his awful taste.

GENTLE READER:

"It's wonderful how he got that texture of your tie, and it has your dignity, but is there something not quite you about the mouth?"

A Sudden Improvement

DEAR MISS MANNERS:

I have had the same podiatrist for about fifteen years, a very pleasant man of uncertain age who has worn a quite obvious hair piece as long as I have known him. He also has been clean-shaven. Recently this nice gentleman had open heart surgery and was away from his office for about four months. Upon his return, I made an appointment and to my astonishment was greeted by someone I scarcely recognized, but who was indeed the same dear man. The voice wasn't different, but the hair piece has been discarded, revealing a mostly bald pate surrounded by a soft, curly fringe (much more attractive than the phony toupee), and a great tan was embellished by a mustache. The whole image was improved by new, stylish gold-rimmed spectacles.

My question is—in such a situation, is a comment appropriate, or does one ignore the transformation? I can't imagine saying, "Oh, I see you're not wearing your toupee now," or "I never *did* like that hair piece, you could *tell* it wasn't yours. . . ." I couldn't decide if it would be unmannerly to comment, or if the improvement should be noted by a compliment.

GENTLE READER:

It is not at all uncommon for people to be absent from their usual circles for a few months and to return looking improved. There was a time, for instance, when it was common for young unmarried girls whose stomachs stuck out to disappear for a few months and come back looking slim. Now one more often sees older people of both sexes returning from unspecified vacations wearing their faces or other parts of their bodies higher than before. No true friend can ever figure out the cause of such a change for the better, except a change of scenery or rest, both of which can do wonders. It is not necessary to supply this observation, however. One should merely mention the improvement. The appropriate compliment is, "Why, you look marvelous! I don't know what it is, but you look years younger!"

Receiving Compliments

DEAR MISS MANNERS:

I find it difficult to accept compliments or congratulations. What should I say that is appropriately modest without seeming to question the judgment of the person complimenting me?

GENTLE READER:

"Thank you." Or, if you feel that is not enough, "Why, thank you very much, how kind of you to say so."

Actually, you already know that. What you don't know, Miss Manners suspects, is how to leave it at that. You then babble on to explain that the achievement was nothing anyone couldn't have done, the article of clothing is old and valueless, and that whatever is admired compares unfavorably with the equivalent quality or possession of the admirer.

To put this under the heading of modesty is absurd. It actually serves to prolong the compliment by treating it as the topic sentence in a speech rather than, as is more likely to be the case, a passing pleasantry. The only advantage of debating a compliment one has received is to reduce the chances of its recurring.

DEAR MISS MANNERS:

What do you say if someone you don't like gives you a compliment?

GENTLE READER:

"Thank you."

Repeated Repetitions

DEAR MISS MANNERS:

When an elderly person tells a joke that has been heard before or repeats something previously said, what should the other person say—"I've heard that before," or "You told me that," or simply act as if it had not been heard before?

GENTLE READER:

It is not only the elderly who tend to repeat themselves, as Miss Manners often says. There is one method of heading off a repeated story, but one must be quick about it. Jump in right at the beginning, and say, "Oh, I love that story," or "Is that that hilarious joke you told us—I've been trying to tell it myself." Sometimes, a "Yes, so you were telling us" works if it is accompanied by an interested expression, as if the listener were waiting for the talker to tell a sequel.

However, often nothing works, in which case you should listen gracefully. We should all be tolerant of the foibles of age; with luck, we will achieve them ourselves.

Conversing with God

DEAR MISS MANNERS:

I'm having a somewhat unusual disagreement with my new roommate on a point of etiquette. We share a dormitory room. It is my habit to pray (silently) each evening before retiring. Whenever I try to do so in our room, however, my roommate throws things at me or chases me out of the building. He says it's rude to carry on a private conversation in the presence of a third party. I say he's full of it. What do you say?

GENTLE READER:

A person who attacks violently one who is engaged in prayer is obviously a great authority on etiquette, whom it would be futile, and probably dangerous, to contradict. However, Miss Manners would point out that your roommate is perfectly free to join into the conversation with the Third Party, provided he observes the convention you do, of doing it in silence.

Eavesdropping

DEAR MISS MANNERS:

Would you be so kind as to advise me in choosing between hypocrisy and non-hypocrisy? My office is so arranged that phone calls (business and nonbusiness) may be overheard by several neighboring workers. I pretend not to hear the content of personal conversations, but I am often tempted to chime in later to give business information to individuals whom I have overheard. Should I pretend that I cannot overhear any call?

GENTLE READER:

Yes. Hypocrisy is a higher form of human behavior than eavesdropping. Besides, you have only overheard one side of the conversation, and that can be misleading. And besides that, such information is more valuable when stored up for private use than when given out freely as if it had been legitimately acquired.

Commands

DEAR MISS MANNERS:

Must you say please to your dog when commanding him to sit? "Sit!" sounds so dictatorial.

GENTLE READER:

How else are you going to teach him to say "Thank you"? If you do not wish to act as a superior to your dog, even "Please sit!" is somewhat strong. What about "Oh, do sit down and make yourself comfortable"?

✿ VOCABULARY

Age

DEAR MISS MANNERS:

My husband and I disagree on the use of the expression "older person." His point, and it is well taken, is that one should not use a comparative form when no actual comparison is being made. I accede that the expression is grammatically incorrect, but it serves a social purpose. No one wishes to be called elderly or (God forbid) a senior citizen. I use "older" to spare the tender feelings of those forever young at heart. What is your opinion please?

GENTLE READER:

Sensitive feelings about grammar take precedence over sensitive feelings about age. If you want Miss Manners' venerable opinion, there is nothing wrong with the word "old," but a lot wrong with the phrase "young at heart," as if there were something bad about having a wise old heart.

DEAR MISS MANNERS:

Kudos to you for your comments on euphemisms for "old." For the past twenty years or so, I have been saying (but no one has listened) that the only unprintable word now is not a four-letter word but a three-letter one spelled o-l-d. Now that this dirty word applies to me, I feel more strongly than ever that it should be cleaned up.

I recently went to buy some specially priced dance tickets (although I disapprove of the whole idea, I'm not above trying to save a few bucks) and asked if they had any old-lady tickets for a certain performance. The nice young volunteer turned on the kind of smile a nurse has for a terminally ill patient and said, "Oh, no. But we do have tickets for the young-in-heart who love ballet!"

Well, she was doing her job and I did want to save that eight dollars, so I didn't spit in her eye.

GENTLE READER:

Miss Manners would probably have to take up another line of work if she advised you to go ahead and spit in someone's eye, but she will at least state that she sympathizes with your desire to perform such an act. The idea that young hearts are the only ones capable of harboring love, while old hearts are fit only for cholesterol desposits, is an insult.

Children

DEAR MISS MANNERS:

My son and his wife have six children. They are all through college, some married, except two girls still at home. One of them is getting married in June. Last night, I said to my daughter-in-law, "Well, how will it feel with only one child at home?" She said, "She is not a child." That was her only reply. I said, "Well, all mothers say 'children' if speaking to one about their family." It wouldn't sound right to say, "Well, how would it feel to have one adult left?" What would be the correct phrase?

GENTLE READER:

The word "child" means offspring of any age, as well as meaning a minor. What is incorrect here is the use of semantic double-talk for the purpose of putting down one's mother-in-law.

"Drapes"

DEAR MISS MANNERS:

A friend of mine always corrects me when I say the word "drapes." She says that is vulgar, and that the right word is "draperies." Which of us is correct?

GENTLE READER:

You are both hopeless. The word for material that hangs on the sides of windows is "curtains."

DEAR MISS MANNERS:

Please stand corrected. The sheer fabric made up to cover a window is named a curtain. A solid fabric made up into window covering or decoration is named drapery.

GENTLE READER:

This is true for commercial purposes, but in ordinary conversation the word "drapery" is never used for anything that covers or decorates a window. All such materials are called "curtains." Please stand recorrected.

Good Greetings

DEAR MISS MANNERS:

What is the difference between "Good morning" and "Good day"? Is there any?

GENTLE READER:

Yes, indeed. "Good morning" is an opener, and "Good day" is a closer. Although "Good morning" can be purely a greeting, to which only the same words are expected as a reply, this function has, for the most part, been replaced by "Hi." Therefore, "Good morning" usually leads to "How are you?" and other such mild conversational excursions.

"Good day," an extremely useful expression, is less often employed. With the proper tone, perhaps expanded to, "I wish you a good day, sir," it means "Get out of my sight this instant" in the language of irreproachable manners.

As the Romans Do

DEAR MISS MANNERS:

When is it appropriate to say *"ciao"*?

GENTLE READER:

When in Rome.

"Ladies," "Women," and "Girls"

People of all sorts of genders are reporting great difficulty, these days, in selecting the proper words to refer to those of the female persuasion.

"Lady," "woman," and "girl" are all perfectly good words, but misapplying them can earn one anything from the charge of vulgarity to a good swift smack. We are messing here with matters of deference, condescension, respect, bigotry, and two vague concepts, age and rank. It is troubling enough to get straight who is really what. Those who deliberately misuse the terms in a misbegotten attempt at flattery are asking for it.

A woman is any grown-up female person. A girl is the un-grown-up version. If you call a wee thing with chubby cheeks and pink hair ribbons a "woman," you will probably not get into trouble, and if you do, you will be able to handle it because she will be under three feet tall. However, if you call a grown-up by a child's name for the sake of implying that she has a youthful body, you are also implying that she has a brain to match.

As for ladies, they come in three varieties: ladies, old ladies, and young ladies. The term "lady" is the most difficult to use. You must not be influenced by having noticed that Miss Manners refers to all of her acquaintances as ladies (or gentlemen). Miss Manners is prim and old-fashioned, which is part of her considerable charm, and can get away with anything. For anyone else to use the term "lady" when "woman" is meant would be vulgar or even insulting.

A lady is someone who adheres to a rather special and graceful standard of behavior, only nobody knows what it is. This makes it great fun for old ladies to set obscure, tricky, and clever tests by which to trap aspiring ladies.

"A lady never goes out of the house without a hat and gloves," is an example of this that put in years of service. What made it so good while it lasted was that it could be used to eliminate every woman who went out on her porch early to fetch the paper and mail. If Miss Manners had to come up with a modern version, she would say that a lady may use an occasional obscene word in exasperation, but never on her T-shirt.

What restricts the use of the word "lady" among the courteous is that it is intended to set a woman apart from ordinary humanity, and in the working world that is not a help, as women have discovered in many bitter ways.

"Lady" is, therefore, a word that should be used sparingly, and never in ways that interfere with a woman's livelihood. Because it should be a term of respect, its potential for sarcastic use is staggering, and snideness is always presumed when the word is used inappropriately, as in "lady lawyer" or "saleslady."

Because respect should be accorded to the aged, an elderly female is called an old lady, not an old woman, unless she is a particularly nasty old thing and you think you can get away with it. "Young lady" is also a special category. A young lady is a female child who has just done something dreadful.

"Pardon Me"

DEAR MISS MANNERS:

Is it true that "pardon me" is the wrong thing to say—that you have to say "excuse me" instead? Obviously, they both mean the same thing, and take the same time to say. What's the difference?

GENTLE READER:

A pardon is more difficult to obtain than an excuse. If you don't believe Miss Manners about that, ask some of the prominent and supposedly influential people who have failed or even managed to obtain pardons. For ordinary transgressions, it is easier to ask for an excuse.

Unmentionables

DEAR MISS MANNERS:

What is the proper and correct term to use when referring to a lady's lower undergarment? Is it "panties" or "underpants"? I've always called them "panties," but recently I've noticed that most of the women I know here call them "underpants" and they laugh at me when I say "panties." Which is correct?

GENTLE READER:

"Panties" is the nickname for "underpants" and, like "tummy" for "stomach," has a certain childish charm. But not very much. Miss Manners is not vehemently opposed to "panties," as she is to "lingerie," a silly way of referring to the perfectly respectable institution of underwear. She loves to drive department store clerks crazy by inquiring for the "Underwear Department" and watching them look puzzled.

"Vase"

DEAR MISS MANNERS:

When is a VASE a VAHZ?

GENTLE READER:

When it is filled with DAH-ZIES.

The Telephone at Home

Suppose the postman arrived during breakfast (more likely dinner, at his rate) and insisted that you leave the table and read your mail immediately? No matter whether a letter consisted of advertising, a leisurely chat from a friend or relation, or a business matter, it had to be attended to that very minute. If you happened instead to be entertaining guests, doing business, taking a bath, listening to a symphony, making love, or any combination of those activities, you would still have to stop everything immediately and devote your full attention to anybody who chose to address you.

This is what most people allow the telephone to do. It has developed into a horrid instrument, always clamoring for attention, and Miss Manners is beginning to think that it ought to be abolished entirely, as it never seems to learn to behave itself. There is that whiny bell. Like a spoiled child, it figures that people will give it whatever it wants just to shut it up. Like weak parents, nearly everybody does.

Miss Manners always has sympathy for people who complain that they are treated rudely by the people whom they telephone. Always, that is, except when they call to say this just when Miss Manners is in the middle of doing something interesting. Miss Manners is always doing something interesting, such as looking out the window at the trees.

Telephoners should not be put on hold indefinitely, made to spell their names more than once, told the person they want is out after they have been asked for their personal histories, hung up on, or subjected to canned music. These people would receive fewer such insults if they would make fewer telephone calls. Telephoning is not the only way to do business. It is not even always the quickest way of doing business. Two people who keep different office hours, either from the nature of their jobs or because they live in different time zones, may easily spend days leaving messages for each other—even more days than it takes to send a letter. Social matters, too, may be better handled by mail. A whispered long distance ''I love you'' is sweet, but a written one keeps forever and may be produced later in court.

The telephone is used not only out of a bad national habit, but because a quick answer is wanted. This overlooks the likelihood that the quick answer may then be regretted, and a second call is necessitated to reverse what one has said. (''I'm so sorry, Rhino tells me he forgot to mention that he had already promised we'd go slumming that night with someone else.'')

It will only be possible to use the mails, with their better manners, if we all promise to answer our letters promptly. The telephone can be reserved for truly urgent matters then, and there can be a stop to that incessant ringing in Miss Manners' ears. Please don't say you have no time to write letters. You will have all those wonderful hours that you used to spend on hold.

Unlisted Numbers

DEAR MISS MANNERS:

A friend of mine has steadfastly refused to give me his unlisted telephone number. While I understand that he works at home and therefore needs quiet, I find it frustrating and insulting that he does not trust me. I would certainly not abuse it.

GENTLE READER:

How do you know? Do you have his schedule, not only of when he works, but when he eats, reads, and thinks? The only insult Miss Manners can find in this situation is the assumption that your friend's life is of so little importance that he should always be prepared to drop what he is doing to answer your summons.

DEAR MISS MANNERS:

I have an unlisted telephone number because I live alone and hate being bothered by calls when I am apt to be in the bathtub or watching a television program. If it's someone I really want to hear from, I do give out the number. But I resent it when people expect me to tell them my telephone number as a matter of course. Can I just make up a number and give it to them?

GENTLE READER:

At the other end of that made-up number lives a person who is lying in the bathtub or watching television, and not anxious to hear from your acquaintances. When people ask you for your telephone number, write down your address.

During Dinner

Dear Miss Manners:

My problem is ludicrous but is causing a rift between my mother and husband. Situation: We are eating dinner and the telephone rings. I answer and state that we are at dinner and ask if I may return the call. My mother becomes offended and thinks my husband dictates my decision to talk or not. Which is correct etiquette—to eat and converse on the telephone, or to excuse myself from conversing? My husband and I both work, so dinner is a time for us to discuss daily events, etc.

Gentle Reader:

Miss Manners is opposed to correcting others, especially one's mother, unless it can be done without hurting feelings, but she can assure you that you have done nothing wrong. Certainly no telephone call, except an emergency, should be allowed to disrupt one's dinner.

Dear Miss Manners:

My father refuses to let me take telephone calls during dinner. I think it's rude to ask people to call back at a time that might not be convenient for them, and even ruder to ignore a ringing phone.

Gentle Reader:

You have a wonderful sense of the courtesies and conveniences due to others. Have you thought of applying these to your father?

Basic Telephoning

Dear Miss Manners:

Could you please remind people of a few telephone courtesies?

1. What is the proper number of rings a caller should wait before hanging up? I dislike the "three-ring phantoms."

2. Who are exempt from introducing themselves as callers? That is to say, "Hi, this is Mary Jane, your mother," is preferable to, "Hi, whatcha doin'?"

3. For social chatting more than five minutes—shouldn't the caller ask the callee whether this is a good time to talk?

Gentle Reader:

1. Six rings are safer, perhaps eight. If you still suspect the person of lurking there, hang up and dial again. This gives the caller two chances to get the number right and the callee an opportunity to get out of the bathtub.

2. Identifying yourself heads off the possibility of your being insulted by the other person's failure to identify you. However, "Mary Jane, your mother," seems excessive; only if there could be more than one person in the role should you add your name. The identification "Your true love" should always have a name to go with it.

3. Yes. 'Bye, now.

On a Names-First Basis

DEAR MISS MANNERS:

Our children are trained to answer the phone, "Smith residence, John speaking." This immediately tells the caller that he has reached the correct number and to whom the caller is talking. It is then, to our way of thinking, only mannerly that the caller immediately identify himself or herself. That the caller who has not identified himself must be asked to identify himself is a breach of manners on the part of the caller. Our children are taught to identify themselves when they are the caller. Are we wrong in our training?

GENTLE READER:

Only half wrong. You are confusing the duty of the caller with that of the callee. A person who wishes to be admitted to another's home, even electronically, should be expected to identify himself, but to announce one's identity first to whoever rings is unnecessary and may even be unwise.

Who Is Calling?

DEAR MISS MANNERS:

When there is a phone call for someone and they're not home at the time, is it the responsibility of the caller to state his or her name, or of the person who answers to ask if they can take a message?

GENTLE READER:

Offering help and asking for help are both acceptable forms of behavior. What you are getting at, Miss Manners suspects, is the matter of extracting information about the telephone calls of a person who is not present. "May I take a message?" is polite, because it allows the answer to be negative. "Who is calling?" is not.

DEAR MISS MANNERS:

Upon answering the telephone with a pleasant "Hello," I am often confronted with the rude response, "Who is this?" The telephoning party has not only ignored my salutation, he or she has imposed on my good nature. One should always retain the option of revealing one's identity to persons of one's own choosing. This is particularly true when one is engaged in telephone conversation, under which circumstances one is unable to discern the intent or character of the inquiring party. I usually just surrender my name, however. Does this only encourage the unmannerly party to repeat his or her offense?

GENTLE READER:

Possibly, although the joys of calling around town demanding people's names are probably limited. The answer to "Who is this?" is properly, "Whom are you calling?"

DEAR MISS MANNERS:

What do you think about people who ask you, on the telephone, "Who is calling?" before telling you if the person you asked for is there?

GENTLE READER:

Miss Manners thinks that they are mouthing your name at a person who is wildly shaking his head and hands at the very mention of it. The same purpose can be accomplished politely by asking the question after expressing doubt: "Let me see if he is in. Who may I say is calling, please?"

DEAR MISS MANNERS:

I must take issue with you on telephone etiquette. You are advising to tell a lie by saying, "Let me see if he is in." If the calling party has any manners, he will introduce himself before asking for his party. I will punish my children if they don't find out who is calling before they give out any information at all. People who do otherwise are making it very easy for would-be robbers, rapists, or other troublemakers.

GENTLE READER:

Miss Manners does not feel that politeness requires anyone to supply helpful information to criminals who are telephoning for appointments. However, "Let me see if he is in" suggests that one is in a busy household where people are coming and going. It is not a lie if one interprets it as the modern equivalent of a lady or gentleman's being "at home to" guests or not. One can be "in" to some people, but not to others.

Screening Calls

DEAR MISS MANNERS:

My son and his wife were visiting for a week with their children. Whenever the phone rang, one of them always seemed to answer for me. If the caller asked for me, they would always question, "Who shall I say is calling?" I take this as an invasion of my privacy. I do not feel it necessary to be identified over the phone, except at a place of business. When a caller asks to speak with "Mary," then "Mary" should be summoned to the phone. As I have said nothing to them, I am hoping you can clarify the subject.

GENTLE READER:

Miss Manners refuses to speculate about whether your relatives are being nosy, helpful, or both. But people's telephone preferences vary so much that she sees nothing wrong with your saying politely, "It isn't necessary to screen my calls for me. I'll talk to whoever telephones." If this were a better world, where callers identified themselves and only one's friends called one at home, Miss Manners would recommend this policy to everyone.

Advice to a Telephone Solicitor

DEAR MISS MANNERS:

In a moment of financial desperation, I recently took a part-time job as a telephone salesperson for a photography studio. I have mixed feelings about the work I am doing. In the past, I have often felt annoyed by the intrusion of the telephone solicitation and have myself responded with rudeness on occasion.

What is your opinion? Is this a reasonable way for a company to promote its product? Is this a reasonable way for a person to earn a—well, hardly a living, but a few needed pennies? More important, what is a reasonable response from the person who answers the telephone? Some people I have called have been happy to have the opportunity to purchase the product that I offer. A number have been gracious and kind, even though they do not wish to buy. However, a few obviously resent being imposed upon and let me know it in no uncertain terms. What would be good manners both on the part of the company that has a product to offer and on the part of the person who is offered that product by telephone?

GENTLE READER:

As you know from your own experience on the other end, it is not polite to burst into someone's house uninvited, by telephone or in person, for social or commercial reasons. Miss Manners advises you to make use of this empathy to excuse people who dismiss you rudely. One is not under an obligation to treat an intruder into one's house with hospitable charm.

If you are to continue in this job, please try to minimize the rudeness that your intrusion represents. You will have done the damage of making someone answer a telephone, but at least state your business as quickly and clearly as you can. Supposedly cute and round-about ways of leading into your sales pitch prolong the offense. Particularly, do not make assumptions about these people's personal lives. It is dangerous, as well as rude. Some day you will call someone from a bridal list whose fiancé has just run away with her maid of honor, or a woman from a maternity hospital list whose baby was stillborn.

Paying for Telephone Privileges

DEAR MISS MANNERS:

How do you pay for a telephone call in someone else's house? It seems such a trivial matter that I feel like skipping it and assuming that my host will make a call in my house some day to even things up, but I've had people offer me change. I feel stupid taking a dime from a guest. On the other hand, I don't want anyone direct-dialing Tokyo on my bill, either.

GENTLE READER:

Miss Manners feels you have two questions here and would like to point out that local and long distance telephone calls are miles apart. For local calls, Miss

Manners feels it is enough to say, "May I use your telephone?" without paying for the service; there are also pay toilets in public, but not in people's houses. She is assuming, of course, that you are using it rarely (the telephone, not the toilet, which is properly used according to need) and not settling in to make your business calls. For long distance calls, it is a simple matter to ask the telephone company to charge it to your home number. Miss Manners suggests doing this in a loud voice, so that the host overhears it and does not have mixed feelings about you from the time you announce you are calling the folks in the old country to the time that his monthly bill arives.

Answering Machines

DEAR MISS MANNERS:

With the advent of telephone answering machines, a problem of etiquette has arisen. What should one do upon reaching one of these electronic marvels? I hang up whenever I reach an answering service, as I hate talking to a machine. I know this is not proper, but what is?

GENTLE READER:

It is perfectly proper to hang up on a machine. In fact, the whole concept of proper and improper behavior does not apply between people and machines. Miss Manners has enough trouble getting people to be polite to one another, without worrying about whether they are treating machines with consideration.

DEAR MISS MANNERS:

I must take issue with your statement that "it is perfectly proper to hang up on a machine." You wouldn't dream of hanging up on someone's secretary, would you? Hanging up on an answering machine is tantamount to hanging up on the person who owns it.

I do a lot of free-lance work which takes me away from home at odd hours. The only way I can stay in contact with business associates and friends is through an answering machine. If someone calls and hangs up without leaving a message, I have no idea of who tried to reach me or why, and have to listen to several seconds of dial tone instead of a friendly voice. Therefore, I maintain that the proper response to an answering machine is to state, at the sound of the tone, a message such as "Hello, this is Anastasia, at Winter Palace, 2362. Rasputin was mad over the cherry cheesecake you served last week, and I wondered if I could get the recipe." If it is worth the trouble to pick up the telephone and dial someone's number, then it is certainly worth the trouble to stay on the line long enough to say who you are. I submit that it is exactly the same, in modern terms, as leaving one's card with the footman.

GENTLE READER:

Miss Manners is sorry to be stubborn, but cannot be persuaded to take an anthropomorphic view of answering machines. "Someone's secretary" has feelings. "The footman" has feelings. Your answering machine does not. Your cat and Rasputin, Miss Manners is willing to argue about.

Toddlers on the Telephone

DEAR MISS MANNERS:

Friends of ours have a daughter who has just learned the joys of speaking. Lately, when I've been speaking to the mother on the phone and little Olga has been in the vicinity and has expressed a desire to speak to me, mother immediately puts her on the phone. I am then obliged to say "Hi!" to which the reply is a knowing, "Hi!" Unless I continue asking questions or otherwise blubbering something to which the reply is never anything but a monotonic blurt, there could be minutes of silence. I have reached the point where I dread calling my friend, for having to experience the above-described delight. I have learned from this and will never attempt such a thing with my future children and friends. Help, if you would be so kind. My friend does not work, so there is rarely an opportunity to talk with her when Olga is not nearby.

GENTLE READER:

Miss Manners is pleased to hear that you have learned from this experience. No one except a grandparent should be expected to hold telephone conversations with people who have not yet learned conversation (as opposed to learning "to talk"), and even they should not be pushed too far. You might try making the child feel important by entrusting her with a message. The message is, "Tell Mommy I said bye-bye."

Busy People and Busy Signals

DEAR MISS MANNERS:

Every day, I call my father, who is quite elderly and lives alone. He knows I will be calling him, although I can't always make it at the same time every day, as my work schedule is irregular. But what drives me crazy is that his line is always busy. I have to call him back over and over again before I get him. He admits that he's just been "visiting" with his cronies, saying nothing in particular, which is fine, except it's very frustrating to me to try to reach him. Suppose there were an emergency? It seems to me inconsiderate of him to keep me waiting when he knows how busy I am.

GENTLE READER:

It will no doubt relieve your mind for Miss Manners to explain to you that an emergency involving the health of your elderly father, which must be what is worrying you most, will not occur while he is chatting merrily away on the telephone. It is quite true, however, that the busy signal is an irritating noise, and most people end up unjustifiably angry with their intended callers who have subjected them to it. This is not logical. One may not take away another person's telephone privileges, even a parent's, for the purpose of keeping him at one's own beck and call.

On Hold at Home

DEAR MISS MANNERS:

Some of my friends have gotten two-line telephones put in their homes, and right in the middle of a conversation they'll break off and say, "Wait a minute, my other line is ringing," and disappear, sometimes for long periods, while I'm left dangling. If they take the time to ask me if I want to hold on, I always say, "No," but most times they don't even bother to ask.

GENTLE READER:

If you have been put on hold without your consent, it is perfectly proper for you to park your telephone receiver on your telephone instrument during the wait. This results in your line's being free when your caller dials your number after having finished with his or her second call. The correct explanation that accompanies this action is, "We seem to have been cut off."

Food on the Telephone

DEAR MISS MANNERS:

A friend called me at home (I did not call her) and proceeded to eat a raw carrot during the entire conversation. I tried to ignore the sound, but I found it extremely unpleasant to have to listen to a series of loud cracks and crunches while talking. Ignoring the question of whether or not it's polite to eat while talking on the telephone (I assume it's not), would it have been polite for me to say, "Call me back when you're finished eating"? I don't like to hear dinner noises unless I am actually there to enjoy the food.

GENTLE READER:

Miss Manners is in complete agreement with you except in the matter of taxing people directly with their social errors. She prefers an oblique line of accusation, such as, "Would you mind calling me back—we have a bad connection. There seems to be a carrot on this line."

A Wake-Up Call

DEAR MISS MANNERS:

I work the night shift and sleep late. Most people know not to call me before noon, but what do I do about the occasional person who means well but doesn't know? If they ask, "Did I wake you?" can I give an honest answer and tell them that they did?

GENTLE READER:

An honest answer? No. Can you let them know that they woke you? Yes. The answer is, "Oh, no, no, no. That's quite all right. What time is it?"

Untimely Calls

DEAR MISS MANNERS:
Saturday morning at five thirty, the phone rang ten, maybe fifteen times until I answered, at which someone called me by name and then said, "Gee, what time is it?" I replied in firm, distinct sounds, "Five thirty AM" and hung up with a powerful sweep. Now I'm wondering if I have lost a friend, discouraged a prank caller, or simply dreamed all of this.
GENTLE READER:
Since you answered the person's question, you fulfilled your obligation and needn't worry about it any longer.

Wrong Numbers

DEAR MISS MANNERS:
A question of etiquette that has been bothering me for many years is, What is the proper response to "I'm sorry, I have the wrong number"?
GENTLE READER:
Miss Manners feels that "That's quite all right" is sufficient, although she realizes that there will always be those who say, "That's all right—I had to get up to answer the phone anyway."

Listening In

DEAR MISS MANNERS:
My big brother keeps listening in on my telephone conversations. I know he means well and is trying to help me, but it surely is annoying. Should I tell him to "bug off, brother" or be more polite and suggest he be more inventive in his curiosity and good intentions?
GENTLE READER:
It is, indeed, difficult to say such a thing to a beloved relative. Tell him Miss Manners says, "Bug off, brother." Unless, of course, you are speaking metaphorically about Big Brother, in which case you may have an interesting law suit.

Calling for Drastic Action

DEAR MISS MANNERS:
In depleting some old personal files, I ran across the attached: "Former Postmaster General J. Edward Day revealed in his book an ingenious way to stop long-winded telephone callers long after they have fulfilled the purpose of their

calls. The painless technique does not insult the caller, for Mr. Day suggests you hang up while you are talking. The other party thinks you were accidentally cut off, because no one would hang up on his own voice.''

GENTLE READER:

Hanging up on oneself is, in terms of etiquette, what suicide is under the law. It is wrong, but impossible to punish. Both are final, if drastic, solutions, but, then, both are apt to be responses to drastic problems.

Voicing Problems

DEAR MISS MANNERS:

I have always had, for a woman, a deeply pitched voice, and now that I've passed the big five-O and with the help of several packs of cigarettes a day, I apparently sound like a tugboat horn in a bad fog storm. Many times a day I have telephone conversations with both men and women addressing me as ''Sir''— ''Yes, sir,'' ''No, sir,'' ''Hold on, sir.'' I've tried, ''I'm a woman in spite of sounding otherwise,'' and ''I know you're attempting to be courteous, but I am a woman.'' No matter how I attempt to handle it, I feel awkward, dippy, am misunderstood, or wind up sounding kind of belligerent and petty. I want a halfway civilized means of handling this goofy thing that is not earthshaking but really causing not only personal but business problems.

GENTLE READER:

Miss Manners considers all etiquette problems earthshaking, and all earth-shaking problems (except possibly volcanoes) to be basically matters of etiquette. Someday, when she has a minute to spare, she will tell the world how to end war and other unpleasantness through observing correct forms of international behavior.

In the meantime, let us consider the matter of your voice. As no one is intending to insult you, you must deal with the honest mistakes of others as courteous disabled people, for example, do with inappropriate but well-intentioned gestures. Actually, you are already doing well, simply calling attention to the error. If you could develop a small chuckle while saying, ''No, I'm a woman with a low voice,'' you could avoid sounding belligerent. Or you could say your first name loudly in the hopes that they catch on that Mary Catherine must be a woman. Of course, if your name is Brooke, this won't help.

Family Relations

The essential thing to know about a family, when predicting its chances of survival in these perilous times, is not whether it is nuclear, multigenerational, single- or double-parented, or tied together by bonds of blood, marriage, passion, or mortgage.

A more useful clue is whether each member of the family who uses up a roll of paper in the bathroom immediately fetches another roll and puts it in place, even if he or she is not planning to return to the house for the rest of the day. Is there, in other words, a prevailing family etiquette?

Miss Manners is horrified when she hears ''company manners'' defined as a higher standard of behavior than family manners. One can always go out and corral a new set of friends to be company, if one has offended the old ones beyond repair. One can begin a new family, too, of course, after one has hopelessly clogged the old one with hurt feelings, and many people do, but it is considerably more expensive.

It strikes Miss Manners as misguided to believe that home is a place where you can relax because you needn't bother to be polite. Home should be a place where you can relax because you know that there, unlike in the rest of the world, no one will be impolite to you. There is enough rudeness in the streets without inviting it indoors.

Here are some of Miss Manners' basic rules of family etiquette:
- Newspapers and magazines may not be mutilated until everyone in the house has had a reasonable chance to see them.
- People do not enter one another's rooms without knocking or use one another's property without asking. However, all such requests should be kindly considered.
- No questions are asked about letters or telephone calls, not even, "I see you got a letter from . . ." or "What'd she want?" All such information is voluntary, with no prompting allowed.
- Under no provocation may the secrets of a family member be revealed by other members outside the family.
- Unless otherwise arranged, everyone shows up at dinner, prepared to make general conversation, and looking reasonably appetizing. As for what you consider appetizing-looking in your relatives, Miss Manners is not prepared to decide.
- Rudeness that is introduced under the name of informality or intimacy is still rudeness.
- True family informality includes the use of first names, even between husband and wife, and the wearing of dressing gowns on Sunday morning, a designation that applies to any period of time when members of the family are home alone.
- Family intimacy means not having to disguise the announcement of one's triumphs or fiascoes with modesty or the pretense that it didn't really hurt.
- Everyone says "Good morning" to all members of the family encountered before noon.
- When preparing food for oneself, one offers to make some for whoever else is hanging about the kitchen.
- A person who did not participate in a given meal or snack should not be expected to clean the resulting dishes.

Principles of Marriage

As befits a highly advanced society, ours has a vast amount of accumulated wisdom on the interesting and crucial subject of Romance. Where to find it, how to encourage it, how to recognize whether it is genuine—all this is discussed exhaustively in our literature. After careful research in the monthly women's magazines and other philosophical journals, Miss Manners has been able to discover only two tenets dealing with how to sustain love, once it has been found, recognized, and acknowledged. It seems that there are infinite ways—not to say techniques or tricks—of conducting courtships, but only two principles of marriage:
1. Don't let yourself go.
2. Don't let yourself be taken for granted. (Or perhaps it's not to take the other person for granted. Miss Manners sometimes reads these periodicals upside down without noticing that she is doing so.)

What these solemn injunctions actually mean, Miss Manners is not sure. The last time she saw them spelled out, they meant that women were not supposed to wear curlers and men were supposed to bring home flowers, but that was a long time ago, before the invention of the instamatic hot curler and the house plant. Even then, these rules troubled Miss Manners. They seemed designed to supply marriage, artificially, with the suspense and tension of courtship.

Now, courtship is a wonderful thing. There is nothing like it for inspiring attractive, new sensitivities and underwear. One tries to look and act one's best, feeling that only that will, perhaps, be good enough for the beloved. There is nothing wrong with carrying that attempt to please into marriage. Miss Manners will go so far as to say that the "best behavior" of courtship, both in looks and manners, is the best starting place for the daily habits of a household.

What disturbs her is the implied threat that lapses—not into rudeness, but into familiarity and comfort—will kill love. People who behave well only under such threats, and there seem to be many who can live together happily only until they marry and erase that threat, don't know much about love.

Any love worth the name ought to be able to indulge the life changes, such as added weight and age, or the relaxation techniques, such as old bathrobes and unshaven weekends, commonly grouped under "letting yourself go."

The entire point of marriage ought to be the luxury of being able to take someone for granted, to know that he or she will always be there, through good times and bad, no matter what. Compared to that, the thrill of wondering whether you will be wanted from one day to the next is rather a crude form of excitement. Miss Manners trusts that none of this will be misconstrued as an endorsement of household ugliness. You know that she believes that manners are even more important at home than in company. If familiarity will breed contempt, there is something wrong. It is the business of the family to be familiar.

DEAR MISS MANNERS:

I am being married this winter. It's a little scary these days, when so many marriages end in divorce. I don't want this to happen to me. You wrote about the importance of being polite to your own family—that it is even more important, maybe, than being polite to acquaintances. Do you have any more etiquette advice for a new husband and wife to each other?

My mother said not to go around in curlers in front of him and that kind of thing, but that isn't what I mean. Anyway, I use hot curlers in the bathroom with the door shut, so that isn't a problem.

GENTLE READER:

No, but how long you stay in the bathroom of a one-bathroom apartment with the door shut might be. However, Miss Manners can do better than that. Sharing and consideration should be obvious. What is not always obvious is that you must always give your spouse the courtesy of not being embarrassed on his or her behalf. Marriage is no excuse for installing yourself as the resident critic of another person's behavior. There is no surer way of ending one than the habit of saying, "You shouldn't have done that" or "Why did you have to say that?" If you resolve not to feel that it reflects on you if he makes an ass of himself, and extract a promise that he will allow you to make an ass of yourself without feeling that it reflects on him, you will be off to a very solid start.

The Hearth

Gather 'round the hearth, everyone, and Miss Manners will tell you stories of how things used to be, back when everyone used to gather 'round the hearth.

Dear Nathaniel Hawthorne, as well as our very own dear energy shortage, is responsible for bringing to mind the simple but great pleasures of the hearth, cut short in Mr. Hawthorne's day by the introduction of the "cheerless and ungenial stove," and in our own by similarly unattractive, not to say nastily expensive, devices. Miss Manners does admit that she takes modest advantage of such contraptions; you wouldn't want her to catch a chill. She also hopes that our modern fireplaces can be used supplementally, to restore former social benefits, as well as to lower the bill.

As Mr. Hawthorne tells it in an essay called "Fire Worship," the hearth of his youth conferred countless blessings on mankind—inspiring love, kindness, patriotism, religion.

The dear man predicted, in 1854, that "social intercourse cannot long continue what it has been, now that we have subtracted from it so important and vivifying an element as firelight." Future generations, he said, "will never behold one another through that peculiar medium of vision—the ruddy gleam of blazing wood or bituminous coal—which gives the human spirit so deep an insight into its fellows and melts all humanity into one cordial heart of hearts. Domestic life, if it may still be termed domestic, will seek its separate corners and never gather itself into groups. The easy gossip; the merry yet unambitious jest; the lifelike, practical discussion of real matters in a casual way; the soul of truth which is so often incarnated in a simple fireside word—will disappear from earth. Conversation will contract the air of debate and all mortal intercourse be chilled with a fatal frost."

Well, was the gentleman right? Does your family gather together in the evening, to warm one another with merry jests and simple truths, or doesn't it? The fact is that modern households have no centers to attract family members, let alone wayfarers, who are considered to be getting a warm welcome if they are squinted at through peepholes and interrogated through doors, rather than shot on sight. Miss Manners does not count mechanical "entertainment" devices around which families may gather.

Nevertheless, there are houses that actually have fireplaces, and Miss Manners recommends that their lucky owners use them as much as possible, in the way that Mr. Hawthorne described, to help restore the amenities whose passing he so rightly mourned. If a fire is lit in the home of an evening, and perhaps supplied with optional extras, such as dinner meat gently roasting on a spit or grill, or a bowl of marshmallows and a supply of long forks for after dinner, perhaps those people who have slunk away into their individual rooms and lives will begin to venture forth once more and reestablish the family circle. Especially if you turn down the thermostat.

Interesting Arguments

DEAR MISS MANNERS:
Do you believe it is proper for parents to fight—argue, shall we say—in front of their children? There is one theory that it is bad to burden them, and another that it's educational for them. Which do you think?
GENTLE READER:
Both. Parents should conduct their arguments in quiet, respectful tones, but in a foreign language. You'd be surprised what an inducement that is to the education of children.

Family Differences

DEAR MISS MANNERS:
On a visit to my husband's family recently, I made a mistake while setting the table. Foolishly, I offered to help my sister-in-law set her dinner table. I put a fork on the napkin and on the placemat. As I completed the setting all around, I noticed the forks had been removed and were on the placemat, and the napkin off to the left of it. I was embarrassed and I said to my sister-in-law, "I know that's the proper way to set the table. I wonder why I put the fork on the napkin?" She made reference to the fact that perhaps it's because that's the way it's done in restaurants. I'll never offer to help again.

The other thing happened at breakfast the following morning. For more than two hours, my husband's brother and his wife talked across the table about people none of us knew. First one then the other would butt in, and there was no way to change the subject or even inject a word from time to time. Now, the reason we try to get together once a year is to catch up on all the news about our children (all grown) and what we've been doing in business, etc. Needless to say, we never got around to that—any of it. Finally, frustrated, we said our polite "thank you's" and departed for home.

I really do not have the time to waste like this, nor do I need to be taught proper place setting arrangement. Seems to me that family gatherings should be easy and relaxed and comfortable. They are in our home.
GENTLE READER:
This is a subject that interests Miss Manners very much. She agrees that family gatherings should be easy and relaxed and comfortable, but is under no illusion that this state is easy to achieve. It does not often come naturally.

What does come naturally, far too often, is the trick of using points of etiquette as darts to express hostility. The putting together of different families—in other words, in-laws—involves mixing people who were brought up with different habits.

There are many different ways to set a table, for example—Miss Manners prefers to center the napkin on the place plate, rather than to follow your sister-in-law's method—and they include a variety of "correct" styles. But one often hears such differences cited as evidence of the superiority of one branch of a family over another.

By your account, your sister-in-law did not attempt to do this. She merely put the final touches on her own table in her own way and even supplied you with a respectable excuse to cover your embarrassment. It is Miss Manners' feeling that you took insult when none was intended. It is certainly the privilege of the hostess to have her table laid in her accustomed style, even if that means building on someone else's work.

Monopolizing conversation, especially in a husband-and-wife act, is certainly inconsiderate. But if you truly believe in relaxed and comfortable standards among relatives, you should be able to speak about this more freely than you would among acquaintances in a formal situation. Being able to say "Come on, Pauline and Paul—you can gossip about the neighbors on the way home; we want to hear about the children" is one of the privileges of family. Following your own prescription, Miss Manners recommends to you taking family gatherings "easily."

Friends and Mothers

Dear Miss Manners:

We are three brothers and a sister whose mother, having been married more than once, is now living, without marriage, with a man who we all feel is below her socially. He goes around the house in his undershirt—that kind of thing. How can we tell her tactfully?

Gentle Reader:

Tell her what? That her gentleman friend doesn't have a shirt on? She knows, she knows.

In the course of growing up, did you or your brothers or sister ever bring home a person you cared about who could perhaps not have seemed to your mother to be exactly what she might have wished for you as a partner? Did your mother ever indicate such a feeling? Probably not. If she did, you would have replied, with high indignation, "I don't care, she's my friend, and I'll choose my own friends, and I don't care about what you think of their clothes" or whatever. Perhaps your mother is old enough to choose her own friends.

Scheduling the Bathroom

Dear Miss Manners:

When many people in the same family have to share the same bathroom, and all have to go off to work or school about the same time in the morning—who gets to go first, and how do you decide how long people can take? This is a major question in our household.

GENTLE READER:

There's no problem answering this question. People should go in order of need and stay there only until that need is met. Now, all you have to do is to define "need," judge the relative needs of your relatives, and enforce this law.

Toilet Paper Altercations

DEAR MISS MANNERS:

This may sound really absurd, but yesterday my mother and sister had a fight —a real fight—about how to correctly take the empty toilet tissue cartridge off the rod and replace it with a new roll. I know I've seen such information published, but I've forgotten where. Can you help?

GENTLE READER:

The correct way to change toilet paper is in private. This way it cannot possibly lead to family arguments, although if people are really spoiling for a fight, perhaps they could argue about the correct way to shut the bathroom door.

Domestic Formality

DEAR MISS MANNERS:

My wife objects if I use her bath towel when mine isn't handy by. Don't you think that kind of "formality" is a bit much?

GENTLE READER:

Certainly not. Your wife is quite right. Marriage is no excuse for that sort of intimacy.

Bad Moods

DEAR MISS MANNERS:

When my father gets in a bad mood, he screams and shouts and carries on over the least little thing. This morning, it was the toaster. The toast wasn't the way he likes it, or at least that's what he said, and he yelled at the toaster. We think he was really mad at Mother, but he didn't say anything to her, just kept banging at the poor innocent toaster. He was completely out of control. Isn't that considered bad manners?

GENTLE READER:

No, and that is not considered being out of control, either. Everyone must shout once in a while, and it is both correct and disciplined to remember then that appliances are meant to be shouted at, but people are not.

✿ ETIQUETTE UNDER STRESS

Jealousy

As a motivating force for unassailably correct behavior, jealousy, Miss Manners has noticed, is not a conspicuous success.

Why is that? Miss Manners should think that people who believe themselves to be on the losing side of romance would endeavor to make their behavior more attractive, not less, to their errant loved ones. And yet the usual procedure is for the person who suspects a waning of interest to adopt a mode of action so outrageous as to supply grounds for dismissal on that basis alone. Miss Manners has always believed jealousy to be a waste of time. She has never known anyone to be the better off for having it. But if you must go in for it, she begs you to observe a few rules of decency.

It is important to identify correctly the object of your ill will. Too many people make the mistake of directing this to the person who got the promotion, rather than the employer who failed to give it out properly, or on the romantic replacement, rather than on the person who did the displacing. It is, in Miss Manners' opinion, pathetic to see two women, for example, engage in a vituperative rivalry while the object of their dispute sits luxuriously on the sidelines, perhaps even urging each of them on in the fight. Disgraceful, indeed.

The correct attitude of one lady to another in such a situation is calm, polite, and somewhat distantly cheerful. And since Miss Manners was talking about motivations for politeness, she will add that such behavior is very worrisome to anyone with rivalrous intentions. Why is she so unruffled—is she really anxious to dump him on me?

As for behavior toward the cause of the trouble, that, too, must be within the bounds of propriety. Faithlessness in one person does not absolve another from ordinary rules of good conduct. Lawlessness, usually in the form of some sort of spying, is not allowable. Miss Manners would even go so far as to say that evidence obtained by such means as opening another person's mail, reading diaries, going through pockets, or making disguised-voice phone calls is not admissible when arguing the original crime. It can only lead to a mistrial in the matter of infidelity, with a new issue, that of unethical snooping, the subject next taken up.

Then there are the modes of behavior that are not exactly unethical, but not exactly attractive either. This includes all material for four-page letters and midnight telephone calls. Ladies and gentlemen do not threaten each other, and they do not attempt to force themselves on each other when they do not seem to be welcome. If this is true in social intercourse, it is doubly true in—in romance.

Miss Manners wishes that she could guarantee that the patient observance of excellent manners under trying circumstances would reinspire errant lovers to know what treasures they are losing. She cannot. But she does promise that no one was ever inspired to fall back in love because of a campaign of unrelenting persistence, or because of a threat of suicide, murder, or financial ruin.

Snooping

DEAR MISS MANNERS:
I am heartbroken because I discovered that my husband has been receiving love letters from another woman, but he keeps changing the subject by saying I had no right to read his mail. Who is right?
GENTLE READER:
You are quite right to seek advice from an etiquette column, rather than a psychologically oriented one. Miss Manners believes that the true value in people is not what is in their murky psyches, which many keep in as shocking a state as their bureau drawers, but in how they treat one another. You are wrong, however, in your dispute with your husband. To be deceived is the natural human condition; to read another person's mail is despicable.

Extinguishing Old Flames

DEAR MISS MANNERS:
My husband and I have been happily married for the past three years. From time to time during those years, my husband's past lady friend has attempted to see my husband. She calls him at the office, and once she came to our home. (We were not at home, but our son told us of her visit.) My husband tells me he has tried to discourage her by not accepting any invitations and by not seeming too friendly over the phone, but she continues to attempt to keep in touch. How can we get rid of her permanently?
GENTLE READER:
The category of etiquette in which you will find the solution to this problem is known, to Miss Manners at least, as Killing with Kindness. Miss Manners, who never believes in being rude, thoroughly believes in the sort of politeness that can drive people away.
Here is a sample of what you can do in this case: Your husband invites the lady to lunch in a nice restaurant. He meets her there, at a table oddly laid for three. He barely pays attention to her greetings, because he keeps looking at the door and at his watch. You arrive. Your husband leaps up from the table, his face alight with pride, and greets you profusely. You greet the lady with enthusiasm and warmth and say how glad you are to meet her, that your husband had been urging it for some time, and you are both so anxious to hear how she

is getting along these days. During the luncheon, you both keep encouraging her to talk about herself while you listen with rapt attention, only occasionally showing embarrassment when you catch yourselves giggling together over a private joke or absently touching fingers on the table or feet under it.

One such lunch should do it.

DEAR MISS MANNERS:

I need assistance in dealing with a modern social entity—the former live-in (not domestic help, although that may have been a part of the arrangement).

My husband of a year and a half and I live in a small town. His former live-in resides here also. Small towns being what they are, we travel in the same social circle, which means we encounter her at least every two weeks at one gathering or another. I feel she still cares deeply for my husband. For the most part, I can handle the situation; however, there are occasions where my strong inclination is to punch her in the nose.

Let me explain. At a gathering, she told me that she had to talk to me, spirited me away from the group, and proceeded to deliver an extended and detailed monologue on her last days with hubby. Those days were close to three years ago. I listened sympathetically and spent the night at the local Holiday Inn, because I was unable to bear the sight of hubby, an unfair transference, I realize.

Her latest escapades, however, are causing me greater distress because they involve my in-laws. Of late, in her monologues, she has taken to referring to hubby's mother as "Mumsie." Most recently, she went shopping with Mumsie and hubby's sister, spending the night in the city at Mumsie's apartment. The whole expedition left me stunned.

Hubby tells me I am being foolish to let all of this bother me. He suggests that I merely walk away when the monologues begin. He further says that I shouldn't be angry with him about the situation, since there is nothing he can do about it. I have countered by saying that I can't walk away because then FLI (former live-in) will know she is getting to me.

With this background, let me ask my specific questions: 1. How can I deal politely and effectively with the FLI's monologues in order to put a stop to them? 2. How do I cope with in-laws who show such insensitivity to my feelings in this rather delicate situation?

GENTLE READER:

Do not—repeat: not—punch her in the nose. This will be correctly interpreted as her having "gotten" to you.

Be polite. Tell the FLI and Mumsie, as often as you can, that each is terribly kind to "take care" of the other. This always convinces people that they have been stuck with bores. Then tell the FLI how very amused you are by all these old stories; how you love hearing about your husband's bachelor adventures, which he can't tell very well because he's forgotten so much and keeps mixing up the characters. You might ask her if she was the one he took to the Riviera.

He needn't help much, but it would be nice if he would interrupt these tête-à-têtes to greet his old girl friend heartily by the wrong name.

Wandering Attentions

DEAR MISS MANNERS:

My husband and I, along with two other couples, went "out on the town" last night. All evening my husband made eyes at a pretty young lady (young enough to be his daughter) sitting directly across from our table. To make matters worse, the young lady enjoyed every minute of the same and reciprocated. This ruined my evening. I wanted to kick my husband and slap the girl's face, but instead I made jokes to my friends about my husband's flirtation.

Question: In the future, how can I handle a situation like this—in a classy way, without looking like an insanely jealous wife? Also, should I let the next young lady know I don't appreciate her participation, or only my husband? Please answer soon—I'm depressed, still!

GENTLE READER:

Please stop being depressed. Miss Manners can't bear it, and besides, you should feel proud of having done—as you say—the classy thing.

This does not mean that she does not sympathize with your position. Trying to look as if you are having a jolly time while the person with you manifests a romantic interest in a stranger is a severe strain on the facial muscles, to say the least. It does not matter whether this "interest" is wicked or innocent. Well, perhaps it matters to the wife. But from the standpoint of manners, it is just as embarrassing for the gentleman to pay a personal compliment to the waitress, under the mistaken impression that this is a form of tipping, as it is for him to send his office key and a bottle of champagne to the next table. If ladies ever behaved that way with strange gentlemen—and Miss Manners prays they will not—gentlemen would soon realize how thoroughly unpleasant it is to be an interested bystander.

Nevertheless, she would not advise you to teach manners to strange young ladies in night clubs. It will be enough if you can teach them to your husband.

Please be careful not to discuss this so as to make it sound like jealousy—an unattractive emotion in a wife, as you have noticed—rather than etiquette. The age of the young lady has nothing to do with it, for example. You certainly do not want to get into such doomed questions as whether she was prettier than you, how he really feels about her, ditto about you, and so on. Merely say that you find such behavior rude and are afraid it makes him ridiculous in the eyes of your friends. Miss Manners trusts you to say this with tact, as well as firmness.

Perhaps he will change this behavior to oblige you. Perhaps he will change it when it is suggested that other people view it as ludicrous and pathetic, rather than dashing and charming. Perhaps not. In that case, Miss Manners suggests that you save yourself this embarrassment again by separating your social life from his. Let him wonder, when you go out to dinner alone with another couple, how the table gets evened out.

Secrets

DEAR MISS MANNERS:

Some time ago, I had a short, tempestuous affair with my wife's boss's wife. There was a lot of anguish involved, and I guess the most excitement I've ever had in my life, although it's hard for me to believe, now that it's over, how reckless we got. We thought we were in love. We even talked about running away together. All of this happened within six months. She broke it off—stopped taking my calls and completely avoided me. For a while, I could hardly get out of bed, let alone work. My wife was incredibly decent about it. She accepted the idea that I was having some sort of nonspecific, middle-aged depression, and was cheerful and supportive without pressing me about the meaning of it. It's thanks to her that I recovered fully.

I think that my wife deserves an explanation. I want to be in the clear with her, and I also am aware that some word of what happened could still get back to her from people who might have seen us together. This woman and I used to meet in a cheap midtown motel, where we often sat in the restaurant, figuring it was not the kind of place where anyone we knew would go. The truth is that we were so besotted that we figured we were invisible and actually held hands in the restaurant, even though we also had a room. At least once, I saw, on the way out from lunch, two women I couldn't place but who looked familiar and were probably friends of my wife.

The trouble is that my ex-great love hasn't told her husband and doesn't plan to. I might mention that my wife is a lousy actress. Whatever she thinks is written all over her face. I don't think she would tell him, if she knew, but he would know that there was something funny going on.

God knows I don't want to make any more trouble for anyone, certainly not now. But it seems to me that my only responsibility now is to my own marriage, and that I no longer need consider the possible consequences to someone who, when you get right down to it, did not hesitate to sacrifice my feelings to save her own marriage. Don't you agree?

GENTLE READER:

No. A secret affair is, by its nature, a secret jointly held by two people. Although you have dissolved this union, you retain joint custody of the secret, and neither has the right to tell it without the permission of the other. That a gentleman may find himself participating in a dishonorable situation does not excuse him from the obligation to pursue the course of honor within that situation.

Middle-Age Crises

DEAR MISS MANNERS:

My husband has just turned forty and I believe is experiencing a mid-life crisis. In February of this year (after an indecisive two years), he took off his wedding ring, said he didn't want to be married anymore, and moved into his own apartment. He further elaborated that a woman friend that he'd known for many years (lunch, etc.) and with whom he'd been having an affair for some time, said she had never loved anyone as much as she loved him. He said he wanted to investigate this relationship further and wanted to find himself, etc., etc., etc. After several weeks, we mutually agreed to see a marriage counselor (a psychologist) separately and then eventually together. We also see each other once a week with our child, age eleven.

The question: He wants to resume sexual relations without any commitment. He says he wants to continue the counseling on a weekly basis to negotiate a truce and he wants to try to make it together again.

What is correct? If my husband is having a sexual relationship with another woman or women, should I, as his legal wife, also have sexual relations with him? Separation—that is, a legal separation—has not occurred. My husband has implied that I'm being a prude by not having sexual relations with him, and am seeking an eye for an eye, etc. He says he wants to move back in with us (me and our daughter) after we have negotiated the truce. The counselor says the decision is up to me.

I feel we should be married again before we resume our sexual relations or before he moves in again. My husband has not said in so many words that he is sorry he caused me pain or that he has totally cut off all relations with the other woman. I feel he wants to have his cake and eat it, too. My husband has said he wants to try to make our relationship work and he doesn't want a divorce or a legal separation. Since we are not legally separated, I am not dating. How would you handle this situation—confusing as it is—correctly?

GENTLE READER:

You have come at last to the right person. It is kind of the marriage counselor to say that the decision is up to you, but whom else should it be up to, pray? You have obviously been too long among people who use sympathetic terms for your husband's behavior and pejorative ones for yours, thus disguising the fact that (1) you were the injured party and (2) you are now in the position of strength.

Thus, when he cuts off intimacy with you, it is called experiencing a crisis and investigating a relationship, and when you cut off intimacy with him, it is called prudery and eye-for-an-eye revenge.

The only valid metaphor in use here is the one of a "truce." Let us look at this in terms of diplomacy. He deserted. He now wants to resume the privileges of citizenship. You have the right to readmit him or to refuse to do so, on the grounds that he has forfeited his rights. You can even assume his tactics, if you want, and declare your own mid-life crisis, a state that he has defined as relieving one of duty to others.

What is up to you, therefore, is not only making the decision, but setting the terms under which you are willing to live. While Miss Manners does not ordinarily tell people when or when not to engage in lovemaking, she will say that no diplomat in his right mind would confer privileges before obtaining agreement on obligations.

Dealing with an Affair

Dear Miss Manners:

I am asking this as a manners question after having given due thought, you may be sure, to the other aspects of it. My husband is having an affair with a longtime friend of mine. I know this for a fact, although they do not know I know, and I intend to keep it that way. Bringing it out into the open would irrevocably damage, if not end, our marriage. I believe if I let it alone, he will get over it, and we can go on as before. She has told me, in the past, about many such affairs she has had, and I'm sure she is not serious about this one.

OK—so how do I behave to him, and how do I behave to her? On the one hand, I don't want to let on that I know, for the reasons stated, but on the other hand, I am no saint, and if I could speed along the end of this by making both of them really miserable, I wouldn't be sorry. They see each other two nights a week and every other Saturday—he is "working late" then, and she keeps her phone off the hook.

The only other person who knows about this is my sister, who has suggested that I openly have an affair myself, which would serve them right. However, even if I knew someone I wanted to do that with, I don't want to leave the children (three, seven, and ten); I know their father is devoted to them. Nor do I want to give him an "excuse." I just want to go on as always, acting natural, but the problem is I can't act natural. So what do I do?

Gentle Reader:

Miss Manners thinks you are quite right not to attempt to "act natural." Behavior natural to this situation would be quite ugly, and thus go against your interests. Yet the agitation produced by your awareness of the situation produces an energy higher than you would have if the situation were normal. The idea is to use this heightened emotion for an effect that would serve your interests, rather than betray them.

What makes people truly uncomfortable is not so much having what others lack, but lacking what others have. Allow Miss Manners to suggest a more subtle way than your sister's of making them jealous of what you are doing two nights a week and every other Saturday. To him, you might let it be known that you and the children are immensely enjoying those free periods you have together. Plan pleasant family activities for that time—building, baking, putting on a play together, or, if you must, even going to the zoo where all the attractive divorced fathers are on Saturdays—which they will babble to him about afterwards, thus making him aware that the time he spends away is the most valuable and memorable part of their childhood.

To her, if you really want to be evil (and why not—it will make you feel better), you might make vague statements with a radiant face that make her believe, without your saying so, that you are spending that same time period with a man who makes you look more thrilled than your husband apparently did. This will pique her; but she will mention it to your husband, to salve his conscience. He will know, from the children's testimony, that it is not true, so it will give him the idea that she has a dirty mind. It will also pique him. Two people in these states of mind are not going to enjoy themselves for very long.

Catty Relatives

DEAR MISS MANNERS:
My father and stepmother's tenth anniversary is next month. I have not spoken to my father or his wife since I moved out, three months ago. My father, however, has written to me several times. My stepmother had kicked me out of the family house because she didn't like my cats. Should I acknowledge their anniversary— and if so, how?

GENTLE READER:
Many relatives who do not get along use etiquette as a weapon with which to fight. Choose your weapon. Either remember their anniversary with a gracious note or present, in the hope that this will make them feel bad, or ignore it, thus giving them the chance to say, "You see? He didn't even remember our anniversary." Miss Manners would not dream of suggesting that you leave a basket with a bow on it on their doorstep, with a kitten or a litter of kittens inside.

On Offensive Odors

DEAR MISS MANNERS:
We have a quarrel about married couples who order different food at restaurants. I can't stand to kiss my husband when he has garlic or onions, which I don't eat, on his breath.

GENTLE READER:
Well, Miss Manners is not going to do it for you.

Visiting

The charming old custom of calling, or paying short regular visits to one's entire acquaintance to thank them for hospitality, mark the milestones of life, and generally acknowledge their existence, has died out of general use simply because it was time consuming, boring, and without content. Eventually, Miss Manners has noticed, it was replaced by television.

In its true form, calling was a lady's principal occupation. Each one chose a day of the week on which she declared herself at home to receive calls, and the rest of the week was spent out inflicting visits on others. Births, engagements, marriages, moves, and deaths required that those who performed them, or their immediate relatives, be called upon. Every guest had to call on every hostess after every party. Then every call had to be returned with a call equal in length but opposite in direction.

It kept the ladies on the streets, rather than off, and rebellion arose. Dear Edith Wharton recalled her mother's day, when "the onerous and endless business of 'calling' took up every spare hour," and how "by the time I grew up, the younger married women had emancipated themselves and simply drove from house to house depositing their cards, duly turned down in the upper left-hand corner [please see p. 509], to the indignation of stay-at-home hostesses, many of whom made their servants keep a list of the callers who 'did not ask,' so that these might be struck off the next season's invitation list—a punishment borne by the young and gay with perfect equanimity, as it was only the dull hostesses who inflicted it.''

For a long time, the drama continued symbolically with the actors absent from the stage. Small strange niceties developed, such as a lady's being honor-bound to be present in her carriage while her footman took the cards—one each from each lady in her family for each lady in the called-upon family, and a card each from the gentlemen in the calling family for every person in the called-upon family—to the servant whose job it was to announce that the lady of his house was not at home.

The virtual disappearance of this crucial servant brought an end to the vestigial remains of calling, everywhere but in a few diplomatic communities where the civilized pleasure of sitting face to face for fifteen minutes with someone with whom you have little in common, perhaps not even a language, is still appreciated.

Otherwise, modern calling has been reduced to the following paltry rules:

1. Real, old-fashioned, in-person calls are paid upon a birth and death and, if appropriate and welcome, on the occasion of an illness. Calling on new neighbors is charming but optional. In all of these cases, one must telephone to make an appointment, but new parents and the newly bereaved are supposed to make themselves available to receive these visits.

2. Hospitality is generally considered sufficiently acknowledged by the offer of comparable return hospitality. The exception is the seated dinner, for which a letter or a telephone call (Miss Manners prefers the letter) is required. Other letters of thanks for hospitality are always appropriate, but not mandatory.

3. Routine social calling is done by telephone. That is, one can call, in this fashion, nearly any time of day and expect, as the ladies plying the avenues in their carriage did, to be received unless there is a specific excuse offered. The facility with which people can be trapped by callers by telephone is, in Miss Manners' opinion, one of the serious drawbacks of modern life. She recommends leniency in accepting excuses by the called upon of not being able to talk, and makes it a point of honor never to recognize the voice of a lady explaining that she is not at home.

4. Dropping in does not exist in proper modern society. Those who practice it should be prepared not to recognize by sight ladies who are trying to establish that they are not at home.

Behind Closed Doors

DEAR MISS MANNERS:

What with the crime rate now, lots of people have those little peepholes in their front doors and refuse to open the door until they've had a look at you. I've even had to stand there while someone who has invited me to come just at that time fusses around behind the door, obviously there but not planning to open up until they've checked me out. I find all this disgusting. What can we do about it?

GENTLE READER:

What do you find disgusting—crime, peeping, or standing outdoors? Miss Manners is happy to deplore any one of these things with you, provided you tell her which one. As for what to do about it, why, you just step back far enough to present a head and shoulders view of yourself and smile in a dignified way.

Receiving while Reclining

DEAR MISS MANNERS:

Are there any circumstances in which one can receive guests while in bed? I'm not kidding, and I'm not talking about sex, either. French kings used to hold court while they were in bed, you know. Obviously, a person in a hospital can receive friends while lying in bed. So why can't I, who spend most of my free time reading, working, or telephoning in bed, ask guests who drop by the house to come upstairs and visit me when I'm comfortably in bed? What's the difference?

GENTLE READER:

A general rule of hospitality is that the host does not enjoy anything that he does not also offer to his guest. The difference between you and a hospital patient is that the patient may safely assume that his visitor does not wish to be given whatever it was that landed him in bed.

Dropping In

DEAR MISS MANNERS:

I live downtown, and people often drop in on me without warning. Some of them are friends, whom I would like to see, others are acquaintances, whom I would like to get rid of—but in any case, the dropping in always seems to catch me at an inconvenient time. How can I convince these people to use the telephone first?

GENTLE READER:

"Dropping in" is an old, warm, friendly, neighborly custom which is properly despised by those on whom it is practiced. Under no circumstances should one let an untimely visitor cross one's threshold. In the absence of a butler to say that one is not receiving, one must say it oneself. "I'm sorry, I can't receive you now," must be said firmly, after which the door must be shut firmly. The unannounced visitor must learn to expect this sort of nonreception. The world would be a better place if we all had butlers again.

House Mouse

DEAR MISS MANNERS:

Some friends of mine have purchased an old town house at an insane price and are "doing it over" with skylights, hanging plants, exposed bricks—the works. They are extremely proud of it and gave a series of small parties after they moved in, to show it off. At the one I was invited to, they took us for a long tour, pointing out every feature. During this house tour, a mouse ran across the kitchen. Several people shrieked, and everybody was terribly embarrassed. The hosts didn't say anything, but it obviously spoiled the whole effect. I felt sorry for them, but what could I have done? Was there any way to cover up after all that screaming we all did?

GENTLE READER:

You could have said, "I'm sorry I yelled, but your gerbil startled me."

Dropping In and Turning Off

DEAR MISS MANNERS:

Some neighbors dropped in while we were watching our favorite television program. I asked them to join us, but they kept talking through it. Who was being rude here—them for talking, or us for keeping the set on?

GENTLE READER:

People have precedence over mechanical contrivances, and therefore you should have turned off the set. However, those who drop in on others unannounced must take what they find, and it can be a lot worse than television. What you have here, therefore, is a rudeness draw.

Calling on New Neighbors

DEAR MISS MANNERS:

Finally, finally, the dreadful people who lived next door have sold their house and moved away, taking their rotten children, their foul dog, and several of my electric appliances with them. There is very little turnover in this neighborhood, so this salvation is more than I had dared hope. It is generally a friendly area, however, and I would like to get off to a good start with the people who bought the house. The real estate agent says they are nice people; how can I be helpful without making them think that my house is an extension of their house?

GENTLE READER:

It is a charming old custom for the residents of a neighborhood to pay calls on newcomers. The reason it is so charming is that the established resident gets an early look at the impossible furniture and worse colors with which the newcomers are ruining a fine old house.

When you perform this gesture, it is useful to be prepared to give out addresses and telephone numbers of shops and services for which the newcomer might ask. Otherwise, you might be tempted to offer to lend your things and "find out" whom to see about what.

It is also wise to refrain from providing the useful service of characterizing the people the newcomer is likely to meet. Tempting as it is to be in there first with the gossip, you should remember that the new person's loyalties are still to be developed. It would be a disservice to your established neighbors to make them feel they had to run *you* out of the neighborhood and call on the people who will replace you.

Peddlers

DEAR MISS MANNERS:

Lately, we have been plagued by people coming to the door selling magazine subscriptions or religious publications or asking for donations. It is a terrible nuisance because they all have long, set speeches, and by the time you've heard them out, ten minutes could go by. Yet it seems rude to cut them off. Is there something I can say before they get going, to save us both time? There's no way I'm going to accept any of their "offers."

GENTLE READER:

This is the old Dagwood problem, in which anything except a firm "No," followed by the shutting of the door, is considered encouragement. If you smile, say, "I'm sorry, but I'm not interested," and close the door immediately, demonstrating that no amount of persuasion will arouse your interest, you will, as you point out, save the other person time as well as yourself. You may consider that a courtesy, if you like.

DEAR MISS MANNERS:

In reference to religious groups who call at your house—one day I told one of them that I hated being rude, but could no longer tolerate them. She said to put a sign or note on the door, "No religious agents, please." I made one with an address labeler and had no more bother. If any do come, I open the door and point to my few little red words and then shut the door saying, "I'm sorry." It works.

GENTLE READER:

It seems a shame to have to warn people off from one's front door, but Miss Manners quite agrees with you that one is not obliged to be open-minded or open-doored to anyone who chooses to appear on one's doorstep. Religious tolerance does not extend to donating one's time to whoever asks.

Comparison Shopping

DEAR MISS MANNERS:

What excuse should one use when visiting a house in the neighborhood—open for sale—when one is not interested in buying but only interested in satisfying his curiosity as to price and furnishings?

GENTLE READER:

"Thank you, but I was hoping to find something with less closet space."

Houseguests

It is easy to be the perfect houseguest. All you have to do is to remember everything you've learned in the last few years about being totally honest, in touch with your feelings, able to communicate your needs, and committed to doing what makes you feel good. And then forget it.

The perfect houseguest is often dishonest, in touch with others' feelings at the expense of his own, able to refrain from communicating his needs, and cheerful about doing what bores him. Contrary to current popular belief, such behavior can be quite pleasurable to those who indulge in it, and leads to fulfillment, happiness, and invitations to beach condominiums, shooting parties, and yachts. However, it takes practice. For example, what do you suppose the perfect houseguest says when asked what time he generally gets up in the morning?

1. "Noon, and I like absolute quiet until then, if you don't mind"; or

2. "Oh, I'm up and around any time—just call me, why don't you, when you're having breakfast."

What do you suppose the perfect houseguest likes for breakfast?

1. "Fresh orange juice, buckwheat pancakes with real syrup, none of that synthetic stuff, croissants with butter and bitter marmalade, not the sweet kind, and good, rich coffee with heavy cream"; or

2. "Oh, anything. What are you having?"

What does a perfect houseguest like to do for recreation? That depends. If the host suggests family relay races, that is what he especially likes. If there are no suggestions, what does he say?

1. "Do you know any interesting people, anybody I might have heard of, you could ask over"; or

2. "Just to take it easy, if you don't mind. I brought a book I've been dying to get into."

And so on through the day, up until bedtime, which occurs when the perfect houseguest has observed that the hosts are looking sleepy. The only critical observation that perfect houseguests may allow themselves is to notice quietly what the household lacks in the way of material comforts—in order that they may purchase that item and send it as a way of thanking the hosts after their visit. What is the reward for all this selflessness? Why, to be invited back, of course, so that he may do it all over again.

Long-term Houseguests

You have all heard what dear Benjamin Franklin said about what happens to guests and fish after three days. He was speaking from the point of view of the host. Miss Manners will now address the problem from the point of view of guests and fish.

Guests and fish tend to hang around where it is possible for them to swim. People who have beach houses or pools sometimes have bursts of generous hospitality, and it is in the interests of the recipients to ensure their not living to regret this. Anyone ought to be able to be a good houseguest for that three-day period, which is why God invented the weekend. One's time is more or less planned, and one's hosts are able to sustain an act of graciousness and calm, postponing weeping over the antique you broke or barking orders at their children, until the house is theirs again.

Long periods require greater variety of emotion, and the considerate long-term houseguest will assist in making his hosts feel at home. Otherwise, he will quickly find that he is. The most helpful way of doing this is to plan frequent absences from the house. These should be announced in advance so that there are no uncertainties about whether the guest is coming to dinner or other family events. If necessary, the guest should invent excuses and go off by himself, to give the family opportunities to cry, argue, or relax in privacy. If, however, unscheduled eruptions take place while the guest is present, the guest should ignore them and disappear. Under no circumstances should a guest take a side in family differences or offer suggestions for improving the family's way of living. All appeals for help must be resisted. Ultimately, nobody wants a live-in family counselor, however sympathetic or fair.

It should be unnecessary to mention that the houseguest should create no additional work for the family. It is his obligation to keep the guest room clean, whether he likes it that way himself or not. Even behind a closed door, a guest room with an unmade bed or newspaper-strewn floor acts as a reproach to the hosts. The guest must share the chores, but not by running about asking "Can

I help?'' and taking no for an answer. By simple observation, one should be able to notice what needs doing, and do it. Preparing meals, cleaning up, baby-sitting, and occasional grocery shopping—selecting what the family likes, and paying for it—are activities that make a guest seem worth keeping.

So do little presents, given at perhaps the rate of one a week. A houseguest is in an excellent position to associate presents with one's presence, not just with one's long-awaited absence. The best present a guest can make after he has left is his silence. This must consist not only of the wonderful silence that pervades the house when he leaves, but of his own precious silence in refusing to divulge the family secrets to others.

Footnoting Fishy Remarks

DEAR MISS MANNERS:
Note a mistake. Samuel Johnson, not Benjamin Franklin, made the comment about fish and guests smelling after three days.
GENTLE READER:
Miss Manners begs your pardon. Dear Mr. Franklin not only made the remark, but at least two variations on it; but, then, so did nearly everyone else, except possibly dear Dr. Johnson. Miss Manners' usual haphazard research reveals that the witticism was first made by Plautus, in about 200 B.C., and was perfected by John Lyly in 1580, but it was also attributed to half a dozen others.

Impolite Houseguests

DEAR MISS MANNERS:
Since moving away from our home state a year ago, we have entertained houseguests on nine different occasions. I was brought up to observe all of what I believe are the proprieties concerning houseguesting: consultation and agreement with hosts on date and duration of visit, the taking of a ''guest gift'' for the home or family, invitation to the host and hostess to dine out as our guests, and a properly gushy thank-you note sent within one week of departure (even if the bed squeaked and the pet dog destroyed our only set of matched luggage!).

Am I incorrect to assume that the aforementioned ''proprieties'' are still appropriate in the name of good manners? Now that we are hosts, my faith in Mother's instruction has been sorely shaken. We have had guests arrive with little notice and stay six days; some (about half) never write thank-you notes; some seem to expect maid service, and since I refuse to perform that service, we have to look at unmade beds and untidy rooms for the duration of their visit.

Is my practice of a guest gift and dinner excessive? Have thank-you notes gone the way of the dinosaur? I would very much appreciate a few words on the current responsibilities of a houseguest, because although I don't keep a checklist in regard to what our guests do or don't do, it would be a pleasure to learn that Mother isn't hopelessly outdated and that she really does know best.

GENTLE READER:

You already know that Mother knows best. You didn't really expect Miss Manners to tell you that Mother is an archaic old bat and those people who come and upset your schedule and your house without so much as asking permission or thanking you are socially up-to-date, and that you should cherish and emulate them.

Your real question is whether you have to tolerate people who behave so badly, if they have been friends whose bad manners were not apparent when you occupied the same city. No, you don't. Cut off relations with the ones who have disgusted you completely. To the ones whom you otherwise like and think you can retrain, you should read the house rules. Anybody you know well enough to invite to stay at your house, you also know well enough to ask, ''When are you coming and how long will you be here?'' or to tell, ''That's not a good time for us,'' or ''I'm sorry we have no one to tidy your room for you so I'm going to have to ask you to do it yourself'' or ''Do you cook? I just don't feel like it tonight.'' For those who will not obey these instructions but whom you still (inexplicably) like, you say, ''How marvelous that you'll be here. I'll make you a hotel reservation, but be sure and save lots of time for us.''

Reciprocating

DEAR MISS MANNERS:

Recently, our family was transferred from a large city to a smaller one, two hours' drive west. Since we expect to return within a year or two, however, we have maintained many social and business contacts in our former home. Our friends there frequently invite us for meals and overnight stays. In fact, because of our small son and our financial situation, we would be unable to stay overnight without this hospitality. The problem is this: how to reciprocate. Our new home is so distant (and the city is uninteresting) that no one ever visits, although we have proffered invitations. I feel that we are imposing on our friends. Please advise.

GENTLE READER:

Technically, you are off the hook, as you have issued invitations to reciprocal visits. Miss Manners assumes that you make these sound more attractive than you have here, emphasizing the pleasure and comfort you can offer guests in your house rather than the dullness of your city, and leaving off the argument about distance before they figure out that it is just as long a trip for you to visit them as for them to visit you.

However, you clearly and commendably wish to find a way to reciprocate that will be of use to your hosts. One does this with presents, whether they are bought, handmade, or performed. You might buy an appliance that would be helpful, or cook and bring a reheatable meal, or plan an excursion with your hosts' children that leaves the parents free time.

Assigning Bedrooms

DEAR MISS MANNERS:

During these days of hazy hedonism and new moralities affecting young and old, I often find myself perplexed. Can you help me?

How do I, appreciating the delicacy of various commitments, plan sleeping accommodations for houseguests who are not married but who appear to be "going together" with some intensity? We have ample room to place guests in comfortable quarters as singles or doubles.

I would be extremely dismayed to discover that I had bedded down two guests in the same room if this pair was not an intimate duo, or if the couple wished to present a facade of respectability, or if they were only platonic friends. How do I tactfully inquire what their status might be, without embarrassment to anyone concerned, and particularly to myself? I have my own attitudes with respect to this subject, but have no desire to inflict these on my guests.

GENTLE READER:

This is a troublesome question for many people in the chaos you describe as "these days," but you have taken two sensible precautions that make the solution easier for you to manage than for most people. First, you have decided not to involve yourself in the morals of your guests. Attempting to direct the intimate activities of one's guests always leads to disaster, even when the hosts are the parents of the houseguests. Only as parents of small children do we ever have the opportunity to try grafting our own moral position onto others. After that, the most we can do to houseguests is to regulate their social conduct. In other words, you can assign people separate rooms, but you cannot insist that they stay in them after dark.

This brings Miss Manners to your second sensible decision, that of inhabiting a house big enough to accommodate guests in a variety of arrangements. This makes it simple for you to put your couples in single, adjoining rooms, and to refuse to worry about where they end up. For those who have smaller houses, or if you feel you must know which rooms are really to be used and which not, you may inquire, as if you were a hotel keeper, "How many rooms will you require?" This leaves you wide open for the smartsy guest who replies, "Oh, just a bedroom, a sitting room, and dressing room," but so be it. You can then suggest a conveniently located hotel.

Rising Time

DEAR MISS MANNERS:

I have some friends with a weekend place in the country. There's nothing much to do there, but it's restful, and I enjoy staying there when they invite me. The problem is that they are late risers, and I get up early. They tell me to make my own breakfast, which I would be happy to do, but the minute they hear me running the water for my coffee, one of them comes out—sort of grumpily—and makes breakfast for me. I've taken to staying in my room, reading and pretending I'm asleep. How should I time getting up so I don't inconvenience them?

GENTLE READER:

Time your emergence from your room with the first sound of running water in the bathroom. That way, you should inconvenience no one (except yourself, of course, because you will find the bathroom occupied).

Making One's Bed

DEAR MISS MANNERS:

I was taught that a good houseguest makes up his or her bed each morning, but what should be done on the last morning of the visit? I can think of four options—to make the bed up as before, to leave the bed unmade, to strip the bed and leave it unmade, or to strip the bed and cover it neatly with the blanket and spread. Which of these would you recommend, for example, during a visit to the parents of a friend, or to relatives you don't know well but who are close to your parents?

GENTLE READER:

The conflict you describe is between image and reality. You wish to show your hosts that you are considerate of them, and yet the more you do to present the appearance of being a considerate guest, the more trouble you put them to in undoing what you have actually done.

Solution One: By leaving a perfect and tightly made bed, you make the most conscientious appearance, but give them the most work, pulling it apart and remaking it with fresh sheets.

Solution Two: By leaving it unmade, you save them work at the cost of your reputation as a guest willing to do his or her own share of work.

Solution Three: By stripping the bed, you are doing your share of preparing the room for the next guest, but you make the room look bad, especially if the mattress is worn. A good guest does not admit to having seen beneath the surface of the household as the hosts have presented it.

Solution Four: By making a pile of soiled linen for the laundry and making up a mock bed with the reusable ingredients, you save the hosts one step of work, and yet leave a nice-looking room. You also do not force them to remake the bed until another guest is expected. At that time, they will have to undo what you have left.

Miss Manners picks option four. Life is full of trade-offs.

Guests Having Guests

DEAR MISS MANNERS:

I was staying with some friends for a week out in the country at a place they have, and a very close friend of mine called and asked if he could drop by because he had some business in the nearest little town. The people I was staying with had plenty of room, but acted funny when I asked if he could stay over. We were college roommates, and it seemed perfectly natural. Was I wrong even to ask?

GENTLE READER:

Guests having guests is like pets having puppies: it is bound to be an unpleasant surprise to those who give them shelter, and should be curtailed as much as possible.

A Hostess' Thanks

DEAR MISS MANNERS:

Recently, I had an out-of-town guest visiting me. While she was here, we had good times together, meeting new people and in general having fun. Would it be appropriate for me to send her a thank-you note for the happiness she brought to me while she was here?

GENTLE READER:

Why does Miss Manners have the feeling that you think it would have been appropriate if your houseguest had written you a thank-you note some time ago, but that she didn't? If your plan is for the purpose of pointing this out to her, Miss Manners may surprise you by approving. This is a classic example of the legitimate use of good manners to make another person feel uncomfortable. On the unlikely chance that you already received the proper letter from her and merely want to reply that you also enjoyed the visit, Miss Manners will simply applaud your good nature and say, "Why, of course."

Stale Bread-and-Butter Letters

DEAR MISS MANNERS:

Conventionally, after a guest has been met at the airport, spent a charming evening, had a luxurious night's sleep, wallowed in bacon and eggs, and is delivered to the airport, propriety calls, not unreasonably, for a prompt and gracious letter to the host and hostess, within two weeks at the outside. After more than two weeks, the letter must include a mumble of apology for the delay, perhaps with an offhand reference to a business trip or some extraordinary press of work. If more than six to eight weeks pass, the excuse must be more specific and impressive: a presidential mission to Nepal or an extended study of diurnal cycles in an abandoned salt mine.

If the letter doesn't go before two months have passed, things get tough. Excuses like a jail sentence or hepatic coma may generate a response that can only embarrass. A popular device under these circumstances is for the guest to write a "second" note which makes casual reference to his previous bread-and-butter letter. This he hopes will lead the gullible recipient to conclude that the bread-and-butter letter was in fact promptly and correctly sent but eaten by the postal service. Actually, this ploy is usable almost indefinitely. Years later, one can encounter the host or hostess at a class reunion, dexterously work the subject around to that elusive letter of gratitude, and then with horror and dismay exclaim, "Do you mean to say you never got my letter? Oh, dear! How awful!"

The trouble with this is not so much that the postal service does not regularly eat letters, or that the ploy is well known (the host may well have used it himself at some time). The principal flaw is that the guest already has a well-established reputation for irresponsibility, unreliability, and procrastination. Even if the letter had been sent and eaten, no one would believe him. So the only viable alternative, as is so often the case, is abject *mea culpa.* "I am indeed irresponsible, unreliable, and given to procrastination. I am a boor. I grovel. But," saith the guest, "at least I am honest."

GENTLE READER:

Miss Manners unreservedly endorses your heroic conclusions about eschewing the facility of involving the innocent in one's own culpability. (Wait a minute. Miss Manners doesn't write like that. Let Miss Manners get a grip on herself. There. Thank you.) However, she would not write a letter whose theme was to acknowledge that she should have written long before. The theme should still be gratitude. You are guilty, but you do not want to put your hosts in the unattractive role of being your accusers. Miss Manners would have written, "What a marvelous time I had with you that weekend in October, 1956. . . ."

House Sitting

Everybody knows how to behave in another person's house when the owner is looking, Miss Manners trusts. Now it is time to learn how to behave in someone else's house when the owner is not at home. This is not an etiquette lesson for housebreakers, although goodness knows they behave badly enough. Miss Manners is addressing this to house sitters.

House sitting ought to be the ideal arrangement between the haves and the have nots. People with property usually lack the confidence to leave it unguarded. People without property usually lack property. The two groups seem made for each other. What prevents house sitting from being one of our major solutions to social problems is the basic distrust that the landed have for the lacklands. People who are temporarily vacating their houses tend not to match themselves up with those who simultaneously are being evicted. They choose, instead, people who were born members of the propertied class, but are temporarily propertyless, through restlessness or youth.

This identification of class presents a difficulty. House sitters who are friends of the house owners, or offspring of such friends, confuse house sitting with houseguesting. These are two different occupations, although the same person may perform both in the same house at different times. A houseguest is supposed to make his presence more desirable than his absence. A house sitter need only be more desirable than those whom his presence is intended to discourage.

However, he must keep the odds on his side. If you leave your house empty during your absence, it is possible that it will be undisturbed, and you will find it just as you left it. If you could be sure of this, no one, except those with very many plants, would need a house sitter. So the amount of breakage, disarray, and snooping done by the house sitter should not exceed the amount likely to be done by housebreakers—after it is averaged in with the possibility of nobody's touching the house.

Neatness counts only when the owner is back to see the state of the house, and therefore house sitters do their straightening on the day before the announced return. They should bear in mind that travel plans do get changed and home owners are given to walking in without notice as if they owned the place. The rules of breakage are not the same as for a houseguest, who need only replace small items if the host fails to protest after the second offer. House sitters must always replace what they have broken, in kind or in money. What is more, they must confess.

Invasions of privacy must be confessed only if they are going to come out anyway. If you have ruined the house owner's reputation with his neighbors or the police, you might just as well tell your side of the story in the most favorable way. If he is likely to meet people you have entertained in the house, their names should be mentioned. The fact that you showed them all the private rooms need not be, as this can be classified as getting lost on the way to the bathroom.

Under no circumstances should a house sitter confront a house owner with information gleaned from the house owner's diary.

Unpleasant Facts of Life

🌹 MAJOR AND MINOR ILLNESSES

Of all the qualities that ladies and gentlemen are most proud of cultivating, the very nastiest is squeamishness. Miss Manners always shudders delicately when she hears someone say, "Eeeeew, I can't bear that," or "Etchch, it looks disgusting." The chances are that the person is bragging about his or her extreme sensitivity, at the expense of someone else's feelings.

That is not to say that Miss Manners is the one who volunteers to gather up her petticoats and kill the mouse with the broom, or to step on the waterbug with her little satin slipper. She does these things with distaste when she has to, and foists them off on others when she can. The squeamishness she finds intolerable is that which concerns itself with human beings.

It is a common and even natural reaction. People have an instinctive revulsion at seeing the ravages of illness or decay, probably from a terror of being infected, whether or not that is a realistic danger. As one who will choose civilized behavior over natural instinct three times out of three, Miss Manners says that this feeling must be stamped out. It should certainly not be admitted, as people do when they confess, "I just can't bear to look at him," or, in a more advanced form, "I'm sure she wants us to remember her as she was," as if they were confessing to fastidious taste.

What they are really talking about is indulging a minor silliness of their own, in order to deny the deepest human claims of people they have cared about when they were strong. Base neglect of the dying cannot be interpreted as refined. This is the one area in which the natural human propensity to grow callous may be used to advantage. If people are not protected in childhood from ministering to their declining relatives, they grow used to the presence of human decay. Soon the unpleasantness is hardly noticed, and one learns that great lesson of valuing people for their positive attributes, rather than focusing on their disabilities.

Patience and compassion develop to take the place of squeamishness. Horror of the situation is replaced by pleasure in continuing to enjoy, as well as to serve, the human being. Self-satisfaction expands into the area that would otherwise have been occupied by guilt. "I did everything I could" is really a much finer feeling than "Eeeeeek."

Colds

The term "common cold" is unfortunately accurate, for most people behave in quite a common manner when ill. It is quite uncommon to be able to handle illness gracefully.

Consider the delicate manner of where to have a cold. Miss Manners is not so much interested in whether you have it in the throat or in the head as she is in whether you have it in the office or at home, on public transportation or at a friend's party. Related to this is the question of sharing one's cold with others. It's so difficult to keep such a thing to oneself, but when one has to spread it around, the choice between giving it to one's own family or giving it to one's colleagues is difficult. For example, the general rule of staying home in bed when one has a cold may not be wise if there are small children there to catch it, and only big adults at work with the sense to shun suffering. In such a case, there are medical considerations as well. A patient who lives with small children may urgently require the sort of quiet and restful atmosphere that only an office can provide.

One does not properly attend social events with a cold, especially if it has an unfortunate effect upon the appearance. Of course, if one has an attractive cold, such as laryngitis, which simply turns one into a good listener, it is hard to resist showing off. The considerate sufferer will go out in company only when absolutely essential and then will make it a point of honor to look as bad as possible in order to warn others to keep their distance. On a crowded bus to the doctor's, for instance, the signal of disease is to hold up a white handkerchief occasionally. (Please don't wave it about. Miss Manners can see it perfectly well from here.) When required to work or otherwise be out against one's will after unsuccessfully pleading illness, it is appropriate to produce wracking coughs, to apply the back of one's hand to one's own forehead frequently, and to moan "Oh, my," softly. This often smooths the way for the courtesy of leaving early.

It is not correct to distribute wadded paper tissue about, sneeze on others, or examine the contents of one's handkerchief. Nosedrops are borderline. Miss Manners does not find the application of nosedrops an aesthetically thrilling sight and would recommend resorting to this only if drastic stage business is required to get across the idea of illness.

Two things are obligatory, no matter how bad one feels:

The first is to appear to listen to the advice of well people on how they get rid of colds. You do not actually need to listen, as you will hear nothing useful, but must look at them attentively with sad, runny eyes.

The second is that if you have been excused, on the grounds of having a cold, from something you didn't want to do in the first place, you must go home and shut your front door, behind which you may enjoy yourself as much as your health permits.

Patients' Behavior

There are considerable social advantages to being hospitalized, and it is too bad that most people who have that opportunity don't feel up to enjoying it. Perhaps if Miss Manners told them all the rules of common decency that they could flout, it would give them a reason to rally.

Outpatient suffering carries no compensating liberties. Contrary to popular belief, "being depressed" does not entitle one to bore people with the causes or symptoms; and no one with a case of What's Going Around should expect anything but resentment from family and colleagues, for having exposed them to it and for making them do more of the work.

Hospitalization, however, confers the official status necessary to legitimize errant behavior. The sick person with a healthy attitude will seize the chance.

At no other time may you protect yourself so thoroughly from people you don't want to talk to or to see. From your birthday parties when your mother made you invite her friends' children you couldn't stand, right through the crowds of friends of spouses, spouses of friends, useful people and pitiful people, every other occasion has its share of people who can't be avoided. But not hospital life. You merely send word that you don't feel up to seeing anyone you don't want to see, or you get your doctor to do it. If they barge in anyway, you sink back on your pillows and firmly close your eyes. If you tried that in your living room, you could be called rude, but not in your hospital room.

You may have heard that it is considered bad manners to discuss your operation, or anything else to do with your physical well-being. That may be true weeks later, at a dinner party, but it does not apply to those still hospitalized. You may, if you wish, spend the entire visit answering the question, "How are you?'' But you may also give a visitor a freezing look in reply, to indicate that such a probe is in bad taste.

And, of course, if the visitor is reminded of her own operation or his once miraculous recovery, you can do your sinking back and closing eyes routine.

A hospital patient has no obligation to keep visitors entertained; on the contrary. When the visitors cease to be entertaining, the host may ask them to leave.

This is a time when people who ask, ''What can I do?'' may, within reason, be told. ''The room is already crowded with flowers—can you bring me something decent to eat instead?'' ''Oh, dear, yes, there are a few books I'd like to read—do you have a pencil?'' ''Well, the hospital gowns are so uncomfortable. Could you pick up some things for me?'' ''I wish I had something to give the nurses.''

The clever patient will then ask one friend to transcribe letters to all the others thanking them for all those favors. And while your friends are thus employed by you, you may sit there and eat your dinner without offering them anything.

So you see, the idea is to think of it as a resort where, with no obligations, you may behave as you choose. If the prices are bankrupting you, the staff is surly, bossy, or uncommunicative, and the food is atrocious—that should help sustain the illusion.

And when you leave, it is perfectly all right to declare, even to those who have devoted themselves to helping you, that you will never, ever enter the place again.

Hospital Attire

DEAR MISS MANNERS:

I am wondering what is the proper way to dress these days for a short stay at the hospital. I am going for overnight only and do not wish to travel with a bag for nightie and bathrobe, mainly because I do not own either. I am accustomed to bathing and then wearing jeans until bedtime. I do not wish to appear freakish but like to continue along in my usual way, which is comfortable.

GENTLE READER:

If you are going to the hospital because you do not feel well, or because you have arranged not to feel well shortly after you arrive there, you should certainly do everything you can to make yourself comfortable. The hospital, naturally, has the opposite goal and may even attempt to put you into a hospital gown, a freakish garment designed to reduce patients to a state of physical and psychological discomfort so that they, when they leave the hospital, will feel better. Who will win depends on how strong your health is at the time.

Directions for a Deathbed Scene

DEAR MISS MANNERS:

Is it proper to invite one's family and close friends to the hospital, preoperation of course, in order to make one's bequests?

GENTLE READER:

The deathbed family gathering is a social event of such drama and excitement that Miss Manners cannot understand why it is so seldom staged in modern times. Perhaps potential hosts don't feel up to it, or perhaps they think of it too late. Miss Manners commends your effort to keep such a vital custom alive.

Here are some guidelines:

1. Be sure to invite friends and relatives who are incompatible, if not sworn enemies. This is no time to consider who will be comfortable with whom. The thought of life's fragility, as demonstrated by you, should keep them from killing one another, and it should give you a sense of peace to watch them all trying to control their jealousy and greed.

2. It is not necessary, in fact it is unseemly, for you to provide any refreshment for your guests. You are feeding them hope, which is what people live on.

3. Keep your bequests vague. "I want to give you my most ancient and treasured possession" is better than "I'm leaving you my baseball card collection." You don't want your actual death to be an anticlimax.

4. Omit none of your guests from your speech. It is an ordinary social convention that no person should be left out, and it continues to apply in the deathbed scene. It is, after all, unforgivable to ask someone to make a special trip in order to be snubbed. In the spirit of vagueness described in (3), you may say, instead, "You, Cousin Atherton, may be assured that I have remembered everything you have done for me since we were children."

5. It is not necessary, after this type of social event, for the host to make a quick exit. You may be happy to hear that it is perfectly correct for you to recover from the operation and, when you have regained your strength, to have a relapse and stage the entire event again, provided you vary the details to keep everyone alert.

Job's Comforters

What a satisfying act of charity it is to visit the sick. One need only pop unannounced into a hospital room, hand out a dripping bundle of flowers, reassure the patient that his or her bath, dinner, nap or whatver need not be interrupted during one's stay, commiserate in some such conventional phrase as "Oh, you look awful!" put things in perspective by reciting the history of one's own greater ills, and offer practical assistance by explaining treatments at variance with what the patient is undergoing that would be more beneficial.

There are those who so much enjoy performing this service that they faithfully visit hospitalized acquaintances with whom they are not moved to socialize during those people's bouts of good health.

Such kindness is not always fully appreciated by those upon whom it is visited. No wonder sick people have an unfortunate reputation for being cranky.

One must humor them, however, so Miss Manners feels obliged to require the charitable to curtail their good offices somewhat to meet the whims of the unhealthy.

The first is that one requests the invitation to make a hospital visit, and accepts no for an answer. Many people who are hospitalized do not feel up to enduring being cheered up. Those who have limitations on their energy or on the number of visitors or time for visiting may prefer to devote these resources to intimates of their own choice rather than the voluntary visitor.

And there are those, notably repeat patients in maternity wards, who regard hospital stays as oases of quiet, not to be marred by social duties. The ideal visit of a nonrelative to a maternity patient consists of first walking by the baby viewing room and then putting one's head into the mother's room and declaring "Yours is the most beautiful baby in the nursery," and then disappearing.

Visits to sick patients should last no more than half an hour, and twenty minutes is ten minutes better. The question "Am I tiring you?" is better not asked, as the likelihood of the answer's being both honest and polite is small.

It is customary, but not obligatory, to bring a small present on a hospital visit. Living vegetation should be self-contained, which is to say that one brings potted plants or flowers in vases. Other presents that hospital patients have told Miss Manners they especially appreciated included bottles of champagne, books, games, body rub for massages, a liverwurst sandwich with a can of beer, and a bottle of gin. It is considered proper not to bring anything that the doctor has declared likely to help kill the patient, however much the patient may appreciate it.

The chief rule about conversation during a cheering-up visit is that it be cheerful. The difficulties of the patient, whether or not they are discussed, must be acknowledged to be the ranking current woes, and it is rude to attempt to top them with one's own or anyone else's tragedies, past or present.

It is the patient who decrees whether the illness is to be discussed and who does all the talking on the subject. It is of surprisingly little comfort to be told that one's sickness is considered by others to be either more serious or more trivial than one has oneself decided that it is. The visitor may either chuckle or cluck-cluck at the patient's description, depending whether it is narrated with humor or with pathos, but opinions, anecdotes, or advice offered by the visitor can only end in conversational disaster.

All patients, whatever their complaint, are to be told that they look "amazingly good." This remark is designed to comfort both the seekers of sympathy and the seekers of reassurance, and must therefore not be elaborated upon under any circumstances.

MESSY EMOTIONS AND MINOR EMOTIONAL DISTRESS

False Cheer

"You wouldn't want me to pretend to something I don't really feel, would you? You don't want me to have to put on an act when I'm feeling rotten, do you?"

Miss Manners is always puzzled by such questions. Her answer is, "Why, yes. Please."

She spends the better part of her life (never mind how she spends the worse part) trying to persuade people to fake such feelings as delight upon receiving useless presents, curiosity about the welfare of the terminally boring, pleasure in the success of competitors, and sincerity in the wish of prosperity for all people, even those who dress offensively. She also expects everyone to give a rousing imitation of having loved the school concert.

What the world needs is more false cheer. And less honest crabbiness.

Miss Manners does not dispute your right to feel miserable, if that is what makes you happy. She has been known to get a bit tetchy herself on days when the air is thick with rudeness, and to have to retire with a cool compress on her fevered brow.

It is when misery starts issuing invitations for company that she objects. To have a dear friend who will occasionally listen to a recital of woes, in exchange for services in kind, is a blessing. To require this regularly, or to impose it upon those who have not volunteered for such tedious duty, is the sin of adding to the total of unhappiness on earth.

The proper place for a person who is out of sorts is out of sight. If one does not feel up to putting on a good act, one should ring down the curtain. Or at least post the notice. Tersely polite warnings, such as "I wouldn't do that right now if I were you, dear," should be heeded.

For many people, however, out of sorts is a geographical location where they set up housekeeping. They may have had a genuine tragedy in their lives, or they may merely enjoy the universal conviction that no one suffers more from the unjustness of life than oneself. Whatever the cause, the air of grievance looks the same, once it has settled on the face.

That is the time to put on a false face.

Please notice that Miss Manners is trying hard to refrain from pointing out that there are people who overcome adversity with courage, bravery, and determination, who turn their attention resolutely away from their own dissatisfactions and toward bettering the lot of others. She has been told that this example is of no use to those who cannot manage that exemplary feat, so she is not demanding true cheerfulness.

Naturally, the more skillful the performance of false cheer, the more pleasing the effect is upon one's public and on that private audience to whom one owes even more. It is also true that the semblance of happiness eventually, by some alchemy of the spirit, turns genuine.

But even the crudest effort is better than tossing one's problems to others, like an unexpected volleyball aimed at the stomach.

The answer to "How are you?" is not "Uhhh," nor "How should I be?" It is not the answer that a gentleman of Miss Manners' acquaintance received when he posed the polite question to an elderly guest at his wedding, and was told, "Oh, not so good since Bill died." (Bill had died eight years previously.)

The answer to "How are you?" is always a hearty, "Very well, thank you; how are you?" A truly disciplined person would never reply anything else, even in a hospital emergency room at midnight.

Sounding the Alarm

"Please come over right away. I need someone to talk to. I'm feeling terribly depressed."

Dear Geoffrey Perfect, who had received this gracious and enticing invitation, looked decidedly low himself, as he plaintively asked Miss Manners, "Do I have to?" He explained that the depressed person was not an especially intimate friend. He pleaded that he would be an unsympathetic listener, as he had already been a reluctant confidant in the activities that predictably resulted in the depression. He wept that he didn't feel like listening to someone else whine. Nevertheless, he was afraid that responding to such an invitation was some kind of compelling human duty.

"That call, 'I'm depressed!' is issued as if it is some kind of civic emergency," he said. "You feel like a rat if you don't rush at the alarm to do what you can."

The Hon. Perfect Pious made a similar inquiry about the emotional problems of his employees, which they felt compelled to explain to him. "I consider myself a reasonable boss," he said. "I know that people might have down cycles in their work, and I try to allow for that. I also think I'm pretty fair about giving people time off for personal problems, so long as they're in good faith about the job and don't abuse it. But do I really have to listen to all the details about those dreadful personal reasons? Frankly, it just makes me angry when they try to enlist my sympathies about how they feel bad because of what their lover did to them. I'd rather they let me believe they were going to their grandmother's funeral."

Miss Manners hereby excuses and, indeed, applauds those who refuse to receive confidences from any except people with whom they have close ties of blood or affection. A person who felt obliged to answer every announcement of depression with his anxious assistance wouldn't have time or spirit enough left to tie his own shoelaces.

A great deal of the trouble lies in the pseudo-dignity of that word "depression." Depression, in Miss Manners' vocabulary, refers to the state of mind brought on by having lost all one's money on Wall Street, or the catastrophic equivalent. It should not be used to refer to a bad mood. If you recognize a bad mood properly, you will realize that the chief thing to be done about it is to avoid inflicting it on others. One keeps away from strangers and warns intimates, "Don't mess with me, I'm in a foul mood," a statement they should take seriously.

When people give this the name of depression, they believe that they are the victims of emotional illness and therefore are entitled to huge amounts of attention and sympathy. This is a mistake. Physically ill people learn, often the hard way, not to expect unlimited interest and sympathy from anyone except those closest to them. It is a notorious breach of manners to bore acquaintances with the story of your operation, and the same should be true about the story of your divorce. Would you call around town to find someone to come and be with you "quickly, because I need someone—I have such a tummy ache"?

DEAR MISS MANNERS:

I have a small circle of loyal friends, and I think I am mature enough to understand how fortunate I am to be thus endowed. My problem is that they always call me when they are depressed, discouraged, angry, bored, or suicidal. My job is demanding, and my day is long. How do I handle their moody, frustrating (and basically selfish) ramblings without estranging them or sending myself over the edge?

GENTLE READER:

We are in the midst of a nationwide depression/inflation of frightening proportions. Everyone who is momentarily blue quickly declares it a great depression and decides that the solution is to annoy his or her friends.

Loyal friends do respond in one another's hours of need, but if these happen every hour, the loyal friends have a right to become suspicious. Miss Manners would like to see the word "depression" taken out of circulation in reference to all but monetary crises, and perhaps for those, too. With its doleful, psychomedical overtones, it lends unnecessary and unhealthy importance to the fleeting downs (as in "ups and downs") of life.

If your friends cannot diagnose their minor ailments properly, you must learn to distinguish their whining spells from their emergencies. A friend who calls because he is out of sorts, at loose ends, at sixes and sevens, or in any other states fitting the excellent folksy descriptions replaced by "depression," should simply be told that you are too busy to talk now. No apologies are necessary. If you occasionally allow him to gripe at you during your free time, you are more than fulfilling the requirements of friendship. You might try cultivating people of normally cheerful dispositions. They make wonderful friends, especially when you feel blue.

Convalescing from a Broken Heart

DEAR MISS MANNERS:

I need advice, please, on the etiquette of dealing with a broken heart in the course of everyday business and social affairs. Having just lost a wonderful man, my world is naturally diminished. While I am handling the situation very well most of the time, I find that at times I am caught off-guard. I have burst into tears in public places, failed to complete work assignments, and lost the thread of conversations in midsentence.

What I need is a way to communicate my present state of withdrawal and vulnerability to friends and co-workers without baring my soul, offering excuses, or asking for sympathy. If I had a broken leg, most people would respond with uncommon decency and expect me to get better as soon as possible so that they could go back to treating me any way they felt like. Do you have any words, Miss Manners, which are as symbolic of a broken heart as a cast is for a broken leg?

GENTLE READER:

The symbol is the heart worn on the sleeve, but Miss Manners does not advise wearing it, as it is much less attractive than a leg cast. In fact, the comparison with the broken leg does not work at all, as you will realize if you think about the questions people address to those in leg casts: "How did you do that?" "Was it your fault?" "When are you going to be getting around again?" "Are you suing?"

You really do not wish to have such questions asked about your broken heart, do you? Perhaps we would be better off using an ailment as private in nature as the broken heart. If you had hemorrhoids, for example, you would excuse yourself when necessary merely by saying, "I haven't been feeling terribly well," and when pressed for details would add only, "Oh, it's nothing really, and I'd rather not discuss it."

❧ DISGUSTING HABITS

"Noises You Can Make," we'll call this problem. Miss Manners is referring, of course, to noises you can make inadvertently, and the proper responses which should be made advertently. There are three categories of such noises:

1. Sympathetic noises. These are noises that evoke sympathy, not noises that express sympathy, such as cluck-cluck, an unharmonious sound which is nevertheless made on purpose, in response to such statements as "My daughter's dropping out of college; she says she's going to major in Life."

One sympathetic noise is the sneeze, and the correct response is, of course, "God bless you," or any foreign equivalent which might comfort the sneezer and which the sneezed-at feels comfortable pronouncing. Another is the cough, to which the proper response is, "Are you all right?" the problem of answering which is supposed to take the person's mind and throat off his cough. These responses are made only to adult sneezers or coughers. If a child sneezes one says, "Don't you have a handkerchief?" and if a child coughs, one says, "Didn't I tell you not to go out without your knee warmers?"

2. Acceptable noises. These are noises such as burping or the sounds accompanying choking, to which the response should come from the noisemaker himself, provided that the choking was not complete, in which case he is absolved of all social responsibility except that of having left his papers in order. Society acknowledges that these noises are made from time to time, but does not dignify them with a response. The offender says "Excuse me," and the subject is considered closed.

3. Unacceptable noises. Miss Manners does not plan to mention them, chiefly because they are unmentionable, but you all know who you are. What they are. At any rate, these are noises that are acknowledged by neither the noisemaker nor the noise recipient, because socially they do not exist. The practice of staring hard at the person next to you when, for instance, your own stomach has given off a loud rumble, is therefore to be condemned on grounds of etiquette as well as morals.

You will notice that there is a noise left uncategorized, namely the hiccup. Technically, the hiccup is not socially unacceptable; nevertheless, people should try to ignore it. A person who is hiccuping has enough troubles, especially if he is foolishly pretending nothing is wrong and trying to prove it by talking soberly in between the hics, without a bunch of crazy people trying to pour water down his throat or clap a paper bag over his head.

Removing Saliva

DEAR MISS MANNERS:
Please list some tactful ways of removing a man's saliva from your face.
GENTLE READER:
Please list some decent ways of acquiring a man's saliva on your face. If the gentleman sprayed you inadvertently to accompany enthusiastic discourse, you may step back two paces, bring out your handkerchief, and go through the motions of wiping your nose, while trailing the cloth along your face to pick up whatever needs mopping along the route. If, however, the substance was acquired as a result of enthusiasm of a more intimate nature, you may delicately retrieve it with a flick of your pink tongue.

Miss Manners can't believe she said that. Please disregard that, and use the more delicate method of resting your cheek momentarily on his shoulder, until his jacket absorbs the mess.

Burping

DEAR MISS MANNERS:

I know that it is good manners and common courtesy to cover one's mouth when coughing or sneezing, but is it also necessary to do so when burping? My husband is irritated if I burp too loud without covering my mouth or trying to cover it up somehow. Is there a polite way to handle burps?

GENTLE READER:

Technically speaking, it is not polite to burp at all. It is strange, but nevertheless generally recognized, that some inevitable natural phenomena, such as coughing, are socially acceptable, and others, such as burping, are not. (Perhaps it is because society recognizes the necessity of breathing but ignores digestion as much as possible.) The correct thing to do, therefore, is to treat the burp as if it were a socially acceptable cough. In other words, cover it up by making your hand into a fist and placing the thumb side against your mouth.

Nose-Blowing

DEAR MISS MANNERS:

What do you do with tissues, after you have blown your nose in them, when you are out in public or at a friend's house?

GENTLE READER:

For such occasions, you employ a cloth tissue, a clever little invention which is a square of cotton or linen that may be conveniently carried in the pocket and reused throughout the day. One should never begin the day without a fresh one of these concealed about one's person. Consider, for example, the difference this would make if you should have occasion to weep in front of others. Weeping into paper is disgusting; weeping into fine linen is romantic drama.

DEAR MISS MANNERS:

Recently, my husband and I were invited to attend a business dinner party at a prominent area restaurant. Although I have severe hay fever, my husband insisted I accompany him. The dinner lasted several hours, during which time I had to blow my nose continually.

My question is this: Was it impolite for me to remain at the table, or should I have excused myself and gone to the ladies' room, although I would have had to have done this dozens of times? I received several demeaning looks from the other guests, so I explained my hay fever was quite uncontrollable. I need an answer, because my husband's company has several of these functions throughout the year, many during hay fever season.

GENTLE READER:

Miss Manners will arouse herself from the state of silly amusement that came on when she pictured guests delivering "demeaning looks" at a nose blower, and remember that nothing connected with human suffering is funny.

Your conduct should be regulated by the desire to create as little distraction as possible with your problem. A woman who gets up from the dinner table a dozen times during one meal would completely mesmerize the guests, leaving them with nothing on their minds but a maddening curiosity to know what was wrong with her. Similarly, a person who is constantly blowing her nose distracts the guests by making them wonder if they are going to catch what she has. Therefore, you were right to explain your illness.

What, then, brought on the demeaning looks? Possibly an unappetizing way of blowing your nose, which distracted the guests from the enjoyment of their dinners. Miss Manners advises you to carry large handkerchiefs (not tissues) and to learn to blow your nose without noise and without exhibiting any interest afterwards in the success of your temporary cure. This may not be clear, but Miss Manners does not know how to put it more plainly without doing distracting things to her own appetite.

Sneezing

DEAR MISS MANNERS:

Obviously, you should use a tissue if you sneeze. But what if you can't get it out of your pocket in time? Is there any way, short of carrying it around in your hand all the time just to be prepared in case you ever sneeze, to avoid having people look at you as if you were a slob because you sneeze without using a handkerchief? I'm not talking about messy sneezes, but small, neat ones that are over when they're over.

GENTLE READER:

As the sneeze comes on, you reach for the handkerchief, and then you get it out whether or not you have managed to outrace the sneeze. Holding a handkerchief in one's hand after a sneeze is the next best thing to holding it over one's nose during the sneeze. It indicates good faith.

Cleaning the Nose

DEAR MISS MANNERS:

How do you clean your nose, if you're not supposed to "pick" it? I'm not trying to be funny—I was told that this is always disgusting, and yet it is obviously necessary.

GENTLE READER:

In manners, as distinct from morals—an icky, messy subject, which fortunately is not Miss Manners' field—the only recognized act is one that has been witnessed. The number of practices, disgusting or exciting, usual or unusual, in which you wish to engage in private is of no concern to society.

Picking Teeth

DEAR MISS MANNERS:

I know that picking the teeth is considered gauche in this country, but other cultures are more sensible about the discomfort of food stuck in the mouth. What do you think?

GENTLE READER:

Miss Manners realizes that dislodging food from the teeth is one of life's great sensual pleasures, and believes that great sensual pleasure should be enjoyed in private.

Perspiring

DEAR MISS MANNERS:

We are a couple of college girls new in town and are concerned with what we view as an imminent problem as summer fast approaches. How does a lady discreetly deal with perspiration?

GENTLE READER:

A lady does not perspire. When dear Orson Welles was married to Rita Hayworth, someone spoke of her as "sweating," and he replied coldly, "Horses sweat. People perspire. Miss Hayworth glows." There is nothing wrong with dewy college girls. Within reason, of course.

Scratching

DEAR MISS MANNERS:

Is it permissible to scratch in public if you have a bad itch?

GENTLE READER:

What would you do if Miss Manners said, "No"?

Cracking Knuckles

DEAR MISS MANNERS:

What do you think of cracking knuckles in public? Do you think it's unladylike or annoying? Please reply immediately, because it is a big issue in my house.

GENTLE READER:

Cracking knuckles is unladylike, ungentlemanlike, unchildlike, and unpleasant. Please insist that everyone stop it this very minute.

Chewing Gum

DEAR MISS MANNERS:

Do you consider it "proper" to chew gum in an office? The office manager where I work is the worst offender, and I feel he sets a very bad example for the rest of the staff. He doesn't chew his gum discreetly, but chomps it very noticeably and flicks it back and forth in front of his teeth, making it visible to anyone he's talking to. I feel that it is annoying, rude, and inconsiderate of others. What do you think?

GENTLE READER:

Gum chewing is another of those pleasures that is never proper. At any rate, the method you describe is, no doubt, repulsive, but the range in gum chewing goes only from slightly repulsive to extremely repulsive. The real question of etiquette here is whether it is proper to correct one's boss. This is something that Miss Manners cannot recommend as being entirely safe, no matter what method you use. If you decide it is worth the risk, at least do it as a group.

Oral Gratification

DEAR MISS MANNERS:

I am writing this letter to take issue with you concerning the answer to the reader who asked if it is proper to chew gum in an office. I am led to believe that by your standards, if he appeared in the office smoking a big black fat cigar, polluting the air, forcing everyone to breathe his smoke, doing irreparable damage to his lungs and mouth, it would be proper.

Everyone is born with an oral habit. A baby will suck on anything from his mother's breast to his finger. As we get older, we substitute other habits for the sucking reflex. Some will smoke the big fat cigar, others cigarettes, still others will chew their nails, pencils, anything they can comfortably get into their mouth. Of all these habits, chewing gum, especially sugarless gum, is the least harmful and even a little beneficial as it does relieve stress and tension. As a practicing general dentist, I tell my patients I would much prefer them to chew sugarless gum than to smoke. I think the time has come for schools to permit their students to chew gum. This might possibly prevent them from running to the washroom or outside between periods for a quick drag.

GENTLE READER:

Miss Manners does not quite follow your logic. If discouraging gum chewing means endorsing cigar smoking, would discouraging face slapping mean endorsing shin kicking? While an oral need may characterize babyhood, adulthood is said to be characterized by different needs. It is also supposed to include a developing ability to control those needs when they are socially unacceptable. What do you recommend in the way of public behavior for people who want to satisfy their anal or genital urges in the office?

Chewing Tobacco

DEAR MISS MANNERS:

In our small office, there is a gentleman who has a habit of chewing tobacco and carrying around a plastic cup as a spittoon. Frankly, I find the entire thing disgusting. Is there any polite and possibly subtle way of letting him know?

GENTLE READER:

Miss Manners, who also finds plastic cups disgusting except at picnics, sympathizes with you, but warns you of the difficulties of changing the habits of grown-ups. Perhaps other members of the office could get together and buy the gentleman a proper spittoon. Or you could announce an agreement that no one would use tobacco in the office. Some people find smoking it as offensive as spitting it.

🐜 POLITICS

Citizen participation is such a wonderful thing that Miss Manners always wants to do something in return for the well-being of people who voluntarily give up their free time to attend civic meetings. The best thing she can think of is to go around from meeting to meeting making motions for adjournment, so that these people can go home while they still have their sanity.

In theory, the best and fairest way to run any public project is for as many people as possible who will be affected by it to gather and freely express their opinions about how it should be done. It's only in practice that this is so dreadful.

In the interest of preserving this great democratic tradition, Miss Manners would like to make a few suggestions for controlling the unfettered self-expression of the people. She is not even going to mention such breaches of courtesy as "Perhaps the gentleman will be kind enough to tell us what his qualifications are for making such a patently ridiculous suggestion?" or "Well, who asked you to move here, anyway?" She assumes that no good citizen would even consider them.

The transgressions she means involve the waste of good time. Here are some matters you might consider before exercising your inalienable right to make known your deepest feelings and convictions:

1. If people do not agree with you, it is not necessarily because they do not understand your position. The reason that the same few people use most of the time at any given meeting is that they entertain this erroneous assumption. Stating your position louder after each statement of opposition occasionally wears down a few of the weaker souls, who drift off down the block, but it does not win the hearts and votes of the majority.

2. Your personal experience is only relevant up to a point, however cleverly packaged in amusing anecdotes. A story beginning "Let me tell you how we used to deal with this problem in Winnetka" is passable, but only once. Extreme caution should be exercised before telling such stories. Anecdotes in which political insight is attributed to your taxi driver, the feelings of a race or ethnic population to your cleaning woman, or in which your child is the authority on matters of education, should never be told.

3. Group therapy traditions notwithstanding, a speech at a public meeting that opens with "I'm trying to figure out exactly how I feel about this" should not be given. A person who finds himself of two minds should consider that one has canceled out the other.

4. There is no disgrace attached to finding that one's thoughts have been adequately expressed by others. Unlike in school, you do not get separate marks for class participation.

If everyone were to keep these few rules in mind, we could all do our civic duty and be home by bedtime. But perhaps Miss Manners would then need to add one more:

5. A short meeting is not necessarily a sign of public apathy.

Civil Disobedience

DEAR MISS MANNERS:
What is the proper conduct of demonstrators at White House demonstrations, and of recipients (targets) of demonstrations?

GENTLE READER:
The first obligation of the demonstrator is to be legible. Miss Manners cannot sympathize with a cause whose signs she cannot make out even with her glasses on. The next rule of conduct is that demonstrators not vent their discontent on passersby, whom they should be impressing with their goodwill and reasonableness. As for the recipients, the proper thing is to resist the temptation to look out of a White House window. Peeking is a mistake when one may wish to declare, the next day, that one was unaware of the demonstration.

Spontaneous Demonstrations

DEAR MISS MANNERS:
How should one comport oneself at a political convention during a so-called spontaneous demonstration (a) for one's own candidate, (b) for the opposition?

GENTLE READER:
The spontaneous demonstration has, as you recognize, a strict code of behavior.
In the case of one's own candidate, the correct form is to jump up and down, waving one's arms and legs, releasing balloons, and tossing straw hats in the air. The facial expression should be dazed delight, the dazed part of which is not

difficult to achieve when one has been more than half an hour at a national political convention, and the delighted part of which is signified by an open-mouthed smile, which, if properly done, signifies a state of pleased idiocy not otherwise seen in this country from one four-year term to the next.

Opposition to the candidate is signified by removing the smile, but keeping the mouth open and limbs still. You would be surprised what a dampening effect this posture—which looks something like that of a person who has just been arrested for jaywalking and has not yet collected his thoughts enough to ask the arresting officer why that gentleman is not engaged instead in pursuing real criminals—conveys.

Rites de Passage

Bar and Bat Mitzvahs, Communions and Confirmations

Bar and Bat Mitzvahs

Something strange happens to children when they turn thirteen years of age, but Miss Manners is not sure she would call it adulthood. Nevertheless, the special celebration of the thirteenth birthday seems as right to her as having New Year's in the crisp, begin-again air of autumn, as the Jewish calendar does, instead of when the roads are already icy and dangerous.

The bar mitzvah, for Jewish boys, and the less traditional (but only fair) bat mitzvah, for girls, carry religious responsibility for the person who is coming of age. But no child should be considered to be legitimately approaching adulthood who has not also mastered some social responsibility. Celebrating a bar or bat mitzvah, whether by receiving the congratulations of the congregation in the synagogue or by being the guest of honor at a hotel dinner-dance for four hundred, is an excellent test of social skills.

No thirteen-year-old should be permitted to begin whining, "But I'm not a child anymore—you always treat me like a baby," let alone to call itself by the dignified title of adult, without having mastered the ability to:

· Accept the idea that no occasion, least of all a social event, is so important as to justify subordinating all claims to the pleasure of one person. While life is often a compromise, parties always are, and learning this early will spare the

Mr. and Mrs. Alexander Wise

request the honour of your presence

when their son

Guy Noah

will be called to the Torah as a Bar Mitzvah

on Saturday, the first of April

at half after ten o'clock

Brookdale Hebrew Congregation

Brookdale, Connecticut

Luncheon following the services

The invitation to a Bar Mitzvah (or to a daughter's Bat Mitzvah) with enclosed invitation card for evening. Divorced parents may issue the invitation alone, together using their current names, or with other spouses, specifying "his" or "her" son. Note that an invitation to religious services does not require a reply, as places of worship are in theory open to all, but that invitations to related social events, including the luncheon at the synagogue, do. For reply wording, see page 447.

Dinner dance

at half after seven o'clock

125 Primrose Path

Brookdale, Connecticut

The favour of a reply is requested

child enormous emotional grief on wedding days, inaugurations, retirement parties, and whatever other milestones are stepped upon.

· Realize that there is a relationship between the financial resources of the family and the amounts of money it can spend. It is difficult to understand that money spent on nonpleasurable items for a child, such as shoes and tuition, have a connection with the amount of money available to spend on things the child actually wants, such as live bands and ski trips.

· Analyze one's family and friends dispassionately in the interests of forming a proper guest list. For example, not being able to stand a certain relative counts for nothing; the only thing that counts is how closely the person is related. There can be a cutoff on the family part of the guest list, but it is made on the basis of how much blood there is in common, not how many interests. While it is true that friends tend to be people one likes, there are often more important considerations, such as how close one's parents are to their parents, or whether invitations were forthcoming to their parties.

· Accept a compliment, no matter how silly. The answer to "What does it feel like to be a (heh, heh) man, sonny?" is a smile.

· Stand in a receiving line looking pleased to see everyone, no matter how detestable. Related to this is the discipline to circulate, in both talking and dancing, without distinguishing between the people one likes and the people one was forced to invite.

· Perform introductions, fully and correctly. No person who cannot introduce to his grandmother the chief troublemaker of the eighth grade, getting the proper sequence and the correct name of each, and entirely concealing terror of what one might carelessly say to the other, can be considered an adult.

· Behave as if age were not the single most distinguishing factor among human beings, and act as if it were perfectly natural to have a room full of people of different generations who are not even all related to one another.

· Write prompt thank you letters, each with an opening other than, "Thank you for the ———"

Miss Manners wishes you to note that this is a minimum list. If, on top of these skills, you can pile some grace and sense, she will promise to consider you a full-fledged human being.

Confirmation and Communion

DEAR MISS MANNERS:

My sister married a Roman Catholic and agreed that the children would be brought up in that faith. My eldest niece is about to take first communion. Can you tell me what to expect, and what my wife and I should do? Do we give her a separate present from her birthday present? What about her confirmation?

GENTLE READER:

Miss Manners takes it that your niece must be about seven, so that her confirmation is four or five years away. In both cases, you will probably be invited to attend services, with a small celebration—at church or in your sister's house or at a restaurant—marking the occasion. Yes, you should give the child a separate present, because the religious milestone is different from an ordinary birthday. The rule about having all such presents strictly religious in nature has been somewhat relaxed, but Miss Manners urges you to remember the nature of the occasion and not give her a doll in a silver jumpsuit who looks as if she could get into church only as a bad example.

Graduations and Reunions

Graduations

Graduations are the perfect preparation for that laughable institution known on such occasions as Real Life or The World Out There. If you can sit quietly in the sun for two hours, listening to irrelevant platitudes with a respectful look on your face, and can survive with dignity the social mixture of your progenitors with your peers, life out there should hold no further terrors.

It is a mistake to think that graduations are held for the benefit of graduates, who therefore should be able to enjoy the celebrations as they choose or even boycott them. Graduations are held to mark the end of the sufferings of people who have been paying staggering tuition bills, nagging about homework until their own lives have no longer been worth living, or despairing that the efforts of their ancestors to achieve a modicum of civilization have been lost under their supervision.

The relief of these people on finding that one of society's most obvious goals has been achieved often borders on the hysterical. Otherwise sensible and reserved parents will attempt to involve their graduating children in odd forms of exhibitionist behavior, and encourage younger siblings to do the same. They will create havoc by taking pictures at every possible moment, and when they are unable to accost strangers to find outlets for bragging, they will exchange such remarks with each other in unnaturally loud voices.

All this must be endured with grace by indulgent graduates. Not looking ashamed of one's parents, no matter where they demand to be shown, whom they insist on meeting, and what they cannot be prevented from saying, is a *rite de passage* certifying the maturity of the graduate.

He or she is not, however, permitted any unconventional behavior. Blue jeans that can be seen below academic robes, protest demonstrations against the school or any of its invited speakers, or any behavior—other than accepting prizes—that distinguishes one graduate from another cannot be tolerated. The graduation ceremony, in all its mesmerizing monotony, was carefully designed to fulfill the fantasies of families, not to enable the graduate to express his independence.

Even the allegedly private aspects, the proms and the parties, carry their family obligations. If you pose prettily beforehand and fabricate a comforting report afterward, it is possible that you and your peers will be allowed a small amount of private pleasure in between.

Satisfying one's family by going along with all their graduation expectations, no matter how silly or embarrassing, is not the graduate's only obligation. He or she also owes something to the educational institution, and that institution owes something to its older alumni—or if it doesn't, it isn't from lack of trying.

Alumni who are using graduations as the setting for their reunions are not always raucous and drunk. However, they are always caught in a mysterious time warp that leads to behavior that can be just as offensive.

Graduating seniors must listen with patient smiles to the questions and comments of alumni who have discovered that the school no longer has curfews, single-sex dormitories, or four years of required Biblical studies. That look will serve them well on job interviews and other such exasperating situations held Out There.

Dear Miss Manners:

I am a senior in high school, and I have a few questions about proper etiquette.

1. Who do I send graduation announcements to?
2. Who do I send graduation invitations to?
3. What is the best way to ask a young lady to our senior prom?
4. What type of tuxedo should I rent?
5. Do you have any suggestions that would make either graduation or senior prom night more enjoyable?

Gentle Reader:

Would it help if Miss Manners solved all your problems at once by keeping you back until you learn grammar? No, probably not. At least allow her to dampen your enjoyment by correcting your questions, before she enhances it by answering them.

1. To whom should I send graduation announcements? Send them to relatives and close friends who you think will say, "Oh, isn't that nice—Adam has gotten through high school," and not to those whose response is more likely to be,

"Oh-oh, do we have to send Adam a present just because he managed to get through school?"

2. To whom do I send graduation invitations? Send them to your closest relatives only. A graduation is a tedious event for everyone whose eyes are not misted with pride.

3. What is the best way to ask a young woman to our senior prom? The best way is "Would you do me the honour of accompanying me to my senior prom?" but it is possible that the best wording will strike her as unbearably funny. You might try the second best, "Would you like to go to my senior prom with me?" In either case, give the date before she has had a chance to answer. This gives her the opportunity to refuse because of a schedule conflict, and that, Miss Manners assures you, is less painful than the blanket "No, not really" she might otherwise give.

4. What type of evening clothes should I wear? Evening clothes, also known as dinner jackets (the pants are assumed), must always be black on black, and the shirts must be white. Men's fanciful evening clothes are unspeakable.

5. No. If you accept all of the preceding corrections and advice, then you can just run along and have a wonderful time, with Miss Manners' blessing.

Presents

DEAR MISS MANNERS:

Just recently, I received a note from my cousin which began, "Bill and I would like to thank you for the graduation gift you gave to Tom." I was beginning to wonder whether Tom had not been taught how to write.

My fears were allayed, however, when I received a canceled check endorsed "Tom Smith." The check had been made out to Thomas D. Smith, as I understood his full name to be from the graduation announcement. The check was cashed by the local liquor store. Perhaps Tom, only eighteen and unaccustomed, we hope, to strong drink, spent the entire sum of twenty-five dollars to sample some of the many varieties available, and as a result was temporarily unable to lift a pen. I wonder if Miss Manners has any comment on all this. Am I being terribly old-fashioned to think it would have been more proper for the young man to express gratitude himself, whether or not he felt any?

GENTLE READER:

As Miss Manners understands it, the phrase "being terribly old-fashioned" is the apologetic way in which people admit to a timid, hopeless desire to be treated with common decency by the young. It is interesting to observe how your cousins are attempting to live a double standard, acknowledging the propriety of your being thanked, but not imposing the necessity for doing so on their son. All this cravenness is, in Miss Manners' opinion, why there is a crisis of manners in the world today.

Of course the young man should have thanked you. (Actually, during a hangover is an excellent time for a nice, quiet activity such as writing thank-you notes, if one can stand the sound of the pen's scratching on the paper.) Generosity and gratitude should always travel together, and since the gratitude is absent, Miss Manners suggests you squelch the generosity.

(For more on presents and thank-you letters, please see pp. 521–523.)

High School Reunion

DEAR MISS MANNERS:

In September, our twentieth high school reunion is planned. What does one wear? It's a buffet dinner with dancing.

GENTLE READER:

Keep in mind the purpose of a high school reunion, which is to give those who would least have suspected it the impression that you turned out to be a success in life, after all. (If you were elected Most Popular Boy or Girl twenty years ago, you still have to show that you were able to translate your early triumphs into modern, adult terms.) Therefore, you dress to look as chic and attractive as possible.

A word of caution, however. The nature of a reunion recreates attitudes of the original time. You will suddenly find yourself and others thinking in clichés you may not have used for years. If you overdo your act, it will be recognized with adolescent cruelty that you are a "show off," "boy chaser," person who "thinks he's so hot," or whatever. So summon up whatever subtlety and finesse you may have acquired over the last two decades—and *then* fix yourself up to kill. Surely you remember how hard you tried to look as if you didn't care whether anyone liked you or not in high school; now you ought to be able to bring that off.

Dark, banker's suit for men; plain dress with one small piece of good jewelry for women. Don't try to imitate the fashion of two decades ago.

College Reunions

Modesty is becoming in all endeavors, but it is essential for people attending college reunions.

Miss Manners realizes that this seems to contradict the purpose of attending college reunions, which is to demonstrate that one has turned out better than anyone expected. Modesty is not intended to prevent this goal, but to prevent it from backfiring.

Bragging is not the only pleasure associated with returning to the scene of one's education, but it is the chief one. Others include walking through classroom buildings knowing that one has no papers overdue, and spending the night in a dormitory without wondering whether one will go through life unloved.

All of these joys derive from the knowledge that one is better off now than one was in college. Merely being in one's late teens is a state from which it is hardly possible not to improve. But colleges tend to be competitive, and improvements will be compared. The entries will be in three categories, Success, Happiness, and Wisdom, as is obvious from the Class Report, which will consist of variations on the following essays:

Success

Life as a designer of household paper products continues to be interesting, stimulating and challenging, with special opportunities for growth in the visual arts as well as in my special interest—people. Having been named Outstanding Promising Junior Citizen in my suburban area was an unexpected honor that I hope to live up to.

Happiness

The high point of this year was the birth of our sixth child, and watching the older ones prosper and grow thoughtful and strong, bubbling with life and learning. Gloria, still beautiful, sensitive, compassionate, and talented, has made our reconverted chicken house into a veritable treasure store of needlepoint, and also finds fulfillment in the candle scenting that she does, for fun and profit, in her dining room office. All of us love to travel as a family and by next reunion we hope to have visited all of America's battlefields and civil disturbance areas.

Wisdom

As we enter our mature years, we gain in self-discovery, awareness of the needs of others, and of our purpose for being on this earth. I continue to be amazed and optimistic as I see our society examining its defects, agonizing over its mistakes, and rising again to meet the challenges before us. On a personal level, I try to live one day at a time.

There will be a fourth type of entry, consisting only of the alumnus' address. That person will show up at the reunion, listening to others and saying nothing about himself. It will turn out, after everyone has gone home, that he has published a witty new translation of Sanskrit poetry, has just completed the leading role in a major movie, is married to a woman whose name is being mentioned for the Supreme Court, and has a son who won the Moscow piano competition and a daughter who is the country's youngest mayor. There is one like that at every reunion. If you keep your mouth shut, people may suspect it is you.

Debuts and Dances

In modern times, it has become fashionable for a young woman, upon reaching the age of eighteen, to signify her membership in adult society by announcing that she refuses to make a debut. This innovation has many advantages over the old debutante system, including being a lot cheaper.

A girl who refuses to come out, like a ground hog under similar circumstances, creates a certain amount of interest; while girls and ground hogs who do come out as expected simply create romantic expectations that they may not be able to fulfill. The wedding announcement of a woman that includes several years of graduate school and professional experience is impressive, but it can easily be put into the perspective of more primitive times if it contains the date of a debut made ten or twelve years previously.

The reason for this negativism on the part of Miss Manners, whose usual custom it is to fight fiercely for the preservation of outmoded rituals (so would you if you were the only person alive who knew how to make correct morning calls from a brougham), is that the surviving debutante tradition often makes a mockery of its original purpose. Bringing young women out presupposes keeping them in beforehand. But that has always been a more or less futile prospect, and it is not the cause of Miss Manners' objections. What distresses her is the atmosphere into which they are brought out.

The original intention was to introduce one's daughter to one's friends, and if they happened to have sons with good prospects, so much the better. In some private dances given by close relatives of debutantes, and in some church or civic groups, where cotillions are organized by members who know one another well, this idea still prevails.

Far more often, the cotillion is run by a competitive committee, more or less in business for the purpose, and it screens debutantes slightly more thoroughly than colleges screen their applicants. The debutante who is accepted is then allowed to bow, as they put it, to an artificial society composed of people her parents don't know and will probably never see again. It is not uncommon to have an ambitious debutante presented to strangers in a strange city by parents who have to add their hotel bill to the already substantial costs.

In such a determindedly organized setting, the presence of young men is not left to nature and what she has chosen to supply in the normal course of events to the adult couples representing society. Each debutante is assigned to scout out what are euphemistically referred to as "escorts," by whatever means possible.

In the interests of providing a shared "stag line" of extra men, debutantes are usually required to dredge up two or three escorts each. Remember that these are supposed to be innocent young girls making their first appearance in the world among eligible men, and then ask yourself how they are supposed to have already acquired—and be prepared to donate to their sister debutantes— several.

Standards are necessarily lowered for this dragnet, and the young men begin to understand that they are at a premium. So for the expense and the trouble of the modern debut, fond parents are able to attach a permanent date to their daughter's youth, have her scrutinized by strangers, and arrange for her to meet a lot of young men who have come to believe that the world owes them free champagne. That is why Miss Manners will not be offended if you decide to skip this particular tradition.

Rules for Debuts

To young ladies contemplating making formal debuts, Miss Manners has an invaluable piece of general advice: Don't.

This need not at all be applied to the question of whether one should go ahead and bow to society, as we say, by which we mean enjoying a little season of having all sorts of people figuratively bowing to the wishes of teenaged girls.

But it is applicable to practically every other question apt to flicker through a debutante's head during that season and is especially appropriate to impromptu suggestions from contemporaries that begin with "I know! Why don't we?"

Manners are of paramount importance for debutantes, because debutantes have most of the responsibilities and problems of brides without the job security.

Like brides, debutantes are prone to feel that no expense should be spared in their honor, that all arrangements should be dictated by their taste and pleasure, that they are to be forgiven any lapse of manners and indulged in any whim because of the specialness of their position, and that everyone else should be

Mr. and Mrs. Geoffrey Lockwood Perfect

Miss Daffodil Louise Perfect

At Home
(line may be omitted)

Saturday, the first of April

at five o'clock

123 Primrose Path

Invitations to a debut. The first is a tea given by the parents, although the word tea is not mentioned; the second is a grand ball given by another grown-up, but the word ball is never used. Even the debutante's name is not used, Mrs. Plue Perfect being extremely strict, but as this tends to make debutantes sulky, the words "in honour of" may be added after "small dance," with the debutante's full name on the next line.

Mrs. Plue Perfect

requests the pleasure of the company of

(space for guest's name to be handwritten)

at a small dance

on Saturday, the first of April

at half after ten o'clock

Society of Early Dames

Kindly send response to
127 Primrose Path

subservient to them for the period of their glory. The only difference is that the debutante antagonizes only one family when she reveals these wishes.

The principle tends to be forgotten that the debut is a presentation by the parents of their daughter to the society in which they move. It should therefore follow that the debut should be in their style of entertaining, that the adult portion of the guest list is as important as the young people's, and that a level of taste acceptable to the parents' notion of propriety be maintained.

Then how come there are so many rock bands, swaggering young men, and abashed adults fading into the wallpaper at most debutante dances? Why, because the parents want, as they say, "the young people to have a good time." Miss Manners is not actually against that. She merely insists on the form of deference to that society to which the young lady is so prettily bending her knees.

The responsibilities of those young people (and Miss Manners wishes to point out that assisting at a sister's debut is a recognized *rite de passage* for young men, and a rigorous one, too) include: presenting only known people as candidates for invitations, acknowledging all other invitations, flowers, presents; dressing properly (no promise by a debutante that an extravagant dress will be later worn as her wedding dress is to be believed); engaging in as many duty dances as ones for pleasure, being hospitable to all guests, regardless of age; discouraging disruptive behavior in themselves and others; and keeping up the fiction that the parents are giving the party.

In addition, the debutante often has the interesting challenge, as the bride does not, of dividing her favor between two escorts. This is an excellent training for the immediate later life. Miss Manners has even seen advice given on how to wear two flower arrangements at once (no, not one on each bosom, but distributed on wrists, waist, and evening bag) and has herself thought of alternating them as tiny nosegays held in the hand, depending on one's dancing partner.

It is when such complications are most pressing that it is most useful for the debutante to remember that her tea or small dance is but a party, that her parents are the social heads of the family, and that the occasion marks her assumption of the privileges and responsibilities of adult society.

A young lady who can do that ought to be able to dangle two or more gentlemen at the same time, even if, like the bride, she of course has no previous experience.

The Debutante's Dress

DEAR MISS MANNERS:

What can be considered proper attire for a debutante these days? My daughter and I have been fighting over this for weeks. Her argument is—as it is for practically everything she wants to do that I find in poor taste, dangerous, or downright bad—"You don't understand, Mother. Times have changed."

Her father and I are giving her cousin and her a small private dance. We did not force this on them; they wanted it. But as long as we're going to the trouble, and including our friends as well as the young people (another fight—she wanted only her set, overlooking the fact that the entire point of a debut is to introduce a young girl into adult society), we would like to do it properly.

I want her to wear a white dress. She wants to wear something ''sophisticated,'' and has shown me, so far, a red dress with rhinestone straps, a black dress with one long sleeve and nothing for the other arm, a layered dress in shades from lavender to bright purple (hideous), and a disgusting green thing that opened to show the legs in front but trailed behind in a short of draggly train.

My son says she is putting me on and will show up looking decent. My real feeling is that she is using these extreme clothes to get me to ''compromise'' by letting her wear an evening dress that would be suitable for an older person and a different occasion. I will not feel right unless she wears a pretty, young-looking white dress, and I know my friends will think it shocking if she does anything else. My daughter simply does not listen to that argument, saying that she likes to be ''just a little bit shocking,'' and that she believes a woman should dress to contrast with what other women are wearing. (Her cousin is wearing a very nice long white dress.) Have ''changing times'' really affected the debut that much?

GENTLE READER:

Miss Manners has observed two changes in the debut that are pertinent to your situation. One you have already assimilated, and the other fits in with your daughter's clothing philosophy, although not, as it happens, her choice of garments.

The big change is that hardly a debutante alive can say ''Of course I hate all this fuss, but my parents are making me do it'' without having her nose grow long. You are the hostess, and you might point out that the dance need not be held if she doesn't like your plans. (You might as well use this argument now, because it is not advisable when you start fighting over her wedding.)

The idea of some contrast in one's appearance to achieve a mild sensation is not a bad one when practiced subtly. The clothes your daughter favors seem likely to overdo the sensation; heart attacks in elderly friends do not enhance a party. What has changed in modern times is that a debutante demurely attired in an innocent white dress is already considered to be an interesting contrast.

Allow Miss Manners to suggest a compromise. White velvet in winter looks sophisticated, and the more severe the cut, the smarter it appears.

Young Men's Responsibilities

DEAR MISS MANNERS:

What are the responsibilities of a young man on the debutante circuit? If any.

GENTLE READER:

The first is to wipe that smirk off your face. The others are to answer all invitations immediately and correctly, to show up properly dressed when expected, to greet the hosts, even though they are not of the debutante generation, to dance with the debutantes, to avoid characterizing the relative merits of the debutantes within earshot, and to refrain from being sick on the premises.

The School Dance

The junior high school dance is, in Miss Manners' opinion, a boon to the social development of young adolescents. In no other way can they obtain those deep emotional scars that make people so interesting later in life.

The true cruelties of the young people's dance cannot flourish in the setting of the old-fashioned and fashionable dancing class, where a thin veneer of civilization is maintained through the vigilance of presiding adults. In the less formal school dance, the police work of the adults does not usually get into the jurisdiction of social niceties.

Therefore, the conscientious parent must do some advance work on the child for his or her own protection. Too often, modern parents assume that their children are too sophisticated to require such guidance. But even years of pornographic research do nothing to equip an unsuspecting child for the frenzied experience of attending his first school dance.

This preparation may or may not include learning how to dance. This is a frill item. What the children need is a quick course in sexual-emotional history.

Dear child (each must be told), you are about to experience a stirring of feelings toward a member of the opposite sex that is universal and natural. What it is, is a desire to be looked down upon by someone whom you feel is better than you are, coupled with a more generalized desire to look down upon people whom you feel are worse off than you are.

Dear child (you must continue), you cannot avoid these feelings, but you must learn to disguise them in order to avoid jeopardizing your present and future social life and therefore creating for yourself even more agony than is already built into the situation.

At a school dance, this works as follows. Two or three children in the crowd exhibit, either from cleverness or accident, an air of self-confidence not normally linked to their age group. All the girls then fall promptly in love with the boy who has this air, and all of the boys fall in love with the girl who does. Just as automatically, they all decide that they despise all the other members of the loved one's sex.

(Many people go through life falling in love on this law, which by definition guarantees unhappiness, but everyone starts out that way. There is no such thing as a thirteen-year-old whose affections have been aroused by the charm of vulnerability.)

The result is that there will be a great deal of slighting going on at this dance, both blatant and in an offhand fashion, as the children make clear their unwillingness to settle for anyone less than the unobtainable ideal. Boys will be heard loudly explaining why they will not ask certain girls to dance, and girls will make public refusals to certain boys who do make that effort.

Dear child (you must continue the lesson), let me tell you something you will have great difficulty in believing. If you indulge in this behavior, it will come back to haunt you. But if you overcome your natural distaste for those of your own level of popularity—or lack of it—you will reap the reward later.

The reason is that while it is extremely common for the desirability of a person to change radically after his early adolescence—sometimes during it, from one year to the next—everyone goes through life with a vivid memory of insults and kindnesses (if any) experienced at those first dances.

The popular boy or girl for whom you lusted from afar may live to bore you silly, which is an excellent reason against early marriage, but the beautiful creature you slighted when she had pimples or he stuttered will be only too pleased to break your heart for you when it gets big. And that, dear children, is why we must learn to be polite to others.

The Dance

Show Miss Manners a grown-up who has happy memories of teenaged years, with its endless round of merrymaking and dancing the night away, and Miss Manners will show you a person who has either no heart or no memory.

Dances for the young were surely not intended to be lighthearted. That is probably why nature always ensures that the couples who enjoy them most—the most popular girl in the prettiest dress matched with the most popular boy in the best car—always come to reluctant parenthood, poverty, and piggishness of appearance.

Those who hope to lead pleasanter lives must endure the ritual of young social agony. To those who have missed out, for lack of invitations, Miss Manners offers the comfort that they are getting off easily and that confessed unpopularity in childhood is an endearing trait in an adult.

If the dance is to be attended in pairs, the rules for ordinary dating apply: that the gentleman make a specific offer for the occasion, with some advance warning, and that the lady may accept or refuse. The difference between a private date and a public dance is that if she plans to show up at the latter with whoever asks her next, the wording of the refusal had better be ambiguous.

More than in general dating, the custom prevails of having the gentleman call for the lady. He also assumes responsibility for her being pleasantly occupied for the evening, claims at least the first and last dances, and fetches her food and drink or accompanies her to get it.

The return responsibility is that the young lady undertakes to occupy herself for much of the time, even if she is reduced to engaging the chaperones in animated conversation.

Miss Manners misses the dear barbaric days when ladies had dance cards on ribbons at their wrists and could schedule their evenings. If juggling one's admirers didn't tax the strength, then inventing names taxed the imagination.

The request for a dance is correctly worded, "May I have this dance?" Miss Manners would not advise the young gentleman to adopt the alternate wording, "Do you want to dance?" and thus suggest the answer, which Miss Manners hopes would remain unspoken, "Yes, but not with you."

Acceptable answers to such an offer are (1) "Why, yes, how delightful"; (2) "I'm so sorry, I promised this dance already"; and (3) "I'm just too tired to dance now." One cannot hop up on the floor with someone else after offering the third excuse, but there is nothing to prevent one's taking another companion for a bit of refreshing air or punch during that time.

Unless cutting in is against the local custom, the procedure is for a young gentleman to tap another young gentleman on the shoulder and spirit away his partner; the second young gentleman is not allowed to offer to tap the first one on the nose for his trouble.

It is a long-established custom on the part of young ladies to encourage cutting in by delivering a soft look over an alien shoulder to the prospective cutter-inner. Waves of distress, however concealed from the cause of that distress, are not permissible.

You will notice that proper behavior encourages opportunities for disaster by having the participants mix and socialize, rather than stay safely anchored to the secure date, however dreary. Like all social customs, this has a purpose. It makes adult social life seem simple and carefree.

Proms

DEAR MISS MANNERS:

I am senior class president at a local college. Our annual commencement ball, an extremely formal occasion, will be held in a few weeks, and I have a couple of questions. What should I do about inebriated guests who lose control? Is there a proper way to ask them to leave without causing an uproar? Finally, a question about what I anticipate will be our worst problem. Certain groups of students have taken to strange dances which degenerate into overt love acts—right out on the dance floor. How can I politely request that such activities not occur at our commencement ball?

GENTLE READER:

Welcome to polite society, where the attempt to fit the chaos of human behavior into the patterns of civilization has always been a difficult, but noble, cause.

No form of nonviolent social life would ever have been possible without law enforcement. Traditionally, this task was divided between the generations. The only reason that guests at Victorian tea dances didn't copulate drunkenly on the dance floor with anything that moved was that they were afraid of (1) the dragons disguised as dowagers and (2) the young ladies who pretended to be terminally shocked and the young men who pretended to be mortally insulted.

You must recruit modern versions of these people. A few of the tougher faculty members should be invited, and a dance committee of students should be convened to decide what behavior will be considered unacceptable, with their decisions made known beforehand to other guests.

When unacceptable behavior occurs, as it will, the offenders should be approached by these people of authority, possibly in cross-generational pairs, and escorted off the scene with determination but no fuss except that which the offenders themselves may unwisely make to call attention to their disgrace.

Courtship

(for Participants, Their Friends and Relations)

Flirtation

Miss Manners resents hearing the word flirtation, the name of one of life's prettiest occupations, applied to the horrid, clerical antics of those anxious to book their lives in one-night segments. A flirt may be audacious, naughty, tantalizing, heartless, or outrageous, but would never be guilty of behaving like a hotel keeper in a fast-turnover joint.

Flirts are, by contrast, happy people who are simply susceptible to additional delights. They flatter the objects of their attention by treating them like the icing on the cake, and not a fast-food meal to be grabbed and devoured because one is starving.

The flirtation is to the compliment what the motion picture is to the snapshot. It lasts longer and it has more words, but it is basically the same idea.

If someone tells you that you are handsome, you do not reply by asking what they intend to do about it. And so it is with flirtation. There must be nothing in it to which the participants are held accountable.

Deep glances, accidental touching, and uncompromising (but suggestive) talk is the stuff of flirtation. The excitement comes from the fact that although both people know what is happening, neither of them is entirely certain because it is all quite ambiguous.

274

Proper flirtation—and it is a proper pastime, or rather an improper one that proper people can properly practice—is an end, not a means. It is not the beginning of courtship, but a different, milder form of romantic activity for those who do not want, for one reason or another, to be courted. That reason can be as complicated as being attracted by someone who, one suspects, would not improve upon acquaintance; or it can be as simple as the fact that one's spouse is seated elsewhere at the same dinner table. Why should only available people have all the fun?

Actually, judging from the lovelorn section of Miss Manners' mail, available people aren't having any fun at all. They're all full of anxieties about where their next liaisons are coming from, and unable to connect their difficulties with their habit of dumping all their psychological problems on each comer, as an introduction.

The tone should be "Ah, had I but met you earlier—had I but known that someone like you existed," as opposed to "How about giving it a whirl and seeing if it works?" It is the essence of bittersweet, a pleasure for the sophisticated palate.

But how can one do this among literal-minded clods? Alas, Miss Manners regrets that flirtation is no longer possible when flirts open themselves to the insult of being held accountable for their actions. People who spoil such sport ought to be punished by being condemned to spend their evenings discussing inflation.

A Reply

DEAR MISS MANNERS:

Your article on social flirting led to a spirited discussion in our household. Our voices, however, were well modulated at all times. There are several questions, purely theoretical of course, that we would like some clarification on.

First, when is social flirting not social flirting?

Second, assuming that the art of social flirting can be learned, how does one not naturally skilled set about developing this social grace?

Third, does your observation match ours, namely that nonflirts tend to marry flirts? That males are seldom bothered by their spouses' flirting, but females nearly always are?

Fourth, what is the proper and polite stance for the nonflirting spouse in the following totally fictional situations: when there are three present, the two flirts and an extra spouse; when the flirting is between one spouse and a member of the restaurant staff during the entire time of a dinner out; when an audience gathers at a party to listen?

Fifth, what is the gracious and appropriate response in the following situations: when an observer inquires, "Don't you mind that your spouse goes on like that?"; when one of the social flirts, at the conclusion of a spirited bout, turns to the nonparticipating spouse and says, "You don't mind if your spouse and I carry on like this, etc., meet to continue our discussion, go (name place) to (name activity), do you?''

I thank my stars that your column came along when it did. I blush to confess that, after considering sulking all the way home, dropping all my attractive unmarried friends, throwing a private tantrum, attempting to flirt myself, I was on the verge of orchestrating a public scene designed to embarrass everyone within a radius of fifty feet the next time my spouse engaged in social flirting. Thanks to your comments that it is only a pleasant social pastime, I can dismiss it from my mind and get back to the weightier business of how to introduce the archbishop to the chancellor's wife.

GENTLE READER:

You will be happy to hear that you may, with perfect propriety, return to your sulking. Your theoretical husband has violated all the laws of decent social flirting, and Miss Manners is revoking his license.

Proper flirtation may not be used as a means of excluding others. It may not be used to entertain others. And it may not be inflicted on those who are required professionally to be polite to others.

The time when social flirting ceases to be social flirting is when plans are made to meet alone later.

Thus, all the examples in your fourth and fifth questions show abuses of flirtation to flout the laws of propriety. The intentions may be innocent—that relief you may keep—but the manners are atrocious.

When a lady's husband's behavior embarrasses her, she does not throw a fit with a fifty-foot radius, blame it on the recipients of his attentions, or duplicate the offensive behavior. His flirting with the waitress, a gross breach of conduct as the waitress may not feel free to reject his attentions, should not send you scurrying for the busboy.

It is the essence of social flirting that no one—*not even the participants*—should be positive that anything more was intended than simple enjoyment and admiration. If you wish, Miss Manners will explain the details to you some day when she is feeling less indignant. Do not force yourself to learn, however, if this occupation is not suitable to your nature.

❧ AGE-OLD PROBLEMS

Diligently as Miss Manners has been doing her research, she has been unable to discover any true innovations in the relations between the genders during the twentieth century. Sex seems to have been invented quite a few generations ago, contrary to the popular belief that it first occurred on the evening after one's own parents' wedding, but that its full potential was realized only when one came of age oneself. Apparently even primitive people long ago managed to catch on to the general idea and even the standard variations.

Therefore when Miss Manners is asked about the horrendous problems arising from Modern Sex, she has a difficult time concealing a weary little smile. The only modern development she has observed is the custom of self-gossip—that is, of making one's own activities so public as to force people who had been perfectly aware what was happening but essentially uninvolved to take stances of approval or disapproval. In Miss Manners' opinion, this contribution has not made the world go around any faster.

Other so-called inventions turn out to be cases of historical ignorance. Take, for example, the "modern" matter of ladies asking gentlemen for dates. Have you never heard of "I find I have an extra theater ticket for Thursday night"? Yet one is constantly hearing of ladies who are puzzled about how to take the initiative and gentlemen who are bewildered about how to respond. Many ladies are unable to take no for an answer, and many gentlemen unable to give it.

The roles of the pursuer and the pursued are well known in society, and there is no excuse for those who have practiced one side to botch things and plead ignorance when playing the opposite part. Miss Manners has no objection to a lady's initiating a social engagement, provided she does so in the dignified, straightforward way that ladies have always appreciated in gentlemen. This means that one suggests a specific date and activity, and is gracious if it is declined. After three separate refusals, one stops asking. Gentlemen should realize that it is perfectly proper to refuse such an invitation politely if one is not interested, and that elaborate excuses need not be given.

Why is it, then, that a lady who knows what it is to be pestered with unwanted attentions does not know how to shrug and accept fate when her advances do not meet with success? Neither continued pursuit nor bitter behavior is gentlemanly, she should know. A gentleman, who knows what a rebuff is, will sometimes yield to the attentions of someone he doesn't really enjoy simply because he feels put on the spot at having been asked. He should know that it is a lady's prerogative to say no. They should both know that sexual attentions should never be demanded or given out of the disgusting notion that they are a return to the person who pays the entertainment bills.

You see, Miss Manners has nothing at all against modern trivial variations on behavior, provided the traditions are observed.

For Young Lovers and Others

DEAR MISS MANNERS:

I am a sixteen-year-old girl. I like this guy a lot, and I am faced with having to tell him how I feel. I can't come right out and tell him, because I'm really the shy type when it comes to this sort of thing. Also, it seems to me that I talk a lot around him. Before I see him, I always tell myself, "I'm not going to talk too much." But no matter what I tell myself, I always seem to run off at the mouth and act silly. Please give me some advice that I can follow, so I can act more ladylike. I don't want him or anyone else to feel that I am a person who doesn't have any control over myself.

Gentle Reader:

The first thing you must learn to control is that impulse to tell the young gentleman exactly how you feel. This is difficult, but to learn it will be of value to you later in life. One reason is that he already knows. Or at least, he has a pretty good idea. Even a gentleman of sixteen can recognize the cause of such heightened behavior as you describe.

If you can teach yourself to tone down that behavior, it would be a good idea. Your task is to make him less certain, not more, about how deeply you care, until such time as you are led to believe that your feelings are reciprocated. Miss Manners is not telling you this because you are a girl who should be ladylike. She would advise all boys, girls, women, and men to put some ambiguity into their behavior in the early stages of courtship. For reasons she does not pretend to understand, the obvious adoration of someone to whom you have not already been forming your own feeling of love produces distaste, rather than reciprocation.

If you cannot teach yourself to get that clear message of love out of your behavior, a skill that requires great practice, at least do not reinforce it with declarations. Cheerful friendliness, along with the vaguest of looks that suggest one's feelings could grow, is the standard at which to aim.

There is no certainty in love, especially these days. Therefore pressing to find out if someone "really cares" is always a mistake. If you have to ask, you don't want to hear the answer. Nevertheless, Miss Manners sympathizes with the wish of ladies—and gentlemen, too—to be assured that their love will be requited before they give it freely. In fact, she considers that the only sensible and civilized way to behave. Handing over your heart to someone who may, for all you know, scream "Yuck!" and drop it in disgust is not a good idea.

The trouble is that the world could easily come to an end if everyone waited for everyone else to speak first. This is why we have developed other ways of knowing, such as the meaningful glance, the small attention, the reduction of conventional distance between bodies (translation: sitting closer on the sofa than the spacing of the cushions), and so on. If these signals are in working order, the romance should progress evenly, so that the person who first says "I love you" is pretty well assured of getting a me-too. If it is progressing slowly, or not at all, the more interested person can, by holding back his or her pace, at least save the embarrassment of dramatic failure. The only way to increase the other person's pace is to slow one's own to a near standstill. Uncertainty and ambiguity are as exciting in courtship as they are tedious in marriage.

Pushy tactics are self-defeating. The real skill, in courtship, is to be able to play just slightly more slowly than one's partner.

Signing Sentiments

Dear Miss Manners:

I gave a girl friend a picture of myself, framed, and now she wants me to autograph it. I don't know why I suddenly have qualms about this—I've certainly written her frank enough letters—but I somehow don't want to put any statement of love out there where others can see it. Is it too mean just to sign my name? Is there anything I can write that would be less compromising, and still not put her off? What would look good to her but not funny to others?

GENTLE READER:

Sign it "Your" with a squiggle at the end, so that she interprets it as a declaration that you are hers, while the others see it as an abbreviated form of the conventional letter closing. Alternatively, you could write a long statement illegibly and tell her it means whatever you think she would find appropriate.

The Secret of Popularity

DEAR MISS MANNERS:

I am almost fifteen years old, and I would be happy if I had a girl friend. Some of the boys in my class date, but so far, I haven't had any luck. My reason for wanting a girl friend is not only what you probably already think. I am talking about a special girl I could talk to all the time. My parents just manage to tolerate me, sometimes not even that. School is even worse. If I had a girl I could tell all this to, I could get along, and maybe I wouldn't mind so much about the others. So far, I'm a long way from it. I go to the school dances, where there are a lot of girls and not too many boys, but when I ask a girl to dance, they'll make some dumb excuse, or the girls give each other funny looks and laugh instead of talking to me. I can't stand much more of that. I don't think there is anything wrong with me. I just don't know what the secret is of being popular, and it doesn't have to be popular with lots of girls. Just one would do if she's the right one.

GENTLE READER:

Many people who are older but no wiser than you also believe one can attract love by looking badly in need of it. This is a mistaken notion. At best, you may attract someone with a social worker approach to romance who will therefore, immediately after making you happy, want to move on. If looking like a problem in search of a solution is not sexually irresistible, looking like someone with a solution is. The secret to popularity is looking as if you had discovered the secret of a happy life, whether or not you have. You may then, once someone has fallen in love with you, have a sudden relapse into misery and expect her sympathy and help.

The Silent Type

DEAR MISS MANNERS:

My boyfriend is very shy, and we never seem to have anything to talk about. On the phone—he calls me every night before bedtime—the silences are awful. Can you suggest something I could say to him?

GENTLE READER:

"Do you have any nice friends?"

Presents

DEAR MISS MANNERS:

My boyfriend and I are getting ready to celebrate our six-month going steady anniversary. He's giving me a present. The problem is that I don't know whether I am "supposed" to give him one also. My mother says that it is incorrect for me to because, as a girl, I am not obliged. I feel somewhat awkward since he has already let me know that he has a gift for me. I don't want to seem ill-mannered. Please let me know the proper thing to do.

GENTLE READER:

Would you and your mother please stop thinking along the lines of "as a girl, I am not obliged"? There really is no such thing as obligatory present giving. (Please see pp. 521–523.) One goes by one's instincts, and yours obviously are to commemorate this momentous occasion. The general rules about presents between unmarried people is that one gives or accepts only what can suitably be returned during a breakup. (Married couples have the courts to help them decide this.) "Take back your mink" is, for example, impossible to say, and therefore it would be inadvisable to give your boyfriend a mink coat. Books, records, and small leather goods such as wallets and keycases are considered to be the proper type of present to be exchanged by those in temporary arrangements.

Intelligent Talk

DEAR MISS MANNERS:

I am very interested in a young gentleman engineer, but am unable to hold a technical conversation with him. Should I obtain a B.S. degree?

GENTLE READER:

You see all those twenty-year-old marriages that are breaking up all around you? Well, those wives are from an era when women educated themselves to be able to understand and talk intelligently about their husbands' careers. The husbands are now leaving them—or they are leaving the husbands—for someone who gives them a fresh new outlook on life.

❧ NEWER PROBLEMS

Displaying Affection

The birds are singing, the flowers are budding, and it is time for Miss Manners to tell young lovers to stop necking in public.

It's not that Miss Manners is immune to romance. Miss Manners has been known to squeeze a gentleman's arm while being helped over a curb, and, in her wild youth, even to press a dainty slipper against a foot or two under the dinner table. Miss Manners also believes that the sight of people strolling hand in hand or arm in arm or arm in hand dresses up a city considerably more than the more familiar sight of people shaking umbrellas at one another. What Miss Manners objects to is the kind of activity that frightens the horses on the streets, although it is not the horses' sensibilities she is considering. It's the lovers', and their future.

Heavy romances—we are speaking of the kind in which the participants can hardly keep their hands to themselves, not the kind in which they have nothing better to do with them—can progress in only two ways:

They can (1) end. In this case, if you have displayed the height of the romance publicly, the public will take pleasure in seeking you out in the depths. Just when you are being very careful not to move suddenly because you have your heart tied together only with bits of old string, it will spring at you and demand to know, "Where's Rock? I thought you were inseparable?" or "How come I saw Hope out with three other guys last night?"

That is not the worst that can happen, however. Romances can also (2) not end. The participants can get married and live happily ever after. Then they are in trouble. This is because one day they will stop behaving conspicuously. Then everyone will notice. The cause may not be that the romance will have gone out of the marriage, but that it will have a home to go to. With more opportunities to express affection, the couple no longer seizes the opportunity to do so on other people's sofas. The other people will then have a good snicker which, unlike the original snickers, cannot be passed off by the loving couple as jealousy. The Duchess of Windsor once said that she hated to have dinner in a restaurant alone with her husband because if they failed for one minute to chatter sparklingly at each other—taking, say, a moment to chew their food, instead—everyone in the restaurant would be saying, "You see? That's what he gave up a throne for, and now look how bored they are."

"I Love You"

DEAR MISS MANNERS:

My boyfriend and I are having an argument about what the response should be when someone says "I love you." He once replied, "Thank you," and I said that one does not say "Thank you" when someone says "I love you." What can one say in response, besides, "I love you, too"?

GENTLE READER:

There is no doubt that "I love you, too," is the only really acceptable reply to "I love you." Acceptable to the lover, that is.

However, making the other person feel good is not, as Miss Manners keeps telling you, always the object of etiquette. If you do not love the person making the original statement, replying kindly could lead to all sorts of dreadful complications, not the least of which is further and even more unfortunate questions, such as "But do you really love me?" or "More than you've ever loved anyone before?" or "How can I believe you?"

One needs, therefore, to make the lack of reciprocation clear while showing gratitude for the other person's good taste. Your boyfriend's suggestion is not bad, although Miss Manners prefers, "You do me great honor." If, however, his object was merely to give variety to the conversation of happy lovers, "Thank you" is a little stiff, as it is firmly attached, in most people's minds, to "You're welcome," and that has a kind of finality that rounds off the conversation, rather than leading it to "Let's run off to Paris for the weekend."

If he doesn't want to keep saying "I love you, too," let him offer one of the many restatements of this remark in every true lover's icky vocabulary. But Miss Manners has never understood why lovers can't keep saying the same thing over and over. They keep doing the same thing over and over, don't they?

A Simple Question

Dear Miss Manners:

I am a twenty-eight-year-old male and have been seeing a twenty-three-year-old woman for almost one year. We work together and see no one else. My problem is that I am in love with her, but she is unable to verbalize any feelings at all for me. She has never had a relationship last for more than a few weeks and says she has never been in love. All of her friends and relatives like me and she is well liked by everyone I know. Many of her friends often say, "When are you two getting married?" She says she cares for me a great deal; but I feel I could very easily lose her. Every six weeks or so, I become depressed and get the feeling I am being used.

Is there a way for me to get her to express her true feelings? Even if they were negative, I would at least know how she felt and I would then have to deal with that.

Gentle Reader:

Yes, there is, but it is so simple that people lose sight of it while they are busy with such complicated things as feeling used, being unable to verbalize, or getting depressed. Ask her: "Will you marry me?" If she says "Yes," it will mean that she cares for you as more than temporary companionship, and if she says "No," it means that she doesn't.

The Rebound

Dear Miss Manners:

My predicament is not new or unusual. I am hopelessly in love with a woman who is in love with another man. For some time, I thought my case was hopeless; however, this spring, I found out her boyfriend is moving away. At first I thought she would be heartbroken, but instead she has been very casual about the situation. My question is, what would be a proper waiting period before asking her out or demonstrating my interest in developing a closer friendship? Also, when I do get her to accompany me out, should I act only slightly interested and pretend not to be overwhelmed by her charm, or should I let her know how I feel about her?

GENTLE READER:

There is no formal waiting period observed by a lady who is bereaved because her boyfriend has moved away. In fact, there seems to be no such waiting period for any kind of bereavement any longer, although Miss Manners did think it in questionable taste when she heard of a proposal being made to a gentleman whose wife had almost, but not quite, completed the formality of dying. So let us abandon the pretense of talking etiquette, in this case, and talk strategy.

Strategically, it is best to be the next romance but one, when following a romance that has come to grief one way or another. It is an unfortunate fact of life that the generous soul who listens to outpourings of anguish, devises ways to distract the unhappy one, takes the midnight telephone calls, and selflessly suppresses his or her own desires in order to devote full time to nursing the beloved back to emotional health—that person gets thanked and dumped when the recovered patient is ready to fall in love again. This is frightfully ungrateful, of course, but it happens all the time. The nurse is associated with the unpleasant atmosphere of the sickroom. Nevertheless, Miss Manners understands that you, having waited out this gentleman, are not prepared to wait for a second to come along and then go along. Also, she knows that every once in a while someone marries the first candidate on the rebound, rather than the second, and that you would be perfectly furious at Miss Manners if this turned out to be one of those cases.

Her advice, then, is to step in now, but to be as little like a therapist as possible. Do not encourage this lady to talk about her woes, do not allow her to treat you sloppily on the grounds that she is not feeling her best, do not be excessively understanding, at the expense of your own comfort. Be a confident suitor, expecting the lady to behave well toward you, and acting cautiously and casually. Miss Manners is sorry to have to tell anyone to be less kind and unselfish than he would like to be, but surely you have heard about nice guys finishing last.

An Intriguing Manner

DEAR MISS MANNERS:

I have not dated since my fiancée broke off our engagement. After sixteen months of not dating, I am interested in going out again. My problem is that young ladies always want to know why I have not been dating. I do not care to explain my previous misfortune, but I do feel they deserve some answer. What is a polite and correct answer?

GENTLE READER:

You have gotten somewhat rusty, in those sixteen months, if you think that the primary object in dating is to be polite and correct, rather than charming and intriguing. Fortunately, there is a way for you to achieve all of these qualities at once, without violating your commendable reticence.

As you are only too aware, a broken heart is a miserably unpleasant thing, making one feel ugly and unattractive, an enormous disadvantage in courting others. However, the idea of a broken heart is quite a poetic one, tantalizing and challenging the next person to heal it by providing a new romance that will make you cease to bemoan the lost one. This only works if it is kept mysterious. If you blab away about the unhappy love affair, you will succeed in conveying only the reality, rather than the poetry. An answer of the ''None of your beeswax'' variety would neither supply the politeness you require, nor serve the more devious purpose Miss Manners is suggesting to you. One that would accomplish both is something along the lines of, ''There was someone. . . . Forgive me, I just can't talk about it. Perhaps when . . . no, please. Can we not mention this again?''

Breaking Up

DEAR MISS MANNERS:

I am interested in knowing what is the proper method of breaking off a relationship. For the past several months, I have been exclusively dating a young lady whom I was extremely fond of. Everything seemed to be going great until about two months ago, when she suddenly seemed to lose interest in me. Every time I wanted to see her, she was busy, etc., until finally I just stopped calling her. I have not heard from her since. What do you think of breaking off a relationship in this manner, and how should it be handled?

GENTLE READER:

What you describe is your basic Kafka Romance Dissolver, and you handled it exactly correctly. Do not be offended if Miss Manners approves of the young lady's behavior, as well.

Naturally, you were hurt and bewildered when your invitations were repeatedly rejected without explanation. Miss Manners would like to point out to you, however, that there is no possible way for one person to end a romance that the other person thought was going great without causing pain and bewilderment. The chief difference between the Kafka method and those more socially approved ones that come with explanations is that the latter engender humiliation, as well as pain and bewilderment.

What, after all, can the explanation be?

''Sure I like you, but I met someone I'm really crazy about.''

''I know you can't help it, but there are a lot of things about you that were beginning to get on my nerves.''

''It was fun for a while, but lately I've found myself getting bored and restless.''

And so on. Rarely, these days, does anyone break off an exciting, stimulating, fulfilling romance to lead a life of service or to save the family through an expedient alliance.

Therefore, all explanations can be reduced to the fact that the other person would rather do something else—sometimes anything else—than continue the romance. Attempts to obfuscate, such as "I love you, but I need room to grow," don't fool anyone.

The patronizing sweeteners customarily added to these explanations are particularly galling. It is easier to bear being denounced as a villain by someone you still love than to be told that you are a "nice person but."

Perhaps you will object that the method without explanation took some time, because its comparative subtlety confused you about what was actually happening. Granted. Nevertheless, Miss Manners maintains that the period of suffering was, in the end, shorter.

The early part, say the first two rejections, was annoyance, rather than devastation, because you did not yet believe it. Then you began to suspect and pay attention; you guessed; you tested the hypothesis by ending your calls; and then you had your proof. Indeed, that period must have hurt.

Consider what that time would have been like had you been spending it discussing the situation with the young lady. As the explanation method spuriously suggests reasons for the whims of the heart, the reaction of the rejected person is always to offer counterarguments. It would have taken just as long and, as the young lady would be forced to escalate her objections to overcome your arguments, the pain would have been more intense.

The true reward comes now. In your memory, you may set this young lady forever as a fool who didn't know how to appreciate you. You needn't carry around the certain knowledge of how little she appreciated you, nor the memory of your having made a fool of yourself trying to argue the matter with her.

Advice to the Rejectee

Falling is always easier than getting back on one's feet, as any water skier can tell you, and so it is with love. Miss Manners has observed that most people can be trusted to behave reasonably well when they have fallen in love and perfectly dreadfully when they have been dumped.

One might protest that it is unfair for the burden of proper behavior to fall on the person who is down, rather than on the one who did the pushing. But so it is. All a person has to do who wants to walk away from a love affair is to walk away. It is surprising how few rejecting lovers understand this. In this day of explanations, it is fashionable for those who no longer love to offer to talk it all over with those whom they no longer love. No worse cruelty ever disguised itself as a kindness.

In fact, the first duty (and only available pleasure) of the rejected one is to reject such offers of help. One ought to reply, as the Republican Party is said to have done to Mr. Nixon when he offered to help with the 1976 election, "Thank you, but I think you've done enough already." Few rejected lovers can bring themselves to do this, however. They always cherish the notion that if they could only make the other understand how they have been made to feel (rotten), that person would come to his or her senses (realize that the old love is true love, after all).

Unfortunately, it never works that way. Otherwise civilized people first take a grim pleasure in watching romantic sufferings that they have inflicted, and then their satisfaction turns to extreme distaste. Unhappiness that one has oneself caused always looks grotesquely exaggerated and disgusting. Therefore, the smartest thing a dumped one can do is to get out of sight, or at least to hide all traces of misery. This is not easy to do, but it is one of those rare instances in which the hardest work brings the greatest chance of success.

Success, in this case, must be defined as making the other person suffer as much as oneself. Miss Manners is sorry—this is not her usual objective in teaching manners—but it is the only way to restore equilibrium. Whether one should resume the love affair after that is another matter. Such suffering is never caused by see-how-miserable-you-made-me-feel. It is caused, as the rejectee ought to know, by the realization that a person who used to love you doesn't any longer. Thus, the proper behavior for someone whose heart is breaking is to be cheerful, not pained; ungrudgingly forgiving, not accusing; busy, not free to be comforted; mysterious, not willing to talk the situation over; absent, not obviously alone or overdoing attentions to others.

Such behavior will have two rewards. First, it will take the sufferer's mind off suffering and begin the recovery. Second, it will make the former lover worry that this supposed act of cruelty was actually a relief to the person it should have hurt. That hurts.

Increasing the Rate of Romance

DEAR MISS MANNERS:

I have been dating a fellow for a year and one half, during which we only saw each other on weekends, due to the distance involved. During that time, we were both basically happy and he told me he loved me. Recently, during our one and only big argument, I brought up ''commitments'' and felt that our relationship should be more integrated after this period of time. His response was that he cared but that something tells him that he wants something different, which would include more freedom and the possibility of dating other women. He wants to be friends. We are still dating occasionally. I can tell that the feelings are still present, but neither one of us has discussed the outcome of our argument.

What do you do when you still care just as much as ever, but now are only seeing him occasionally, not knowing if in between times he is seeing others? I feel that if I give him an ultimatum and question him, he'll know it bothers me. Do you think the advice in your article about being a cheerful loser would still apply when they tell you they care? I would appreciate any advice that could be given because the situation is driving me crazy and I'm just not sure how to handle it.

GENTLE READER:

Of course the situation is driving you crazy. The slow jilt is bad enough, but it is at least clear that one must not hang around waiting to get the last possible twitch of torture. When there is real hope that a slow courtship, rather than a slow jilt, is what is going on, the response is more difficult.

You are actually doing quite well. Miss Manners knows that it is fear, and not understanding, that keeps you from blurting out, ''Why can't you make a commitment? Don't you love me? If you really loved me, you'd want to,'' and all those tedious remarks. Whatever the motivation, the action required in this situation is no action. A commitment is made when both people want certainty. Pressing an unwilling person to make a commitment is giving that person the certainty without extracting it. It thereby removes his incentive of securing certainty by giving it freely. Miss Manners apologizes if this sounds like the old keep-'em-guessing routine. She is well aware how exhausting, degrading, and debilitating such antics are for the sure and loving heart. That is why God invented marriage: to give people a rest. Miss Manners wishes you the best and only asks that should you live through this courtship to marriage, you appreciate certainty and not start whining about how there is no more magic in your life.

Modern Romance

Dating

All the dear little gentlemen who are now asking Miss Manners for the rules of etiquette for dating claim to have possessed this knowledge once, but to have forgotten it. Miss Manners doubts that.

If you were once taught proper dating behavior, there is no reason that a few decades of marriage and an unpleasantly contested divorce should have knocked it out of your head.

Here, then, are the basics of dating manners for teenaged gentlemen. The ones who happen to be over forty may substitute the word children for parents when studying how to treat the young lady's family.

There are three possible parts to a date, of which at least two must be offered: entertainment, food, and affection. It is customary to begin a series of dates with a great deal of entertainment, a moderate amount of food, and the merest suggestion of affection. As the amount of affection increases, the entertainment can be reduced proportionately. When the affection *is* the entertainment, we no longer call it dating. Under no circumstances can the food be omitted.

A well-planned first date, for example, might consist of theater, a concert, or the movies, followed by a light snack, after which the dating couple lock eyes significantly and then part. In the middle stage, the entertainment may be encompassed into the food part, as in an evening spent at a restaurant or picnicking, and the expression of affection increases. In the last stages of dating, food comes last, but is needed in greater quantities.

But let us return to the earlier stages of dating, when practitioners of the custom display the most uncertainty. This is the point at which conventional patterns should be strictly followed as a safeguard against the premature expression of frank emotion.

To begin with, a specific invitation can, at worst, inspire a specific refusal, while a general invitation may bring on a general refusal. The reply to "Would you like to go to the circus with me a week from Thursday?" may be negative, but it is bound to be more bearable than a negative reply to, "Would you like to go out some time?"

Upon acceptance, the lady is told the details of the evening. She needs to know the hours she will be missing from home, enough information about where she will be to satisfy the other occupants of that home, and what the appropriate dress will be.

Gentlemen still pick ladies up in these early stages, and they still make pointless conversation with the other inhabitants of the house. The purpose of this is to reassure the lady's parents (children, roommates) and to give them some basis for understanding her evaluation of the date afterward. That is why the conversation must be pointless. Pointed conversation, about politics or automobiles, for example, does not reassure them and will be used against you later. If you feel at ease at this time, you are doing something wrong.

The hours of the date are respected at this stage. You pick the lady up when you said you would, and you bring her home when you said you would. You enter the house afterward only on enthusiastic urging, you take care not to disturb the other inmates, and you depart before it has occurred to the lady that it would be advisable.

The younger gentlemen are no doubt wondering now why all this politeness and gradualness is necessary, and why they can't just frankly get on with it. Miss Manners would be greatly obliged, therefore, if the elder gentlemen would explain to them the principle of the prolongation of pleasure.

Social Segregation

Imagine how astonished Miss Manners was to be asked about singles bars. Why, Miss Manners has never even set foot in a sandwich bar, let alone a singles bar, and wouldn't know what to order.

Nevertheless, the question seemed a sensible one: "Now that the segregation of people by age and marital status has made the personal introduction obsolete, how does Miss Manners meet gentlemen of honorable intentions without resorting to such degrading alternatives as single bars?"

To begin with, let us leave Miss Manners herself out of this, and also the intentions of gentlemen of her acquaintance. It was not Miss Manners who raised the problem. However, she does acknowledge that it can be a legitimate one.

She is also forced to acknowledge that it is a social, rather than a romantic, problem. As the question states, society is segregated now by age and marital status. There are two quite distinct classes of people today—not Rich and Poor, but Looking and Not Looking. The overwhelming occupation of the population seems to be looking for a mate, which leaves those who are mated nothing to do but macramé. That is why the latter are so anxious to discuss what is wrong with their relationships: so that they can break up and start all over again.

There must be a solution to all of this, and Miss Manners has it. The singles must stop being so single-minded. Those who are looking must stop looking as if they are looking, so that others will have to look after them. Perhaps that is not clear. Well, in an ordered society, singles as well as doubles are part of a network of social ties and obligations. Single people must then invite happily married former roommates to dinner, visit ailing great-aunts, take the children of friends to the Museum of Natural History, and pay calls on hospitalized relatives. Right now, they tend to skip such attentions on the grounds that there is no payoff.

What they don't know is that they will then give a new interest in life to the recipients of these attentions. The former roommate's spouse will produce, on the return dinner, an about-to-be-divorced friend whose reentry into the market hasn't yet been posted. The great-aunt will scheme to pair her grandniece with her late husband's grandnephew. The children will reciprocate by issuing invitations to dreadful school plays directed by undreadful, unmarried teachers. The patients will gather up strength to ring their bedside bells to summon eligible doctors and nurses.

This is the way society used to function. Did you ever hear of a singles' problem before the singles decided that they would solve their own problems?

The Proper Pickup

DEAR MISS MANNERS:

As a newly single male in my mid-thirties, I am somewhat confused by the proper etiquette, if there is one, in indicating to a woman with whom you are not acquainted, for example in a bank line, that you find her attractive and would like to make her acquaintance, say, over a glass of wine. Do you, Miss Manners, feel ill at ease when approached by a strange male in such situations? Is there a nonboorish way to accomplish this? I would appreciate it if you would respond forthwith and have decided not to go into a bank until I hear from you.

GENTLE READER:

Miss Manners dislikes being approached by strange men in banks, particularly after she has withdrawn money. Even before this transaction, an overture made to a lady waiting in a bank line does seem connected with the expectation of her coming into money soon.

What you are really asking is whether there is a proper way to make a pickup. Certainly. There is a proper way to do everything, and usually several improper ways. Pickups, to seem respectable, must be contrived to seem accidental. No lady wants to meet a stranger whose object is to meet a strange lady, because such gentlemen tend to be rather—well, strange. You must begin by choosing an unlikely place. A bar, for instance, or a beach, is a likely place; an unlikely place is one in which your emotions could be presumed to be engaged in the business in hand. In that respect, the bank is a good choice. Traffic court might be even better.

You begin by attempting to engage the lady in conversation on a relevant topic, on which you may reasonably expect to discover mutual sympathies. If the business ends before the conversation does, you may suggest continuing it nearby, again in the least romantic place possible. After that, what you do will be your own business.

Here, for example, is an attempted bank pickup:

"Oh, no, it's the teller who counts on his fingers. I've had him before. . . . Oh, well. I'm not going to jump lines again. Every time I do that, the guy with the Other Window Please sign spots me and slams it on my fingers just when I get up there and I'm endorsing my check. . . . Did you get a three-cent service charge on your statement last month? No? Well, I did. It's not the three cents I mind; it's the fact that if I change my records, they'll correct it two months from now when I've forgotten, and I'll have some three-cent credit there messing up my books. . . . Really? But how long have you banked here? . . . Well, you see, that's it. You haven't given them a chance yet to mess you up. Don't worry, they will. . . . I suppose I should, but it's like changing lines, you always end up with the same problem. . . . Oh, he is? Isn't that interesting? Well, I sympathize with bankers' problems these days. It isn't easy. I mean it's not just the crime problem, but finding competent people, and then finding people who will stay and want to do a good job. I'd be interested in what a man like your father has to say about that. I have a cousin who wants to go into banking and his mother thinks it's too risky. Do you mind if I ask you a couple of questions? Look, let's not get in people's way here. There's a coffee shop down the block. It wouldn't take a minute. . . . That's very nice of you. . . . I'll just wait here while you get your money."

Matchmaking

DEAR MISS MANNERS:

Recently I arranged a blind date between two very dear friends. Believe me, I had only the highest intentions for their happiness. However, believing, as you do, in the delicacy of one's sexual feelings, cravings, and demands, I had no idea that such a match was unlikely. One of the parties, though, is now revealed to be homosexual. How should I advise the other friend?

GENTLE READER:

Why would you want to give up just when it's getting so interesting? Rest assured that a matchmaker is not supposed to have pretested the product, and therefore has no responsibility for its performance.

Coming Out

DEAR MISS MANNERS:

How ought a well-bred person to respond when an acquaintance "comes out" (in the contemporary sense of making public one's sexual tastes)? I once received such a revelation in a Christmas card, and for months I was at a loss as to what to write back. I felt obliged to make an intimate revelation in return. What should I have done?

GENTLE READER:

Whenever anyone makes a sexual revelation of any nature to Miss Manners, she always replies, "How nice for you." Miss Manners sometimes gets into trouble that way, when she hasn't paid close attention to the particulars of the revelations. However, it is not as much trouble as one can get into playing "Can You Top This?"

A Social Disease

DEAR MISS MANNERS:

I do not consider myself to be a promiscuous person, but recently, much to my dismay, I learned that I have contracted a social disease. The man from whom I received this dubious honor was a passive carrier, so he was unaware of his condition. Since he is not from the area, I called him to inform him of the problem. Is it wrong of me to expect some kind gesture from him? Maybe some get well flowers or even a note? I'm not sure how modern etiquette would deal with this situation, so I'll be eagerly awaiting your response.

GENTLE READER:

Modern etiquette does not have a specific rule to cover the social situation you mention, but it is Miss Manners' experience that traditional etiquette has a rule for everything. The one that applies here is that a note or flowers or both would be a charming way to apologize for having inadvertently caused another person discomfort.

Nomenclature

DEAR MISS MANNERS:

What can you do after accidentally calling your present lover by your former lover's name?

GENTLE READER:

Seek a future lover. Such a mistake is easy to do and impossible to undo. Why do you think the term "darling" was invented?

Propriety

DEAR MISS MANNERS:

I'm sure you're aware of the confusion of "male-female" roles in courtship these days. I, for one, am particularly confused. You see, I was rather a, uh. sexually free young lady, starting at fourteen.

The problem is that I don't know the "proper" way to act on a date because I have never before attempted to be "proper." What does one say? Can one get personal? Do you kiss and hug on the first date? How soon is it OK to ask a man over for dinner? Obviously, I don't know the etiquette and I am so tired of those shallow, quickly ended relationships. Actually, I'm a bit frightened of men—will this one and the next reject me, too? I have been told that I "try too hard" and "fall too fast," so I'm trying to restrain myself.

GENTLE READER:

Welcome to the world of propriety. We have more fun here than you may have been led to believe, just as the world of promiscuity, as you have discovered, offers less fun than you may have been led to believe. Like fast food, it tends to be of poor quality and may leave you with worse problems than the hunger it was intended to quell. So stop gobbling and learn to prepare something decent. It takes time and effort, but the preparation can be fun in itself and the results will be better.

No getting personal. No hugging and kissing. No come-over-to-my-place. Your feelings of fright are the correct ones, not your ones of c'mere, honey. In the proper world, romance is supposed to develop out of friendship. A gentleman and a lady both pretend that they are cultivating each other for common interests, shared humor, or whatever—and then they both act surprised when passion strikes them like lightning. This shock is considered exciting by proper ladies and gentlemen, who regard instant matings, based on the idea that we all have standard parts that may be fitted together interchangeably, to be dull as well as distasteful. You will find that rejection by a friend who does not become a lover is less painful than rejection by a lover who does not want to go on to become a friend.

Now, are you willing to try? Can you act friendly to a man while being reserved enough to discourage either emotional or physical intimacies? Can you treat him as a pleasant enhancement to your life, and not the answer to your prayers? Miss Manners doesn't want to upset you by too quick a transition. But can you hold out until the second date?

Juggling Gentlemen

DEAR MISS MANNERS:

I am single and have male guests in my home quite often. What I need to know is if it is proper to answer the phone farthest away from my guest in case it may be another man, or is it rude? I would also like to know what to do when an uninvited man comes to the door while another is in the house. It seldom happens, but would I go outside the door and partially close it behind me, or simply tell the intruder just what I thought of his unscheduled call in full view of my guest and shut the door?

GENTLE READER:

One does not desert an invited guest to entertain an uninvited one, by telephone or in person, regardless of gender. A telephoner should be told that you will return the call later. A caller, unless he would enhance the visit of the original guest, may be told politely that he has called at an inconvenient time. Ladies who are conducting simultaneous romances with several gentlemen cannot be too careful about such niceties.

Providing for an Unexpected Guest

DEAR MISS MANNERS:

What should a lady keep on hand for the comfort and convenience of a gentleman guest who may be spending the night unexpectedly? An extra toothbrush? Shaving equipment? Perhaps a comfortable bathrobe? Slippers? Should I keep them in different sizes (small, medium, and large)? I'm only interested in being a gracious hostess.

GENTLE READER:

Yes, Miss Manners can see that. But what are you running there? Or rather, as Miss Manners deals in manners, not morals, what do you want to appear to be running? Suppose you were overcome with passion while visiting and were then offered a wide choice of sizes and styles in nightgowns?

Even the most gracious hostesses, and that is what you say you aspire to be, offer their house guests nothing more than a fresh toothbrush, towel, soap, and perhaps a good book to read if they get bored at bedtime. If you think your gentleman guest might be embarrassed to leave your house unshaven in the morning, you might keep a fresh throwaway razor designed for women on hand, and tell him it was a spare one of your own.

The One-Night Stand

DEAR MISS MANNERS:

I am almost embarrassed to ask this question. I expect you won't like it. It's just that a friend called me up yesterday to complain about it, and it's fresh on my mind.

Occasionally, when one is an adult single person in the big city, one has a, ʼah, liaison with a member of the opposite sex whom one does not know very well. It's customary in such things to exchange telephone numbers afterward, and it is here that the problem arises. My friend and I agree that it is the proper, well-brought-up thing to do to call the other person afterward, merely to query idly after their well-being and tie things up, as it were. A postcard would serve the same purpose. However, she has recently had a series of brief relationships where the gentlemen in question never called again, and in at least one case, never returned her call after she left a message.

Is my friend being totally unrealistic to expect these men to call her? Are they being boorish cads to give her a peck on the cheek in the morning and never show their faces (or voices) again? If one has a pleasant and enjoyable time at dinner, or some similar social function, a telephone call thanking the hostess is taken for granted. Why do so many people ignore it when the hospitality extends overnight? Or is this merely an antiquated convention, another way of expecting unrealistic behavior from innocent acquaintances? I am not asking for pronouncements on the morality of such interpersonal engagements, since I'm afraid they must be taken for granted in modern life, but rather for your opinion of proper conduct afterward.

GENTLE READER:

The social event to which you refer is, Miss Manners believes, known as a one-night stand. It is by no means a recent invention, but it is a comparatively short time since it was taken up by people, such as your friend, who wish to put into it the nuances of social niceties. There are therefore no widely recognized etiquette rules in connection with it. Another problem is that it is, by definition, practiced with people whom one hardly knows, and whose standards of behavior may surprise one unpleasantly. Please do not take it as a moral pronouncement if Miss Manners advises some preliminary acquaintanceship before one has the right to assume that a person will behave as one would expect. You would not invite a man to dinner if you had not observed that he had mastered the rudiments of polite behavior.

Miss Manners is afraid that you do not understand the meaning of the ritual you claim to have practiced. The night stand, whether it is of the one- two- or three-variety, does not, by its very nature, require social continuity. You are confusing it with an entirely different social tradition called courtship. Miss Manners cannot find your young men remiss, provided that they met the basic requirements of the night-stand act.

On Hope

DEAR MISS MANNERS:

I have been enlightened by your august self as to the fact that one-night stands are not to be confused with courtship. I now know what to expect from a one-night stand, but the identifying characteristics of the latter still elude me. Does anyone still fall in love? If they postpone thinking about sex for two weeks or more, should one begin to worry about their psychic or hormonal tendencies?

GENTLE READER:

The stages of courtship were best described by dear Marie-Henri Beyle, who had an interesting career as a writer under the name of Stendhal, but whose primary occupation was falling in love. The succession of admiration, fantasy, hope, doubt, and what he calls crystallization—in which a plain human being appears dazzling through the eyes of a lover, as a plain twig does when covered with crystals in the salt mines of Salzburg—as described in his little book, ''On Love.''

Neither Mr. Beyle nor Miss Manners pretends that tremendous periods of reflection are needed to run through these stages. On the contrary: Nothing is as inimical to passion as the slow, sensible weighing of practicalities. But the rapid calculation of practicalities is not inducive to falling in love, either. The expediency of thinking ''Well, why not? This will suit the needs of us both, and we needn't make an undue fuss about it'' is equally chilling to romance whether it concerns an early-nineteenth-century arranged marriage in France or a late-twentieth-century one-night stand in America.

The customs of courtship vary in time, place, and class. But they are always based on the desire to secure the affections of a person one believes to be too perfect to be reasonably attainable, not a person whose most conspicuous characteristic is convenience.

Living Together

It has come to Miss Manners' attention that not all ladies and gentlemen who live together in pairs are husband and wife, or even brother and sister. While Miss Manners would never dream of inquiring into anyone's living arrangements, she is always pleased to hear of increased sociability in the world.

However, it seems that these people have a problem. They don't know what to call each other. The terms "husband" and "wife" are not accurate; nor are "fiancé" and "fiancée," which lead to questions these people do not wish to entertain. "The person I live with" is not only unwieldy, but it ends in a proposition, where these arrangements tend to start.

Miss Manners has long endeavored to avoid this problem by inquiring querulously why people need to declare their sexual affiliations at all. Why can't they simply introduce one another by their names?

For further identification, why can't they use the traditional system, which recognized three categories of relationships: marriage, engagement, and just-good-friends? There is nothing new about sex, many of our ancestors having practiced it, and the last category has long served those who followed their emotions rather than the law.

Miss Manners prefers such a general catch-all, simultaneously respectable and intelligible to all, to such infinite subdivisions of romance as were identified by the young of the 1950s, who had such rigid social and anatomical definitions as "going in the same crowd," "dating," "going together," "going steadily," "going steady," "being pinned," and "being engaged to become engaged," for their premarital activities.

However, she has finally conceded that a term is needed for couples who reject legal sanction for their union but demand social sanction. She asks for your help, Gentle Readers. (She also asks that you not bore her with explaining the comparative quality of marital and nonmarital relationships, especially when using the term "honesty" or asking the nonsensical question of what difference a piece of paper makes. Miss Manners has a safe-deposit box full of papers that make a difference.)

She must set down certain rules for this search. The word must be simple, sensible and dignified, appropriate for public, daytime usage. It must not describe graphically the private purpose of the liaison, which is none of society's business. But it should not be so conventional as to be easily confused with other existing relationships, thus casting an implication of sexuality onto them.

Allow Miss Manners to illustrate these principles by explaining her objections to the terms that she has heard proposed.

"Paramour," "lover," "the person I share my life with," "significant other," "meaningful associate": These are too vivid. If you imagine a long-married person introducing his or her spouse to you as "my lover," you will understand, as your gorge rises, Miss Manners' distaste. Such terms are also bound to be at least occasionally inaccurate during the normal ups and downs of life. Miss Manners once heard the term "my fondest friend" proposed to a lady in need of a term for the gentleman with whom she lived, and the lady replied, "But actually, I can think of people I'm fonder of."

"Mistress": This suggests some financial arrangement favoring the lady, and what, pray, is the corresponding term for the gentleman involved?

"Roommate," "housemate," "live-in friend": These are infringements on the meaning of a different relationship. A roommate is a person who tells one's parents that one is asleep when one is actually keeping scandalous hours, and who leaves hairs in the sink.

"Companion," "partner": Similarly, these carry confusing connotations. A companion is an impoverished but genteel person who has taken a situation traveling with someone elderly, rich, and cranky in the hope of increasing that person's friction with his or her legitimate heirs and thus figuring prominently in the will. Miss Manners used to favor the term partner, on the grounds that it represented "marriage partner" without the marriage, but has become convinced that it is the proper property of cigar-smoking gentlemen who suspect each other of cheating on the books, and of those who come from a part of the country where they pronounce "How do you do?" as "Howdy."

"Consort," "co-vivant," "comrade": Each of these conjures an irrelevant image in Miss Manners' mind. Consort suggests Prince Philip permanently assigned to walking three paces behind his wife. Co-vivant sounds like someone who will cook only with expensive copper pots. Comrade, etymologically impeccable, as one Gentle Reader pointed out, because it derives from the Latin *camera* for "chamber," has come to be associated with people who think it their patriotic duty to report you to the authorities.

"Comate": This is etymologically disastrous. One meaning is that of companion, but another, if you will take the trouble to look it up, as Miss Manners did, is hairy.

"POSSLQ": This term, the acronym for Persons of Opposite Sex Sharing Living Quarters, invented by the Census Bureau, is a possible winner. People do have an antipathy to newly invented words, however—there are still many who object to the practical "Ms."—and this is not an easy one to spell. Miss Manners is therefore reserving judgment.

"Uhmmer": Another possible winner, this has a natural origin, from popular usage, as in "This is my daughter's uhm . . . uhm . . . uhm."

In her heart, Miss Manners believes that a more nearly perfect term exists, and she is waiting for a kind and Gentle Reader to send it to her.

The Bonds of Friendship

DEAR MISS MANNERS:

I am separated from my husband, and my gentleman friend has, so far, escaped the bonds of matrimony. Our problem is that we do not know how to refer to one another on those rare occasions when first names of the standard terms of endearment just won't do. Am I his mistress (he insists I am, but I thought that referred to the female friend of a married man; besides, it sounds too tacky for my taste). Is he my lover? Personally, I am quite satisfied with "friend," on the premise that the rest of it is nobody's business but our own, but in the interest of domestic tranquillity, I promised him I'd check.

GENTLE READER:

There are several accurate ways in which you and your gentleman friend could explain your relationship to casual acquaintances. "Pamela is Buster McClintock's wife, but she showed up at my place once at two AM and has been there ever since," or "Eldred and I have been together for three years now, but so far he has escaped the bonds of matrimony." Miss Manners does not see how either of these explanations would add to your domestic tranquillity, although they certainly would liven up the lives of others. The beauty of the term "friend" is that it is ambiguous.

Ceremony and "Congruence"

DEAR MISS MANNERS:

I received a troublesome invitation last week, and I need your advice. Two former college friends sent a silk-screened card inviting me to "partake in a ritual celebrating the congruence of their lives." Knowing the couple makes me doubt very much that this is a wedding, yet I think it is something more than the exchange of friendship rings. Just what are my social duties in this case?

Do I congratulate them, and if so, on what? What sort of gift does one send for a congruence, and how should one dress for the occasion?

GENTLE READER:

Miss Manners had hoped that the plague of social originality among lovers had been stamped out, but here it is flaring up again. If it were Miss Manners who had been invited, she would go in a chiffon pastel dress and garden hat and send them a silver chafing dish. The other dignified approach is to play tourist and write, "I am afraid that I am not familiar with the customs of your faith. Would you be kind enough to explain to me exactly what you are doing?"

Extended Nonfamily

DEAR MISS MANNERS:

How do you like this one: my daughter is twenty-six, and lives with a divorced man exactly my age and his twenty-two-year-old daughter who has an adorable eight-month-old baby girl. At this stage in my life, I can't think of anything I want more than a grandchild—I baby-sit this "semi-step-great-grandaughter" (or whatever she is besides being simply darling), but this isn't exactly what I've had in mind. And talk about making introductions when my daughter and I are out to lunch or shopping with the baby—whew! It's one of the few times I'm almost rendered speechless. Any suggestions?

GENTLE READER:

Whew! is right. If you attempt to explain this relationship to people you meet while out lunching or shopping, the baby will probably grow up and move away before you finish talking. Miss Manners suggests you curtail the introduction to merely, "And this is Baby Snooks," or whatever. People will naturally assume that you have kidnapped this child for complex psychological reasons or hope of financial gain, or that she has selected you for her nursery Adopt-a-Grandparent work project. But so what? She will grow up learning that you can't explain everything to everyone, which is a valuable lesson in life.

Pieces of Paper

DEAR MISS MANNERS:

It will soon be exactly a year since my lover and I moved in together. Neither she nor I ever has any intention of getting married, which we consider unnecessary for many reasons, but we will probably be together a long time, maybe even permanently. I would like to surprise her by celebrating our first anniversary. What would be appropriate to get her? I looked up wedding anniversary suggestions and found that the first is considered the "paper anniversary." Would this apply to our situation?

GENTLE READER:

No, no, no. That is for married people only! Don't even think of it! *Stop that.* (Wait. Miss Manners is sorry she got hysterical. You know how tolerant Miss

Manners usually is about young love, or old love, for that matter. It's just that you unmarried people have bored her to death talking all the time about how you "don't need a piece of paper to love each other," so don't expect her to let you have any paper now. Besides, there ought to be some thrills attached to marriage only.)

Correcting Mistaken Assumptions

DEAR MISS MANNERS:

How does one handle possibly disapproving visitors to a nonmarital household? Such visitors as poll takers, charity collectors, and friendly neighbors, etc., may initiate a conversation; and, in the course of the talking they begin to refer to the household sharer as "your husband" or "your wife."

Such a reference puts the sharer in an awkward position. Should a reply like "Mr. Jones and I are not married" be given? Is it polite to include any further explanation, like "We've known each other for eleven months" or "We are waiting for his divorce to become final" or "We live together but we don't share the same bed"?

GENTLE READER:

The greatest benefit of civilized society is that respect for others also relieves people of the responsibility for the habits, morals, or errors of others. Thus, a poll taker, friendly-or-otherwise neighbor, or Girl Scout cookie vendor has no occasion to approve or disapprove of your living arrangements. Similarly, you have no responsibility for that person's assumptions about you. The explanation that you and Mr. Jones are not married because you are already a bigamist, your grandchildren disapprove, or you don't know each other well enough is superfluous. Explaining your bedding habits to whoever rings the doorbell is gratuitous, to say the least. If you should encounter this person later and he says, "But I thought you and Mr. Jones were married," you may then say, "I am afraid you were mistaken," or, if you prefer, "You thought wrong, buddy."

Delicacy

DEAR MISS MANNERS:

My boyfriend will be moving into my apartment as soon as his lease is up. We will be sharing everything, and I want to do what is proper. I have been accustomed, when living alone, to hanging up my things that I wash out every night on the shower curtain. I don't know if it's right, though, to have my lingerie all over what will, after all, be his bathroom, too. Not that he hasn't seen it before, but my mother says it isn't right. I said I'd ask Miss Manners.

GENTLE READER:

Miss Manners says you should ask your gentleman friend. Miss Manners never interferes with intimate actions performed in private by consenting adults.

Sharing a Guest Room

DEAR MISS MANNERS:

When my son and his girl friend come home to visit, they expect to share his bedroom. I know they are living together at college, but I don't feel right about it in my house. My son says I'm being Victorian.

GENTLE READER:

No, you're not. The Victorian solution, employed with great success at English house parties, was to put illicit couples in separate rooms, but to ignore nocturnal traffic in the hallway.

Marriage

(for Beginners)

Engagements

The engagement, that sweet time before an emotional commitment is turned into a legal commitment, is, of course, a trial period. The reason it is such a trial is that a couple who can get through an engagement, with all its etiquette land mines, ought to find marriage a cinch. The failure of so many young marriages, however, leads Miss Manners to suspect that these people are not enduring sufficiently rigorous engagements and are doing their fighting after marriage, when it can take a nastier turn.

The popular belief that sex and money are the two subjects that couples split over is erroneous. People who love each other don't break up over such trifles. They must learn to handle the explosive subject of conflicting etiquette. For example, a situation where one marriage partner is feeling playfully amorous and the other is taking the bar examination in the morning is an etiquette problem of dangerous proportions.

Here, then, is a checklist of etiquette fights an engaged couple should have, so as to be ready and tired enough for a peaceful marriage. Miss Manners is presuming that the couple is well suited and in love, and that fortune and their families are smiling upon them.

Six Months Before

· Fight over whether wedding is to be formal or informal.
· Fight over what is meant by "formal" and "informal."
· Fight over size of wedding.
· Fight over whether seventy-five people can be considered a small wedding.
· Fight over whether silver and china fit into your way of life.
· Fight over whether silver and china are a better investment than stereophonic equipment.

Three Months Before

· Fight over whether anybody can really tell the difference between engraving and raised print.
· Fight over whether relatives who had bitter divorces should be invited, as well as their former spouses.
· Fight over whether wearing a white wedding dress will be worth enduring the sneers of people who believe these must be accessorized by intact hymens.
· Fight over whether the mother of the bridegroom should be forced to wear a type of dress she dislikes in order to be visually paired with the mother of the bride, who finds that style flattering.

Two Months Before

· Fight over the discovery that bridegroom's family has not only exceeded its quota of guests, but has provided a list using initials instead of names and terms such as "and family" for children.
· Fight over whether guests' requests to bring their current love interests should be honored and who is going to tell people that their small children will not be welcome.
· Fight over slurs made toward relatives who sent cheap or tasteless presents.

One Month Before

· Fight over whether it is the bride or the bride's mother who is at fault because elderly friends are beginning to complain that their presents have not yet been acknowledged.
· Fight over whether the seating arrangements should be done according to tradition or according to who is speaking to whom.

One Week Before

· Fight over the failure of some guests from each side to answer invitations and about who is going to prod whom so as to provide accurate numbers to the caterer.

• Fight over how much luggage is to be taken on the wedding trip.
• Fight over the wisdom of marrying a person now discovered to be short-tempered, stylistically alien to one's own tradition, and completely absorbed in petty details to the exclusion of any intellectual or romantic activity.

At the Wedding

• Fight over whether the ceremonial kiss should demonstrate enthusiasm for the marriage or protect the bridal makeup.
• Fight over whether it is each other, the wedding guests, or the photographer who deserves the bridal couple's chief attention during the reception.

This is only a minimum list, and every young couple should feel free to make additions that express their personal relationship. For example, there are people to whom a wedding reception means dainty tea sandwiches and champagne only, and others for whom no wedding is recognized by God unless everybody present is groaning audibly and able, through the bounty of the hosts, to go home sick. If the mothers' dresses fight appeals to you, you may expand it by attempting to force all grandmothers to match, which could stir up a great deal of irascible excitement.

The important thing to remember is that no one rule of etiquette is as essential as the general atmosphere of conflicting standards. People who have conscientiously fought out all such matters during the engagement will find themselves only too grateful to be living happily ever after.

The Proposal

DEAR MISS MANNERS:
I am totally in love with a beautiful woman whom I would love to marry. The only thing is, she does not really like the idea of marriage, although she says she loves me. Could you suggest a secluded, romantic place for The Question? How might I persuade her?

Also—her parents are fantastic people but they complain that I never talk when visiting. I'm fairly well educated, but when they discuss matters such as old friends, and places they have been, I have very little to offer because the subject matter is something I know nothing about.

GENTLE READER:
A gentleman of Miss Manners' acquaintance recently expressed to her his alarm that a return of romantic manners would put him out of business. He said he has been getting marvelous responses by such simple courtesies as bringing ladies flowers or sending them candy, because gentlemen rarely do these things anymore. If these techniques again became commonplace, he feared, he might have to bestir himself to think of something better, and probably more expensive, in order to keep his lead.

However, we have not yet reached this point, and an old-fashioned, little-used convention might still work for you. Are you ready?

1. Arrange the lady on a sofa.

2. Kneel in front of her. (That should put her into shock. If she is still able to talk and says something like, "What do you think you're doing?" simply smile mysteriously.)

3. Pull out of your pocket a small velvet box with an engagement ring inside. That should put her back into shock, giving you the opportunity to perform the next step, while you are still holding the box.

4. Say, "I can't live without you. Will you marry me?" Got that? Not "I think we might make a go of it," or "My mother says she's tired of telling her friends that you're my 'fiancée' after ten years and wants to know when we're going to get married," or "I've talked to my tax consultant, and I think we can get married without getting hit too badly."

5. Open the box, take her hand, and put the ring on her finger.

6. Congratulations. You are now engaged.

Miss Manners does not guarantee this. The lady may actually not want to marry you. But by this method, it may take her a while to recover and remember that.

In any case, it should solve your conversation problems with her parents. If she accepts, they can now be asked about their friends in terms of how these people can be identified at the wedding or what they are likely to give you for a wedding present, and places they know can be discussed in terms of appropriate-ness for a wedding trip. If you are refused, you will have the consolation of not having to make conversation with the parents any longer.

Choosing the Ring

Dear Miss Manners:

The girl I plan to marry and I both love old Hollywood musical comedies and romance movies, and I would like to surprise her by "popping the question" on my knees and pulling a boxed engagement ring out of my pocket. I know it's corny, but I think she'll love it. My sister says she doesn't think girls really like that kind of thing and ought to be allowed to select the ring themselves. But to tell you the truth, I can't spend too much on the ring, and the idea of letting her loose in a jewelry store to buy whatever she likes scares me. Is the surprise a good idea, or isn't it?

Gentle Reader:

The surprise is lovely, provided it is she who is surprised by the question and not you who are surprised by the answer. There are two things you should know in order to prevent your being surprised: whether the jeweler will take the ring back, and whether the intended intends to take you.

The Ring

DEAR MISS MANNERS:

Is it necessary to buy my fiancée an engagement ring?

GENTLE READER:

No. Nowadays, it isn't even necessary to marry her. We do everything by the dictates of the heart these days, which accounts for the astounding divorce rate.

On (Or Off) the Engagement Ring

DEAR MISS MANNERS:

Is it true that once you put on an engagement ring, you should never take it off? I take mine off every day before I wash dishes or bathe, and put it on in the mornings to wear during the day until I come home.

GENTLE READER:

Miss Manners just loves symbolism, especially diamond symbolism, but still, a sensible person must make a distinction between the symbol and the thing symbolized. Removing your engagement ring on the occasions you mention should not cause a rupture in the engagement or marriage unless the donor of the ring is repeatedly asked to fish it out of the plumbing into which it has been carefully swept upon leaving the finger. Other occasions on which you may wish to remove the ring are when breaking the engagement or when visiting the pawnshop.

The Bridegroom's Ring

DEAR MISS MANNERS:

I hate the feeling of wearing a ring and never wore the class ring I was pressured into buying. Now my fiancée wants me to wear a wedding ring. I know it will drive me crazy if I do. I could accept it, of course, and then not wear it, but I'm afraid that would be a worse hassle eventually than the one we're having now. Her argument is, how are other women going to know I'm married if I don't wear a ring?

GENTLE READER:

You might shout out the information while fighting desperately to save yourself from their determined advances, if this, as her argument suggests, is a major problem in your life. Surely, you concede that she need not wear a ring, either, to be married. However, if you two can't find something more important than this to fight over now, perhaps you should not be getting married.

The Future Bridegroom's Parents

DEAR MISS MANNERS:

When a young man asks a woman to marry him, what should his parents do? Should they call the future bride up and perhaps take the couple out to dinner to celebrate their engagement?

GENTLE READER:

What the bridegroom's parents have to do is comparatively easy; it is what they have to refrain from doing that is difficult. It is their duty to initiate the relationship between themselves and the bride and her parents. This is better done by inviting the bride and her parents to dinner in their home rather than taking them out, as they will be madly curious to see how the bridegroom has been brought up.

DEAR MISS MANNERS:

Our son is planning to marry a girl from another city, a distance of four hundred miles. What are our responsibilities? We have met his fiancée, but not her parents. Do we (a) call them and invite them to visit us? (b) call first and then visit them? (c) wait for them to call us? Any visits must be overnight stays because of the distance. However, we have three other children at home and cannot offer house guests a private bath and other conveniences conducive to privacy. If they come to visit, would it be proper to accommodate them in a nearby hotel? If yes, should we pay the bill? Also, if we visit them, should we expect to stay with them or arrange our own accommodations?

GENTLE READER:

If you choose (c), you may wait forever. Society has changed since the rule about the parents of engaged couples was invented, and no one has bothered to revise it to meet such outrageous situations as engagements between couples whose parents live four hundred miles apart. This has resulted in a great deal of confusion and hurt feelings that are better saved for the wedding.

Miss Manners will now come to the rescue. Here is the old rule: The young man's parents call on the young woman's parents. ("Calling" referred to the now defunct custom of arriving at their doorstep for a short surprise visit that would not inconvenience them because everybody was always calling on everyone else all the time, and therefore it was no surprise at all.)

Here is the new rule: The young man's parents initiate the relationship by telephoning or writing the young woman's parents and expressing their desire of becoming acquainted. The details of the two meetings are then worked out with the help of two people who are in a position to know what would be most convenient for each household—the young couple. All you have to do, then, is to call or write the other parents and say, "we're so pleased. Daffodil is such a lovely girl. We're anxious to meet you, and would love to have the pleasure of entertaining you here." Assuming that Daffodil has warned them about your limited bathroom facilities, they can accept or counterinvite you to their hometown. In either case, saying "I'm afraid we don't have room to make you comfortable, so I've made a hotel reservation for you nearby" is proper. Paying the hotel bill of your guests is charming if you can easily afford it but if not, don't worry about it.

Clashing Manners

DEAR MISS MANNERS:

I am engaged to be married, but there are moments I think it will never work out—usually when I am with my fiancé's family. I have been brought up to expect certain things from people and it seems at times they have no manners at all. They think I am picky and stuck-up, with no warmth at all. Help!

GENTLE READER:

Ah, so you are planning to be married. Please allow Miss Manners to wish you happiness by attempting to deflect you from the misery you are wishing on yourself.

Marriage, my dear, is the formation of a family from two existing families. The two are likely to have different standards of behavior, which can cause friction. When it is said that marriages are easier between people who come from "similar backgrounds," that is not a euphemism for money, religion, or race, but an accurate warning about clashing manners. Generally, one family has stricter standards than the other. The stricter side refers to the looser as having "no manners at all," and the looser to the stricter as being "picky" or "stuck-up" or having "no warmth at all."

That there exist many different standards is not, in your case, the point. The point is how to create a harmonious marriage out of disparate elements.

You cannot ask your fiancé's family to conform to your standards, or your family to his. He is your best guide to explaining his family's motivations and what they expect from you—you should be listening to him on this, and you are not—as you are about yours. What you can expect of him is to reach an agreement with you about standards for the new family—you, him, and your future children. Do not be shy about establishing compatibility in manners as a prerequisite of marriage. Many foolish young people think that if they can establish physical compatibility, the manners will follow easily, whereas it is more likely to work the other way around.

Preplanned Nonparenthood

DEAR MISS MANNERS:

At a beautiful engagement party which we gave for our daughter and her fiancé, they went around telling all our friends that they never plan to have children. We were horrified. It isn't that we don't understand that they are young (twenty-two and twenty-three) and maybe shouldn't have children for

quite a while; and it isn't that we're anxious for them to provide us with grandchildren. We just think their statement was in poor taste. If they do have children, those children are going to think they were unwanted. Also, what must our friends at the party have thought of such a declaration?
GENTLE READER:

It is never charming to announce your reproductive plans socially, but Miss Manners does not think that your friends will remember the statement with anything except amusement should the couple later change their minds. Didn't your daughter announce to you, a decade or two ago, that she was never going to get married because boys were so icky?

Engagement Presents

DEAR MISS MANNERS:

Is it correct to give a present to my friend for an engagement announcement party? I know that some of her friends will be having showers for her later, and then there will be the wedding present. It will be too expensive for me to do it all. What do you suggest?
GENTLE READER:

Your question is not so much whether engagement presents are correct—presents are nearly always correct, with or without occasions—but whether they are obligatory or even customary. The answer is no. Engagements are rarely long enough nowadays to permit of two shopping expeditions. Therefore, Miss Manners suggests you concentrate your thoughts and money on the wedding present, which you may send any time during the engagement.

DEAR MISS MANNERS:

Our daughter has recently become engaged, and the young man's parents have given them a set of table linens as an engagement present. Is it necessary for us to give them an engagement present, too? We plan to present them with something nice as a wedding gift, but you know how easily engagements are broken. For instance, who would keep the linens if the wedding never comes off? Would it be better for us to give her a shower, with a smaller, shower-type gift?
GENTLE READER:

Nothing is certain in this world, least of all anything having to do with romance, and Miss Manners understands your caution. (One of these days, she is going to announce a new rule that couples must return all presents unless the marriage lasts a minimum of six months. She is still working on the details, such as what if the present is slightly used by then?)

Engagement presents are already safe, because they must be returned to the givers if the wedding does not take place. You cannot give your own daughter, or anyone related to you, a shower. There is nothing to stop you from giving her an eggbeater, or whatever you consider to be a shower-type present for an engagement present, but perhaps you will feel more generous now that Miss Manners has promised you that you will get it back.

Bridal Showers

DEAR MISS MANNERS:

I often have the chance to give bridal showers, and love doing so. A problem often arises with the invitations. My mother says that I should send them to friends and relatives who live out of town or state, just to be courteous. I feel that a shower is only for those who live near and that the others will give their gift at the wedding or send a congratulatory note, with a possible gift. Postage is so high, and invitations aren't cheap, either. What do you say?

GENTLE READER:

Miss Manners hates to go against the judgment of mothers pleading for courtesy, but she has to say that you are correct. Perhaps your mother is confusing the courtesy of inviting people to wedding without presuming to anticipate whether they will be able to attend. One does not do that with lesser parties. A wedding is considered to be enough of an event to make a trip worthwhile, but a shower, however pleasant, is not.

DEAR MISS MANNERS:

Last week I attended a wedding shower for my niece. After the gifts had been opened, the hostess presented her with a package that she said contained the "most important gift of all." It was an ornately wrapped package. The accompanying note read "The Secret of a Happy Marriage." When my niece opened the package, she found two items: a pair of pink underpanties with the words "Spank Spot" printed across the seat, and a wooden paddle, bearing a cartoon drawing of a woman across a man's knee being spanked and the label, "Wife Trainer." When my niece unwrapped the package and disclosed its contents, the ladies all laughed and applauded. I was shocked and appalled and made no attempt to conceal my displeasure. I informed the hostess that I thought her "gift" was in extremely poor taste. To my surprise, not only did she and other women in the room take me to task for having no sense of humor, but so did my niece. They claimed this kind of "ceremony"—as they called it—is very common these days. When I left (shortly after), my niece was being urged to put on the underpants and let the hostess "see if they worked."

Miss Manners, I have seldom experienced anything so upsetting. I found the gift itself degrading, the behavior of the women unspeakable, and my niece's attitude inexcusable. But my niece still thinks I was rude, and even her mother feels that I overreacted. So, please tell me: Was I wrong to act as I did, and is this, in fact, something that happens these days at showers?

GENTLE READER:

If this is what showers are like, remind Miss Manners to stay indoors.

Let us separate the taste questions from the etiquette questions here. If you met a woman in a vulgar dress, it would not be proper for you to tell her what you thought of it. Her vulgarity would not excuse your rudeness. Miss Manners is certainly not going to dispute the poor taste of this present. She doesn't even want to know whether we are talking about masochism or about dirty joking. It doesn't matter.

The reason it doesn't matter is that it is now considered rude to criticize the sexual preferences of consenting adults. This is, indeed, a changed custom. In more enlightened eras, it was considered perfectly natural for the elder women in the family to tell the bride what they considered to be appropriate sexual behavior.

Yes, you were rude to express your condemnation of their behavior. You should merely have excused yourself from this distasteful scene, especially if the highlight of the entertainment was to be, as Miss Manners gathers, the spectacle of the hostess beating up the guest of honor. Nevertheless, your niece is equally guilty of expressing disapproval of your behavior. The best thing would be to call it a draw, with apologies exchanged by all.

The Mother and Daughter Talk

DEAR MISS MANNERS:

My daughter is getting married soon, in a big church wedding. We thought it was charming that her young man asked my husband's permission to have her hand, even though they have been living together for nearly two years. During the wedding festivities, his family will be staying with him at their apartment, and my daughter will move back into her old room at our house. The thought of her there, among her doll collection, old teddy bear, and childhood books (which I am saving for her children, the first of whom is expected in six months) touches me and I would like to hold the traditional mother-daughter talk with her about sex the night before the wedding. Do you think this would be superfluous?

GENTLE READER:

Oh, no. Surely you remember reading her those childhood books aloud. Was your mutual pleasure lessened just because you both knew how the story came out?

Breaking an Engagement

The solemn rule that one must never break an engagement just because something better has come along does not, of course, apply to engagements to enter into holy matrimony. A person who would break an engagement to dine for reasons other than sudden death is a cad, but for an engagement to be married, the excuse "I don't know, I just don't feel like it" will do.

Miss Manners does not mean to suggest that breaking such engagements is not a serious, delicate matter. When doing so, one cannot be too careful of the tender feelings of those most concerned—the caterer, the bridesmaids, and the mother of the bride.

When one is jilting one's publicly affianced, it is only fair to do so at the convenience of that part of society that has become involved. This comes to mind because Miss Manners was told a story about a perfectly dreadful bride. It seems that she canceled the wedding while all her friends were busy scraping up the money to pay for the bridesmaid dresses she had chosen and then, when everybody thought it had all died down, upped and married the man without their attendance. That last act wiped out any possibility of sympathy for a panicked young girl who suddenly sees herself ruining her life and bolts. What remains is someone whose caprice stuck her closest friends with bills for dresses they didn't want.

Let us consider how such a case should be properly handled. One evening, three weeks before she is to be married, Daffodil Perfect tears her eyes away from her forty-page check list of Things the Bride Must Do and takes a hard look at Jonathan Awful, her betrothed. She never noticed before how his dinner tends to remain on the tip of his mustache. Life with him, she realizes, would be as flawed, or as cloudy, as the diamond he gave her.

As a considerate member of society, she immediately finds out how many of the wedding commitments are irrevocable. If the disadvantages are outweighed by the refunds, she cancels it. If she then notices that Jonathan does not look as heartbroken as she had imagined, and decides to uncancel him, she re-schedules the wedding with the original participants at a date convenient to them.

Suppose, however, that the revelation occurs two nights before the wedding. What does the considerate bride do? Miss Manners would never advise a woman to marry someone she doesn't like just because the arrangements have been made.

But even the social mortification of calling wedding guests, packing up the wedding presents to be returned, and breaking the news to the prospective spouse must be endured, in preference to living unhappily ever after. Society may miss a good party, but it will not have to endure listening to the story of the divorce.

Announcing a Broken Engagement

DEAR MISS MANNERS:

My wedding invitations were mailed on Saturday morning, and on Saturday night I broke my engagement. It was to have been a large, formal wedding, so there will be lots of people receiving engraved invitations which must now be recalled. How shall I do this? May I use the envelopes from the announcements?

GENTLE READER:

Miss Manners wishes to congratulate you on your good fortune. This is not a reference to the departure of your young man, with whom Miss Manners is unacquainted, but to the fact that you have the engraved announcements at your disposal. Miss Manners suggests you correct them with a pen, so that they will now read:

Mr. and Mrs. Geoffrey Lockwood Perfect
have the honour of announcing
that the marriage of their daughter
Daffodil Louise
to
Mr. Jonathan Rhinehart Awful, 3d
will not take place

Weddings

You, out there in Brideland, you sweet thing: Are you planning your wedding so that it will be perfect in every detail? Do you expect it to be the happiest day of your life? Miss Manners sincerely hopes not.

Few of those who prattle about that "happiest day" seem to consider the dour expectations this suggests about the marriage from its second day on. They don't realize that a wedding reception is basically a large party, and is therefore not perfectable because there are too many variables, not to mention too many people who one thought would not accept. At any rate, someone whose idea of ultimate happiness is a day spent at a big party, even spent being the center of attention at a marvelous big party, is too young to get married.

This notion of a wedding persists, often working directly against the purpose of a wedding, which is to create a new family, and not to put cracks and strains in old ones. Miss Manners' advice to young brides is to plan weddings that will be pretty and festive, but not to attempt to make them grand on a scale unrelated to the rest of their lives, and not to expect them to be perfect. Many an otherwise lovely bride has turned ugly attempting to create a "dream" occasion and to make everyone else conform with her conception of their roles in it.

A warning that one has strayed too far afield is an excessive preoccupation with everything's being done "right." Weddings are rare events in most people's lives, and Miss Manners has no objection to the participants' seeking advice on correct form. She dispenses such advice herself, right and left. But if one needs professional direction—not just help or advice—in every aspect of the wedding, it may mean that one has wandered into completely foreign social territory and should think about heading home. One's wedding should be a heightened version of one's best social life, not an occasion for people to attempt to play grand and unfamiliar parts in a fantasy play.

Another warning about expecting a perfect day is that this carries a built-in potential for disappointment. (There are adults who go through life expecting other people to make their birthdays perfect for them, and if you ever meet one of these, watch out. Nothing will ever be enough for them.)

What Miss Manners wishes all brides is not the happiest days of their lives, but jolly gatherings of family and friends, in which they are the object of general admiration, but everyone has a good time. They will then have some happiness left over with which to live happily ever after.

Uncertain Location

DEAR MISS MANNERS:

Please help me! My daughter was brought up in the area where we still reside. However, she has become a legal resident of a southern state, where she attended a university for the last four years.

She has now become engaged to a young man whose family reside in· the town in which the university is located. They are talking about getting married in the next several months. I told my daughter that I want to give them a lovely wedding, which I would like to have here. All I wanted to know from them was what kind of a wedding they wished. I was told in no uncertain terms that it is "their wedding" and therefore they intend to have it in the southern town where her fiancé's family resides, primarily because it would be very inconvenient for her fiancé's relatives and friends to have to come up here and stay in a hotel. Naturally, I am expected to travel 1,200 miles several times to make all the arrangements and, of course, pay for the wedding. Never mind the inconvenience to me or our relatives. She also claims they just bought a book which states that the bride and groom decide where the wedding should take place. I never heard of such nonsense.

GENTLE READER:

Miss Manners has, but more accurately than your daughter, who has confused two types of weddings. One is the traditional wedding of a young woman marrying from her parents' house, so to speak. Such a wedding is given by the parents of the bride in their hometown. The other is the wedding of an independent woman who has already left her parents' home. In neither case is the geographical statement to be taken literally; there is nothing to stop a thirty-five-year-old tycoon who lives on two coasts at once to consider that she is symbolically leaving her parents' protection at her wedding.

However, no woman who speaks to her mother "in no uncertain terms" can be considered to be under her parents' protection. Miss Manners therefore believes your daughter is entitled to put on her own wedding, wherever she chooses. Naturally, this means that she will make all the arrangements, including the minor matter of meeting bills.

The graceful thing for you to do, in the interests of family harmony and respect for your daughter's rights, is to inform her that you will be pleased to attend—as a guest, of course, not a hostess—whatever sort of wedding will make her happy.

The Proper Time

DEAR MISS MANNERS:

June used to be the traditional time for weddings, but customs are so different now. Is there any preferred date for weddings in modern life?

GENTLE READER:

It is preferable to hold them after the divorce and before the birth of the baby.

A Bored Bridegroom

DEAR MISS MANNERS:

My fiancé refuses to take an interest in the arrangements for our wedding. There will be about two hundred people, one hundred from his side and one hundred or slightly more from mine, with a reception in our families' country club. There is a lot of work to do, and I don't mind that so much, but it worries me that he is so bored by it. Is this a bad sign?

GENTLE READER:

No. While a bridegroom is not actually superfluous at a wedding—most states require one before issuing a license—he is all but superfluous, and need not be as enthralled by the preparations as the stars. However, this tendency might bear watching. If his lack of interest interferes with his participation—in other words, if he doesn't attend the wedding—that would be a bad sign.

INVITATIONS AND ANSWERS

Original Invitations

DEAR MISS MANNERS:

I need your help in interpreting the wording of this invitation:

Mary Jane Doe

and

Stephen Michael Roe

invite you to share the joy of the beginning of

their new life together

when on Saturday, the fifth of July

at three o'clock

they exchange marriage vows at

Union Methodist Church

The bride and groom invite you to join them in a buffet dinner reception following their marriage.

I understood this to be an invitation to a reception only, and therefore did not attend the wedding ceremony. This led to an angry confrontation, and if I was wrong, I wish to apologize to the family members. To what was I invited?

GENTLE READER:

Heaven only knows. A wedding is a solemn, public ceremony, and Miss Manners hates to think what these people contemplated doing in church to create new life and joy, let alone to share it. This illustrates the reason for Miss Manners' fervent rejection of the "originally" worded pseudo-formal announcement. It is vulgar, in its assumption that this wedding is somehow more joyous than others, and it is open to severe misunderstanding. (It is also redundant, as is the silly phrase "buffet dinner reception.")

You owe no apology. In any case, a ceremony held in a church is theoretically open to the congregation and it is not therefore customary to reply that one is, or is not, attending; what requires an answer is only the invitation to the private social event following.

Now Miss Manners will tell you how your friends should have worded their invitations. The most impressive invitation begins: "Mr. and Mrs. Geoffrey Lockwood Perfect/ request the honour of" and then there is a space of several lines, followed by "presence at the marriage of." The blank is filled in with the possessive form of the full names of the people invited (no more than two to an invitation), written by hand. But why, you ask, should I go to all this trouble? (That is why these invitations are so impressive, Miss Manners answers.) But how, you continue, do I fit the names of my friends who are living together into that little space? That is a more difficult question, and Miss Manners will delicately sidestep the issue by giving you permission to use an equally correct, all-purpose form:

Mr. and Mrs. Geoffrey Lockwood Perfect
request the honour of your presence
at the marriage of their daughter
Daffodil Louise
to
Mr. Jonathan Rhinehart Awful, 3d
Saturday, the fifth of June
at twelve o'clock noon
Our Lady of Propriety Church

The reception invitations are engraved on separate cards, slightly smaller than the wedding invitations:

Reception
immediately following the ceremony
The Racket Club

R.s.v.p.

By omitting these cards in certain envelopes, one may trim the feeding list, thus simultaneously inviting and slighting a portion of the guests.

At Home Cards

DEAR MISS MANNERS:
Do people still put "at home" cards in with wedding announcements? What is the purpose, and what is the correct wording?
GENTLE READER:
The traditional reason was to let people know where they could call upon the newly married couple after the wedding trip, and the traditional motivation was to let tardy present-givers know where to direct their offerings after the wedding.
Now there is a better reason, which is to let everyone know what the bride

Mr. and Mrs. Geoffrey Lockwood Perfect

request the honour of your presence

at the marriage of their daughter

Daffodil Louise

to

Mr. Jonathan Rhinehart Awful, 3rd

on Saturday, the first of April

at twelve o'clock noon

Our Lady of Propriety Church

Brookdale, Connecticut

An invitation to a wedding, with a card enclosed for the wedding breakfast. Divorced parents may issue the invitation alone, together using their current names, or with a current spouse, with "their daughter" corrected to read "his daughter," "her sister," "their niece," or whatever. The bride's last name is included if it differs from the host's.

Wedding Breakfast
immediately following the ceremony
123 Primrose Path
Brookdale, Connecticut

The favour of a reply is requested

The pleasure of your company

is requested at the wedding reception of

Stacey Awful

Vice Admiral, United States Navy

and

Trevor Nuisance

Major General, United States Army

on Saturday, the eleventh of November

at six o'clock

Fort McBoom Officers' Club

R.s.v.p.
General Nuisance
Cannonball Barracks

Invitation to a wedding reception,
with ceremony card enclosed. The
phrase "the honour of your
presence" is used for religious
ceremonies; for home weddings,
those taking place in clubs or
hotels, and for related social
events, the proper phrase is "the
pleasure of your company." The
variations used here, such as the
absence of hosts and the use of
military titles, may, of course, be
used when the main invitation is to
the ceremony. This form is used for
an intimate ceremony, followed by
a large reception.

The honour of your presence

is requested at the marriage ceremony

at half after four o'clock

The Memorial Chapel

Fort McBoom

Mrs. Plue Perfect
accepts with pleasure
the kind invitation of
Mr. and Mrs. Perfect
for
Saturday, the first of April
at twelve o'clock noon

Acceptance of a wedding invitation on "house" paper, which may be used by anyone in the house, including the guests, for formal letters.

Mrs. Perfect used to copy out more of the invitation, putting, instead of that one lonely word "for," four extra lines reading, "to the wedding breakfast of their daughter/ Daffodil Louise/ and/ Mr. Jonathan Rhinehart Awful, 3rd," but she is now forced by her arthritis to use the modern form.

To decline the invitation, one would substitute "regrets that she is (they are) unable to accept" for the second line, and add the adverb "very" before the adjective "kind" in the third line.

and bridegroom have decided to call themselves—his surname, hers, a combination, or an invention. The old form was engraved on a heavy oversized visiting card:

Mr. and Mrs. Jonathan Rhinehart Awful, 3d

After the first of April   129 Primrose Path

A practical new one might be:

Ms. Alexandrina Awful

Mr. Ian Fright

After the 29th of February   127 Primrose Path

Those Who "Request the Honour"

DEAR MISS MANNERS:

My fiancé and I are selecting our wedding invitations, and we don't know how to word them. The bride's parents are paying for the catering. The groom's parents offered to pay for the rehearsal dinner. The bride's parents offered to invite the guests to their house after the mass. My fiancé and I are paying for the hall, cake, marriage, license, flowers, music, and drinks. Who gets the honour of inviting the guests on the invitations?

GENTLE READER:

You are making the common, and often justified, assumption that honors are always for sale. In this case, they are not. The bride's parents issue the invitations. However, the tradespeople issue their bills to those who have indicated a willingness to pay them.

Stepfather of the Bride

DEAR MISS MANNERS:

My mother divorced my father fourteen years ago, and remarried. I came to love my stepfather very much, and I never really considered my stepdad as not being my real father, since he has raised me since I was five years old. I never really saw my real dad, and that never bothered me, because I was quite content with my stepdad.

My stepfather is even going to walk me down the aisle, because I asked him, and I wouldn't want anyone else to do it. But how do I go about filling out the invitations? I want my stepdad's name down, and my mother says it can't be done that way. My real father and stepmother are invited to the wedding also.

GENTLE READER:

Having been right once, in marrying such a nice man, your mother cannot expect to be always right. In this case, you are—by all standards of kindness as well as strictest etiquette. The correct wording is:

Mr. and Mrs. Horace Drew Contentment
request the honour of your presence
at the marriage of her daughter
Pamela Jean Larue
& c

Titles on Invitations

DEAR MISS MANNERS:
My daughter will be getting married in September. She has a Doctor of Veterinary Medicine degree, and is therefore "Dr." as is her husband-to-be.

My question is, do I use her title in inviting the guests to the marriage of my daughter (I am a widow) as Jan Lee, Dr. Jan Lee, or Jan Lee, D.V.M.? Also, how do I title Tom? It is very possible Jan will opt not to use her title on the invitation, but I would like to know the correct way if she decides to use it. Also, she is keeping her own name (what else is new?) and I don't know what to do about stationery for her. These should be our biggest problems.

GENTLE READER:
Miss Manners knows from sad experience that the way to turn this into a big problem is to put forward her own prejudice against using titles socially when it is not necessary to do so. ("But I worked hard to earn it!" they all scream. All right, go ahead. But you worked hard for your money, too, and shouldn't be flaunting it.)

On a formal wedding invitation, the bridegroom does need a title with his name, so you would use Dr. here instead of Mr. The bride does not, as only her given names appear, unless her last name is different from that of the person issuing the invitation (you). If she absolutely refuses to do without the "Dr." it must be used with her full name. Do not—repeat not—use the initials, except on her business stationery. Please persuade her to omit any reference to her education on her social writing paper; this may be engraved with her maiden name, as she will continue to use it socially.

Instructions for Invitations

DEAR MISS MANNERS:
Please tell me what is the proper way to stuff wedding invitations? Etiquette books and local stationers have given me conflicting answers about whether it is correct to put all the enclosure cards (reception card and response card) inside the invitation itself, or simply on top of the invitation, before inserting into the inner envelope. Also, do I use the tissue paper provided, even though the reason

for it is no longer valid? If so, where does it go? The invitation opens like a greeting card and is blank inside.

While on the subject, is it correct to use response cards for certain cases? I realize it may be insulting to assume the recipient will not R.s.v.p. with a handwritten note, but, as is typical in the small town where I will marry, my parents are having a sit-down dinner and need a fairly accurate head count. At twenty dollars per head, it seems too risky to rely on good manners.

GENTLE READER:

Please listen carefully, because this is going to sound like instructions for making paper monkeys out of bubble gum wrappers, as translated from the Japanese.

Fold the double-sheeted wedding invitation in half again, engraved side in, and insert it into the inner envelope (the one without the glue), with the fold side at the bottom, and the top of the invitation facing the reader who has the flap of the envelope facing him or her. Put the extra cards, writing also toward the flap, in the center of the main invitation. If, however, the invitation is small and does not need folding, the cards go in front of it, which is to say, closer to the rear of the envelope.

Tissues are provided to prevent the engraving from smearing after the folding. You may include them, but you don't need them if the cards are in between. You don't need them if it's not real engraving, either, but in that case you may want them for motives Miss Manners will not mention.

Miss Manners hates response cards, although she admits they are widely used. Her feeling is that someone too rude to answer by hand will probably also fail to take the trouble to mail the card, so there goes your stamp, as well as your head count. Nevertheless, she sympathizes with your problem. Another solution is to telephone the missing people a week before the wedding and ask them whether you will have the pleasure of their company. If that doesn't shame them, nothing will.

Addressing Invitations

DEAR MISS MANNERS:

I heard someplace that I shouldn't put "and Family" or "and Guest" on my wedding invitation envelopes. Well, how else do I let them know everybody is invited? Also, why do I have to use two envelopes? It seems like a waste to me.

GENTLE READER:

Using "and Family" on your invitation is its own punishment. You cannot then complain if your sister-in-law's dog disturbed the ceremony, and you didn't know where to seat your bridegroom's best friend's stepgrandfather's new friend. The word "family" can be very broadly construed where free champagne is involved, and those who use "and Guest" on their invitations are courting disaster.

If you care enough to invite people to your wedding, you will find out each one's name and use it. You need not send an invitation to every man, woman, and child. You may send married (or otherwise cohabiting) couples a single invitation, and you may even include, beneath those of their parents, the names of daughters living at home, as in:

Mr. and Mrs. Jonathan Rhinehart Awful, junior
  The Misses Awful
                    129 Primrose Path
                         Brookdale
                      Connecticut

Their brothers, "The Messrs. Awful," should be sent a separate invitation, even if they live at the same address. It is best not to include more than two adults in one invitation.

It is a treat for children under about age thirteen—if you really want to invite them—to receive a separate invitation addressed "The Misses and Messrs. Awful."

The purpose of these two envelopes is to protect the invitation from the ravages of the modern postal service, now that invitations are no longer hand delivered by footmen. That they may also make the invitations too fat for modern letter-sorting equipment is beside the point.

Titles and full names are used on the outer envelope; the street address, city, and state are written out in full, in black or blue-black ink, each on its own line (see example above). The inner envelope has the titles and surnames only.

There is, of course, a good reason for all of these rules: they make the writing of proper thank-you letters seem simple.

About Engraving

DEAR MISS MANNERS:

It's not the money, but I think it's silly to have our wedding invitations really engraved. It is virtually impossible to tell the difference between engraving and good raised printing, and it seems a waste of money to pay for something extra that doesn't even show. My fiancée disagrees with me, but she can't give a valid reason. Can you?

GENTLE READER:

Yes. The world is full of nasty people who examine the backs of wedding invitations and run fingernails over the front in order to tell whether the thing was properly engraved. Miss Manners is one of them. However, she wishes to point out that anything usually engraved is equally properly handwritten—engraving merely being mass-produced handwriting.

The Double Wedding

DEAR MISS MANNERS:

My two daughters became engaged to two young men within a week of each other, and they want to get married within the year. I have always promised the girls the kind of wedding they want (big), but I never thought they would want them at the same time. Is there any way I can marry them both off properly without taking out a second mortgage?

GENTLE READER:

The solution to your problem is the double wedding, one of the few cases in which tradition and practicality join forces. Issue one invitation, either with a normally worded invitation for each bride on either side of the inside of a double sheet (please see p. 322), or in the following form:

Mr. and Mrs. Geoffrey Lockwood Perfect
request the honour of your presence
at the marriage of their daughters
Viola Brentwood
to
Mr. Alexander Dashing
and
Daffodil Louise
to
Mr. Jonathan Rhinehart Awful, 3d
& c

The ceremony itself proceeds either as two individual weddings with extra people hanging around (in which case each bride can be maid—or matron—of honor to the other, presuming they are still speaking to each other after doing all the double planning), or as one large ceremony with each part repeated twice. In the processional, the older sister (with retinue) comes down the aisle on her father's arm, followed by the younger sister (with retinue) escorted by her brother, uncle, or other unoccupied male. If this precedence gives the unfortunate impression that the older bride is rushing down the aisle to beat her younger sister to the altar, don't blame Miss Manners. She does not make up these rules.

Marathon Wedding

DEAR MISS MANNERS:

Because of religious preference, our two daughters are being married at different churches, on the same day. One wedding is at three, and one is at five. We are giving a joint wedding reception that evening. Both grooms are from out of town and the respective families and friends are not acquainted.

We plan to send one invitation for both weddings. The printing would be on the inside folio. The left inside page would be for one couple, and the right inside page for the other couple.

Some people feel this would be in poor taste, as it would obligate the recipients to give gifts to both couples, even though they might only know one couple. Others say, not so. On the other hand, if we use separate invitations, how will we handle the surprise of finding a second bride and groom at the reception? Also, how might we send the reception card with a separate invitation?

Gentle Reader:

You are planning quite a day. You will soon realize, if you do not already, why there isn't a great body of precedent for holding two separate-location weddings on the same day.

However, Miss Manners thinks it sounds like great fun for your guests, and would encourage you to include everyone for the entire marathon. (Miss Manners hopes people will have the sense to send presents only to the bridal couple they know, understanding that they are being included at the other wedding only because it is part of the festival.)

The double invitation you suggest, on facing pages, sounds sensible. Acknowledge the custom for a one-location double wedding by having your elder daughter's wedding occur first, with the invitation on the left-hand page (please see p. 329).

You need include only a reception card with such an invitation. However, if you decide not to invite everyone to both ceremonies, make your chief invitation one to the joint wedding reception and enclose separate cards for the appropriate ceremonies.

Invitations, Expenses, et cetera

Dear Miss Manners:

How many weeks or days in advance should you mail out wedding invitations or hand deliver them? Exactly what are the bride-to-be's responsibilities for wedding expenses?

Gentle Reader:

Wedding invitations should be mailed three or four weeks before the wedding is to take place. This gives people time to worry about what they are going to wear and how much you will expect them to spend on a wedding present. Any more time is unwise, as it will enable them to speculate on whether the wedding will actually come off.

In theory, the bride has no responsibilities other than looking radiant (and showing up) and no expenses, because those are being met by the bridegroom (license, ring, flowers, and clergyman's fee) or being taken care of by the bride's parents, who give the wedding. In practice, she had better be prepared to help with them all if she does not want her parents to wash their hands of her before they give her away.

"Get Me to the Church"

DEAR MISS MANNERS:

Please help me to correct my fiancée and her mother on a point of etiquette. I have generously refrained from interfering with their preparations for our wedding thus far. Regarding invitations, however, I dared to speak my piece: guests must be sent maps if they are to find the church. Aimless wandering about will not do. My fiancée and future mother-in-law, however, insist that the insertion of maps ruptures the formality of the invitation, sending our wedding into the depths of boorishness. Should I return to passive acceptance of the rampages of two women gone mad?

GENTLE READER:

It may reassure you to know that this particular form of madness—the abandonment of all common sense in the desire to conform to a concept of rigid correctness in matters on which there is, in fact, nothing at all written in stone— is nearly universal, but temporary. It is possible that if you lie low, you may find yourself ending up with a wife and mother-in-law as sane and reasonable as they were when you first suggested the relationship.

It is also possible that you will find yourself being married in an empty church. Miss Manners sees nothing wrong with including small, neat maps, but if that drives them madder still, you might suggest a seperate mailing of maps —or just do one yourself.

A Formal Acceptance

DEAR MISS MANNERS:

What is the correct way, these days, to answer a formal, engraved invitation?

GENTLE READER:

What do you mean, "these days"? Are you suggesting that just because modern life is chaotic, you can get away without a beautifully handwritten formal reply with all the lines neatly centered? Do you know how much it cost those people to have that invitation engraved? Do you think they want to hear your cheery voice on the telephone saying, "Sure, why not?"

Oh, all right. Miss Manners will shorten the task for you slightly, **but not** much. You may write that you accept with pleasure, or regret that you are unable to accept, your friends' kind invitation for whatever date it is—and you don't have to repeat in the reply the time, place, or bride's name. You still have to write the thing out, though. And get those lines centered!

(Please see illustration, p. 324.)

The Correct Response

DEAR MISS MANNERS:

I got a wedding invitation with an answer card enclosed for me to fill in my name under "Will attend" or "Will not attend." Does this take the place of a handwritten reply?

GENTLE READER:

Never. It is meant to, however. Miss Manners finds such cards an abomination and invites you to help foul up the systems of people who try it. Use your own letter paper to write a conventional formal reply. This will be too big for the filing box in which the hosts are keeping track of who is coming and who isn't, and thus drive them crazy. Maybe then they will learn to behave better by the second wedding.

❧ ANNOUNCEMENTS

Announcements or Invitations?

DEAR MISS MANNERS:

We are being married at the courthouse. What I want to know is, how do I let all my out-of-town relations know I'm getting married? I want them all to know about it, but my mother says it is tacky to send announcements because they are not being invited to anything. I am having a small reception at my parents' home for close friends. I would like to send something to let them know, but what do I send, announcements or invitations, and should I send them before or after?

GENTLE READER:

Getting married is still considered a perfectly respectable thing to do, and there is nothing "tacky" about announcing that one has done so. That is, in fact, the purpose of wedding announcements. The purpose of wedding invitations is to invite people to attend the wedding. Invitations are sent before the wedding to those whom you wish to attend, and announcements are sent after the wedding to those whom you wish to inform.

Delayed Announcements

DEAR MISS MANNERS:

My marriage was a quiet one, occurring as it did during the terminal illness of a close family member. Now, more than a year later, we are moving to a new house, and I would like to take the occasion to let friends know we are married,

Mr. and Mrs. Jonathan Rhinehart Awful, 3rd

have the honour of announcing

the marriage of their daughter

Alexandrina Grace

to

Mr. Ian Fright

on Saturday, the first of April

Nineteen hundred and eighty

Our Lady of Propriety Church

Brookdale, Connecticut

Announcement of a wedding
with enclosed at home card.

At home cards traditionally
omitted the name, but that
was when people could figure
out the bride's new name by
adding a Mrs. to her
husband's name, as shown
on the announcement.

Ms. Alexandrina Awful-Fright

Mr. Ian Fright-Awful

will be at home

after the fourth of July

127 Primrose Path

Brookdale, Connecticut

along with the new address notification. I retain the use of my birth name at all times. What wording can you suggest for a card that would provide all the information without suggesting inadvertently that I hereafter wish to be known as Mrs. John Doe?

GENTLE READER:

Please do not attempt a formal-ish, third person announcement card. The situation is too complicated, and, what with all the strange arrangements being announced these days, the possibilities of misinterpretation are staggering. A personal note can be dashed off quickly on a card: "John Doe and I, who were married last year, are living at—" with the address and your full signature. (Get John to write the half that go to his friends.)

Which Parents Are Announced

DEAR MISS MANNERS:

Recently my brother shared wedding vows, and we read of his wedding as it was printed in the paper. Our parents are divorced and both are remarried. When they printed his announcement, he listed his parents as the first set—the mother and father of his birth. There was no mention of the two remaining parents of equal importance. Was this proper?

GENTLE READER:

Yes. A wedding announcement is not intended to be like a list of movie credits, where everybody who had a hand in the production is named. There is also a distinction between an announcement submitted to a newspaper and an announcement mailed to those friends who were not invited to the wedding. In the announcement submitted to a newspaper, the people making the announcement may include a stepparent of the bride's, although her other biological parent is also listed, but the bridegroom's original parents are listed merely as a matter of information, as they are not giving the wedding. A mailed announcement to friends gives the names only the people who gave the wedding and the couple whose wedding it was.

❧ WEDDING PROCEDURE

When is the correct time for a bride to get prenuptial jitters, who should be present, where should each person stand, what should they wear, and does this event require a separate present?

This is the only ingredient Miss Manners can imagine that has not yet been codified into the marathon of wedding events recommended by florists, photographers, social consultants, and other such well-wishers.

Of course, the more subevents there are in a wedding, the more opportunities for squabbles between the two families and among their members over those two major issues—who controls the procedure, and who pays for it—that Miss Manners has never succeeded in convincing anyone are unrelated.

Far be it from her to interfere with such a sacred tradition as the founding of family feuds, so here is a schedule of possible activities from the arrival of the wedding party until the departure of the bridal couple.

Two Days Before the Wedding

1. Bachelor dinner, given by the bridegroom to provide his friends with an opportunity to entice him to behave in such a way that the bride will call off the wedding.

2. Bride's luncheon (or tea or dinner), given by the bride to provide her friends with an opportunity to complain about the color of the bridesmaid dresses and the quality of the groomsmen.

One Day Before

1. Bridesmaids' and ushers' dinner, given after the rehearsal for all members of the wedding party, including clergy, and, if possible, out-of-town guests. Traditionally given by the bride's parents or godparents or close family friends.

2. Rehearsal dinner, which takes the place of the bridesmaids' and ushers' dinner and is identical to it, except that the bridegroom's family pays for it, an increasingly popular custom, especially with the socially and financially exhausted parents of brides.

Wedding Day

1. Bride lives out all her royalty fantasies by acting spoiled at the expense of parents, sisters, and friends as she gets dressed. Bridegroom, separately, endures jokes at his expense by his parents, other relatives, and friends.

2. Wedding ceremony is performed, a necessary event although it allows for the least leeway, except to very young relatives who may use the opportunity to make innocent but loud remarks which are interpreted by the congregation as dirty. In the processional, the bridegroom and best man come in sideways, and down the aisle come, in order, the ushers, bridesmaids, ring bearer, flower girl, and bride with father; or, in a Jewish wedding, bridegroom flanked by his parents after the ushers, and bride, flanked by her parents, after the bridesmaids or flower girl. In the recessional, the bride goes on the arm of the bridegroom, followed by attendants, bridesmaids first, or paired off with male attendants.

3. Wedding breakfast (which is to say lunch) following morning wedding, or reception (which is to say tea) following afternoon wedding, or dinner (which is to say dinner) following evening wedding.

a. Receiving line so everyone can tell bride she looks beautiful and then mess

Processional

Altar

Recessional

Receiving line

THE PROPER ORDER IN WHICH A BRIDAL PARTY ARRIVES, ENDURES AND RECEDES FROM THE WEDDING. (_In the receiving line for the wedding reception, fathers are optional. To exercise the option, insert the father of the bridegroom between the mothers, and the father of the bride on the bride's right._)

up her makeup. In the receiving line, the hostess, who is the bride's mother, greets guests first, then the bridegroom's father, the bridegroom's mother, the bride's father, the bridal couple, and the bridesmaids. The fathers may agree to get themselves drinks instead.

b. Eating, which may include a full meal. At a seated wedding breakfast or dinner, the bridal pair sit together with their attendants at one table, while the parents (again with bride's mother as hostess and bridegroom's father as ranking male guest) sit at another table with the priest, minister, or rabbi and his or her spouse, the grandparents, and other close relatives. Toasts are made (to the bride by the best man and anybody else who wants to, including the bridegroom; unless the bride offers return toasts to the bridegroom and her parents, she will never get any champagne) and the bride and bridegroom cut the cake together and try to feed each other bits of the same piece without ruining their clothes.

c. Dancing, first by the bridal couple, then each with the opposite sex in-law, then with their own parents, then with the best man and maid of honor, then with whoever asks.

d. Ancient and disgusting rituals, such as the bride's throwing the garter to the groomsmen, a custom from the days when the attendants helped the couple change out of their wedding clothes, so to speak; and throwing the bouquet to be caught by a bridesmaid who is already engaged, or tired of being asked when she is getting married.

e. The couple, having donned travel clothes, depart in a shower of fertilizing rice, rose petals, or confetti, in an automobile which their friends have ruined with wedding graffiti.

Day After the Wedding

The couple sometimes shows up to continue the festivities. This must be discouraged, no matter how long they have lived together and how short a time they have off from work. Enough is enough.

Symbolism and Ceremony

It is never too soon to plan your wedding, especially if you have already met someone you like. But if you plan your wedding to be spontaneous, original, honest and open, a dramatic presentation of your own personal love story, beliefs, and aspirations, Miss Manners will not attend. Miss Manners sees enough bad plays as it is.

All the world loves lovers except, of course, the people who were married to them when they fell in love. But love is no excuse for inviting people to a popular pageant and treating them, instead, to amateur theatrics about sex and philosophy. When people write their own wedding ceremonies, it is generally with the belief that the standard ones are boring or hypocritical (not to mention the crazy idea that *The Prophet* is better than the Bible). This is a basic misunderstanding about the nature of ceremony.

Miss Manners has no objection to bridal couples' doing some discreet editing of the standard ceremony, omitting details they find offensive, such as obeying and giving away. Certainly the innovation of including children from previous unions who will be underfoot in the new one is important. But they should bear in mind that symbols are intended to apply generally to the social function of the occasion, and are not clues to private behavior. The bride and bridegroom should not use the occasion to announce that they have considered themselves married already, belittling the social and legal sanction they are now receiving. It is rude to brag about your sex life at a public function.

Traditional ceremonies, whether civil or religious, express hopes and ideals; they do not make realistic predictions. Statistically, it may be true that it is likely to be the bride and bridegroom's subsequent feelings, not death, which do them part. But that is no excuse for making lukewarm vows to stay together ''as long as we both shall wish.'' How would you like to hear a President of the United States take an inaugural vow to uphold the Constitution as long as it doesn't interfere with his political plans?

The long, droning parts of the ceremony do not, in fact, bore the wedding guests. These merely give them time to enjoy appropriate thoughts for the occasion, such as ''What does she see in him?'' and ''What does he see in her?''

Arranging the Family

Should the bride's grandfather's live-in girl friend be sent a corsage? Is the matron of honor allowed to be pregnant? Must the bridegroom's mother and stepmother sit in the same pew, and if so, does the father sit between them? Suppose the bride has twelve friends who want to be bridemaids, and the bridegroom doesn't have enough male friends to supply as many ushers? Does the bridegroom's son sit at the bridal table, or at the parents' table? After the bride has danced with the bridegroom, her father-in-law and her father, can she dance with her mother's husband, who helped rear her, before she dances with the best man?

This is a sampling of the kind of question Miss Manners gets. Being a good sport, she usually answers them. (Some sample answers are: Yes, no, why not, it depends on if they speak, and oh, go ahead.) There is a limit, however, and Miss Manners thinks she may have reached it. Such silliness has got to stop. The supposition behind these questions is that a wedding is a set piece, with rigidly prescribed roles, that the wedding party must be ruthlessly cast to fit the parts, and, as is the way of the theater, too bad for those who won't do.

What is the historical precedent for this series of tableaux? Miss Manners, being a scholar, is aware that wedding customs are a jumble of evolving traditions, and that even the proper Victorian wedding was much more a part of the bride's family's own style of entertainment than an abstract law of correctness for all. In fact, the only wedding custom with a pretense to long tradition and universality, that of public checking up on the consummation of the marriage, seems to have been dropped. Miss Manners can't think why.

The pattern that so many modern brides apparently have in mind can be traced to Hollywood, California, circa 1948. According to this, the bridal couple are not allowed to have stepparents, children, more than one grandmother apiece, or more than one grandfather between them. The small size of the family cast was compensated by the number of places available in the wedding party for friends, provided these friends were young, unmarried, and of uniform height. This is a manageable group, and any director can arrange it into decorative patterns.

So what happens if you have more people than you need for some roles, such as mothers, and fewer for others? Dear brides, you rewrite the script to fit the company. You group your relatives as makes sense to you and them, in terms of their closeness to you and toleration for one another, and you arrange a wedding party that includes your friends, whatever their size, shape, and number.

If you complain that this is not correct or traditional, Miss Manners will come around and check up on you the next morning.

Pomp and Circumstance

DEAR MISS MANNERS:
After two and a half years of living together, our daughter is getting married to this man. She is young and has not been married before. Her groom-to-be is older, divorced, and of a different religious faith. Under these circumstances, how is a wedding properly conducted?

GENTLE READER:
Under which circumstances? Do you suspect that there is a special color of wedding dress symbolizing that the bride has been living with the bridegroom for two and a half years, and distinguishing her from a bride who has been living with her fiancé for six years, one who has only been parked out front with him all night, or one who has been courted by correspondence? Would an older bridegroom wear an older suit than a younger bridegroom? (Possibly.) Should it be old enough to let everybody know that this is its second wedding?

The answer is that these people may have a conventional wedding—or not, as they choose—and need enlist the consent of a clergyman only if they want it to be a religious ceremony in the faith of one or the other.

Delayed Wedding

DEAR MISS MANNERS:
How does one get married after living together for more than two years? My fiancée and I feel that a traditional wedding would be tacky. Actually, we would just as soon slip off and get married privately, and let people know later. However, that ignores the people for whom weddings seem to be designed— the parents and other relatives. Have you any suggestions that might help our planning?

GENTLE READER:

You will not take it amiss, Miss Manners hopes, if she emits a small giggle over the modern world. You are confident that living together is respectable, but afraid that a wedding might be tacky.

The tackiest thing about any wedding, in Miss Manners' opinion, is very traditional. That is the assumption that the bride doesn't know exactly what is going to happen later. People have been chuckling over this for centuries and feel disappointed when they know it isn't true. Otherwise, there is nothing in a public wedding that is inappropriate to the marriage of a well-acquainted couple.

An Overdue Wedding

DEAR MISS MANNERS:

My niece is getting married next month in a long white dress after living with the man three years and having two children. Do you think this is proper? One little girl will be flower girl. Having a reception afterwards, too.

GENTLE READER:

This event comes under a particular category of "Proper" known as "High time." In this area, there is no time for quibbling over dresses or other accessories. Go and wish the couple joy. You cannot accuse them of rushing into matrimony without due consideration.

The Blushing Bride

DEAR MISS MANNERS:

Our daughter is being married soon in a formal ceremony, although she is, only too obviously, I am afraid, pregnant. It's a long story, and perhaps you will think her father and I are wrong to allow such a public wedding when everyone knows the situation, but it is what she wants. Anyway, my concern is that people do not laugh at us. She says it is nothing to her friends, but her father's and mine are still not used to such things. For instance, wouldn't people think it ridiculous for us to throw rice at the bridal couple, symbolizing fertility, when everyone will be able to see that that has already been assured?

GENTLE READER:

You could throw minute rice, symbolizing that things are happening any minute now. Miss Manners prefers the paella or pilaf approach: The more good things in your symbolism the better, but don't examine it too closely.

Jewish Customs

DEAR MISS MANNERS:

I am being married at home, in a Reform Jewish ceremony, and I am somewhat uneasy about some modifications of traditions that my mother is suggesting.

If they were really as common as she says, why is she always saying that it isn't necessary to bother the rabbi about them?

The first is, is it really all right to have the chupah made out of flowers? I have always seen cloth ones, but my mother and the florist say any canopy will do. The second question is about the ring. My engagement ring is part of a set, and the wedding ring is an odd shape to fit around it, and is set with diamonds. I know that only a plain, gold, unbroken circle is traditional for Jewish brides and wonder if the fancy one will seem frivolous. I know I should have thought of this earlier, but it bothers me. The last question is about breaking the glass. My mother tells me it is customary to substitute a light bulb, since it is wrapped in a napkin anyway and no one can see it, and that the bridegroom has less trouble crushing it under his heel to ensure good luck.

GENTLE READER:

What luck do you expect to have with a husband who can't be trusted to smash a glass? Please use a real glass. Do you think God can't see inside a napkin? Anyway, the gesture symbolizes the destruction of the temple at Jerusalem, not luck.

Miss Manners will approve the floral canopy if you ask for a plain gold ring to receive at the wedding, saving the diamond one for whenever you feel like wearing it instead. Not only is the symbolism of the plain ring beautiful, but it won't tear your stockings in everyday use.

For the processional in a Jewish wedding, please see p. 335.

Expenses

DEAR MISS MANNERS:

I am a sister of the groom-to-be; my best girl friend, whom I introduced to him, is the bride. The bride's parents are not very well off. They live comfortably, but can't afford the big wedding that their daughter wants to have. She wants my parents to pay half of the expense, but my parents don't want to, because six people fighting over the way the wedding is going to be would really be a hassle. My mom and dad said they can use some of the wedding gifts to pay for the wedding, but my brother doesn't want to. My friend, the bride, thinks it is old-fashioned to be this way.

My mom and dad said the bride's parents should have a wedding they can afford. They suggested cutting the list by a third, to cut down the cost.

So here is my question: Are they old-fashioned, and is my friend right?

GENTLE READER:

Certainly, the concept of living within one's means is an old-fashioned one. Miss Manners hopes you do not imagine that she considers the term old-fashioned to be pejorative.

In this case, it appears that your friend has little choice. The expenses of the wedding are properly borne by the bride's family, and they are unable to pay the sum she is demanding. She has also failed in her attempts to extract payment from your parents, and even to get the consent of her future husband to take over their mutual funds, actual or anticipated, for the purpose.

Unless she is willing to come up with the money herself, she will have to have a wedding in the standard of living to which she has been accustomed.

And it seems to Miss Manners that a marriage in which the feelings of the future parents-in-law and the judgment of the bridegroom have been sacrificed to a luxurious fantasy would be a shaky investment.

✿ THE FAMILIES

Stepparents

DEAR MISS MANNERS:

My parents are divorced and both are remarried. I would like to include them all, parents and stepparents, in my wedding equally. How do I do this, and in what order, without hurting anybody's feelings? What do I put on the invitations and announcements, and who walks down the aisle with me? My father is paying more of the cost, but my mother is contributing, too.

GENTLE READER:

Miss Manners is beginning to think that each member of a family should hire an agent before there is to be a wedding, so that questions of billing and roles may be worked out in a businesslike manner. Otherwise, you are bound to get not only hurt feelings, but overcrowded casts. Perhaps you could do two performances of the wedding, with a different pair in the role of parents each time.

The sensible alternative is to choose one couple as hosts, who will have their names on invitations and announcements, and one father to walk you up the aisle. You might have one father and one mother do that. (It is a Jewish custom of particular charm to have both parents accompany the bride—and both of the bridegroom's parents accompany him—and it is beginning to spread to gentile weddings as a replacement for the anachronism of the father's "giving the bride away.")

For example, you might have your mother and her husband (or your father and his wife) issue the invitations, all four receiving guests after the ceremony, and your original father (and original mother, if you wish) accompany you up the aisle.

Your emotional ties and the civility or lack of it among these people are legitimate considerations when you make your choices. Miss Manners urges you only not to offer these parts for sale on the basis of who contributes most to the wedding costs.

Who Giveth This Woman?

DEAR MISS MANNERS:

I am twenty-two years old and about to be married. My father died when I was a child and my mother, who never remarried, died two years ago. Since her death, I have lived for the most part at college (I graduated last month) and have spent summers and holidays with my grandparents, my father's brother (he is my only uncle), and my two older brothers, both of whom are married. Ours is a close-knit family and all of its members have been important in bringing me up and in helping me—financially and emotionally—through the difficult times following my mother's death.

Because my family is so important to me, I want to be married "from the family"—in other words, I want to be "given away." But by whom? Does someone have a traditional claim to the right to do the honors? I would hate to have to choose among my brothers, uncle, and grandparents only on the basis of personal preference, because I would be miserable if my choice made someone unhappy. If there is a traditional preference, my problem will be solved.

GENTLE READER:

Miss Manners supposes it's of no use to tell you to choose whomever you feel closest to. You love them all, equally, don't you? That's why you are making Miss Manners choose, isn't it?

There is no formal order in this case, but you might consider the question of who, in the old-fashioned sense, is the head of the family. It would be your grandfather, if you are thinking in terms of the clan, or your elder brother, if you want to have someone from your nuclear family.

When the Bride's Mother Gives Her Away

DEAR MISS MANNERS:

My daughter is planning her wedding. She has asked me, her mother, to walk her down the aisle. I have raised her by myself since she was two years old. I got married four years ago to a wonderful man. He has been a good stepfather to my daughter. Her father hasn't been in her life much since the divorce—he is remarried and living about six hundred miles away—but my daughter loves him in spite of his absence and has decided to ask me to give her away, because she doesn't want to hurt either her father or stepfather by having one of them give her away. She said if I didn't give her away, she would prefer her stepfather, as he will be the one who pays for the wedding, and her dad would be third choice. She talked to the minister, and he said it would be all right. My second question is, if I do walk her down the aisle, what do I wear?

GENTLE READER:

Miss Manners thinks it is a charming idea for you to escort your daughter in positive acknowledgment of the fact that you were the sole parent who reared her. Obviously, you do not dress as the Father of the Bride; nor do you dress as a sort of senior bridesmaid, although you may want to choose a color that will not actively clash with the attendants' dresses. The usual Mother of the Bride dress is lace or chiffon, in beige, blue, yellow, or pink, and makes the Mother of the Bride look fat. Miss Manners hopes you can find a pale, dressy dress that doesn't.

Flowers for the Family

DEAR MISS MANNERS:

We recently attended a wedding where the groom's stepmother and bride's stepgrandmother were not given corsages. To me, this looked bad. What is your opinion?

GENTLE READER:

The number of people who are expected to be distinguished with floral arrangements at a wedding has multiplied over the years, at the instigation of the flower industry, no doubt, to include mothers and grandmothers of principals, as well as their attendants. However, the number of mothers and grandmothers per bride or bridegroom has also multiplied considerably. Miss Manners' opinion is that it is silly to have one bridal couple with what look like four mothers and eight grandmothers. Limiting these decorations to the original relatives—or eliminating them (the flowers) altogether—seems more sensible.

When the Bride's Parents Are Divorced

DEAR MISS MANNERS:

Would you kindly inform me, my wife, and her daughter as to who should dance at the parents' dance at the daughter's wedding?

My problem is this. The daughter's real dad is divorced and is going with another woman. He left a lot of sore spots and hard feelings during the married years and very sore spots during the divorce proceedings, and left a real financial responsibility on my wife's shoulders. She does not want to have anything to do with him—much less to dance with him. The daughter stated she'd like her real dad to dance with her mother at the dance. Let me point out to you, Miss Manners, that the mother and I are married and I am the bride's stepdad. The mother and I agree that we should do the parents' dance at the wedding.

GENTLE READER:

Miss Manners quite agrees with you. If, considering all these various sore points, you and the mother manage to be polite and charming to the father during this family occasion, you will be making enough of an effort to please the bride. If she dances with all her fathers (one, father-in-law; two, biological father; three, stepfather), she will be too busy to notice.

Seating Sequential Families

DEAR MISS MANNERS:

In this day of sequential marriages, I have an etiquette question for multiple parents of the groom. Jeff and I have been married two years and Jeff's son, Tyke, is planning to be married. Tyke has a mother and two stepmothers. He's been close to all three. He also has a grandfather, grandmother, and stepgrandfather on his mother's side. All will probably attend the wedding, and all are relatively simpatico except the grandparent trio. The wedding will involve expensive travel for all. My question regards seating arrangements at the wedding and rehearsal dinners. What arrangements are called for by proper etiquette?

GENTLE READER:

What do you mean by "proper etiquette"? Do you imagine that there exists, somewhere, a stone diagram indicating the correct placement of sequential spouses according to some staid tradition? How many people do you figure that such a chart will allow in each collection of parents or grandparents?

Or, as Miss Manners hopes, are you asking her what would be a sensible and gracious way of distributing these people at dinnertime, so that they are not likely to be insulted either by the arrangements or by one another? There are many families, nowadays, chock full of people who do not correspond to the little figures on wedding charts for receiving lines, pew assignments, or dinners. Some people try to cut the families to fit the charts—Grandpa can't bring his fiancée, and Mother is told she can arrive with her third husband but may not invite the second one who did so much car-pool duty on behalf of the bridegroom.

Miss Manners calls this the Procrustes School of Etiquette. He was the ancient Greek gentleman who, you will recall, stretched short guests on the rack or chopped off the feet of tall guests to make them fit his bed.

In any case, parents are decidedly secondary characters at wedding festivities, the bride, bridegroom, and their attendants being the stars and featured players. (Who pays the bills has nothing whatever to do with the matter.)

You may put parents and grandparents in front pews, you may have mothers and even fathers in receiving lines, and you may have a parents' table at dinner, seating the clergyman or woman and spouse there, and the grandparents, too, if you wish. If they are amicable—and Miss Manners believes they have an obligation to seem so, on such an occasion, however they may really feel—put them all there. The bride's chief father acts as host, with the bridegroom's chief mother at his right; the hostess is the bride's chief mother, with the bridegroom's chief father at her right.

By "chief," Miss Manners generally means the original parents, whoever they may now be attached to. However, a stepparent with whom the bride or bridegroom has grown up would not, according to good sense and affection, be replaced by a parent who, say, disappeared at birth. Where there are hostile feelings, obviously you must separate antagonists. A simple and gracious solution at the dinner is to have several small tables, with one parent or grandparent, or one current couple serving as hosts at each table.

Fatherly Concerns

DEAR MISS MANNERS:

My father, who is a widower, is planning to attend my wedding with his girl friend, who is a widow. My brothers and I like her very much and consider her part of our family at this point. They have not discussed marriage with us, but have vacationed together. They have been together about two years.

My questions are: Is it proper for my dad and his girl friend to be at the "head table" with my fiancée's mother, whose husband is deceased? Would it be acceptable for my dad and his girl friend to stay together at the hotel where most of the guests will be staying? (He lives out of town.) They have always stayed together at hotels when visiting here.

This situation has created some friction within our family, and I need help in coping with this potential crisis. I would prefer to have both of them at the head table and don't object if they stay together at the hotel. Some other people in my family evidently object to their staying together.

GENTLE READER:

Let us call the lady your father's "intended." This is a slightly slangy word for Miss Manners, but she admires its ambiguity. This will confer on her a quasi-official status that will make it easier for you to carry out your admirable and hospitable intentions toward your father's companion. It would also make it simpler for your prospective mother-in-law to explain to her side of the family whom she has seated at the bridal table.

The bride's mother, as hostess, is the only person whose consent you need for this public question; your side of the family are merely guests. As for the private arrangements, they are no one's business at all. What your father and his intended intend to do after the wedding is over, and where they intend to do it, is not a proper family question.

❧ THE BRIDEGROOM'S PARENTS

DEAR MISS MANNERS:

Our son is getting married at an informal lawn wedding. I believe there will be a picnic-type reception afterward. I would like to know the proper things to do on my husband's and my part. Immediately upon learning of our son's wedding, we gave a dinner in our home for the parents of the intended bride. What else is expected of us? Wouldn't a long dress for the mothers be wrong for an informal wedding? Who gives the bachelor party? Should there be a rehearsal dinner? If so, who gives it and who pays? Would it be wrong for us to offer to pay for anything, like the cake or the food?

GENTLE READER:

The chief duty of the bridegroom's family is to take orders from the bride's family. Some people find this a difficult task, but it is cheaper and less time consuming than the tasks assigned to the bride's family. Thus, the cake, other food, and even the length of your dress come under their jurisdiction.

Your side may run three side events, one obligatory and two optional, that you have already properly identified. The social overture to the bride's family, which you have performed, is required. The bachelor's dinner is not necessary, but if it is given, it is given by the bachelor, a.k.a. the bridegroom. The rehearsal dinner has become a customary way of the bridegroom's family taking the responsibility, financial burden, and the wedding party away from the bride's family on the night before the wedding when they are apt to have as much, or more, than they can handle. Please see p. 335.

Rehearsal Dinner

DEAR MISS MANNERS:

My husband and I have a serious situation facing us. Our son, twenty-nine years of age, is being married and we were just informed that it is our duty to give a rehearsal dinner for the wedding party. There are sixteen in the wedding party, plus, we're also told, we must invite the various spouses or mates of the individuals participating. My husband and I are living on a fixed income, and in today's inflation, we cannot come up with any solution of how we can get around this issue of feeding thirty-two people because of "tradition." Our son tells us we're not up on wedding etiquette. Miss Manners, will you please help us in this plight?

GENTLE READER:

Tradition, indeed! Miss Manners has no patience with people who invoke etiquette for the purpose of bilking others, especially if they happen not to know what they are talking about.

The tradition, you may inform your son, was always that the bride's parents gave a bridesmaids'-and-ushers' dinner or, more likely, a tea after an afternoon rehearsal. Only in recent decades has it become usual for the bridegroom's parents to give a rehearsal dinner for the wedding party (including the clergy and all spouses) in order to free the bride's parents from this obligation at a time when they are already harassed beyond human endurance, and to create a role for a family that was traditionally nearly invisible at the wedding, namely the relatives of the bridegroom.

In any case, prolonged carousing the night before a wedding is a terrible idea. Miss Manners suggests you give a tea party after the rehearsal, tea and cucumber sandwiches being both festive and cheap. Or you could do the traditional thing and let the bride's family worry about entertaining all these people.

Housing the Bridegroom's Family

DEAR MISS MANNERS:

First I would like to say that being the father of two girls and no sons is very expensive and somewhat unfair around wedding time. When my older daughter was married a couple of years ago, almost everyone was local and no lodging was needed. Now my younger is getting married in June, and her fiancé is in the Marine Corps and his relatives are from far away. I would think that my obligation would be to make reservations for them, but my wife says that we are obligated to pay for their motel rooms. I haven't been able to find out which way is correct.

GENTLE READER:

Indeed, it is unfair to be the father of a bride, as opposed to the father of a bridegroom, but not quite that unfair. You get to pay for everything connected with the wedding and the reception, with the exception of the clergyman's fee and the atrocious bills run up by the ushers, and for everything the bride wears and has bought before marriage to wear later, except the wedding rings.

You are not responsible for the support of the bridegroom's family, even during the wedding festivities. It is thoughtful to make a convenient reservation for them, but not necessary to pay their bills. The only hotel bill you will have is if your family is unable to persuade local friends what fun it would be to have the bridesmaids stay with them.

THE ATTENDANTS

The Matron of Honor

DEAR MISS MANNERS:

My eighteen-year-old granddaughter, who'll be nineteen when she gets married, really wants me to be her matron of honor. I am sixty-seven and will be sixty-eight at wedding time, and am also very fat and short. I will lose some weight by then, but can't slim down all that much, as it would look uglier than fat. I believe the groom will go along with her. My question: What is proper in this case? She does have a fourteen-year-old sister who will be bridesmaid and does not wish her to be maid of honor. We will appreciate your opinion.

GENTLE READER:

Miss Manners' opinion is that it will be a charming wedding, and an unusually good marriage, too, judging from the values of the bridal couple. People who understand that there are qualities more worth honoring than youth and beauty will probably achieve the happiness they deserve.

Proper Presents for the Wedding Party

DEAR MISS MANNERS:

What are the proper presents to give bridesmaids and my fiancé's ushers? Is something so untraditional as a good book—different books for each, of course, according to their tastes—all right instead of things like bracelets and cuff links they may never use?

GENTLE READER:

Are you trying to give these people something they might enjoy, or are you trying to do the proper thing by them? Books, at best, are only read, but useless, monogrammed silver objects that cannot be returned serve to remind one of the occasion of their presentation every time one sees them tarnishing away, unused. Cuff links and bracelets are all right, since everyone has too many of them, but silver golf tees or toothpaste tube squeezers are ideal.

Bridesmaids

DEAR MISS MANNERS:

Now don't get me wrong. I am really a very proper person. So forgive me, Miss Manners, if my voice becomes shrill as I tell you this story.

My roommate was engaged to be married a year ago and asked me to be her bridesmaid. I tried my best, Miss Manners, really I did. For an entire year I chauffeured her around to photographers, addressed invitations, and planned menus. (Are salmon toasts suitable for a three o'clock reception, or is it more fashionable to have pink cottage cheese molded into the shape of a lamb?) I was forced to buy a hideous red bridesmaid's dress trimmed with cotton strawberries for eighty-five dollars. Red shoes to match for thirty-five dollars. And in July, I spent twenty-five dollars on a bridal shower after I found her copy of Emily Post tactfully left open to the page which stated that this was my social obligation. But I drew the line when she told me to buy four pink plastic midget carnations for my hair at eighteen dollars a pair. No, I said, and stood my ground. No? She was incredulous. Hadn't I agreed to be her bridesmaid? Didn't I understand that it was her inalienable right to deplete my bank account of its entire contents, to render me poverty-stricken in the name of propriety? Tell me, Miss Manners, did I behave badly? I fear that I am unfit for polite society.

GENTLE READER:

Or vice versa. Miss Manners congratulates you on your social fortitude. Miss Manners herself would have cracked before you did, at the pink cottage cheese, to be exact.

DEAR MISS MANNERS:

Last winter, I was invited to be an attendant in a close friend's wedding to be held this summer. A mutual girl friend recently returned to town, and the prospective bride immediately began spending all her time with her. I now rarely get to see the bride at all. I was horrified, but not surprised, when the bride-to-be told me that she had previously promised her recently returned friend that she could be in the wedding party. And now, she says, this friend keeps pestering her about being in the wedding (I don't believe this), so she adds, why don't you hold the guest book instead of being a bridesmaid. Besides, the prospective bride says, ''It would be awkward for you because your boyfriend can't be in the wedding party, and wouldn't have anyone to sit with in church.''

GENTLE READER:

As the bride seems to recognize a peculiar social form known as the Retroactive Previous Engagement, it seems to Miss Manners that you are at liberty to have one of these yourself, to go to a less awkward place, where you and your boyfriend could sit comfortably together, as that is what seems to worry the bride. Of course, you could also be gracious, ignore the bride's dreadful blunder (all she would have had to do would have been to increase the number of bridesmaid-usher sets), and preside over the guest book.

The Junior Bridesmaid

DEAR MISS MANNERS:

My fiancé and I are getting married soon. My future sister-in-law is nine years old, and we are having her in our bridal party, but have a question. Is she too old to be a flower girl? I thought she was, and am having her as a junior bridesmaid. The only problem is that I haven't got an usher to walk up the aisle with her. Could I still have her as a junior bridesmaid? Who would she dance with at the reception?

GENTLE READER:

Miss Manners approves of using one's future family in the wedding party, and the younger they are, the more they appreciate it. The general rule is that flower girls and pages should be still in the *Awwwww-aren't-they-adorable* stage, which is to say, under about eight. What you have here is a junior bridesmaid.

It is not necessary to marry this young lady off, even symbolically. If there is no appropriate young man to be a junior usher, so be it. Even if there were, male wedding attendants precede female ones down the aisle in the processional, and when they escort them up, as it were, after the wedding ceremony, are hardly noticed because everyone is craning to see the expressions on the faces of the newly married couple. Your junior bridesmaid may walk by herself in front of the paired attendants during the recessional, or take the arm of an adult usher. Whom she dances with at the reception is her lookout.

(For alternate recessionals, please see p. 335.)

🌹 RECEPTIONS

Greeting Guests

DEAR MISS MANNERS:

My daughter is having quite a nice church wedding, and we have rented limousines to take us from the church to the hotel where the reception will be held. I know that we will be busy having pictures taken of the receiving line at the reception, so I would like my husband and me to have some time to greet our friends after the ceremony is over, before we get too busy. The limousine man says we can't do this at the church; that it's not right. We are paying him by the hour, so it's not his problem, but he claims that it isn't proper etiquette, but that we must greet our friends at the hotel room. Is that really right? If so, why?

GENTLE READER:

Yes, it is, and the reason is that you cannot receive guests formally at something at which you are not the hosts, namely a religious ceremony in a church. It is God's Church, and therefore He or, by extension, His clergy, alone may receive people after a religious service.

Feeding the Multitude

DEAR MISS MANNERS:

My son is getting married about two hundred miles from where we live. They are sending out invitations to our family, relatives, and friends. My question is, if you invite people to your wedding and it is two hundred miles away, shouldn't the reception consist of more than cake and plain punch? After a little protesting, they finally agreed to have turkey salad sandwich loaves. I even offered to help pay expenses, but that is all they want. I say you shouldn't invite people to your wedding when they have to travel that distance unless you are going to provide a meal.

GENTLE READER:

You have to realize that the food at a wedding is of such emotional significance that practical considerations, such as feeding people who have been driving all day, have nothing to do with it. Overstuffing is an important part of many people's idea of a wedding. Unless people groan at the very sight of the buffet table at the reception, or at the approach of still another course at a wedding dinner; unless most of the conversation consists of "No, no, I couldn't," and "Can you imagine what this must have cost them a head?" and "I didn't even see the crab legs over there''; unless a junior bridesmaid gets sick and a grand-parent has to be led to a chair and fanned—the wedding has not been a success. Others are of the cucumber sandwich and two glasses of champagne persuasion.

Miss Manners does not favor one tradition over another, but advises against trying to win converts from such deep convictions. Take a hotel room in town, and invite your side over to eat after the wedding. You will have a good time laughing among yourselves at the skimpiness of the bride's family.

Wedding Cake

DEAR MISS MANNERS:

Most wedding cakes are so vulgar, with all the overly fancy trimming, and I would prefer to have a perfectly plain cake. My fiancée, who generally has very good taste, and who agrees with me about keeping the rest of the wedding simple, says that would look ''cheap'' and wants one of those several-tiered monstrosities. She has forgotten that she once told me a story about being a flower girl and looking up at her cousin's cake which had a bride and groom on the top, and probably that's what she really wants but is ashamed to admit it. This is such a dumb argument, but it makes me wonder what else she is keeping from me in the way of secret ickyness.

GENTLE READER:

Who are you, the Mies van der Rohe of the pastry shop? Wedding cakes are supposed to be vulgar. Go buy yourself a doughnut to satisfy your aesthetic sense, and let her have that wedding cake.

Liquor

DEAR MISS MANNERS:

I'm in a bind as to how I can suggest to the parents of my future son-in-law that if they want an open bar type of cocktail hour before dinner at the reception, they should spend for it. They are quite able to do this financially. My husband could pay for it, but we agree that we should not have to spend for something we don't like, especially since it is quite unnecessary. We do not drink, and neither does my family. I was thinking of serving a punch or beer.

GENTLE READER:

It is unfortunate that in weddings, as in divorces, money is often used as a weapon when hostilities have nothing to do with cost. In this case, you say there really is no financial problem in paying for the drinks. Why, then, do you wish to stick the other family for a bill for an occasion for which you are the hosts?

The answer is that you don't like having to entertain people who drink. This is clear when you say that there is no need for liquor because your family does not drink—as if you were not equally obliged to be hospitable to the family into which your daughter is marrying. If your convictions prevented you from presiding at an event where liquor is served, Miss Manners would support you in explaining politely to the other set of parents that you could not violate this policy. However, you have made it clear, by bringing up the matter of money, that this is not the case.

Miss Manners is afraid that it is too late to pretend that it is; you should have thought of this earlier. Allowing some of your guests to drink but refusing to pay for it cannot be passed off as a moral position.

Reducing Expenses

DEAR MISS MANNERS:

Recently an acquaintance invited my husband and me to her wedding. This was quite a surprise, since I have heard that she was complaining about the cost of said wedding and the fact that she would have to spend two dollars to feed each person. She succeeded in getting this amount reduced to a dollar and fifty cents and has reportedly invited one hundred and fifty people. In addition, she has borrowed the wedding gown from the matron of honor, and has asked two guests to help, one to cut and serve the cake and one to pour and serve the punch. I have also been told that there will be a cash bar at the reception. What is your opinion of a person with such a limited budget inviting so many people? Is it proper to invite guests to your wedding and then ask them to serve as waiters and waitresses? Is it proper to expect your guests to buy their own libations?

GENTLE READER:

It may surprise you to hear that what you call serving as waiters and waitresses is, under the odd verb "to pour" (as in recruiting friends to pour tea at one's tea party), a traditional honor. Nor is there anything wrong with borrowing a wedding dress or inviting many people. However, you may be relieved to hear that selling drinks is disgusting. By serving them tea and homemade cake, she could be perfectly gracious within the limits of the budget.

Toasts to Oneself

DEAR MISS MANNERS:

My fiancé and I have been in one continuous whirl of parties practically since the day we got engaged. We are also having a large wedding, and there will be several parties before it. Mind you, we are not complaining. It's hectic, but it's fun.

My question has to do with being toasted. Someone is always proposing a toast to us, or sometimes just to me. People seem to think that champagne is the only fit drink for us now—and, again, I'm not complaining about that, either. But last night I got a little high, and started telling funny stories about the time I almost ran off and got married to a boy who got arrested, soon afterwards, for stealing cars. That is, I thought these stories were funny. Nobody else did. There were a few forced laughs, and my fiancé turned white. In short, I think I had better stop drinking so much at the prewedding parties, or there won't be any wedding party. Yet I know there is nothing more gauche than refusing to drink a toast. What shall I do?

GENTLE READER:

Fortunately for you, there is something more gauche than refusing to drink a toast, and that is drinking a toast to oneself. Since you are the object of all these liquid good wishes, all you have to do—in fact, all you should do—is to sit there, hands in lap, and smile demurely while everyone else drinks to you. You are supposed to be sufficiently drunk on happiness. If you can manage a blush, that is nice, too. It is only after the toast is completed that you may join the guzzling, or not, as you see fit.

When England's Princess Margaret Rose was considerably smaller and more adorable than she is now, she was said to have asked her father what he sang while everyone else was singing "God Save the King." The answer to your question is the same as the answer to hers: Try to look gratified and dignified, but under no circumstances should you join right in.

Wedding Questions

DEAR MISS MANNERS:

I am a single, twenty-five-year-old professional woman who will soon be participating in my younger sister's wedding, the family's first. Faced on this occasion with the inevitablity of parrying personally objectionable inquiries about the duration of my single state, how might I respond without appearing needlessly rude? Also, may the bride's attendants wear wrist-length gloves at a morning summer wedding?

GENTLE READER:

Questions such as "And when are you getting married?" do not deserve to be answered. (Questions about wrist-length gloves do, and the answer is yes.) If you do not wish to be needlessly rude, a resolve Miss Manners admires, your reply should be a smile, the statement "Oh, I don't know," and a change of subject.

A Postwedding Reception

DEAR MISS MANNERS:

My son is being married out of state. The bride's mother is having a lovely reception. She asked me not to invite more than eight guests, as she will be inviting eight also. My husband and I have many new friends and business acquaintances who should be invited. We therefore plan to have a large post-honeymoon reception, inviting two hundred guests, including the parents and family of the bride. Can you advise me about the invitations? Do we invite these people separately, or would it be proper to enclose an invitation along with the formal wedding invitation? Do we print announcements of the wedding and enclose our party invitation? I want to do the proper thing, but it is physically impossible to invite the large number of friends, relatives, etc., to the out-of-town wedding.

GENTLE READER:

Indeed, a delayed reception, such as you propose, is the correct and gracious solution to the bride's family's space limitation problem. But you must be careful not to seem to be passing this off as part of the original wedding festivities; it is, instead, a charming but different tradition, namely a reception in honor of a newly married couple.

Your invitations should not be sent with the wedding invitations or with wedding announcements, both of which are issued by the bride's parents. For a reception such as you describe, the form is:

In honor of

Mr. and Mrs. Jonathan Rhinehart Awful, 3d

[or, less formally] Daffodil and Jonathan

Mr. and Mrs. Jonathan Awful, junior

request the pleasure of your company

on Saturday, the eighth of May

at eight o'clock

The Racket Club

🌹 PHOTOGRAPHS

Memory, to the best of Miss Manners' dim recollection, used to be an interesting and original thing. It was eccentric in what it selected, skipping the obvious in favor of the curious. One's wedding was often a blur, while moments containing nothing more than the touching of fingertips may have been framed in gold. A child's first birthday may have disappeared, while a babyish look of trust may have gotten itself accidentally bronzed. An exotic trip may have faded, while the picture of a domestic moment continued to burn brightly.

Naturally, all of this was possible only before the widespread use of the camera. Now that every family has its official record maker, there is no room for wispy memories in the world of indisputable snapshots. Life is no longer something to remember. It has become, as we say in the media business, a photo opportunity. Baby is not allowed to take his first step when he first feels brave enough to attempt it: he must wait until his parents have loaded the camera. Here Miss Manners must step in. Miss Manners is the patron goddess of all social events, and a lot of family events as well. She is therefore in a position to tell all professional and amateur photographers that they may record such events only if they allow the events to take place.

A wedding in which the bride and bridegroom pose for photographs kissing, eating cake, standing with their wedding party, standing with their parents, cutting cake, eating ice cream, standing with the out-of-town guests, drinking champagne, throwing bouquets, and otherwise following a photographer's schedule of expected events is not a wedding.

A holiday trip in which members of the party are required to spend their time standing in the hot sun in front of tourist sites is not a vacation. A birthday party in which celebrants are instructed when to open their presents and to blow out candles on cakes is not a party. These are merely photo opportunities.

Now, Miss Manners does not wish to incur the outrage of all camera enthusiasts, knowing, as she does, that they are armed. Therefore, she wishes to suggest a compromise by which photographers may save such activities for the albums, without having to destroy the activities in order to do so.

One way is the truly "candid" picture. A candid picture is not, as many people seem to believe, a photograph in which a bride has been instructed to feed cake to a bridegroom who, in turn, has been instructed to eat it. There is also the true photo opportunity. The old set-up photograph, done at a crucial moment between the bride's last hair appointment and the wedding ceremony, well served the true purpose of wedding photographs, which is to give the couple's descendants something to laugh at years later.

Posed photograph sessions at weddings are so notoriously abused that Miss Manners would ban them entirely, relying for all the "formal" pictures on the advance sessions, and trusting to catch-as-catch-can for the rest. On vacations, the best posed session would be in the airport with all the luggage, a time that does not interfere with anyone's pleasure and is apt to be beautifully typical of the trip.

Otherwise, those who aspire to record life photographically must be made to realize that they must not interfere with the natural course of life and record things that would not have taken place otherwise. There is little enough improvisation left in life as it is.

Joint Portraits

DEAR MISS MANNERS:

Does a formal bridal portrait have to be just of the bride alone? I have seen some, with announcements and in people's houses, that show the couple in a formal pose—I'm not talking about the candids of her feeding him wedding cake, or anything like that—instead of just the bride in her wedding dress, and it seems to me that it makes much more sense. After all, they're both getting married, aren't they?

GENTLE READER:

It is true that many modern couples have the notion that the bridegroom is as essential an ingredient of the formal wedding as the bride. Miss Manners wouldn't mind this so much in matters such as photographs if she didn't know where that kind of thing leads. It leads to husbands' thinking that they have as much right as wives to play starring roles in the delivery room—that's where it leads.

Placing Parents in Pictures

DEAR MISS MANNERS:

What is the correct way to picture the bride and groom and parents and grandparents when the parents have been divorced and have remarried, so that there are then three sets of parents? Is it improper to picture the bride's mother and father together, since they now have different spouses? Or does one take two sets of pictures?

GENTLE READER:

Miss Manners remembers when people got married because they wanted to. Then bridal couples started saying that they were getting married for the sake of their parents. From what Miss Manners has been able to observe, weddings are now held for the convenience of photographers. Nevertheless, there is no "correct" or "incorrect" order for the taking of wedding photographs. Some divorced couples are friendly enough to climb into the same photograph together, and others are not. If you must have pictures posed in parallel groups, Miss Manners advises ascertaining the wishes of the bride's parents and respecting them.

❧ THE WHITE DRESS
(*and Other Bridal Symbols*)

DEAR MISS MANNERS:

I am a twenty-year-old female who has never been married before, and I am planning to be married soon. I was wondering, is it proper to wear an all-white wedding dress with all the trimmings? I know that is supposed to signify purity, but, like most of the population, I am not a virgin! Is this proper in this day and age?

GENTLE READER:

Is what proper? Not being a virgin?

What is most improper, in Miss Manners' opinion, what is, in fact, indecent, is the widely held notion that the wedding dress is supposed to reveal to all the world the condition of the bridal body inside. If that is the object, one might as well wear a see-through dress (of Alençon lace, of course).

Here is the correct Bridal Color Code, or the Wedding Guest's Guide to Identifying Brides by Their Plumage. (However, as you point out, bridal conventions are sometimes disregarded by some or most of the population.)

hat or veil

least formal

Afternoon

Formal

Garden or second wedding

most formal

Brides maid ...make up your own costume to fit

mother— sure of only one thing — she'll wear her pearls

flower girl

LADIES' WEDDING CLOTHES. *The bride's style of dress is determined by the degree of formality of the wedding, rather than the time of day. Most formal is a high-necked, long-sleeved dress with train and long veil. A less formal wedding dress may have short sleeves, some or no train, and be worn with a hat or flowers in the hair. At second and other informal weddings, a dress or suit is worn with a hat or flowers. The couple's mothers and the female guests should wear long dresses only at evening weddings of some formality, but the bridesmaids wear long dresses if the bride does and should try not to complain that they hate them.*

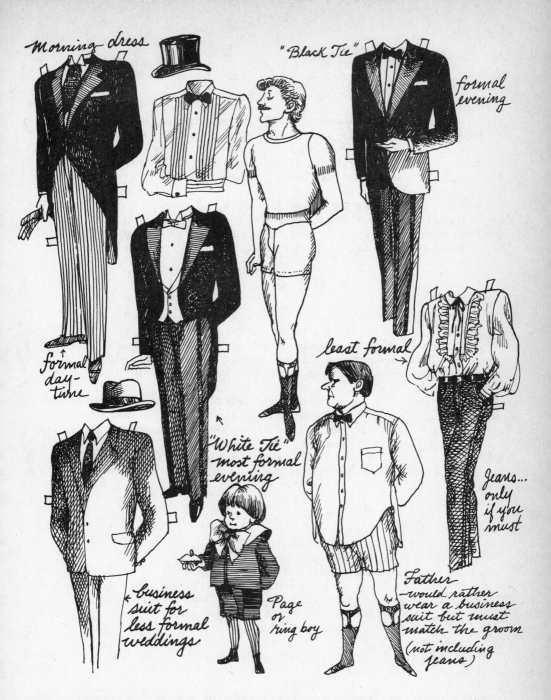

Morning dress

"Black Tie"

formal evening

formal day-time

least formal

Jeans... only if you must

"White Tie" most formal evening

business suit for less formal weddings

Page or ring boy

Father — would rather wear a business suit but must match the groom (not including jeans)

GENTLEMEN'S WEDDING CLOTHES. *The bridegroom's clothes are dictated by the time of day and by the bride. The most formal, when the bride wears a dress with a train and veil, are morning dress for daytime weddings and white tie for evening. Black tie may be worn at an evening wedding, and a blue, black or grey business suit for an informal wedding at any time of day. The jeans are there only to show what no nice girl should marry.*

The fathers and the groomsmen dress as the bridegroom does. It is a mistake to attempt to distinguish the bridegroom by his clothes. The bride can usually tell which one he is, and no one else much cares.

Brides come in two models: Young and/or inexperienced, and mature and/or experienced. The former wears white, the latter something more subtle *or* more befitting her station *or* more sophisticated. The experience referred to is not the one you and so many others assume; it is marriage. If you do not believe that marriage is an experience in itself, above and beyond lovemaking—well, then, you should be wearing white, because you have just proved how pure and innocent you are.

The effect of the white dress should be fresh and sweet—an effect that is not usually what women who are older and wiser want to project. The difference is what makes people cry at first weddings, and smile at subsequent ones, smiles being infinitely more complicated than tears.

Wearing Glasses

DEAR MISS MANNERS:

Do I have to wear my glasses to my wedding? I can't see without them and have never been able to tolerate contact lenses, but I think I would look prettier without them, and they seem inappropriate with the wedding veil and cap I am planning to wear. Is it all right to look different for that one day?

GENTLE READER:

If your fiancé does not recognize you without your glasses and you cannot properly identify him without your glasses, it seems to Miss Manners that you are running a dangerous risk. If members of the bridal party promise to guide you properly through the ceremony, you might chance it. Miss Manners advises putting the glasses back on for the reception. It's one thing not to recognize one's new husband, but it would be rude not to be able to recognize one's old friends.

A Black Tie Wedding

DEAR MISS MANNERS:

What are the proper clothes for a black tie wedding? Of course, the ushers and the best man will be in black formal wear, but what about the bridegroom? Should he wear white tie to distinguish himself from the other men? And what about the guests? What do they—both men and women—wear? Suppose the wedding is in the afternoon?

GENTLE READER:

There is no question of that. Wearing black tie during daylight is no way to start a marriage. The cutaway with gray, striped trousers is formal daytime wear.

As for the black tie evening wedding, all adult men at it, in whatever relationship, wear the same clothes, although guests can also get away with dark business suits. There is no need to distinguish the bridegroom; he is the one marrying the bride.

Women guests wear dinner dresses (as opposed to ball dresses), which are generally long, although every once in a while we have a season when de-designers pretend that short, very fussy dresses are just as formal.

🌹 WEDDING GUESTS

". . . and Guest"

DEAR MISS MANNERS:

I am a widower in my sixties and receive wedding invitations, some of which are marked with my name only, and others with my name "and guest." Both contain R.s.v.p. cards requesting "Number of persons attending————." Am I allowed to bring a guest if the invitation is marked with my name only?

GENTLE READER:

Certainly not. A wedding should not be treated as if it were a public institution, like a disco, to which one can bring an anonymous date. If the hosts make it that, you may take advantage of it, but please don't institute this practice on your own. Besides, you might decide you like the maid of honor better than anyone you already know.

Guests Bringing Guests

DEAR MISS MANNERS:

We have encountered an unexpected and appalling problem regarding un-married wedding guests. It seems that every one of the singles we've invited—and they range in age from twenty to sixty—believes that of course their "friend of the week" is invited. We, on the other hand, have always believed that only the honor of the presence of those persons actually listed on the wedding invitation envelopes was desired. How about a lesson in wedding etiquette?

GENTLE READER:

You do not need a lesson, as you are quite correct about only those actually invited being invited. Your question is really how to teach your friends a lesson.

If you find yourself unable to be so firm, there is one rule about wedding guests that allows for some flexibility, and Miss Manners suggests invoking it: If a person has become formally engaged to be married without the hosts' realizing it, that person may ask to be allowed to bring the fiancée or fiancé to a wedding. Suppose you reply to the request of bringing someone by declaring, "Oh, are you engaged? How marvelous! I didn't know that! What a wonderful chance to tell everyone at the wedding!" If the prospective guest then retreats in embarrassment, denying the engagement, you may say gently, "Oh. Well, in that case, I'm afraid I can't ask you to bring a date. We'd love to meet him (her) on some less formal occasion."

When Children Are Not Invited

DEAR MISS MANNERS:

My daughter and her fiancé do not wish to invite anyone under sixteen to their wedding reception. Is there any polite way to express their feelings to family and friends without causing any hard feelings?

GENTLE READER:

There is no polite way to issue negative invitations. Neither is there a polite way to accept invitations that have not been issued. Address your invitations to the adults whom you wish to invite, without mentioning their children. If they inquire whether they may bring the children, explain your policy. Miss Manners hopes you appreciate the difference between committing a social error yourself and merely responding to someone else's error.

Uninvited Guests

DEAR MISS MANNERS:

I'd just like to know how one is supposed to cope with responses that include uninvited guests. Children, in particular, were excluded from the invitation to my daughter's wedding. Two guests asked the bride about bringing the child ("Never before excluded from the parents' coming and going"). Another guest (single guests were invited to bring a friend/companion) added two friends to the number of dinner guests to expect.

I'm probably allowing my mind to distort this out of proportion—but am I wrong to resent this behavior? What is the best, mannerly way to handle such situations?

GENTLE READER:

If Miss Manners feels like weeping when she hears of how rudely people attempt to impose on those whose only crime is to invite them to a wedding—and Miss Manners isn't even in the emotionally wracking throes of putting on a wedding—how can she call your resentment wrong, or even out of proportion?

Do not listen to the pleas of parents claiming that umbilical cords have not yet been broken at any social event; these are the very parents who will permit their children to whine during the ceremony. Nor should you allow any guest to run his or her own party-within-the-party with a guest list not chosen by you. Even allowing single guests to bring their own friends is more than Miss Manners would do.

The answer to how to deal with these outrageous requests is: firmly. "I am so sorry—we are simply not having children," or "No, I'm afraid we're only inviting our own dear friends." Do not allow these people to blackmail you by threatening their own refusals. The answer to that is, "Well, I'm so sorry you won't be able to come. It would have meant a great deal to all of us to have you there."

Wedding Conflicts

DEAR MISS MANNERS:

My sister-in-law advised us a long time ago that her daughter would be married month after next, and recently she told us the exact date. It is a very large affair with the ceremony set for noon and dinner, etc., ending about five thirty, in New Jersey. A few weeks ago, my daughter-in-law's aunt told her that her son is having a religious wedding ceremony in Long Island on the same date in the late morning, and naturally, would like them to be there. They were married by a judge a short time ago.

Question: How do my son and my daughter-in-law solve this problem with the weddings at approximately the same time, several hours' driving time away, when both weddings involve first cousins? They will have their three-month-old baby with them, whom everyone wants to see, including the baby's great-grandmother in her eighties at the New Jersey wedding.

GENTLE READER:

Miss Manners' concern is about the type of life to be expected of someone who, at the age of three months, is already torn between two urgent, conflicting social engagements. If Miss Manners were starting out life with such a problem, she would write charming notes to both families pleading her inability to attend weddings because of infancy.

Your son and daughter-in-law should be old enough to know that in these cases one honors the commitment made first, and questions of great-grandmotherhood, previous marital status of the bridal couple, or New Jersey vs. Long Island are irrelevant.

A Double Standard

DEAR MISS MANNERS:

I have heard that it is wrong to say "Congratulations" to the bride—that you can say it to the bridegroom, but are supposed to say "Best wishes" to the bride. Why is that?

GENTLE READER:

Because of inequality in the marriage laws.

Civility to Inferior Connections

DEAR MISS MANNERS:

I have a troubling problem on my mind. I come from a well-to-do and well-respected family. My brother has already married respectability. But my sister is going ahead with a marriage to a dense-headed man whose family has a history of marrying money. We are having a very, very fashionable wedding. To make a long story short: How should I treat his rather interesting family?

GENTLE READER:

"With condescension," is obviously the answer you have in mind. No doubt you are asking Miss Manners how to pass this off as politeness. You are in luck, because the best way to be condescending in such a situation is to be excessively polite. If you ignore these people at your very, very fashionable wedding (Miss Manners wonders how much the caterer charges for each very), you will expose yourself to justified criticism. You must hover graciously over these people whom you so dislike, steering them gently about by the shoulders and enthusiastically introducing them to everyone. It will be clear to all exactly how you feel about them.

By the way, congratulations. If your sister's fiancé's family has a history of marrying money, he must be quite rich.

What Guests Wear

DEAR MISS MANNERS:

My friend's daughter is getting married in a few months. I had heard that mothers of the bride and groom should not wear white or black to the wedding. But I thought that rule went out with "white signifies virginity." Anyway, the bride's family is all upset because the groom's mother is wearing white. I also had intentions of wearing white. My friends and I would like to know the restrictions, if any, on black and white worn by the mothers of the bride and groom. Also should guests follow the same rules?

GENTLE READER:

The mother of the bridegroom should not wear white to the wedding, whether she is a virgin or not. Neither should any of the guests. Nor should any of the mothers of guests wear black; this rule, too, is unrelated to physical characteristics that are none of anybody's business. Black signifies mourning. No woman should show up at a wedding at which she is neither the bride nor a mourner wearing white or black. Those in deep mourning should not attend weddings. Those in second mourning may wear beige, gray, or lavender. (Please see pp. 694–695.)

DEAR MISS MANNERS:

Quick! I need your opinion. Is it in poor taste to wear a black hat to a friend's wedding? It's really sharp-looking, and will be worn with some color (my dress will be white or red).

GENTLE READER:

Miss Manners dearly wishes you were going to a funeral instead of a wedding. It's not that she wishes your friends any harm—it's just that practically nobody wears a black hat to a funeral any longer, and it's so nice and respectful. She doesn't think yours will do any harm at a wedding, if it's very sharp-looking and your dress is very red. One does not wear a white dress to a wedding. It looks as if you were competing with the bride.

Reason over Rules

DEAR MISS MANNERS:
I have been invited to a wedding next month, when I will be seven and a half months pregnant. I have a black maternity party dress—is it proper to wear that?

GENTLE READER:
Marriage, childbirth—there is a whole cycle of life behind this question, isn't there? Miss Manners pictures you, in your charming dilemma. Having been a bride once yourself, you are sensitive to the dress violation of wearing black to a wedding, and thus lending a sort of bad witch appearance to an otherwise light event. At the same time, you have your child's future to consider. What sort of a heritage will a child have whose mother squanders her money on a party dress she will wear only once?

Miss Manners' feeling is that while it is incorrect to wear black to a wedding, it is insane to invest good money in another party maternity dress. Use the black as a background color, adding a light coat, shawl or scarf to disguise it, if not you.

Long Dresses

DEAR MISS MANNERS:
May I wear a long dress to an afternoon wedding?

GENTLE READER:
Certainly, and best wishes to you, my dear, for your future happiness. (Miss Manners is assuming you are the bride. A wedding guest would of course not dream of wearing a long dress in the afternoon.)

Guests's Services

DEAR MISS MANNERS:
Eight months ago, I wrote to my first cousin's wife, asking her to play the organ during my wedding. She replied that she would be happy to, and that she requests only a baby-sitter for her daughter. Now, four weeks before the wedding, she called stating how all the music was set, and that as usual, the service would be a wedding present. She said that my only cost would be to pay for her flight to the Midwest. If this cost was to be too expensive, and if I was able to find a less expensive organist, she would understand.

I responded with a letter, stating that I had never intended her as only a participant, but as a welcomed guest at the wedding. Furthermore, as the distance was so great, I would not have ever asked her for that sole purpose. Furthermore, I was able to contact a local organist, so if she wishes to come, to please come as a guest only. Also, I apologized for the misunderstanding. Was this the correct thing to do?

GENTLE READER:

Indeed it was, and Miss Manners trusts that you have learned from the experience never to ask your guests to donate their professional services. Now please tell your photographer friend just to come as a guest and have a good time, because you have hired someone to take the pictures.

🌹 WEDDING PRESENTS

(and Thank-You notes)

When bridal couples invite those who are dearest to them to share the public solemnization of their happiness, they may be sure that all their cherished friends and relatives are having the same thoughts: Do we owe them a present? How much do you think we have to spend? Can't we get away with less? How much did they spend for us?

In a society that uses the terms "free gift" and "mandatory donation," it is not surprising that the exchange of presents is treated as an unpleasant commercial transaction, while impersonal fees are disguised as voluntarily given presents. Miss Manners once tried to step into the Metropolitan Museum of Art in New York after having discovered that there was no admission charge—only to be detained by an employee who admitted that one could enter "free," but explained that that could only be done after one made a voluntary donation to the museum. Miss Manners naturally inquired as to the meaning of such a voluntary donation.

"What do you want to give?" this person countered.

"A wing," replied Miss Manners, and was explaining that unfortunately she had not yet saved up the cash to carry out this wish, when she was interrupted with the information that intentions aside, she must give.

That is voluntary gift-giving in commercial life. In social life, however, there is no such thing as an obligatory present. You do not owe your friends anything just because they are getting married. Nevertheless, it is customary that when one values people enough to want to participate in occasions that are important to them, one is moved to express this emotion in some tangible form.

Get that? In other words, if you do not attend a wedding to which you have been invited, or merely receive an announcement, or attend only the ceremony and not the reception, you are not considered involved to the extent of, say, a silver bud vase. However, if you want to partake in the couple's bliss and also their champagne, this restraint would be inappropriate. The same principle may be applied to other occasions. You must care enough about people to want to gladden their hearts with a token of your esteem if you accept their overnight hospitality, celebrate Christmas, their birthdays or graduations with them, or expect a large inheritance from them.

One's Presents at the Reception

DEAR MISS MANNERS:

If I bring a wedding present to the reception, shouldn't the bride open it while I'm there? I have had presents pushed aside, which hurt me. I choose things carefully, and would like to see the pleasure on their faces.

GENTLE READER:

Please don't bring presents to weddings or wedding receptions. Please. Let us stamp out this unfortunate practice.

For one thing, the bride and bridegroom cannot take the time from their guests to open presents. For another, they (or their parents) must then figure out how to get the present home, or carry it with them on their honeymoon. For still another, the pleasure on their faces, at, let us say, receiving their fourth Crock-Pot, is best enjoyed in privacy.

Addressing Presents

DEAR MISS MANNERS:

Please advise me on the proper way to address the name on a gift to be sent ahead of time to the home of the bride-to-be. Is it "Mr. and Mrs. Joe America" (name of the groom-to-be) or Jane Doe? Need an answer soon.

GENTLE READER:

The custom is to address all prewedding presents to the bride-to-be, and those sent after the marriage to the couple. Nowadays some people may take offense at this, as a sign of inequality. Nowadays some people will take offense at anything. However, sending people presents goes a long way toward mitigating any offense.

An Indelicate Idea

DEAR MISS MANNERS:

My fiancée's parents have offered to give us a large wedding with all the trimmings, but they are agreeable to going along with the small simple one that we really prefer. Is there any delicate way we can suggest that we could really use the several thousand dollars they were willing to spend on us but now don't have to? I say "we," but the truth is I first need a delicate way to suggest this to my bride.

GENTLE READER:

It is not a very delicate idea, is it? If Miss Manners were to invite you to dinner, would you ask her to send you the grocery money instead and then pride yourself on having saved her the trouble of preparation? Often, parents will state frankly the limits of their resources and ask the bridal couple whether the money should be spent on the wedding or on a present (which sometimes *is* the money). But it is quite another thing to have such a suggestion made by the hopeful recipients.

Great Expectations

DEAR MISS MANNERS:

I am soon getting married and will be sending wedding invitations to a lot of out-of-town relatives. Would it be proper to enclose a card stating my patterns that I have picked out in crystal, china, silver, etc.? If this is proper and not too aggressive, how can I word the card and not appear too forward?

GENTLE READER:

Any indication that you make a connection between wanting certain people at your wedding and expecting presents from them is improper.

Charitable Expectations

DEAR MISS MANNERS:

Since my fiancé and I are both in our late twenties and have been working professionals for some time, we really are not lacking in any of the material comforts. What we would prefer to do is let those of our friends and relatives who might offer us wedding gifts know that we would prefer that they make a donation to a charity we've selected which has great meaning for us. Can we do so tastefully? And if so, how?

GENTLE READER:

Yours is the most altruistic of the many letters Miss Manners receives from people who want to have some control over the selection of presents they expect. Others ask, "How can I let them know I want money instead of some crummy toaster?" or "Instead of giving us pieces of silver we won't use, why can't our friends get together and pay our mortgage?" Then there are the people who either sympathize with their friends' problems of buying presents or profoundly distrust their taste, and want to say "No gifts, please" on their wedding invitations.

What Miss Manners must tell all of you, regardless of your motives, is that there is no tasteful way—not even any moderately decent way—of directing present giving when you are on the receiving end. Contrary to general belief, present giving is never required. It is traditionally associated with birthdays, Christmas, and weddings, but cannot be used as an entrance fee to related festivities. You must pretend that you invite people because you want to celebrate important occasions with them, and you must seem pleasantly surprised when they give you something. To act as if it is such standard payment that you can acknowledge your expectations is rude-rude-rude.

Perhaps what has confused you is the business gimmick of the bridal registry, by which engaged couples inform stores of their tastes in the hope that their friends will come in, get this information, and act on it.

There is just enough distance between the giver and the receiver to make this a passable practice. The bride and bridegroom do not actually instruct their friends—they only tell their preferences to a neutral business establishment. And the present givers only receive the information if they ask for it.

Another practice that has confused you is that of bereaved families who ask that "contributions" be made to a charity instead of flowers being sent to them or to the funeral. This is also a borderline case, most practical when there are huge numbers of mourners and it is known that there will be more than enough flowers. (Notice to florists: Miss Manners adores flowers and believes that they are an important, symbolic part of a funeral, but too many of them, sent to the bereaved family's house, can be oppressive.)

However, we were talking about weddings, not funerals, and the charitable donation idea is appropriate to the latter, not the former. Your wedding guests should not have to "memorialize" you with a charitable contribution in your name. If they want to remember you charitably, they can invite you for dinner. So the answer is no. Miss Manners knows you mean well, but you must take what people decide to give you, looking grateful that they went to the trouble to get you anything at all. And *then* you can exchange it.

Fishing for Presents

DEAR MISS MANNERS:

We work in an office where two employees are getting married to each other this summer. Since announcing their engagement, they have been dropping hints regarding presents they feel would be appropriate. For instance, they have said that they would not mind if someone paid off one of their charge cards, or they would not be insulted by cash. They have chosen a china pattern and have informed us that it is on sale at one of the area's department stores and have even told us when the sale ends. Invitations, engraved or oral, are still forthcoming, consequently we do not know if we are invited. Also, the prospective groom has been hinting broadly that he would like a bachelor's party.

Since they have been living together for quite some time, one would expect a quieter transition to wedded bliss, yet they are turning this occasion into a thinly veiled excuse for soliciting gifts. Being somewhat older than this couple, we are unsure whether their conduct is now considered proper and would like to know what response, if any, you would suggest the next time hints are dropped.

GENTLE READER:
It is improper to drop such hints, but downright foolish to feel that you have to pick them up. Let them lie there, right where they fell flat.

Displaying Wedding Presents

DEAR MISS MANNERS:
What is the best way to display wedding gifts?
GENTLE READER:
By putting them to their intended use in the bridal couple's home, for guests to admire or not admire as they wish. Miss Manners cannot say that the custom of displaying wedding presents at a wedding reception is vulgar, as it has been done for generations, but she can say that it is barbaric. The curiosity of one's friends as to one's china and flatware patterns is probably not overwhelming, and the only feeling satisfied when a bride sets up a dry goods department in her house is curiosity about who spent what. This is a nasty instinct and ought not to be indulged.

Obligatory Thank-You

DEAR MISS MANNERS:
When is a written thank-you note for a wedding gift not necessary?
GENTLE READER:
When no wedding present has been received.

Prompting Thank-Yous

DEAR MISS MANNERS:
Two months ago, I received three wedding invitations and purchased each a gift. I still haven't received a thank-you. Have any rules changed with regard to sending a thank-you note?
GENTLE READER:
No, the rules haven't changed, but neither, unfortunately, have the brides.
Successful love creates an exaggerated feeling of worthiness, which leads all brides to believe that it is reasonable to expect everyone whom they, their parents, and their parents-in-law know to spend large amounts of time, effort, and money sending them presents, but that it is outrageous to assume that they can spare the three minutes each it would take to acknowledge these presents.
Therefore a little ritual has evolved, to teach brides that most valuable of life's lessons: that generosity should always be encouraged.
As the unacknowledged donor of wedding presents, you are in exactly the right position to get this training going. Telephone the bride's mother or, if

your connection is to the bridegroom, his mother, and say gently, "I know how busy Alexandrina must be now, setting up housekeeping, and I don't like to trouble her, but I wonder if you could just make a discreet inquiry for me. I'm so afraid—you know how stores are these days, and I don't have to tell you about the postal service—I'm worried that my little package might have gotten lost. Could you just find out if she got the china service for twelve I sent two months ago? I don't want to make her think she has to take the time to write or anything—I just want to know if she got it, because otherwise I'll have to have it traced, so I can let the insurance company know it was lost."

As you can see, this speech, a traditional one, is designed to drive Alexandrina's mother crazy. She knows that you know that Alexandrina and Ian set up house together three years ago, and if there's any housekeeping done by either of them, nobody's seen any signs of it yet. By going to her, you have made it clear that you have traced the reason for Alexandrina's having no manners. Because you are voicing a practical concern and because you have placed yourself in the faultless position of a generous person who expects no return, she can't offer any defense.

So she murmurs that "the young people have been so pressed with all the festivities and settling down to their new life that I'm afraid they've been terribly remiss," and she promises to speak to Alexandrina about it.

Does she ever. You can probably hear the reverberations in your own living room. If it is the bridegroom's mother you have talked to, the scolding is administered in sweeter tones, or perhaps it is delivered through the bridegroom himself, who will be asked to "make her" write the letters. (This is a true no-win situation and the bridegroom, if he is clever, will then write the letters himself. However, this will only ensure that the recipients will refer to him and his wife from that moment on as "poor dear Ian and that girl.")

In any case, you will soon have a stilted letter thanking you for "the lovely present," but not informing you whether it was appreciated, exchanged, or broken, or even whether they know that you were the one who gave them the china. Your satisfaction should come from knowing that you have participated in a significant romantic tradition.

Absent Thanks

DEAR MISS MANNERS:

Our son was recently married to a lovely young woman and they appear to be quite happy and well suited to each other.

I realize the above paragraph says a great deal of importance and I should be pleased. I am—except for the fact that our daughter-in-law never thanks us for any gift. This rankles. I would never confront her about this, and am reluctant to mention it to our son, as I would hate to start any contention between them. And yet the thought and planning of any future gifts leaves me cold. How shall I handle this?

DAL

Dear Aunt Patience,

Rhino and I are thrilled with the magnificent silver sugar shaker you sent us. It adds not only beauty and dignity to our table, but amusement, too, as some of our friends who are both ignorant and daring have not waited for the berries to be served, but have shaken it over their meat. "This could only have come from your Aunt Patience," said one, and we were proud to say that it had.

Rhino joins me in thanking you for your kindness. We look forward to having you in our new home.

Love,
Daffodil

A letter from a bride, thanking the giver of a present. This monogrammed paper can be used for any private correspondence. It would be perfectly proper for the bridegroom to write such a letter on his monogrammed or initialed paper, but he refused.

GENTLE READER:

It is all very well to say that love is more important than thank-you letters, but your letter shows that you know in your heart that they are both important. It is Miss Manners' experience that an absence of thank-you letters, usually due on wedding presents, is the singlemost cause of alienation of affection between brides and their in-laws.

Please clear this up before it rankles you into some terrible family breach. You may address your complaint in a kindly way, either to your daughter-in-law or to your son. Do so on the next occasion for present giving. "Kimberly, dear, I never know what to get you," you say, patting her hand maternally. "I would so like to find something that pleases you, but you've never said a word about any of my presents and I'm so afraid you don't quite like them but are too polite to say so." (The son version goes "Jonathan, dear, I'd so like to give dear Kimberly something that would really please her, but . . .")

A Frank Thank-You

DEAR MISS MANNERS:

I enclose herewith the text of a recently received thank-you note, and wonder what you think of the bride's forthright frankness. Do you consider this the *nouvelles mercis?*

> *Dear friends:*
> *Thank you so much for the beautiful vase. Unfortunately, it was the seventh one we received, so we did want you to know—and we hope you won't mind that we exchanged it in order to complete our china pattern.*
> *We send our love to you, etc.*

GENTLE READER:

It isn't the bride's frankness that worries Miss Manners—it's her brain. If one has seven vases, it should not be difficult to figure out how to exchange six of them, while letting the seventh represent, to each of the seven donors, the one that was kept. Miss Manners hopes that this couple is not planning to have children.

Rules for Thank-You Notes

DEAR MISS MANNERS:

My daughter was recently married. Most of her gifts arrived after the marriage, and we have had notes engraved Mr. and Mrs. John Doe, which she had intended using to write her thank-you notes on. However, we now question whether she can correctly use stationery that is engraved with both their names. If it is acceptable, does she close with just her name or both their names? If joint stationery is not acceptable, what would be your suggestion?

GENTLE READER:

Miss Manners understands the temptation to use informal cards or notes for this occasion, because they have less space on them to fill, and to sign both names. However, this must be resisted. The letters should be written on letter paper which may be engraved with her married name. They should be signed only by the letter writer. Otherwise, the day will come when Mrs. Awful starts signing her letters "Love from Kimberly, Rhino, Lisa, Adam, Jason, Kristen, and Fido," and at least one of them is not going to have authorized the sentiment. It is perfectly acceptable 'for her to write "Rhino loves the electric shrimp deveiner" without consulting Rhino.

. . . But No Thanks

DEAR MISS MANNERS:

How should thank-you cards—the good white ones that usually have "thank you" in gold script on the front—be properly used?

GENTLE READER:

Over Miss Manners' dead body. If you can't take the trouble to write out the words "thank you" yourself, you do not deserve to have anything for which to thank anyone.

Presents of Money

DEAR MISS MANNERS:

I recently got married and received between two hundred and fifty and three hundred gifts; two hundred and fifty or more were money, so I had pre-printed thank-you notes made, along with my invitations, and sent them out. A few family members felt that I should have written in each and every one to thank them for exactly what was given. This meant that I was supposed to write thank you for X number of dollars. I felt that this was in poor taste. Who is right?

GENTLE READER:

Nobody. Everyone is wrong. You are wrong, because you should have written each person a letter. It's a lot of work, and might take you a while, but if some-one has taken the trouble to write you a check, you can take the trouble to write that person a letter. Your family is wrong about having to mention the sum. The most gracious way is to do the present selection that the giver should have done in the first place, and then thank that person for the object. "Robin and I had been longing for a" (statue for the front lawn, Scotch tape dispenser, or whatever would approximate the buying power of the cash) "and you made it possible for us to rush right out and buy it."

Admittedly, this taxes the imagination of the bride, especially if she is receiving several such presents. In that case, the person may be thanked for an "incredibly generous" (over $500), "extremely generous" ($100 to $500), "very generous" ($50 to $100), "kind" ($25 to $50), or "thoughtful" (under $25) present.

A Delayed Present

DEAR MISS MANNERS:

Two of my friends, M. and S., were married almost three years ago. Because of my laziness (of which I am very ashamed) and because I never found an appropriate gift (they are very opinionated and choosy individuals), I have failed to give them a wedding present. My problem is that M. and S. separated several weeks ago. I believe that their chances of getting back together are slightly less than the proverbial snowball's. Thus, my dilemma. If I give them a present while they are separated and having marriage problems, they and other people may believe that I am making sport of their situation. However, if I do not give them a gift, I continue to look cheap. M. continues to question me frequently on when I am going to give them a gift. What should I do? Since I am closer friends with M., would it be appropriate to give him a divorce gift in lieu of the wedding present? I do not plan to get married in the near future and do not expect a wedding present from either M. or S.

GENTLE READER:

Miss Manners thinks you are wise not to plan a marriage in the hope of receiving a present from M. and/or S., as you see what good it did them. It is not generally known, but nevertheless true, that all presents are voluntary, including wedding presents in cases where the couple keep careful records of who spent what on them. (Please see pp. 521–523.) Thus you are obligated to give them neither a wedding present nor a divorce present. However, your feeling that you are appearing to be cheap, reinforced with the constant reminders to that effect on the part of your friend, indicate that you wish to make an appropriate gesture. Under the circumstances, Miss Manners suggests that an appropriate present would be one that is easily divided between bride and bridegroom, such as twin candlesticks, lamps, or decks of cards.

The Trousseau

The Bare Essentials

DEAR MISS MANNERS:

I'm confused by the lists of household "necessities" in the bridal magazines. What are the minimum essentials a bride needs to begin married life?

GENTLE READER:

A bridegroom.

Silver

If you believe that stainless steel is just as good as silver, you are too young to get married. Miss Manners urges you to put off having children until you mature. If it turns out to be congenital lack of sense, it should not be passed on to innocent children.

Young couples who think that silver is impractical should be told a few rough facts about what has happened to its price over the years before they attempt to discourage their relations and friends from giving them silver as wedding presents. Affordable presents are more likely now to be individual forks or spoons, rather than place settings, but there is still no opportunity like a wedding to get the basic pieces. In fact, it is the single most striking argument Miss Manners knows against the what-difference-does-a-piece-of-paper-make theory.

Miss Manners' idea of a basic place setting is slightly different from that of silver flatware manufacturers. Hers is the large knife, large fork, small fork, and oval tablespoon, with small knife as the choice if there is to be a fifth piece. Teaspoons are properly used only for coffee and tea, and those confining themselves to the basics are not likely to use their silver at family breakfast or to give tea parties. The tablespoon may be used for soup, as well as dessert. The small fork is used for salad, dessert (you run out and wash it during the cheese course), and luncheon, and may also fill in for the fish fork or the fruit fork before you acquire those luxuries. The small knife is also used for luncheon and, of course, for courses other than the meat course, at which the large fork and knife are used.

After one has a service of place settings, Miss Manners advises getting the teaspoon, the butter knife, and the fish knife and fish fork. Next in usefulness are the demitasse spoon (which certainly needn't match the table silver, as demitasse is served in the drawing room, but Miss Manners prefers those that do not say "Souvenir of Atlantic City"), the fruit knife and fork and, if you have leftover money and go in for that sort of thing, the oyster fork, the iced-tea spoon, the bouillon spoon, the grapefruit spoon, or whatever else you can find.

In the time of great financial boom—Miss Manners is thinking of the Industrial Revolution—all kinds of strange implements were invented, and if you are rich and clever enough, you can set a table on which, as a lady of Miss Manners' acquaintance says of her inherited silver, it is not clear whether dinner is to be served or a hysterectomy performed.

Silver is marked with the three initials of the bride's maiden name. This is particularly practical these days, when silver lasts much longer than her average marriage.

A carving knife and fork, two large serving spoons, perhaps one of them slotted, another large fork, and a small ladle are the basic serving implements, to which you can then add a soup ladle, a flat cake server that can also be used for quiches and such, asparagus tongs, grape scissors (nobody ever uses them, but Miss Manners adores them), large fish knife and fork, and so on. Why some people think they need special forks for serving cold meats Miss Manners doesn't know, but then, not everyone understands why she needs asparagus servers.

As a secret tip, Miss Manners confides that sterling silver does not wear out. Therefore, buying it second hand, whether it is modern or antique, makes a great deal of sense. There is nothing quite so grand as setting a table with the kind of old European silver which is engraved on the back, thus giving your guests a terrible shock when, not knowing that those pieces are correctly placed with the fork prongs and spoon bowls facing the tablecloth, they conclude that you have set the table upside down.

Tea and Coffee Sets

DEAR MISS MANNERS:

Can you help us resolve a lively debate about the proper use of the waste bowl in a coffee service? At a recent elegant dinner party, one guest was certain that it should be used to hold hot water that has been used to "preheat" the cups. Another was equally certain that the dregs of one cup of coffee are poured into it before the cup is refilled. Our hostess was very uncertain, and admitted that she does not use hers for fear of doing so improperly. This seemed to us like the waste of a good bowl.

GENTLE READER:

Quick! Stop! Please! Oh, good heavens, why didn't you call for help earlier? *You are using a tea set to serve coffee.*

Actually, Miss Manners can think of no good reason why you shouldn't. She just doesn't want to spoil that lovely party by siding with one friend against another. Surely if you are all equally wrong, no one can feel hurt.

It also explains why there is a waste bowl or, as it is sometimes so elegantly called, a slops bowl. This is for the dregs of tea. A coffee set consists of three pieces: a coffee pot, a sugar bowl and a cream jug; a tea set has five pieces: a teakettle for boiling water, a teapot for the tea, a milk pitcher, a sugar bowl, and the waste bowl. (Miss Manners is not counting trays, tongs, caddies, strainers, and such, any more than she is counting the teaspoons, until after the guests leave.) If you can subtract, you can figure out how your hostess can have a passable coffee set, free.

DEAR MISS MANNERS:

Look at this ad for silver. You see how contemptuously it says, "Still using a teaspoon for coffee . . . really?" Then the part about this wonderful new invention, the sterling silver coffee spoon, $19.95 each, "Not as large as the conventional teaspoon that slides off the saucer. Nor as tiny as a demitasse spoon. But just in between. A sterling jewel, proportioned and balanced to look beautiful with today's taller coffee cup." And so on. It makes it sound as if anybody who would use teaspoons with coffee, which is what I've always thought proper, isn't fit to mix with decent folks. OK, Miss Manners—do I have to run right out and buy coffee spoons? Is that what you are doing?

GENTLE READER:

Miss Manners has other things to do first. One of them is to search her personal history to discover whether spoons sliding off saucers has been a major inconvenience in her life. Another is to ask herself what in the world "today's taller coffee cup" is. If it is the kind of big old mug people put their faces into in the morning before they wake up, it would only be embarrassed if you gave it a silver spoon because it wouldn't know what to do with it. It would probably try to solve the problem by pushing the spoon off the saucer, which may be where that problem came from—although, come to think of it, mugs don't have saucers.

Teaspoons have little enough employment as it is, considering that they are sold as an essential part of the "basic place setting," without being deprived of the job of stirring full-sized cups of coffee. Coffee is properly served in a large cup only at breakfast or at tea parties, and considering how many people use mugs at breakfast and live comparatively full lives without giving tea parties, that is hardly a full-time job for the teaspoon. Demitasse cups and spoons are used for coffee that follows lunch or dinner. The teaspoon also gets to stir tea, of course, and to help out with the grapefruit or jam if no specialized spoon is available. Many people use teaspoons for dessert, but that is incorrect. Do you have big oval tablespoons for dessert? If not, don't let Miss Manners hear any more talk about needing coffee spoons, or she'll push you off the saucer.

DEAR MISS MANNERS:

What on earth is a "runcible spoon"?

GENTLE READER:

A runcible spoon is the instrument used by the Owl and the Pussycat to eat mince and slices of quince when they went to sea in a beautiful pea-green boat. It is a large, slotted spoon with three thick, modified fork prongs at the bowl's end, and a cutting edge on the side. According to Miss Manners' Aunt Grace, the spoon was fashioned after Mr. Edward Lear named this object for his poem. Miss Manners believes this with all her heart, but has trouble proving it, as neither dear Mr. Lear nor Aunt Grace is with us any longer.

DEAR MISS MANNERS:

Can you use grape scissors for any function other than cutting grapes?

GENTLE READER:

Not unless you pay overtime.

Demitasse Spoons

DEAR MISS MANNERS:

Are demitasse spoons useful?

GENTLE READER:

Does a duck swim?

Miss Manners is not going to consider the possibility that you are serving full cups of coffee after dinner, or that you are asking people to stir their proper thimblefuls of coffee with great big old teaspoons. She is therefore left to believe that your question is whether tiny spoons have any function other than their primary one.

Some people collect them. Miss Manners is not sure what the thrill is in that, but sees no harm in it and acknowledges that it is a cheaper hobby than collecting Impressionist paintings.

If the spoons are not silver, they may be used as egg spoons. Silver does not go well with eggs, but the tiny spoon is more appropriate for eating boiled eggs from the shell than the ubiquitous teaspoon. This means that the demitasse spoons would be working both early morning and late night shifts, but you could give them alternative Thursdays off.

Demitasse spoons are also good for eating yogurt when you are on a diet.

An Unidentified Silver Dish

DEAR MISS MANNERS:

How can you tell whether a small silver dish is meant to be used as an ashtray or as a candy dish?

GENTLE READER:

If it has ashes in it, it is being used as an ashtray. If it has neither candy nor ashes in it, but you see no other place besides the carpet to deposit the ash on your cigarette, it is an ashtray. If it belongs to you, you may declare it whatever you wish.

China

DEAR MISS MANNERS:

The china pattern I selected has a bewildering variety of plates, ranging in diameter from five inches to ten and a half, and of course the saleslady tells me that no well-stocked household could do with less than ten of each. Maybe someday I'll get around to all that, but would you tell me, in the meantime, what each one is for, which are more useful than others, and whether it is better to start with, say, four complete place settings or eight incomplete ones?

GENTLE READER:

It depends on whom and what you like for dinner. Assuming that you would prefer simpler meals and more friends—although Miss Manners has no grounds for making such an audacious judgment—start with these basics:

Dinner plates. Those are the largest ones, and you will need one for every person you have to dinner.

Luncheon plates. Get the eight-inch ones, so that you may use them not only as the main plate at breakfast or lunch, but also as salad plates, dessert plates, tea plates, and for serving first courses such as fish or pâtés. Of course, if you use them for fish, salad, and dessert at the same meal, you will spend on soap and kitchen help the amount of money saved on buying dishes.

Bread-and-butter plates. These are five or six inches, and may also be used for serving fruit or as underliners for bowls.

Two-handled bowls with saucers. These may be used for cereal, gooey desserts, and all soups, provided you promise Miss Manners that you will put aside your first earnings to buy wide, rimmed soup plates for formal dinners and small bouillon cups for lunches.

Tea or coffee cups and demitasse, each with the appropriate saucer. Teacups are slightly smaller and thinner than coffee cups, but unless you serve both coffee and tea, your guests will never be able to compare the cups and accuse you of having the wrong ones. There is no use trying to pass off your regular coffee cups as demitasse, however, no matter how large you claim your breakfast cups are.

Glass salad plates and dessert plates may be used with china dinner plates, and serving dishes can be silver, pewter, stainless steel, or a plain china.

You can cut down on the amount of china you need by entertaining only at formal dinners, where soup bowls, bread-and-butter plates, and coffee cups are not properly used, the respective replacements being soup plates, the tablecloth, and demitasse. If that leaves you eating your own breakfast and lunch straight from the refrigerator, don't tell anyone Miss Manners recommended it.

Glass

Always wishing everyone the best, Miss Manners is usually quite generous with your money. She feels wise and good-hearted when she urges you to have silver flatware, rather than stainless steel, and linen napkins instead of paper. Even cries of economic disaster do not deter her; she merely bolsters her position by saying that silver on the table is better than money in the bank, and linen napkins last longer than paper.

When it comes to glasses, however, her conscience begins to assert itself. Miss Manners is perfectly capable of rhapsodizing sincerely, not to say poetically, about the beauties of crystal. But if you ask her point blank to justify the cost of extensive and expensive glasses, she could only mumble, ''They're pretty.'' They also either gather dust on the shelves because nobody drinks anything except white wine and soda, or they make troublesome fragments at the bottom of the dishwasher.

So, although Miss Manners finds it reassuring to see five glasses neatly arranged above her knife at a dinner table (for sherry with the soup, white wine with the fish, red wine with the meat, champagne with the dessert, and water so she won't slide off her chair), she admits that one can live decently on only one wine and water.

A large, stemmed glass and a slightly smaller one will fill (and be filled with) these needs. If you have a second, still smaller, wine glass, you can use the larger for red and the smaller for white. (It is as cheap to impress your guests with two wines as with one of which they will drink twice as much.) A third, smallest, wine glass used for white allows you to serve the Burgundy in the largest and claret in the middle one, a situation not likely to come up.

Sherry glasses, you may be surprised to hear, are for sherry, although Miss Manners would not refuse a late afternoon offer of the topaz liquid if it were served in the regular wine glass, rather than the Y-shaped one. Wide-rimmed champagne glasses are for whipped desserts and frozen daiquiris, as well as one's daily ration of champagne. Tulip-shaped champagne glasses are snazzier, in Miss Manners' opinion, but not as versatile. One can also have fat-bowled glasses on short stems for brandy and teensy glasses on weensy stems for liqueurs. However, sticking one's face in the former and snorting, or tossing the content of the latter down one's gullet are bad form.

Unstemmed glasses have all sorts of names for themselves. They insist that they are highball glasses or old-fashioned glasses or iced tea glasses or fruit juice glasses. Don't believe them. They are either big glasses or small ones. The tall ones are used for mixed drinks, iced tea, low-calorie pop, high-calorie pop, the children's milk, and the children's beer. The short ones are for straight liquor and the following morning's fruit juice.

It may aid you in saving money to know that having many types of glasses for complicated drinks shows an interest in bartending that is not quite nice. Miss Manners doesn't recommend stirring your guests' drinks with your fingers, but a bar full of liquor-connected tools and devices is vulgar.

You should also know that if your glasses are reasonably thin, hardly anyone can tell the best crystal from more durable crystal, or sometimes even from plain glass. At least, they can't by candlelight. When they get to the store the next day, to replace the fragile glass of yours they broke, they will find out the difference.

Marking the Trousseau

DEAR MISS MANNERS:
What monogram does an engaged girl use on her trousseau sheets and towels —the initials of her maiden name or her married name?
GENTLE READER:
The old-fashioned custom was to use the initials of her maiden name, and the modern bride will find that there is a lot of sense in this rule, as the trousseau will then see her through any number of marriages. Marriages don't tend to last as long as they used to, but, then, heaven knows that sheets don't, either.

Linens

DEAR MISS MANNERS:
When I was a little girl, my great-grandmother gave me her hope chest and now that I am thirty-four and all my relatives have given up hope, I am actually getting married. My great-grandmother is long since dead, and even my mother said she never thought she'd live to see the day. But anyway, my mother once promised to fill the chest with linens when I became engaged. I plan to hold her to this, although she claims that the decision, by me and the man I have been living with for six and a half years, that we might as well get married, is not her idea of a proper engagement. While we fight over that, would you mind settling the next issue, which is bound to be: What does a proper linen trousseau consist of?

GENTLE READER :

Do you mean to say that you are going to send Miss Manners out of the room to count the sheets and towels, while such an interesting fight as you are having now is taking place? Oh, all right. She's going, she's going.

The linen trousseau is subdivided into Bed, Bath, Kitchen, and Table, of which Table (surprise!) is the most interesting.

Table linens

It is well known that no bride can enter matrimony with her head held high unless she has a damask tablecloth and twelve dinner napkins, each twenty-four inches square, to match. It is well known that the bride never uses these items until her silver wedding anniversary, and that someone then promptly justifies her caution by spilling red wine all over them. Nevertheless, the cloth should be monogrammed diagonally high on one corner, and each of the napkins on the part that will show when the sides are rolled under and it is centered on the service plate.

A linen luncheon set, consisting of a tablecloth and smaller napkins (about fifteen inches square), is also needed for those elegant lunches that every bride rushes home from work on weekdays to give for seven of her closest friends. Linen or cotton table mats and napkins may be used for breakfast. An endless supply of teeny-weeny hors d'oeuvre napkins are necessary, as guests always put them in their pockets.

What about the wipe-off mats, brightly colored cloths and napkins that don't show stains, imaginatively used designer sheets for the table, and bridge-size cloths that the bride will actually use? She buys them herself; those are not part of the trousseau.

Bed linen

Six sheets for every bed and three pillowcases for every head (meaning six for a double bed) are the minimum and naturally they should be monogrammed. Hemstitching, which rips off like perforated toilet paper, is nice, too. Miss Manners allows only white sheets, and prefers that the monograms be in white, as well.

Naturally, each bed needs a silk or muslin blanket cover, and a bedspread. Miss Manners likes blanket covers to be monogrammed, but never bedspreads. Don't ask her why.

Again, all that permanent press, jungle-patterned mix-and-match junk you use for sleeping in, and the fitted, quilted things you use to avoid making the bed, are not properly part of the trousseau.

Bath linens

The most important items here are the linen face towels and linen hand towels, none of which are ever used, even by the guests. You are also allowed to have terry-cloth bath towels and washcloths, which are used, although what a respectable person does with those small terry-cloth towels always sold to match, Miss Manners cannot imagine. Monogramming terry-cloth strikes her as silly, unless you are a hotel with untrustworthy guests.

Kitchen linen

Linen towels are needed to keep up the pretense that the bride will never put her fine china and crystal into the dishwasher. They have no other use. Rough towels and potholders are quite useful, however, which is why they do not belong in a proper trousseau.

Household Atrocities

To keep a house in which every object, down to the smallest bibelot, is in perfect taste, is in shocking taste. No house can be truly elegant unless it contains at least half a dozen atrocities of varying sizes and uses. This must not include the residents, however.

Such an apparent attack of madness on the part of Miss Good Taste herself is not to be confused with the unfortunate notion that a house should have the look of being "lived in," or, as Miss Manners terms it, "slovenly." If disorders were indeed sweet, we could solve the teenage summer unemployment problem by leasing adolescents out as decorating consultants.

It is rather in the selection of furnishing that care must be exercised to include enough dreadful items to avoid the appearance of being mercenary, heartless, and socially aggressive.

The discriminating person always has on hand a few things that could not possibly have been chosen for their aesthetic value, thus emerging as a person of tradition and sentiment.

For those who find it difficult to commit taste errors, here is a small list of horrible things from which to choose. If one does not come by them naturally, it may be possible to purchase them at yard sales.

Child-made Objects

No household, even one that is blessed with no children, should fail to have at least one item whose provenance is clearly Arts and Crafts Hour at a school or camp. Ceramic ashtrays, a favorite present from children to parents they never noticed don't smoke, are good, as are yarn pot holders, because they are relatively permanent. Things made out of cardboard, straws, and pipe cleaners tend to disintegrate, although not so quickly as one would like. Artwork must be rotated on the standard exhibit space (the refrigerator door), because it is found in such prodigious quantities.

Hideous Presents Donated by Adults

These should be displayed and cherished in proportion to the sacredness of the bond between giver and receiver, divided by the number of miles they live apart. Thus, wedding presents from friends may be quietly returned, but a spouse's poor choice should be tolerated unless you are willing to exchange the giver at the same time. Inviolate are presents from one's servants. We are not all as fortunate as the lady whose faithful butler returned from a trip to his ancestral land of Egypt with an electrically lighted sphinx for his employer's living room, but we should all be as wise as that lady, who considered what her friends would think if she kept it, considered what the butler would think if she expelled it, and gave it a place of honor. One can always make new friends, but a good butler is not easy to find.

Souvenirs

This category includes sports trophies, wedding albums, framed awards, family photographs (as long as they do not include famous people), and items pertaining to happy vacations (as long as they are not of the sort that could only have been stolen from public accommodations). No member of the family should be allowed to contribute items from more than one of these categories to the general decor, and they must all be kept in places that indicate the owner's embarrassment for having them at all. The powder room walls are an excellent place for awards, the photographs go in the master bedroom, and the trophies are used as doorstops in the guest room.

What Miss Manners does not want to see are awards hung in the library, children's artwork professionally framed and put in the drawing room, wedding albums on coffee tables, photographs of any member of the family shaking hands with the President hung anywhere at all, or any restaurant or hotel property, including matchbooks. The ostentatious display of bad taste is in extremely poor taste.

Dealing with New Relations

Referring to One's Husband

DEAR MISS MANNERS:

What do I call my husband?

GENTLE READER:

Probably "honey." How would Miss Manners know? Possibly you are asking what to call him when referring to him in conversations with other people. Use his name, or, if you have trouble remembering names, refer to him as "my husband." What are to be avoided are terms that suggest you know him too little or too well, such as "Mr." or "lover."

Only the Names Have Been Changed . . .

DEAR MISS MANNERS:

Recently, I had a discussion as to the proper and legal name when one married. Does a new bride retain her maiden name and discontinue the use of her middle name? Is either correct? I would appreciate your printing this for the sake of discussion.

GENTLE READER:

Miss Manners would not even presume to call any of the combinations of maiden, married, or hyphenated names one now sees ''incorrect.'' However, if you ask what we staid, fastidious, super-proper ladies have traditionally preferred, it is to ''change'' the last name. In other words, one retains one's first and middle name, and changes the surname of the father for that of the husband.

Names-in-Law

DEAR MISS MANNERS:

My soon-to-be-married son refuses to call his fiancée's parents Mom and Dad. He claims they aren't his parents, which is true, of course. His future in-laws do not want to be called by their first names. Things are at an impasse, with my son avoiding the issue whenever possible by not calling them anything. When necessary, he uses Mr. and Mrs. with the surname. This doesn't seem friendly to me. Any suggestions?

GENTLE READER:

That impasse you describe runs across the country, and therefore a great many married people address their parents-in-law as Um. The truth is there is no satisfactory solution. Those who use some variation on ''Mom'' and ''Dad'' are forever having to explain, to third parties such as their own spouses, whom they are talking about. Some people consider first names too familiar and Mr. and Mrs. too distant. Other unsatisfactory solutions your son might consider are combining the parental title with the given name or surname. Thus you get ''Mother Agnes'' or ''Father Jones,'' which reek of convent school.

The compromise Miss Manners prefers is to let the older generation choose, on the grounds that whatever discomfort your son feels about their preference he can make up for by some day imposing his on his unwilling son-in-law.

Work

Applying for Jobs, Raises, and Fees

DEAR MISS MANNERS:

It's not as easy as you imagine to be polite while you have to scrounge for a living. You give me a surefire way of getting rich quick, and I promise to behave perfectly from that moment on.

GENTLE READER:

Very well. Think of a business that particularly caters to some legitimate need of people who live alone. There must be nothing about it that suggests recreation —not even music playing in the background. The atmosphere should be no-nonsense, utilitarian, and eminently respectable. Then devise some way of keeping all of your customers waiting. Service should be delayed just long enough to get people grumbling to one another, but not long enough to make them walk away in disgust. You should aim at having a good-sized group of unmarried people standing together with a common practical purpose and nothing to do but to talk to one another while they wait. Miss Manners realizes that she has just described a laundromat, but perhaps you can think of something else.

The Job Interview

Having devoted her life to extolling the virtues of modesty and quiet charm, Miss Manners feels bound to admit that these are not wildly successful qualities to exhibit in job interviews. Few employers are seeking models of self-effacing gentility to reward with responsibility and money.

In Miss Manners' day, there was no conflict between being ladylike or gentlemanlike and seeming competent and efficient, because ladies and gentlemen did not seek jobs. The respectable solution, for aristocrats short on cash, was marrying for money. Now honest labor is appallingly chic, and everyone needs a set of business manners, as well as social ones.

The best job applicant is one who is able to sing his or her own praises without embarrassment, confident enough to steer an interview away from inappropriate areas, and persistent. When you would demur, socially, with "Oh, it was nothing, really," you would, in business, say, "I graduated with honors, had the best sales record in my last job, and left because I felt the job wasn't really using my abilities." When you would tell a prospective host, "I would be simply delighted to be there," you tell a prospective employer, "I think your company would benefit from my contribution." To a dinner partner, you might say, "Why, yes, my husband is the one over there with the blond mustache, and we have four beautiful children from three marriages"; to a personnel person, you say, "Well, I really don't think my personal life will have any bearing on my work."

Crispness replaces flirtatiousness; showing that you know the other person's business is not nosy but intelligent; and stating one's capabilities is the mark of the able worker, not of the bragging bore.

There is one social skill that can serve as your strongest asset in a job interview. In private life, it makes people fall in love with you and seek you for purposes ranging from honored dinner guests to spouse; and in business, it helps more than any other single qualification, with the possible exception of being the owner's eldest child. That is enthusiasm. A look of vitality and happiness, an interest in the world and an eagerness to participate in life, is what is called charm in the social milieu; but in the working world it is called competence. One may practice such a look. It is chiefly done with the eyes. If they can be made to shine radiantly, the rest of the face will automatically compose itself into the properly attractive expression. Practice staring into the mirror as if you have fallen madly in love. Most people have little difficulty with this when they have thought it over. Such a look, accompanied by short, to-the-point remarks about one's native abilities, one's invaluable experience—not only in previous jobs, but in volunteer work, education, and hobbies—and one's deep interest in the work being done by the company to which one is applying, convinces an employer that what you can do for him is more important than what he can do for you.

It should make the face look so intelligent that it can see the wearer with dignity through such shabby interviewing tricks as being deliberately kept waiting while the employer takes a personal telephone call, or being badgered to take a drink when one knows one shouldn't. It should make refusals to disclose one's present salary or discuss how long one might stay on the job seem businesslike, rather than weasly. It is also useful, because you needn't change it when going from the office out to dinner.

Dress in an Interview

DEAR MISS MANNERS:

I will be going for a final interview with an airline soon. Question: Should I wear a suit or would a dress and jacket be sufficient? Also, are there specific colors that might work best?

GENTLE READER:

You do not say whether you are applying for a job as a mechanic, a pilot, a stewardess, or an executive at this airline, but the general rule about dressing for job interviews is to look like someone who already has the job. Thus, you would either wear dark coveralls, a blue suit with a white shirt, a red-white-and-blue dress with matching jacket, or a dark three-piece suit.

Reservations on Recommendations

DEAR MISS MANNERS:

I am in the embarrassing position of having been asked to write a letter of recommendation for someone I can't honestly recommend. I don't want to be cruel and prevent his getting another job—what am I saying? I desperately want him to get another job. That would save me the trouble of firing him. But I don't know if it's right to stick the next person by misrepresenting his qualifications.

GENTLE READER:

Ah, the great moral conflict in life—honesty or kindness? Miss Manners tends to choose kindness, feeling that there is quite enough honesty in the world, but this is an occasion for compromise. Sometimes one can avoid writing a letter of reference, saying, "Perhaps you could find someone who would be able to write you a stronger letter than I could," or "I don't feel I know enough about your qualifications." Those take care of the troublesome student, or an acquaintance's nephew.

When failure to write any letter would be a blot on the person's career, something must be produced. The object is to suggest severe problems without zapping the person. The tone to take is: "He probably has lots of talents that would come to light in a situation where skills such as alphabetizing correctly aren't needed."

Raises

DEAR MISS MANNERS:

What is the most effective way to apply for a raise? I don't want to be impolite and brag about myself, but the truth is that I deserve the raise and am not going to get it unless I ask for it pretty forcefully.

GENTLE READER:

The most effective way is to mention politely that your employer's chief competitor has just offered you a job at twice the salary. There is, however, some risk involved in this method. One, he might congratulate his competitor the next time he sees him, and two, he might congratulate you on the spot.

Therefore, Miss Manners advises the more subtle method of using your own authority to establish that you are worth more than you are getting. Do not fear you are being impolite. What is called bragging in the social world is called self-confidence in the business world. Length of service, devotion to the company, and faithfulness in performing one's duty are valid reasons for having one's salary gradually increased, but these dogged virtues rarely inspire employers to provide rewards. If you add to them proof of imagination and energy in the performance of your tasks, you are more apt to suggest that you would also have the imagination and energy to place yourself better if you were not satisfied. In the working world, as in teenaged romance, the person treated best is the one who might be lost, not the one whose feelings would be most hurt.

Please note that Miss Manners believes in citing worth, rather than need, as the reason. The reason that $100,000-a-year executives with paid-off houses and grown-up children are worth the money to their companies is that they all possess the skill of proving to junior employees that they are not nearly as needy as they plead they are.

Fees

DEAR MISS MANNERS:

One of the things I do for a living is to give lectures. I don't get rich on it, but I give audiences their money's worth, and I have worked up some good speeches that people seem to enjoy.

Word gets around, of course, and I am often asked by small groups, such as clubs and professional organizations, to give luncheon speeches or answer questions at their meetings. But often, when I accept, I find that they have no intention of paying me!

Perhaps I should bring it up when they invite me, but I assume that they know I am a professional, and it seems crass to demand payment while they are telling me how wonderful they've heard I am, how much everyone is looking forward to hearing me, and so on. These same people wouldn't dream of offering me the services or goods they sell for free, of course.

GENTLE READER:

Nor would these people be embarrassed to put price tags on their goods or send out bills for their services. All you have to say is, "What is your budget for speakers?" or "Why, I'd love to; do you know my fee?" Remember that selling one's time is not necessarily a shameful transaction, depending on what one spends that time performing.

When All Is Said and Done

DEAR MISS MANNERS:

When you have engaged a speaker for a meeting and you have paid him in either money or a gift, are you still expected to write him a thank-you note?

GENTLE READER:

No amount of money (Miss Manners is unsure how one can be ''paid'' with a ''gift'') can assuage a speaker's need to be told that he or she spoke well. Do not grudge anyone this, whether or not it happens to be the case. After all, didn't the speaker say you were a wonderful audience?

Office Etiquette

The young ladies were plotting revenge. Perhaps one of them might coax the office colleague to repeat his suggestive remarks to her when, unbeknownst to him, their superiors were listening. Or one of them might agree to the assignation he suggested, only to show up at the hotel room with all their office mates. That should cure him, or others in the office who seemed to believe that female workers were designed for their amusement. Miss Manners, to whom the young ladies came for final approval, was tempted to let them go ahead. Miss Manners has too much to do, what with setting out the tea things and all, to save gentlemen, or perhaps she should simply say men, from the natural consequences of their bad behavior. People who make obscene remarks should be prepared to be struck back at, one way or another.

Yet Miss Manners began to feel an unnatural twinge of sympathy for those gentlemen who, caught in changing times, may not realize that what they consider gallantry is considered obscenity by young ladies today. Mind you, Miss Manners is entirely on the side of the young ladies. Overt sexuality, when there is no reason to suppose it is welcome, is not gallantry. People who do not have a well-developed sense of when flirtation is welcome and when not, should not play that subtle game. In any case, talk of hotel rooms is not flirtation.

Nor is it proper to assume that young ladies always welcome favorable appraisals of their bodies. "We are not here to please the men in the office," de-

396

clared the angry young ladies. "We're workers, too, not decorations, let alone sex objects." It is true that it was once the custom for such remarks—mild ones, such as telling young ladies that they looked pretty or had lovely eyes—to be made even in the most impersonal situations.

Elderly gentlemen brought up in this atmosphere sometimes assume that the greater freedom women have today means that they can not only make such remarks, but that they can make even freer remarks. They are incorrect. They are going to get socked in the eye one day, and the next time Miss Manners is not going to help them.

Harassment

DEAR MISS MANNERS:

You have been so helpful (and, of course, correct) in the past to those of us who still don't quite understand how equal rights for men and women could be dangerous. We beg to impose once again.

Upon earnest study of the sayings of Chairman Phyllis Schlafly, notably in testimony before the Senate Labor and Human Resources Committee, we are horrified at our past errors and extremely nervous about future gaffes. We feel confident you will guide us in charting a correct course through the troubled waters of Ms. Schlafly's Sermon on the Hill.

On sexual harassment: "Virtuous women are seldom accosted. . . ." This has an eerie ring of the Calvinist doctrine of predestination. Is our virtue documented only by the absence of propositions? Once pinched, is it all over for us? "When a woman walks across the room, she speaks with a universal body language that most men intuitively understand." Help! Why aren't we given this intuition? Will the ladylike gait we all polished as teenagers be safe? Should we now affect the movements of stevedores? Does Miss Manners have a male relative or friend who will interpret for us?

On paid employment and affirmative action: This one's a bit easier, but we still need your advice. Ms. Schlafly reminds us that motherhood is ". . . honorable and the most socially useful of all careers." She further reminds us that a homemaker is one whose ". . . cash wages . . . amount to significantly less than her husband's." Widowed, deserted, or divorced mothers of dependent children may have some difficulty meeting this ideal, but the rest of us know we can somehow keep our earnings below those of our husbands (as well as those of most of our male colleagues). However, those of us who lose our virtue by means of the uninvited pinch are next liable to have a raise or promotion thrust upon us (see "discrimination against virtuous women"). Others of us, provided we are "less qualified," will surely be offered a job in place of a man, though it is not clear we would be paid as much (see "affirmative action").

Can Miss Manners show us the ladylike way through this swamp?

GENTLE READER:

Swamp it is, indeed, muddied by ignorance and not a little dirt.

Surely we all agree, you, Miss Manners, and the lady you quote, on the importance of ladylike behavior. But many who prattle of this do so without understanding the social context in which such traditions evolved.

Certainly, no lady is ever accosted improperly, in the work place or any other place—because no gentleman would do such a dastardly thing. If one who is not a gentleman—namely, a cad or a villain—should venture to do such a thing, the full wrath of the society, including all gentlemen, ladies, and the majesty of the law, should act immediately to expel this person. An injured lady will naturally call any transgression to their attention as quickly and loudly as possible.

The notion that financial inequality should exist between husbands and wives has no basis in civilized tradition (although, of course, one always hears whispers of gentlemen of embarrassed means attaching themselves to heiresses). In the upper classes, no one would have dreamed of doing useful work to get money, no matter how badly it was needed; only among the crassest social climbers did the division of labor exist, whereby the husband earned money while the wife, keeping her hands clean of that, devoted herself to society and the arts. Dear Edith Wharton mused how "gold-fever" had ruined the luncheon parties of her youth, where the men were as much at leisure during the day as the women. In the lower classes, also, men and women espoused this principle, sharing the amount of toil and starvation not only between husbands and wives, but also with their children.

Please do Miss Manners the favor of telling your friend to cease putting the claim of propriety and virtue on the manners of cads, villains, and social climbers.

Beginning a Working Affair

DEAR MISS MANNERS:

I trust that Miss Manners will not find this inquiry too indelicate to comment on.

I am a successful young bureaucrat who, half a year ago, was fortunate enough to be able to hire an exceptionally well-qualified personal secretarial assistant. She has performed beautifully and contributed greatly to my ability to achieve great recognition in serving the people of our nation. Fortunately or unfortunately, my feelings of appreciation and respect for her are now, I detect, taking on romantic characteristics. As I have not expressed these feelings, I have no idea if she shares them—and would probably be unable to "read" any subtle indications on her part due to my shyness.

What, if anything, should I do, and how should it be done? The options I see are business-as-usual, frank revelation and discussion, or gradual encouragement of her to indicate her feelings and take action. I am not a seducer. At present, I have a barely satisfying marriage. I do not want to lose my assistant as a result of some foolish action on my part. But I am unable to choose a course of action between my normal tendency to suppress such feelings and taking a chance on something which could be very fulfilling. Would Miss Manners please suggest what and how she thinks I ought to do?

GENTLE READER:

Thank you for your consideration in assuring Miss Manners you are not a seducer, but actually that was not her worry. Who seduces whom seems rather a moot point, these days.

Who hires, fires, and promotes whom is somewhat clearer. The reassurance Miss Manners would like, for herself and for your assistant, is that you are not a harasser. You realize, of course, that no matter what happens, you will only hurt the one you love. If she returns your sentiments and the romance progresses happily, she will be subject to the criticism of colleagues who will refuse to believe that you admired her performance before noticing anything else about her. If she rejects you, or you come to want to end a romance with her, she will have difficulty separating her personal problems from her personnel problems. Miss Manners does believe that the best thing to do would be nothing. However, she does not believe for a minute that this is the sort of advice anyone ever takes.

Presumably, your assistant understands the hazards she will face if she accepts your suit. So what Miss Manners is most anxious about is that you should present that suit in such a way that it is clear that she is free to reject it, if she chooses, without fearing that it will affect your professional relationship. Paradoxically, "frank discussion" will not achieve this. The franker your protestations, the more threatening they will sound. What you must do, as you would know if you were in the diplomatic branch of government service, is to provide her excuse for her, and then wait to see if she takes it or not. Your marriage is an excellent excuse, as you may have noticed on other occasions. If you declare your interest and then add, "But I understand perfectly if you feel you can't get involved because I'm married," you will give her the chance to look at you regretfully and say, "No, I wish I could, but I don't feel it's right."

But if she says, "So what? So am I," you're in business.

Proper Dress

DEAR MISS MANNERS:

The girls in my office wear clothes to work that are close to being indecent. Some years ago, I got into a fight over the wearing of pantsuits to the office and lost—in fact, there were threats to quit, and my own wife finally turned against me. So I hesitate to say anything now, but I am proud of the business I built and want to have the place look businesslike, not like the lounge of a nightclub. Lately, the smarter ones have wised up on their own. Two of them have started wearing nice blouses and suits with stockings, and I thought maybe I could use them to influence some of the others to dress better. How can I do this subtly, without getting into another fight?

GENTLE READER:

By promoting them to executive positions, where they can serve as role models for the other women.

Security

DEAR MISS MANNERS:

I have worked for the same firm for over twenty years. In the last few years, since everybody got so crime-conscious, they have had a "security system," which means that you are supposed to show your employee pass every time you enter the building, which is at least twice a day for me, in the morning and at lunch, and sometimes more often, if I have to see someone outside the building. Most of the guards just wave me in, including the security chief, but there is one who insists on seeing my pass every time and once made me sign in as a visitor when I had run outside for a minute, leaving my jacket, and therefore my wallet and pass, inside. I thought this was deliberate rudeness, but it's one I can't officially complain about (I tried) because he is "only doing his job." Once this guard had to stand there while his chief waved me through, and I enjoyed that, out of all proportion with the situation. When there are two guards on duty, on each side of the hallway, I, of course, go for the one who recognizes me, but as the desks are several feet apart, I can't very well cross over if I have headed for the wrong one. You see, I am not by nature a rude man. But I would like to have some way of indicating my disapproval of the letter-of-the-law harassment.

GENTLE READER:

Show your pass without turning your head to the guard who requires it, while turning pleasantly to the other guard and saying, "Good morning" or "Good afternoon" in a friendly manner, thus indicating that you recognize one as a human being, but do not recognize the other, who never seems to recognize you.

Shame

DEAR MISS MANNERS:

Some months ago, the head of the department I work in singled me out for praise on a certain report. Obviously, I should have told him right then who had written it. There were reasons at the time, which are too complicated to go into now, that I felt I couldn't. Anyway, the credit bolstered my position at a time I needed it, and no real harm seemed to be done. I certainly never lied about anything, and I had, indeed, made some suggestions on the report.

My problem now is that the same department head is down on the woman who did write it, saying that she is not really pulling her weight. This came up because he found out that she takes off on Wednesday afternoons to take her son to the orthodontist. I pointed out that she doesn't go to lunch that day and stays late after she comes back, so that no work time is actually lost. But then he just said, "All right, but what does she do around here, anyway?"

It was too late for me to mention that report, but I did, and still am doing, what I can to defend this woman as a hard worker.

The question to you is that I would like to do something nice for this woman, something that shows real, human feeling, because, even though I'm already doing what I can for her professionally, I feel kind of guilty about the whole thing. I thought of sending flowers or a box of candy, but my wife thinks these might be misinterpreted or would embarrass her. She says that you know everything, so you would know just the right thing to do as a gesture of good will.

GENTLE READER:

Indeed. There is one thing that Miss Manners does not know, and that is the nature of this malady, so much among us, called Feeling Guilty. It is spoken of the way gout was by Edwardian aristocrats—as an affliction of the fortunate, perhaps born of overindulgence but something to be proud of nonetheless, its pain compensated by its fashionableness.

The feeling you describe sounds to Miss Manners, not like feeling guilty, but remarkably like an old one called Shame. Shame is a truly nasty feeling that one cannot gaily confess to one's friends because, unlike guilt, shame is the direct result, to anyone not utterly beyond redemption, of having done a shameful act. The only way to avoid shame is to forgo acting shamefully. The only way to get rid of it is to undo the shameful act.

Flowers will not help, in this case. You must go to the department head and say, "You asked about what she did—she wrote that report you told me you liked so much." It is your good luck that he will probably think you are being generous, but you must do an honest job of convincing him to take this statement at face value. Then you will feel better. And you can send the flowers to your wife.

Coffee

DEAR MISS MANNERS:

Somewhat enlightened corporations have installed, in dingy surroundings called canteens, machines which dispense something that is passed off as coffee. One procures this liquid by putting coins into a slot. Should one put in more money than required (the current rate is twenty cents) one's change is returned to one (one hopes) through an aperture somewhat below the slot. Recently, Miss Manners, I deposited a quarter in the slot. While waiting for the machine to fill my paper cup, I heard the change cup receive two coins. Putting in my eager fingers, I found that my "change" included the nickel, which I had anticipated, *and a quarter!* My question, Miss Manners, is this: May I properly (or improperly) keep the unexpected twenty-five cents?

GENTLE READER:

Miss Manners believes that this form of gambling is prevalent in most states, even in those in which racier forms are illegal. It is therefore Miss Manners' impression that you are ethically entitled to whatever coins come out of the machine, with the understanding that the odds are against you. Miss Manners once enjoyed quite a winning streak in an office canteen similar to the one you describe, and was crestfallen when her luck changed and coffee, as the machine claimed it to be, was produced instead of quarters.

The Delights of Tea

DEAR MISS MANNERS:

I am a tea drinker in a coffee world. Ordinarily, this poses no problem, but on occasion I must attend meetings where coffee and doughnuts—alas, no tea—are served. Although I am generally outspoken, I have not yet confronted my colleagues with my dilemma, mainly because I am the only woman in the group. Should I speak up and further distinguish or possibly alienate myself from the group?

GENTLE READER:

Miss Manners is a cucumber sandwich eater in a doughnut world, so don't think she doesn't sympathize with you. But if one wishes to stress one's willingness to work with other people, regardless of gender, one keeps special requests to a minimum, or presents them as if one were the spokeswoman for a faction, as in, ''Perhaps we should provide tea at the next meeting for people who would prefer it.''

Presents in the Office

DEAR MISS MANNERS:

When you receive a present from all your friends in the office and you thank them in person, should you send a thank-you note too?

GENTLE READER:

First of all, you didn't thank them all in person. You forgot two people who were sick that day, the new person who you assumed hadn't contributed, and the one who was out of the office. There was one whom you thanked twice, and you thanked profusely someone who said he had been hit for office present collections three times that month and wasn't contributing another dime. Second, such presents are usually given on momentous occasions—you have just been married, or had a baby, or been promoted or been asked to resign voluntarily—and should be acknowledged with a letter. Address it to the staff, and word it suitably for bulletin board posting.

The Boss's Wife

DEAR MISS MANNERS:

In a boss and wife relationship with the employees (thirty-five female, five male), after the boss has introduced her and she treats them in a gracious but not gushy manner, who takes the next steps toward further friendship? It has always been my feeling that being too friendly with employees clouds one's objectivity. I am open to a little more than just greetings, but I don't want to push myself on them. Should I initiate further friendship or should I let them voluntarily offer it?

GENTLE READER:

The chief thing to remember about the boss's wife's position is that she is the boss's wife. You may be sure that the employees remember it—or if they forget it when overcome with jolly sociability, they remember it later when they wake up in the middle of the night. You must therefore be aware that they are unlikely to take the initiative in advancing the intimacy of social relations with you, and also that they will feel obliged to go along with whatever you suggest. It is not pleasant for people to have close social relationships where there cannot be equality. For the sake of the employees, as well as your own, Miss Manners suggests not pushing the friendliness beyond office-related social activities.

The Office Party

The ideal office Christmas party starts before lunch, with an invitation issued by the boss. The exact wording of this invitation should be: "Why don't you take the rest of the day off?"

This is the simplest and pleasantest invitation that a person in authority can issue. It does not require engaging a caterer, and it does not leave the office littered with plastic cups and personnel problems. It costs nothing and delights everyone. Nevertheless, many people persist in the notion that office parties spread goodwill among co-workers. Annual experiences to the contrary never seem to dislodge this often fatal error.

Miss Manners' mean-spirited approach to professional merrymaking is actually part of an increasing hostility to the entire concept of business entertaining. From the formal diplomatic dinner to the salesperson's after-hours drink with a client, she finds it an intrusion on the worker's private life and an insult to the concept of good business. It is Miss Manners' belief that most people make their professional decisions on the basis of their best judgment, unclouded by an ecstasy of gratitude brought on by the offer of a free drink. She also feels that disguising the business relationship as friendship produces more dangers than rewards. A person who behaves disgracefully at a party ought to lose his friends, perhaps, but not his livelihood.

In the case of an office Christmas party, blurring the class lines is always a mistake. The fraudulent attempt to pass off people of different ranks and degrees of power as a bunch of jolly equals can only lead to trouble. Take, for instance, the matter of "There's something I've always wanted to tell you." Such things, whether they involve how you feel about the shortcomings of a superior or how you feel about the personal attractions of an inferior, are always better left unsaid. That is why you didn't say them all year, isn't it? Remember?

How much nicer was the old tradition of emphasizing the distinctions of rank, with false cheer instead of frank exchange. By this system, the worker says a few words about the privilege of working there, and the boss distributes praise along with a-little-something-extra-in-the-check.

If partying is required, a paternalistic or maternalistic version is best, with the employer paying for the treat and the employees responding by being on their best behavior. Perhaps they can be asked to bring their immediate families to the office, and the children may be allowed to examine the premises, while the adult relatives are told how valuable is the contribution of their particular wage earner. Perhaps this is too wholesome and unsatisfying a way for some people to celebrate Christmas with their co-workers. Well, remember that unexpected half-day off Miss Manners suggested as the ideal celebration? She never said you had to go directly home and spend it trimming the tree.

The Bonus

DEAR MISS MANNERS:

I work in a rather close-knit office. We rarely see our boss, since he has retired to enjoy the profits which we work to produce. Four times a year, we receive a bonus out of the company profits. The others see this as a gift and send thank-you notes to the boss. I feel we are entitled to these bonuses and that they only serve to cut the profit margin anyway. I have not sent any thank-you notes. (I wonder if he even reads the others?) Am I wrong?

GENTLE READER:

Miss Manners always believes in sending thank-you notes. It encourages people to give more.

Leaving Gracefully

DEAR MISS MANNERS:

I work in a small department. I am, in fact, planning to leave the job in a few months. My boss and my co-workers have no knowledge of my plans as of yet. I have not communicated much to them recently, because I realized that when I try to talk to them, they either can barely mask their boredom or proceed to tell me how I am young and therefore ignorant of the ways of the working world. This, of course, does not inspire my confidence in or loyalty to them.

Now, my problem: When it does become time to break my news, I know that they are going to feel betrayed and hurt because I have not confided in them all along or asked for their guidance and counsel. How do I manage to defend myself without breaking the rules of civility, against the inevitable onslaught of their attempts to make me feel guilty for keeping my own counsel?

GENTLE READER:

Miss Manners cannot understand why you would want to leave a job where everybody is trying so hard to make you feel incompetent, ignorant, sneaky, and guilty. However, you do not need to tell her the reason, and you need not tell one to these people, either. The reason for not announcing a new job until it is time to give proper notice of leaving the old one is always that it had not yet become "definite."

Entertaining Isn't Very Businesslike

Business entertaining is rather a curious term, Miss Manners has always thought. What is amusing, pray, about having to work overtime and to pretend that it is just the same as having a real social life with real friends?

Nor is she convinced that it makes the business world go around any faster. Miss Manners spent years of her life attending diplomatic parties, for reasons she has forgotten, and the only useful result she could see was to maintain modest citizens, such as Miss Manners herself and members of the international diplomatic community, in a style of nineteenth-century lavishness complete with eighteenth-century furniture, none of which even the richest can now afford.

That is a worthy cause, of course. If it were not for expense accounts of one kind or another, we would all have to live within our means and what would become of the champagne industry? But the common justifications—that business entertaining generates goodwill, makes informal exchanges possible, and is necessary to keep up with one's rivals—merely mean that one must do it because it is done. It seems to Miss Manners that any sensible business can be conducted directly, that goodwill does not prevent bad business, and people can as easily blunder as ingratiate themselves in pseudo-social circumstances.

Having said that, Miss Manners will now turn her attention conscientiously to the business of business entertainment. Lunch in a restaurant is by far the best way to do this, as many people resent carrying business over into hours usually devoted to families, friends, or sitting in a hot bath with a good book. There is no excuse for being late to a business luncheon, short of having been run over on the way there. Everyone is "busy" and "rushed" in the middle of the day. The person who proposed the luncheon insists upon picking up the check; gender is not a factor, and any suggestion that it is should be cheerfully ignored.

For business dinners—unless they are held among people who are going back to work afterwards, in which case they are treated as lunches—it is customary to invite the spouses or their equivalents as an acknowledgment that the event will be occupying private time. If these people have any sense, they won't go, anyway. For that matter, the employees should be able to regard these activities as optional overtime.

Large-scale business luncheon or dinner parties will succeed in the proportion that they imitate real social events. Correct invitations, a prominent guest of honor or important occasion as an excuse, good food and drink, and a decent amount of general conversation help to lull people into thinking that they are there because they want to be, not because they have to be for the sake of their careers.

The business cocktail party is a bastardization of an already unnatural form (or rather, natural, if one is to stay with the metaphor). People are at their most greedy and ungrateful when appraising cocktail parties, even when the hosts are friends. So the best chance for a business to impress them is to entertain on a scale not usually available to the guests—the food, the drink, the place where it is held. After all, this is, as Miss Manners said, the real attraction of organization-sponsored entertainment.

Anyone who attempts to have fun in the usual social way—overeating, overdrinking, heavy flirting—would be jeopardizing his or her career. So enjoy these occasions, but just don't have a good time. That is what friends are for.

Colleagues' Companions

How generous many businessmen are in their hospitality. Miss Manners has often wondered at the businessman's capacity to lavish time and expense accounts on people who are then likely to work against him as a fifth column among his clients and associates. These are the wives and sweethearts of businessmen—we are discussing businessmen's wives here, not businesswomen's husbands—sometimes invited along to parties or restaurant meals of a professional nature. The host encourages this because he knows that an evening a couple spends at such a party will be counted by them as going out, rather than working late; or because he knows that he is not likely to entice his prey away from a dinner date and find him in a pleasant frame of mind.

But by the time a host has finished being what he considers charming to the lady, the chances are that he has developed an enemy. After being patronized, ignored, or both, the lady will express an opinion where it will do the most harm. If the couple are in the habit of raking over the people they meet—one of the great intimate pleasures—she may only say, "That twit on my right asked me my name three times and still didn't get it right." A less outspoken lady will do more insidious damage by remarking vaguely, "Oh, I don't know, there was just something I didn't quite trust about that man."

How does a well-meaning businessman achieve this result at his own expense, so to speak? By assuming that the lady does nothing of importance herself—or challenging her to prove that she does. By refraining from boring her with business, turning away from her when that is discussed, and searching for topics he presumes to be more suitable when forced to converse with her.

Such rudeness cannot be classified as garden variety antifeminism. In fact, Miss Manners has noticed that taking a superior tone toward wives—she has rarely heard of it happening to businesswomen's husbands—is a common fault of men who profess to espouse equality, and is sometimes also practiced by professional women.

Gentlemen of the old school are less likely to offend, having been trained in politeness to ladies, whatever they really think of them. In spite of what these gentlemen's own daughters may confide afterward about their father's porcine tendencies, such gentlemen may select the correct approach automatically. That is to treat the guests who are there through marriage or its equivalent the same as the guests who are there through their jobs. It is to assume that if the lady took no interest in the work being discussed, she would have let the gentleman attend alone.

Everyone occasionally attends an event connected with the achievement of a friend or relative. The graceful way to do this—whether it is a fiancé's business lunch or a child's school assembly—is to minimize one's own identity and exhibit supportive interest in the other person's. Miss Manners does not approve of the "I'm-someone-too!" approach to getting attention at such a function. When there is equality, both spouses know how and when to be the accompanist. But they retain the right to feel insulted when deprived of the dignity of this function by people who act as if they must be too insecure or uninformed to take an intelligent interest in the proceedings.

Businesswomen, Businessmen, and Business Dinners

DEAR MISS MANNERS:

I am an unmarried businesswoman. I am occasionally invited out to dinner with out-of-town executives and their local managers. I have not accepted their invitations because I am uncertain of the etiquette that would be proper in a situation in which I would be the only female member of the dinner party. Although these gentlemen can be as sober as judges during business hours, they are quite capable (I hear) of really letting loose during evening hours. However, I know my male counterparts have sometimes come away from the table with valuable information—"shop talk"—that can be used to our company's benefit.

Should I invite a date to accompany me to such a dinner in order to retain respectability and keep weird ideas out of the head of some gentleman who's half swacked by the time the salad is served? This is a nagging problem, as my male counterparts may or may not invite their wives along. In either case, they do not become subject to the raised eyebrow or leering-look routine. Should I conduct these semi-business, semi-social evenings as I would a well-organized business meeting? It seems to me that one should try to strike a balance between being either too loose or too straitlaced. What should I do if one of the gentlemen leers or makes suggestive comments? What should I wear to such an event —a business suit or a dinner dress? Of course, either outfit would be conservatively cut. Should I meet the gentleman at the restaurant or allow them to pick me up at home? When I travel out of town on business, am I expected to invite my hosts out to dinner? This problem is easier, because then I could invite their wives as well.

Your advice on this matter is going to be appreciated—not only by me, but also by our managers who, despite the advances in the women's movement, are chary of allowing their female subordinates enough rein to become involved in such situations.

GENTLE READER:

Miss Manners would dearly love to see "semi-business semi-social" entertaining abolished, for the very reason that it presents so many unpleasant possibilities. However, if businessmen have them, businesswomen must, and unfortunately they must protect themselves against men who try to give them the business.

The surest way to make people behave is to make them aware that many people will know about it if they don't. Yes, invite their wives, if you can. Yes, bring an escort if you can. If neither is possible, you might bring along a junior colleague and explain that she is making a report on what she is learning. Or ask a friend to pick you up at the restaurant after dinner. Another method is to find an opportunity, such as your out-of-town dinner, to establish social contact with the wives of these gentlemen and to mention, if a gentleman makes improper advances to you, that you hope to be talking with his wife soon. Threatening blackmail while smiling and being sociable is an indispensable business technique. In your dress and arrangements, you should treat the occasion as a pleasant, informal extension of the work day, not a date. They do not pick you up at home, and you do not dress up. It is unfortunate that businesswomen must protect themselves, but it is wrong for managers to concern themselves with the problem. They will only use it as an excuse for not promoting women. If one attempts to discuss the problems, however sympathetically, ask him what he does to protect the chastity of his male subordinates.

When the Lady Pays

DEAR MISS MANNERS:
As a businessman, how do I allow a businesswoman to pay for my lunch?
GENTLE READER:
With credit card or cash, as she prefers.

Embarrassed Businessmen

DEAR MISS MANNERS:
I want to be fair and reasonable, but there are some things I can't get used to about the "new manners." Specifically, I am embarrassed when a woman I am lunching with grabs the check. Some of them do this quite aggressively. I am talking about business lunches, of course, although the way things are going, this may well spread to social occasions. My company is perfectly willing to pay for any business lunches I consider necessary, and my lunch partner does me no favor by making a show of paying for me herself. What is the woman's real objective here—to prove she's my equal?
GENTLE READER:
Yes.

Lunch with Colleagues

DEAR MISS MANNERS:
Is it proper for a married woman to have lunch with one of her male co-workers?
GENTLE READER:
Yes, provided that he is not her husband. A woman who meets her husband for lunch in a restaurant is only inviting scandal. Everyone will assume they have met downtown for the purpose of visiting a lawyer.

Business Correspondence

"Esquire"

DEAR MISS MANNERS:

When I was a young man, I worked for a very distinguished book publisher. To be sure that everyone knew he was distinguished, this publisher addressed all his male correspondents as Joe Doe, Esq., rather than Mr. Joe Doe. I am rather fond of this quaint English custom, but notice that it has now gone out of fashion, except for expensive lawyers who call themselves Esq. on their stationery. That strikes me as silly. But I like to use this form of address on envelopes of letters I write. Does that make me seem affected and conspicuous?

GENTLE READER:

If you understood the true English usage of ''esquire'' you would, indeed, seem affected and conspicuous, as no two Englishmen seem to agree on this. It has to do with legal designations of younger sons of peers, eldest sons of knights, crown officers, and so on. Some American lawyers, who adore such tangles, have jumped in and appropriated it for themselves, which is quite selfish considering how many American lawyers are women. In England, ''esquire'' is used widely and indiscriminately these days, and Miss Manners advises Americans to let them have it.

"Esquire" for Women Lawyers

DEAR MISS MANNERS:

Some of the men in my office are feeling incorrect after I challenged their assertion that women may not properly use the title "Esquire." They have even expressed some willingness to part with a portion of their hard-earned salaries in their insistence that "esquire" is incorrect for women. I am eager to assist them in their divestment of funds, so I decided to write you, the ultimate authority, to find out what is correct. (The men have decided to accept your decision, although some of them feel you are not completely serious.)

We are familiar of course, with the medieval origins and usage of the title in England, but this differs from American usage, does it not? As I have always understood it, the title in the United States carries none of the significance of the English usage (i.e., a title for anyone with the social position of a gentleman), but is instead used mainly by persons in certain professions, such as lawyers and justices of the peace. I have certainly seen it used by women, although for the life of me, I can't figure out why any woman would want to encumber her name with this particularly anachronistic and pompous borrowing from her male counterparts.

GENTLE READER:

Miss Manners agrees with you that the use of "esquire" among male lawyers in this country is anachronistic and pompous, but she will explain to you why female lawyers similarly encumber themselves. It is because it is a not uncommon experience for people of the female gender who are recognized as the ultimate authorities in their fields, and on whose weighty decisions the disbursement of hard-earned salaries may hinge, to be nevertheless taxed with being "not completely serious."

If the Name Is Known

DEAR MISS MANNERS:

Please settle a disagreement that has recently come up in our office. I was asked to type a letter addressed to a firm we have done business with, encouraging them to do more business with us. The person who dictated the letter insisted I used "Gentlemen" for the salutation, even though the letter was addressed to the company, and made to the attention of a female vice-president of the firm. I, and all the other female employees of this firm, thought that this practice was incorrect and would offend the woman to whom the letter was directed. The gentleman who dictated the letter insists that it is grammatically correct, and she should not be offended in the least. We are not extreme advocates of women's liberation, but found this practice disrespectful.

GENTLE READER:

Miss Manners has seen a lot of nonsense running around masquerading as correctness, but your dictator has topped it all with his assertion that it is grammatically correct to address a woman as "Gentlemen."

If he can't get either her gender or her number right, why doesn't he try using her name? The form "Gentlemen" was invented for the awkward but frequent business situation in which the names and genders of recipients of a letter are not know to the writer. Miss Manners prefers "Mesdames" for that purpose, assuming that any males in the organization will understand that they are meant to be included.

If Miss Manners is addressed as "Dear Customer" in commercial correspondence, she replies to "Dear Merchant."

DEAR MISS MANNERS:

Some years ago, I was taught that the only proper salutations for business letters addressed to large institutions and not individuals were "Dear Sirs," "Gentlemen," and "Dear Sir or Madam." The first two are unacceptable because inaccurate and sexist, and I consider the third stilted and Victorian. Since at the time I was not writing business letters, the matter did not trouble me. In my present situation, however, I have (a) considerable business correspondence with persons of unknown sex, (b) a continuing dislike for the forms once taught me, and (c) very little acquaintance with women who approve of being called "madam." I need a form of address that is correct, not antiquated, and that offers no possibility of offending the recipient. Would you please suggest one?

GENTLE READER:

What is wrong with being stilted and Victorian? Your letter has left Miss Manners, who has not been able to help being stilted and Victorian all her life, sobbing quietly into her cambric handkerchief. So you see, one cannot be sure of writing anything that offers no possibility of offending the recipient.

Miss Manners would also like to know what is wrong with the term "madam." "Madam President," "Madam Secretary," and "Madam Prime Minister" are quite attractive titles, and not the less respectable because those who hold racier administrative positions have also employed it. As you were taught, the only proper salutations when the name of the person to whom you are writing is unknown to you are "Dear Sir," "Dear Madam," and "Dear Sir or Madam." If your sense of prose style prevents you from using the last of these, Miss Manners hopes you will alternate between the first two.

DEAR MISS MANNERS:

My sweet bride and I see no reason for you to be ashamed because, in a brief lapse, you could offer nothing better than "Dear Madam or Sir" to those who wish not to offend the unknown recipient of their letter. May we suggest "Dear Friends"? We assume that there are enough nice people about that the chances are reasonably good that, if we met, we might be. At any rate, the "Dear Friends" signals good fellowship and sets a proper tone.

We remain perplexed when forced into correspondence on ugly matters; "Dear Knucklehead" or "Hey, ratface," seem in poor taste, and may well be counterproductive.

GENTLE READER:

Miss Manners is perplexed when you call it setting a proper tone to anticipate friendship with an unknown person. One might just as well go the whole way and imagine falling passionately in love with one's unnamed bank representative, for example, and therefore address that person as "My Own Darling."

As for insulting a person in the salutation—why, that takes the fun out of the letter proper, does it not?

Miss Manners' solution to adjusting the conventional salutation to an age in which women are as likely to be in business as men, is to use "Mesdames" or "Dear Madam," under the assumption that a well-run business is run by women. If she sends a letter of complaint, she uses "Gentlemen" or "Dear Sir."

Closings

DEAR MISS MANNERS:

I write occasional business letters. What is the proper complimentary closing? Many are to people whom I do not necessarily respect; that lets out "respectfully." "Yours" is obviously out; I am most certainly not. While I hope I am almost always sincere, "Sincerely" seems to be out of place in a business letter. So does "love," whether agape or filial. How about just "very" or how about nothing?

GENTLE READER:

How about "Yr. most humble and obedient servant"? How about not being so literal? Miss Manners signs herself "Very truly yours" to business people and "Sincerely yours" to acquaintances—believing that "sincerely" alone is as close to nothing as "very" alone—and has not yet been required to surrender herself to any of them.

The Telephone in the Office

It is not in the nature of Miss Manners' business to have sudden emergencies. She does not carry that curious item called a beeper in her beaded bag when she goes out to dinner, just in case she should be wanted by someone at another dinner needing to know if it would be proper to ask for thirds. Nevertheless, Miss Manners is aware that the air about her is crackling with the great game of business telephoning. As she understands it, the person placing a call, however trivial or postponable its contents, must exercise all possible ingenuity to get through. Furthermore, the more difficult it is—if the recipient is, say, on vacation and in the shower and also taking another call at the time—the greater the triumph.

It is always the object of the person being called to avoid the call. But while he or she may use fierce people and treacherous machinery to put off the caller, it is not considered fair for the callee actually to be out of range of a telephone. By leaving numbers everywhere, carrying that beeper, and installing telephones in all vacation house landscapes, one is considered to be giving the caller a sporting chance.

Miss Manners has always thought all this a dreadful nuisance, and has remarked how much more quickly and efficiently business would be accomplished if people wrote and answered letters, instead of papering one another's offices with telephone messages. However, many people seem to enjoy this pastime more than working, so Miss Manners will confine herself to setting a few rules. She will address them to the caller and the callee's interference person, since the game is over if the caller gets directly to the callee.

If the caller has used an interference person to go directly to the callee, he cannot also play the part of the evader of calls. If a secretary tells Miss Manners that she has a call from someone who does not come on the line immediately, she offers her apologies for having answered the telephone at an inconvenient time, and rings off.

The caller must state his or her name and business, although "It is personal" or "I'm returning his call" do not require elaboration. The callee gets a chance to judge from the name whether these claims are hoaxes.

The interference person is allowed a certain number of questions about the name and business. These must be brief and tactful, to avoid sounding like an interrogation to scare off the undesirable, which is, of course, what they are.

"Would you spell your name, please?" is reasonable; "What was your name again?" is not because, of course, all information is written down immediately. "Does she know what it is in reference to?" is more polite than "What is it about?" And prolonged interrogation is permissible only when it is plausible to suggest that someone else might be better able to handle the business.

If this seems to give the advantage to the caller, it is because Miss Manners hasn't yet shown how easy it is to be honestly unreachable. You know that it is rude to take a telephone call while you have a person present doing business with you. Putting previous callers on "hold" is also rude, unless your telephone plays tunes to them while they wait, in which case it is unspeakable. It should also be understood that concentrating on one's work may require you to avoid interruptions, and that being at home or on vacation or sick is an acceptable excuse for not taking business calls. By combining all of these situations, it can become possible to develop a universal policy of receiving messages instead of calls. Placing the calls you choose when you choose will give you long peaceful hours in which to conduct business in writing or in person. It will also give you time for the frustrating task of trying to reach other elusive people by telephone.

Those Who Work for Others

Democracy is a perfectly wonderful idea, Miss Manners fervently believes, provided it does not give the help funny ideas. It is difficult to feel the proper patriotic passion for equality while being sassed by one's inferiors.

If this does not seem an appropriate sentiment for one who adores the Fourth of July, it is only because the terms Miss Manners uses may be subject to misunderstanding. She yields to no one in her love for America as a land of opportunity. The only quibble is over what we want the opportunity to do.

Miss Manners does not believe there is any such thing, anywhere, as a classless society. But she has noticed that talent, intelligence, and perseverance seem to be randomly distributed in the population, without respect for money, let alone race, religion, or sex. Therefore she sees democracy as a system that allows people to change classes, according to their abilities. As many people will, at least temporarily, occupy the lower part of the structure, she believes that they ought to do it gracefully and well. Dear Mr. Jefferson, adorable Mr. Franklin, and others who so enjoyed pleasant living did not intend, with their services to the common man, to make all of us behave as if we were common. Nor did they intend, in a country where the most honored people are called public servants, to dishonor the idea of service.

Yet the idea has gotten around that there need be no hierarchy in the job structure. And since there obviously is—one need only check one's paycheck—

416

people in the service jobs seek compensation by behaving with inefficiency and surliness to those whom they are supposed to serve. The worst offenders are not those who are stuck in such jobs, but the people—such as college students with temporary jobs—whose upward route seems clearly marked.

The widespread use of first names, sports clothing, audio recreation, and other attributes of "informality" in the work world has assisted in the illusion that no one really needs to perform a service for anyone else. The results is that badly paying jobs are badly done.

Miss Manners has not failed to catch the irony here. She is not unsympathetic with the ambitions of workers to be paid their worth; only with the determination to scale down the performance to worthlessness.

People in service jobs—waiters, clerks, parking lot attendants, taxi drivers, whatever—do not prove, by being inefficient and rude, that they are meant for better things. They merely show that they can't properly handle the jobs they have, many of which can be done with cleverness and skill.

Miss Manners' idea of democracy is a society in which the lower classes practice the kind of graciousness that will fit them perfectly for upper-class positions.

A Reply

DEAR MISS MANNERS:

As a person who performs and who has performed "services"—secretarial, clerical, and so forth—I am much too full of bitterness and resentment against those people (probably people like you, I'll wager) who enjoy the idea of a "lower class" of workers to whom *they* have the right to be rude, to be sympathetic to your view that "people in the service jobs seek compensation by behaving with inefficiency and surliness to those whom they are supposed to serve."

Yes, I have been the victim of some surly people in service jobs—clerks who stand there watching me wait at the counter and don't come over to help me, and so forth. But I have also noticed how those who are being served—doctors, lawyers, professors, professional people in the upper brackets in particular—show rudeness toward their "inferiors" as your snobbish expression puts it. They really believe that those lower on the pay scale do not deserve to be treated with dignity and respect.

I am a college graduate who worked service jobs while in college, and I have always been a lady. Therefore, I have never been anything but gracious to everyone, whether they be college professors or trash collectors. I have noticed, however, that the professional "upper class" people are notoriously lacking in any genuine good manners or graciousness, unless they are courting the attention of someone who can assist them in moving higher up the economic ladder. Now, lest I be guilty of generalizations (as you are, I hasten to add), not all people in the "upper classes" behave like that. I have found the utmost grace in many groups of people—even doctors and lawyers, believe it or not. With that, Miss Manners, I leave you to your snobbery.

GENTLE READER:

Ah, you have not heard the half of it. Miss Manners' snobbery is such that it follows the nineteenth-century practice of classifying doctors, lawyers, artists, professors, and businessmen in the serving classes. In other words, all of us who work for a living are in a position of service when our work brings us in contact with the public. Your doctor and your lawyer, if they but knew it, are as obligated to be pleasant to you as your waitress and your automobile mechanic. As this includes just about everybody in America, who, you may well ask, are the members of the upper classes, and are they exempt from polite behavior?

In a democracy, we all get an opportunity. You, as patient, client, customer, are being served and should be served well, by working people. And what keeps it imperative that you treat them graciously is *noblesse oblige,* the sternest master of all. One last generalization, from your Miss Manners: There is no snobbery like that inspired by those who aspire to the lower classes.

Domestic Service

It used to be the custom for ladies to gather in a corner of the drawing room to speak, in hushed tones, of the Servant Problem. Now that they can shout it from house to house without any danger of being overheard by servants, the fun is gone.

What pleasure there used to be in comparing the gaucheries and debaucheries of the lower orders, as observed at close range by those who could only stand and be waited upon. It was a fine time, too, for ladies of Miss Manners' profession, who wrote exquisite essays on the three daily costume changes required of the parlor maid, and sly, hypocritical reassurances to the hostess who attempted to feed eight people with only a cook and a waitress to help.

It wasn't that the Servant Problem went away, just that the servants did. The reason for this was that it had never really been a Servant Problem so much as an Employer Problem. Hushed tones or no, the servants found out from the employers' attitude, to say nothing of their wages, hours, and responsibilities, that they could serve their own best interests elsewhere. One can say that the servants served the employers right. Human dignity is better served when each individual is able to be self-sufficient, which includes both earning one's bread and making the sandwich.

However, it is not practical for everyone to do each and every task of daily life. The hope remains that someone else will perform the services you cannot personally manage—for love or money. Fewer people are willing to do it for love these days. They found that they were running into the same problems as the servants: lack of appreciation, ready money, time off, and job security. Miss Manners would like to resolve this unfortunate situation, because she has always wanted to write about the correct attire for footmen. Her revolutionary suggestion is that service jobs be treated as being as important as we say they are when people perform them for themselves.

A woman who keeps her own house clean is considered to be a model for others. A person who cooks for his or her friends is thought of as warm and creative. A father who spends time caring for his children is deemed a paragon. Why, then, are people who clean, cook, or care for children professionally at the bottom of the vocational ladder?

Let Miss Manners review briefly for prospective employers of servants what a decent job is. It is, at most, five-day, forty-hour week, with overtime pay for time over. It has vacations, sick leave, and a pay scale providing increases for merit, experience, and cost of living. One should also be able to earn respect, which means using one's own judgment about managing the assigned tasks, and not being accused of stealing every time something has been misplaced.

These principles apply to hiring a cleaning woman for part-time every other week, as well as to running a household full of servants. It is the only way to solve the Employer Problem; and the only way Miss Manners will ever be able to plunge into that exciting argument about whether the butler should stand behind the host or the hostess at dinner.

Respect

DEAR MISS MANNERS:

I am an elderly woman. I clean house for several families. The people for whom I work pay me well. They treat me well. They all tell me I do a fabulous job. So why am I writing to you? Just one thing mars all this for me! They all call me (unasked to do so) by my first name. I should have stopped this at the start, but I didn't. I don't mind that—a great deal—but how do you think I like being introduced to their relatives and friends—"Mrs. Ryan, this is my housekeeper, Hilda"? Their children also call me by my first name.

I have been told by others (younger than I) that they, too, resent this first name business. My children were brought up to use surnames unless asked otherwise. I like to think of doing housework as a reputable profession. I really like my employers and try to be trustworthy and do a good job. I am older than any for whom I work. Please write about the etiquette of this.

GENTLE READER:

It is an oddity of tradition that occupations that are of real use in the world, such as yours, have been accorded less respect than many that are of no perceptible use whatever. Miss Manners is in full sympathy with your desire to be addressed by title and surname, as befits your age and business relationship with your employers.

Please keep in mind, however, that they are merely going by tradition and do not mean to insult you by using your first name. (For traditional ways of referring to household staff, please see pp. 609–611.) There are, in fact, women in your job who, being used to that tradition, are uncomfortable at being addressed otherwise. In such a transition period, it is the person being addressed who should make the choice. Miss Manners advises household employers to ask their employees, when hiring them, what they prefer to be called. As you say, it is too late for that in your case. Nevertheless, you must make your wishes known. Knowing that they are simply using an old form from habit, you should, when announcing the change, assume goodwill on their part.

You can put it something like this:

"Mrs. Awful, there is something I have been wanting to tell you."

"Yes, what is it, Hilda?"

"Well—that's what it is. I have never felt comfortable with your calling me 'Hilda.' I'm not a young girl, you know, and I feel entitled to the respect of my age and my occupation." (Then you put in the rest about how you try to do a good job, and generally feel that your employers treat and pay you well. Say everything that you put into your letter.)

Mrs. Awful will then be covered with embarrassment. She will protest wildly, "Oh, Hilda, I never meant any disrespect," and then she will realize what she just said and get even more embarrassed. But eventually, she will learn. And you will have performed a service, not only for yourself, but for all working women.

Entertaining Labor

DEAR MISS MANNERS:

We are having a lot of work done in the house, and I feel funny sitting there eating meals while the painters and electricians are working nearby. I'm not saying that I'm willing to cook for them, and anyway, the ones that are there all day bring their own lunch pails. But I can be having my lunch, sometimes with a friend who's stopped by, and we're at the table while the men who are doing over the kitchen are standing around, and I feel as if I ought to ask them to sit down and at least have a cup of coffee. I don't really want to, as lunchtime is when I do my reading if I'm alone and if I have a visitor I'd rather talk to her, but doesn't it seem snobbish not to ask them to join us?

GENTLE READER:

It would be snobbish to ask them to join you. Such an invitation presumes that you believe that you, whose walls are peeling and whose wiring is a mess, who don't even have a functional kitchen, are the social equal of honest laborers.

False Friendship

There seem to be a great many incompetent people in the world named Hi. Miss Manners has observed that a person who announces brightly, "Hi I'm Ron" or "Hi I'm Cindy" is about to make a perfect nuisance of him or herself, and will furthermore prove utterly inept in whatever station God has seen fit to place him.

Hi the Waiter forgets the vegetables, can't remember who got the chicken, and appears at the most thrilling moment of the tête-à-tête to ask, "Is everything all right?" Hi the Airline Clerk tells you that the plane is now being serviced for your convenience, but can't tell you how many more hours it will be before it will leave or whether there is another way to make your connection. If Miss Manners ever complained that the world was an impersonal place where no one cared if you lived or died, she takes it back. It is now a personal world where no one cares if you live or die. False friendship and instant intimacy seem to go with a complete lack of concern for the person at whom they are directed. The idea seems to be that spreading a pseudo-social air will make it seem rude to complain that the job isn't being done.

Miss Manners realizes that innocent people are caught in this, being made to Hi themselves, as waitresses may also be required, for example, to wear suggestive uniforms. Sometimes people force a fabricated conviviality on those who are not in a position to reject it—asking the doorman to address them by their first name, inquiring the cleaning woman's political views—because they are uncomfortable with the master-servant relationship, failing to understand its mutual dignity.

Such "informality" is not universally appreciated. Restaurant patrons may prefer to converse with the people they asked to dine with them, rather than to get to know the person who is waiting on their table. Your cleaning woman may prefer to get on with doing your floors and go home, rather than to suffer your company. Miss Manners loathes being addressed by her first name ("Miss") by those with whom she is not intimate. Such social promiscuity destroys the pleasure and value of friendship. Rather than encouraging human warmth, perverting its usages for business purposes spoils them for their true and special purposes.

It damages the business world. It robs the working person of his or her dignity. "If you and I are friends, why do I have to wait on you? But if I can be on equal terms with friends of my own choosing, it doesn't matter if I perform a service for wages." It destroys the effectiveness of the job and the dignity that would otherwise come of doing it well. Chumming around is, in itself, a job, and rather a whorish one, taking up time and energy that might otherwise be spent in performing a necessary service well, and taking pride in doing so.

The Role of the Waiter

DEAR MISS MANNERS:

I am an actor looking for my first professional engagement. In the meantime, I am supporting myself as a waiter—something actors have traditionally done. This is really my first paying job, and although I don't plan to make a career of it, I would like to do it well. Can you give me some suggestions?

GENTLE READER:

Allow Miss Manners to congratulate you: you do have your first acting job. Good waiters have always been great actors, and the best of them go on to more difficult roles, such as those of maître d'hotel, butler, or King Lear. There is not much competition, as most waiters and waitresses nowadays believe in "acting natural," which is to say that they don't know how to act.

The mechanics of the part you may learn on the job (although attention to Miss Manners' rules of meticulous table service will put you ahead of most people in the field—please see pp. 498–499), but you must work on motivation and character.

This means showing the pride of a person who performs his job well, and the dignity inherent in gracing a well-defined position. In plain language, you do not behave as if you are trying to show that you are just as good as the people on whom you are waiting, by chummy or surly demeanor. The waiter who joins in the conversation or snaps at the patrons is clearly saying that he feels defensive and inferior. The one who executes his task with an impenetrable air of detachment and impersonal efficiency conveys that he is flawless in handling the role—and therefore probably also excellent in a variety of other roles, professional and social.

Taking Blame

The mental health industry in this country, also known as the Feel Good Business, has put a massive effort into reducing the Gross National Guilt. But in so doing, it has only increased the distressing amount of unresolved blame that is going around.

Nobody is taking any blame for anything any longer. The new battlecry is "It's not my fault." Perhaps it's not. But Miss Manners, who believes that collective civilization is more important to the public happiness than a lot of little satisfied psyches bumping up against one another, does not like the result. She believes that if each one of us were to accept graciously a small portion of blame, it wouldn't all be hanging there, clogging up the air.

Example: Mrs. Ipswitch receives, in her department store bill, an offer she cannot refuse for a bottle of hair goo, "free" with the purchase of a related product. She duly fills in the form that will avail her of this unprecedented commercial opportunity. Some time later, a package arrives, containing the free product, but also a bottle of shampoo for red-headed people, when Mrs. Ipswitch had clearly ordered the shampoo for blue-headed ladies. There is a delivery charge that Mrs. Ipswitch had not noticed. Attempts to reach the department store by telephone fail, a fact that puzzles Mrs. Ipswitch as she is always being deserted at store counters by salespeople who prefer to answer the telephone. Mrs. Ipswitch packs up all the hair products and goes to the store. The shampoo counter is part of a vast cosmetic department divided by brands and populated by idle salespeople, all of whom refuse to have anything to do with Mrs. Ipswitch's problems because these come under the jurisdiction of the one occupied salesperson on the entire floor.

Mrs. Ipswitch grows increasingly fidgety as she waits to be waited upon. When her turn comes, she recounts, in her soft voice that is the delight of six grandchildren, two elderly beaux, and the staff and patients of the hospital where she pushes a bookmobile, the ills that have been perpetrated on her. The salesclerk maintains an unpleasant silence. She then informs Mrs. Ipswitch that she cannot read the sales slip pasted on the package, so she must assume that Mrs. Ipswitch was charged for the red shampoo, which is cheaper, and now must pay extra for the blue. Mrs. Ipswitch requests that the delivery charge now be removed, as she was forced to make a trip to the store to complete the purchase. The clerk refuses to do this.

Mrs. Ipswitch cracks. After sixty-seven years in which she has never said anything harsher than telling the fat pigeons in the park to allow the thin ones to share the breadcrumbs she brings, Mrs. Ipswitch goes bananas. At this point, the salesclerk decides to give Mrs. Ipswitch a lecture on etiquette, of which the theme is that the ills recited are "Not My Fault." Whatever has been done to Mrs. Ipswitch—by the person who packed the wrong product, those who should have answered the telephone, those who make the rules about delivery charges and about territorial division of the cosmetics department—has not been done by this particular clerk. "Don't yell at me, lady," she says coldly. "It's not my fault."

Perhaps not, as Miss Manners acknowledged earlier. But there is a greater human issue here, which is that Mrs. Ipswitch has to yell at someone. It would not hurt the clerk nearly so much to take the blame as it would Mrs. Ipswitch to swallow her indignation. Miss Manners believes it is the salesclerk's duty to identify with her offending employer, repeating "I'm terribly sorry" as long as necessary for Mrs. Ipswitch to recover.

So Miss Manners' advice for today is: Take some of the blame. If you are the fifth wrong number at City Hall whom a person has been connected with, say, "I'm so terribly sorry." If you are the driver of a bus, apologize for the bus that passed by the person for whom you are stopping. If everyone takes a little blame, there will be less of it going around.

Taking Calls

DEAR MISS MANNERS:

What do you think of a store clerk who leaves you right in the middle of writing up a purchase, in order to answer the telephone and take an order for someone who isn't even there?

GENTLE READER:

Miss Manners thinks that is the same clerk who puts the telephone on hold, when you are the one calling, in order to pretend to take the order of someone who is in the store. Between the two systems, a clever clerk is able to avoid the hurly-burly of the marketplace entirely.

Bargaining

DEAR MISS MANNERS:

We sell antiques, with the prices plainly marked on them. Our policy is that the prices are fair and firm—and yet people keep trying to haggle with us, asking "What is the best you can do?" or "What would you really take?" after we have told them the price. Once we had an Italian customer who said, "What is your final word?" and I said, "It's 'arrivederci.'" What is a gracious way of telling people that their attempts at lowering the prices are not appropriate, without making customers lose face?

GENTLE READER:

What your customers need is proof that the policy applies to everyone and is not simply a bargaining strategy you are using on them. Assuming that you think a "Fixed Prices" sign slightly crude for your type of business, Miss Manners suggests you find an oddly framed, dusty old sign saying this in French or Italian. The words are similar enough for anyone who speaks English to understand them, and yet you can seem to be displaying it as a curiosity. The customers will forget to lose face because they'll feel flattered at the assumption that they read French or Italian.

Salesmen

DEAR MISS MANNERS:

I was so embarrassed when my husband and I walked in the salesperson's office to sign contract papers. The salesman just shook hands with my husband and as I gave my hand, he was sitting down. He and the rest of the people there saw me pulling my hand back in shame, so he tried to put forward his hand, but it was too late. It looked like he just didn't want to shake hands with me in the first place! If I had known his attitude, I wouldn't have made a fool of myself. Please give me some tips on avoiding such embarrassments in the future.

GENTLE READER:

The person making a fool of himself was not you; it was the salesman, who was rude to a lady as well as inept with a customer. The embarrassment and shame should therefore be his, and the best way Miss Manners can help you prevent such situations in the future is to help you accentuate such embarrassment so that the salesman will try to avoid it in the future.

You do not say what you were buying, but let us assume it is an automobile and that the salesman was making the unbusinesslike assumption that all cars, even those to be driven by women, are sold to men. The most effective way of riveting his attention to his mistake is to say to your husband, "Darling, I changed my mind. I've decided I really don't want to buy this car, after all. But don't worry, I'll find you something you like." If you don't want to go that far, either with the assumption that your husband will fall into the role or with boycotting something you do want to buy, you might amend this to something like, "Is there a salesman here who deals with women customers? Since we are buying this together, I would feel more comfortable with someone like that." If you say this sweetly, it will make your point, especially if the salespeople work on commission.

Tellers

Although she abhors rough behavior, Miss Manners is reconciled to the idea that bank robbers must be treated with as much severity as can be mustered. What she does not understand is why the employees of banks do not apply a different standard of etiquette to their customers.

Presumably, the problem is that they cannot readily distinguish between the robbers and the customers. Perhaps that is true; yet Miss Manners fancies that when she goes to her bank with her stockings where they belong, rather than over her face, and attempts to make a deposit with a check rather than a quick withdrawal with a scrawled note, she should be given the benefit of the doubt. But she has heard that appearances can be deceiving, and that one cannot be too careful these tricky days.

This is where politeness could help. It is possible, in a bank or any other business establishment where identification is important, to follow security procedures while maintaining an air of civility. If the customer is then proven to be dishonest, one can always adjust one's manner back down to rudeness. Adjusting it up, from rudeness to deference after a suspected thief has been proved respectable, is rarely successful.

Take the statement, "We can't find a record of your account." That line, which is delivered almost automatically to everyone who arrives at Miss Manners' neighborhood bank, can be pronounced as if to say, "Please bear with us in this freak accident, as disgraceful to our standards of efficiency as it is inconvenient to you." The usual delivery clearly says, "Thought you'd pull a fast one, didn't you?"

There was a time when banks liked to characterize themselves as "friendly." That seems to Miss Manners a bit excessive. One should find one's friends and one's toasters in more appropriate places. But it is possible for the representatives of a bank to be moderately pleasant without violating the bank's security— or even while carrying out its routine precautions.

It's easy to pretend to recognize a regular bank customer—the name is on the check, see?—while actually checking identification. The idea to convey is: We know you and trust you, of course, but have instituted careful practices to protect your money from unscrupulous people, and are disciplined to follow them without exception.

It can be pointed out that the customers themselves do lots of rude things short of armed robbery. They try to jump lines or keep switching them like highway lanes, they forget to fill out forms until arriving at the head of a line, and they add up their figures wrong. In no business, however, is that an excuse for the working people to behave badly. We all get our turn in life to be unreasonable customers. (One should, of course, skip the turn.)

In the meantime, banks could relieve some of the crankiness by marking clearly what business is performed at each window, so that customers don't waste time in the wrong lines, and by admitting that their twenty-four-hour machines are really twenty-three-hour machines so that customers know when these will be out for servicing and where the nearest working machine is.

Honesty, they will find, is the best policy, or at least the second best. Right after politeness.

Doctors

Doctors have so much in the way of the world's riches that it is not necessary for them to have manners as well, many people believe. These people tend to be doctors.

Miss Manners does not mean to say that the world is not full of charming doctors. Those who specialize in social events often have lovely manners. But the ordinary rules of the profession are set up in a way that enables, one may say compels, the doctor to treat his patients rudely as a matter of routine.

Patients are exasperating people, Miss Manners is aware. They inevitably have some complaint or other, they want to talk about themselves, which is always a bore, and they show up when they're not feeling well, which might make them cranky. Not the sort of people you would think of to enliven a dinner table. Nevertheless, many doctors are forced to deal with these people, and could do much to make the encounters less jarring. To do this will require two adjustments in the way the medical profession is regarded, in comparison to other professions.

First, there must be recognition that there are other services offered in the world that are of comparable value, and that some of these are actually performed by patients when they are not occupying medical facilities. Second, there must be an acknowledgment that doctors are not entitled to the adulation, presumed omnipotence, and consequently, the arrogance of automobile mechanics. A doctor who remembers that his patient has his own mantle of dignity—which is admittedly not easy to think about a naked person clutching a sheet and wearing an alarmed expression—will not be patronizing in his form of address. He will not call patients by their first name while expecting to have his own title used, and he will not object to explaining what he means when it is not clear to someone whose education has been in a different field. He will do his best not to keep these people waiting for his services, because he will understand that their time is, to those whom they serve, as valuable as his. If there is inevitable waiting, he will warn the patient, at least as well as an airline might do, of how long the delay is likely to be. He will not keep music playing in his waiting room, knowing that patients may be people who have work or thinking to do in times of enforced idleness. (You will notice that Miss Manners has used the pronoun ''he'' about offending doctors. This is because she has observed women doctors who behave better. That may be a statistical error.)

Doctors and automobile mechanics have in common the necessity of dealing with complicated and unpredictable machines whose owners have little idea of how to care for them or what has gone wrong when the things won't work properly. The mechanic is justified in refusing to share with the owner any information about what he will do, when he will have it done, and how much he plans to charge. The client can, after all, jolly well walk until he is given his car back.

Not so, in the case of the doctor's patient. By necessity, the patient must be present when all the tinkering is done, and cannot get by on other equipment during the servicing period. It is incumbent upon the service person to tell him—without giving away the entire contents of an expensive medical education—how the repair job will be handled.

DEAR MISS MANNERS:

Please chastise presumptuous medical assistants who address patients by their given name. Thrice in a week, I have been the victim of this gaffe. Perhaps the physicians are simply poor administrators or lack the time properly to instruct their employees. Perhaps the employees are simply dense or densely simple. My example (''Thank you, Miss Crimp'') and cold looks availed me nothing. I feel it inappropriate to go further, exceed the bounds of good form, and chide the offenders, especially as they have power over my body. Miss Manners, rescue us all from that sad deterioration in standards. It may be that the transgressors are not too far lost to civilities to learn the gravity of this offense and mend their ways.

GENTLE READER:

The trouble is that we have here two deteriorations, or at least two low points. One is the increasing use of first names in situations that are not social, and the other is the insufferable old habit many medical workers have of calling patients by their first names while themselves expecting to be addressed with their titles. Fortunately, the cure in both cases is the same. If Miss Crimp, or Dr. Botchitt, says, ''How are we today, Hortense?'' one replies, ''Why, just fine, Millie; *and you?*'' Those being rude for medical reasons will then stiffen up and understand. Those without a medical excuse may never understand.

Nurses

DEAR MISS MANNERS:

My mother had to spend the final year of her life in a nursing home. My sister and I spent most of our hours for the first week at her bedside, helping her through a difficult loss—of her preferred autonomous life at home. A couple of months later, I journeyed to that city to pay her another visit, and I went into the nursing home, a good one with liberal visiting hours. The staff were always kind and helpful, and considerate in many ways of all the patients. My mother had been known always to her friends and neighbors of her age as "Mrs. Jackson," and to her relatives and intimates as "Ellen," her middle name. I was aghast to find that twenty-two-year-old aides would invariably come in and say to my eighty-year-old mother, "How are we feeling today, Margaret?" using her first name, which she had never used.

What to do? I was concerned that if I said, "My mother's name is Mrs. Jackson," they, or some of them, would just take it out on her when my sister or I were not present. I said nothing, because I saw it as a no-win situation. Was there a way to win?

GENTLE READER:

Miss Manners is determined to find a way, having no intention of spending her old age being cheekily patronized by those who recognize no gradations of intimacy or respect. What makes the battle difficult, as you recognize, is that the intentions are probably good, although the effect is dreadful. Those who believe in instant and universal informality generally mean well, although they will never understand the joy of real warmth that is allowed to develop naturally and therefore slowly.

In this case, you should simply have explained to the offenders that your mother was used to being addressed as Mrs. Jackson and preferred it. They would put it down to hopeless old-fashionedness, but so be it. Miss Manners cannot believe that otherwise kind, helpful, and considerate professionals would hold it against an old lady to prefer old ways, much less retaliate against a patient for any reason.

Journalists

DEAR MISS MANNERS:

I attended the Democratic convention four years ago as a guest. There was often an incredible amount of pushing and shoving. I noticed that most of it was done by the reporters—especially the TV reporters. Don't they teach manners in journalism school?

GENTLE READER:

Waddya mean? Out of Miss Manners' way, you.

Actually, as the only known surviving mannerly journalist, Miss Manners feels called upon to explain journalistic manners. You seem to have noticed that there aren't any. But there is a rationale behind this which may help you to understand, if not condone, being hit in the skull with a hand-held camera. Journalism is a sacred trust on behalf of The People and their Right To Know. Surely you have noticed this while reading *People* magazine. Therefore, each journalist who shoves you thinks of him or herself as representing the millions of people who will be reading or watching whatever that person is able to gather. When millions of people are trying to get where you are trying to go, naturally you are apt to get somewhat trampled.

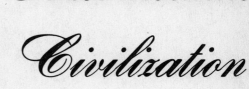

Intermediate Civilization

Prominent hostesses are frequently asked for a "secret of success" for a perfect party. They always reply, "Good food and interesting people."

Some secret. It's like the universal "beauty secret." If you could ask Cleopatra hers, she would reply, "A balanced diet and hardly any makeup—just a touch of blusher and maybe mascara for a really big evening out." They all say that. Miss Manners suspects this has something to do with the folly of asking people their secrets, and expecting them to tell. People who tell on demand wouldn't have any secrets, would they?

Now, do you want to know the secret of giving a successful party? Miss Manners does not deny that interesting people and good food are better at a party than dopey people and spoiled food, but they are not the secret. Interesting people can have dull spells, or they can all try to be interesting at the same time, which is a social disaster. Good food can go unappreciated because of allergies or calories.

The secret is to create the proper atmosphere. Contrary to popular belief, a good party atmosphere is not "relaxing," but the opposite. It should be full of tension. Tension is what makes people sparkle at parties, because they are trying to live up to the occasion, to make a lasting impression on one another, and to be invited back. The proper amount of social tension will make the interesting people put forth their best efforts, and the dull people strive to be at least ingratiating. Who knows, it may even inspire them to be interesting.

One does this by notifying people in advance that this will not be the same old get-together, but a special occasion. Requiring them to dress up, rather than to "just wear something comfortable," is one way of reminding them, while they are still in the shower, that they are expected to make an effort. When they arrive, the house should look as if it expected the players to be worthy of the setting. Fires (in the fireplaces—unless you are after a really startling effect) and flowers are the usual way of doing this.

Then you may have the "interesting people"—provided, of course, that you fill in with enough people who are not interesting, but charming. The definition of charming is a person who is willing to listen attentively to someone else being interesting. The principle of a proper mix of people is that they must be interesting to one another. You ensure this by inviting people who are in different professional fields, but at the same level of achievement, so that they want to impress one another, and inviting people who would enjoy flirting with one another. These are the human equivalents of fire and flowers.

Don't tell anyone.

The Voice of Experience

DEAR MISS MANNERS:
If you had to give a single piece of advice to a couple who want to break into society, what would it be?
GENTLE READER:
"Don't bother."

Types of Parties, Some Stunning and Others Ghastly

The impulse of expansive hospitality is such a charming one that Miss Manners would like to encourage it by showing how one can make hospitality somewhat less expansive. Ah, er, cheaper.

For while it is true that no form of social entertainment is quite so enjoyable as the "little" dinner party of ten people, five courses, and three wines (unless it is the private Aegean cruise, which is also a pleasant way to see one's friends), this kind of thing now runs into a considerable amount of grocery money. Nor does Miss Manners quite believe all those articles about clever, thrifty cooks who make perfect soufflés Grand Marnier out of discarded orange crates.

A simpler solution, it seems to her, is to invite people to visit you when they're not hungry. One cannot say, "Do come by some time when you're stuffed"; but one can learn to socialize at times other than the dinner hour. Six to eight o'clock at night is exactly when most people are getting ravenous, which is why the cocktail party has had to turn into a buffet dinner, and why you will find after a "wine and cheese party" that all the paper doilies under the cheese have been eaten.

Four o'clock is much better. Bread and butter, cucumber sandwiches, cookies, and tea will satisfy most people at that hour, and if they are also given an iced cake, one inch square, and a thimbleful of sherry, they will consider themselves to have been treated lavishly. (For more extensive directions for tea parties, please see pp. 435–437.)

There are other times, morning, noon, and night to be exact, when most people actually prefer eggs, breads, and salads to higher-priced staples. There ought to be more weekend breakfasts and luncheons given, anyway. Dinners represent a greater effort on the part of the guest, as well as on that of the host. One feeds the children first, dresses up, turns the children over to another keeper, and goes out, committed for three hours or more. But a breakfast or luncheon invitation can be a welcome short break in an otherwise busy day, and children should be encouraged to come along (and then encouraged to "go out and play").

Light food also looks luxurious late at night, because even the greediest people know they are not really entitled to a midnight supper. The way to get people to your house for a midnight supper is to invite them to something beginning at nine thirty or ten—dancing, for example, or an amateur concert given by friends who are good enough to be bearable but not so good as to become unbearable. Or one can invite them to supper after a movie or play that they and you are attending.

For a really chic and cheap party, suppose you find out which of your friends have opera tickets the same night as you do and invite them to come home with you afterwards, adding "We'll dress," which means that you are dictating the importance of an event for which they have paid. You then allow them to kick off their evening shoes and feast on scrambled eggs and cold wine. The least they can do in return is to invite you to vacation with them in the Aegean.

Cocktail Parties

DEAR MISS MANNERS:

I give elaborate cocktail parties, which I take care to make a treat for my guests. There are always lots of different kinds of food, which I prepare myself, and a hired bartender who makes all kinds of drinks. I usually have about forty people. And yet I am finding, more and more over the years, that they behave badly—not just a few, but almost all of them.

I am not talking about getting drunk, which doesn't happen often. But listen to this: Most of them don't bother to answer the invitation, even to regret when it says "regrets only." I never know who's going to come, and whether they will bring extra people I've never heard of. If I'm not right at the door, they start drinking without bothering to find me and greet me. Not as many people smoke as used to, but those who do have put out their cigarettes in my plates, glasses, and even on the coffee table itself. I direct them to leave their coats in my bedroom, but have found people getting into other upstairs rooms, not always on the best of behavior. Some people leave without saying good-by, and most people don't think of inviting me back. For days after a party, I find glasses and dirty plates in odd places—under the sofa or on the porch. I have also discovered things missing, from napkins, which could have been taken accidentally, to onyx egg decorations, which couldn't have.

The reason I entertain is to give pleasure to others and frankly to build myself some sort of social life. If I am doing something wrong, to make people treat me so badly, I wish you would tell me what it is.

GENTLE READER:

It is giving cocktail parties. The large cocktail party, such as you describe, is the least personal entertainment one can give in one's house, and has come to be considered a public event. The behavior you describe, while rude, is the way people behave in night clubs, coming and going when and with whom they choose, stealing souvenirs, and feeling entirely free from obligation. This is not terrific behavior for public accommodations, either, and perhaps some of your friends are hopeless. Others may behave better if you invite them in small groups, as if you truly wanted to spend time with them, not merely to keep them from stealing your eggs.

DEAR MISS MANNERS:

Am I obliged to serve huge amounts of food when I invite people to a six to eight evening cocktail party?

GENTLE READER:

You have an obligation not to take up your guests' dinner hours without feeding them.

DEAR MISS MANNERS:

I would like to have a wine-and-cheese party, but since I have never attended one, I'm unsure of the proper procedure. How many different wines and cheeses are served, and are they cut into cubes or slices? Also, I cannot justify buying twenty-four wine glasses for the occasion, so would the plastic champagne variety, that can be purchased in a liquor store, be acceptable?

GENTLE READER:

Never attempt to slice wine, which is about as unacceptable as . . . as forcing innocent people to drink from plastic glasses, particularly silly hollow-stemmed ones that think they are hot stuff. At the simplest wine-and-cheese party (as opposed to the so-called wine tasting, which is usually a disaster), you need serve only one kind each of red wine, white wine, sharp cheese, and mild cheese. You needn't even cut the cheese if you provide boards and knives for each, and biscuits on which to dump the shreds. Cheap glasses are, in the long run, cheaper than plastic, the long run being your second wine-and-cheese party.

Afternoon Tea and High Tea

DEAR MISS MANNERS:

I should like to begin having tea on a daily schedule with friends stopping in, with or without invitations. A couple of questions do require answering: At what time is "teatime," and should coffee be offered or placed on the table?

GENTLE READER:

Miss Manners adores afternoon tea, from "Oh-do-join-me-for-a-cup" to royal receptions for three thousand people. She would advise you to get some practice in the former before attempting the latter. There are few more charming ways to spend an afternoon than to sit, surrounded by fine china and friends, wolfing down scones and bringing up epigrams.

She commends you for attempting to revive another venerable tradition, that of being "at home" to friends in the afternoon, but she must caution you that even the most accomplished hostesses of Miss Manners' day did not attempt it more than once a week.

If you wish to test the water before jumping in even on a weekly basis— and water for tea should always be boiling—invite people for a specific day, writing:

Tea

Tuesday the seventeenth

four to six o'clock

in the lower left corner of your visiting cards. Later it may be "Tuesdays, four to six o'clock."

Place on a tray a large silver or copper kettle over an alcohol burner, and a tea caddy, with the teapot, cups (which have been warmed with boiling water), teaspoons, a slops bowl, a tea strainer, a milk pitcher (cream overpowers a dainty cup of tea), a bowl of lump sugar, little plates, and napkins. Tea is made in the drawing room, in full view of the guests, so get it right.

The proper method is this: Rinse the teapot with boiling water. Give your teaspoons a chance to do the job for which they were trained by putting in one teaspoon of loose tea (tea is claustrophobic and hates being stuffed into little bags) for each tea drinker, plus one. Now pour on the rapidly boiling water. There are few things worse than tepid tea. The boiling water comes from the kettle (with more always ready in the kitchen) and used water and dregs of tea are dumped into the slops bowl.

When the tea has steeped for about four minutes, ask your guest of honor how she takes it. Using the strainer, pour straight from the pot for strong tea, and dilute it from the kettle for weak. Then add sugar (the reason for using lump sugar is so you may ask the traditional "One lump or two?") and milk, according to her taste. Some troublemakers prefer lemon to milk, and you may put slices in a glass dish on the tray, but you are only encouraging them.

When this ritual is performed, the guest takes her tea from the hostess, or if there is a gentleman present he takes it to her. She then takes a plate, napkin, and a modest selection from your platters of hot breads, tiny sandwiches, cookies, and a slice of whatever luscious cake your cook has baked that day.

If you become addicted to this form of entertaining, you may need to move on to stronger doses, such as the reception, which is tea served in the dining room. The tea service is placed at one end of the table, and the teacups, napkins, plates, forks if needed, and a larger supply of tea food (at least two of each kind mentioned above) go in the middle. At the other end stands an urn of chocolate, bouillon, or more often lately, to Miss Manners' dismay, coffee. You may ask friends "to pour," that is, to serve the tea and chocolate for you, as you move among your guests. Being asked to pour is an honor just short of knighthood.

However much this may sound to the contrary, a tea is an informal party, and your guests may wear whatever they normally wear when out in the afternoon. To Miss Manners "informal" means the flowered dress, pearls, gloves, and picture hat one wears between lunch and dinner; others may be in the habit of wearing street clothes. The hostess unfortunately may not wear a hat, another advantage to being a guest now and then.

The traditional time for tea is four o'clock, which is perfect if you have your afternoons free. However, coffee is only one of the sad things that has happened to tea over the years. Some people have the idea that there is something more important to do in the afternoon than sip tea and eat buttered bread—such as earning a living. If you have friends who work, Miss Manners suggests that you schedule your tea on a weekend or at a time convenient to them on their way home, when you could give them yet another variation, high tea, so as to replace, rather than interfere with, their supper. High tea is more substantial in all matters of food and drink than afternoon tea. It could include a whiskey and soda tray. Along with the dainty foods traditional to afternoon tea, there are soft boiled eggs, sausages, sardines on toast, kippers, chicken livers, and such. While some unscrupulous restaurants try to make afternoon tea sound more "high society" by calling it high tea, the word "high" is actually related to "It's high time we had something to eat." As social events go, high tea is lower on the scale than afternoon tea, because the chances of being fed dinner are small on a day you are given high tea. In that respect, it is like the "cocktail-buffet," than which there are few lower social events.

(For a description of a tea service, please see p. 378.)

Pouring Tea

DEAR MISS MANNERS:

Which is correct, to pour milk into tea, or tea into milk? I have an aunt who pours cream into her coffee, but puts milk in the cup first when she is having tea. What about lemon?

GENTLE READER:

What about your aunt? Has she ever been a nanny? According to dear Evelyn Waugh, "All nannies and many governesses . . . put the milk in first," which has given rise to the disparaging remark, "She's rather milk-in-first, darling." Class indications aside, a lady of Miss Manners' acquaintance wonders how one would know how much milk to put in first, as she judges her tea by the color.

Thinking people everywhere put the lemon in the cup first.

Surprise Parties

DEAR MISS MANNERS:

Do you like surprise parties?

GENTLE READER:

As a guest, certainly. They are an excellent way of catching a friend when he or she is emotionally and often physically unprepared to attend a party, and thus embarrassing someone under such a guise of friendship that is impossible for that person to express outrage without sounding churlish. As a guest of honor, Miss Manners loathes surprise parties, for the identical reasons.

Housewarmings

DEAR MISS MANNERS:

I will be moving into a new house soon and would like to have a housewarming party. I was told that it is wrong to give yourself a housewarming party. Would it be better to send out open house or housewarming invitations? Please answer soon because we are about ready to move in.

GENTLE READER:

Miss Manners is answering as fast as she can, and hopes that your movers, painters, electricians, and plumbers show you the same consideration.

You were told wrong. A housewarming is correctly given by the people who own the house. You may call it whatever you want. Miss Manners heard of one given by the new owners of a house in which a famous sex scandal had taken place, and it was called a housecooling, because the house was hot enough already. All housewarmings are also "open house"—which means only that they are given in a cocktail party sort of way, but generally for families rather than just adults—although not all open house parties are housewarmings.

DEAR MISS MANNERS:

Is it proper for parents of new house owners to lay the plans, extend the invitations, serve as hosts, or express appreciation for any gifts given for the occasion?

GENTLE READER:

It is not. If you aren't old enough to warm your own house, you aren't old enough to have one.

DEAR MISS MANNERS:

There was a terrible fire in our neighborhood which, thank God, did not spread to our house, but the people three doors down had extensive damages. I mean their house was practically just a shell when it was over. Well, they've rebuilt, and are moving back in, with all new furniture—they were insured—next month. In a sense, they are starting out with a new household, still lacking a number of things, and are moving in afresh, even though they were our neighbors for eight years. Do you think it would be nice if we gave them a housewarming party?

GENTLE READER:

You may give a party, but would you please think of another name for it, for social as well as emotional reasons.

Dessert Parties

DEAR MISS MANNERS:

I have a question about table setting. When I have my bridge club, I serve dessert and coffee only. What is the correct way to set the table? It is a rather formal affair, and I use my good china and sterling.

GENTLE READER:

"Dessert only" is an unfortunate term for a useful form of entertainment. The difficulty is that the negative wording suggests the absence of other courses, rather than the richness being offered. What you should avoid, in your table setting, is the suggestion that the guests have missed the first three courses. The way to do this is to align it with a self-sufficient form, namely tea. If you put out your best things in a buffet arrangement patterned on a formal tea, you will be emphasizing the positive virtue of your offering.

Pot Luck

DEAR MISS MANNERS:

I would like to know what you think of the problem of leftovers at a pot luck supper/dinner/dessert/brunch. Is the hostess supposed to scrape the remaining food into her own storage containers and then wash or rinse the guest's bowl or serving dish for her to take home, or is she supposed to send the guest home with a dirty pot of remaindered baked beans to put on the back seat of the car? Is the hostess entitled to the food if it looks good and she could use it tomorrow? I have seen a near fight develop when the hostess wanted to keep a shrimp salad under the guise of washing the dish. The guest who brought the shrimp salad thought it was rather expensive and wanted what was left herself. What is the correct approach to this problem?

GENTLE READER:

It is never correct for two people to fight over a shrimp salad. (Lobster, yes.) Nor is it correct to assume that a person whose house you have visited is capable of performing the task of washing another person's plate in the hope of being allowed to keep the table scraps. In the circumstances you describe, the hostess, busy anyway at the end of a party with saying good-by, should firmly hand each dish to its owner. If she does not do so, a guest can certainly assume that the most considerate thing she can do is to remove her dirty dish from the premises.

Bring Your Own

DEAR MISS MANNERS:

At a Bring Your Own Bottle (BYOB), who drinks what? Can you taste anything on the table, or must you stick with your own bottle? Who provides the mixers? Who gets to keep the leftovers?

GENTLE READER:

Miss Manners has the feeling she would not be very good at a Bring Your Own Bottle party. She would probably wander about as if she were at a picnic, saying, "Won't you have a drop of my port?" and "Do have some of my rye," generating a jolly spirit of sharing that would have everyone pie-eyed in no time. The selfishness of everyone's being glued to his own bottle would be too much for her. One solution to the problem, which Miss Manners assumes is a financial one, is for the hosts to provide inexpensive wine instead of providing the mixers. Another is for all the bottles to be parked without private ownership, and the resulting collection to be used as if it were the hosts' bar.

The conventional BYOB arrangement is that guests take their own bottles home with them, having shared their liquor with the hosts, whose contribution is the mixers, the premises, and food. However, Miss Manners is beginning to get upset at squabbles at cooperative parties. The reason such events exist is to allow sociability among people who cannot, for reasons of time or money, entirely sponsor parties individually. If you are going to fight over the scraps of food and the dregs of liquor, Miss Manners is going to confine each of you to your own home and there will be no more parties until everyone is in a better mood.

Television Parties

As a social activity, having guests over to watch television ranks, in Miss Manners' opinion, just below inviting people to run down to the corner to see if it is raining.

Why would anyone invite real guests to watch electronic "guests" talk to a canned "host"? Surely the living host-guest group has to be better than that. One's own guests seldom wave their books in your face and demand that you buy copies. However, Miss Manners recognizes that there are certain state occasions, such as the presidential election and the Super Bowl, when one seeks one's fellow humans to share disaster or to enhance one's own triumph with their misery.

If Miss Manners tells you how to give a television-watching party on these occasions, will you promise always to snap off the television set when you have guests on ordinary days?

The guest list is important for the election or sports party. This is a good time not to invite one's friends who have a predilection for violence. Highly excitable people who prefer red wine to white are also to be avoided by hosts with white velvet sofas.

Mild range of opinion can be interesting, if it is kept in bounds. What is even better than an articulate but tolerant person with the ability to explain his views reasonably is a guest who is physically capable, for short periods of time throughout a long evening, of watching without eating. Otherwise, a host could easily serve the equivalent of four suppers during a hotly contested election.

Television food needs to be safe, manageable, and digestable. Any nursery school teacher's aide who is in charge of snack time can give you the general idea, although that drink menu probably needs to be supplemented. It's just that people who consume nothing but beer and the contents of cellophane bags until the polls close in Hawaii are not happy people when the election is called, no matter who wins.

The key, however, is to have more than one center of interest. The television set and the food table are two, and a second set, perhaps turned to a different channel, would be a third. The point of this is to get people moving before their limbs petrify, and to separate the lecturers from the commentators. (Miss Manners is not suggesting that any provision be made for those who want to watch in silence. They should stay home.) Talking back to a television set is an acceptable exercise, and all that some people get. But two forms of conversation are possible, and those who practice one are apt to be annoyed at the intrusion of the other. At one set, you should aim for a discussion group on the material being watched—how the election is going in relation to one's own predictions, or how one would oneself have played the game. The other is on how it is being televised—the commentary, personalities of announcers, and such.

If no permanent damage has been done to anyone's digestion or friendship at the end of many hours of television watching, the event can be counted as a success.

TV Party

DEAR MISS MANNERS:

I am having friends over for dinner during the airtime of the political convention. Would it be rude to watch it on television during dinner, or should I plan to serve dessert in front of the TV?

GENTLE READER:

While it is sometimes expedient to require one's guests to eat from plates balanced on their laps (the semibarbarous custom known as the buffet dinner), expecting them to do so in the dark shows a lack of consideration for both your guests and your rug. Miss Manners suggests confining this practice to dessert, and confining dessert to a food that is as tasty when picked up off the floor as it is from a plate. Apples, rather than zabaglione, for example.

The Charity Ball

The charity ball ranks second only to the cocktail party as an event that people who attend regularly profess to dislike. And yet there are those who believe that the rich know nothing of the rigors of self-sacrifice!

Miss Manners does not indulge in the popular vulgarity of comparing the menus, clothes, and social practices present at charity balls with those customarily enjoyed by the objects of the charity. A good benefit is beneficial both to the benefactor and to the beneficiary. It not only raises money for the unfortunate but, by roping off the bountiful in their ballrooms, protects the poor from the misfortune of being visited by them, as was once the custom, and getting money diluted with advice. Ballgoers are enriched, not only with the satisfaction of having done a good deed with photographers present, but by being allowed to participate in an ŏbsolescent ritual.

The private ball, in its day, was a fine work of anthropology. Miss Manners cannot understand why it is that so few people these days choose to maintain private ballrooms in their homes, which they can open to their four hundred closest friends once a year. A warm heart, two orchestras, enough food, champagne, and footmen to keep continuous service open until three in the morning, and an awning and carpet for the street are really all that is needed to give people several hours of pleasure and the opportunity to end and begin romances with their entire social circle watching. The public ball is just not the same thing, no matter how hard well-meaning committee members try to reproduce the spirit of the grand hostesses of yesteryear by saying, "Let's make sure those dreadful Piffles don't get an invitation."

Nevertheless, it is the only opportunity the average person with the above-average income will have to wear full evening regalia, including whatever grand jewels remain after those whom they encounter on the sidewalk while going in to the ball have had their pick. It is therefore incumbent on ball organizers, Miss Manners believes, to simulate a pleasant social event for the benefit of the ticket buyers. Instead, she has found, most public balls combine the crushing, noise, and surly service of a discotheque with the self-congratulations, entertainment level, and commercial breaks of a televised awards show. Instead of thanking one another for having worked so hard while requiring the guests to listen and even applaud, the committee members might spend the time doing the duty of hosts—greeting those whom they know at the door, introducing people, rescuing those who get stranded, and so on. They might see to it that there is room to dance, a place to take a flirtatious walk or to make good an escape from an unwanted partner, music that everyone can dance to, and which even allows the human voice to be heard by a nearby human ear. (You don't want it to be possible for the human voice to carry to a third person; no sensible person tries to have a sensible conversation at a ball.) They might refrain from bragging about getting favors, prizes, decorations, or whatever free. The rule ought to be that if the donor requires oral acknowledgment, not just a discreet program note, his donation is not free, nor worth accepting. In fact, all the time should be devoted to amusing the guests—which can best be done by allowing them to dance, mix, chat, sit down, walk around, and even eat when they wish. (Miss Manners prefers buffet suppers at dances, rather than plates of congealed food dealt out by bossy waiters.) Actually to give a good time to people who pay dearly to attend—now that would, indeed, be an act of charity.

Invitations and Replies

If Judgment Day were scheduled for tomorrow, the question most people would be worrying about today would be, "Can I bring a date?"

The kaleidoscopic state of love these days has left everyone uncertain about who goes with whom, including, sometimes, the parties concerned. As always, it is the innocent who suffer most from these couplings and uncouplings. Miss Manners is referring, of course, to hosts and hostesses. If you invite an impossible person for the sake of getting his marvelous spouse, you will be informed that he will come, but not she. If you have finally captured the perfect mate for a lonely friend, that friend will insist that he bring someone of his own choice along. There are roommates who hate being invited together, because it should be obvious that they are trying to lead their own lives, and roommates who are furious about being invited individually, because it should be obvious that they are inseparable.

People who try to get a specified number of people to their dinner tables in alternating genders will soon want to drown themselves in their centerpieces. There are times when Miss Manners despairs of any form of social life except opening one's home like a discotheque, admitting people with whomever they bring, and simply cutting things off at the door when it gets too crowded.

Let us try, however, to salvage a semblance of order by defining what is a social unit of two and what is not. The most likely couple is the one that is

443

engaged. But they must be engaged in the sense of having decided to get married, not in the sense of not knowing how else to explain themselves to their parents. Engaged couples *must* be invited together, but the reward is that they nearly always appear together.

(For the application of this rule to wedding guests, please see p. 361.)

Less certain is the married couple. While they must be invited together, they must, if necessary, be accepted singly. It is considered offensive, for instance, not to urge a woman to attend by herself just because her husband is out of town. One also may find that the couple has separated or divorced since last seen the previous week. In that case, the one who answers the invitation is the one who is urged to attend alone.

People who are living together as lovers, whatever their genders, are generally offended if not invited together. However, it is up to them to make themselves known as a social unit, as in, "Oh, Perry and I always go out as a couple."

The most grateful of all to be invited to the same gathering are illicit lovers, and the more dangerous the situation, the more thrilled they are to be treated conventionally. You may not want to countenance such relationships, but if you do so, even perhaps providing a cover excuse, they will cherish you as do no other guests. The least grateful are the single people involved only in transitory alliances, who nevertheless will not trust your ability to provide entertaining company, but insist on bringing their own dates. This practice should be discouraged. With all the couples one has to allow for, the least single people can do is to appear singly. Otherwise, they will have no one but themselves to blame when they come around whining that they have such a hard time meeting anyone new.

On Impulse Inviting

The ancient Greek laws of hospitality are the ones to which Miss Manners still subscribes. A host's duties to anyone under his roof are sacred, no matter how anxious he may be to polish him off, for reasons related or unrelated to the visit.

However, if the Greeks had followed Miss Manners' rules of preventive hospitality, they would not, she suspects, have had to give their guests such expensive hints as fully manned ships.

Not everyone needs to know preventive hospitality. Some people are naturally careful about the invitations they issue, and others enjoy promiscuous socializing. But a surprising number of people are subject to hysterical fits of hospitality, in which they issue invitations ruinous to their every comfort, with mad insistances that these be accepted.

"Let's all go over to my house!" they cry, just as the fatigue of an evening's round of merriment hits them. "Come on—I won't hear of your going home this early. I'm right near by, and I'll whip up something delicious in a jiffy." "Don't be silly—you're not going to stay in a hotel," they declare to acquaintances who speak of coming to their town to look for jobs and houses, however long that might take. "I have all this room, and it won't be any trouble at all. I'll hardly know you're here." "Why, we've been talking about going to Mexico, too!" they scream brightly to people who are part of the ties they had been scheming for months to get away from for a complete rest. "Let's rent a van and all go together." To anybody who will listen, they say, "Come by any time—any time at all, we'd love it," when they had planned to get some work done at home.

These are the people who go to pieces when their privacy is invaded. If you think they look bad, you should see their spouses. Miss Manners' attitude is that it is better to bar the door to unwanted guests than to back them out through it. She therefore believes in strong measures to break the invitation habit: Never issue invitations on the spot to people you have just met. Instead, find out where to reach them, which is just as flattering, and do not call with a specific invitation until you have slept on it.

No invitations to spend more than three hours under one's roof should be issued without the consent of all of those who dwell under it, if they are to be responsible for entertaining the guests. If one spouse cannot think why the Awful family should not be asked to spend their spring vacation in the guest room, the other ought to be able to. And if neither of them can, the children, who have met the Awful children, may have some information to contribute.

It is not more gracious to issue open-ended invitations than timed ones, and besides, it is insane. "Please stay with us till Thursday" and "We're free Sunday between four and six, and would love to see you" are perfectly respectable offers of limited hospitality. They do not result in the hosts' sneaking off to write Miss Manners desperate letters begging her to tell them how to get their guests to leave.

Accepting with Pleasure

DEAR MISS MANNERS:
Would Miss Manners please tell me, once and for all, what is the correct way to answer a formal invitation?
GENTLE READER:
All right, Miss Manners will tell you, but she is under no illusion that it will be once and for all. Ann Landers has to keep telling you not to sleep with anyone before marriage, doesn't she, and then what do you go and do? Now pay attention:

> Mr. and Mrs. Perfect
> accept with pleasure
> the kind invitation of
> Mr. and Mrs. Hoping
> For Saturday, the twenty-third of November.

These gracious words are handwritten and each line is centered on plain white or ecru paper. You will notice that Miss Manners does not consider it necessary

Mr. and Mrs. Jonathan Rhinehart Awful, 3rd

request the pleasure of the company of

at

on

at   o'clock

R.s.v.p.

129 Primrose Path

An all-purpose invitation on which one fills in the name of the guest, the type of event (dinner, tea, reception), the date and the time. The "R.s.v.p." may be crossed out and replaced with "To remind" for a second round.

Vice Admiral Stacy Awful-Nuisance

accepts with pleasure

Mr. and Mrs. Awful's

kind invitation for

Saturday, the Third of February

at eight o'clock

General Trevor Nuisance

regrets exceedingly

that he will be unable to accept

to repeat, in the answer, every gruesome detail of the invitation, such as the fact that there will be dancing, that it will take place in a club because their house isn't grand enough, or that they have palmed off their daughter Lucretia Marie. This is called modern, streamlined living.

A Correct R.s.v.p

DEAR MISS MANNERS:

Which is correct, "R.S.V.P." or "R.s.v.p."? I have seen both on properly engraved invitations.

GENTLE READER:

If Miss Manners told you all the improprieties she has seen on allegedly properly engraved invitations, it would curl your hair. "R.s.v.p." is correct. It stands for the imperative sentence *"Répondez, s'il vous plait."* If you were to write this in English, you would put, "Kindly give me an answer," not "Kindly Give Me an Answer." Possibly you would put "KINDLY GIVE ME AN ANSWER!" but Miss Manners does not believe in shouting.

"Répondez, s'il vous plait"

DEAR MISS MANNERS:

I disagree with your use of "R.s.v.p." *"Répondez, s'il vous plait"* is not "Kindly give me an answer," but "Respond if you please." Therefore, saying "If you please" leaves it up to the recipient to respond or not. So, in fact, using R.s.v.p. means you can either inform the sender, or not. Does this mean the use of R.s.v.p. is a waste of time? Also, what about the few who know the proper meaning of R.s.v.p.—are they to be condemned if they don't respond?

GENTLE READER:

The surest way to be condemned socially is to take conventional phrases literally. *"S'il vous plait"* indeed means "if you please," but there is no option about complying. Try responding literally to such conventional phrases as "How do you do?" "Please make yourself at home," and "Feel free to call me any time if there is anything I can do for you," and see how far you get. If there is doubt that your prospective guests will understand "R.s.v.p." you may just as correctly write, "The favour of a reply is requested" (note English spelling, which doesn't make sense in America—there is remarkably little logic in social matters).

Breaking Various Engagements

You may have heard that a California judge ruled that a young man who was stood up by a young woman with whom he had a dinner and theater date was not entitled to compensation for his time and expenses. You may think that this means you may break any social engagement you choose without notice. You think wrong.

Judge Richard P. Figone of the San Francisco Small Claims Court may have been correct when he ruled that "the promise to engage in a social relationship for one evening in exchange for affection and/or one evening at the theater is unenforceable under the law of contracts and torts." He should have consulted Miss Manners before he went on to write that "the promise to attend a social engagement is always conditioned by the promiser's ability or disposition to attend the event." Not always. There are social engagements that may be broken, and those that may not.

For example, a time-honored method of indicating that you do not wish to fulfill an engagement to be married is to fail to show up at the altar. It is a dramatic and effective way to indicate that your ability or disposition to go on has changed. It is quite another thing to fail to show up at the altar if you have promised to be a maid of honor or a best man. That would be truly unforgivable.

In the matter of dinner engagements, the following may not be broken under any circumstances short of sudden death : seated dinners for ten people or fewer, dinners at which you have been requested by the hosts to help entertain a difficult guest, and restaurant meals when you have promised to meet one other person and cannot notify him or her that you will not be there, leaving that person to sit there playing with the napkin for everyone to see. As for theater engagements, it depends on how hard it was to get tickets.

DEAR MISS MANNERS :
How much of an excuse do you need to break a social engagement after you have already accepted? Does it depend on how well you know the hosts? I mean, of course, that you can tell a close friend that you got a weekend invitation and don't want to stay home just for one night's dinner, but that someone you don't know as well should probably get a more urgent excuse.

GENTLE READER :
There is no surer way to get to know someone less closely than to confide that something better has come up than the engagement with him. Miss Manners was once forsaken by a guest who cited the opportunity to participate in a weekend encounter group. Can you imagine anyone's thinking it was more important to bare her soul to strangers than to use the material for its amusement value at Miss Manners' dinner table? Naturally, the offender was struck from Miss Manners' list.

The direness of the excuse should correspond to the size, structure, and nearness of the event. At one extreme, you would have a wine and cheese party two months off, and at the other, a seated dinner the following evening. For the latter, the best excuses are extreme illness or death, preferably one's own.

DEAR MISS MANNERS :
I know you're not supposed to break one date when a better one comes along. I went by this rule when I was dating because my mother drummed it into me, and I think I missed out on some terrific opportunities while I dutifully enter-

tained the drips. Virtue isn't always rewarded. Anyway, now I'm married, and my husband and I love to go out. We don't feel bad about breaking a date to go out to eat with another couple if someone else invites us to a dinner party, because that seems to be a different level of engagement, if you know what I mean. But what about canceling one dinner party to go to another? Is there any socially impeccable way of doing this?

GENTLE READER:

Only one. The correct wording is:

> Mr. and Mrs. Alexander Dashing
> regret extremely
> that an invitation to the White House
> prevents their keeping
> their previous engagement for
> Saturday, the seventh of March

(For refusing to go, at the proper refusal time, please see p. 599 [excuses].)

No Answer

DEAR MISS MANNERS:

Recently, I invited ten people to dinner, and only two out of the total replied. Was I correct in waiting until the last possible date and then phoning them to see if they had, in fact, received the invitation? I felt very awkward in doing this, and it was then too late to invite other people. Could you please explain the purpose of a reply, i.e., to allow time to invite others, do shopping, preparation, etc.? I find the total lack of a reply quite rude, but may be out of touch with small town etiquette.

GENTLE READER:

Interesting, how people who have been the object of rudeness tend to turn apologetic. Miss Manners refuses to adopt that sort of humility herself and explain to people why they should answer their invitations. Those who cannot figure it out probably wouldn't be able to find their mouths with their forks, either.

If you must socialize with such people, Miss Manners suggests that you invite them over the telephone in the first place, and extract an answer on the spot.

Estranged Couples

DEAR MISS MANNERS:

Will you please advise me how to address invitations to a couple who are separated, when you wish to invite both, each with a friend or escort? They are living at different addresses.

GENTLE READER:

It should be an exciting party. Write to each separately, at each separate address, and state your invitation and the fact that it includes the opportunity for each to bring a guest. It is, of course, common courtesy to inform these people that they will be confronted with—and exposing their accompanying guests to—their estranged spouses, but Miss Manners understands that doing so may ruin the fun you have planned for the evening.

"And Guest"

DEAR MISS MANNERS:

I want to issue an invitation to a man who is living with someone, and to indicate that he may bring her. Should I write "and guest" with his name?

GENTLE READER:

Certainly, presuming that her name is Guest. The way to write it is:

> Ms. Theodosia Guest
> Mr. Alexander Dashing

If Guest is not her name, find out what is.

Who Invites Whom

DEAR MISS MANNERS:

Am I being silly and old-fashioned to be upset when my husband's married female colleague invites him and me to her and her husband's home for dinner without writing or telephoning me? Likewise would the same rule of etiquette apply regarding an unmarried female secretary who invites my husband and me to her party without personally writing or phoning me?

GENTLE READER:

Yes, you are being either silly or old-fashioned, but Miss Manners can't tell which from your letter. If it is the fact that the invitation comes from a female that upsets you, you are being silly and should cut it out. If it is the fact that the invitation should be made to the female in the family, you are being old-fashioned, and while Miss Manners is always happy to see lack of progress, it is probably a losing battle.

A Solution

DEAR MISS MANNERS:

Recently, my wife and I gave a dinner party for younger couples in my office. To our surprise, we discovered that many of the married couples use different names. For example, it was not Mr. and Mrs. John Smith; it was Mr. John Smith and Ms. Lydia Brown. The problem was how to address the invitations.

We solved the problem in the case of each of the female office members by addressing the envelope only to her, and stating on the invitation, ''We hope that you and your husband will be able to join us for dinner,'' etc. In the case of each of the male office members, we addressed the envelope only to him, and included a similar message in the invitation. We would like to know whether this was an appropriate way of handling the situation. Or should we have addressed the envelope to Mr. John Smith and Ms. Lydia Brown?

GENTLE READER:

Either is correct, but your solution is particularly good because it emphasizes your wanting the office worker, whether or not the spouse can attend. In fact, it's so clever, Miss Manners wishes she had thought of it herself.

Excluding Children

DEAR MISS MANNERS:

I am in desperate need of etiquette advice! I'm planning a party in two weeks or so, and I don't want any kids. Is there any proper way to send out invitations to people and at the same time indicate that adults only are invited? I don't want everyone angry at me, but I don't want a bunch of little brats to ruin my party, either.

GENTLE READER:

No well-bred person assumes that anyone whose name is not written on the invitation is invited, and therefore to specify no children, you would be assuming that your friends would commit an error unless you head them off. That makes it tricky, doesn't it? Miss Manners suggests that you send out as formal and grown-up an invitation as possible—none of this WE'RE HAVING A PARTY stuff in green with pictures of cats on the cards—and let the word ''cocktails'' figure prominently on it.

Last-Minute Additions

DEAR MISS MANNERS:

A friend invited me and my wife to bring our granddaughter to her country home for dinner. Granddaughter and this friend are alumnae of a prestigious eastern college. There are fifty years between the dates of their graduation.

A year later, I arranged a luncheon party in a restaurant for the four of us. Granddaughter is attending graduate school in our city. The evening before the luncheon appointment, granddaughter telephoned: A young woman from her hometown had come unannounced to visit her. Would it be all right if she were to bring this friend to lunch?

I was confused. I felt that the two alumnae should not have their mutual conversational interests diverted. I offered the opinion that under the circumstances, we ought not to invite the young lady. (There was no problem in providing her with lunch in my granddaughter's apartment.) What is your opinion about such a situation? Who should have been favored, the older alumna or the un-announced visitor?

GENTLE READER:

As you well know, age, both of the alumna and of the luncheon engagement (as opposed to the age of your granddaughter's commitment to an unannounced visitor), take precedence here. While there was nothing wrong with your decision, Miss Manners questions whether it was, in fact, in the best interests of your contemporary. The luncheon was not an alumnae meeting—you and perhaps also your wife did not attend the college—nor a first meeting for the purpose of discussing the college. As a return invitation, it suggests that your friend and your granddaughter enjoyed meeting each other the first time. Perhaps the elder lady might have enjoyed widening her acquaintance still further by meeting her new friend's friend, which is always a flattering request.

Going Alone

DEAR MISS MANNERS:

My husband is not interested in meeting and socializing with other people. I'm involving myself in church and have met wonderful people. I find myself receiving and refusing invitations to include my husband for dinners, seasonal parties, quiet get-togethers, etc. He feels as if I'm imposing on him people of whom he has no need.

Where do I stand socially? Should I resign myself to nursery school mothers and women's church groups? Have you any suggestions on how to encourage some socializing with adults from time to time as a couple? Should I go it alone as if I were single, not dating other men, obviously, but attending parties alone?

GENTLE READER:

Miss Manners attributes the high divorce rate to the custom of considering married couples to be socially inseparable. This is an excellent reason for conducting your own social life, independent of your husband, but if you need another reason, it is that this gives you lots of interesting material with which to entertain your husband privately afterward.

However, if you reciprocate invitations with dinner parties, your husband should not absent himself.

Gay Couples

DEAR MISS MANNERS:

Today's society is certainly permissive, which enables me to bring a gay male date to family, social, and business functions. However, there is always a question as to introduction and seating arrangement. My date is explained as a "friend," and we are seated as far away from each other as possible. It seems there is a limit to society's acceptance. What is the proper seating arrangement and introduction? And could you please give further etiquette rules governing the behavior of gay couples in the family, social, and business functions, and also the behavior that should be extended by the host, hostess, and other guests?

GENTLE READER:

If you wish to be accepted by society, you must learn to obey the conventions of society. Miss Manners is not referring to your taste in sex—that is not, and has never been, the business of decent society. To avoid such meddling, society recognizes only three relationships—the marriage, the engagement, and the friendship. If you and your date are not married or engaged, you are friends. The same rule applies to heterosexual couples. People who arrive at and depart from a social function together are not seated together. The rationale is that if you had wanted to talk to each other all evening, you could have stayed home.

What is it that you want? To be introduced as lovers, with some explanation provided to the company at large about your feelings for each other? To sit together and chat, if not hold hands, instead of socializing with other people?

People who live together should be prepared to mix with others when they go out, and their pleas of being in love—Miss Manners also hears such bragging from married people occasionally—only make her wonder why, then, they don't refuse all invitations and stay home and enjoy themselves.

The Numbers Game

DEAR MISS MANNERS:

Do you have to invite the same number of men as women, or does it matter if you have more of one sex or the other?

GENTLE READER:

It depends on what sort of activity you are inviting them to engage in. If the activity is to be conversation, it doesn't matter.

(For seating at a formal dinner, please see pp. 481–483.)

Inviting One's Physician

DEAR MISS MANNERS:

The doctor and I have a pleasant, bantering relationship, and I think I would enjoy seeing him socially. Is it all right for me to extend a dinner invitation to him?

GENTLE READER:

Only if you do so with your clothes on.

Spontaneous Invitations

DEAR MISS MANNERS:

I am a frequent victim of those who do not deem the refinement of prior notice necessary.

I am not against spontaneity. If I meet my neighbor on the stairs and she informs me that in two hours she is going to see *The Invasion of the Plantar Warts* at our local cinema, and I may come along if I want to, I am not asked to alter well-laid plans. But when Aunt Ethel (by marriage) wakes me out of a deep sleep and tells me that she and Uncle Fred are in town and my husband and I had better be halfway around the beltway in a few hours in the house of strangers, and it is a holiday and we went to bed late and we have dirty hair and we had already made other plans, she is not behaving in a manner that will lead to a felicitous conclusion. "I want to see you, and you two never come to where we are (Ultima Thule)," she whines. Yet she has been in town since the previous day, and within reach of apparatus with which to make a local call, even. By her failure to call us earlier, she deprives us all of the pleasure of seeing each other (though no one really wants to see Uncle Fred). I cannot count the number of times when friends have called to say they were nearby and were we going to be home. What if we were not? We would have to wait another year or two to see them. For those who cannot afford long distance calls, there is the stamp, which is cheaper. Please urge your readers to use it.

GENTLE READER:

Indeed, Miss Manners will so urge them. She also urges you to use the spontaneous refusal, which is the appropriate response to the spontaneous invitation. It goes something like this: "Oh, we would have adored to see you and Uncle Fred—isn't it rotten luck that the one time you were free is the time we simply can't? Promise that next time you're planning to come you'll remember to put us on the top of your advance notice list!" (Note two Miss Manners essentials in this statement: 1. Hypocrisy; 2. Absence of specific excuse.)

For a Good Time

DEAR MISS MANNERS:

Could Miss Manners please help in the invitation wording for a "good-time" thirty-year party? The celebration is thirty happy years on the job. It is meant to be a gathering (like a reunion)—more than two hundred of longtime work associates, and a very few close friends outside of work departments. It will be held in a private hall, with a sit-down dinner and dancing.

The desire is for the guests to feel welcome to come "to a good time," a "good to see you" gathering (at no expense to them). A receiving line is not planned. Neither is entertainment.

Does this sound simple and congenial for a "happy time"? Could you please help in the wording for a "carefree, fun-loving evening"?

GENTLE READER:

It sounds to Miss Manners as if you have carefully planned the party so as to give people a good time. A sit-down dinner with dancing is an excellent and comfortable way to let people who have worked together enjoy themselves, and having no entertainment is extremely wise, as it will allow people to enjoy the chief purpose of a reunion, which is conversation. However, you cannot advertise in the invitation how good the party is going to be. Telling them it is to be a "good time," "happy time," or "fun-loving evening," is like killing off a joke by prefacing it with "This is so funny—you'll love it." The normal human reaction is to think, "Oh, no I won't." Call it merely a thirtieth anniversary celebration and a reunion. The fact that they are invited as guests, and not expected to buy tickets, will alert them that their host is anxious to see them and to give them a delightful evening.

Avoiding Birthday Presents

DEAR MISS MANNERS:

We're giving a party a few months from now, celebrating my sixtieth and my mother's ninetieth birthday. They fall about a week apart. I don't want the invited guests to feel obligated to give gifts. My mother, especially, doesn't want gifts. What is the most tactful and effective way of handling this: .

1. Don't say anything on the invitations about its being a birthday party.

2. If the invitations say it is a birthday party, put "no gifts" in some form on the invitation.

3. Enclose a separate note with the invitation conveying the no-gift message.

GENTLE READER:

Although Miss Manners sympathizes with your motivation, she is opposed to conveying the message "No gifts" on an invitation in any form. Therefore, Miss Manners chooses your first solution. It will be all the more fun to announce the birthdays at the party.

Inquiring into the Guest List

DEAR MISS MANNERS:

When invited to a party, I always like to know who else is invited, so I can be mentally prepared to meet them. Is it improper to ask the hostess who else will be there?

GENTLE READER:

This would depend on whether you ask before or after you accept the invitation. Discovering a previous engagement after you hear that the hostess is asking her high school sorority sisters whom she hasn't seen in years is decidedly bad form. To announce heartily, "Oh, won't that be fun!" and then add offhandedly, "Whom else are you asking?" seems to Miss Manners to be within the bounds of politeness. It is, in fact, helpful to hosts to have their guests supplied with just enough information about one another to enable them to begin conversation. Guests who have to do this for themselves sometimes offend people when they ask "What do you do?" and have it interpreted as a challenge. Hosts who do this in front of the guests have the occasionally impossible burden of being simultaneously flattering and informative.

Miss Manners was once fascinated to receive a reminder card on the back of which the hostess had listed the other guests and their occupations. Even more informative are such confidences—one could not commit them to paper—as "To tell you the truth, he's never done anything in his life, but I asked him because he's such a delicious gossip and knows everything about everyone." The only problem that a prospective guest might have in taking the initiative in this is that the guest list might not yet be complete. The response, if the hostess doesn't seem to know yet who else will be there, is to be flattered that she took care to secure you first.

Thanks for a Deadly Time

DEAR MISS MANNERS:
Just how necessary is it to return an invitation? Periodically, when my husband and I are invited to dinner at the house of a work colleague or a casual acquaintance, we spend a dull, uninteresting evening. The atmosphere is friendly, but the group just doesn't hit it off and conversation lags. Are we absolutely obliged to invite our hosts at these gatherings to our house for dinner—and face another ho-hum evening?
GENTLE READER:
Then they'll ask you back, and you'll feel obligated to ask them back and . . . don't you see years of dreadful evenings ahead of you? Of course you do. That's why you asked the question. Perhaps your hosts do, too. Somebody has to call a halt to this nonsense. Most of us hardly have time these days to see people we already like, let alone people we might come to like, let alone people we don't like and who probably also find us dull.

Miss Manners trusts that you wrote these people immediately after their dinner, thanking them for a lovely time. Unless you are known far and wide for the number of parties you give, leave it at that. They will never know if you realize how ill-suited you are to one another, or if you are just among the increasing number of people who find they don't have as much time as they used to for entertaining, and who keep meaning to get round to giving the perfect little dinner one of these days.

The Subtle Snub

DEAR MISS MANNERS:
If you visit people several times and they do not repay calls; you write letters and get no answers—I say the people are giving you a message. My family disagrees. Will you please advise the proper etiquette?
GENTLE READER:
Look at it this way: If such people really want to maintain a relationship, there are many things they can do. They can explain that something has prevented them from seeing you but that they truly want to, they can also extend invitations, they can call and protest that their neglect should not be counted as a lack of interest. If they don't want to have anything to do with you, what more

can they do to show this than exactly what they have done? Miss Manners believes that it is essential to proper, dignified behavior to know how to accept a snub graciously.

Reciprocating

DEAR MISS MANNERS:

If the Browns invite the Smiths for dinner for a particular evening without suggesting a date that is mutually convenient, is it up to the Smiths to do the inviting in the near future? Does this let the Browns off the hook, so to speak?

GENTLE READER:

Having made one social overture, the Browns have established their desire to offer hospitality to the Smiths. They may do so once more. If the Smiths wish to establish social contact, they may issue an invitation after refusing the first, or after the second. If, as your comment about the hook suggests, these people do not really care for one another, they may all forget the whole thing right now with no one's feelings being legitimately hurt.

Returning a Non-Invitation

DEAR MISS MANNERS:

Please tell me how one goes about wrecking the nerves of the host of a party to which one has not been invited. It is of note that the host was recently given a party in his honor in my home. Of course, I wish to appear as magnanimous as possible. What is an appropriate remark, if any, to make when unexpectedly running into the host? If I am planning a party in the near future, should the host be invited or not?

GENTLE READER:

If you want to be magnanimous, you will assume that the party you heard about was not considered sufficiently grand by its host to be the one to repay you for your hospitality and that he is saving up to be able to do this in appropriate style.

However, you did not say this; you said that you wished to *appear* to be magnanimous. The remark on meeting unexpectedly could be, "Oh, I've heard your apartment looks just beautiful now. I'd love to see it some time." The invitation to your next party could be issued by saying, "Do come—I know you don't have much time to entertain, but I'd love to see you."

New Friends and Old

DEAR MISS MANNERS:

Some people whom I don't like finally lured me to their home by inviting a couple whom I had always wanted to meet. Now that I know this couple socially,

I would like to include them at my next dinner party. Frankly, the people who introduced me to them wouldn't fit in. I seem to recall that there was an old rule about not inviting new people unless you also invite the people through whom you met them, but I don't know why or whether this is still in effect?

GENTLE READER:

Yes, it is, but you need invite them only once. The purpose is to clothe the art of social climbing with some decency, so that the act of acquiring new friends is not directly linked with the related act of dropping old ones.

Procedure

🌹 CORRECT DEPORTMENT FOR LADIES AND GENTLEMEN

Ish o'Clock

DEAR MISS MANNERS:

Is "five-ish" socially correct form? If so, until what o'clock does "ish" embrace?

GENTLE READER:

"Ish" has come to be acceptable for spoken, although not written, invitations. It is extremely tricky, however, because the meaning varies with the hour and the nature of the invitation, so perhaps Miss Manners had better set out a timetable.

Five-ish for tea means five twenty PM, while five-ish for drinks means between five thirty and six fifteen.

Six-ish for drinks means six forty-five, but six-ish for "an early supper" means one should arrive at seven and will be fed at seven thirty.

Seven-ish for "a drink" means seven ten, but seven-ish for dinner means one should arrive at seven thirty and will be fed at nine.

Eight-ish for dinner means one should arrive at eight fifteen and will be fed at nine.

There is no nine-ish.

People who expect their guests to show up at specific hours should not ish.

Flowers

DEAR MISS MANNERS:

I entertain often, in a formal way, and am justifiably known for my cooking, beautiful table settings, and so on. I do not think I overlook any detail for my guests' comfort and enjoyment. However, I cannot always say that the reverse is true.

The thing that annoys me most is people showing up on my doorstep with bunches of loose flowers that they just hand to me in a soggy mess. I am then expected to leave the front door, where I should be available to greet other guests, go into the pantry, find the right vase, fill it with water, arrange the flowers, find a place for the flowers in the living room—and you may be sure that I have already arranged the living room perfectly, with flowers where they are needed. It seems to me that this is very inconsiderate of my time and of the duties I should be performing for my other guests during this time-consuming period. Isn't it proper to send flowers to a hostess either in the afternoon, before the party, or the next day to express appreciation? And don't you think it's more thoughtful to send arranged flowers in a vase, rather than a box of cut flowers or, worse, a bunch bought on a street corner?

GENTLE READER:

When Miss Manners entered the advice business, she knew that some day it would break her heart. As dear Nathanael West warned in his *Miss Lonelyhearts*, mass exposure to the insoluble suffering of this world can drive one to despair.

Now you've done it. Miss Manners doesn't know if she can bear to go on living in a world where people such as you—for surely, no problem is unique—are plagued with the untimely floral offerings of their friends. What to do? Miss Manners, although she is herself groping for the strength to go on, will offer one last timid, faltering suggestion to help you in your time of need: Why don't you just keep a filled vase in the pantry on party nights and dump whatever you get into it?

Edible Presents

DEAR MISS MANNERS:

I like to bring gifts of food to anyone who has invited me over for an evening, but I am often looked at with dismay by a hostess who seems to assume that she has to serve whatever I brought, right away. I really mean her to keep it for herself later. Are there any rules about what it is OK to bring, and what is not?

GENTLE READER:

It is necessary that the food itself agree with your intention of its being enjoyed by the hostess after her guests have left. This means that it must be something that does not require any immediate attention on her part. Food that is leaking, sizzling, or mooing when presented is out. It is considerate to offer food without a time limit on it—preserves, herbs, freezable breads. The exception is home-grown tomatoes, which are always welcome.

Presents of Wine

DEAR MISS MANNERS:

It is common practice for dinner guests nowadays to bring gifts of wine. The wine may or may not be appropriate for the hosts' menu, and may or may not be any good. Does courtesy require that the host offer to serve wine given in this fashion at the meal to which the donor has been invited?

GENTLE READER:

Only presents of Chianti brought to the spaghetti dinner parties of impoverished graduate students need be consumed when and with whom they appear. Otherwise, it is presumed that the host will provide all the goodies and that the guest's reward is emptying the host's larder and cellar. All one has to say, when accepting the wine, is "Why, how lovely. We'll think of you when we enjoy this." The fact that one plans to enjoy it in one's salad, with plenty of olive oil to counteract the taste, need not be mentioned.

Background Music

The adage that Silence Is Golden has never been more true, in Miss Manners' opinion. Its value is rising astonishingly every day, and it is getting correspondingly harder for most people to have any.

By silence, Miss Manners means something you can hear a bird tweet in. As if the hum of the mechanical world and the blather of the human world were not enough, individuals and industries have combined to produce a constant stream of nasty noise masquerading everywhere under the inappropriate name of music. Restaurants, hotel lobbies, and shops are wired for sound. Hand-carried radios take care of the streets and buses. In private houses, the choice is usually between the informal, or lower-class, sound of unattended television sets or the fancy sound of mild classical music used as a "background."

(It has been objected that many fine pieces of music were written for the purpose of providing a background for the activities of patron-hosts and their guests. If Mr. Handel does not mind making Water Music while your guests are slurping their wine, Miss Manners will reluctantly permit it.)

Miss Manners is not even going to tell you what the medical consequences probably are to steadily assaulted ears. The fact is that all this noise is rude. It is rude to the captured audience of half-listeners, and what is more, it is rude to the music.

Music worth listening to is worth listening to, which is why symphony concerts provide the world's dullest "visuals," a huddle of people in black and white, sawing and blowing away. If you want something to look at while you listen, you can go to the opera and watch people stab one another, or go to the rock concert and watch them stab themselves with their instruments.

What you cannot do is put conversation or thought in the foreground and music in the background. Noise-producing industries have studies to prove that ''background music'' soothes (as on airplanes before takeoff or other antics) and stimulates (as in factories and hen houses). Whichever it is, it is an impertinence for public services or private hosts to attempt to manipulate the feelings of their customers or friends.

If you really want to soothe and stimulate a guest, what is wrong with sherry? The chief results of piped-in noise, as far as Miss Manners can see, are self-absorbed salesclerks who don't attend to their customers and half-shouted conversations that ought to be nearly whispered. We have gotten so used to it, that silence has come to be considered somewhat frightening—an admission of social failure, or the world's being empty. It is now possible to make anyone confess anything—not by torture, but by looking at them in silence for so long that they will tell all, just to break it.

Here are some suggestions of other things to throw into silences while you are (please) tapering off noise:

A naughty smile.

A satisfied look around the room, pausing at each face.

A thoughtful expression.

An appreciation of the sound of ice clinking in glasses, crackling fireplaces, or rustling leaves.

Words, produced by a mind that has had the quiet in which to think.

Couples Together

DEAR MISS MANNERS:

How much attention does a man have to pay to his wife at a party? Mine always gets upset if I leave her to talk to others, but if I spend the whole evening talking to her, or even just hanging around her, we might just as well stay home. Does she have a right to feel hurt if I expect her to fend for herself while I do the same?

GENTLE READER:

It is graceful for a man to make a few conspicuous gestures of solicitation for his wife upon arrival at a party, such as helping her off with her coat and seeing to it that she gets a drink. This gives others the idea that he values her and will encourage them to try to find out why, thus freeing him to talk to someone more interesting.

Guests in the Kitchen

DEAR MISS MANNERS:

I have several friends who are gourmet cooks, and I enjoy eating at their homes. But I never know what to do when the host goes into the kitchen. Should I follow him to be sociable? Or stay in the living room doing—what? One friend of mine got really irritated, it seemed to me, when I went into his kitchen to continue our conversation; another friend just kept shouting at me while she was in the kitchen and I was in the front room, until I felt I should go in there so she could converse without going hoarse. What would you do?

GENTLE READER:

Ask. By all means, you may ask Miss Manners, since Miss Manners knows everything, but you might also ask the individual cook if you should go into the kitchen or not. Some people enjoy entertaining in their kitchens, while others prefer that their guests not observe them sticking their fingers into the food, licking the stirring spoons, and other such maneuvers that good cooks perform.

DEAR MISS MANNERS:

What are my husband and I supposed to do when we are the only guests, and our host goes into the kitchen, saying he doesn't need any help with the cooking? We get left in the living room. May we inspect the bric-a-brac? Should we follow him anyway and keep offering to help, or stand in the doorway, making conversation? I have the feeling he really doesn't want us there, but it seems odd for us to make conversation to each other.

GENTLE READER:

Every couple should have a topic ready for such situations. The best ones are extremely distant—"How should we do over the house when the children are grown?" "What would be good second careers for us if we went back to school after retirement?"—because they are generally more graceful than discussion of recent situations, such as, "Did you pick up the things I asked you to on the way home?"

The Bathroom

DEAR MISS MANNERS:

I read recently that Charlotte Ford and Nancy Tuckerman and Letitia Baldrige, who have written etiquette books, say it is wrong to disturb your hostess by asking her where the bathroom is because she is busy with her party duties. They say it's better to ask a waiter. Do you agree?

GENTLE READER:

It is certainly the rule for guests who are inquiring at leisure out of idle curiosity about the layout of the house. When Miss Manners asks such a question, however, she is not fooling around. Therefore she asks the person most likely to know, and not the rent-a-butler. Miss Manners believes that a hostess who is too busy to deal with her guests' most basic needs deserves the consequences.

On Guest Towels

DEAR MISS MANNERS:

My daughter is thirty-two years old, single, and has a very nice town house. There is a half bathroom on the first floor and another in the finished basement.

Even when she has a cocktail party of twenty-five guests, she will put only one (clean) terry hand towel on the towel bar. She will not even allow a box of attractive paper guest towels to sit on the top of the vanity next to the wash bowl (where there is plenty of room). Is she correct to use only the one towel, or should she have more?

GENTLE READER:

It is elementary that if one has several guests, one should have several guest towels. The vehemence of your daughter's refusal to acknowledge this must strike you as peculiar and illogical.

And so it is. But you have to understand that the guest towel is, in American society, a fetish item, strangely respected and venerated even by those in whom no other sign of respect for the property of others has ever been manifested. It is easily possible to give a party for twenty-five people, each of whom may visit the bathroom at least once, and end up with an untouched rack of guest towels. Did they not wash their hands? Did they blow dry them, or wipe them on their clothes or on your curtains? You'll never know.

Why did they refuse to use the guest towels? Perhaps because they were warned not to use them in their childhood homes and have failed to make the transition to full-fledged guesthood. Perhaps from the silly reluctance to "be first" that has guests staring stupidly at untouched buffet tables, walking around the block until other guests arrive, or torturing their hosts by not leaving when the party should be over. Miss Manners is not really interested in the psychological justification; most people keep their souls so untidy. By giving them a terry towel, your daughter is providing her guests with a pseudo-family towel, which therefore supposedly does not participate in the taboo put on guest towels.

Miss Manners has a simpler solution. Before giving a party, put a row of fresh guest towels on the towel rack in the bathroom. Then wash your hands, dry them on one of the towels, and place the used towel, in a crumpled state, at the edge of the rack. This is not easy for most people. It requires courage and daring. But your first guest will be able to be the second to use a towel, and, whatever any of your guests decide to do with their wet hands, you will have set them a brave example.

Curbing Guests' Curiosity

DEAR MISS MANNERS:

I have only one bathroom in my apartment, so of course my guests have to use it. I try to keep it clean when company is coming, which is not easy, because I take my shower just before they come, after finishing cooking. How much of my personal stuff must I put away, out of sight? My toothpaste? My shaving equipment? More intimate products? My girl friend's shower cap?

GENTLE READER:

All of it. It is amazing to Miss Manners how much amusement and interest people can get from the ordinary contents of a drugstore shelf when they are transferred to a friend's bathroom. The least you can do is to make them pay for the satisfaction of this unwholesome curiosity by the embarrassment of having to open someone else's medicine cabinet.

Buffet Directions

DEAR MISS MANNERS:

Which direction should one travel when filling a plate from a buffet table—clockwise or counterclockwise? And at what point of the table do you start? Six o'clock?

GENTLE READER:

Six is a little early. It is wise to start where the plates are, and to quit when you hear the people in line ahead of you saying, "That looks like that mousse again." You will find that the usual pattern requires you to go clockwise, although large buffet tables are set out in a mirror image fashion, so that one may pick either side and march in the direction of one's choice, still coming out with the same results as those who chose a different path. If one is really hungry, one may nibble discreetly as one goes along, thus clearing the plate at the same time one is refilling it, which may be kept up indefinitely or until the hosts wise up.

Rearranging Ladies

DEAR MISS MANNERS:

Quite often, my mother is involved in club meetings, church functions, etc. After the business is completed, the ladies adjourn to a separate room for lunch, cake, coffee, or whatever. Everyone seems to like taking a seat closest to the entrance, causing most of the ladies to squeeze through cramped space, around girdles, and over toes to get to a place at the table. Other than knocking yourself out to be the first into the room, can you give us a solution? Rearranging the furniture is also out.

GENTLE READER:

One rearranges the ladies, girdles and all, with some tactful comment. If "I wonder if you would join us over there?" doesn't work, you might try, "Who is that lady way over there in the corner in that shocking dress?"

Madame Defarge Did

DEAR MISS MANNERS:

Can I knit during social events? I like to keep busy when a few of us get together for coffee, but sometimes people think I'm not paying attention to what they are saying.

GENTLE READER:

Miss Manners knitted all through classes at Wellesley, and at the end of four years ended up with an education and a sweater both of which were serviceable but somewhat smaller than she had imagined. Whether you can manage both is something only you know. Miss Manners advises you only not to explain to friends that you wish to do something useful while listening to them.

Providing Transportation

DEAR MISS MANNERS:

My husband and I disagree on how to respond to a frequent demand: we live in the city and own a small car that we use only when very inconvenient not to do so, for example, to attend parties in the suburbs. Almost inevitably we are asked to give other guests without a car a lift home. Unfortunately, these are usually the people we've enjoyed meeting the least. Although this is really no big inconvenience, we feel as if we cannot refuse; thus our freedom to leave when we choose or to stop en route home is hampered. Can we politely refuse these requests? If so, how? Or are we being mean to even think of refusing?

GENTLE READER:

Well, you are being a tad selfish by bragging about how little you use your car and then not wanting to help others cut down on the use of cars. It is not hard to accommodate others without giving up your freedom. It is, after all, your car. You could say, "We'd love to give you a ride—we'll be leaving in about another hour, probably," thus leaving the petitioners the choice of waiting or of seeking earlier or later departures with others. Or you could say, "Certainly, if you don't mind waiting while we stop for a snort on the way home." Flatly refusing to give people lifts is the privilege only of people whose cars never break down.

Departing

DEAR MISS MANNERS:

Is it true that the guest of honor must leave a party first because no one else is supposed to depart before that? It seems unfair. When a party is in your honor, you are likely to be having a better time.

GENTLE READER:

This is exactly why one must allow the others to go home. Being honored is enjoyment enough for one evening.

Speeding the Parting Guest

If hospitality is a divine obligation, it certainly has an immediate earthly reward. Miss Manners is referring to that sublime moment when one's guests all go home. If they ever do.

Anyone who has prepared a meal for others and set out clean implements with which it can be eaten, who has performed the feat of looking around his or her own living room at his dearest friends while managing to recite their names correctly, and who has spent an evening encouraging others to tell their best stories which he already knows by heart, deserves a treat. The treat is to remove his shoes and eat up all the leftovers.

This can be done only if the guests depart. It is nearly impossible to manage both giving guests a good time and getting them to budge promptly. No thoughtful host should be without his own resources for speeding the departing guest.

According to the *Analects* of Confucius, as summarized by dear Harold Nicolson, an ancient Chinese guest was amply provided by his host with clues on when to leave. "When visiting a superior, it is permissible to ask leave to retire when the host either yawns, stretches himself, looks at his watch, or 'begins to eat leeks or garlic as a cure for sleepiness.'" Sir Harold noted in *Good Behavior*. Unfortunately, yawning and stretching are considered unsubtle in our society. Watch looking is borderline; watch shaking is out. Now that last suggestion—there is a wonderful idea. Miss Manners also admires Mr. Max Warburg, the Hamburg banker who is reputed to have concluded his entertainments by looking at a clock and declaring, "Why, you naughty clock, you're driving my guests away!"

For simple, modern good manners, Miss Manners recommends that the host merely arise at the proper time and, with a grateful smile and outstretched hand, say, "You were so very, very kind to have visited me." The key part is the stance. Few guests can remain planted in their chairs while a host or hostess is standing in front of them, beaming with smiles.

SOCIAL DISASTERS

DEAR MISS MANNERS:

This may sound silly, but I'm serious. When someone suffers a particularly embarrassing accident in front of you and many others, what is the socially appropriate response? My husband and I got into an argument about this. We recently visited Boston, and while we were there, we attended a large party where everyone was elegantly dressed. At the party, a lady in a low-cut gown tripped, stumbled, lurched across a table, falling face first into a bowl of guacamole dip, and in the process "popped out" of her top. After an initial stunned silence, practically everyone in the room burst out laughing, even though it was obvious that the lady was terribly embarrassed. Then the hostess rushed over to help her and ushered her upstairs.

After we left the party, I cricitized my husband for laughing and told him I thought it was very bad manners. But he said that it was not impolite for people to laugh at something like that as long as they meant no harm and didn't "overdo" it. I said it was inconsiderate of the person's feelings to laugh at all. He said it's the social custom. Could you settle the argument?

GENTLE READER:

What do you mean "something like that"? Miss Manners doubts that there is anything in the world like an elegantly dressed Bostonian lurching across the room and diving face first into a bowl of guacamole dip while simultaneously disengaging her bodice from her bosom. Therefore, Miss Manners has a wee bit of trouble preparing a general rule for dealing with this eventuality. Nor, if she were your husband, would she attempt to justify a reaction on grounds other than direct cause and effect.

One might try to ignore a less spectacular accident. If, say, it were avocado dip, rather than guacamole, and the lady had merely trailed her sleeve in it, one could pretend not to have noticed. To pretend not to notice a performance such as you have described—even if it were humanly possible—would be to suggest that the lady did it all the time and her friends have gotten used to it. It is far better to comfort her later by telling stories of your own about hilariously embarrassing accidents you have survived.

Medical Emergencies

DEAR MISS MANNERS:

Please tell me the proper behavior for host, hostess, and guest when one or the other suffers a heart attack, stroke, or has a miscarriage during a party. I assume the correct thing would depend to some extent on the size of the gathering. Should house guests who are not relatives or close friends leave (or be thrown out)? Should guests at a large barbecue stay and eat? On what grounds can one cancel a party at the last minute? I would rather not go to the house of someone whose kid has the flu.

GENTLE READER:

Flu, heart attacks, and miscarriages are all acceptable reasons for canceling large parties. If they should occur when such a party is already under way, you are right in assuming that the party is over.

One small point of etiquette that you neglected to inquire about is how to treat the victim of sudden disaster. Allow Miss Manners to suggest that it is quite proper to take such a person to the nearest hospital, however much this may dampen the festive spirits of the other guests. These people may then, if they wish, hang around under the guise of "waiting to hear how she is" and may quietly consume the remaining barbecued ox while doing so. If, however, there is a medical reason for not moving the ill guest, healthy guests are expected to remove themselves from the immediate scene unless they can be of some genuine practical assistance. House guests need not leave the premises entirely unless their rooms are needed.

What you think the size of the gathering has to do with anything, Miss Manners cannot imagine. It is as improper for seven carefully chosen dinner guests in formal clothes to watch the eighth one having a miscarriage as it is for a cocktail party comprising a year's worth of social obligations.

Screaming

DEAR MISS MANNERS:

Is it possible to be guilty of being rude when you absolutely can't help it? Let me give you some examples. The first has to do with an incident in which everybody treated me as if I had made some terrible error, but I only reacted naturally. It was at a party, and I was sitting in a steel and leather chair. The arms were steel; this is important. We were having a buffet dinner, and a woman I'd been talking to in the buffet line took the seat next to me, in another chair just like mine. In order to continue our conversation, she drew the chair up exactly next to mine, pinning my arm, which had been dangling over the arm of my chair, between the two steel beams. It hurt like crazy, and I screamed. She then said, stupidly, "Did I hurt you?" and of course I said yes. Even if I hadn't, it was plain from the red mark on my arm that she had done considerable damage. How it got to seem like my fault, I don't know, but I saw people glaring at me and shooting her sympathetic looks as I rubbed my arm. I can tell you other examples, but they are all pretty much the same. Each time, I have cried out in pain before I even thought about it. As often as not, the person who does it doesn't even apologize, so I'm not sorry that I let them know, in this perfectly natural way, that they did something wrong. The party incident bothers me, however. What should I have done? After all, I didn't decide to yell; I just did.

GENTLE READER:

Natural instinct only excuses you so much in polite society. Etiquette, after all, is the imposition of civilized behavior over the chaos of instinct.

In society, we occasionally consider the motive. What might be an obvious insult—a direct blow, than which one can hardly deliver more of an affront—is not taken as such if no offense was truly intended. Your acknowledging an injury when none was meant is as bad as swallowing an intended insult. Granted that you could not help crying out, you must then reply to the stupid question by saying, "Oh, no, no, I'll be all right. I was just startled." The red mark will belie this, of course, but that only makes you seem the more saintly in your forgiveness. In any case, there's not much point in making the other person remorseful when there is no way that that person can repair the injury. Miss Manners does acknowledge that the scream is helpful in obtaining the necessary apology. This apology is what should bring forth your denial. If none is forthcoming, you may leave the scream as your final remark.

Guests in Undress

DEAR MISS MANNERS:

Recently, a very dear friend and I gave a party. Nothing elaborate; just snacks and drinks for some thirty people. Our problem arose when one of the guests brought a friend. We did not mind an extra person here or there; on the contrary, we enjoy meeting new people. However, this young man decided, once inside the house, that it was too warm, and promptly removed his shirt. Apparently, he thought this gesture reeked (if you'll pardon the expression) of machismo, and was a marvelous way to get the women to swoon. Needless to say (but I will say it anyway), he was wrong. The majority of us were, to say the least, fairly repulsed by his actions. As hostess at this gathering, I did not like to see one individual make the others feel so uncomfortable, but I was at quite a loss of what to do. Finally, I took him aside, gently explained the situation, and, as politely as possible, asked him to please put his shirt back on. Was I wrong in doing this?

GENTLE READER:

You are right to feel an obligation, as hostess, to see to the comfort of your guests. Explaining that you were having a formal evening, that clothes were being worn, was perfectly acceptable. If you wished to make the offender particularly comfortable, too, in any temperature, you might have hinted that the ladies found his déshabille "disturbing."

Property Rights

DEAR MISS MANNERS:

Early this spring, we sat on the front veranda with a couple of dinner guests. It became cool, and I lent a new white sweater to the better half. I think she inadvertently wore the sweater home. She has an almost identical sweater. How can I ask her to check her closet without seeming to accuse?

GENTLE READER:

There are two matters here on which Miss Manners is not quite clear. 1. Did she have "an almost identical sweater" before you lent her yours, or is that what she has now? 2. What is it you are trying to avoid "seeming to accuse" her of doing?

Miss Manners is puzzled because she suspects you of stating the problem in social euphemisms. Miss Manners adores euphemisms, and if you want to practice them on her before using them on your friend, that is fine. But Miss Manners needs to know—and you can be quite frank with Miss Manners, who never breathes a word of anything to anyone—whether your problem actually is: I lent a friend my sweater and she stole it from me and wears it now as if it were hers. You see, if you really believed that she had inadvertently kept it, all you would have to do is to say, "Do you still have that sweater I lent you? I could use it if you don't need it," and she would return it. There's no rudeness involved in "seeming to accuse" someone of having been forgetful. Do that anyway, even if you think it wasn't inadvertent, because that would accomplish the same purpose, while saving face for her. That is what euphemisms are for.

Spilled Coffee

DEAR MISS MANNERS:

While engaged in animated conversation at a dinner party recently and holding my coffee cup momentarily motionless in an elevated position, I did not notice that I was holding it tipped at an angle, until shouts of alarm from several other guests made me aware that the cup was dripping rapidly (but fortunately, directly above its saucer). Feeling embarrassed at this faux pas, I meticulously picked up the saucer with my other hand, and carefully began pouring its contents back into my coffee cup, at the same time resuming my conversation. Almost immediately, however, I was startled by a cry from my hostess, and discovered to my astonishment that while I was still pouring, I had again inadvertently allowed the cup to tip, and now both the cup and the saucer were dripping directly onto the table.

My hostess was very angry, and I was understandably quite upset by this situation, considering that my intentions were only the best. Miss Manners, do you think that I deserved a public rebuke? Or, in a time when good conversation is so rare a commodity, do you not think that my hostess was unseemingly rude about this unfortunate incident? Also, what should I reply to wags who are now telling me that I can't handle drinking and talking at the same time, and should consider entering national politics?

GENTLE READER:

Why not enter national politics? You seem to take naturally to mistaking a well-meant warning against pursuing a course of disaster for a personal rebuke, and to feel that being a good talker and meaning well excuses you for making a mess of things.

Falling Asleep

DEAR MISS MANNERS:

From time to time, I give small dinner parties in which we talk about politics, art, theater, or other people, and they are anything but boring. I have a very dear friend who now and then falls asleep after dinner, in the middle of my party. Should I give her coffee, instead of the Sanka she always requests? She is not old. I have talked to her about this problem, and I know she feels bad.

GENTLE READER:

Nearly everyone has, at one time or another, fallen asleep at a public or social event, or watched someone else do so. But while it is common, natural, and blameless, it nevertheless cannot be tolerated. It cannot fail to suggest boredom, even though that seldom is its cause. It also falls into the spinach-in-the-teeth category of actions that cause more humiliation in the doer if he or she is uncorrected, than if it is pointed out at the time. (Please see pp. 94–95.)

You must wake up your friend. Perhaps not with substituting coffee for decaffeinated liquids without her knowledge—Miss Manners is against administering stimulants to the unsuspecting—but with a word or an elbow. If no one else has observed your friend's mental departure from the party, you could grab her arm or nudge her, under the pretext of passing her a mint or brandy. If you cannot get near her without causing a disruption, call out her name and then draw her into the conversation, as in, "Marabelle! We were just saying how many wonderful presidential candidates there are to choose from this year. What do you think?" Vague questions are best, you see, because even an alert person can be excused for replying, "Well, um, I don't rightly know."

A Reply

DEAR MISS MANNERS:
Your advice to the hostess whose friend falls asleep after dinner—that she should quietly nudge or whisper him awake—may be correct as far as manners are concerned, but you didn't really deal with the cause of the problem, which is probably medical. There could be many causes of uncontrollable sleepiness after eating—the sugar in the dessert, for instance, or breathing difficulties—and it is extremely important that the person find out why he has this problem and does something to control it. A truly good friend would not only minimize the embarrassment when this happens, but afterwards urge the person to get to a doctor.
GENTLE READER:
You are quite right, and Miss Manners appreciates your calling her attention to her lapse from alertness.

Somnolent Limbs

DEAR MISS MANNERS:
My leg fell asleep at a dinner party. I didn't want to make a fuss, and so I just sat there pinching it, but that didn't help, and I was in agony. Would there have been a polite way to handle this problem?
GENTLE READER:
Some medical emergencies take precedence over the ordinary rules of polite behavior. It depends not on the seriousness of the illness, but on how socially acceptable it is. Nothing would excuse your head's falling asleep, but the leg might squeak through. You could have waited for a pause in the conversation, announced calmly to the hostess, "I'm afraid my leg seems to have gone off again," and, with her permission, amused the guests by stamping around the dining room table until you had effected a cure. A more subtle solution would be to rub the back of the knee (yours, not your dinner partner's) to get the blood moving again.

❧ APOLOGIES

People who boast that they "never apologize, never explain," or who claim that "love is never having to say you're sorry" ought to be ashamed of themselves and admit it and ask forgiveness.

Now that the duel is illegal, the apology is the only way left to settle many disputes without getting blood on the sofa. A humble speech, a graceful letter, a box of flowers, a duplicate Etruscan vase to replace the one you merrily knocked over to dramatize a story—what fault will these not erase? Well, Miss Manners will tell you. One day, a lady of her acquaintance asked what she should do after she and her husband failed to show up for a small, seated dinner party that a kind friend was giving in their honor. The engagement had simply slipped their minds, and the thought of these good people standing about as the food congealed, waiting to do honor to cherished friends who never bothered to show up, was beginning to interfere with their sleep.

Miss Manners was quick to realize that there was only one thing this couple could do. That would be to change their name, move out of town, and take up a life of anonymous service to others. It is a course of action Miss Manners nearly followed herself, when a rare Anthony Trollope volume, lent to her by a kind stranger from a complete, matched, and cherished set, disappeared from her desk. (The volume returned and confessed to having merely hidden to tease Miss Manners, a trick it had learned from observing her spectacles, and that is the only reason your Miss Manners is able to be with you today.)

So there are, indeed, unforgivable social sins for which there is no need to apologize because no apology would ever be adequate.

Ordinary crimes of forgetfulness—as the dinner engagement might have been if it had been a large party, or served from the buffet, and if the absent guests had not been guests of honor—should be redeemed by an excess of thoughtfulness. One bombards the offended person with abject words, spoken and written, and with flowers until that person is exhausted enough to soften.

The only excuse, as in so many acts better left uncommitted, is temporary insanity. To say "I was terribly busy" is another insult, meaning, "I had more important things to do than to take time or effort to think of you."

"That was such a dreadful, hectic time that I went out of my mind and neglected the very things that mattered to me most" is more like it.

The best apology for material damage is material. But "Can I pay for it?" is no help, said, as it is, with the knowledge that it will bring a protest, however insincere. "Who does your reupholstering?" or "What is your crystal pattern?" or "Who is your antiques dealer?" is infinitely more reassuring. In these cases, the bother, as well as the cost, should be assumed by the wrong-doer.

Dear Aunt Patience,

    I shall never forgive myself for that awful scene I caused at your house last night. Daffodil says I should be drummed out of the family and she is quite right. I had no idea who that young lady was, and I don't know what possessed me. I only hope some day to regain your esteem.

                   Sincerely yours,
                   Rhino

A note of apology.
This is a man's informal, monogrammed card, for short, informal letters.

Exclamations of "Oh, no, don't give it another thought" on the part of the offended hosts should be steadfastly ignored. After all, those are the same people who were just saying to you, "Oh, don't leave yet, it's early"—just as if they meant it.

Borrowing and Losing

DEAR MISS MANNERS:
Recently I borrowed seven sheep from a dear friend. They were to have mowed my lower lawn, but somehow they went out into the lane in the woods. When my dear friend came to collect them, there were only six sheep. My problem is, how do I compensate him for his lost sheep? I offered to pay him, but he refused. Then I sent him a gift certificate for one hundred dollars, but he returned it. I feel awkward about this large loss, for which I am responsible. What do you suggest?
GENTLE READER:
A leg of mutton? Or how about offering to baby-sit for his children? That ought to do it.

On the Weak Smile . . .

DEAR MISS MANNERS:

What is the proper reply when someone says "Excuse me"?

GENTLE READER:

A weak smile. The way to perform a weak smile is to raise the corners of the mouth without moving the center part of the lips, which remain closed. The length of the weak smile depends on the magnitude of the act for which the excuse was requested. For example, if a person has asked to be excused for burping, the weak smile in response should last only a fleeting moment, as did the burp, one hopes. If he is asking to be excused for breaking a porcelain vase that your great-grandfather brought back from China, the weak smile becomes fixed. This is to distract attention from the expression in your eyes as you stare at the fragment of china on the floor.

. . . And the Hollow Laugh

DEAR MISS MANNERS:

Now that I have mastered a "weak smile," I find that I have need for a "hollow laugh." Can you please tell me how to do it?

GENTLE READER:

Ah, the hollow laugh. Yes, indeed, it is a most useful social skill indispensable for responding to tasteless jokes, excessive kidding, and other unacceptable forms of behavior. Miss Manners will be glad to teach it to you.

For the hollow laugh, you first smile with the lips wide open, displaying all of the forward teeth, while the rest of your face registers a puzzled look. You then force up from the throat a noise that does not resemble a genuine laugh, but rather imitates the words "Ha ha" or "Huh huh" that writers use to transcribe the sound of a laugh. When these words have been emitted, leave the open smile hanging there for a moment, as if you had forgotten about it, and then abruptly close the mouth into a solemn expression.

Embarrassment at the Embassy

DEAR MISS MANNERS:

At a formal embassy dinner, I was gesturing to make a point and accidentally knocked the meat tray from the waiter's hand, splattering an entire line of guests, including my dinner partner, who was wearing white. I feel terrible. Is there anything I can do to make amends?

GENTLE READER:

Renounce your social ambitions. You might just as well, under the circumstances.

When One Has Had Too Wonderful a Time

DEAR MISS MANNERS:

What do you say to a hostess the next day when you don't really remember how you behaved at her party? Maybe you were perfectly all right, in which case you don't need to apologize, and in fact, doing so would only call attention to something you got away with concealing, if you know what I mean. But maybe you weren't OK, in which case you ought to say something if you want to be forgiven and invited back some day. How about just "I had a wonderful time?" Is that neutral enough to be grateful-sounding without going into details?

GENTLE READER:

Well, no. She may be already aware, perhaps more aware than you, of how wonderful a time you had. The apology, if indeed you owe one, is likely to be needed in connection with the effect your wonderful time had on the rest of the party. How about saying to her, "You were magnificent"? That covers anything from her simply being a good hostess to her having tolerated your bad behavior.

Dinner Parties

Truly Formal Dinners

Is it possible, as Miss Manners has been hearing lately, that there is a general yearning to return to formality? She can scarcely restrain her excitement. But perhaps she has misunderstood. Miss Manners has always had trouble with the word ''formal,'' because to her it means white tie, as opposed to black tie, which is ''informal.'' (''We're not dressing,'' once meant dark suits, but is a phrase Miss Manners wouldn't have dared use in the last two decades.)

But if we are truly to have formal dinners again, Miss Manners begs that they be done right. Slipshod ways have crept in everywhere, with the most unlikely people absurdly claiming that they want their parties to be ''fun'' or their guests to feel ''comfortable.'' If that is the object, Miss Manners, for one, would just as soon stay home.

To begin with, Miss Manners wants all formal dinner invitations and responses to be on paper. She never wants to see an engraved telephone number again. Nor does she ever again want to see the abominable designation ''and guest.'' Everyone must be invited by name.

There is to be no skimping on the paperwork. She wants seating charts in the hallway, so that guests may study them before having to face the assemblage, cards with each lady's name put into a little envelope bearing the name of the

478

gentleman who is to be her dinner partner; and place cards on the table. This system may involve a great deal of writing (but why else are so many people studying calligraphy these days?) but it gives the guests a sporting chance to fake remembering one another, avoid their dinner partners before dinner and, for the adventurous, to sneak into the dining room before dinner and improve their lot.

Miss Manners also wants to see menu cards on the table, and she wants them back in French, a time-honored affectation. Classical Athenians wrote their menus in Doric. A little mental exertion before eating is good for you.

She expects the table to be set with a white or off-white tablecloth in damask or lace, rather than the now-traditional flowered bedsheets. People who give formal dinner parties have no business being clever and creative. The centerpiece should be flowers flanked by candles, with small dishes of candy and fruit placed strategically and symmetrically. People who attend formal dinners should not require conversation pieces.

The guests should be announced as they first arrive, wives before husbands. Miss Manners is aware that this is reversed when the man has an official title, but has never liked that. She believes the two systems could be reconciled by giving all such titles to women.

She expects the guests to arrive by eight minutes after the appointed time, and be allowed another twenty minutes for a drink before the butler announces, "Dinner is served." (Actually, Miss Manners prefers his saying to the hostess, "Madam is served.") Too bad for anyone who isn't there. People who give formal dinner parties should have learned ruthlessness.

She expects there to be identical platters and footmen (even if it is hard to find identical footmen these days) for each four to six guests. This is the only way to have proper Russian service (explained on pp. 498–499). She does not want to see filled coffee cups being offered after dinner, with the liqueurs and the cigars, to the gentlemen in the smoking room and the ladies in the drawing room. The coffee must be poured.

But wait! Make that the smokers in the smoking room, and the ladies and gentlemen in the drawing room. That other form of separation was silly. There is no sense in being a slave to tradition.

🌹 THE GUEST LIST

The public sport of ruining people's lives by discovering their diaries or introducing their love letters into court is gone. Few people write such things anymore, and as it has become the custom to deliver such information about oneself orally and voluntarily at social events, one could easily suppose that there are no written personal secrets in existence.

This is not the case. The most fastidious people still record information that would, if discovered, cut them off from decent society. Miss Manners is referring, of course, to the party book, in which one keeps the names of one's friends under the classifications one has given them as guests. Such a record is as useful as it is dangerous. In it may be noted guests' violent allergies, to food or to specific people, but the heart of it is a system that enables one to put together an interesting party. Risking ostracism, Miss Manners will explain her system, not only to show off how magnificently organized she is, but to illustrate what makes a good combination of guests.

You may have heard of "A" lists and "B" lists. All experienced hosts classify their friends this way, but only the clumsy ones allow their guests to know, from looking about a room, which they are on. (A gentleman of Miss Manners' acquaintance has the misfortune to live next door to a good friend who frequently entertains in her patio and has, through long, careful window observation, discovered that, much as he enjoys the parties to which she invites him, they are not her first rank ones. He has chosen the wise course of ignoring this information.)

The A list should consist of what Mrs. Perfect calls "sparklies." These are people who, through their private status or through their talented efforts, can "make" a party. The greatest artist of the day could fill this position silently, for instance, or a nonentity could do it with consistently brilliant conversation.

The B list, like the ideal middle class, should consist of solid citizens with a strong sense of duty. The duty is to listen to the sparklies and to be able to carry a reasonable amount of good conversation.

Then there is a C list which, like poverty, one is always trying to eliminate but can't. These are the social obligations—incurred through sloppy acceptance of their hospitality, ancient friendship from which the interest has disappeared, or the pleas of A- or B-listed friends—who do not earn their dinner.

Miss Manners then cross-files these lists by occupation and level of achievement. One's friends tend to be from a limited number of fields. The question of achievement level is not snobbery, but the fact that people who are striving for advancement—a category that naturally includes almost all young people and even some people who ought to be enjoying their high status but can't stop striving—rarely give themselves over wholeheartedly to theoretical and disinterested conversation.

In the well-planned dinner for ten, there should be (taking out the host and hostess) : two sparklies from different fields, four solid listeners and contributors from assorted professions, one charity case, and one mystery guest whose classification will not be clear until after being auditioned at this dinner. Laurel resters should, on the whole, be kept separate from ladder climbers, unless the latter show extraordinary talent as listeners. All sparklies make as dull a party as all audience. Unless occupations are mixed, you will hear nothing but shop talk.

Since a good party is such a mix, your best friends will never know what you consider them. Provided, of course, you keep your jaw and your desk locked.

Gender and the Dinner Table

DEAR MISS MANNERS:

As a single lady who includes married friends in dinner parties in my home, I am puzzled by the frequency with which I hear married persons planning to invite "a few other couples" to their dinner parties. I find this particularly distressing in light of the fact that the speakers are often those whose weddings occasioned my most extravagant expenditures in Bloomie's fine china department. Although it has long been been my understanding that unescorted single ladies need not be invited to parties where the entertainment is planned around group sex or the Superbowl, I was under the impression that dining in most private homes these days does not require a mate. Am I mistaken?

GENTLE READER:

Miss Manners certainly hopes you are not mistaken, or a great many people would starve to death, at least socially. The Noah's Ark dinner party is a mistake of long standing (or floating) however; soon, Miss Manners hopes, it will be left high and dry.

Placing dinner guests in an alternating pattern of boy-girl-boy-girl around the table was traditionally considered to be as important and decorative as the pairing of candlesticks and saltcellars on the table. Hostesses kept careful lists of "extra" men and women to be matched, which was a great deal of trouble, so they found it easier to choose friends who had made themselves into prepackaged sets, or what we call marriages.

Nowadays, marriage no longer guarantees the sanctity of the matched dinner table. Husbands and wives thoughtlessly unmatch and rematch themselves without consulting the wishes of their dinner hosts, and even married people who remain together are claiming the right to be accepted socially by their friends when their spouses are not accompanying them. Therefore, the difficulties, which formerly affected single ladies who were not welcome without escorts, single men who were expected to "fill in" at a moment's notice, husbands and wives who were disinvited when they had to admit that a spouse would be out of town—this group of people who were regularly insulted for the sake of keeping the dinner table matched has been expanded to include practically everybody.

Perhaps it is time for the givers of dinner parties to weigh the pleasures of a symmetrical table against the pleasures of being hospitable. Miss Manners, who is by no means immune to the joy of a well-ordered table, nevertheless votes for hospitality.

As a single hostess, you can do your part by entertaining your friends, married, single, or others, in whatever state they are available to you. Do not punish them by banishing them from the dinner table to the living room, where the mixture of genders will not be noticed—simply arrange them around the table in terms of compatibility, rather than sex. By doing this, and by letting it be known to your married friends that you can enjoy an evening with them without their having to provide you with a potential sexual partner, Miss Manners hopes you will be an example to all.

. . . An Opposing Viewpoint

DEAR MISS MANNERS:

Recently I was invited to the home of a good friend of mine for dinner. The food was delicious, the table setting elegant, but the guest list consisted of three couples and me. I am a single woman, never married, and have broken up with my most recent romantic entanglement only a few weeks ago. Eating dinner with all those happy people sitting next to their loved ones affected me rather badly, but being a mannerly sort of person myself, I waited until I got home before becoming horribly depressed.

The question arising from this situation is twofold: namely, did she act properly in inviting me at all when she knew the situation, even though we are good friends; and how do I explain to her that although I value her company and appreciate the invitation, I'd rather not attend under such circumstances? I don't necessarily want her to fix me up with some dinner partner, but the inclusion of at least one other single person, whether male or female, in the party would have avoided my discomfort. Would I be wrong to bring it up to her as a confidence, or what?

GENTLE READER:

How can you call this woman a good friend, when she was so dreadfully insensitive as to invite you to an elegant dinner party with delicious food and cheerful people? Why didn't she fill her house with other depressed and lonely souls, so that you can find yourself a new liaison, or, at the least, commiserate over the dinner table with others who feel as sad as yourself? In Miss Manners' opinion, your friend's mistake is believing that you valued her friendship. (She should also not have seated couples adjacently at the dinner table, but that is a technicality that pales before your more glaring problem.)

Your mistake is in believing that the way to romance lies in pursuing it singlemindedly. Ironically, it is the people who most enjoy a variety of social relationships whom others are always wanting to introduce to their eligible friends and relatives. Miss Manners is at least glad that you had the discipline to conceal your depression at the dinner party. There is nothing quite so unattractive as a morose whiner. Happy couples and fascinating single people tend to react the same way to such behavior.

Filling In

DEAR MISS MANNERS:

I must be the last person in the world who still gives seated dinner parties for eight people at which I expect my guests to come on time, in the couples that I invited—no last minute dropouts or additions on the plea of sudden divorce or falling in love—and I still seat them man, woman, man, woman around the table. It's not easy these days, as you know, but I'm in there trying. People do say they enjoy my parties very much, so they must feel it's worthwhile to cooperate with my rules. Occasionally, however, people have iron-clad excuses for dropping out at the last minute—I mean like extreme illness, or a death in the family. I try not to hold it against them. My question, though, is what to do about getting others to fill in at the table for them. I find that six people is not as good for conversation as eight, and anyway, by that time, I have already cooked for eight and it seems a waste to have empty places. If I invite people the day before the party, or even the day of the party, do I have to pretend that it's a last-minute party and that I'm inviting everyone at that time? I'm afraid if I do, they will assume that it's casual and informal, which it's not.

GENTLE READER:

This is one of those rare social situations when a more or less honest confession is actually more flattering than a hollow lie. The correct last minute invitation is worded as follows: "If you weren't such a dear friend, I wouldn't be able to ask you a very great favor. I have a rather difficult dinner tonight, and some people I was hoping were going to make it sparkle have just been called off on an emergency—would you be an angel and fill in? It would make all the difference."

If accepted, this invitation is followed, within the month, by an invitation to the filler-in, in which you offer a choice of dates for a dinner that you plan to build around him or her.

🌹 AT TABLE

Old Family Silver

DEAR MISS MANNERS:

My husband inherited some silver for the table from his family. It's a service for ten, very old and rather pretty (although hard to clean). The monogram belonged to his great-grandmother, and has no initials in common with ours. Also, it's marked on the wrong side. That is, the letters are engraved on the backs of the forks and spoons, instead of on the fronts. Why would that be? Should I have my own put on the front, where they can be seen, or what? I'd like to show it off to best advantage.

GENTLE READER:

You are headed smack in the wrong direction by attempting to pass off your inherited silver as new. Miss Manners does not suggest you go so far as to adopt the English insult, "The sort of people who buy their silver," but notifies you that such an expression exists, in the hopes of making you appreciate what you have. Fortunately for you, everyone will notice this when you learn to set your table as this silver was intended to be placed—with the fork prongs and spoon bowls facing down, so that the initials may be seen. Because this is rarely done in this country, you will undoubtedly be asked questions by those who wish to point out that you have set your table backwards. That will give you the opportunity to explain that you have old family silver. For this purpose, you must learn what each initial stands for, and a charming anecdote or two about the original owner. Your only danger, in this triumph of status, is that some people will lump you with the sort of people who buy old silver and make up names to go with the initials.

Carving Knife

DEAR MISS MANNERS:

How do you feel about the use of an electric carving knife for roasts, or poultry shears for birds, at the table when guests are present? I like the ritual of carving at dinner, and there's no problem when it's just the family and we use the everyday things. But when we have company, my wife likes to put out a silver carving knife and fork in our pattern, and they are of no practical use whatsoever, no matter how many times I try to sharpen them. What always happens is that either I say nothing and hack away and get furious and make a mess, or I put out the things I need while she isn't looking, which makes her angry. What do you think we should do? Which is more important, that the guests know we have two pieces of silver, or that they get their meat sliced right?

GENTLE READER:

They both seem to be important, and therefore Miss Manners has outlined a small scenario to be memorized and performed for company by you and your wife. We will call it "Great Moments in Carving." When the scene opens, the table is set with the silver carving fork and knife. The husband and wife are all smiles. As the action begins, the husband attempts to make an incision in the meat. There is a dramatic pause. He looks across the table at the wife—not reproachfully, but thoughtfully. Think of two surgeons in the operating room, communicating with their eyes because the lower parts of their faces are hygienically covered. He speaks first: "Do you think perhaps I should use the electric knife for this?" She considers, while the audience sits silent and spellbound. "Yes," she says slowly, "I believe you're right." They exchange a look of satisfaction after one of them fetches it, and another such look when it slides successfully into the meat. Properly enacted, this drama should leave an alert audience with the knowledge that the couple owns a silver carving set, and also that they are a smoothly functioning team, careful to use the exact tools they judge necessary at the crucial moment. Of course, they will also be left with the thought that the meat has turned out to be tougher than the hosts anticipated. Miss Manners may have to do a new second act finish on this play.

Silver Wine Goblets

DEAR MISS MANNERS:

We have received six silver wine glasses for our last wedding anniversary. Would it be proper to use them when serving wine at a formal dinner, or are they really just for show?

GENTLE READER:

Miss Manners does not believe in keeping useful objects from their use unless they have, as in the case, say, of an Etruscan vase, outlived their usefulness and may be put on a shelf to be respected in old age. Metal and wine are not, however, the happiest of combinations. The silver could lend an undesirable flavor to your wine; it also conducts temperature and could, if filled with chilled wine, give your guests quite a shock. Your glasses could be given a new use in which they could also be prettily shown off. You might put trailing flowers in them and use them at intervals along the dining room table for decoration.

Placing the Napkin

DEAR MISS MANNERS:

Would you please tell me the correct side, when setting a table, to place the table napkin? Years ago, when I worked as a servant, I was taught to place the table napkin on the left side, but I have now been told that this is incorrect.

GENTLE READER:

In formal service, the napkin is centered on the service plate before the first course is placed on the table, with the hope that each person will remove his or hers before the soup plate lands on top of it. In modern practice, however, the first course may well be on the table when people come to the table, so that no one in a servantless household has to make that extra scoot around as the conversation is starting. In that case, the napkin is placed to the left, next to the forks, as centering it in the soup would be impractical.

The Art of Napkin Folding

DEAR MISS MANNERS:

I have, if I may say so, a talent for folding napkins into interesting shapes, such as fans and flowers. I have seen this done at restaurants, but never in anybody's house. Is there anything wrong with this for dinner parties? I feel it makes the table look more festive. Someone told me that it was an old-fashioned custom not only to do this, but to put bread—a roll, I guess—into the folds of the napkin. Would you approve of this?

Gentle Reader:

Would Miss Manners discourage a talent like that? Yes, indeed, making napkins stand up is an ancient art, lost in the hurly-burly of modern living—or so Miss Manners had thought. They certainly used to have buns hidden in them. Perhaps you should be cautious about that little surprise nowadays, however. People would not expect it and are apt to be dropping them, like marbles, from all sides of the table.

The Finger Bowl

Dear Miss Manners:

Please explain the finger bowl. I have not used any, but I am considering it, because I often serve messy foods, and it sounds like a sensible, practical idea.

Gentle Reader:

Actually, it is not. Correctly used, the finger bowl is a charming touch of no practical use whatsoever. When service is of a degree of formality to require finger bowls, the food is never messy enough to require them. If you want to clean off your guests before dessert at an informal meal, offer them warm, damp, small terry-cloth towels, served with tongs from a wooden tray.

Miss Manners must not get unpleasantly practical herself and forget that what you asked her to do was to explain the finger bowl. Very well. It is a small, individual bowl, usually glass but sometimes silver with a glass lining, half-filled with water in which small flowers or flower petals are floating. No lemons, please. It arrives on the dessert plate. For formal dinners, dessert service paradoxically consists of a lot of different things all stacked up together, just the way you told the children not to clear the table. On the plate from which dessert is to be eaten are a crocheted doily, the finger bowl, and, on each side, the dessert fork and spoon. The guest is then expected to set the table properly, placing the finger-bowl and doily to the left, and the fork and spoon on either side of the remaining plate, before taking dessert. What the guest does not do is use the finger bowl as a sink. At the most, one can dab one fingertip in it, but many people consider even that vulgar. Finger bowls are not for people who cannot tolerate anachronisms.

(For formal service of the rest of the meal, please see pp. 498–499.)

The Party Drama

[*Opening Scene. The stage is set for a party, with small bowls of flowers about, and a tray of sparkling glasses to one side. The host and hostess, beautifully dressed, are discovered sitting side by side on the sofa.*]

Host: Are you sure you told them seven thirty?

Hostess: Of course I did. You heard me. I even sent out reminder cards with maps in them.

Host: Maybe you told them next Saturday.

Hostess: Oh, stop it. Make me a drink, will you?

Host: Let's wait till they get here. What'd you do with my book?

Hostess: I didn't want it lying around. Stop eating all those nuts. You know how fattening they are, and we're having a big dinner.

Host: It's ten after eight. What time were you figuring on sitting down?

Hostess: Well, I thought eight thirty, but we're obviously not going to make it. What do you think—nine? I better turn down the oven. It's going to be all dried out.

Host: Is there anything I can eat?

Hostess: Come on, don't spoil the tray.

[*Doorbell rings. Curtain down. Four hours pass. In the closing scene, the room is littered with coffee cups, brandy glasses and guests.*]

Hostess: Would you like some more coffee?

Guest: Oh, no thank you.

Second Guest: I guess it's a little late, dear.

Hostess: Oh, no.

Host: How about a drink?

Guest: Well, just a little one, perhaps.

Miss Manners is ringing down the curtain on this scene right now, because it is never going to come to an end. If you will make the effort to believe that between these two dreary scenes there was a great deal of jolly activity and witty dialogue, she will explain how to direct this drama properly.

If well played, the opening will convey the irritation experienced by the hosts, and the ominous warning about what is happening to the food. In the last scene, it should be clear that the party has resulted in a stalemate. The guests want to go home, the hosts want them to leave, but nobody is moving.

This is because it is widely and mistakenly believed that to be the first to arrive at a party or the first to depart is a violation of etiquette, punishable by three weekends in traffic court.

The fact is that you can do your hosts no greater favor. They, you will realize from studying the first scene, were obliged to be ready to receive guests at the hour they stated. They are not having a good time sitting around a clean room refraining from eating, drinking, and by some connected law of nature, conversing. (The same couple may be in the habit of chattering to each other brilliantly day and night. It is impossible for anyone to converse in a party-ready room before a party.)

Nor do they want even the most successful party to go on until it is a burden to everybody involved.

Here are these scenes correctly played.

[*Opening. It is seven thirty-five. The doorbell rings.*]

Guest: Good evening. (*Note: Such lines as "Am I the first?" and "I hope I'm not too early" have been taken away from this player, by force if necessary.*)

[*Closing. Although everyone is lounging about, one guest stands up with a smile.*]

Guest: It's been a marvelous evening, but I'm afraid I must go now. (*Note: Phrases such as "I have to work tomorrow" or "I have to drive the baby-sitter home" have been cut on grounds of inanity.*)

Host: Oh, do stay. It's early. How about another drink?

Guest: Oh, no thank you. Good night. I had a wonderful time.

[*Exit. Applause.*]

Cocktail Hour

It is some years now since Miss Manners made it a rule never to attend social events at which she would be expected to stand up. Thus, Miss Manners misses out on a lot of good conversations about how awful cocktail parties are because she doesn't go to cocktail parties, which is where these conversations are held.

There are other advantages to attending cocktail parties, of course. They are an excellent opportunity to meet all the people your friends don't like well enough to invite to dinner. And where else do you get a chance to eat a whole meal of anchovies and raw cauliflower?

However, this is no excuse for the trick of inviting people to dinner and then treating them, instead, to a long cocktail party followed by a midnight supper. Such an event is usually scheduled to begin at seven thirty or eight. Drinks and finger food are served, but taken moderately, for the first hour, by guests who have been led to believe that they will soon be plied with wine and fork food. After that time, some of the smarter ones begin to understand that they have been duped and go after the celery leaves. Meanwhile, the hosts aren't budging.

The excuse hosts give for this outrageous behavior is they can't plan to serve dinner on time because their guests won't show up on time. Guests who have caught on to this then arrive later and later, and so the error is perpetuated. It is the hosts who must correct this situation. It was their idea to stage the event, luring people from their own kitchens. The guests are helpless—it is impossible to pack a sandwich into an evening purse. The hosts might begin by issuing a warning with the invitation. "We eat rather promptly" might be ominously added when the time of the dinner is stated. The cocktail hour must then be severely limited to the hour from which it gets its name. Forty-five minutes would be better. Each prompt guest should have time for one and a half drinks and three canapés. Then dinner should be served, while everyone is still young enough to enjoy it.

What if guests haven't arrived by then? Well, the old rule was that you wait fifteen minutes after the appointed hour for a man, and twenty for a woman. In the interests of equality, we might make it seventeen and a half minutes for each. And if some persist in being later, the rest of you may split the resulting extra desserts. Late comers may be welcomed with an apologetic, "We knew you wouldn't want us to wait." When you are invited out, you may ask, "What time do you plan to sit down?'' and if the answer is an unreasonable one, either decline the invitation or fortify yourself before going.

Serving a Delicate Dish

DEAR MISS MANNERS:

I pride myself on my cooking and love to give elaborate dinner parties at which the timing of the food is very important. It drives me crazy that people just won't leave their drinks and come to the dining room when I tell them to. Last weekend, I had a fish soufflé as a first course, and by the time people finished their drinks and conversation, it was a mess. Not ruined completely, and they all pretended to marvel at it, but, believe me, it didn't look the way it would have if they had come into the dining room when I told them to. I was seething, but my husband says that people are more important than food, and if they were having a good time, I shouldn't have even tried to interrupt them.

GENTLE READER:

Like all generalizations, the idea that ''People are more important than food'' depends on the circumstances. Many people are more important than fruit cup, for instance, but very few, in Miss Manners' opinion, are more important than fish soufflé. In any case, it is not the guests who decide what time dinner is to be served; it is, first, the cook, and second, the hostess or host. As you are both, you must take command. Instead of timidly standing in the doorway and begging people to ''Come in to dinner, please,'' you must announce this in a tone that means business. If there is no general move in your direction, march into the room, grab the man who is to sit on your right, and march him into the dining room with you. If there is still no response, go and get the man who is to sit at your left. If no one else follows, the three of you may eat all their fish soufflé.

Seating Arrangements

DEAR MISS MANNERS:

Last night we went to a dinner party at the home of some neighbors we've never visited before. They have a big dining room, and it was all fixed up with candles and everything, so I asked the hostess where I should sit. She said, ''Oh, just sit anywhere,'' and so I did. Then the host said, ''No, I'm sitting there''—it was a sort of oval table, so I couldn't tell what was to be the head of it—so I moved. I picked another place, but then we were told to get up to get our food from the buffet table, and somebody else sat down in that place. So then I took my plate and sat down again—you notice that this is now the third time I've tried to sit down and have dinner—and guess who comes and sits next to me? My wife. I know married couples aren't supposed to sit next to each other at dinners, but I didn't know she'd been sitting there and was now up getting her plate filled. I got fed up when the hostess noticed where I was and said, ''Oh, you two can't sit next to each other,'' and my wife sat there as if she wasn't ever going to move. But I still was nice, and I said, ''OK, where do you want me to sit?'' and the hostess said, ''Oh, sit anywhere,'' and when I looked at her—this is now the third time she or her husband had made me move—she said, ''I mean anywhere else.'' So I took my plate and went and sat in the living room. Would you mind telling me what the hell ''Sit anywhere'' means?

GENTLE READER:

It means that the hostess has not taken the trouble to finish planning her dinner party. There is a mistaken notion that this omission is a sign of merry insouciance on the part of the hosts who would not dream of failing to orchestrate every other aspect of the party. If the hostess cannot carry the seating arrangement in her head so that she can give you a decent answer to your decent question of where you should sit, she ought to use place cards.

Two Tables

DEAR MISS MANNERS:

I am having a dinner party, strictly for couples, and there are eighteen people invited. My question is, how do I set up the seating arrangements? We will have two tables. One consists of five couples, and the other will have four couples. It is a buffet-style dinner, but I wish to have assigned seats. Do I sit at the larger table across from my escort, or does he sit next to me, or what?

GENTLE READER:

You sit at the head of the larger table, and he sits at the head of the smaller table. The idea when arranging more than one table is to prevent the guests from having any suspicion that there is an A table and a B table. There is, of course, but you must do everything you can to avoid letting the guests find proof.

You will naturally want to seat the gentlemen whom you consider most important next to you, and you may do so, provided you put their wives (or mates—Miss Manners is not sure what you mean by ''strictly'') at the other table. You put the ladies you consider most important next to your escort, and their husbands or mates at your table. That way, when couples try to talk on the way home about the ''better table'' at which they failed to be placed, they will either be contradicted or convinced that the prestige of the family, at any rate, has been recognized.

Enduring a Separation

DEAR MISS MANNERS:

Why must married people be separated at dinner parties? I enjoy sitting next to my wife.

GENTLE READER:

Oh, good for you. Perhaps you can put your dining room table against the wall and sit together in the privacy of your home, if you both consent. It is delightful for a married couple to want to sit together during dinner, but, like some other marital pleasures, this one should be enjoyed in private. At dinner parties, married couples must be separated because they tell the same stories, and they tell them differently.

Turning the Table

DEAR MISS MANNERS:
What does the term "turning the table" mean, and how is it done? Is it, in fact, still a social custom, or is it archaic?
GENTLE READER:
Turning the table is one of those marvelously civilized customs invented by our ancestors who knew, in their wisdom, that no one person should be forced to endure the conversation of the same individual for an entire dinner party. Conscientious hostesses still practice it, although they must pretend they do not, because now we are all supposed to believe that spontaneity is best and that anyone is fascinating providing you get to know him well enough.

Whereas in the old days a hostess could perfectly well confide to Mr. Crawbeard on her right that she was now planning to talk to Mr. Fiddlediddy on her left, she must now be more subtle. Say Mr. Crawbeard has been explaining to her, from the soup course until halfway through the roast mutton, the troubles he has been having with his automobile. She should then turn to Mr. Fiddlediddy, who hasn't heard a word of this because he has been busy making plans for slipping away after the dinner with Mrs. Boltenbrook on his left, and says in a loud voice, "Don't you agree, Simon?" If he has any sense of propriety, he will agree, after which he and his hostess may begin a conversation on any subject they choose, while Mr. Crawbeard asks the lady on his right how many gallons she gets per mile, and Mrs. Boltenbrook begins sizing up the gentleman on her left.

❧ THE MENU

DEAR MISS MANNERS:
I am, if I may say so, a superb cook and an even more advanced eater. So are many of my friends. I would like to give an old-fashioned dinner party, with lots and lots of food. I know that eight- or ten-course meals used to be served at formal parties, but I don't know what all the courses were. If you will list them for me in order, I will promise to prepare, serve, and eat them all, correctly.

GENTLE READER:

Miss Manners is taking you at your word. There were fourteen courses.

1. Oysters or clams on the half shell. Fruit or caviar may be served instead.

2. Soup, giving each guest a choice of clear or thick.

3. Radishes, celery, olives, and salted almonds.

4. Fish, served with fancifully shaped potatoes and cucumbers with oil and vinegar.

5. Sweetbreads or mushrooms.

6. Artichokes, asparagus, or spinach in pastry.

7. A roast or joint, as we say, with a green vegetable.

8. Frozen Roman punch, to clear the palate and stimulate you to go on.

9. Game, such as wild duck or little birdies, served with salad.

10. Heavy pudding or another creamed sweet.

11. A frozen sweet. It is a nice touch to have tiny crisp cakes with this.

12. Cheeses, with biscuits and butter. Or you may serve a hot savory of cheese, which is more filling.

13. Fresh, crystallized, and stuffed dried fruits, served with bonbons.

14. Coffee, liqueurs, and sparkling waters.

Each course requires its own plate and flatware, and as only three knives and forks are permitted on the table at the start, the others must be brought in with their courses.

Miss Manners offers this only as a basic list; you needn't consider yourself limited to it.

(For complete Service à la Russe, please see pp. 498–499.)

(For correct table setting for a formal dinner, please see pp. 119–122.)

Noncarnivorous Guests

DEAR MISS MANNERS:

My husband is a vegetarian; I am not. When we are invited to dine at the home of friends, I maintain that my husband should inform our hosts-to-be that he does not eat meat. I know that when I entertain, I am always disappointed to learn that a guest cannot eat what I have prepared when it is too late to do anything about it. My husband, on the other hand, is perfectly happy to eat salad, bread, and any vegetable, and does not like to have people feel that they need to go out of their way to alter the menu on his behalf; he feels that if he tells them that he is a vegetarian, they will feel obliged to accommodate him. What is the socially correct thing to do?

GENTLE READER:

The socially correct thing for a guest to do is to be perfectly happy eating salad, bread, and any vegetable; the socially correct thing for a host to do is to refrain from being disappointed when a guest does not, for any reason, consume everything that is offered.

Suppose the other guests call, too, and announce themselves as being on the Scarsdale diet, kosher, allergic to seafood, and on the grapefruit diet. Is their hostess expected to be a short-order cook?

The Salad Course

DEAR MISS MANNERS:

Why, in all my travels through Scandinavia and France as a youth, was I served the salad after the entrée was eaten, while here in the United States, it is served and eaten before the entrée?

GENTLE READER:

The Europeans were following the conventional order for dinner courses, one that Miss Manners still prefers. However, one more usually has salad served first in America for one or all of three reasons:

1. Some people believe it is better for the digestion or for the figure to fill up on salad first.

2. In California, which always has to do everything differently from normal people, salad is served first.

3. Restaurants serve salad first in order to give people something to eat besides bread while they are cooking dinner. Many people copy this because they believe that restaurants epitomize correct service. This is an error.

"Too Good to Eat"

DEAR MISS MANNERS:

It is a matter of pride to me that food looks as good as it tastes, and I certainly enjoy being told that an aspic, or, especially, one of my fancy desserts, looks spectacular. But the way people put it, usually, is "Oh, I'm not going to spoil this—it looks too good." I know they mean well, but I'm standing there, holding a platter out to them, and they don't do anything until I've said, "Go ahead" over and over until I lose my patience. It's heavy, after all, and I have to go around the whole table with it. How do I convey the idea to the first person that I made it to be eaten?

GENTLE READER:

By saying, "Well, I hope you'll change your mind," and moving on to the next person. By the time you get back to the first person, after everyone else has been served, the problem, if not the dessert, will have disappeared.

Bread and Butter

Imagine that you have a committee to help you accomplish some task. A few people are on it just for show, and others, of whom you expected much, have proved unreliable. However, there is one person on whom you can always count, who is consistently helpful, cheerful, and unlike the others, troubles you for a minimum of expenses. You are delighted to see this person every day, and often extend invitations to lunch or breakfast or perhaps tea, at which you enjoy making a special fuss. It is only when it comes to big, important, formal dinners that you have some qualms. There you prefer to have your showy people, and either exclude the good soul, or try to improve on his or her appearance, or arrange, at least, that the spouse of this person doesn't have to be there.

Isn't that shabby? Did you ever hear of anything so ungrateful and plain mean? That, Miss Manners is obliged to tell you, is the way you are supposed to treat bread and butter.

We all know that there is no better food on this earth than good bread and butter. It delights your nostrils, appeases your hunger, and keeps you company in restaurants while fancier types keep you waiting. It is always able to make itself ready for you on short notice and is careful not to abuse your budget. No better companion can be found for breakfast, luncheon, tea, or between meals. Yet you are not supposed to have this faithful friend at your best dinner parties. Miss Manners would hardly blame you if you haughtily declared that you would follow no such rule that insults your most loyal daily companion. If, however, you are one of those who is willing to compromise between fashion and friendship, Miss Manners will tell you how to do it.

Like other happy couples, bread and butter must be separated at the dinner table, and their happy home, the bread and butter plate, razed. Butter is never directly invited to the formal dinner table, although it sometimes slithers in, having cozied up to the asparagus in the kitchen. The bereft bread, if it meets a more chic partner such as caviar or anchovy sauce, may appear in the canapés before dinner. If it is willing to be toasted and cut into bits, it may show up on the surface of the soup. The bolder ones just walk in, naked and dry, at this time. Tiny slices may sometimes slip onto the fish platter if they hide under tomato or cucumber slices. During the cheese course, a time at which the guests are on their third or fourth wine and not paying careful attention, it may stride in, in the form of biscuits, and sometimes it even sneaks the butter on its back.

What, one cries, about croissants? English muffins? Hot cross buns? Fresh-baked French, Italian, or your-own-oven loaves? Garlic bread? What about sweet cream butter that has been curled into delicate patterns or pressed into luscious shapes? Are these to be banished in favor of costly, complicated, and often less satisfying dishes?

Certainly not. Bring all your thick slices of hot fresh bread to breakfast, swimming in gently melting butter. Bring out their favorite little plates and butter knives at luncheon, for the prettiest rolls and most cunning curlicues of butter. Decorate your tea table with elegantly thin and crustless slices of buttered bread. Enrich your family suppers with the most dashing garlic-smothered loaves. Just make sure to shove them all ruthlessly out of the way when you want to impress your dinner guests.

For more on bread at less formal meals please see pp. 126–127, 144; tea, pp. 435–437.)

Hazardous Meal

DEAR MISS MANNERS:

Why don't people put warnings out when they serve spicy food? Personally, I hate it, and I don't think it's fair to dish out some fiery concoction to an unsuspecting person who doesn't know what hit him until the tastebuds have been burned off his tongue.

GENTLE READER:

The warning should come with the invitation. Miss Manners feels that all unusual, let alone cruel, forms of entertainment should be so labeled in advance.

🌹 CORRECT SERVICE

With One "Servant"

It is of no use for Miss Manners to indulge herself by describing how to serve a dinner when there is a ratio of one footman to every two guests. The fact is that many people don't have any footmen at all these days, because, among other reasons, fine, strapping young men no longer seem to aspire to such a position. If one does have them, they probably came packaged with their own instructions, and have their own squadron leader, a.k.a. the butler, the last person in the world besides Miss Manners who takes a lively interest in arguing such questions as whether to remove finished plates gradually or when everyone has concluded a course.

If one does not have supporting troops, either in the household or rented for the evening, one is generally advised to pretend to be utterly crazy about informality, and give lots of picnics, pot luck suppers, and children's birthday parties. You are not supposed to be allowed to expect your guests to shower and change before arriving in return for a fine meal, served in comfort, at which they will have an opportunity to talk to their hosts without following them to the kitchen.

However, it is possible to serve such a dinner with what we can either call one servant or admit it is the cleaning woman coming in for an extra evening at time-and-a-half, or an indentured teenaged member of the family. This can be accomplished with a minimum of training, say one fifteen-minute rehearsal, plus kindly worded promptings from the table. It assumes that the host and hostess will perform the advance labor and graceful tasks that may be done among their guests, and that nobody is expecting perfect, silent, and rapid service.

The host serves drinks from a tray in the drawing room, discouraging smart-alecky requests by saying something like ''Will you have whiskey, gin, or tomato juice?'' instead of ''What would you like?'' The hostess uses the maneuver of passing a tray of canapés to regroup people according to her ideas of compatibility.

While the guests are seating themselves in the dining room, the helper makes a first, furtive appearance—in the drawing room, where he or she quickly removes all the dirty glasses, including the one under the sofa.

A four-course dinner is possible if the food has been planned for easy service. The first course should be soup, oysters, or fish in ramekins—something that may be properly portioned in the kitchen and brought in individually. Next is the main course, a meat or fowl that has been carved and arranged on a platter with potatoes or rice and, if there is room, a vegetable. Otherwise, to avoid a special trip for serving the vegetable, it may be served in another course, as a broccoli soup, say, or a green bean salad. The third course is the salad, and possibly also cheese. The fourth, dessert, is something that looks pretty on a serving dish and may be passed, such as a mousse. All this has been prepared beforehand, and only courses one and two need be kept hot. All the helper needs to know is how to arrange the food on platters, and how to serve:

Food is always served to the left of each guest, unless the guest announces left-handedness and asks to be served from the right. The first person served is the woman at the host's right, and then the service may either go clockwise skipping the host and taking each person in turn, regardless of sex or place of residence (in other words, getting the hostess on the way around), with the host last; or counterclockwise, ending at the host. There are two schools of thought about the side from which plates are removed, both schools sparsely attended. Miss Manners prefers removing dishes from the right.

If the table has been set with place plates, which may be any large dish differing in material or pattern from the dinner plates, the helper has only to bring in the individually served first course dishes and put them on top. It may be done two dishes at a time, if Miss Manners isn't looking.

Upon hearing the signal of the hostess, a bell or a foot buzzer on which she has been careful not to place the leg of her chair, the helper appears carrying one dinner plate, preferably a warm one. He or she removes the first course dish and place plate of the first guest and substitutes the dinner plate. It takes a while to do this eight or ten times, but the guests may chat among themselves to pass the time, and the conversation is likely to be friendlier than if two at a time had been attempted and guests are dipping their napkins in their water glasses to remove the soup stains from their clothes. The meat platter is then passed to each guest. Sauces that are served separately may be passed from guest to guest. Wine may be poured by the host, who, according to this plan, isn't going to get any food for a while, anyway. It is expedient to observe the strict rule about not having butter plates on the dinner table. With four courses, you should be able to skip bread without anyone's starving.

As the individual dinner plates are removed, a fresh plate is substituted for the salad, and the salad platter (not bowl) then presented to each guest. However, the salad plates are removed before any dessert plates appear. This is the time for a general clearing up of salt and pepper, forks people forgot to use, and the larger crumbs. As we are not attempting finely tuned service, "crumbing" with napkin or scoop is not necessary if the helper will remove any conspicuous bits of garbage, such as cubes of beef Stroganoff.

Then we come to the tricky part, which is the dessert. (We are not attempting finger bowls. The helper has carried in the filled soup bowls without disaster, but let us not push our luck.) A dessert fork and spoon are placed on each dessert plate, and the combination put in front of the guest. The helper then passes the dessert. If the guest is unfamiliar with the nicety of placing the dessert silver on the plate—the host and hostess should, of course, set a good example—the helper will have to glare at the guest before the guest does the proper thing of putting his fork at his left and his spoon at his right.

At the conclusion of this meal, the hostess, who has not yet had to leave her guests, is given the coffee tray in the drawing room by the helper, who is then free to go upstairs to do his homework. It is, of course, a nice touch if the helper then washes all the dishes and silently puts them away, so that the hosts find an immaculate house as they close the door on the last guest and remove their shoes. However, we are trying to deal in reality.

The Hostess Alone

DEAR MISS MANNERS:

I do not have a maid. When I cook dinner for my guests, is it proper to leave the room repeatedly while checking the food in the kitchen? I'm speaking of times when my husband is not here to entertain guests. I feel uncomfortable doing this, as well as serving at table, such as bringing the soup in bowls, yet I don't see how else it could be done. Unless the answer is that all hosts should have partners. But there must be a way to conduct little parties if one is alone.

GENTLE READER:

You are certainly correct that, as there are two essential functions for a hostess to perform, feeding and talking, it is easier to have two people to perform them. If you have a child in the house old enough to walk, grab that. The quality of their talk is unreliable, but they make adequate servants and can often be persuaded to work merely for the opportunity to eavesdrop.

It is, however, possible to provide good meal service alone. Presuming that you have already figured out that you cannot serve food that requires a great deal of last-minute attention, "family style" service will keep your absences during dinner to a minimum. This means that the filling of plates is done by the hostess in full view and speaking distance of everyone, from the table itself or a nearby service table or tea cart. This should be viewed cheerfully as the only opportunity one has to show off to one's friends one's soup tureen or one's ability, or lack of, at carving.

Service à la Russe

It is a dreary convention of the modern etiquette business that the arbiter of manners assume that her followers are so modest in ambition or means as not to employ servants, at least not of proper training or in sufficient numbers.

Miss Manners is fed up with all this timidity and egalitarianism. Wouldn't you like to know how a dinner is properly served, whether or not you live to eat it that way? Miss Manners would like to tell you.

The place setting for each guest is called a cover, and it consists of a service plate (silver or china will do), all the necessary flatware except that for dessert, and stemmed glasses for water, and two or three wines, with the champagne.

On the service plate is the rolled napkin, with the place card on top; and above the plate is an individual saltcellar, ash tray, nut dish, and the handwritten menu.

To the right of the plate, from outside in, are the oyster fork nesting in the bowl of the soup spoon, the fish knife, the meat knife and the salad knife or the fruit knife; to the left, also from outside in, are the fish fork, meat fork, and salad or fruit fork. But, you protest, can't I eat both fruit and salad courses? Yes, yes, of course, but it is considered bad form to have more than three knives or forks on the table, so the salad or the fruit equipment is brought in on a tray when that course is served.

After the guest has been seated and removed the napkin, the oyster plate is put on top of the service plate; and when that is cleared, the soup plate (not bowl) is put on the service plate. The latter two are then removed together, with a heated plate put at the place. The rule is that a filled plate is always replaced by an empty one, and no place is without a plate until just before dessert.

(Don't you love this already? Aren't you ready to head for the employment office to recruit the personnel? Ask for someone who understands service à la Russe.)

As a filled plate is never put before a guest, the fish and meat courses must be served from platters. It is up to each guest to take notice of how many people each platter is expected to serve (one footman starts at one side of the table, while another starts opposite, with identical platters) and estimate his or her portion. No seconds, folks.

Before the dessert, everything is removed from the table except the wine and water glasses. (No, not the tablecloth and menus. No wonder it's so hard to get help nowadays. Who wants to work for a smarty?)

The table is then discreetly swept clear of all crumbs, except, of course, those who are invited guests.

Dessert (which may be subdivided into ices, sweets, and fruit, but never mind because the most you will ever see is the sweet, which may or may not be ice cream) comes next, followed by a fruit and cheese course—as Miss Manners was saying, the dessert plate is brought in with a doily on top, a finger bowl on top of that, a fork balanced on the left side of the plate and a spoon on the right.

The guest removes the doily and finger bowl, parks it to the left of the plate, and places the fork and spoon on either side of the plate before dessert is served. That, Miss Manners supposes, was the begining of self-service. And as that brings us around full circle, you will excuse Miss Manners, who is going into the drawing room for coffee.

(For the menu for a formal dinner, please see pp. 491–495.)

Waiting to Begin

DEAR MISS MANNERS:

I was brought up to wait for the hostess to begin before I started eating. Occasionally now, I am told by a hostess who has not yet been served herself, "Oh, please go ahead before it gets cold." I recognize that as a legitimate suspension of the rules, and even do it myself, sometimes, when I have guests. But what I can't handle is having my own guests just go ahead and start eating the minute they are served, without being asked by me to do so, because some of them do and others just sit there politely. If I don't start eating, even though some of the male guests might not yet have their food, I seem to be rebuking those who did; but if I do, I feel rude on behalf of those who have waited or who haven't been served yet. What is the polite way of doing this?

GENTLE READER:

The polite way of rebuking guests who have begun to eat without authorization is to say to them, "Oh, please go ahead," etc., while their mouths are full. The polite way to hedge, without rebuking anybody, is for the hostess to pick up her fork and hold it poised without putting it into her food.

(Please note that at parties with individual tables, someone must take the lead or nobody will be able to touch anything.)

Refusing Wine

DEAR MISS MANNERS:

I was always told that it was rude to cover your wine glass to stop wine you didn't want from being poured, but I saw a museum exhibit on manners that says this rule is as wasteful as "spraying a pig with Chanel No. 5." Was the rule just a way to show off, and should it be abandoned?

GENTLE READER:

Indeed, it was not wasteful, as the unspoken part of the rule was that all wine left untouched on the table belonged to the butler. You see that this is the opposite of piggishness. Dear Douglas Sutherland, in his book *The English Gentleman's Child,* offers his father's counterattack, which was to instruct the butler to "pour the wine over the offender's hand until it was removed."

Putting Out Candles

DEAR MISS MANNERS:

Who blows out the candles after a dinner party, and when? Does the hostess do it, and if so, does she do it after the guests have left the dining room, or while they are getting up from dinner?

GENTLE READER:

Miss Manners is amazed to hear of a household that is not equipped with a candle extinguisher (a snuffer cuts the wick, rather than snuffs the flame) and must depend on the windpower of the hostess. Ordinarily the candles are put out after the guests have left the dining room. However, Miss Manners has found that many guests refuse to budge after a good meal, and an effective way to speed them along is to extinguish one candle on the table, with the implied threat of leaving them in the dark. Besides, Miss Manners has a pretty candle extinguisher and likes to show it off.

Social Correspondence

Writing is such a useful social skill that Miss Manners is surprised that more people don't bother to learn it. She appreciates the fact that our school systems are overloaded with the task of teaching creativity and adjustment, but some of the happy people it turns out might enjoy writing if they tried it.

By writing, Miss Manners means the ability to compose a few clear statements and write them clearly, by hand. Such mechanical wonders as typewriters, telephones, greeting cards, and computers have not eliminated the need for writing by hand.

If you cannot master writing, you will:

Begin married life with the enmity of all four parents, whose friends' presents have not been acknowledged properly.

Not be able to get married in the first place, because you will be unable to address the invitations.

Find that your autograph becomes worthless at auction, because nobody can figure out whose it is.

Spend a lot of time having silly telephone conversations.

Discover that your family has been reading your diary from the typewriter ribbon.

Have to go to the expense of having your menu cards for formal dinner parties engraved.

Decrease your Christmas list, as people who couldn't read the signature on your cards stop reciprocating.

Never again be able to look in the eye some people for whom you care, because you didn't write them condolence letters when you know you should have.

Consider the difference, in time spent and effect achieved, between written and nonwritten methods for performing such a simple task as thanking a hostess for a dinner.

Written version: Grab clean paper, write, "Dear Olga-Marie,/What a marvelous dinner that was. The bean sprout soufflé was magnificent, and Sidney Mobile was as fascinating as you promised"; look for stamp, look up ZIP code, mail. Time: two minutes. Effect: hostess gets a touch of happiness among her bills.

Nonwritten version: Dial telephone, hang up, work up pitch of anger over fact that line is busy, try again, have conversation:

Guest: "Hey, that was a terrific party last night."

Hostess: "Well, I'm so glad you could come." (aside) "I don't know, dear, somebody from last night. Be with you in a minute."

Guest: "It was just great."

Hostess: "Thank you."

Guest: "Thank you for asking me."

Hostess: "Well, it was good to see you."

Guest: "It was good to see you."

Hostess: "Well, I'm so glad you could come."

Guest: "Oh, I was delighted to. Say, there's something I've been meaning to ask you. . . ."

Actually, there was nothing the guest was meaning to ask the hostess, having just spent the previous evening with her, but the guest can no longer bear the sound of his own inanities and doesn't know how to get off the telephone. Time: twenty minutes. Effect: Hostess decides that wit apparent previous evening must be credited to her own wine cellar.

You may notice that the silly statements of the telephone conversation are really no less original than those of the letter. That is the secret of handwritten sentiments and the reason that they are still considered necessary, and not just by finicky old snippets (mentioning no names).

Writing makes the most conventional statement, which would look dopey if printed, seem dignified. This is especially useful, as life's most important occasions are expressed in conventional phrases. Nobody ever felt cheered by the warmth of a card with "My Sympathy" printed in silver scrolls, or traced a typed "I love you" with a trembling finger. On the other hand, statements printed on T-shirts probably cannot be used in court as evidence against you.

Letters That Should Not Be Written

"Persons without a sense of humor always write long letters," observed dear Sir Herbert Beerbohm Tree, the great actor, "and I have noticed, too, that all madmen write letters of more than four pages. I will not venture to assert that all persons who write more than four-paged letters are mad. Still, the symptom should be watched.''

As Miss Manners recalls, dear Sir Herbert was referring to dear George Bernard Shaw when he spoke of madmen without humor, but nevertheless it has always seemed to her an observation of remarkable truth. We are all quite mad and humorless upon occasion, and we all seize those occasions to fire off letters of four pages or more. The symptom should indeed be watched.

Miss Manners encourages, even begs, people to write letters. She spends much of her life urging you to write business letters instead of arranging oral duels between your secretary and somebody else's about who is going to get on the telephone when; to write charming little notes to bolster the generous impulses of those who have offered presents, hospitality, and favors; to pen such simple sentiments as ''congratulations'' or ''I love you'' rather than waste time looking for commercial greeting cards to express them for you; and to conduct the interesting transactions of your life in such a way as to leave plenty of material for your biographer, perhaps even enough for a separate volume of letters, rather than a collection of little pink telephone message slips.

She recognizes, however, that there are some letters that ought never to be written. Most of them happen to be four pages long.

All letters that begin, ''Never in my life have I been subjected to such . . . .'' fit into the category of letters that ought not to be written. So do all letters that begin, ''You may not be aware of it, but I have feelings, too.'' (Miss Manners would go so far as to say that all people announcing, ''I'm a person, too,'' should be strictly avoided, at least until they have managed to pull themselves together.)

Letters explaining God's feelings, how they happen to coincide with the letter writer's, and what God plans to do to the receiver of the letter should not be written. These carry double violations, as they are traditionally nine pages long and have extra writing up the margins of the lined yellow paper on which they are written.

Threats in general, name calling, and other insults are not worth writing, because their effect tends to be humorous, rather than frightening. Letters correcting the information and grammar of others should probably not be written, but at any rate should not be written in high sarcasm, because they are bound to contain errors of their own.

It is not a good idea to write letters that make clear the existence of a relationship that the receiver has not confided to other people at the same mailing address, such as her parents or his wife.

Miss Manners would be remiss if she did not pass on to you a suggestion about what to do if you find yourself seized with the desire to write one of these letters. She turns again to dear Sir Herbert, who said, ''One of the most alarming signs of insanity, it has often seemed to me, is that of writing to the newspapers (invariably more than four pages) to prove that Hamlet was mad, and that Bacon wrote Shakespeare. . . . I am satisfied that many of the learned commentators have only been kept out of lunatic asylums by the energy which

ANDREA DORIA

Dear Daffodil,

    You seem to have forgotten, or perhaps you just don't care, that today is my birthday. Separated or not, I am still your husband, although I suppose you have forgotten that, too. I don't think you ever realized that I am a person, as much as you. I have feelings, too, you know, and

A letter that should not have been written, on paper that should not have been used once the passenger was no longer on shipboard.

they have expended in the harmless occupation of discussing these two kindred subjects in print.

"In many cases it has proved a most valuable safety-valve."

Writing Paper

A "stationery wardrobe" is something Miss Manners has been dearly longing to have, ever since she first heard the term. She thought it meant dresses that didn't play the trick of looking too short one year and too long the next and that didn't capriciously change their fit through the years.

If poor Miss Manners were able to spell, she would not have made such an embarrassing mistake. It turns out that a "stationery wardrobe" is the commercial term for what ladies and gentlemen refer to as "writing paper."

By that definition, Miss Manners has an ample wardrobe:

Cards, in the proper ladies' size, engraved with her name; fold-over "informal" cards with her name engraved on the front and little lined envelopes; flat cards, once known as "the new informals," with her name engraved on the upper center and her address above it on the right, also with little lined envelopes;

White double-sheeted paper with her monogram engraved in gray, to be used for serious letters written in black ink; cream double-sheeted paper with her monogram engraved in brown, to be used for frivolous letters written in brown ink; unmarked double white sheets for very grave letters indeed;

Large single sheets with her engraved address for business letters and the use of anyone in the house including guests; unmarked sheets for the second pages of such letters;

Red-bordered paper for Christmas letters; black-bordered paper for mourning (a leftover, rather than anticipatory item); and unbordered paper for lists and memoranda.

Perhaps you begin to see, as Miss Manners suddenly does, why all this is called a wardrobe. It is because it is full of expensive things one never uses because they are impractical, have gone out of fashion, or because the occasion for using them will never arrive. There is, for example, no modern justification for cards, more's the pity. (Miss Manners agrees with dear Nancy Mitford in refusing to call them "visiting cards" or "calling cards" on the grounds that those are what a dog leaves. On the grounds.) Even diplomats rarely pay formal calls anymore in America, where they could do nothing else including sleep if they followed the prescribed rounds. If you send enough flowers to justify keeping a supply of cards on hand, you are probably up to no good.

The unmarked sheets for second pages of business letters are useless because only crazy people write business letters of more than one page. The way to get unmarked paper for writing notes to yourself is to cut off the back of a double sheet after you have ruined the front sheet with an ink blot.

Miss Manners does not approve of gimmicky printed "memo" pads, writing letters from home on office or hotel paper, or filling in your own name on printed or partially engraved invitation or reminder cards. Here is what she recommends as a basic, tasteful wardrobe for all occasions:

Necessary: A large single sheet, unmarked or with an address, for the personal and business letters of everyone in the house.

Optional: A double sheet, plain or with a monogram, for a woman's personal letters of various degrees of formality; a single sheet with a man's full name and address if he wants it.

Useful: A postal-card-sized, thick card, with a woman's or couple's name and address, that can be used by itself for quick notes or in an envelope for invitations or notes with presents.

Smashing: A formal invitation card and matching reminder card, engraved with one's name and address, if one gives formal parties. Other written invitations may be issued in letters or on the cards.

There, now. Look at all that money Miss Manners has saved you. As a return favor, please invest it in the quality of the paper and of the engraving—or printing, if it is clear, frank printing. Engraving costs more initially, but subsequent orders, once one has the die, are much cheaper. Don't think Miss Manners can't tell the difference. She may not be able to spell, but she has a very sensitive fingertip.

Appropriating Paper

DEAR MISS MANNERS:

When you talk about proper stationery, I think you are putting your readers to an unnecessary, and sometimes actually counterproductive, expense. My law firm, for example, has beautiful letterhead paper, properly engraved in a way of which even you would approve. I find it does for almost all my needs; that, in fact, people pay more attention to such letters than they would to the complaints, for example, of an ordinary person on paper with just a name or street address. Hotels also provide impressive stationery, and using that— good hotels give you a generous supply you can take home with you—is beneficial to them, because of the advertising, as well as to the person who saves himself needless bother and expense. Why don't you advise your readers of this?

GENTLE READER:

Oh, that's not necessary. You should see Miss Manners' mail. At first glance, you would think that she is constantly carrying on important legal business or being thought of by people in the midst of the most luxurious trips. The misappropriation of writing paper to give a false impression has caught on very well, without any help from Miss Manners.

She thoroughly disapproves of the practice. Using your professional letterhead paper to conduct personal business suggests, fraudulently, that the full weight of your employer is behind your every private transaction. When you try to create the impression that the ire of your law firm will be felt if the vacuum cleaner part you ordered is not delivered soon, any simpleton can see that it is a bluff.

> *Mrs. Geoffrey Lockwood Perfect*

A woman's card. This is engraved with her formal name, which may be her husband's, or her own name in full with the title of Miss, Ms., or her medical, military or noble title. There may also be an address engraved in the lower right corner.

A man's card. No address is used, unless he moves into his club, in which case its name is engraved in the lower left corner.

> Mr. Geoffrey Lockwood Perfect

> GEOFFREY LOCKWOOD PERFECT
>
> PERFECT PRODUCTS
> 18 COMMERCE STREET
> BROOKDALE, CONNECTICUT   (203) 555-1212

A business card. No title is used before the name, although the person's position, such as "President," may appear below his name. The name of the company, its address and telephone number may be given, but its motto, cable address and six branch offices' addresses should be discreetly omitted.

A diplomat's card.

> *Perfect Pious*
> *Ambassador of the*
> *United States of America*

For the art of turning the corners of cards to convey secret messages, see page 509.

As for hotel paper, Miss Manners believes that it, like the soap, towels, and bedspreads, was meant to be used in transit by people who do not have their own such articles with them. A person who writes from his home town on paper from a distant hotel gives the recipient a vivid picture of his thriftily packing away in his suitcase whatever he thinks he can carry out of the hotel without being arrested. Miss Manners' favorite vision is created by a woman who has been for years using the paper of a famous ocean liner on which she once traveled. The ship is no longer in service, and when Miss Manners sees its name on a letter, she has a charming picture of the writer diligently keeping up her correspondence from the bottom of the sea.

Cards

The best card game in town has been busted up. Miss Manners has been left with some terrific cards in her hand, and no opportunity to play them.

Such cards are of bristol board and have engraved on them one's name and, in the case of a woman or unmarried man, one's address. The game was to run about town, leaving them on everyone, for purposes of welcoming, congratulation, condoling, thanking, taking leave of, or any other excuse for ringing other people's doorbells. Formal calling, when properly done, was a social form combining the maximum of effort with the minimum of communication.

In its way, this was the perfect social event. Strange that it should have died out. The custom survives, barely, in the diplomatic corps, where the necessity of acknowledging one's colleagues, at posts where there may be well over a hundred missions, is believed to promote world peace, in that it keeps the diplomats from engaging in more active diplomacy.

For private individuals, the card may still be used to enclose with flowers or presents, or to bear little messages, such as "Looking forward to Saturday," or to mark one's place in a book. There are those who say that the corners are excellent for dislodging luncheon remains from the teeth, but Miss Manners wouldn't know.

Naturally, only the very best engraved cards will do for any of these purposes. Women's cards should be 3⅛ inches by 2½ inches, give or take an eighth of an inch; and men's, oh, say 3¼ by 1⅝. Names and social titles are used, so that the sender looks friendly by crossing out the title in ink when the card is used.

Initials are never used on cards, and suffixes, such as junior, are spelled out in full. The card of a married woman or couple uses his name, so that one can stare at "Mrs. Hendrik Thinglebottom" without realizing that behind it lies Sally Wretzle, the airline president. In other words, these cards are uninformative, expensive, and useless. Miss Manners is extremely fond of them. Her honest advice to anyone tempted to order them is to invest, instead, in the comparatively new invention of the oversized card, a nonfolding version of what used to be called an "informal" card. The size should depend on the latest postal regulations, as the Post Office Department hates little cards and keeps making rules demanding larger and larger mail. This card is engraved with the name or joint name in the top center and the address in smaller letters in the upper right corner. It has room on it for notes, invitations, or replies to these.

Smaller cards have become the tool of business people who want to give their names to new associates in a more formal way than a lapel button reading "HELLO! I'm Gerry, your waiter." However, most business people mistake the card for the résumé, and try to cram on it such details as telex address, telephone numbers of four branch offices, and the company's motto and logo. The proper business card contains only the person's name, title, company name, one address, and one telephone number. This is quite as much as anyone needs to know about a stranger before deciding whether to extend the relationship. Besides, cards with too much engraving all over them make messy bookmarks.

Turning the Card

DEAR MISS MANNERS:

What is proper business card etiquette? Is there a way of folding the corner of the card to let the receiver of the card know how the card was left?

GENTLE READER:

Funny you should ask. Miss Manners occasionally brags about being the last living person to know the code of card turning, and then waits in vain for someone to say, "Well, then, what is it?" The code was not intended for business cards, but social cards, which are hardly used now that people imagine they have better things to do with their time than to ride about in their carriages all morning, paying calls on one another. So you may as well amaze and delight your business acquaintances, as well as mystify them, by turning cards on them.

There are four statements you are able to make just by bending little bits of pasteboard. They are, with their French names: *visite*, meaning that you have appeared with the card in person; *félicitation*, meaning that you congratulate the recipient; *congé*, which announces that you are leaving town; and *condolence*, which is, of course, an expression of sympathy.

Turn the upper left corner of the card for *visite*, the upper right for *félicitation*, the lower right for *condolence*, and the lower left for *congé*.

If you promise to revive this custom, Miss Manners will permit you to get funny with it by, say, turning both bottom corners for "Too bad, I'm leaving you" or both right corners for "Congratulations on your loss."

It is possible to express the same sentiments in abbreviated writing: "p.p.c." means "*pour prendre congé*," or " 'Bye, 'bye, you will see me no more." But that is making it too easy, don't you think?

Cards for Children

DEAR MISS MANNERS:

I have encountered a problem which other mothers may be facing and I do believe your expert opinion would be much appreciated. The situation is as follows: My young son, Elliott, age three, attends a lovely, very proper, private preschool. At the end of the school term, he wanted, as most generous youths do, to give his teacher a remembrance. We purchased a small but appropriate gift, and Elliott and I enjoyed the wrapping and making of a delightful construction paper note with his name drawn in his own dear hand.

However, Miss Manners, when little Elliott returned home, he was most distressed. It seems most of the other children had their own engraved cards to include in their gifts. Little Elliott had only his hand-drawn token. My question is—should I have little Elliott's cards engraved for him to include in future gifts? I do want to spare him every embarrassment. I need your answer as soon as possible, as little Elliott is invited to a small afternoon birthday party requiring a gift, and the question of the appropriate enclosure will again arise.

GENTLE READER:

For heaven's sake, do you realize there are children in the world starving who don't even have printed cards of their own, let alone engraved? Little Elliott has obviously fallen into bad company, although his own instinct for bribery indicates that he was a rotten apple to begin with. Save your anguish on his behalf. You will need it later.

Informals

DEAR MISS MANNERS:

Please tell me about the size, paper, printing (or engraving) of proper informals today, since the size of envelopes that can be mailed has changed. What is the choice of paper, color, and printing versus engraving? As one of the old school who had calling cards and informals engraved, we kept the metal form for using again. I see much printing now. What is correct?

GENTLE READER:

You said the magic word: proper. There are many designs now for writing short messages, which are neither proper nor improper. One can, for instance, have large cards in some pale color with one's name and address printed on them, and use them as postal cards or insert them in envelopes. These are rather attractive and very practical.

A proper informal card, however, is engraved in black ink on white rag paper. An improper one is a close variation of this—printing instead of engraving, or different colored ink or paper.

Every time Miss Manners discusses sizes for informal cards, the Post Office changes its regulations. The fold-over card, with one's name on the outside, is funny-looking in a large size, so it is more usual now to have a single card with one's engraved name centered at the top. In the fold-over version, one's address, in smaller lettering, was in the lower-right corner. On the new, single card, one's address is engraved on the upper right-hand corner, and one's name centered, slightly below that line. They must be at least three and a half inches by five inches.

In using your metal plate, the old address can be waxed out, and a new one put in. Engraving is an example of a principle of old school thrift: The initial expense of having the plate made is justified by its long usefulness.

DEAR MISS MANNERS:
Kindly advise me as to the correct way to mail my lovely and expensive informals, now that the ever-amazing Postal Service will no longer mail the smaller and more unusual letter sizes. Should I insert the informal and its envelope into a larger envelope, or grit my teeth and pay a highly inflated postage fee?
GENTLE READER:
Please do not grit your teeth. It cannot be good for them, and the sound bothers Miss Manners something fierce. Not that she doesn't appreciate the provocation given you by the Post Office in banning that useful social missive known as the informal. This is the same Post Office that some years ago made regulations that banned the personal or "visiting" card from the mails. It obviously does not understand the need so many citizens have for a card on which one can write only a few well-chosen words ("So sorry about last night!") and sign one's informal name ("Peaches"), knowing that one's full name ("Mrs. Bilkington Hazard, 4th") is there in all its glory.

One can send a postcard, of course. Imagine the above message sent on a postcard with a view of the seaside resort to which the sender has fled until the ignominious happenings of the previous evening should have been forgotten. A better choice is the alternate type of informal, invented when the Post Office made those first unpleasant rumblings. (Please see pp. 508–509.)

When you run out of your informals, Miss Manners suggests using the same engraving plate to have single-card informals made. But how are you going to run out, you wonder, if this person doesn't stop running on like that without answering your question? A good point. The answer, as you suspected, is to put the informal in its own envelope, and then into a larger, mailable envelope.

Penmanship

DEAR MISS MANNERS:
Must personal letters be written by hand? I type my letters because my handwriting is so bad people won't understand them otherwise.
GENTLE READER:
Yes, but you then expose your bad spelling, don't you? Miss Manners is appalled that penmanship is no longer taught in the schools, and advises you to go

immediately to a remedial writing class. In the meantime, type the letters in which you wish to convey information, such as the ones in which you threaten to sue appliance stores, and handwrite your letters to friends, thanking them for the egg poachers or sympathizing with them because their rich aunts died. In those cases, the fact of writing is more important than the information.

Ink

DEAR MISS MANNERS:

I am feeling very incorrect because I do not have black or blue-black ink, nor white letter paper. I have only green ink. Please tell me what I can do.

GENTLE READER:

Save up all your letters all year long and answer them at Christmastime.

Stamps

DEAR MISS MANNERS:

If I get an uncanceled stamp on a letter that comes to me in the mail, is it ethical to pick it off and use it again myself?

GENTLE READER:

No, but when you do, watch out for the Frank Lloyd Wright stamps. The lines in the Guggenheim Museum behind his head make it difficult to tell if the stamp was canceled or not.

Carbon Copies

DEAR MISS MANNERS:

My daughter-in-law doesn't write to me: she "carbons" me. That is, she writes frequent letters to my other daughter-in-law, who was, in fact, a college friend of hers and the one who introduced her to my younger son, and then she sends me carbon copies of those letters. I don't want to seem unreasonable about this, and I know that in large families, people might need to send around copies of letters because they just don't have time to write everyone individually, but in our case, it is just me and the two boys left, and it hurts me never to get a letter that isn't secondhand, except twice a year, on my birthday and Mother's Day. It seems to me that she could copy out the family news twice, without seriously cutting into her leisure time. I suppose you agree with her and think I'm being a difficult mother-in-law.

GENTLE READER:

Not at all. Miss Manners, who is difficult herself whenever it is politely possible, also dislikes carbons of letters. She once received a carbon of a letter to Dear Abby. Her feeling is that it brings families of any size closer together if, instead of writing everything the same way to everyone, one writes a different short piece of news to each. That way, in almost the same amount of time, one provides everybody with gossip for trading purposes.

A Reply

DEAR MISS MANNERS:

When the woman complained about the carbon copies of letters her daughter-in-law sent her, you overlooked a big question: Why was the daughter-in-law expected to write to her at all? Why isn't the son writing to his own mother? This seems to me to be a typical example of expecting the wife to do all the work—and then complaining about her on top of it. The only fair thing would be to have each person write to his or her own parents. Then there couldn't be any complaints.

GENTLE READER:

Oh, yes there could, but at least they wouldn't start out with unpleasant remarks about how the person was brought up.

Jailed Correspondents

DEAR MISS MANNERS:

I have a friend who is in jail (never mind how he got there), and I would like to stay friends. The trouble is that he writes me four and five pages of letters nearly every week, and is always asking me when I can come visit. In the first place, I don't have the time, and in the second place, I don't want to be that good friends. Once I explained that I can't come often because I have soccer practice, and he went into a whole big thing about how lucky I am that made me feel bad. I try to act normal with him, but it doesn't seem to work.

GENTLE READER:

No, it doesn't, quite. Miss Manners once, in arranging such a visit, asked, in her usually charming way, "When would be convenient for you?" The jailed gentleman replied, graciously, "Oh, any time. I'll be here."

The answer is that jail is not a normal situation, and anyone in it has probably noticed the fact. A friend who is in prolonged trouble—it could also be a nervous breakdown, or a drawn-out divorce—cannot expect others to curtail their lives accordingly. You need only explain that you will write and visit when you can, and then do so.

Keeping Love Letters

DEAR MISS MANNERS:

Where is a safe place to keep love letters? I don't want a moral lecture, just an answer. The relationship is over, but the letters are very beautiful and mean a lot to me. I can't keep them at home for obvious reasons, and I can't continue to keep them at the office, either, because he still works for the company (he was transferred out of town) and there are a lot of snoopy people here.

GENTLE READER:

The only safe place to keep damaging letters is in the fireplace, between burning logs. Miss Manners does not expect you to follow her advice in this matter; no one ever does. That is what used to make divorce cases so interesting. Now that no-fault divorce is becoming popular—its place in sensationalism having been taken by no-marriage divorce—you may at least be comforted that your letters will go no further than the discoverer and everyone he can manage to tell by word of mouth.

✿ ADDRESSES, OPENINGS, AND CLOSINGS

Addressing Couples

DEAR MISS MANNERS:

When is it correct to address mail to "James and Mathilda Jones," rather than "Mr. and Mrs. James A. Jones?" I confess that the former method circumvents charges of sexism, yet it raises questions of informality and excessive familiarity. Please clarify the current thinking.

GENTLE READER:

It is only too true, as your letter makes clear, that we live in times when the possibilities for unintentional insults are limitless. Miss Manners considers both styles of address you mention to be acceptable, but agrees that each will probably offend some people before they even open the letter. Miss Manners suggests that you either stop worrying about this silly form of insult catching, or hand deliver your letters, in which case you may write "Mr. and Mrs. Jones" on the envelope.

DEAR MISS MANNERS:

I am so worried I just don't know what to do. I have recently received a perfectly gorgeous Wedgwood vase for a wedding present. (Jasper and I have been married two weeks.) The gift was sent by two friends of Jasper's parents, a doctor and a sales executive. But (Lord help us all in this new age) the doctor is the woman!

My problem is how to address the thank-you note. Mr. and Mrs. Roger Thornburg can't be correct—it simply does not recognize the woman's professional status—and Mr. and Dr. Roger Thornburg simply does not make any sense. I suppose to recognize the status of each, I could put both names—Mr. Roger Thornburg and Dr. Loretta Thornburg—but my neighbor tells me that way would indicate they are simply "Living together." I certainly would not want to do that.

It has now been ten days since I received the gift, and I feel dreadful for not having sent a note yet. Please answer as soon as possible. I have never delayed sending a thank-you for so long.

GENTLE READER:

Lord help us, as you so aptly say, in this new age. Miss Manners does not know, any more than you do, the personal preference of the Thornburgs. It is possible that they go by the old standard of not using the woman's medical title socially, and would be insulted if you did so. It is possible that they go by the new standard of using medical titles for women, and would be insulted if you did not do so.

It is possible that they are so unbearably touchy that they would manage to be insulted even if you used both their names and both their titles, and would wave your envelope about furiously, screaming, "So she doesn't think we're married, does she?" Miss Manners tends to doubt that. With the same last name, they are either married or brother and sister, and neither is something of which to be ashamed. If it were true, she would not worry about it, on the grounds that they were incapable of being satisfied. So go ahead and address them as "Dr. Loretta Thornburg and Mr. Roger Thornburg." It is also possible that these are nice people who would never dream of your returning their kindness with insult, and wouldn't much care what you put on the envelope so long as they could learn, from the contents, that you and Jasper are pleased with the Wedgwood vase.

Doctors and Doctorates

DEAR MISS MANNERS:

Several women doctors I know are extremely sensitive about being addressed socially as "Doctor." One of them is married to a "Mr." and another to a Ph.D. I created a furor by sending them cards addressed to Dr. and Mr. What is the correct way to do it?

GENTLE READER:

Illicit love has given us, if nothing else, the two-line method of address, which may also be applied to married couples with different titles or names. The doctor and Mr. may be addressed as:

Dr. Dahlia Healer
Mr. Bryon Healer

and the doctor and academician, if he uses his title socially, which not all holders of doctorates do, as:

Dr. Dahlia Healer
Dr. Bryon Healer

or as:

The Doctors Healer

or as:

The Doctors Bryon and Dahlia Healer.

DEAR MISS MANNERS:

My husband and I are both Ph.D.s and not fussy about how we are addressed. I mean, we don't make a big thing about being called "Doctor." Our friends just write our first and last names on letters, without any title, and that's fine. Older people usually address us as "Mr. and Mrs.," and that's fine, too. But a cousin of my husband's addressed us as "Dr. and Mrs.," and that's where I draw the line. It seems to suggest that my Ph.D. doesn't count as much as his.

GENTLE READER:

Miss Manners supports the old-fashioned usage, which means that only medical doctors, not Ph.D.s, use "Doctor" socially. (Please see pp. 71–73.) However, she is in agreement that the form of addressing you and your husband should be uniform.

Salutation

DEAR MISS MANNERS:

When you address an envelope, it is correct to say Mr. and Mrs. John Murphy, using the man's first name or initial. When you write your note on the inside, you usually say Dear Mary and John—or should you say Dear John and Mary? We've had a discussion about whether it is correct to use the man's name first, or the woman's.

GENTLE READER:

The woman's. Miss Manners refuses to get into the discussion of why, because if the minute explanations go beyond the conventional into an exploration of possible reasons and symbolism, there is going to be big trouble.

Closings

DEAR MISS MANNERS:

My son learned in school to sign all his letters—even the ones the class wrote to the President—with "Your friend." I think it sounds insincere when he writes it to anyone but a real friend, and as a matter of fact, he and his friends don't write to each other, anyway. What should I suggest to him that would be more realistic?

GENTLE READER:

If conventional letter endings were expected to be sincere, we would not be able to use such a convenient form as "Yours sincerely"—let alone "Yours very truly"—and would all have to sign our business correspondence with "Cautiously yours." "Your friend" is for small children only; you must warn him to turn sincere and true by age ten.

DEAR MISS MANNERS:

I am seeing a young man—how shall I say?—intimately, but not yet necessarily seriously. I would not be sorry if it turned out to develop into something permanent, but we are not at that stage at the moment. At any rate, he has now had me twice to visit his parents, who have been very lovely to me. I am fond of them quite aside from my relationship with their son, and am grateful for their warm hospitality. In writing them thank-you notes, I would like to express my affection, but I am afraid that if I signed my letters "affectionately" or "love," they might get the idea that I am presuming on the relationship— that I, in other words, have expectations of coming into the family. This would not be a good idea to plant at this time. How about "cordially?"

GENTLE READER:

Please, no. "Cordially" in a letter closing is a word that Miss Manners, and other authorities before her, particularly dislike. In the 1922 Emily Post, it is singled out as being a "coined" word that is both "condescending" and "pretentious."

Conventions were invented specifically to allow a person to retreat from having to make choices in situations open to misinterpretation. "Sincerely yours" is a perfectly good closing, neither cold nor warm. Miss Manners quite agrees that this is not the time to suggest that you feel like a daughter to these people, and she would rather see you err on the side of formality than of intimacy.

GREETING CARDS
AND CHRISTMAS LETTERS

Greeting Cards

DEAR MISS MANNERS:

I buy greeting cards from certain veterans' and charitable organizations. In one box, I found the usual birthday and get well cards, and also congratulations cards. I always thought that those were for graduates and people getting married. Now I notice they also say "Congratulations to you"—as if for one person only. That leaves the married ones out, and also they never look like cards to be sent to a graduate. Can these congratulations cards be sent to someone on his birthday?

GENTLE READER:

It is one of the ambitions of Miss Manners' life, one of the futile ambitions, she should say, to get people to write letters or even short notes expressing their feelings. A handwritten sentence, such as "Congratulations on your graduation," is so much kinder than any printed sentiment. It is less expensive than buying cards, and easier than the effort people put into selecting a card that says what they want to say, when all they had to do was say it directly.

No matter. It is a hopeless cause. Congratulations can as well apply to birthdays as any other pleasant milestone, and "you," in the English language, is both singular and plural. Don't bother sending Miss Manners a printed card reading "Thanks for the advice."

"Get Well"

DEAR MISS MANNERS:
Is it considered proper to send a "get well soon" card to a Christian Scientist?
GENTLE READER:
Certainly. A Christian Scientist may disagree with you about treatment but, as Miss Manners understands it, has no objection whatever to the prospect of getting well.

Christmas Cards

It is not the junk mail from business concerns that Miss Manners minds so much as the junk mail one's relatives, friends, and acquaintances send out under the impression that they are conveying good wishes for holidays.

The Christmas card, or the ecumenical holiday season card, is a fine institution if properly used. The custom of taking time at the end of the year to keep in touch with those whom one does not ordinarily see or write to is a charming one. However, signing one's name to printed inanities, or mimeographing a composition in which one brags about one's petty triumphs over the year, is not keeping in touch. Keeping in touch means writing one's sentiments with one's very own hand. These may be a full letter, or only the words "Merry Christmas," but one must write this oneself.

At Christmastime, there are many different types of paper and cards that may be used for this purpose. Miss Manners, who is ordinarily strict about the colors of papers and inks, gets giddy enough at Christmas to enjoy the use of red or green, in inks, borders of cards, and lining of envelopes. She would even allow pictures in good taste, which may sometimes include those of one's own family. To those who feel that the Hi-There Greeting Card Co. has perfectly captured their feelings in one of its limericks, Miss Manners will only add the requirement that they nevertheless write out a message, however brief, between the poesy and the signature.

Now comes the question of to whom these cards should be sent. The Post Office is obviously straining beyond its powers already, just trying to deliver people's Social Security checks, so perhaps some restraint should be used.

Miss Manners considers it superfluous to mail holiday wishes to those whom one offers such wishes to face to face, although one certainly may if one wants to. At the other end of the list, she suggests crossing off people whom one would no longer recognize if they fell over one on the street.

What remains is the people one actually knows and likes, but cannot see or write to often during the year because of problems of time or distance.

It might help to consider the extent of such people's interest. In some cases, they might find it sufficiently pleasant just to know that they are remembered. In others, there may be an eager audience for family news. It is unlikely, however, that anyone's interests extend to three pages of single-spaced purple mimeographing. Furthermore, such Christmas letters are usually highly biased bits of reporting, rarely containing the sort of juicy news that is of real general interest. They tend to run to the children's new teeth, rather than to Mommy's new lover.

The final word Miss Manners offers on the subject of dignity in Christmas cards is the plea that they be properly addressed and properly signed. This rules out the use of such catchalls as "and family"; if you can't address people by their proper names, then you address the card to those whose names you know, asking to be remembered also to "the children" or "your father."

The signature on a Christmas card should include a last name, and the envelope a return address. The only excuse for leaving them off and thus forcing your friends to play guessing games is the hope that the mystery will encourage them to drop you from their list before you drop them from yours.

The Christmas Letter

DEAR MISS MANNERS:

OK—what is really wrong with mimeographed Christmas letters? I know a lot of people make disparaging remarks about them, but suppose you have a lot of friends and can't possibly sit down and write each one a separate letter? Isn't the newsletter once a year actually a good way of informing people about your activities? I would find it helpful if, instead of looking down on this, you set some rules about how to write them. Our Christmas list has more than one hundred names on it, and I don't know any other practical way of letting our friends know what has happened to us—about our month at the beach house, Junior's new braces, my husband's promotion, and so on.

GENTLE READER:

Far be it from Miss Manners to look down on anyone so fortunate as to have more than a hundred friends so close as to be awaiting the news about your son's teeth. You will forgive her if she suggests that so high a degree of intimacy is not often maintained on the basis of a mass mailing once a year.

In other words, the trouble with mimeographed letters is that they are almost inevitably inconsistent with the relationship between writer and recipient. Friends and relatives who have a genuine interest in the details of your family life deserve some personal attention. If they can get through the year without wondering where you spent the summer, the chances are they are not burning to know now. And to bombard casual acquaintances with full accounts of your lives is to satisfy curiosity they may not feel.

So much for why Miss Manners dislikes the idea. Now to answer your question about how to do it. First, make the thing legible. Most of them are smudgy. Next, refrain from bragging. You wouldn't stand up at a party and shout

"Lauren was made cheerleading captain!" or "We bought a boat!" or "We went to Maine last summer!" or "I got a raise!" Confine your "news" to more or less public matters—"We've moved to Colorado," "I've finally finished law school," "Annabelle has joined the Army"—and state them neutrally. The exception is that births, engagements, and marriages include mention of the family's pleasure in them—although, come to think of it, why haven't these close friends of yours been notified of such important events at the time that they occurred?

Another rule is to refrain from offering your philosphy, politics, or general wisdom gleaned from life. If the urge overwhelms you, it is better to write leaflets and hand them out to strangers on the street, than to offend your friends by giving them unsolicited advice.

Finally, sign the letters with your own sweet little hand. Surely you can manage that much for close friends. Better yet, write a few words, even if they are only "Have a merry Christmas." Better still, put those words on a blank card and put them in the mail, just to show your friends that you think enough of them to take a minute for each alone. Christmas cards are the only form of correspondence in which one person can take the liberty of signing for another.

When signing a card, please, Miss Manners begs you, err on the side of more information, rather than less. This means including your surname to nearly everyone but close blood relatives, and even making it clear which names belong to the parents and which to the children. You'd be surprised how many people stare blankly at such signatures as "Lisa, Adam, Kimberly, and John" without knowing which of these people, if any, is a dear pal.

The signature form Miss Manners prefers is:

Jonathan and Kimberly Awful

Lisa and Adam

The parents are the ones with the surname. The man's name is written first to follow the "Mr. and Mrs." order, or because the woman has done the signing and therefore puts herself second. If the man has signed for both, his name should be second. Children are listed by seniority. The family pet is not listed at all. He is expected to handle his own social responsibilities.

Not Sending Cards

DEAR MISS MANNERS:

I do not wish to send Christmas cards. What is the procedure of handling this? Should I tell relatives and friends before they send them to me and make me feel guilty?

GENTLE READER:

Of the three activities you mention—sending Christmas cards, notifying everyone that you are not sending cards, and feeling guilty—sending cards seems to Miss Manners to be the least trouble. However, there is nothing wrong with doing none of these activities.

Presents

Presents are never given because they are felt to be obligatory, but because people enjoy expressing their affection and appreciation in a tangible form. You choose a present when something catches your eye and suggests itself as a source of delight for a particular person. When you receive a present, your pleasure in it and in the feeling it symbolizes obliterates any awareness of its material worth.

Do you believe this? Miss Manners is trying to. People keep interrupting her by asking if they have to give something to this person or that, how little they can get away with spending, how they can get others to give them something they want rather than something of that person's choosing, and what do they do about people who give cheap presents or none at all. What a nasty, troublesome business it all seems to have become. Miss Manners is beginning to think that nobody deserves to get anything until we all manage to get greed under control.

Miss Manners will now answer those calculating questions, and then she wants to hear no more of them:

If you care enough about a person to spend Christmas or some personal occasion (birthday, wedding, graduation, anniversary, and so on) with him or her, it is customary to give a present. If you care, but will not be participating in the celebration, it is still nice to send a present. If you don't care at all, but the other person seems to expect you to, perhaps has sent you an announcement, you may send a warm letter and no present.

You should realize what Miss Manners is doing for you in saying this. She is allowing you to cut from your Christmas list those with whom present exchanging has become an empty gesture and is relieving you from investing more than a few kind words in a wedding, for example, that doesn't mean anything to you. She expects you to ignore the fact that some presents that you expect will not arrive.

This is another extremely important point. No one has a right to expect presents, and, therefore, attempts to choose them—manipulating others into buying for you things that you want to buy for yourself—are inappropriate on any occasion. Does this mean that Miss Manners is a curmudgeon opposed to little children writing their wishes to Santa? Well, yes, as a matter of fact. It is charming for a person who wants to give a present to find out, by whatever subtle means, what the other person would like; it is not charming for the recipient to volunteer the information to whoever will listen.

If you get something you absolutely don't want, you may quietly exchange it, donate it to charity, or give it to someone who would appreciate it. You cannot moan over the loss of money involved, which could have been applied to something else.

That brings Miss Manners to her final word on the subject of budgeting presents. One spends a reasonable amount in terms of one's own resources—not the resources or hopes of the recipients—to get as nice a present as one can. What does "nice" mean? It means that you never give anything below your own taste level—something you wouldn't want, but suppose is good enough for others. It means that the present must be thoughtful, whether you made it for free or spent a lot; that it was chosen to please that particular person.

The one rule about money is that you not overwhelm someone by giving something so valuable as to be inappropriate to the relationship or occasion. But, then, a well-bred person, not being aware of cost, wouldn't notice it if you did.

In Miss Manners' philosophy of present buying, the following ideas should be rejected:

1. The present that exactly reflects the interest of the person to whom it is given, such as giving a bug collector the latest book on comparative feelers, or a jogger the new designer bag for collecting sweat.

2. The present of a promise of service: twenty nights of baby-sitting with your menage, or eleven certificates for pruning your hedge.

Miss Manners' reasoning on the first is as follows: The person who has a specialized interest knows more about it than the present giver. Having already cast his or her eye on all the bug books or jogging equipment, he has already, from superior knowledge, approved some things and rejected others. If your choice is something he has wanted, the chances are he has also acquired it, even if it meant mortgaging the children, your true expert being something of a fanatic. If he has not done so, it is probably because he has considered the object and scorned it.

As for those certificates for services to be rendered during the year, they are indeed charming and cheap to give. The reason they are cheap is that both the donor and the recipient know perfectly well that they are not collectable. Just wait until that muggy day when your dear friend lets you know that his hedge needs trimming.

Having delivered herself of these dampening options, Miss Manners might be expected to announce that one should give money or "gift certificates." Wrong again. Miss Manners objects to money as a present on the grounds that the recipient knows exactly what you paid for it. The charming equivalent of giving money is to give something that is easily returnable, and not to seem to stare at your friend's mantelpiece on New Year's Day, as if you were wondering where it was.

A more positive approach is to select something among those things of which one cannot ever have enough. In this case, you are paying attention not to the expertise of the receiver, but to his or her style. What falls into this category? Bottles of wine, diamonds, and homemade cookies.

Disappointing Presents

Accepting a present graciously is not much of a problem when the present turns out to be tickets for a Caribbean vacation. In that case, Miss Manners trusts you to emit the proper cries of surprise and joy, to place your hands over your face in the classic posture of one who is overwhelmed, to place your arms around the donor in another classic posture, and to confuse, in your expressions of gratitude, the attractions of the gift with those of the giver.

What if the surprise is not of the pleasant variety? Can Miss Manners trust you to behave properly when given a present that disappoints you?

From greediest childhood, we build up so many expectations about presents that the chances of being let down are statistically higher than those of feeling unworthy of the bounty showered upon us. You can guess, of course, that Miss Manners' general rule in such instances is to fake the reaction she has described for you in detail. The ability to look delighted when not—now that is truly a gift. You should, of course, modify this until it is plausible. But Miss Manners will also allow a form of, shall we say, constrained delight, to be used in cases where it is possible to warn the giver, without outright hurting of feelings, that more care another time might produce a better result. This reaction consists of a wide smile made with closed lips, and accompanied by a bright-eyed but sober look. The words are, "Why, how nice!" Promise Miss Manners that you will not employ this to encourage more expensive presents—only more appropriate ones.

Here is a brief guide to disappointing presents, with notations as to which deserve unrestrained gratitude, and which constrained gratitude:

Useless Presents

Unrestrained: handmade ceramic ashtray from child to nonsmoking parent.

Constrained: silver cigarette case from longtime lover to person who has never smoked, especially if engraved with wrong initials.

Useful Presents

Constrained: equipment for baking bread at home to mother who has just reentered job market.

Unrestrained: Crockpot to ditto, who had hoped for attaché case.

Tasteless Presents

Unrestrained: knitted toilet seat cover from person who has knitted covers for all own toilets.

Tasteful Presents

Constrained: Coffee table book on antiques from person with formal old house to one who has glass house with high tech furniture.

Unacceptable Presents

Furs, jewelry, yachts from person one doesn't know very well.

This calls for a third response. The mouth curves in a half-smile of regret before and after the protest, but the eyes shine.

"What Did You Bring Me?"

DEAR MISS MANNERS:

Can you give me some suggestions for gifts for children? My husband and I spend the winter in Florida or the Caribbean every year, and shopping for the grandchildren there has gotten to be a pain. If we bring them back clothes, either they don't fit or they don't like them because they're not what all the other children are wearing. (Of course not—if they were, they wouldn't be souvenirs of a trip to a different place.) If we get toys, they already have them. If we buy curios or decorative items, such as weavings or pictures, they're not interested in them. Whatever we bring, they are disappointed with. And yet the first thing they always say when we walk in the door is, "What did you bring me?" There are four of them, ranging in age from three to nine and a half.

GENTLE READER:

Why, pray, do you wish to bring presents to these children? Surely not to see the childish delight break on their merry little faces. Your duty, as a grandmother, is not to feed their insatiable and ungrateful appetites, but to cure them from the multiple rudeness of "What did you bring me," which combines greed with insensitivity.

The ways in which grandparents can teach manners to children, when the parents do not, are limited. You cannot train them to behave well in general, but you can insist on their doing so to you, which will not only make your life more pleasant, but inform them that there are higher standards of behavior than those with which they are familiar at home. If you have your grandchildren as house-guests, or perhaps take an older one on a trip with you, you can insist that your preference in manners be observed. Miss Manners considers this of sufficient importance to suggest to you that you think of ways to include these young people in your life under such circumstances.

When you are visiting them, you cannot impose rules different from those permitted by their parents. But you can, and should, refuse to cater to the attitude suggested by their demand. Children should learn that they must pretend not to expect presents, to the extent that they must look surprised at the regular birthday and Christmas offerings, and even more so at such less traditional occasions, such as the return from a trip. They must also learn to look pleased with whatever they get. And finally, they must treat the giver as if what pleases them most about the present is the thoughtfulness of the giver, because however much they love things, they love people more. This is a difficult order for a small child, and no less important because it is not true. If they learn to behave as if it is, the better sentiment will gradually merge with the basic lust for possessions, and make finer persons.

Therefore, Miss Manners is going to answer your question by recommending the toughest present you can give, although it has the advantage of being cheap: nothing. Brave their disappointment by ignoring it, until it becomes clear to them that the valuable thing you have brought them is the presence of their grandparents. When they have been shocked into understanding this, give them the present of an excursion with you, or a visit. Then, when they have learned to control themselves and at least to fake an interest in you, you can resume, on an irregular basis, bringing them presents. By that time, you should have gotten to know them, as well, and therefore you will be better able than Miss Manners to judge what would please them.

Presents from Beaux

DEAR MISS MANNERS:
What, these days, is considered to be the kind of present that a respectable girl can accept from a young man? In my day, it was only candy, flowers, or books, but I suppose that has changed. Is it all right now for a young woman like my daughter to accept expensive presents when she is not engaged? What about clothing—should that be only after an engagement?

GENTLE READER:
Whenever Miss Manners hears the phrases "these days" and "in my day," she knows there is trouble. You and your daughter are squared off across the generations, you standing tight-lipped, trying to hold your ground, while she taunts you with the passage of time. Oh, dear. What is all this over? A fur coat? A condominium? A gold compact?

No, it's probably over a digital watch. That is what has changed, "these days."

The old rule is that a lady never accepts anything personal or expensive from a gentleman to whom she is not engaged. In other words, anything that she can't give back, either because it would be embarrassing to remove it or because she couldn't bear to part with it, should not be accepted. A lady who is engaged may accept expensive presents from her fiancé, but not ones that suggest he is supporting her. A diamond necklace is now acceptable, for example, but a utilitarian object, such as a sweater, is not.

These rules still apply, although Miss Manners feels obliged to mention that they were not always strictly obeyed. Another thing that has not changed is what a lady who accepts an expensive present from a gentleman is expected to do in return.

No Presents

DEAR MISS MANNERS:

I am about to go into retirement and wish to stop sending gifts, due to insufficient retirement income. I am a godmother to two girls (same family) and wish to stop sending birthday and Christmas gifts after both girls pass age twenty-one. How do I not hurt the older girl's feelings by continuing to send the younger girl gifts but not any to her?

GENTLE READER:

By explaining the situation to her. If *her* feelings are hurt by the fact that *your* income is insufficient, then this girl's godmother has neglected her spiritual education.

Unwanted Presents

DEAR MISS MANNERS:

What could be done with holiday and birthday gifts that are of no value or use to the receiver? I have in possession several gifts that I can't use. Several years ago, I read that it's only proper to give unworthy gifts to charity for resale, but with garage sales so popular, I'd give it a try myself.

GENTLE READER:

Properly speaking, there is no such thing as an unworthy present, so you may dismiss what you read about disposing of them. The minimum use that a present has, no matter how dreadful an object it is, is to please the giver with the mistaken notion that you appreciate it. If you are clever, you may keep this misconception alive through your thanks, while quietly ridding yourself of the offensive object by returning it to the store whence it came, selling it, or giving it away. The only thing to make sure of while doing any of these things is that the person who gave the present is unaware of this transaction. Do not have him at your garage sale.

Price Tags

DEAR MISS MANNERS:

What is your opinion of people who purposely leave the price tag on gifts in order for the giftee to be aware of the generosity of the giftor?

GENTLE READER:

That the least they can do is to scream as the person is opening the present, lean over and pull the price tag off, and drop it into a nearby ashtray, where it can be left, to be examined at leisure by everyone.

DEAR MISS MANNERS:

I have been corresponding recently with a young lady who attends the same university as I. For my birthday, she was kind enough to send me an amusing card; therefore, as her birthday approached, I naturally attempted to reciprocate. Unable to locate a suitable card, I wandered into a bookstore. I chanced upon a remaindered copy of a recent critically acclaimed novel, and I soon found myself outside the bookstore, having purchased a clothbound book and intending to present it in lieu of a greeting card.

Should I "forget" to remove the price tag from the book? Clearly I do not wish for her to think that I am so boorish as not to know that one removes all indications of price from a gift before presenting it. In addition, I have a natural desire not to appear miserly. I fear, however, that it would appear gauche to present a gift which seems much more considerable than a mere greeting card. I am also somewhat fearful, owing to the shortness of our acquaintance, of appearing to place more weight on our acquaintance than she does. My mother taught me that one always attempts to make the gifts one gives to friends of equal worth with the gifts given one. Due to the circumstance under which the book was purchased, however, the two presents—the greeting card and the book —are in fact of comparable value. I can think of no graceful way of informing her of this, save by "forgetting" to remove either the price tag or the sales slip.

GENTLE READER:

Have no fear. Miss Manners always thinks of graceful ways of doing disgraceful things. In this case, she is particularly happy to be of help, as you have learned the basic lesson so well at your mother's knee: Although no nice person ever indicates or acknowledges what a present received or given is worth materially, it is polite to keep exchanges even, and not embarrass people by upping the ante. Most children would tax their poor mothers with the inherent contradiction in this lesson, but that is because the young think that life should be logical. Do not leave the price tag on your book, or the sales slip inside. Instead, write a short note with the present saying, "I hope you didn't read this when it came out—I am an habitué of remainder bookstores, and when I saw this, I thought you might like it."

Plastic Covers

DEAR MISS MANNERS:
Would you please tell me the proper way to give sheets as presents? I often give sets of sheets as wedding presents or for housewarmings, and never know if I should remove the plastic cover and the pictured enclosure. If I do remove these, it may cause problems if the person wants to return the sheets, but at the same time, it seems a bit crass to leave them on.

GENTLE READER:
Miss Manners feels you are taking a defeatist attitude about your presents when you anticipate their being returned. If you had the courage of your convictions, you would have the sheets monogrammed. However, that was not your question, was it? As long as the price tag is removed, Miss Manners does not see what is crass about leaving the plastic covering. As for the picture, it seems harmless but unnecessary, as most people can figure out on their own how sheets work.

Personal Presents

DEAR MISS MANNERS:
I often perceive in your guidelines unresolved and potentially explosive issues that have been swept under the rug by today's gentry, or paraded in the guise of etiquette. Trusting your expertise to be upright and right-on at the same time, I direct my question to you. I will know, by your response, whether I am to be considered militantly feminist, outrageously gauche, or simply inexperienced if I carry out my plan.

Mother always warned me that gifts bestowed by a beau should never refer to the bedroom or related activities thereof. This includes such articles as: negligees, lingerie, bathrobes. By the same token, I have found a lovely satin bathrobe/smoking jacket which I would like to give my beloved. My dilemma is: Would I be flagrantly ignoring a hard-and-fast rule, or am I wandering onto the rocky road of changing social morals?

GENTLE READER:
Miss Manners never, ever sweeps dirt under the rug; she prefers to gather it up and plant flowers in it. In your case no such effort is necessary. This is one of these rare occasions in which tradition, conscience, and personal preference all agree. The choice of whether to be militantly feminist, outrageously gauche, or simply inexperienced (Miss Manners would choose one and three with an extra plate of eggrolls) may be avoided.

Your mother said you should never accept articles related to the bedroom. You should listen to your mother, and listen carefully. She never said you shouldn't give such presents, did she? Anyway, your beloved should not be smoking in bed. Tell him that Miss Manners said it is dangerous, and that he should wear his smoking jacket in the smoking room.

Forgotten Presents

DEAR MISS MANNERS:

I brought two nice gifts from Europe (value about thirty dollars) for a friend who house-sat for us in our absence. My return and presentation of the gifts coincided with her decision to move to another city, and she left them on our living room coffee table. Even though she visited the house four more times, the largish items remained in the place where she left them and she never said a word. She has now moved away. I don't really feel like storing them for her until she remembers them a year or so from now—if she does.

GENTLE READER:

Perhaps your house-sitter has come to feel that your house is a second home for her. This sentiment should be discouraged. As you are not obligated to give the same present more than once to the same person, you might present them to someone else and cultivate a confused look in case she ever asks you for them.

Decent Dress
for Ladies and Gentlemen

"What shall I wear?" is society's second most frequently asked question. The first is, "Do you really love me?" No matter what one replies to either one, it is never accepted as settling the issue.

The only sensible answer to the clothes question is one that Miss Manners learned long ago, when she was confined to a women's college dormitory, an educational experience if ever there was one. In that establishment, everyone asked "What shall I wear?" all of the time so that, once dressed, they could go out and ask the other question.

"Wear your yellow silk, dear," a wise young woman used to reply each time the question was asked. It spared her a great deal of idiotic conversation about other people's wardrobes and how they felt about each item. However, Miss Manners is willing to discuss categories of dress. The terms in current use are Formal, Informal, Semiformal, Don't Dress, and Optional. None of them means anything.

Once, some of them did have meaning. Informal meant black tie, or what some people now call Formal, and Don't Dress meant dark suits, or what other people now call Formal. What Semiformal is, Miss Manners has never discovered, although it gives her a vivid picture of someone in tails with unmatched pants. Optional is, of course, the same as saying nothing at all, but trying to make it sound organized.

You will notice that Miss Manners always explains the specifics in terms of men's clothes. This is because the difference between a woman's most formal dress and her second most formal dress is whatever she wishes to make it, while the difference between a man's is down there in black and white, even before he gets the statement from the rental agency. For that reason, invitations that mean white tie or black tie come right out and say so. No other designations should appear on invitation cards, because they will only confuse the issue.

Ah, you say, but then, what do I wear? Miss Manners knew you were going to ask that. You have been invited to a dinner that has one of the above meaningless designations on the card, or no instructions at all, and your yellow silk is at the cleaners. The general rule here is custom. In many communities, everyone knows that "Just wear anything" means anything from the designer salon, or else anything from the floor of your closet, and "We're going to dress up" means either that we're all going to look smashing, or else we're all going to comb our hair. If you don't know, you ask. The trick is to ask a question that can be answered. "What shall I wear?" is not such a question. Hostesses all think that it's charming to answer, "Oh, anything," and then let you turn up in jeans when everyone else is in diamonds, or the reverse. A slightly better question is, "What are *you* going to wear?" but the answer is likely to be "Oh, probably a caftan," and you won't know if it's an heirloom or a bathrobe.

Miss Manners suggests questions such as "Do you mean jeans?" or "Should Alphonso wear a tie?" or "Are long skirts being worn?" Not only do such questions yield more information, but they sound less whiny than "What shall I wear?"

Informality

It is with inexplicable pride that people describe themselves, their homes, and their dinner parties as "casual" or "informal." From the tone of voice in which just about everyone says, "Oh, of course, it's to be *terribly* informal," or "We're *always* casual," you would think that America now is like the court of Louis XIV, and that they, alone, have introduced some spontaneity.

Properly, "informal" means "black tie," as opposed to "formal," which is "white tie," a rather charming style now kept alive chiefly by magicians and pianists. Instead of either one of those, we now have a dreadful thing called "black tie optional" for occasions before which one is expected to wash one's ears extra carefully, and for all other occasions, a worse style that others are calling "casual" and "informal," by which they mean that they don't plan to take any trouble.

When Miss Manners longs for a bit of style in daily living, she is by no means thinking only of styles that were associated with the rich. Until recent times, both rich and poor people distinguished between their work clothes and "Sunday best," between meals on the run and company dinner, between the back room and the front parlor. This distinction was not an affectation, but a special effort made out of respect for an occasion, or aesthetics difficult to maintain daily. Recently, we have had a member of Congress complaining that he is expected to go to the trouble of wearing a necktie to the United States House of Representatives. Miss Manners understands that a member of this institution may know better than she whether that is a place to be treated with respect, but would expect him at least to gloss this over in public, as do his colleagues. The excuse that people use for being sloppy is that this is more comfortable. Actually, people often feel better when they are uncomfortable, which is why high heels were invented. Miss Manners was once asked whether dress at her own dinner party was to be "Formal or comfortable," and, given such a choice, replied, "Informal, but uncomfortable." Informality does not necessarily produce comfort. Miss Manners is infinitely more comfortable eating her dinner at a properly set table than jauntily perched on someone's rug.

When it is truly a matter of acute discomfort, Miss Manners is not opposed to the entire society's agreeing to make certain changes in conventional dress or furnishings. For example, Miss Manners always thought the stocking or panty stocking a fetching garment for springtime, autumn, or heated ballrooms, but a menace in really cold or hot weather, and she is delighted at the spread of the "city sandal," which may be worn barefoot in summer, and the leather boot, which may be worn with heavy knee socks in winter. She would even be willing to listen to arguments in favor of replacing the necktie—if another formal daytime standard were universally adopted.

What she opposes is defying prevailing standards. Once the society has agreed what is proper—as in the cases of the boots and sandals, but not yet the neckties—Miss Manners expects people to observe this in public places. Even if it's only the House of Representatives.

Elegance

DEAR MISS MANNERS:
Would you comment on the decline of elegance? The fashions today look like rejects from a garage sale.
GENTLE READER:
Elegance in fashion didn't decline: it stopped short the day Worth stopped providing wardrobes to the heroines of Henry James's novels, who traveled seasonally to Paris for this purpose.

A Lady's Gloves

It is some years since the extraordinary notion got abroad that summer clothing should be less restrictive than winter clothing, because the weather tends to be warmer in summer. Before that, people used to look crisp and correct in the heat, although of course they were dropping like flies. Now look at them. Good taste in light clothing now means not wearing a T-shirt on which a licentious invitation to the general public is spelled out across the chest.

Miss Manners misses white gloves.

There is little use in pretending that white gloves are still alive. Even those who loved them best have only to open their glove boxes and look at all those gloves one used to have, lying there in limp but dignified silence, to know that they will never again lead the merry, busy, flirtatious life of old.

For those who missed this era, it may be necessary to explain that white gloves were a hand covering. There were white gloves of various lengths for various occasions, but the ones for summer were what was called wrist length, and they were properly worn every time one stepped out of one's house, except to pick up the newspaper, and, possibly, to go to the beach. Then there was the matter of when the gloves were to be worn, when they were to be carried, and when it was appropriate to do one of each. This fascinating and complicated problem kept a great many people worried and anxious who might otherwise have applied these emotions to such problems as "Am I really happy?" or "Is this the true me?"

People who had a literary turn had an advantage in this matter, because *Little Women* contains the formula for dividing one clean pair of gloves and one dirty pair between two women so that each is wearing a spotless glove and carrying in that hand something which cannot be examined.

Properly gloved, there was no situation that a lady could not carry off. Miss Manners saw this demonstrated some years ago at a fashionable bullfight in Madrid, when a triumphant matador tossed his trophy, a freshly severed ear, to Grace of Monaco. That lady, who is not called Serene Highness for nothing, was wearing her Minnie Mouse gloves, and thus was able to receive a hairy, bloody ear of bull as a lady should. Now, isn't that better than being comfortable?

Recycling Cotton Gloves

DEAR MISS MANNERS:

All right, I'm sorry, too, that white gloves are no longer worn in summer because I also have a drawer full of them. But what do I do with the ones I have? I hate to throw them out.

GENTLE READER:

Cotton gloves may be worn for gardening, baiting fish hooks, or preventing the wearer from scratching chicken pox. They may also be kept in the drawer against better days to come.

Designer Clothes

DEAR MISS MANNERS:

Could you give me some taste guidelines about designer clothes? I am now in a position to upgrade my wardrobe, having taken a new job with a much improved salary, and am at an age, twenty-eight, where I feel I should dress nicely.

The clothes I can now afford, and which I like best, are the "designer boutique" sort, frequently bearing the initials, insignia, or the name of the designer. I understand you object to this, but I don't quite understand why. I am not above letting people know that I care to dress well. Is there anything wrong with a good designer putting his signature on work he is proud of? Please tell me why you consider this in bad taste, if you do, and whether I am likely to be embarrassed in wearing such things before others who may feel as you do.

GENTLE READER:

The worst instance of embarrassment in connection with such clothing was suffered by Miss Manners herself, who found out that a lady of her slight acquaintance whom she had been addressing for years as "Mrs. Klein" wasn't a Mrs. Klein at all. How was Miss Manners to know? By every indication, the woman's name seemed to be Anne Klein and that of her husband, whose T-shirts she apparently often wore, to be Calvin Klein. Miss Manners, indeed, thought that the family names were emblazoned somewhat exaggeratedly on their clothes, but assumed they had had bad experiences as children, when their mothers forgot to sew name tags on their clothes for summer camp.

It turned out that the Kleins were unrelated artisans whom this woman was helping to advertise by allowing space on her body to call attention to their work. Miss Manners does believe in encouraging good craftsmanship, but finds this method excessive. She, herself, and most people who appreciate good dressmaking and tailoring, can recognize quality without having to read the label on someone's sleeve or bosom or worse.

Monograms

DEAR MISS MANNERS:

I certainly agree that it is vulgar to wear "designer" initials or their names on your clothes, particularly as some of these people sell franchises, and no more designed the clothes than I did. I do like, in contrast, the effect of having my own initials, or monogram, on my things. Could you tell me, please, where—that is, on what items of clothing—it is considered tasteful to have these?

GENTLE READER:

It is faultless to have your initials, or your entire name, on the lining of your sable coat, embroidered in thread the same color as the lining. Initials may also be put on handkerchiefs, leather goods, and men's shirts. A servant girl who has married into the peerage is excused if she wants to have a coronet embroidered on her underpants.

Provenance

DEAR MISS MANNERS:

My cousin is always asking me where I got the suit I am wearing, or who designed my dress. She is a completely different size and type from me, and is definitely not asking because she wants shopping tips. It's only curiosity, probably to get an idea of how much I pay for my clothes. Frankly, I don't want her to know. I wear good clothes, but I buy them at discount stores or factory outlets, and sometimes I don't even know the brand name. I don't care, either. This questioning annoys me. I told her so, but she said I was being ridiculous, that it's a compliment to be asked who designed your clothes. Is it?

GENTLE READER:

Only in the sense that "Who taught you to kiss so good?" is a compliment. Both suggest that no talent of your own could account for your success.

❧ DAYTIME DRESS

Morning Dress

DEAR MISS MANNERS:

Is it necessary to dress to go out on the porch in the morning and pick up the paper?

GENTLE READER:

It depends on what you mean by dress. Hat and gloves are no longer considered necessary for such an excursion, but it is customary to be covered in such a way as to be able to pick up the newspaper without oneself making news in the neighborhood.

Sans Brassieres

DEAR MISS MANNERS:

What do you think about bralessness?

GENTLE READER:

Bralessness is a subject Miss Manners hardly thinks of at all. Good taste, in clothing, depends on a delicate balance of appropriateness to the individual, the occasion, and the fashions of the time. There have been times and places where showing an ankle was considered indecent, and others when going nude was not. Miss Manners herself aims at delicately suggesting a slight daringness and awareness of fashion while confirming her basic old-fashioned ladylike air. This is difficult enough, without her attempting to meddle in the closets of others.

Adjustments

DEAR MISS MANNERS:

I have an embarrassing problem with my clothes that I also see other women having. My shoulders are fairly narrow, and my bra straps keep slipping down my arms. It isn't too obvious under most clothes, but it is very annoying. Is it ever proper to discreetly adjust your straps while in public? I see some women pull their straps up even in the office, while others just tolerate it until they get to a private place. What do you think?

GENTLE READER:

Some clothing emergencies are attractive and others are not. Tightening an earring, for example, can be a lovely gesture, but reaching inside one's front and giving a yank to an errant brassiere strap cannot. At sewing shops, you can buy tiny grosgrain ribbons with snaps on them to sew inside your clothing and hold the straps in place. This will leave your hands free to adjust your stockings.

Straightening Seams

DEAR MISS MANNERS:

Have you seen the new seamed stockings? I'm crazy about them, but my mother remembers wearing them—she even remembers drawing lines down her legs with eyebrow pencil during World War II when "nylons" were impossible to buy—and says it was a bore always to be straightening the seams. I read in a fashion magazine that straightening the seams is sexy, but it doesn't say how to do it gracefully. My mother says adjusting lingerie is not sexy, just sloppy looking.

GENTLE READER:

Your mother probably knew what it was to have to straighten a girdle, and may you and future generations be spared from ever finding that out. Rearranging one's stockings is an activity of recent origin for respectable women wishing to make themselves conspicuous, as something was certainly needed to replace the dropped lace handkerchief. Here is the method for straightening seams of stockings: Look shyly over one shoulder, while extending the corresponding leg six inches backwards. Lower the eyelids, while slowly pushing the hand down the leg—remembering to keep the posterior tucked sideways and under—until reaching the heel. Then move the hand slowly back up along the line of the seam, undulating it under the pretext of straightening the seam.

A Reply

DEAR MISS MANNERS:

In talking about stocking seam straightening, you commented, "Your mother probably knew what it was to have to straighten a girdle, and may you and future generations be spared from ever finding out." You really must be some kind of Women's Lib Kook! Too bad your mother didn't tell you that even fashion models wear girdles to give their dresses a smoother look! Who wants to see idiots like you let it all hang out!! A lot of women without girdles look like the south end of a hippopotamus going north! Even skinny women from the rear look like a bowl of Jell-O being shook! With women like you advising them, no wonder we see girls pregnant without being married.

GENTLE READER:

Miss Manners may not be skinny, but at least she does not have the impression that girdles prevent pregnancy.

Dress Codes

DEAR MISS MANNERS:

While staying at a delightful mountain resort in southwestern Virginia, a question came to mind regarding the appropriate attire for women. Upon arrival, we were presented with a card which indicated that gentlemen were required to wear "jackets and ties" during evening hours. My wife was not certain as to what was to be expected on her part, inasmuch as the written request made no mention of an equivalent dress requirement for female guests. What would be correct attire for women under such circumstances?

GENTLE READER:

Neither Miss Manners nor your resort is going to fall into that trap. Many public accommodations, including some very self-confident restaurants, tried, in the 1960s, to prescribe dress codes for women, prohibiting them from wearing "slacks" or "trousers" or "pants." Were they ever sorry.

It simply can't be done. Fashion changes too quickly for anyone to be able to say for long what constitutes correct female dress for such places. The best unisex rule would be "Sports clothes not permitted," but even that could be argued way past dinnertime. People at such establishments have had to fall back on the fortunate distinction that while clothes may have to make the man, you can tell a lady just by looking.

Propriety and Pants

DEAR MISS MANNERS:

I am confused by changing fashions. I remember when it was considered dreadful to wear pants—some restaurants wouldn't even admit you—and then it became all right. But now it seems to be going back again, or am I wrong? My question is: Is it still considered proper to wear pants to a luncheon?

GENTLE READER:

For a gentleman, always. For a lady, local custom varies. Miss Manners got sick of the fight over pants long ago—it was raging on a level with fights over lengths of hair for men, which is a poor excuse for a good fight. Miss Manners also has a pretty good idea that most people are well aware of how they can dress to shock or to conform; which they wish to do is up to them. If you are truly anxious to be safe in this case, Miss Manners assures you that no one will think a skirt improper.

Fur Coats

DEAR MISS MANNERS:

I bought a fur coat this year. It's not a terribly expensive coat, as fur coats go, and I got it on sale. I feel it is a better investment than buying a new cloth coat every two or three years, as this should last me quite a while. But I am really tired of people kidding me about wearing a fur coat. What can I say in reply to cracks about how much it must have cost, it's making me such a grand lady, and so on?

GENTLE READER:

A lady always explains a fur coat by saying that she suffers terribly from the cold. This shifts the focus from her presumably bulging bank account, which is vulgar, to her presumably aristocratic frailty, which is not.

Fur Stoles

DEAR MISS MANNERS:

I have a mink stole and only go to church or weddings occasionally. I'm wondering what is the proper place to wear it and with what sort of clothes?

GENTLE READER:

A mink stole is the most difficult of all fur clothing to wear. You can soften the drop-dead message of mink by claiming that you wear a mink coat only for warmth, or by tossing your mink jacket over bluejeans as if it were merely old and practical. But you can't claim a mink stole is keeping all of you warm, and you can't pretend you got it for rugged sportswear.

Therefore, you must obey the rules about wearing it, or risk looking as if you are using a minimum of pelts for the purpose of maximum showing off. The stole should be worn over dress clothes, whether they are dresses, suits, or evening dresses, in the evening, in slightly chilly weather. You should also wear with it a facial expression suggesting that you almost grabbed a sweater instead, but were afraid that wouldn't be warm enough or dressy enough for the occasion.

Fur-Lined Coats

DEAR MISS MANNERS:

I have a fur-lined raincoat, which is very practical, as it is cozy inside on dreary days, while the outside is waterproof. But you won't believe the problem I have in connection with it. When a man holds my coat for me, he always holds it backwards. In other words, he picks up the coat, meaning well, but convinced that the fur belongs on the outside, he will hold the outside toward me and wait for me to get into it. What can I do?

GENTLE READER:

Well, you can crawl under his extended arm and snuggle into it backwards, facing him with a foolish smile on your face. Or you can say, "I'm sorry, it's the other way around."

Bathing Suits

DEAR MISS MANNERS:

Would you say something, please, about the general appropriateness and attractiveness of one-piece, as opposed to two-piece, bathing suits? I'm no prude, but it does seem to me that aesthetic standards, as well as those of, shall we say, minimal decency, are being violated all the time on our public beaches.

GENTLE READER:

Miss Manners quite agrees with you. If gentlemen realized how much more mysteriously alluring they looked in two-piece bathing suits, instead of the present one-piece models, they would toss fashion aside and return to those modest and becoming fashions of old.

Children's Bikinis

DEAR MISS MANNERS:

We are vacationing in Florida this winter, and my seven-year-old daughter wants a bikini. Many of her friends wear two-piece suits, but I think it's in poor taste at their age. Would you settle this for us?

GENTLE READER:

Poor taste is displaying one's bosom. Displaying one's lack of it is poor judgment.

Fire Attire

DEAR MISS MANNERS:

For several years now, I have occupied a succession of high-rise apartments, and in each of them this problem of mine has come up. Specifically, what is the correct attire for those little impromptu social hours under the lobby chandeliers during a fire in the trash chute? These occasions invariably occur well after midnight, so that one leaps from one's bed to attend the festive gathering.

My feeling is that one's dress should be adequately covering but informal. I generally wear a navy blue nylon pajama and matching coat, and tennis shoes. Last time, I spent an agreeable hour chatting with (1) a young man clad in running trunks and running shoes; (2) an executive type in a business suit with vest, carrying a briefcase; (3) a young lady in a scarlet caftan, her head swathed in a brilliant yellow towel. Her accessory was a brown grocery bag that contained a live cat.

Gentle Reader:

Your instincts are correct, but, then, so are everyone else's, as fires are classified socially with come-as-you-are parties. However, Miss Manners' instinct would be to avoid the man in the three-piece suit. A person carrying a briefcase at midnight is up to no good.

On the Gentleman's Handkerchief

Dear Miss Manners:

Can the handkerchief in a gentleman's breast pocket ever be used?

Gentle Reader:

The handkerchief is in the breast pocket, where everyone can see how clean it is, to indicate that (1) the gentleman owns one; and (2) the gentleman does not sneeze. In the case of true gentlemen, Miss Manners takes the first for granted and does not believe the second. Therefore, she prefers that the handkerchief be kept in the trouser pocket and taken out when needed. A truly fastidious gentleman may wish to take it out three seconds in advance of need.

Maintaining Fragile Ties

Dear Miss Manners:

What would you have thought if you had seen me at lunch today, in an expensive restaurant, pouring club soda on my tie because I had gotten soup on it and was more interested in saving the tie than my reputation?

Gentle Reader:

That it wasn't going to work. Reputations are sometimes salvageable, but ties rarely are.

Children's Dress

Dear Miss Manners:

When do children dress up these days, and what are children's dress-up clothes now? I want to send my goddaughter a dress, but I've never seen her wear one.

Gentle Reader:

Children have two styles of dress these days. One, which consists of velvet dresses for girls and velvet suits for boys, is worn only to performances of ''The Nutcracker.'' The other, which consists of rags, is worn for everything else life has to offer. Miss Manners does not condone this, but that was not your question.

Uniform

DEAR MISS MANNERS:

We attend a small, coeducational, private school. We bear the awesome impediment of wearing the same clothes to school every day. (We do change the articles themselves. The "style," or rather lack thereof, is, however, constant.) We would like your opinion of such a uniform. If you could also address another related issue—the question whether we should have a "non-uniform" day, when students dress formally but not in adherence to the uniform regulations—our gratitude would be abysmal.

GENTLE READER:

Miss Manners believes that doing away with rules for the young takes all the fun out of life for those in the rebellious years. She feels that even one free day violates this. Besides, students who are not required to wear uniforms all look so drearily identical in their T-shirts, jeans, and sneakers. At least in uniform, your teachers can tell you apart.

School Clothes

DEAR MISS MANNERS:

I am in the sixth grade and I will be going to junior high school next year. I've been telling my grandma and sister that I will be wearing dresses next year and I won't be getting all muddy from playing in the field. But my friends will think I'm weird if I wear a dress all the time. I want to look nice at times, but I'm comfortable in jeans. I'm confused.

GENTLE READER:

Of course you are. The conflicting pleasures of dressing up and messing up have been confusing older women than you through countless decades and fashions. In the sixth grade, you are old enough to defy the conventions of your grandmother and sister, but not old enough to defy the conventions of your friends. That will come later. In the meantime, Miss Manners suggests that if you wear jeans to school and adjacent mud fields, you will look all the nicer by contrast when you dress up for social occasions.

Hats

DEAR MISS MANNERS:

Where does one wear a hat these days?

GENTLE READER:

Same as always: On the head. (Whoops. You'll have to pardon Miss Manners, who occasionally gets giddy after a full day of this sort of thing.) The proper answer is that the occasions for wearing hats, for both men and women, are the same as always, but the purpose is the opposite. One used to wear a hat with daytime clothes to be conservative; it is now done to be shocking.

DEAR MISS MANNERS:

I need your advice concerning the wearing of hats. I have recently purchased a charming chapeau that I dearly love. However, because ladies' hats have not been extremely popular as of late, I want to know when and where it is proper to wear them. Can I wear a hat with a pants suit? Can I wear my hat indoors at a luncheon or dinner? Obviously, I wouldn't wear it at the theater, but is it correct at other social events? Can I wear it to church?

GENTLE READER:

Miss Manners is willing to love your hat dearly, sight unseen, because she missed hats so dreadfully during that famine you describe. That time, incidentally, goes back to before the invention of pants suits, and there is therefore as yet no correct way of wearing a hat with a pants suit. (As with high heels and pants, once unthinkable, its time may come.) The general rule is that if the hat looks as if you had it built, it may properly go to daytime functions; if it looks as if it just landed in your hair (tiny bits of feathers, sequins, or whatever), it goes out at night.

The reason Miss Manners adores hats is that they have so much to say; you bear this out by describing yours as "charming." In order to decide where to wear it, you must listen to just what it is that your hat is saying so charmingly. There are charming little hats that say, "When God created me, He did a fine job, and I am grateful for that," and these hats may be worn to church. Charming little hats that say, "Why, hello there," are better left for later in the day.

A lady certainly may wear a hat inside church, a restaurant, or anywhere else during the daytime. The exception is a function in her own house, where hat wearing would suggest that she had some place better to go, unlike her guests. It is gentlemen who must take their hats off indoors, although they are finding it difficult these days, because they don't have any hats, either.

Lawyer's Hats

DEAR MISS MANNERS:

What is the proper attire for a young female attorney making her maiden argument before the Mississippi Supreme Court on a May afternoon? I was wondering if either a hat or gloves would be appropriate. Also, if I did wear a hat, at which point should I remove it: before entering the chamber, or before beginning the argument?

GENTLE READER:

It was at some nice court down South that Bella Abzug began the practice of wearing hats, after tiring of being mistaken for a lawyer's secretary. Miss Manners recommends not only a hat and gloves, but opera-length pearls and an expression that indicates one will not be messed with. Such assets should certainly not be abandoned before the judgment is reached. After winning the case, however, you may toss the hat once into the air before replacing it and exiting in triumph.

Cowboy Hats

DEAR MISS MANNERS:
  A certain lumpish fellow of my acquaintance contends that it is not a breach of etiquette for a man to wear a cowboy hat indoors. He states that cowboy hats are unique in this regard. My mother was always a proponent of the Mrs. Paul W. Bryant, Sr. school of thought on this subject. (You may recall that when Bear Bryant was asked why he didn't wear his trademark hat in the Astrodome, he replied that it was because his mother taught him that a gentleman doesn't wear a hat indoors.) To your knowledge has there been a special papal dispensation or whatever the equivalent is in the world of etiquette for cowboy hats?
GENTLE READER:
  Mrs. Bryant's rule certainly applies to cowboys who wish to behave as gentlemen and, Miss Manners would like to add, to gentlemen who wish to disguise themselves as cowboys, a proliferating breed. For example, a person wearing a cowboy hat, along with a gray suit and lizard boots, in a city office building elevator, is not excused from removing the hat—no, not even if he is wearing the complete cowboy suit, with fringed jacket, jeans, and spurs that he got for Christmas. However, a genuine cowboy, wearing cowboy clothes and going about his cowboy business, does wear his hat everywhere. In other words, it is not the hat but the head that defines the man, oddly enough.

Shoes

DEAR MISS MANNERS:
  What is the proper way to walk in high-heeled shoes?
GENTLE READER:
  Left, right, left, right, left, right.

White Shoes

DEAR MISS MANNERS:
  I wonder if you would be kind enough to settle a dispute which is causing much discussion and unkindness in the office where I work. The question is when to begin wearing white shoes. I am, of course, not speaking of baby shoes, tennis shoes, or nurses' shoes, which are always appropriate for the respective wearers—but white calf, patent, or linen ladies' dress or street shoes or sandals. Some New Englanders have declared it a substantial gaffe to wear them any

earlier than Memorial Day, some Georgians have said April first is not too soon.

GENTLE READER:

Miss Manners would like nothing better than to tell you to go ahead and wear your white shoes. Miss Manners herself has a favorite dress which goes only with white shoes but cannot be worn in summer because it has long sleeves.

Alas, Miss Manners also has principles. White shoes may be worn only after Memorial Day and before Labor Day. Otherwise, you will develop warts on your toes.

A Reply

DEAR MISS MANNERS:

I read with some concern your ultimatum about not wearing white shoes before Memorial Day, since I have been wearing cream-colored shoes on slightly formal occasions (church, theater, concerts) since spring began. You'll be gratified to know that on these occasions, I also wear a dress and spring blazer. I've noticed that most other women have adhered to wearing their brown and black winter shoes. Now that you have been so wonderful as to dicate when to and not to wear white shoes, would you please clarify this matter of when to wear cream-colored shoes?

GENTLE READER:

Nothing is ever black and white, except the rule that white shoes may be worn only between Memorial Day and Labor Day. Nevertheless, there are some gray areas, which include everything cream-colored.

If you can call your off-white shoes cream, bone, beige, or taupe, you may wear them whenever you like. However, if they are merely dirty white shoes, clean them and put them away until Memorial Day. If you are being married in a white dress, you may wear white shoes. In fact, you may not wear any other color shoe, not even sensible brown and white spectator pumps. A white satin bridal slipper should not be open-toed in case the bridegroom is seized with the desire to drink champagne out of it. This is a messy way to start a marriage. White shoes may be worn year-round in resort areas. However, if you live in a resort area, you may want to observe the regular rules, which originated in places of erratic climate, first to give yourself some variety, and second to distinguish yourself from the tourists.

White in Winter

DEAR MISS MANNERS:

I am a lady who cannot bring myself to wear white shoes before Memorial Day (nor after Labor Day). Fortunately, I am not a nurse. The dictum is inscribed within my mind somewhere near "Do not murder." Although I see many women (ah—but I am a "lady," as I noted) sporting this color already, and its allowability would delightfully complement my spring wardrobe, I just can't do it. Am I hopelessly outdated?

GENTLE READER:
Is the law against murder outdated?

Dark Clothes

DEAR MISS MANNERS:
I promise you, I didn't start wearing white shoes until Memorial Day, which you said was the first possible time to do so, regardless of the weather. My question now is, when do I start wearing dark things? I wouldn't dream of changing from summer clothes until you tell me to, but I would appreciate your letting me know in advance, as we get a lot of snow here and I'd hate to be left standing here in my white shoes and sundress, waiting for your answer.

GENTLE READER:
Labor Day is the first day for wearing fall clothes, but the only people who do so then are the candidates for the Miss America title, and do they ever look silly, running around on the boardwalk in their wool suits in all that heat. White shoes may not be worn after Labor Day, but for full fall regalia, please wait for the first cool day.

Boots

DEAR MISS MANNERS:
I always wear knee-high boots to work in this mushy weather, but if I keep them on all day, my feet sweat. So I bring along a bag with a pair of shoes in it and change when I get there. My question is, how do I pull off my boots gracefully, while everyone is watching? My knees always seem to be rather far apart, if you know what I mean, while I tug at the heel of the boot.

GENTLE READER:
There is no graceful way to take off boots. Miss Manners suggests the following: Enlist a friend. Hand over one booted foot to that friend—by putting the foot out behind you. The friend, facing away from you, takes the boot between his or her legs and pulls. This is far from graceful, but it has a faintly sporty look, which will do for the office.

❧ EVENING CLOTHES

Gloves

DEAR MISS MANNERS:

What are "eighteen-button gloves"?

GENTLE READER:

These are white gloves that come above the elbow and make a riveting show when the wearer slowly peels them off before she can take a drink. They are called "eighteen-button" because they have three pearl buttons at each wrist.

DEAR MISS MANNERS:

No doubt this is a stupid question, and I am demonstrating my unfitness for respectable society, but *why* doesn't a pair of eighteen-button gloves have eighteen buttons on it, or even eighteen buttons a glove, for a grand total of thirty-six?

GENTLE READER:

Yes, indeed, this is a silly question, because everybody knows that there are buttons and buttons, and while eighteen-button gloves have three small pearl buttons each at the musketeer (which everyone knows is the opening at the wrist), there are, indeed, eighteen buttons on each in length. That button is a standard of measurement of approximately one inch. The approximate part is because it is a French standard of measurement.

If you begin measuring at the base of the thumb, you will find that four-button gloves end about the wrist, eight-button below the elbow, ten-button above the elbow, and twenty-six button, the longest, up to the armpit. Naturally, this system only comes out right on French arms.

DEAR MISS MANNERS:

Since we're geared into high fashion now, what about the etiquette of gloves? A lady with standards shouldn't take off her gloves when shaking hands, should she?

GENTLE READER:

Indeed not, unless she is a lady subject to uncontrollable bursts of enthusiasm for direct human contact, in which case Miss Manners prefers the naked hand-shake to the promiscuous and noisy kissing of near-strangers. Truly unforgivable behavior when wearing gloves consists of eating, drinking, smoking, and saying, "Pardon my glove."

Gentlemen remove their gloves when shaking hands. Please do not expect Miss Manners to justify this discrepancy on any basis of logic, morality, or equal opportunity.

Cocktail Hats

The cocktail party is a perfectly dreadful social event, and Miss Manners was planning to ignore it in the hope that it would go away. However, while Miss Manners is impervious to the charms of mixed drinks, stuffed eggs, and the conversation they inspire, she suddenly finds herself being seduced by the new cocktail hats.

There is nothing new about the new cocktail hats, of course. After half an hour in the attic, Miss Manners produced three tiny confections of velvet and veiling, just right for perching on the forehead, at an angle as precarious as possible without the hat's tumbling down onto the nose, in the very latest style. That was easy. The question with which Miss Manners has been struggling is whether it is necessary to endure the trial of attending a cocktail party in order to have the pleasure of wearing the cocktail hat.

It is, after all, not only Miss Manners who dislikes cocktail parties. People who give them profess to dislike them; they invite lots of people they dislike enough to avoid inviting to dinner; and the people who attend them all stand around telling one another that they hate cocktail parties.

So, sparing herself some pain (Miss Manners is a dedicated researcher on your behalf, but no martyr), Miss Manners chose a pleasant tea party for her experiment—as it had the cocktail party characteristics of being a late afternoon gathering in which several people stood up, but not the usual, offensive attributes of being held on a weekday during the dinner hour.

Now, Miss Manners is quite aware that nobody wears cocktail dresses to cocktail parties. For some years now, it has become quite unfashionable to lead a life in which you are at liberty to go home and change your clothess at five in the afternoon. It leads to being thought of as not serious, enterprising, or sufficiently sensitive to the general human plight. Therefore, Miss Manners was not surprised to see the other guests in turtleneck sweaters and tweeds. She was unpleasantly surprised to find them not acting surprised to see her with black veiling on her nose, apparently choosing politely to assume that she had come from some sort of flashy funeral.

Miss Manners satisfied herself by this endeavor that the cocktail hat will probably never belong at the cocktail party, let alone that one must attend a cocktail party in order to wear a cocktail hat.

The question which remains is: Where may the new cocktail hats be correctly worn? (Mind you, we are talking about cocktail hats, not hat-hats, which are a more substantial item having to do with larger dimensions and felt, and which Miss Manners also hopes to be welcoming back one day.) Miss Manners is not willing to condone cocktail hats being worn with either daytime or evening clothes, both of which mistakes she has observed in the merchandising of these hats. Since we have already dismissed the cocktail dress as being without redeeming social purpose, this doesn't leave much, does it?

It leaves a certain type of suit, variously known as the dinner suit, the theater suit, or the little suit. Or the little theater suit or the little dinner suit. "Little" is a refined way of calling attention to how expensive something is, as in "my little dressmaker" or "our little place in the mountains." The little suit is usually modestly slim and dark and hideously expensive. This may be worn, oddly enough, to a restaurant or theater, and the cocktail hat may be worn with it to these places. Do not worry about the cocktail hat's blocking anybody's view at the theater. It is too small and too strategically placed to blind anyone, except, of course, the person wearing it.

DEAR MISS MANNERS:
What would be appropriate attire for a gentleman accompanying a lady to theater, assuming she has chosen to wear something simple and classic topped off with a small, black, veiled hat?
GENTLE READER:
A cocktail hat is sufficient decoration for any two people, and therefore the gentleman should think of himself as background material and dress accordingly. If he does not wish to wear wallpaper, a dark suit will do.

Specifying Dress

DEAR MISS MANNERS:
I received a formal invitation from the Secretary General of the Organization of American States to a reception, and it says, in the lower right-hand corner, "Dark business suit/Long dress." As a matter of fact, I was planning to wear a business suit anyway. What did they think I would wear to a diplomatic reception—my jogging suit? It looks peculiar to me, if not insulting. I've seen "Black Tie" and "Informal" written on this type of card, but never "Dark business suit." What are they afraid of?
GENTLE READER:
Men in white silk suits and Panama hats with evil political intentions.

"Black Tie Optional"

DEAR MISS MANNERS:
I know it is improper for an invitation to include "black tie optional." However, I would like to have those guests who own formal attire wear it. In my past experiences, formals were worn only when I included the above wording. Would it be in very poor taste?
GENTLE READER:
It's the "optional" that is objectionable, for being weasely, when you really mean that you want your guests dressed alike. Those who do not own dinner clothes may rent them, or may have the common sense to understand that the option exists of wearing dark business suits.

A Gentleman's Evening Clothes

DEAR MISS MANNERS:
Is an off-white dinner jacket acceptable?
GENTLE READER:
Not to Miss Manners, but, then, Miss Manners is so unbearably finicky about men's evening clothes that nothing is acceptable to her but the strictest black, winter or summer, and the very plainest of stiff white shirts. It is her belief that a dull satin stripe up the side of the leg is quite enough sartorial excitement for any gentleman at any formal occasion, including his own wedding. This is not the prevailing opinion. The world is full of fanciful clothes, in odd colors, with strange black margins on the lapels, and blossoming ruffles, that are passed off as "formal wear" for men. Compared to these abominations, the off-white dinner jacket seems very restrained. Miss Manners is almost too worn out from the other horrors to protest against it. But, since you have asked her opinion, it is that she prefers black.

DEAR MISS MANNERS:
What do you think of ruffled shirts in bright colors for men's evening dress?
GENTLE READER:
That is the sort of thing Miss Manners tries very hard not to think about at all.

Evening Watches

DEAR MISS MANNERS:
My grandfather used to say that a gentleman never wore a watch with evening clothes. Is that true—or was it ever? I certainly see men looking at their watches at formal occasions, such as charity balls.
GENTLE READER:
The formal ball, these days, certainly inspires watch watching. Your grandfather, however, would have understood that there is watch watching and watch watching. He told you—you were only half listening, weren't you?—that a gentleman never wore a wrist watch with evening clothes. The act of looking at a wrist watch denotes businesslike impatience, unsuitable for social functions. The act of looking at a pocket watch, however, is a graceful gesture denoting respect for the night as a time in which sooner or later every civilized person ends his revels and goes to bed. It is an act of which your grandfather would have approved.

Hats for Gentlemen

DEAR MISS MANNERS:

What is the difference between a gentleman's top hat, and an opera hat?

GENTLE READER:

The opera hat, like some gentlemen Miss Manners has observed at the opera, collapses.

❦ JEWELRY AND OTHER ADORNMENTS

Watches

DEAR MISS MANNERS:

Help! My fiancé has asked me to select a watch for him to give me as an engagement present. (I am never on time, and this is a sweet way of reminding me.) He is quite, in fact very, well off (and nice, too!) so I have no need to think about cost. In fact, the ones I am considering cost thousands of dollars, but I am afraid that some, which have faces in different jewel colors, might strike his friends as nouveau riche. (I was his secretary, so I have to be careful.) I thought I would get diamonds, because my engagement ring is a diamond cluster, and I will be wearing it with a diamond wedding ring. I have seen some where the face is surrounded by diamonds, and some where the face is made of pavé diamonds. Which do you think is in better taste?

GENTLE READER:

Nothing is in more exquisite taste, in a woman of modest circumstances who is marrying a rich man, than the protestation that she does not care much for jewels and would prefer something simple in gold with his initials and the wedding date engraved on the back.

This does not strike Miss Manners as being your style. However, allow her to urge it, anyway, in the case of a watch. A watch case that is heavily encrusted with jewels is never appropriate. It is too elaborate for daytime wear, and an obvious watch of any kind is not worn in the evening, when people are supposed to pretend they are not keeping track of the time. Also, with all the diamonds you plan to be wearing on your finger, a diamond watch would make your hand look as if you had left it outdoors and it had frozen over. Do not be inhibited by the idea that expressing a preference for simple things will be held against you later. The charming tastes of an impecunious fiancée are unrelated to the standards of a rich married woman.

Pearls

DEAR MISS MANNERS:

My husband recently gave me a strand of pearls, matinée length, and I also have a strand in the short, choker style. My question: When are pearls appropriate? I tend to wear them only in the evening, but it seems a shame to leave them in my jewel box so much of the time. May I wear them to the office with, say, a silk blouse and wool suit or velvet blazer?

GENTLE READER:

Certainly. Pearls are almost always appropriate, which is the endearing thing about pearls. They adore being worn and are said to react, in gratitude for this attention, by picking up the skin tones of their owner. For this reason, many rich women wear their best pearls tucked into their nightgowns. It would be easier for Miss Manners to tell you when pearls are not appropriate, than when they are. Never wear pearls with your bathing suit.

DEAR MISS MANNERS:

My fiancé gave me a double-strand pearl necklace as an engagement present. I would be much happier having the pearls in one long necklace, opera-length. What do you think about the delicate question of my having the pearls restrung?

GENTLE READER:

What Miss Manners thinks is that pearl necklaces must have odd numbers of strands—one, three, five, and so on, depending on how long your neck and deep your purse. Having learned this rule in Japan or some place, she makes it a firm tenet of her life. Therefore, Miss Manners thinks that restringing the two strands into one is not only permissible but imperative. Perhaps, however, what you are really interested in is what your fiancé will think when he sees you have tampered with his jewels. In that case, why don't you ask him?

Phi Beta Kappa

DEAR MISS MANNERS:

Where and when is it correct for a woman to wear her Phi Beta Kappa key? Men can wear theirs on a vest or as a tie clasp, but it is difficult for a woman to wear one without looking tacky. I worked as hard as any man for that key, and feel I'm also entitled to wear my accomplishment with pride. But where?

GENTLE READER:

Miss Manners is surprised that this question is not coming from a man, complaining that women can wear their Phi Beta Kappa keys on chains at the neck or wrist, or as brooches, but that it is difficult for a man who may not use a tie clasp and knows that it is tacky to hang from a watch chain items that properly belong secured at the end of the watch chain—the opposite end from the watch

—in the pocket. A woman can easily wear this symbol of accomplishment, but a man has a harder time, even though he may have worked as hard for it.

Bracelets Below the Waist

DEAR MISS MANNERS:

Should an ankle bracelet be worn inside hosiery or outside? Is one or the other correct, or a matter of personal preference?

GENTLE READER:

An ankle bracelet should be worn on the arm, where it should call itself a bracelet. If it insists on leading a lower life, it should do so on the beach, where it can do no harm to stockings from within or without.

Hair

DEAR MISS MANNERS:

I cannot understand why the hair stylists of this world won't do anything about this long sloppy hair on girls and letting it go on forever. We always have to see them brushing their hair away from their faces and having to eat with them in diners, etc., it's a sickening sight.

GENTLE READER:

It will take Miss Manners a moment to collect herself before answering you. She is shocked and upset and even has a tear or two to brush away from *her* face before she can trust herself to think. You see, Miss Manners has very long hair herself. She doesn't wear it down at her age, but she always thought it proper for young girls to do so, and never worried that hair stylists or other free-lance critics, such as yourself, were policing the streets, looking for visual offenders. If you must, please try to remember: It's the girls who bob their hair who are fast.

Flowers to Wear

DEAR MISS MANNERS:

Where does a corsage look best?

GENTLE READER:

In the refrigerator. Miss Manners thinks the custom of giving and wearing fresh flowers is charming, and hopes that florists or individuals will learn how to fix them for this purpose without adding so much in the way of ribbons and extraneous vegetation as to make the wearer look like a banquet table with a centerpiece. An arrangement meant to be attached to the bosom with a sharp, pearl-handled weapon is fated to be crushed by the wearer's coat or dance partner. Wrist ones, attached with the sort of bands hospitals use for the speedy identification of anesthetized patients, do not fare much better. Small bunches that can be simply pinned in the hair or on the lapel would be more practical, as well as attractive. However, if you do plan to wear a First Circle Winner arrangement, Miss Manners at least begs you to wear it right side up. Turn those little flowers' faces up to the sun (or the moon if you are wearing them at night). (Flowers hate hanging upside down by their toes. It makes the chlorophyll rush to their heads.)

Lipstick

DEAR MISS MANNERS:

Bright red lipstick is coming back into fashion. I am considering wearing it sometimes, just for fun, although I've never worn anything but lip gloss on my mouth before. How do you keep it from getting all over napkins, forks, and such? Doesn't it make a mess?

GENTLE READER:

Why do you think it went out of fashion in the first place? If you think the forks look messy, you should have seen the freshly kissed gentlemen in those days.

Cologne

DEAR MISS MANNERS:

A female at work informed me, when I showed her a cologne I had purchased, which she liked, that when a gentleman enters a room, his cologne shouldn't be smelled until after he has departed. This I did not know—if, indeed, there is any truth in it. I myself, as a young man, twenty-one, believe in looking sharp at all times, but never to overdo anything, which includes the amount of cologne one should wear. Please help me out in this mind-twisting matter.

GENTLE READER:

No, no: the rule is that a gentleman's cologne (or a lady's perfume) should never *precede* him into a room. It does not follow that it should remain behind when he is gone. Perhaps it would be less confusing to say that a gentleman's cologne should never occupy a room that the gentleman is not occupying.

Ever After

Divorce

One day, when Miss Manners was tidying up, she came across an entire set of discarded manners. They had to do with second weddings, and Miss Manners had permitted them to fall into disuse when she noticed that second marriages were, as a rule, tending to be more sensible than first marriages.

Why, she reasoned, should first-timers be allowed to put so much money and valuable etiquette into creating memories they will try to forget, and experienced people be advised to be quick and inconspicuous about something they might like to remember? Thus, she abolished furtive second weddings, and set out fresh rules for festive ones. (Please see pp. 572–575.)

But someone has to use those old rules. It would be a frightful waste to throw them away, and it is one of Miss Manners' principles that tradition should be preserved, even if it has to be taken to the dressmaker's and altered.

In her wisdom, she has made over the old second-wedding rules to apply to divorces. There seems to be a basic fairness in there, somewhere.

Here, then, are the new rules:

It is in bad taste to issue formal announcements of a divorce. When you must notify people, do so by letter. This is also an excellent way of using up paper marked with obsolescent names.

No big parties are given, but some quiet celebrations may take place with relatives and intimate friends. The legal ceremony should be attended by as few

557

people as possible, and afterward it might be desirable to share a drink. Parties afterward, if one wants them, should be quiet and restrained (as opposed to boisterous and conspicuous).

Dress should be conservative—suits for both ladies and gentlemen at their divorces, and conventional party clothes for the social events.

Children are naturally deeply involved in the occasion, both emotionally and logistically, but should not be present at any events. They should certainly not be in any formal supportive role. In private sessions, they are told what is about to happen, never asked or consulted as to whether it should (as nobody listens to their decisions, anyway, they should feel innocent of any responsibility); and they are kept entirely apart from the public part of it.

The couple should not expect presents, although those same close relatives and intimate friends may certainly choose to give presents. The basic principle is that one does not give household presents to people who may be presumed to have acquired the basics.

However, if this is, indeed, the occasion for a person's starting a fresh household from absolute scratch—Miss Manners has heard that this is sometimes the case—it is charming for friends to indicate their wishes for happiness in a tangible way. Strictly speaking, one does not hold showers in connection with such an event, but Miss Manners would be willing to look the other way if a close circle were to organize a similar gathering privately.

You see, she really must insist on the proper tone. One may radiate quiet happiness, but that all-out triumphant air is not in good taste.

In compensation for this restraint, Miss Manners is, you remember, suspending the stricter rules for subsequent weddings. Thus, those who cannot wait for full-scale celebrating need only move to the next milestone.

ANNOUNCEMENTS AND DISCUSSIONS

Behaving Well or Badly

DEAR MISS MANNERS:

How many times have I sat at my breakfast table while some woman friend my age (forty-seven) has wept and said, "I never thought it would happen to me." And all the while I would be thinking, "Yes, but it really won't happen to me!"

Of course it has. My husband of twenty-five happy (I thought) years has left, maybe to come back when he's had his fill of "freedom," maybe not. I can't stop him from making a fool of himself. But I want to know how to avoid behaving foolishly myself.

You see, while I've tried to be helpful to those women who've been crying at my table, and I always started out sympathetic, I found that after a while I began to resent them. I suppose this will come home to roost now, and people will treat me the way I'm sorry to say I have treated others—first pledging support, and then gradually dropping them. I can't tell you why, or exactly what it is. One friend of mine took to the bottle. I've had close friends who became different, somehow, after their marriages broke up. I don't want this to happen to me. I haven't done anything wrong, and there is no reason I should lose my friends.

My sister-in-law (who thinks her brother has behaved disgracefully) counsels me to take the opportunity to think more of myself, have a good time, maybe even "have a fling." She says I've been devoting myself to others all my life, and now's the time for me "to be selfish." I'm willing to try, but I don't know how to go about it. How can a woman who is gray-haired, a little stout, and used to being a reliable helpmate, compete in this modern world?

GENTLE READER:

Easily. The world is crammed with people who do know how to be selfish, who have no trouble thinking of themselves all the time, and who are eagerly in search of good times and flings. How can they hope to compete with someone who has a lifelong habit of being kind and unselfish?

Here are some things not to do. Perhaps you will recognize some of them as common symptoms of divorce, which, exhibited by your friends, contributed to your decrease of interest and sympathy in them:

Do not overdraw on the amount of sympathy to which one is entitled at a difficult period of life. Even with a close friend or woman in a similar position, try to limit your complaints and be sure to accompany them with a semblance of true interest in the vicissitudes of the other person's life.

Beware not only of the bottle, but of the telephone, which many people reach for with the same desperation, and overuse with the same self-indulgence and sloppiness.

Do not bristle with eagerness to have that fling. The glitter in the eye that advertises sudden availability is not attractive.

Do not dye your hair. This is the first gesture of the newly unattached middle-aged woman and, like the ditto of the male, which is buying a red sports car, it does not have the dashing effect that is intended.

What should you do? Continue to be a warm and cheerful person (even if you have to fake it for a while), making your interest and experience available to a widening circle of acquaintance, without dwelling on immediate benefits to yourself. This should make you quite a rarity nowadays, and there will be those who will appreciate it.

Family Loyalty

Loyalty to members of one's family before outsiders is a matter of decency, morality, and principle, the principle being that one should never snitch on one's sister because she knows too much about one.

Today's question is: Is there family loyalty after divorce? Yes, there is. But before you ask Miss Manners indignantly if she realizes all the terrible things your former spouse did to you, let us talk about the reasons for family loyalty so that we can consider whether it should still apply. (Even then, Miss Manners doesn't want to hear what that awful person did to you. Dear Count Tolstoy notwithstanding, it is Miss Manners' experience that all unhappy families are alike.)

Suppose, instead of former spouses, we were talking about siblings. Siblings do not even have the responsibility of having once chosen each other and may never have been tied by bonds of affection, even for an instant. So why must they be loyal to one another?

First, because one must tell one's secrets somewhere, or one will burst. If the family is, by definition, a safe place, one will be less tempted to go around proposing idiotic deals such as "Let me tell you something—but you must promise never to breathe it to another soul."

Also, many family secrets are right there for the observing, on the telephone, bathroom shelf, or elsewhere, and without the protection of loyalty, there is no privacy. Obviously, reciprocity is a motivation for keeping one's mouth shut.

The other reason is that bad-mouthing one's relatives is an exceedingly unattractive characteristic, making one's own mouth look worse than one's relative. It is known as: If she would say something like that about her own brother, what would she say about me?

Both of these motives apply to divorced people. Saying disloyal things about one's former marriage partner is not only dangerous, in that it invites retaliation from one who is bound to have lots of ammunition, but it makes the speaker sound embittered. Must one then forgo the pleasure of revenge? Not entirely. In insisting that you say only kind and loyal things about a person to whom you were once married, Miss Manners is not excluding the possibility of ruining that person's reputation with a few well-chosen and kind words.

For example:

"Good heavens, it certainly wasn't his fault. He was trying the best he could; you have to give him credit for that, even if it didn't work."

"She's such a nice woman, you know. I kept telling myself that that ought to be enough."

Announcing Divorce

DEAR MISS MANNERS:

What is the correct way of announcing that I am divorced? Do I send out cards (and if so, how are they properly worded)? Can I give a party? Hire a billboard? Shout it from the housetops? I don't want to do anything in poor taste, but I am delighted with my new freedom and want to let people know about it.

GENTLE READER:

This will come as a shock, but society's laws about which events one may rejoice over and which one may not do not necessarily correspond to the true feelings of the participant. For example, if your nasty, crotchety, quarrelsome, critical old great-uncle dies and leaves you a fortune, you must try to look solemn, if not actually grieved. If your fourteen-year-old daughter is having a baby, you are supposed to act delighted. You may call this hypocrisy. As a matter of fact, Miss Manners calls it hypocrisy, too. The difference is probably that you don't consider hypocrisy one of the social graces, and she does. In any case, one does not brag about a divorce, however much personal satisfaction it may bring one. There is no formal announcement. Anything along the lines of hiring an airplane to write it in the sky is considered to be in poor taste.

Naturally, you want everyone to know. Miss Manners appreciates that. If you can write notes announcing a change of name or address and explain in them that it is a result of your recent divorce, that is a solution. You may even give a party, provided that the excuse is not the divorce itself, but a result of it, such as a party to show off your newly redecorated house, even if the redecoration is only the fact that you have put your clothes in both bedroom closets after emptying one of them of someone else's clothes.

Failing this pretext, you must be alert for opportunities of working the news into conversation. This is not difficult. If someone says, "Tell me, how have you been?" You may answer, "Well, I think everything is settled down now, since the divorce." Miss Manners urges you, for the sake of propriety, to keep a straight face.

Informing Relations

DEAR MISS MANNERS:

My one-and-a-half-year marriage ended in divorce. My relatives passed the word around, but I think not everybody knows. I got distant from them because there is "no divorce in the family." Eight months after, I got married again; but never told anybody, afraid of what they would think. Now, I just became a mother. How can I straighten things up?

GENTLE READER:

Well, you could keep going the way you are, and let them read the basic facts of your life in your obituary. Or you could just burst in with an important current announcement, presuming that they are already in possession of the previous ones, but providing re-caps on request. For example, you can write everyone that you and Lester have just produced a baby girl, and then, when someone says, "I thought your husband's name was Hiram," you reply, "Oh, heavens no, Hiram and I were divorced ages ago and I was remarried the following year—I thought you knew." What is to be avoided is making direct announcements of marriage and birth at the same time—"Just wanted to tell you that Lester Mickel and I got married and we have a darling baby girl."

The Reaction

DEAR MISS MANNERS:

What is the correct thing to say to someone who has just told you of his impending divorce?

GENTLE READER:

Miss Manners used to say, "Oh, I am so sorry," until a lady replied, "If I'm happy and he's happy, what are you so sorry about?" Miss Manners was forced to acknowledge that a quiet "I wish you the best" is more appropriate.

Taking Sides

DEAR MISS MANNERS:

My sister and I are close. Our husbands have become friends over the past twenty years. Now my sister and her husband are experiencing a long and unhappy, but not yet legal, separation. Although my brother-in-law has lived with his girl friend throughout the separation, he and my sister still profess a desire for reconciliation. How do my husband and I conduct ourselves without offending my husband's right to friendship, my sister's wounded feelings, and my loyalty?

GENTLE READER:

If your sister and your brother-in-law make their separation legal, you and your husband may certainly entertain them separately with whatever partners they may have. There are too many such disruptions now for anyone to expect others to take sides in their separations. If, however, you pursue this fair-minded policy now, during the trial period, and there is a successful reconciliation, they could easily, in their new harmony, transfer residual feelings of ill will to you. Worse, you could get stuck with the friendship of the now-deserted girl friend. At that rate, you would always have at least one weepy person in the house. It seems to Miss Manners that a temporary policy of blood over friendship would be practical.

A Divorcée's Rings

DEAR MISS MANNERS:

I am a divorced woman—mother of five—married twenty-six years. I have a lovely diamond wedding ring and engagement ring. Is it ever proper to wear these after divorce?

GENTLE READER:

What you have on your finger falls into two categories: jewelry and symbolism. Confusing the two leads to foolish acts, such as tossing perfectly good gold into a river because the giver turned out not to be so good. If you continue to wear the rings in the conventional way, you will retain the symbolism of marriage. Many widows want to do this and it is conceivable that a divorcée, divorced against her wishes or principles, may also want to do so. It is discouraging to prospective suitors, which you may or may not want to be. Retaining the jewelry without the symbolism is another matter. The engagement ring may be worn as is on the right hand and reclassified as a dinner ring, and the wedding ring may be worn on the right hand, perhaps with other bands, as a guard ring. You could also have both rings reset.

Retrieving the Ring

DEAR MISS MANNERS:

I have been dating a man for more than a year, and we want to get married. The problem is that his ex-wife has the family ring that his grandmother had given him.

Is it proper for the ex-wife to keep the ring or should she return it, since it is a family heirloom? I talked to my boyfriend about this, and he says he gave it to her and seems scared to ask for it back. He told me that he would gladly give her the money that it would be worth, but he has not spoken to her on this issue. I feel somewhat resentful here, although I realize that a divorce is painful and hard for both parties involved. I don't know why she should keep the ring when it would mean so much to me to have it and have a part of his family's history.

Miss Manners, what is the proper procedure here, as by all means I want to do what is right and correct for a young lady who wants to get engaged. I plan to stay with this man for the rest of my life, not just a few years like his first wife.

GENTLE READER:

Miss Manners could recommend to you that you consult a lawyer, who will explain that your husband has no legal right to this ring, but it would be cheaper and more interesting for you to read *The Eustace Diamonds* by dear Anthony Trollope for an understanding of the complications involved in the term "heirloom," which you use so freely.

That, however, is merely the legal thing to do. The proper thing, which you say you want to do, is for a young lady who wants to get engaged to avoid making it clear to the gentleman that of all the intimacies he has enjoyed with another before he met her, the only one that bothers her is the one involving jewelry.

✿ CHANGING NAMES AND HABITS

Miss, Mrs., Ms., or Mlle?

DEAR MISS MANNERS:

I have a question about forms of address. It is not uncommon for women today to reassume their maiden names following divorce. Indeed, it seems a considerate gesture if one's husband proposes to remarry five minutes after the decree becomes final. Resumption of one's own name eliminates many of the confusions that naturally arise from their being too many Mrs. Soandsos around. It takes no time at all for one's acquaintances and professional associates to accustom themselves to a change of name. This process can even be helped along by the simple expedient of ordering a few monogrammed sweaters and wearing them quite frequently during the early weeks. A more difficult problem is posed by selection of the correct form of address. I have always found Ms. appropriate for business purposes, but I do not care for its use in social situations. The term appears either rude or coy. If one is going to mingle with people socially, it seems to me that they have a perfectly good right to know. What are you: Miss or Mrs.? One is, of course, prepared for the odd gaffe. The true dimensions of the problem did not come home to me until I enrolled in a French course and was asked point-blank by the instructor if I were Madame or Mademoiselle. I explained my difficulty, and he pronounced gallantly that I was, of course, Mademoiselle. All very well in that setting. The fellow was not only French, but a diplomat.

This remedy does not carry over so easily to my personal life, which is conducted almost exclusively in English. How are my children to introduce me to their friends—as Miss H.? This seems ridiculous. As Mrs. H.? Clearly not. Ms. H.? Most children have far too well-developed a sense of natural dignity to use the word Ms.

May I propose adoption of a new form of address, the only one that I have felt thoroughly comfortable with in my brief experience as a divorcée returned to her family name? From here on out, let all such American ladies be known as Mademoiselle. It is easy to say, unlike the word Ms.; properly used, it would define one's position as clearly as Miss or Mrs.; and then it has an upbeat quality, a certain *je ne sais quoi*, a cachet that would be welcome to the entire population so addressed.

GENTLE READER:

Mademoiselle Manners sait quoi. Elle sait that your enchantment with the romance of being addressed in French has blinded you to how silly it sounds in English. If your children introduced you to their friends as Mlle H., you could not blame the youngsters if they assumed that you were the governess, if not the *au pair* girl.

If it really matters to you, you might consider moving to a French-speaking nation, such as France. However, you will find that as you grow older, you will increasingly be addressed there as Madame, regardless of your marital status, on the same assumption that your French diplomat made: that young ladies should be single and old ones should be married.

A less drastic solution would be to go to medical school, so that you may be addressed as Dr. H. And a less drastic one still would be to get over your prejudice against Ms. (if you can learn French, you can learn to pronounce Ms.), as it was invented as "a new form of address" for just such problems as you describe. In any case, Miss is preferable to Mrs. in this situation, as it was increasingly being used as an all-inclusive business term before Ms. came along.

DEAR MISS MANNERS:

I have recently been divorced. I am very uncertain as to my title for mail, credit cards, etc. I was taught that "Mrs." means "the wife of," and so it seems wrong to use Mrs. with my first name. Of course, we know there is Ms., but I have mixed feelings on that. I am a woman in business and also a mother.

GENTLE READER:

If we know there is Ms., why don't we use it? Why is it that the people for whom this is the best solution—the only solution, in fact, as Mrs. is indeed incorrect with a woman's first name—have mixed feelings about it instead of unmixed relief?

The truly correct style is to combine Mrs. with your maiden and last names (Daffodil Perfect who married and divorced Mr. Awful becomes Mrs. Perfect Awful) but few people use it nowadays.

✿ THE SUCCESSORS

Why so many nuclear families explode is not anything Miss Manners cares to study. There are too many people in the field already, and Miss Manners has noticed that anyone who stands too close is apt to find something flying into his or her eye. What Miss Manners prefers to do is to wait until the dust settles and then to study the new elements that have been formed, and their relationships. It isn't easy. Miss Manners has been asked the following questions in recent weeks:

· My son's ex-wife has remarried, and of course she is no longer my daughter-in-law. But I often see her because she has custody of my grandchildren. How do I introduce her to my friends?

· I grew up with the daughters of my mother's second husband. My mother and their father are no longer married, but we are still on affectionate terms. They introduce me as their "brother," and I have been introducing them as my "ex-stepsisters." Are they exaggerating, or am I being too precise and cold? We all have a half-sister in common, and we all call her our "sister."

· I often have dealings with my wife's ex-husband, because he is the father of the children I live with. How do I refer to him when we make travel arrangements and so on? We get along fine, and I want a pleasant term.

All of these people are trying to avoid the harshness of saying "ex." "Ex" is so final, and these relationships are obviously continuing, or there wouldn't be any problem. The other prefix they don't like is "step." This was given a bad name by the publicity attached to the unfortunate home life of Cinderella, although dear Edith Wharton refers charmingly to "the steps" resulting from various marriages of her characters in *The Children,* that marvelous jet-set novel written before such people had ever set foot in a jet.

Other terms could be invented. One could refer to "the children's bio-daddy," as a gentleman of Miss Manners' acquaintance suggested, or to "my sisters once removed." Another gentleman of Miss Manners' acquaintance calls his younger step-brother and -sisters collectively, "My father's second litter." Miss Manners believes in recycling old words and rescuing them, if possible, from bad associations they don't deserve. Many kind people who devote their lives to children they didn't foist upon the world resent the name of stepmother or stepfather, which suggests that they hand out poisoned apples.

In some cases, the relationship can simply be briefly described: "The mother of my grandchildren," "the father of my stepchildren." In others, it is not necessary to define the relationship exactly and, unless those so designated object, there is no reason why the terms "brother" and "sister" cannot be used for the variations on this relationship. Provided the whole thing doesn't get out of hand and we all wander around sounding like a vast revival meeting. Wouldn't it be rather sweet to hear one grown man refer to another as "the father of my children"?

Introductions

DEAR MISS MANNERS:

Miss Manners has discussed how to introduce one's ex-relatives to friends when they are still on good terms. I thought it would be better if the mother-in-law introduces her grandchildren's mother as "This is Jane. She was my daughter-in-law, but now she is my friend." The brother can introduce his ex-step-sisters as cousins without hurting their feelings. For a new friend, the term "cousin" will suffice. The husband can just introduce his wife's ex-husband as "Jane's first husband." What does Miss Manners think about my suggestions?

GENTLE READER:

Must you spell out all these severed relationships? Miss Manners shudders to think how the current daughter-in-law would be introduced.

A *Civil Reunion after a Civil Suit*

DEAR MISS MANNERS:

This is going to be a new one, even for you. My wife's ex-husband has invited us "for tea"! You have to understand that this was not a friendly divorce. As a matter of fact, he sued for adultery, after having put detectives on us. We have not spoken in eight years. But now he's remarried, and wants to be "civilized." So now comes this invitation, on an engraved "Mr. and Mrs." card. I suppose his wife is curious to meet his ex-wife, and the trouble is, my wife is curious, too, to see his new wife, and wants us to go. How are we supposed to act?

GENTLE READER:

Happy. This is a competition, in which the idea is to show whom fate thought it right to reward, after all. Your job is too look at your wife with the same expression that the detectives caught on your face eight years ago.

Sour Grapes Flambé

DEAR MISS MANNERS:

My ex-husband is coming to our daughter's wedding and, as a matter of fact, giving the bride away. Fine. My daughter wants it that way, and I have no objection. But he wants to bring that bimbo he calls his new wife, who is not much older than our daughter. The divorce was very difficult. She is the one who took him away from me. I held on for a long time, thinking he would get over it. My friends and pastor had explained to me that it is natural for a middle-aged man to panic and have a little fling—but this one went on for three years, and I couldn't take it any longer. I have seen him once or twice since, and have managed to be dignified, but do I really have to see her? My daughter, although she sided with me, seems to be friendly with them, and thinks she should come. If so, do I have to be polite to her?

GENTLE READER:

As a point of etiquette, one cannot exclude a spouse from a wedding invitation or any invitation for which people are invited in couples. A marriage is a marriage and creates a social unit, regardless of whether it was achieved through kidnapping, as your account suggests. The wife's bimbohood is irrelevant.

However, Miss Manners cannot help noticing a flaw in your perception of who has injured you by dissolving your marriage. It is an old and ugly trick of society to pit the women against one another in a difficult situation and excuse the men even if, as seems to be the fact in your case, the women don't even know each other. Miss Manners thinks it would be helpful to consider this so that you may be in more of a frame of mind to work on your real question, which is: How can I triumph over my successor in front of all my friends and relations?

By acting triumphant. How does one act triumphant? Not by being haughty,.

as is your inclination, but by being generous. There is nothing like the full gratification of one's wishes to convince one that the world is a delightful place and
all the people in it just as adorable as they can be.

Suppose it had been your fondest wish to unload your husband so that you
could pursue a clandestine relationship with a man so important that his identity
must remain secret, or to exercise your genius as a scriptwriter, or whatever.
But because of your kindheartedness and your realization of how incompetent
he is to fend for himself and how difficult for a woman to tolerate, you despaired
of ever ridding yourself of his tiresome presence.

Along comes a woman eager for the job. But your conscience will not let you
jump at the chance. She is too young to know what she is doing. How can you
use her ignorance to stick her with this burden? Yet, she insists. Well, you have
tried your best to save her. Now it is your turn to live. Such a woman would
greet her ex-husband's new wife with charm and care, just managing to suppress
an air of triumph that would reveal the happiness and relief she has in her
postmarital life.

It is not an easy role to play. However, one is on stage, like it or not, at an
event such as a wedding, and the alternative is to play an embittered woman
who has lost what she wanted.

Naming New Relationships

DEAR MISS MANNERS:

Recently, a particularly pugnacious friend, Lise, and I got in a debate over
the proper title for one of her relatives. A few years ago, Lise's mother died and
after a year, Lise's father remarried. My friend and I both agree that her
father's new wife is her stepmother. However, I say her stepmother's mother
is now her stepgrandmother. Lise denies this, since her original maternal grandmother is still alive. Lise claims as long as her real grandmother is alive, she
cannot have a stepgrandmother. I say that Lise is selfish and crass to insist on her
original grandmother's death before she can have a stepgrandmother. Please tell
us who is correct so we can cease our petty bickering.

GENTLE READER:

Be gentle with your friend Lise. Coming from a home in which steps are engaged only for positions that are already vacated, she does not have the modern
child's understanding of the complications of step relationships and the possibilities for exploitation that they represent. If she did, she wouldn't dream of
turning down an applicant for the position of grandmother.

The number of stepparents one may have is limited only by the activities of the
original parents. They are additions, rather than replacements, to the original
relatives. Lise would, no doubt, properly recognize that her mother, although
deceased, remains her mother. She is certainly entitled to a maternal stepgrandmother, in addition to her maternal grandmother. A child who has both
parents remarried can easily collect eight grandparents and the corresponding
birthday presents.

Collected Photographs

DEAR MISS MANNERS:

I have a wall in my dining room where I have each of my sons' graduation pictures. Under each picture I have that son's wedding picture, and under each of these, a picture of their children. Everyone thinks it is such a novel idea and how nice they look. Here is my problem. My oldest son was divorced. He has now remarried a woman with one boy. What do I do about them? I can't take down his first wife's picture since she is the mother of my grandchildren. His second wife and her boy also come over. How can I arrange something so as not to hurt her feelings, either? They are all eight-by-ten pictures.

GENTLE READER:

Congratulations: your picture collection has now moved into the now fashionable style known as eclectic. Miss Manners, who is very orderly, sympathizes with what has happened to your careful symmetry, but is afraid that people take precedence over wall decorations and one must face the fact that a great many families these days are eclectic.

THE CHILDREN

Dear child, of course you want to tell your mommy simply everything, don't you? You certainly don't want to keep back any little secrets from your very own daddy, do you? The question is: Do you want to tell Mommy everything you know about Daddy, and do you want to share with Daddy all of Mommy's little secrets?

Whatever else divorce may be for children, it is a severe etiquette problem. Miss Manners is always hearing grown-ups wail about the difficulties of maintaining social relations with mere friends when they are partners in a divorce. She thinks at least equal consideration should be given to the diplomacy problems of the descendants of such people. Whether they are big or small, residents or visitors in their parents' homes, these children have to consider such problems as:

1. How much can I cater to one parent's curiosity without betraying the privacy of the other?

2. How much free rein can I give to my natural discussion of what I see, hear, and think without getting myself involved in my parents' feelings about each other?

3. How can I observe special occasions, such as my birthday, graduation, or wedding, with both parents present and not have the event taken over by their drama, rather than mine?

4. How can I play off one of them against the other to my own advantage?

Most children have a natural instinct for number four in this list, and Miss Manners is not going to abet them. But in numbers one through three, they need all the help they can get. You may expect Miss Manners to come out in favor of discretion, as she normally does. Indeed, she would suggest to the grown-up offspring of unhappily divorced people that details about money, sex, or any other possible area of irritation—and in a rousing divorce, anything can qualify —be withheld when possible. But it is not always possible for grown-ups, and never really possible for minors. One cannot maintain a semblance of normal family life while constantly trying to censor one's conversation. Nor should children of any age be expected to curtail the great events of their own lives to pander to the sensitivities of their parents. Not having succeeded in one's own marriage is no excuse for spoiling the wedding of one's child.

Naturally, Miss Manners expects all parents to realize this, and control their own behavior accordingly. Naturally, Miss Manners realizes that they often will not and sometimes cannot. What can the children do to encourage them to be civilized? They can do nothing. If one parent seems to be abusing the other, a child who stares stonily back and does nothing will serve to remind an adult not to risk a good relationship by dwelling on a bad one.

Confused Children

DEAR MISS MANNERS:

I am feeling incorrect. What am I supposed to do if my mother and father get a divorce? How are my brother and sister and I supposed to react? Do we have to pick a parent to live with? If we don't get or pick the other parent, do we get to see that parent a certain day or many days a week? If one parent asks us to do one thing and another parent another thing, which one do we listen to and why? Why does my brother, age six, hate my father so much? Please give me the answers because I can't figure them out for myself and I need the advice.

GENTLE READER:

There is no reason for you to feel incorrect, now or in any confusion that may arise from your new situation. It is a common mistake for those who have been put in an awkward situation by others to take upon themselves the responsibility for the awkwardness. Perhaps your brother's hatred is a feeling of resentment against the disruption of family life. Justified or not, it is likely to pass.

The fact is that all three of you children still have two parents. Whichever one you live with most, you will still be the children of the other. It is unlikely that you will have much say about when you will live where (but if you are consulted, Miss Manners urges you to go against your natural inclination and pick the one who makes irksome rules for you, not the one who lets you do whatever you want).

Your duty is to treat both of them with respect, and to obey the house rules of the one whose house you are in at any given moment. Miss Manners is sorry to spoil the game of But Daddy Lets Me Do Homework with the Television On or But Mommy Lets Me Eat Whatever I Want, but she considers these games incorrect behavior.

Adult Visitors

DEAR MISS MANNERS:

I am a divorcée with two small children. I would occasionally like to have a friend spend the night, but the one time I tried it, the children asked all kinds of rude questions at the breakfast table in front of him. While I don't want to lie to my children, I didn't want to embarrass my friend, either. I don't like to tell the children they can't talk freely, and I'm not sure they would shut up even if I did. Am I failing in my duty to my children if I insist on their being polite to a guest?

GENTLE READER:

Your duty to your children is to teach them the basic fact of life, which is that everyone occasionally does things that he or she does not wish to explain.

Marriage Two
(Prerequisite: Marriage for Beginners)

❧ SECOND WEDDINGS AND ON UP

It is becoming the custom now for people who are already grown-up to get married.

Wedding etiquette has always been based on an assumption of youth and innocence on the part of the chief participants, and this is what gives traditional weddings their peculiarly bittersweet appeal. Grown-ups were not expected to get married, or at least to have any fun doing so. Miss Manners doesn't see why not. Weddings between people who are well acquainted not only with life, but with each other, should be fascinating occasions.

They should be equally festive, but different. Grown-ups should not make themselves silly by following procedures designed for children. There is nothing wrong with an adult birthday party, for example, but the participants do not wear Mary Janes or short pants, and do not play Pin the Tail on the Donkey (Spin the Bottle is another matter) or pop balloons. It is still possible to have a good time. One's last marriage may be far greater cause for celebration than one's first.

Let us consider some of the differences between grown-up and child marriage couples. Grown-ups usually have children, toasters, grown-up friends, flatware, formed tastes. Grown-ups usually do not have friends who will dye shoes to match or wear colored dinner jackets; the sense of permanence required to have towels monogrammed; parents who say, "Oh, what the hell, go ahead. We want this to be something you'll remember all your life."

Grown-up women do not look cute in white tulle or organdy candy-box wrappings. For grown-up brides, regardless of previous marital or other escapades, hats, flowers, or hair are more becoming than little princess wispies. It is stretching the imagination far enough to suggest that the father of a young girl has had any hand in disposing of her hand, but the idea of a father's giving away a grown woman is ridiculous. The close relatives whose cooperation adult bridal couples most need are their children. If anyone is to be given a role in the ceremony, it should be they.

The pretense that a wedding means that a fledgling is leaving the nest is also even less plausible than for youthful marriages, and therefore Miss Manners believes that it is inappropriate for grown-up brides to have their parents issue their invitations for them. As that is the form for the traditional formal invitation, Miss Manners prefers skipping that approach altogether—rather than altering the wording to make it sound as if the couple is giving itself away—and writing real letters:

> *Dear Rosemary,*
> *Philpott and I are being married on Saturday, June twentieth, at four o'clock at the Town and Suburb Club, and we would be so pleased if you would be with us. . . .*

If the couple simply cannot stay away from the engravers', they should issue invitations to the wedding reception as they would to another formal party (please see p. 574).

The effort of writing out the invitations is compensated by the reduced necessity of writing letters after the wedding to thank someone for the lovely electric wall ornament. No one has to fork over more than one major present, so it is not necessary to give them for multiple marriages. Grown-ups getting married not only don't need electric hot plates and linen towels, but are likely to be in dispute over which of them should throw away his or her set. Only intimates, who know what might be useful and pleasing, and who take pleasure in the idea of making these people presents, need bother.

Of course, the chief advantage of being a grown-up is that one can do what one wishes, including disregarding all sensible advice.

Types of Weddings

DEAR MISS MANNERS:
Is it proper to have a large wedding your second time around? I was married for a short time. My ex and I had a very small wedding. My fiancé has never been married before, and I don't think it would be fair to him if we couldn't have a large wedding. I wish the first marriage had never happened. Also, can I wear a white dress and invite my relatives who were at my first wedding? I see no reason why I cannot! Please advise. I have been divorced two years.

GENTLE READER:
Miss Manners recognizes three general categories of weddings in which the

Dear Alexandrina:

Brian Botchitt and I are being married here at the house on Saturday, the twenty-ninth of February, at four o'clock. We very much hope that you and Ian will be with us for the ceremony and a small reception afterwards.

Affectionately yours,
Aunt Tracy

An invitation to a second wedding. Really, this should be written on the bride's monogrammed paper or her formal house paper, but this bride prefers the modern custom of having one paper for private and professional use. Such a paper could have used the title "Miss" or "Ms." Paper marked with a married woman's formal husband's name and address is properly used for her household business correspondence only.

bride is either not at her first wedding, or not in her first youth, or both. They are:

1. The Snicker-Proof Wedding. This is the low-key wedding prescribed by advisers who provide new brides with schedules of things they must do from the minute of engagement until the consummation of the marriage, for the greatest possible lavish, knock-'em-dead display—and curtly tell veteran brides to do everything "quietly," as if enjoying getting married more than once were brazen. If you marry in a small chapel or judge's chamber, wearing a navy blue suit with a flower pinned on the lapel, have no one but your and his parents present, and celebrate afterward with a luncheon that nobody else in the restaurant can tell is bridal, you will violate no one's standards of propriety.

2. The This Time We Know What's What Wedding. This can be small or large, but it is distinguished in its festivity by less formality and more sophistication than the blushing, veil-covered bride conveys. It does not mimic a first wedding, but replaces some of its fixtures with advanced good taste. The bride does not wear a standard wedding dress, but something more party-ish in a flattering color; she is not attended by a girl chorus, but by a real friend or by her own children; she does not have her parents send engraved cards, but herself writes a charming letter inviting each guest.

3. The I Got Cheated Last Time Wedding. This is the wedding in which the bride says the heck with what people say—I've always wanted a dream wedding with all the trimmings, and by God, this time I'm going to have it. If you want to do this—and Miss Manners takes it that such is your inclination—then simply follow the directions for a first wedding.

Of the three types, Miss Manners much prefers the second, which combines appropriateness with joyousness. However, she understands a yearning for the third, and only cautions you to cultivate an air of self-mocking humor about it, rather than keeping a straight face. And she warns you that the less generous of your acquaintances will cluck about it's all being frightfully improper. Don't let it bother you.

Wedding Dress

DEAR MISS MANNERS:

My daughter, aged twenty-eight, is marrying for the second time and she wants to have a church wedding this time. Would you please tell me what the differences are between a first and a second wedding? Should she wear a veil and have her father give her away? What color dress should she wear?

GENTLE READER:

The chief difference is in the amount of judgment the bride is assumed to have about what she is doing. It is not customary to have her given away as new, and therefore she is not gift-wrapped in white dress or veil. Miss Manners is not hysterical about the enforcement of this somewhat tasteless symbolism, as some people are, but the conventional bridal dress for a second (or fifth) wedding is a pastel dress or suit with a hat.

Many people think that a white wedding dress is the packaging for an unused bride, which gives them a good snicker at most weddings. This is not true; it is true, however, that it is conventionally associated with a first wedding. Wearing off-white, which is practically the same thing, for a second wedding may prevent the snickers of those who believe in the sanctity of this rule. Then again, it may not. People always seem to be snickering at weddings these days over one thing or another.

Guests' Clothes

DEAR MISS MANNERS:
Help! I'm getting married for the second time. A private garden ceremony will be followed by a reception given two weeks later. I'm having trouble with the invitations that will be included with the announcements. I prefer dressy dress, since my long wedding dress will also be appropriate to wear to the reception. I just consulted a book of etiquette that says to use "Black tie" for evening attire and "Informal" for dark suits and dresses. Black tie seems to mean tuxedos, which I don't want, and informal in this day and age could mean Levi's and sports shirts to some people, which I don't want! Any suggestions? The reception will be given at 7:30 PM.

I have a second question: Should my invitations read "a reception" or "a cocktail party" or just what? A cold buffet and wedding cake will be served. There is the possibility of dancing. I'm concerned about the wording because I don't want my guests to feel obligated to bring or send a wedding gift yet, at the same time, I don't want to say "No gifts," either.

GENTLE READER:
A bride may dictate to her fiancé, her parents, and her future parents-in-law what to wear to her wedding and what to do, but she is expected to show some faith in the good taste of her friends. Miss Manners agrees with you about not stating "Informal" or "No gifts"; the most you can do is to set an example of formality in your invitations (please see pp. 320–324), and hope that they will follow the usual practice of dressing nicely and not bringing presents under their arms. This is one reason you should not refer to the event as a cocktail party, which sounds racy, while we all know that marriage is not. "Reception" is the polite term for a late afternoon party with liquor.

Who Pays

DEAR MISS MANNERS:
I have a problem. Our divorced daughter is marrying a divorced man. They are planning on having a meal after the church ceremony and a week later is the reception. What are our responsibilities in regard to footing the bills for the meals? Do we offer to pay for both, or neither?

GENTLE READER:

Miss Manners hopes you did not neglect, on the occasion of your daughter's first wedding, the ceremony of saying, "OK, kid, that's it. From now on you're on your own." It is a practical tradition these days. No, you are not responsible for paying for festivities related to a second wedding, although it is charming to do so. For that matter, the same is true of a first wedding. These decisions are usually based on the desirability of the bridegroom, as assessed by the bride's parents.

Presents for a Second Wedding

DEAR MISS MANNERS:

I would like to know if it is expected or necessary to buy wedding gifts for second and third marriages when the others ended in divorce. My husband says yes and I say no. We are invited to both second and thirds.

GENTLE READER:

This sort of thing has got to stop somewhere, especially with the price of silver being what it is today. Since your romantic friends show no sign of stopping, Miss Manners suggests that you do. Presents need not be provided for second or third weddings.

🌹 STEPCHILDREN

DEAR MISS MANNERS:

Could you give some advice on throwing a family engagement party—the family being my children and my fiancé's children. We are going to put together a his-hers-theirs family—he has custody of one of his three children, I have both of mine, and we are going to have at least one child of our own before we get too old to cope—and feel that this is the time to start. It frankly hasn't been easy. His son refuses to accept me as a permanent fixture, and keeps pretending that I am just passing through Daddy's life so there is no need to get my name right; my daughter can't stay off his lap, and my son alternates between vying for my fiancé's affections with his own son, and ignoring all of us. And then there are the two children who live with their mother and will be with us on holidays—I never know whether they are going to be sweet as pie with me, or hostile.

We haven't told any of them that we have definitely decided to get married, because we want to do it all at once and make a festive occasion of it. This family is going to need some sense of tradition to keep it together, and this could be one of these times. I thought we would make our surprise announcement first, and then let everybody say how they feel about it. But we thought we could have a fancy cake and sparkling grape juice in wine glasses. Do you have any suggestions for this new type of engagement party?

GENTLE READER:

Yes. Plan a different form of entertainment. The cake and the grape juice sound fine, but for heaven's sake, don't ask all these various children to tell you how they feel about your engagement. They might do so.

Surprise engagement announcements should be made only to people who will act delighted and can afford to do so because the new arrangements will not affect their lives. (Surprises can also be pulled on those whose discomfort will increase your pleasure, such as former spouses and sweethearts.)

The parents and the children of newly engaged couples have the right to be informed of the news in private, so that they can air their uglier feelings about the situation—and the individuals—before having to work themselves up into some expression of festivity. Each of you should tell your own blood relatives separately, taking care not to make the common mistake of putting the matter as a question that their inclinations will help decide.

Then have the party, each warning your own relatives to behave as if they were delighted for the sake of the others. If everyone at the party is pretending to be pleased, you should be able to enjoy your sparkling grape juice and cake, and will have set the proper tone for future ceremonial occasions.

Including Children

DEAR MISS MANNERS:

I am writing on behalf of our daughter, who has two daughters by a previous marriage (ages seven and eight and a half years). This is the second marriage for the man she plans to wed, and he has no children. What role, if any, would her daughters play? It will be performed in church, with the reception in the church basement. They will have one couple as attendants.

GENTLE READER:

The most destructive etiquette rule there ever was barred children from their parents' subsequent weddings. It has now been largely abandoned, but Miss Manners cannot imagine anyone with any sense ever having followed it. (This is not to be taken as general license for throwing strict old rules to the winds. If each person used his or her own common sense about every rule of etiquette, the world would be a sloppy place to live in, and how would Miss Manners earn her bread?)

The children should play as large a part as they wish, which also means that a wish not to participate should be respected. Such a wedding is, after all, the beginning of a new life for them, as well as for the bride and bridegroom. Although second weddings do not usually include great troupes of wedding attendants, however many children there are should be added to the basic two —maid of honor and best man—or be allowed to fill those parts. Your two young granddaughters could be flower girls, or one could be a flower girl and the other a ring bearer.

If they don't want to be that deeply involved—and there are sometimes peculiar feelings among children in these cases that go against the natural instinct for glamour—they could simply stand with their mother at the altar, or they could sit in the front pew with you. Even if there were twelve children from six previous marriages, Miss Manners would still recommend putting them into the picture.

Stepchildren in the Wedding Party

DEAR MISS MANNERS:

I have encountered what I believe to be a rare problem in the relationship between my ex-husband and myself. Until now, the distance between my home and his has been an asset, as it is a two-hour drive and keeps him from becoming overly involved in my life. My nine-year-old daughter has been asked to be a junior bridesmaid in his wedding. I know that the bride and groom will be too busy to drive four hours on a trip to pick up my daughter and another four after the wedding, bringing her home. When I expressed this concern to my ex, he explained that my husband and I will be invited to the ceremony, thus solving the transportation dilemma.

We are the parents of three young children, one a nursing infant. A trip out of town for a weekend will be a major project for us, as well as a considerable expense. This occasion is very important to our daughter, however, and she is looking forward to it. I would certainly enjoy seeing her in a wedding, although I did not hold the groom in particularly high regard and do not relish the thought of going to his wedding with all the inconveniences it will involve. Do you have any suggestions on how I can handle the situation gracefully and provide my oldest child with the pleasure of this occasion?

GENTLE READER:

What is the fun of divorce and remarriage if it does not provide you with many extra relatives to perform family tasks? Your ex-in-laws fall into this category, as does, you will find, the new bride. One way of using them on this occasion would be to ask a grandparent, aunt, uncle, or cousin of your child's (on her father's side) to provide her transportation. Another is to call your child's future stepmother and ask her to suggest other transportation. Miss Manners is sure that if you explain to her that you would adore to go to her wedding, that you would find it an absolute scream to watch your former husband being married again, she would assist in saving you the inconvenience of the trip.

Stepmothers

DEAR MISS MANNERS:

With Mother's Day coming up, I would like to know who is responsible for buying gifts for the stepmother of small children. My sons are "four parent" children living with their mother, but very much in contact with their father and stepmother. I have, in past years, provided gifts for their stepmother and grandmother, from them, for Mother's Day.

Is this the proper thing for me to do? Do you have any suggestions to help ease the edge of inflation in regards to these "special days"?

GENTLE READER:

You have missed the point about Mother's Day presents on two counts, and both of these mistakes are costing you money.

1. The present should be provided by the child according to his ability. Naturally, if you are providing your former husband's second wife with a present appropriate to your income level it is going to cost more than if the child, assessing his allowance, chooses, say, a sachet or a prettily wrapped chocolate.

2. The most appropriate presents for such occasions are made, not bought. This is therefore a marvelous opportunity for you to encourage your child to choose presents from among the wealth of refrigerator art, ceramic whatnots, and two-inch-square woven pillows that every parent with custody has around the house.

Anniversaries

Marking Many Anniversaries

DEAR MISS MANNERS:

What are the proper gifts for different anniversaries? I mean like the paper anniversary, wood, silver, and so on. I've seen various lists, but they often disagree.

GENTLE READER:

A couple married for twenty-five years (to each other) may celebrate a silver anniversary and give or be given silver presents. At fifty years, they may celebrate a golden anniversary. A lady who has occupied the same throne for sixty years may celebrate a diamond jubilee and sell souvenirs, such as china plates with her profile painted on them. Miss Manners regards any such designations for lesser milestones as being silly. If you wish to accept the dictums (or dicta) of various self-serving industries and believe that the eighteen-month anniversary means new back tires for the car while rotating the others, go right ahead.

A First Anniversary Party

DEAR MISS MANNERS:

My daughter and her husband were married in the courthouse last fall. We didn't have time for a shower or any kind of celebration. We are Roman Catholic, and they didn't want to wait for all the preparations of marriage. They only received a few gifts from close relatives. My side says, no party, no gifts. This keeps eating at me, no nice memories for them, and I let the relatives down. I can't shake the feeling of not having anything. Would it be all right to have some sort of gathering for their first wedding anniversary? If so, what would you suggest? I feel they lost out on so much and let the relatives down without a wedding celebration. I was just wondering, before it is too late.

GENTLE READER:

It *is* too late for a wedding reception; the first thing to do is to face that. You cannot, out of a feeling of family obligation or greed for missed presents, pretend that this is a wedding. However, it is a perfectly delightful idea to give this couple a festive anniversary party which can be practically indistinguishable from a delayed wedding reception—one given, say a week or two after the ceremony. Then, if your family decides it has gotten its money's worth of drinks, people may decide to give the couple anniversary presents.

Overly Exciting Anniversaries

DEAR MISS MANNERS:

Every year on our wedding anniversary, my husband likes to wear some strange outfit to dinner to remind me that my "real husband is not so strange at all." One year he was Mickey Mouse; another year, he was Sinbad the Sailor. It's funny, sure, but I think it should be a time for romance and tenderness. It's especially embarrassing when we celebrate with another couple. Is his "act" ill-mannered when we invite someone else over? How can I tell him without hurting his feelings? What should I do?

GENTLE READER:

Miss Manners hesitates to suggest "doing" anything that would interfere with such an exciting marriage. If there were any husband a woman would have to decide to love uncritically or to leave immediately, it would be a husband who dresses up as Mickey Mouse. If you have any desire to celebrate one more anniversary with this man, Miss Manners recommends that you declare it a costume party and wear a polka dot skirt, white gloves, and black ears.

Renewing Wedding Vows

DEAR MISS MANNERS:

Next year, we will celebrate twenty-five years of marriage. I am thinking of renewing our vows, but I'm at a loss to know all the procedures. Our children are twelve and fourteen years, so they are too young to give a party for us. Please send information on church etiquette and everything.

GENTLE READER:

The chief thing to bear in mind when planning such a ceremony is that it marks a continuation of your marriage, rather than a reenactment of its beginning. While you should invite the same people there who witnessed the wedding, you should not attempt to look or act like the couple you were twenty-five years ago. Anyway, Miss Manners thinks that the pledges of a couple who have been married for twenty-five years are infinitely more moving than those of people who don't know what they're getting into.

You may ask the same clergyman to perform the ceremony, or your present one to repeat the original service. And you should have the original wedding party there.

But you are now a grown-up couple with children. Include them in the wedding party. Dress festively but appropriately to your age. And entertain your friends afterward as grown-ups do, by giving a party in your own house. Invite them by letter.

Golden Threads among the Silver

DEAR MISS MANNERS:

We have just been married fifty years. When we celebrated, I wore a gold dress which I had made; my husband was in a rented suit. My question is: My daughter-in-law will be married twenty-five years soon. Would it be proper for me to wear my gold dress at the party?

GENTLE READER:

You show a very proper delicacy about not wanting to outshine your daughter-in-law's silver presence with your golden one. Perhaps that is why people in your family seem to stay together. However, Miss Manners thinks it would be quite charming to display the tradition of marital stability, so rare these days, that your dress represents, and your daughter-in-law, if she is as considerate as you deserve, will agree.

Toasts

DEAR MISS MANNERS:

We are giving a surprise thirtieth wedding anniversary party to my brother-in-law and his wife. I must make the toast. Is it proper to thank everyone for attending, and can you give me an appropriate toast for the occasion?

GENTLE READER:

Toasting the guests for having made the effort to attend a party is Miss Manners' idea of excessive humility. She believes in having as few toasts as possible, and hold the butter. The best toast for a wedding anniversary is still, ''To Esmeralda and Gideon!''

The Wedding Dress

DEAR MISS MANNERS:

After all these years, my wedding dress still fits! Do you think it's all right if I wear it to my golden wedding anniversary party? I haven't yet tried it out for my husband.

GENTLE READER:

It depends on how well both of you have worn over the years. The desired effect is that of a woman of your age, whatever it is, in a becoming dress with sentimental attachments. As you neglected to consult Miss Manners when you were married, she does not know what type of wedding dress it is, but warns you that sweetheart necklines were not designed for grown-ups. Check with your mirror, but not your husband. If he advises against it, it will only set you thinking that the romance has gone out of the marriage.

Performing

DEAR MISS MANNERS:

My husband and I are celebrating our fiftieth anniversary this June. I would like my party to be a fun affair, in which all will participate.

Twenty years ago, I was active at charitable functions and I pantomimed an opera record. I was considered fairly good and was asked to repeat it several times. I would like to perform at my own party, but my daughter thinks it is not proper since I am the hostess. Could you please advise me on the correct procedure since I am anxious not to spoil a beautiful party.

GENTLE READER:

It is considered fair to warn guests when there will be performances of amateur talent at innocent-sounding social events. Miss Manners is in favor of such gatherings, and urges you to arrange a party where you and others can display their abilities. But she agrees that it is unfair to spring this on un-suspecting people when you are not only the hostess but an honoree; in other words, where you already have a double claim to center stage.

Thanking Hosts

DEAR MISS MANNERS:

Our children are giving us a large party for our fiftieth wedding anniversary soon, and they are going to quite an expense (which we didn't want them to do —at least not so much) and now I'd like to show our appreciation for their trouble by doing something in return. Can you suggest what we can do? We have four children, three in Wisconsin and one in Germany, and would like to give them each the same thing if possible. I do not like to show favoritism at any time, so I am very puzzled as to what to do or say. I presume there will be toasts at the party, and again I don't know what would sound proper besides "thank you."

GENTLE READER:

Nonfavoritism does not preclude showering them with favors, orally and otherwise. A graceful reply to the toasts would be to wish your children the same happiness they have given you. A thoughtful token of appreciation would be a family photograph, framed in silver if you wish, with a message of appreciation to each child individually.

Distributing Decorations

DEAR MISS MANNERS:

We are about to give a very large family party, celebrating my grandparents' sixtieth anniversary. All ages will be there. We have ordered a huge cake representing, in icing, various milestones of their lives. My question may seem silly to you, but I know from experience at my children's birthday parties that it will come up. It is, who gets the fancy decorations on the cake when the cake is distributed to be eaten? Whenever my children have parties, I try to see that there are enough icing roses or whatever, so that every child gets one, because otherwise there are a lot of hurt feelings. At a party this size, it's not possible. But I bet all the children and maybe even some of the adults are going to say they want this figure or that. Should I (I'm acting as hostess) just say, "No, they go to Grams and Gramps because it's their day?" and then pile all the trimmings on their plates?

GENTLE READER:

Yes, if you want to save yourself the trouble of celebrating their sixty-first anniversary. Those things taste dreadful. Miss Manners approves of serving them as food to children, because children are hardy sorts and this is a perfect way of teaching them that some of the most beautiful things they see will turn out to be disgusting inside. However, if your grandparents have not yet learned this, they may squeak by without having to. If Miss Manners were serving this cake, she would not entertain any special orders, but would smile blandly at all requests, perhaps answering, if pressed, "It's all white meat."

Silver Presents

DEAR MISS MANNERS:

Our children are planning to give us a twenty-fifth anniversary party. Is there a nice way to make an invitation asking them not to bring silver pieces? We really wouldn't use most of it, and I'm not crazy about it, anyway. We would much rather take a trip.

GENTLE READER:

As Miss Manners has often observed, there is no nice way to suggest that you do not want presents, as it always comes off sounding like "Don't try to kiss me because I won't let you." In this particular case, the price of silver being what it is today, Miss Manners suspects you may have less of a problem than you anticipate. If you do get silver, however, do not complain. You can go a long way on it these days.

DEAR MISS MANNERS:

We are planning a party for our twenty-fifth wedding anniversary. Friends and relatives will expect to bring gifts to the party, but we don't want or need the usual assortment of bric-a-brac which is given for anniversary gifts. We really need our sofa recovered! How can we properly and nicely say on our invitations, "Please no little gifts. There will be a bank at the door for coins for a new sofa cover and an anniversary card for you to sign"?

GENTLE READER:

Even thinking of using a family celebration and a party for your friends as an occasion to make others pay for household repairs is improper. Miss Manners is horrified. She wishes she had caught you twenty-five years ago, when you needed to be told, as many brides do, that it is greedy and vulgar to manipulate the anticipated generosity of your relatives and friends. While it is true that people who attend weddings and anniversary parties usually give presents, it is not true that such donations are tickets of entrance to the event. They are (in theory) a purely voluntary expression of goodwill and affection from those who share your joy, and are chosen by their taste and sense of what you might like, in consultation with their bank statements.

Any suggestions from you, unless specifically requested by an individual guest, are improper. This includes a ban on stating "No gifts" because, although less greedy than the attempt to pick one's own present, this also assumes that some sort of payment is taken for granted. If you did not learn as a bride to look surprised and delighted at all manner of horrible bric-a-brac, it is high time you did.

The "Money Tree"

DEAR MISS MANNERS:

My topic is the "money tree." My husband's oldest brother and his wife recently celebrated their golden wedding anniversary. Prior to the actual date, my husband's niece forwarded an announcement of the anniversary with the information that there was to be a "money tree" to which we were free to contribute.

My husband and I discussed, at great length, the proper thing to do, and we decided to send a check for ten dollars. A few weeks later, we received a thank-you note from my husband's sister-in-law in which she thanked us for our ten dollars but indicated that many had sent gifts of twenty-five dollars and fifty dollars. We are totally at a loss whether we erred in sending any amount, or perhaps should have sent more than we did, or just what is the proper thing to do.

GENTLE READER:

If the "money tree" is in questionable taste, there is no question at all about the taste of holding a shakedown, such as you describe. The improprieties are many here, but you have not committed them. Your sister-in-law never should have known the amount you contributed, as it should have been presented to her and her husband as one lump sum with the names of all contributors but not the amounts they gave, or better yet because it should have been used to buy a present larger than individuals might have given. In any case, a thank-you letter does not properly contain the information that your present compares unfavorably with others.

Party Presents

DEAR MISS MANNERS:

We understand your point about not putting "No gifts please" on our fiftieth wedding anniversary invitation. But if some of our guests do bring gifts, what is proper? Do we open them at once, later on in the evening before all the guests, or the next day in private? We don't want to embarrass the guests who don't bring gifts.

GENTLE READER:

This is precisely why bringing presents to parties, unless they are children's birthday parties or bridal or baby showers, where opening them is part of the entertainment, is a terrible idea. Any other presents should be sent, so that a person who is trying to give a party or get married or whatever can have her hands free. If people bring things anyway, thank them and put the packages aside while you are greeting other guests. If you are very busy, open them after the party and write a note. If there is a moment in which you can open such presnts inconspicuously, do so and thank the giver quietly. And *then* write the note.

Advanced Civilization

Protocol

In their infinite wisdom, our forebears decided to save Miss Manners a great deal of trouble by declaring that the American way would be that of dignified but strict simplicity. Thus there are no elaborate court rituals to be taught, nor subtle gradations in postures of humility. The only instruction Miss Manners has for Americans who bow or curtsy is "Get up" (unless they are performing artists, in which case it is, "Get up before you hear the rattle of car keys").

She can teach you in minutes the basics of addressing all of our high public officials.

High American officials are addressed by their job titles, and the only trick is to know which titles are used alone (governor, general, judge) and which are preceded by "Mr." or "Madam" (president, vice president, secretary, under secretary, speaker, ambassador, mayor). The Supreme Court, an equal opportunity employer, recently dropped its "Madam" or "Mr.," making the title simply "Justice Wise," although Miss Manners does not understand why "Madam Justice" would not do.

In many cases, one needn't know an official's name to address him or her with utmost respect, a convenience under a system where glory is fleeting. Surnames are, however, used with the title of senator, and may be with governor or mayor; and when there are numerous holders of a title, such as United States

591

PERFECT PRODUCTS
18 COMMERCE STREET
BROOKDALE, CONNECTICUT

IAN FRIGHT
VICE PRESIDENT-PRODUCT DEVELOPMENT

The Honorable
Marjorie Stately
Governor of Connecticut
Hartford, Connecticut

Dear Governor Stately,

    I really must protest the outrageous

GEOFFREY LOCKWOOD PERFECT
SUITE 16, CRUMBLES BUILDING
TOWN SQUARE
BROOKDALE, CONNECTICUT

The President
The White House
Washington, D.C.

Dear Mr. President,

    I really must protest the outrageous

*Letters to dignitaries,
written on different
but correct types
of business paper.*

BRIAN BOTCHITT, M.D.
324 MEDICAL BUILDING
BROOKDALE, CONNECTICUT
———
(203) 555-1212

The Honorable
Janet Elizabeth Tuff
Mayor of Brookdale
Brookdale, Connecticut

Dear Mayor Tuff:

    I really must protest the outrageous

BANK OF BROOKDALE
BROOKDALE, CONNECTICUT

GREGORY AWFUL
HEAD TELLER

The Honorable
Perfect Pious
House of Representatives
Washington, D.C.

Dear Mr. Pious,

    I really must protest the outrageous

representative or assistant cabinet secretaries, they are addressed by surnames with social titles only Mr., Ms., Dr., etc.). In writing to all of these people, (except president, vice president, or chief or associate justice), it is safe to use three lines: The Honorable/Full Name/Job Title.

There are no consort titles in America—no, not even "First Lady," a term lacking in official recognition, in addition to sounding about as silly as you can get. The only difference between addressing officials' wives and private female citizens is that they use only a surname, not the husband's given name, with the title of "Mrs." Officials' husbands, never having used their wives' given names, retain their own.

See how easy it all is? Now let's take a turn around the room and say hello to everyone: "Good evening, Mr. President; hello, Mr. Vice President, everything all right? Why, Mr. Justice—whoops, I mean Justice Fairminded; Madam Secretary, how nice to see you; Mr. Speaker, nothing new I hope?; Madam Ambassador, how are you?; Senator Aegis, I've been hearing interesting things about you lately; Governor, you're looking great; Mr. Mayor, everything all right?"

Over there? Why, that's Mr. Smith, Mrs. Jones and Mr. Brown. He's an assistant cabinet secretary, she's a member of Congress, and he's a spouse.

What's that? You want to know how to introduce all these people to one another and in what order?

Oh, don't worry about that. It's easy; they already know one another. And those who don't, fake it.

Curtsying

Royal personages are like any other personages, only more regal. Their prerogatives include being called charming when they are civil, witty when they are pleasant, handsome when they are presentable, and astute when they are informed. They are entitled, by heredity and custom, if not by divine right, to have all their weddings referred to internationally as storybook romances, and all public meals in which they participate as feasts fit for a king.

However, they do not have the right to receive physical obeisance from American citizens. Miss Manners has had to issue the decree many times now that American ladies should not curtsy to royalty, and still there are those who do so at every available opportunity. They are in error, not only in the matter of world etiquette, but of geography, physics, and ancient and modern history.

Miss Manners will now graciously explain the matter once more, after which there will be no further disobedience from her subjects.

Bending the knee is the traditional gesture of an inferior to a superior. We bend our knees to God, or whatever it is that we worship—debutantes traditionally curtsy to Society, for example. The curtsy is but one form of the gesture of adoring a sovereign. Other kingdoms have their subjects touch their foreheads to the ground or kiss the ground as royalty passes.

Thus, those who believe that curtsying demonstrates their own high social rank or breeding are mistaken. Their geography is faulty if they think that

THE PROPER WAY TO ADDRESS DIGNITARIES. *Note that it is often not necessary to know the names of high-ranking people in order to address them correctly. One can greet a president ("Mr. President"), a queen ("Your Majesty"), or a pope ("Your Holiness") without the bore of learning which is Bloody Mary and which Good Queen Anne.*

bending down will elevate them; the notion that there is a law of physics stating that what goes down must come up is erroneous.

As for history, Miss Manners considers that the matter was settled by the philosopher Callisthenes, who disabused Alexander the Great of the notion that the Persian custom of groveling to royalty could be established in Macedonia and Greece. According to an occasionally broken chain of information (Callisthenes' clerk, Stroebus, told Aristotle, who told Plutarch, who told Miss Manners), Callisthenes "stoutly stood against kneeling to the king, and said that openly, which the noblest and ancientest men among the Macedonians durst but whisper one in another's ear, though they did all utterly mislike it: where he did yet deliver Greece from open shame, and Alexander from a greater, bringing him from that manner of adoration of his person."

(Miss Manners does not want to hear from scholars pointing out that Plutarch also characterized Callisthenes as grave, sour, and not very pleasant. He was, nevertheless, right on this issue.)

If you require more recent history, there is that matter of the war that we Americans fought to free ourselves of subjugation to the British crown. And for absolutely up-to-date history, by Miss Manners' standard, she has a report from a Gentle Reader of an encounter between that lady's mother and dear Queen Victoria after which, the American not having been instructed on what to do, the sovereign kindly informed her, "You need not curtsy, but turn and walk out."

How, then, do we Americans properly treat royalty? With the dignity and respect we naturally show to heads of state and other foreign officials. Our traditional form of greeting is to shake the hand.

This gesture is not interchangeable with that of the curtsy, as the State Department tried to suggest when obfuscating the matter during the last go-around, claiming that the word curtsy being derived from courtesy, it signified no more.

Your government should not have to inform you that the word courtesy derives from behavior in the courts of royalty, which is no business of ours.

"Your Ex—"

DEAR MISS MANNERS:
    What do you say to a man who has recently lost his throne? Or who lost the presidency, for that matter?
GENTLE READER:
    Presuming that you wish to be polite, but also to refrain from making a political statement, Miss Manners suggests, "History will record your true worth." Please note what a versatile statement this is.

First Ladies

DEAR MISS MANNERS:
    I would like to comment on a form of rudeness, not to me personally, but to all Americans, if they only realized it. This is the habit that so many people have of

talking freely about our public figures. Specifically, at the moment, I am talking about the things one hears about Mrs. Ronald Reagan. I hear people who say that she is a cold person, or she spends too much money on clothes, things like that. My point is that not only does it seem disrespectful, but that these people really know nothing about her real personal life, in spite of all the junk written about her. She strikes me as a warm, dignified, ladylike woman, who really cares about her husband, and I think it's very rude for people to keep making personal remarks about her. Don't you?

GENTLE READER:

Actually, these are not personal remarks at all. It is traditionally said about each president's wife that she is a zombie with no thoughts of her own and slavishly subservient to her husband, and that she is the only brains in the family and has controlled his rise to satisfy her own ambition; that she is laughably dowdy, and that she is extravagantly and heartlessly chic. As these remarks do not vary with political party or individual, they should not be taken personally. Besides, if you were to stop the God-given American right of criticizing the personal attributes of public figures, you would also have to stop characterizing someone you admittedly don't know as warm and devoted.

Kissing Cousins

DEAR MISS MANNERS:

What do you think of the behavior of a president of the United States who is always going around kissing everyone? I know that baby kissing is an old American custom among politicians. But President Carter did a lot more than that. There are always pictures on the front page of him kissing, or at least hugging, this world leader or that. Presumably, they like it. But what about someone who doesn't? When he kissed Jackie Kennedy Onassis at the Kennedy Library opening, she was obviously offended and pulled back. I read that she showed "royal displeasure."

I think there is some confusion here of what is the proper kissing behavior for presidents and others, such as another president's widow, or just members of the public. If there were agreement on the etiquette, at least you wouldn't get such a public conflict. Would you set down the rules, Miss Manners? What are the old customs, and what should the new ones be? What's the American thing to do? Was Jackie being impossibly "royal?"

GENTLE READER:

No, actually, President Carter was behaving royally, although he may not be aware of it, and Mrs. Onassis, in her unwillingness to kiss someone she didn't love, was behaving in the American tradition, although she may not have been aware of it. There are two royal traditions involved here, one of which applies to what you described as baby kissing, and the other to what one might call the cousin-kissing.

Physical contact between common people and their ruler dates from the reign of Edward the Confessor, when the touch of the king was said to be empowered with the ability to cure disease. This was known as Touching for the King's Evil, and continued to be a practice long after, although the cure rate was never verified by medical statistics. (Dear Dr. Johnson was the last person to be so touched.) Nowadays, you see people, notably at airports, making great efforts to be touched by the president, apparently feeling that there is some magical power in it. These people were not necessarily ill beforehand, but they exhibit strange behavior afterward, such as grabbing their right wrist with their left hand and saying, "He shook my hand! He shook my hand!"

Kissing among the rulers of the world (or their widows) is another matter. This is connected to a convention that all the sovereigns of the earth are of one family. Sometimes in history, when you have had a particularly family-conscious monarch who has set about finding thrones for all his or her unemployed relatives—Napoleon, for example, or Queen Victoria—this has been pretty nearly true. But it is meant spiritually, rather than literally. The correct salutation on a routine business letter from a king of one country to a queen of another and hers to him would be "Madam My Sister" and "Sir My Brother." (You may not have occasion to use this within the week, but Miss Manners thought you might like to know.) If they are actually blood relatives, this is indicated separately, as in "Madam My Sister and Cousin." When the president treats other heads of government as if they were family, he is acting within that tradition.

Miss Manners' preference is for the American tradition known as Keep Your Hands and Mouth to Yourself.

🌹 THE WHITE HOUSE

Dining at the White House

When Americans say, "The White House Belongs to all The People," they mean that they feel entitled to be invited to dinner there, whether or not they have shown any kind feelings for the host.

The value of such invitations, among those who occasionally receive them, is not in the expectation of seeing magnificent clothes and jewels or hearing the political secrets and sparkling conversation of the country's most interesting citizens. The people you are likely to meet are distinguished by the size of their political contributions, and what they are busy doing is stealing souvenir matchbooks and menu cards and looking to see who is famous. The only state secret you will hear is that the president feels a deep and personal friendship for whoever happens to be that week's guest of honor.

(This perhaps unpleasant, but not unpatriotic, cynicism on Miss Manners' part is at least nonpartisan. She has been watching the scramble for White House matchbooks for the last six administrations.)

The value of the invitation is that one can cancel one's previous engagement by saying, "I'm afraid I must go to the White House that night." If necessary, one must make a previous engagement hastily for the purpose of doing this. (For the proper form of this perfectly correct snub, please see p. 450.)

Here are some other things you need to know about attending a White House dinner, but other advisers are afraid to tell you for fear of sounding disrespectful:

The correct form for declining an invitation to the White House if one doesn't feel up to it because one is secretly planning to endorse a rival candidate publicly is:

Mr. and Mrs. Benjamin Mobile
regret that owing to the very grave illness
of Mr. Mobile
they will be unable to accept
the very kind invitation of
The President and Mrs. Eagle
to dinner
on Wednesday, the fifth of November

However, it is no longer the practice that only extreme illness or death prevents otherwise well-bred citizens from accepting a White House invitation. Any important event or geographical distance is considered a sufficient excuse. One need only substitute "distance from the city" or "wedding of their daughter" for the illness in the above example. What is rude is to refuse and then to brag that it was really disapproval of the president's stand on some issue that motivated you. This only points out that you didn't take this stand publicly before, or the president would not have invited you.

Dress as you would for a dance at a conservative country club: black tie (white tie is making a comeback on certain occasions) and nonadventurous long dress. Anything unusually magnificent or chic will make you look as if you are trying too hard to be noticed. Unfortunately the Secret Service no longer checks whether the proper length gloves are being worn.

You needn't rent a limousine if you don't happen to have one lying around the garage. Many people drive their own cars, and parking space is provided on the Ellipse.

Don't forget the enclosed admittance card, which will be tested by machine to see if it is a forgery. Of course your face is your passport—until you try to travel on it.

You will be told by an aide that the husband should precede the wife in the receiving line but this is only if he is the reason for the couple's being invited. If the wife is the office holder, she should go first. However much the president and his wife express delight at seeing you, they are not anxious to talk to you during the receiving line. Say "Good evening" and move on.

Don't worry about minor points of etiquette, because the staff (many of whom

The President and Mrs. Eagle

request the pleasure of the company of

Mr. and Mrs. Awful

at dinner

on Tuesday, December 7, 1982

at 7:30 o'clock

Black tie

On the occasion of the visit of

His Majesty

Handsome V

King of Magicland

An invitation to the White House with surprise follow-up.
The names of the guests, which are in the same style as
the engraving, are handwritten.

Mr. and Mrs. Jonathan R. Awful, III

will please present this card at
THE SOUTHWEST GATE
The White House
December 7, 1982
at 7:30 o'clock

NOT TRANSFERABLE

MR AND MRS JONATHAN R AWFUL, III
129 PRIMROSE PATH
BROOKDALE, CONNECTICUT

THE PRESIDENT AND MRS. EAGLE REGRET THAT HIS
MAJESTY HANDSOME V WILL BE UNABLE TO VISIT THE
UNITED STATES AT THIS TIME BECAUSE OF THE REVOLU-
TIONARY CIRCUMSTANCES NOW EXISTING IN MAGICLAND.
THEREFORE THE DINNER IN HIS HONOR AT THE WHITE
HOUSE ON TUESDAY, DECEMBER 7, 1982, HAS BEEN
CANCELLED.

THE SOCIAL SECRETARY THE WHITE HOUSE

have been hired for the night) and social aides are accustomed to steering people through. If a social aide asks you to dance after dinner, it is not because you are popular.

It is not only gauche, but useless to try to have a substantive conversation with someone you might not otherwise meet. Anyone that much more important than you will relentlessly return penetrating questions with comments on the weather, dinner, and entertainment.

It is not true that no one may leave before the president retires. Many a president who loves to dance all night has been left there—first by crotchety Supreme Court justices, then by a tolerant First Lady, and finally by everyone else except the three least important but best-looking women at the dinner.

If your invitation is for ten o'clock, eat a good dinner secretly in your kitchen. You have been invited as a secondary guest, to the after-dinner entertainment only. But you needn't mention that detail when describing to friends later what a glittering and glamorous dinner it was.

Is Protocol Necessary?

Thinking she knew all about the above-the-law attitude in the Nixon White House, Miss Manners found herself freshly shocked during the film of Charles Colson's autobiography, *Born Again*. About to set out for a state dinner at the White House, the then counsel to the president answers his wife's questions about protocol by saying, "Honey, the way you look, you can break all the rules of protocol you like."

As the ensuing dinner is not shown, Miss Manners is unclear about how much license Mrs. Colson was able to take on the strength of her blond pageboy and chiffon dress. Did she, for example, go bounding upstairs with President and Mrs. Nixon and their guests of honor to drop in on the private reception customarily held before their appearance to other guests in the East Room? Did she brush aside any of the feebler Supreme Court justices to step into the receiving line before her husband's rank permitted? Did she mischievously change around the place cards to find herself a more compatible dinner partner?

Miss Manners remembers those Nixon administration state dinners and does not recall their being characterized by breezy informality. In fact, Miss Manners was left with the impression that the same people who later confessed to having broken the law were the ones most careful not to transgress the slightest rule of rank in front of their boss, let alone to allow their underlings to ignore their rank in the interests of spontaneous fellowship.

Miss Manners also often hears this sort of hypocritical bad-mouthing of protocol by those who enjoy it most. In fact, the attitude strikes Miss Manners as designed to draw possibly envious attention away from that enjoyment. It is like complaining about the terrible burden of being rich.

Protocol is etiquette with a government expense account, and is not to be sneered at. (Some people try to sneer at etiquette, too, but Miss Manners is putting a stop to that.) If one is to have several hundred people to dinner at the taxpayers' expense, as presidents often do, it is necessary to impose a pattern

Mr. and Mrs. Jonathan Rhinehart Awful, 3rd
have the honour of accepting
the kind invitation of
The President and Mrs. Eagle
to dine
on Tuesday, the seventh of December
at seven thirty o'clock

A reply to an invitation from the White House. (For declining such an invitation, see page 599.)

Heraldic devices are rarely used on American writing paper, and this crest (without the full coat of arms) has been questionably assumed by the Awfuls.

on the event for organizational purposes, or the place will end up looking like a children's birthday party. The White House often does anyway, what with people madly grabbing menu cards as party favors. If that pattern corresponds to certain known rules, so that people know what is expected of them, and has some ceremony and tradition to it, so that it is pleasant and attractive, so much the better.

Calling on the President

DEAR MISS MANNERS:

I am invited to a White House dinner, and I heard that it is proper to leave cards for the president and the First Lady the next day. Is this true?

GENTLE READER:

That was once, indeed, the charming custom. Unfortunately guards are now instructed to transfer to a psychiatrist anybody who approaches the White House exhibiting what they consider bizarre behavior.

Speaking of Unmentionables

DEAR MISS MANNERS:

Some time ago, a lady was dancing with her male friend at the White House and her underslip dropped off on the dance floor, and the lady just kept dancing as if nothing had happened. Was this the proper thing for the lady to do?

GENTLE READER:

Actually, such events have happened several times to several ladies in Miss Manners' memory, which gives rise to the suspicion that the White House inspires a desire to "make history," or that the elastic industry is in deep trouble. As to your question of the proper response when one loses an undergarment at the White House or another respectable establishment, yes, the thing to do is to ignore it. A general rule of etiquette is that one apologizes for the unfortunate occurrence, but the unthinkable is unmentionable.

The Toasts

DEAR MISS MANNERS:

In an account of a White House dinner, I read the toasts were offered at the beginning of the meal instead of the end. The reason given was so that people who give the toasts need not feel nervous all through the meal, but, being through with the task, be able to relax. What do you think of this, Miss Manners?

GENTLE READER:

The practice has now been dropped. The people who give toasts at White House dinners are the president of the United States and his guest of honor, a head of state or a head of government. Any president or prime minister or queen who is unnerved at the prospect of giving a small speech, to the point of not being able to enjoy his or her food, is in the wrong business.

Doggie Bags at White House Dinners

DEAR MISS MANNERS:

I read in a newspaper story that Mrs. Jacob Javits, the wife of the New York senator, was at a White House dinner and used her evening purse as a doggie bag! It said that she wanted to bring some of the fancy dessert, a marron mousse with chocolate trimmings, home to a friend who had read about the dessert beforehand and wanted to taste it but wasn't invited to the party. I've heard of doggie bags at restaurants, but at the White House? Apparently she told everyone what she was doing and coolly put the dessert in her purse. Would you like to comment on her manners?

GENTLE READER:

No. A person who has put a marron mousse into an evening bag has suffered enough.

Inaugurations

DEAR MISS MANNERS:

What does Miss Manners consider the proper behavior for Inaugural festivities, especially the Inaugural Ball? Correct and formal? Friendly and equalitarian? Gracious but aloof? Restrained but enthusiastic?

GENTLE READER:

Defensive, actually. Welcome to Washington. This must be your first Inauguration.

Inaugurations are jolly events and Miss Manners loves them, but they do not lend themselves to any of the gradations of behavior you mention. You are thinking coronation, when you should be thinking football weekend. If you can be cheerful about messy weather, failed transportation, spectator events one can't see, social events composed mostly of elbows, drinks acquired after massive physical exertion only to be spilled on one's best clothes, and the realization that one will never find those whom one had hoped or planned to see, then you have nothing to worry about. Provided you are not the person being inaugurated, of course.

The Average Citizen

DEAR MISS MANNERS:

You know how presidents sometimes go around visiting "average citizens" every once in a while, to get their opinions? Well, this may sound silly, but I keep wondering what would be the proper thing to do if the president came to visit me. I don't mean what opinions to give—I have plenty of those. What worries me is the protocol of it. Let me explain. I don't want to be disrespectful, but I don't think any president should be either, and I think that's what it is to go around calling people "average." Maybe you would think I am average— I work hard, have a decent job, have a wife and two children, live in the suburbs and keep up with what's going on. I have trouble making ends meet like everyone else, but have never been in trouble. And yet I think of myself as an individual, something special, not "average." If the president visited me, how could I make that point without being disrespectful?

GENTLE READER:

By saying, "Mr. President, it is a great pleasure for me to meet an average president."

❧ THE DIPLOMATIC CORPS

Diplomatic Dress

DEAR MISS MANNERS:

At a posh hotel in Washington, I picked up a leaflet advising people on official life in Washington. My wife and I were combining a business trip with some socializing, and had the chance to go to an embassy party given by a country that my firm does business with. We were looking forward to this, not having been to an embassy party before, and read what it said in the booklet which was, in part, "Morning coats with striped trousers are seen more frequently at afternoon receptions and cocktail parties of the diplomatic corps than in most other segments of Washington society, but business suits may be worn to such functions with security." I thought it would be fun to rent the striped pants outfit, even if I didn't need them, because we were only doing this once. Fortunately, there wasn't time. When we got to the party, I realized that I would have made a fool of myself—not a single man, including the ambassador and several other ambassadors who were there, wore anything but a plain suit, such as men wear to parties at home. My question is: Was this a cut-rate party, or even a cut-rate country, we were dealing with? When do diplomats wear "morning coats with striped trousers"?

GENTLE READER:

In cartoons and drawings accompanying suggestions that the foreign service is not as serious as it ought to be. However, a serious diplomat would read such instructions as the ones you quote more carefully and note the following:

It says "afternoon receptions and cocktail parties," but since embassies no longer give receptions and cocktail parties that are over before 6 PM, when such clothes may no longer be worn, who's to say that people wouldn't wear them if they did? Also, it says they are worn "more frequently" at diplomatic functions than at those of "other segments of Washington society." As they are never worn in "other segments," but were at the State Department gathering following President Kennedy's funeral, the statement is correct; once is more frequent than never.

The Diplomatic Wife

DEAR MISS MANNERS:

I don't know whether or not you would care to comment on a matter of State Department etiquette. My question concerns the practice of "potluck" social occasions. For example, to honor the wife of the American ambassador who is departing from a post overseas, the wife of the deputy chief of mission invites the ladies of the official American community to a luncheon. She requests them to R.s.v.p. and to indicate what food or wine they will bring. The DCM's wife claims to be acting for the group as a whole. She is not the hostess. She is merely providing her residence and organizing the luncheon. The reason given is that it would be too expensive and too much work for one person to handle, but that if everyone contributes, the result will be a lovely party, with no undue burden on anyone.

There is invariably at least one proud cook, who painstakingly turns out a good dish, but most contributors think, "It's not my party, why go to a lot of work and expense?" So picture, if you will, a buffet table laden with several varieties of hamburger and tuna casseroles, lettuce and tomato salads, and, for dessert, a choice of cakes from the commissary's current stock of mixes. Because there is an excess of food (each person is instructed to bring enough to feed six), each woman must carry home the leftovers in order to retrieve the serving platter she brought it on.

Potlucks seem to be a new but increasingly popular practice. Thirteen years ago, when I first accompanied my husband overseas, no one had them. Not everyone resorts to them now. What do you think of this? What should I do if I disapprove? Or should I not disapprove? Are potlucks now a common practice among Washington hostesses or wives of private business executives in the United States? Are they somehow a product of women's liberation—i.e., the husband's position does not obligate the wife to entertain?

GENTLE READER:

The potluck party is a natural result of the potluck personnel policy long followed by the State Department and many business organizations in recruiting people to do their official entertaining.

Potluck personnel works as follows: A man is hired for a job that requires an extensive amount of entertaining, and he is expected to bring along whatever he has in the way of wife, ready or not, to do the social half of the job, free. If he brings a tuna fish–type wife, it is held against him.

Some years ago, foreign service wives understandably rebelled against this involuntary volunteer labor, and the State Department agreed to cease requiring nonemployees to perform its work. Did it then hire people to do the job?

No, it left the ranking wife at each post knowing that the job had to be done, but no longer able to enlist the junior wives to assist her. If you are the wife of a junior officer, you may now easily walk away from this problem by declining the invitation. However, Miss Manners asks you to feel some sympathy for the women who are stuck with the job, and understand that people who continue to carry the responsibility might show undue enthusiasm for potluck suppers and commissary cakes. It would be even more helpful if women in such situations did not turn against one another, but asked themselves and their husbands' employer why the situation exists. Is this extensive entertaining necessary? Should people who do it be compensated? Should they at least be given adequate professional assistance?

And is tuna fish all that bad?

The Flag

The best way to display the flag of the United States is on the front of one's limousine, with siren-flashing automobiles containing police and other security escorts placed just to the front and the rear of one's car. This shows that not only do you respect your country, but that the feeling is mutual. However, there are also ways in which the ordinary citizen can use the flag to display his love for his country.

Flag etiquette is extremely complex, and the first rule is to avoid international offenses in the use of the flag that could lead to war or other unpleasant reactions. For example, it is correct to burn a flag that has become tattered beyond repair, but it is wise to choose the circumstances of this ritual carefully and to know in advance the political positions of any chance witnesses. Although it is widely believed that the flag may not be flown after sunset, this is not strictly true. Like its citizens, the flag can flap about freely during daylight, but should stick to well-lighted areas if venturing out at night.

Emotions about the flag should not be flown higher than the flag itself. For example, people who feel that a flag that has touched the ground must be destroyed, or that there is a question about whether a flag may be washed or dry-cleaned (it depends on the material—to shrink the flag is an unfortunate sign, especially for the person in charge of the laundry), are violating what the flag stands for. It stands for, among other things, good old American common sense. Nor is it respectful to use the flag to imply that others are less fully American than one is, oneself. Miss Manners does not approve of using the United States flag as personal adornment, whether in the lapel or the seat of the pants, if the intention is to provoke an attack from one's fellow citizens. It is one thing to fight for the flag and quite another to use it in order to start a fight.

The Large Household

The Household Staff

Why it is that so few people nowadays keep full household staffs, Miss Manners cannot imagine. Do they prefer searching for parking spaces to having a chauffeur? Would they rather surrender their clothes for indefinite periods of time to cleaning establishments than keep a laundress? Are they content to be done in by any strange criminal off the street rather than by the family butler?

Surely there are many who would reconsider if they knew how smoothly life can go when the servants outnumber the family, two or three to one. That is, provided that the servants don't notice that this ratio is also a favorable one for revolution.

One housewife could accomplish all these tasks, of course. But because Miss Manners is a devout believer in good working conditions for household workers, with strictly observed hours, days off, vacations, and sick leave, she recommends employing a sufficient staff so that no one is overburdened.

This should consist of:

Pantry Department

· The butler, who supervises this department and sees to it that meals are properly served, flowers arranged, silver polished, wine treated with respect, and the downstairs halls, including the door and the telephone, properly covered.

In poor households, he must serve the meat and the wine at dinner, but in more favorable circumstances he need only stand behind the chair of the lady of the house, waiting to receive orders for the troops. The butler is addressed by his surname, with or without the title of Mr.

- The footmen, who actually perform the duties of serving, answering telephones, and cleaning up. In equal employment opportunity households, this work may be performed by waitresses. They are addressed by first names.
- Parlormaids, who are responsible for the drawing room, the library, and delivering breakfast trays to ladies in dishabille. A Gentle Reader (and letter writer) recalls that in Victorian days "housemaids and parlormaids had to have appropriate names, for example: Jane, Sarah, or Alice; but names like Violet, Priscilla, and Katherine were definitely not used and were substituted with one of the suitable names. Parlormaids in a higher position were called by their surnames—they valet the gentlemen, too, so were considered more masculine." In equal employment opportunity households, this work may be performed by parlormen.

Kitchen Department

- The cook, who cooks. The cook may be addressed as Cook.
- The kitchen maids, who do the dirty work of the kitchen. In E.E.O.H.es—oh, never mind.

Upstairs Department

- A lady's maid, who keeps the clothes and hair of the lady of the house in order, dresses her, draws her bath, listens to her cry when the master is behaving badly again, and delivers her love letters directly to the person for whom they were intended. She has a surname only.
- The valet, who does the same for the gentleman of the house. He has a surname only.
- Chambermaids, or housemaids (or men), who keep the upstairs clean, orderly, and appropriate to the hour—that is, they draw the shades and turn down the beds at night, and undraw them and turn them up again (in the better households they take the beds apart completely in the morning). See parlormaids.

Laundry Department

- Laundress(es) (launderers), who are responsible for the cleanliness of all clothes not immediately occupied by their owners. That is, if the lady spills soup on her bosom, the lady's maid mops up, but if the lady takes the blouse off, the laundress gets it.

Outdoor Department

- A chauffeur, who drives the car, keeps it clean and repaired, and keeps out of trouble with the law, especially when he is in the car alone and pretending that it is his. It is best to have two chauffeurs, one for day and one for night.
- The gardeners, who, under the supervision of the head gardener, keep the out-

door property in order and provide flowers for the house and vegetables for table.

· The gamekeeper, who—never mind what the gamekeeper does.

Miscellaneous

· The housekeeper, who battles for control of the household with the butler and the cook. She is addressed by her surname, usually with the title of "Mrs.," whether or not she is married.

· Companions, governesses, tutors, nannies, and nurses, who occupy positions above the servants but below the family members, which means that they tend to be lonely. Fortunately, someone always falls madly and inappropriately in love with them, except for the nanny. She may be addressed as Nanny. The eligible ones are addressed as Miss or Mr.

· The people who perform all of the above tasks on Sunday afternoon—the lady and gentleman of the household. Servants must arrange among themselves to let these people do the work occasionally. Otherwise, they get spoiled.

Guards

DEAR MISS MANNERS:

I invited a very prominent person for dinner—I prefer not to say who. The person arrived with two bodyguards. My question is whether I am expected to feed the bodyguards, and if so, where? In the kitchen or in the dining room? I am afraid this is a very new etiquette problem.

GENTLE READER:

Nothing is new to Miss Manners, who has seen it all. This problem previously existed in the form of personal maids and valets who might or might not accompany guests on house visits. At a good-sized country house, the servants' dining room could always accommodate more, but it was considered polite to inform one's hosts how many people one was bringing along.

Bodyguards, if announced in advance, should be provided supper in any convenient place away from the main party; if not announced, they may be offered whatever refreshment is available in the kitchen. This is perfectly proper, and need not cause you embarrassment when the bodyguard reappears, at your next social function, in the role of fiancé of the lady he was guarding. At that time, one simply moves his place into the dining room.

Chauffeurs

DEAR MISS MANNERS:

I read that the president of Italy has decreed that his chauffeur should not wear a chauffeur's cap or gloves, in order to set a "simpler style" for his (the president's) administration, and to symbolize a cutback in expenses for official cars. Do you approve of this?

GENTLE READER:

Miss Manners does not approve of forcing one's servants to violate the conventions of their trade in order to make the employer look democratic.

Celebrity and Publicity

Are celebrities people? Must they be treated with the ordinary courtesies accorded to human beings?

Miss Manners, who believes in treating all living creatures with kindness and consideration, must nevertheless answer this with a yes and a no. Public figures who voluntarily seek publicity cannot claim that they are entitled to the courtesy of privacy enjoyed by private figures. The problem then becomes defining a public figure. The Supreme Court has been fussing around with this far too long; Miss Manners will simply have to do it herself.

An individual who has marketed normally private aspects of his or her life for financial or psychological profit is not, in Miss Manners' opinion, entitled to run around grousing about how rude people are for being curious to know more.

Example: Lisa Adventura, the singer, has long been making the rounds of television talk shows, discussing why she did not feel the need to marry the father of her children. On her recent wedding trip with a recent acquaintance, fans approached her and her new husband wherever they went, some of them asking quite personal questions, others taking photographs or requesting autographs. She is citing this, on the talk shows, as an example of the bad manners of not letting people lead their private lives free of annoyance.

Example: In Jonny Rapide's autobiography, of which he was the coauthor, it was explained what it takes for an athlete to get to the top. Now people are insinuating that he is past his prime, and keep asking him whether his age has slowed him down and whether he is commanding less money than he used to. He has said bluntly many times what he thinks of people who ask such prying, personal questions.

Example: Senator Howard Aegis' graceful wife and lovely children have been his best campaign workers, always ready to open their home and their hearts to constituents and television cameras so that everyone can see what a wholesome family man the senator is. Now the scandalmongers have discovered the other household that Senator Aegis maintains. He is outraged; as long as his private life does not interfere with his duties, he says, it is none of anybody's business.

Miss Manners is never going to defend anyone who annoys ordinary people by asking them personal questions or forcing unwanted attentions on them. Miss Manners is also always prepared to protect extraordinary people from this curiosity—people who, in the course of pursuing legitimate or illegitimate occupations, such as science, dance, or assassination, have incidentally become famous.

Being a celebrity is an occupation that—however one arrived at it—provides certain rewards in exchange for the surrender of one's privacy. Miss Manners does not presume to judge people who chose to expose themselves; she merely refuses to allow them to condemn others who point, stare, or request details.

The Privilege of Rank

In a democracy such as ours, any ordinary citizen can cherish the hope of someday reaching the point where he or she will not have to endure being treated as the equal of an ordinary citizen.

Our principles do not grant privilege with rank, but our nasty little hearts crave it. Being able to ignore traffic or other laws, never having to wait in line, always getting the best table, not having to pay for many goods and services— these are deemed the rewards of success, and not just by our ruling class of politicians and talk show hosts. Miss Manners was shocked to hear of an astronaut's illustrating how far he had come from celebrity status by reporting that on the anniversary of his moon shot, a policeman had actually given him a ticket for a traffic violation.

This isn't democracy, but it isn't noblesse oblige, either. Miss Manners knows of no more magnificently aristocratic statement than, "Oh, please, don't do anything special for me—I just want to be treated like everyone else." Compare the ring of it with, "Do you know who I am?" an unfortunate question that suggests its own answer.

Miss Manners brings this up not for the fun of lecturing her betters (her what?), but because the practice has sifted down through the society until there is hardly anyone who can't pull rank on someone, and also because for sheer offensiveness, having an airplane held or claiming kinship with a friend of the mayor's beats coughing in the soup any time. Those of lower status resent those who pull rank; people of equal status who don't, resent those who do; and those who do, resent those who could but don't, on the grounds that it is ostentatious to pass up a chance to elude the ordinary annoyances of life. You see what a mess this makes. Wouldn't it be better if we all agreed to abide by the rules and confined our ambitions to achieving wealth and immortality?

Miss Manners doesn't usually offer incentives for good behavior, beyond that of choking with the sense of one's own goodness, but there is an advantage in refusing perquisites, or, more precisely, a disadvantage in accepting them. This is known as the Nya-Nya Factor.

Each of these little conveniences is achieved at the inconvenience of people of lesser rank. Because of the nature of the privilege, they are not achieved anonymously. People demand to know why that individual is allowed to go to the head of the line, or they take a good look at the license plate of the car that is allowed to park illegally day after day. They then wait until the position that engenders this status disappears. In the case of politicians and entertainers, they may even have an opportunity to help this natural process along. Even absolute rulers are abruptly subject to these reversals, as recent history has shown us. Then comes the most terrific and satisfying nya-nya.

That is why it is a good, not to say becoming, idea for the people of rank to emphasize their obligations rather than their privileges. It is one attribute of success that everyone has unlimited opportunities to practice in advance.

Accepting Awards

Suppose you win an Academy Award.

All right, then, suppose you don't. Statistically, your chances of not winning are probably greater, even if you are a member of that segment of the population called Movie Stars. If you don't win, though, Miss Manners needn't worry so much about your being able to handle it properly.

The job of a loser, at the Academy Awards or any other lottery, is simple. (Not easy: simple.) You need only smile radiantly while saying that you honestly feel that the winner deserved it more, and then smile shyly while saying that you are sufficiently thrilled with the honor of having been nominated. If you can manage both of these convincingly, you deserve an Academy Award.

Accepting an honor is more complicated. Many people can't even accept a compliment without making the giver deeply regret ever having uttered it. The formula for both begins with, "Thank you." These are easily pronounced words, not difficult to memorize. And yet they are often omitted while the flustered recipient makes a colossal mess out of the optional second part of the response. The second part can be either (1) humility or (2) explanation. A small dose of one will do, but certainly not both. If there is any doubt, it is better to omit this section entirely.

An example of reasonable humility is "Thank you—my mother made it," and of a reasonable explanation is "Thank you—actually what I did was to transpose the violin part for trumpet." Anything along the lines of, "Oh, this is nothing; I can do much better" or "The idea goes back to when I was a little boy and we all used to get together and make up stories . . ." is not.

The odd fact is that praise and awards always look bigger to the person receiving them than they do even to those bestowing them, let alone those looking on and wondering at the choice. People who issue a Checker of the Year Humanitarian Award, and anyone who bothers to attend the presentation, should expect the recipient to be humble and awed, but owing to some perverse quirk in human nature, too much gratitude gets them to thinking that something that overwhelming to the winner was probably not quite deserved.

Here are some guidelines for those who find that their chores include accepting an Academy Award:

1. Look pleased and grateful, but not hysterically so. The person who bursts into tears and sobs that this is the greatest moment of his or her entire life is overdoing it.

2. Thank two or three key individuals and perhaps a supportive group, but not your parents, grade school teachers, and everyone else who has ever touched your life. That suggests that you are crediting those people with having created something magnificent (you).

3. Understand that you are being honored for one ability and not for being a general national treasure, and therefore keep any utterings of wisdom to your profession, instead of sharing your politics or philosophy of life.

If you can't manage all this, you might want to consider losing, instead.

Picture Oneself

DEAR MISS MANNERS:

What do you think of people who display photographs of themselves with famous people? Is it too show-offy? I had my picture taken with our senator, and I don't know what to do with it. I have seen clusters of such photographs in people's living rooms or, more often, in offices. You know—signed pictures of celebrities, or pictures of the host shaking hands with some famous person. Should I put this one out where people can see it? If so, where?

GENTLE READER:

Miss Manners considers such displays unfortunate on several grounds. 1. It suggests that you have established a category—for which celebrities, but not friends, qualify—of those whom you consider worthy of having their likenesses contribute to your decor. 2. It shows the extent of your acquaintanceship with people in that category. 3. In the case of people who do have a large collection of such pictures, it requires some shifting about, as the subjects of the pictures go in and out of office or fashion, and that invites unpleasant comment. Therefore, Miss Manners suggests that you not display the photograph of you and your senator, unless he is equally likely to display the photograph of you. The exception to all of the above rules is an autographed portrait of the late Queen Mary, which always looks appropriate on a piano.

Speaking with Speakers

DEAR MISS MANNERS:

A number of prominent people come to speak at our club, and to enjoy a social hour with us afterward. We have general interests, and have had people in widely different fields, some of them quite famous, such as authors who discuss their books. I think it only right to bone up on whatever field it is before meeting them—but I have noticed that other people don't bother. Don't you think it is only polite to be able to talk to them about their interests?

GENTLE READER:

Yes, if you understand that their chief interest is whether the local bookstore has stocked copies of their book. Otherwise, the rule is that people who are not yet prominent like to talk about their fields, while people who are prefer to talk about how bad the airline and hotel service is on speaking tours.

Remarks to Writers

DEAR MISS MANNERS:

Last night I ran into a classmate of mine whom I haven't seen in ten years. I know he's a writer now, but I didn't feel I could say anything about his new book because I haven't read it and he would be sure to find that out if I tried to talk about it. And yet I feel I should have said something, if only because he didn't mention what he was doing and seemed to be waiting for me to acknowledge that I knew, if you know what I mean. What is the right thing to say to an author when you can't honestly say "I loved your book"?

GENTLE READER:

Few people, and no writers, have such high standards about compliments as to accept only those that will pass a rigorous test for veracity. Miss Manners' experience is that an author will accept with joy any remark except "How many have you sold?" or "Did you know it's being remaindered now?" or "I'd love to read it—please send me a copy."

Public Exposure

The old rule about publicity was that a lady should allow her name to appear in the newspapers only three times: when she is born, when she marries, and when she dies. This is no longer workable. Miss Manners herself may have already exceeded her quota, and she hasn't yet used up all her events.

A modern rule might be: A lady never gets married, gives birth, or, if possible, dies on television—even if she is offered a free refrigerator for doing so. The principle of ladies' and gentlemen's not conducting their lives in full public view is especially important in an era when fame has replaced fortune as every schoolchild's goal. Do they want to be tycoons, that respectable old American dream? No, they want to be celebrities. There is some confusion between the two, as it has been perceived that fame leads directly to such fortune-making opportunities as book contracts, lecture fees, and photograph sessions in which the subject can keep the mink coat.

Nevertheless, the lust for notoriety now goes far beyond such considerations. Almost anyone will, if asked, publicly discuss his or her depressions and adjustments, and give away sexual details and family recipes. If you think that's bad, look at the people who aren't asked. Surely a major cause of antisocial acts these days is the hope of their being widely recorded.

This, in turn, has led to the bizarre notion that publicity, as our most valuable commodity, ought to be distributed as a reward and withheld as a punishment. ("Why do we have to keep hearing about that teenager who murdered his family, when there are so many good teenagers who haven't done anything?")

Miss Manners supposes that this indecent interest in exposure has something to do with a general feeling of anonymity in the world. If one's neighbors don't know one by sight, perhaps it drives one to seek recognition elsewhere.

Isn't it strange, then, that we all agree that publicity does not bring happiness? Nor does the public truly admire that creature we call a "personality"—a personality being something less than a person, blown up to look like more. The highest compliment we can give to such a figure is to assert that it is actually very "real" or "human."

How much easier, and more ladylike and gentlemanlike, it would be if people did not work so hard to puff themselves up so that they then have to work themselves back down to human size. That energy is, among gentlefolk, supposed to be used to win recognition from those who really have a chance to see and judge one—relatives, friends, colleagues, and acquaintances. It is a matter of working, not on one's image, but on what modestly used to be called one's reputation. It lasts longer.

Off the Record

DEAR MISS MANNERS:

My husband has taken quite an important new job, and I was the subject of a lengthy interview about our so-called life-style. I assure you that I will never do that again. I have never been so embarrassed in my life, nor felt so betrayed. A nice young woman came to my house, and I gave her tea and then, because it grew late, sherry and some beautiful little sandwiches and cakes (from a party we'd had the night before). We chatted about many things, including her boyfriend, and got quite friendly. I thought of including her at our next party, because we have some quite interesting people, and it might make another story for her. You can imagine my horror when I saw that she had violated the spirit of the visit by printing every little thing I said, even little things about our new friends in high places, which look insulting in print.

It is true, as she said when I complained to her boss, that I had not specified that anything was "off the record." I didn't think I needed to, because I assumed that she had the good sense to know what was proper for her article and what not. I was not, after all, holding a press conference: I was acting as hostess in my own drawing room.

I wish you would say something about this particular form of rudeness. Personally, I plan to reply to any press question in the future, no matter what the circumstances, with "No comment." I may sound abrupt myself then, but at least I'll be safe.

GENTLE READER:

Not necessarily. Miss Manners remembers another lady in your position making just such a resolve, the result of which was that after dancing with the president of the United States at the Inaugural Ball, a reporter asked how she had enjoyed the dance, and she replied, "No comment."

Miss Manners feels you would be better advised to learn the difference between friends and working people. It is true that the same people can be both at different times, and also that a great deal of money and effort is put into blurring the distinction to gain professional advantage. Your safety, as you call it, would be in learning to see clearly through that blur.

Your interview was not a social occasion. You tried to make it seem so, with your tea and leftovers, in the hope that you would inhibit your visitor with the restriction people have when they visit their friends socially, to speak well of them afterwards. The interviewer added to the social air, to the extent of chatting about her own life, in the hope that you would feel the conversational freedom of a hostess among friends. The evidence shows that you were taken in by her ruse, but she was not taken in by yours.

Miss Manners cannot condemn her for not having the good sense to censor the remarks you did not have the good sense to refrain from making.

The ability to distinguish between business being conducted in social settings and a true social life among real friends will be of enormous value to you, not only now, but later in life. Have a good time, with your "new friends in high places," but learn which ones turn into real friends and which ones you see because of mutual professional advantage. This will save you the trouble, when your husband no longer holds his position, of moaning about the fickleness of those whom you value only because of their professional positions.

Being on Television

DEAR MISS MANNERS:

Because I have been active in certain community projects, I have been asked to appear on a television talk show along with some people who have long opposed what I am doing. There is one man in particular who has attacked me violently, and I rather dread being on television with him. He can be amazingly suave and almost convincing when he states his case. I know it's full of errors and sophistry, but it sounds so reasonable when he talks. My question is this: How can I argue with him on television without seeming rude? He has a kind of exaggerated old world courtesy when he deals with me face to face, and I don't want to look uncivilized. On the other hand, I sure don't want to look as if I have the weaker case. Because mine is the humanitarian view, I ought, by all rights, to be more sympathetic. I'm afraid of forfeiting that by getting angry.

Also, this will be my first time on television, and I'm nervous in general— quite without the dislike of meeting my chief adversary—probably because I don't know what to expect. How early should I get there? Will they make up my face? What clothes should I wear? Should I prepare a statement and memorize it? Will I get a chance to rebut inaccurate statements made by others? Should I be prepared to roll off statistics to support what I say? There must be some sort of etiquette that has developed rules for what to do and what not to do on television.

GENTLE READER:

The rule, Miss Manners regrets to say, is that good manners make bad television and vice versa. If you forget everything you know about restrained behavior, substantiated conversation, and deferring to others, you will be a great success. Perhaps you will forgive Miss Manners for not watching this exhibition, however.

When the television people instruct you to be "lively," "spontaneous," "controversial," and full of "energy," what they mean is that you should feel free to ridicule others, interrupt, toss off opinions from the top of your head, argue with cleverness rather than evidence, and display intolerance for any opinion but your own. The person who tries to make a complicated point or to prove something with statistics or prepared examples, is, in the simple vocabulary of television people, "boring."

Bragging about your achievements, touting your latest venture, and telling self-aggrandizing anecdotes are classified as "humor," and outrageously insincere flattery—telling everyone "You're the greatest"—is called "charm." Mock courtesy, in a tone of satirical derision, is very effective. All this pains Miss Manners, but she would not be doing her duty if she did not tell you these dreadful facts.

Now, there are a few techniques of polite society that *will* be useful to you. These she can relate in less sadness.

Arrive on time. But bring a book, because the time given will be much too early.

Dress simply. Black or white will not do, but something very plain in a bright color is effective. Don't try to make your clothes interesting: that job should be done by your face.

Powder your face so it will not shine, but do not otherwise attempt to change it much from your normal appearance. Television cameras are subtler than they used to be, and most local programs do not bother to make up the "guests."

Whenever possible, look at the camera, not at the person to whom you are talking. It represents the person to whom you are really talking: the viewer. Look at it with liquid loving eyes and passionate intensity. This is where a background of disciplined social politeness really pays off. You wouldn't think it difficult to look at a black box with breathless admiration and interest if you had trained by directing such a look at the faces of some of the dinner partners Miss Manners has had at formal dinner parties.

The Traditional Interview

DEAR MISS MANNERS:

What is the etiquette for staff members of agencies such as the Department of Human Resources, hospitals, reformatories, etc., when interviewed for an exposé?

GENTLE READER:

The conventional procedure is to tell everything one knows at the time of the interview, and then to say afterward that one was quoted out of context.

Interrogating Someone Politely

DEAR MISS MANNERS:

I would appreciate your thoughts on the manners of reporters. My quandary comes from the dilemma of being polite, on the one hand, and asking the probing questions necessary to developing a good story, on the other.

GENTLE READER:

Miss Manners does not consider any profession to be an excuse for rudeness, even journalism. It is Miss Manners' experience that asking questions in a sweet and simple way, with a sympathetic expression on the face, is a good way to elicit startling information from people who feel they must spell things out for people who look dumb.

Pressing Events

DEAR MISS MANNERS:

Don't you think it's rude the way the press gathers around a house where there has been a gruesome murder? How do you think the family feels?

GENTLE READER:

That is what the members of the press are trying to find out for you.

Model Manners

DEAR MISS MANNERS:

Look at the way the model is sitting in this department store advertisement, with her knees apart and her feet going every which way. I find many of these pictures offensive, and have written to the stores about it, but they never seem to care enough to do anything about it.

GENTLE READER:

Miss Manners was deeply offended by this advertisement when she noticed that it asks two hundred and thirty dollars for a daytime dress that looks like a bathrobe. Mentioning this to the stores never seems to make them do anything about it. As for the model, Miss Manners has enough trouble making real people behave.

Play

🌹 CULTURAL EVENTS

Instances of rowdy behavior in popular public gathering places are multiplying. People have simply got to learn to behave themselves if we are to continue to assemble peaceably. Habitués will, of course, recognize that one such place is the opera house.

A gentleman of Miss Manners' acquaintance was recently assaulted on the head by an elderly party wielding a rolled-up program. This vicious attack was explained by the perpetrator as punishment for the gentleman's having stood during a standing ovation, thus blocking his attacker's view of the curtain calls. The same gentleman was once chastised by a person holding a season ticket next to his because his "clap has too sharp a sting."

Another gentleman and a lady of Miss Manners' vast acquaintance got into a nasty tangle during *The Magic Flute* with a chronic whisperer who later attempted to justify her behavior by explaining that she was narrating the stage events to a blind musicologist. Whether the musicologist's enjoyment of the event was enhanced by being told that a man dressed in green feathers and a bird cage had just walked on stage is an open question, but in any case, that of the people nearby was not. Miss Manners herself was once glared at, if you can believe it, for laughing at comic lines and business during *The Barber of Seville*.

So it is high time for us to agree on the rules. Miss Manners is prepared to issue them:

There shall be no talking, eating, rustling of papers, or prolonged coughing during an opera. Those who feel obliged to perform one of these actions must leave the auditorium.

However, one is permitted to enjoy the opera, particularly at those prices. Enthusiastic clapping and laughter at appropriate times is acceptable. At curtain calls, standing ovations are permitted, as are booing or shouting "Bravo!" provided one uses the correct endings and does not shout "Bravo!" when one means "Brava!" or "Bravi!"

There shall also be separate regulations for arriving at and departing from the opera house. People who arrive late should not attempt to sit until there is a break in the music. But it is perfectly all right for anyone to leave when the program has been concluded, skipping encores and curtain calls; those who wish to stay must simply let them pass.

Let us all understand this. Miss Manners remembers when many cities had no opera house, and does not wish to see them taken away because we don't know how to use them properly.

Distractions during the Overture

DEAR MISS MANNERS:

As a music lover, I never fail to arrive at an opera house or concert hall well before the time given for the performance to begin. A fat lot of good it does me. Not only do things often start late, but I am trampled to death by late arrivals. Some theaters have policies about not seating anyone during the music and others do not. For example, I rarely get to enjoy a full overture for all the people walking on my feet to get to their places. What do you think is a good policy, and how does someone who cares about manners, but also about music, behave when already seated while others traipse in at their leisure? You're not going to tell me I should stand up to let them pass, are you? I feel I'm doing more than is humanly possible when I just refrain from giving them a good smack on the backside as they pass.

GENTLE READER:

Miss Manners sympathizes with you; she does not believe that operas have overtures in order to provide inconsiderate people with incidental music to find their seats by. She heartily endorses the strict rules that some halls and theaters have against seating latecomers until there is a natural break in the program. It is impossible, however, for an individual member of an audience to be the sole keeper of such a policy. Stabbing violators in the backside under cover of darkness only adds to the distractions it seeks to eliminate. You must put your case to the management, but in the meantime, you must put your knees to one side of your seat to let these people pass.

Curtain Calls

DEAR MISS MANNERS:

I am terribly upset about some people's deplorable conduct at the conclusion of a recent opera. Barely had the final curtain touched the stage, the opera stars not yet gone forward to take their bows, and throngs of what I consider extremely rude patrons started a fast exit up the aisles, supposedly to beat the crowds to the doors, parking lots, or after-theater suppers.

My being able to rise and applaud the players on stage is as much a part of an enjoyable evening at the opera as the actual performance, but when six people push their way past me to make their exits, and a near platoon is en route from the front rows, I am personally angered and goodness knows what the performers must think seeing a sea of backs.

I cannot believe that this is proper conduct, but I am at a loss on how either to halt this exodus or to appease my anger. Would you please help?

GENTLE READER:

Well, actually, no. Miss Manners prefers to make things worse.

Courteous as it is of you to feel that your appreciation is as important a part of the evening as the opera itself, Miss Manners cannot believe that most opera lovers share your opinion that clapping must be accorded the same respect as music.

In fact, as a violent opera lover herself, Miss Manners (who just loves violent operas) endorses the lively school of audience reaction, rather than the genteel one that you represent. Uniformly respectful applause is the result of ritualizing the experience of attending an opera to the point that no real expression of opinion is permitted.

This codification is more prevalent when opera going is treated as a tedious civic or social duty, than among people who find opera exciting. Miss Manners is far too shy to shout boo or bravo (with the proper endings, depending on gender and number of singers being addressed), but she recognizes that you cannot permit one without the other, and that both are sanctified by operatic tradition.

Perhaps the answer to the booing problem is to recommend the Italian equivalent of "you stank!" with proper endings, of course.

A less conspicuous method is to applaud when pleased and withhold applause when displeased, or to leave the theater when unable to applaud. If Miss Manners were an opera singer (and she has all the qualifications but voice), she would prefer the occasional excesses of enthusiasm when ecstatic fans pulled her carriage through the streets (even if it also meant occasional obviously misguided disapproval) to hearing the same tepid politeness for her triumphs and her failures.

Miss Manners would like to ask what you do after a truly terrible opera. She has sometimes sat enthralled through five-hour performances and stayed, tapping her little hands until the last person has left the theater, but has also gone staggering out after an hour and a half that seemed a lifetime of torture.

In any case, the opera is over when the curtain comes down. It is not rude to leave the opera house then, and there may be many reasons for doing so, even aside from terminal ennui. One may have a train to catch, a baby-sitter to let off duty, or a rendezvous backstage with the tenor.

For these reasons, you will never succeed in halting the exodus. But there is no reason you cannot stand and show your appreciation while others leave. If you are the only one remaining to do so, it will be even more appreciated.

Shh-ing

DEAR MISS MANNERS:

I believe in shushing people who talk during concerts. I didn't pay to hear them blabbering. Yet a friend who went with me told me I was being rude in telling people to shut up. It seems to me that what rudeness is, is talking during music.

GENTLE READER:

Both are rude. The polite thing would be to say to the noisy person, "I beg your pardon, but I can't hear the music. I wonder if you would mind talking more softly?" By the time you have said all this, a third party will utter a loud shush, thereby accomplishing your purpose without sacrificing your manners.

Romance in the Audience

DEAR MISS MANNERS:

I should like to bring to your attention a matter which I believe deserves your censure. I refer to couples who are so "close" that they totally obstruct the view of the person who sits behind them. I am far from the enemy of romance. And I have only sympathy for those so enfeebled that they need to lean upon each other, although in that case, one can think of institutions more appropriate to the circumstances. I don't like to spend $12.50 to look at the back of someone's head.

GENTLE READER:

Romance and getting a clear view of what is going on are opposite experiences, but should not be irreconcilable. Perhaps you could suggest a compromise, such as, "Excuse me, but I wonder if you two would mind holding hands instead."

Culture for Children

DEAR MISS MANNERS:

Last Sunday, my wife and I attended a concert where our enjoyment was considerably marred by the family with two small boys sitting directly behind us.

Despite their parents' almost constant hushing, the boys whined, talked loudly, sang, and drummed their feet against the back of my wife's chair until their father mercifully removed them, midway through the Bach Cantata. I think that it is a fine thing for parents to want to expose their children to cultural experiences, but must this ruin these same experiences for others? Do you have any suggestions or guidelines for parents who want to take their children to concerts, plays, and movies?

GENTLE READER:

Miss Manners is grateful that you phrased the question as you did, rather than demand, as many people would, that children be kept away from civilized entertainment and be condemned to watch cats chase mice across the screens of popcorn-infested shopping center theaters until they are of a proper age to watch bloodletting.

It is her opinion, after some experiments in the field, that children do not have innately rotten taste, but put up with children's entertainment only because they have never been allowed to view anything more interesting. If you put together all the ingredients that naturally attract children—sex, violence, revenge, spectacle, and vigorous noise—what you have is grand opera. You are right, however, that children must be properly prepared for such treats. This must be done in several stages:

1. Making them feel left out. Mama and Papa should get dressed up and giggly as they prepare to leave their children home with a cold television set and dash off to fun at the concert hall. Requests to come along should never be snapped up. The proper answer is:

"Don't be silly. You wouldn't understand it, and you'd just spoil it for us. There probably won't be any other children there. Anyway, you know what tickets cost these days? It would be a big fat waste of good money for something you wouldn't appreciate. Now, you be good little children. We'll be home in a couple of hours—unless we decide to get a bite afterward some place. Now, don't whine. This kind of music is really sophisticated, and it's for adults only." If this is said with a mixture of condescension and obvious anticipated pleasure, the children should be begging to go. When you get them to their knees, lean heavily on the objection that they are not familiar with the music, or whatever the cultural treat is to be. They will then agree to cooperate in the next step:

2. Making them familiar with the program. The best way to teach them a piece of music that is to be played is to let them call up the local good music station and make a request. This is more fun than playing records, not to say cheaper, and will especially make an impression if the station mentions the child's name. Of course, the station may begin to tire of playing the Bach Cantata, and then you can switch to records, or picking it out on whatever instrument you or the child plays, or humming it. Plots of operas or of classical plays should be told as bedtime stories. Being able to recognize a tune or a theme will make the event comfortably familiar, rather than chillingly alien.

3. Teaching them cultural center etiquette. You must include the tedious reminders not to kick or comment, but these may be hidden among the finer and more interesting points of behavior: not clapping between movements, the

mechanics of standing ovations and of encores, the feminine and plural endings of "bravo," and so on. If a child feels privileged to go, understands what is being done, and knows how to behave—even knows enough to catch misbehavior in others—he or she will be hooked on high culture for life.

In the Rows

DEAR MISS MANNERS:

When passing along a row of seated people at the theater, for instance, or in church, how many times is it necessary to say "Excuse me" as you work your way to your seat?

GENTLE READER:

Once for each person passed, plus one "Oh, dear, I am so sorry!" for each person stepped on.

DEAR MISS MANNERS:

When I have soft drinks at the movies, I often have to get up about halfway through the picture and excuse myself. The people in my row seem annoyed when I go past them, first in leaving and then in returning. I only block their view for a minute. Is this inconsiderate of me, really?

GENTLE READER:

Perhaps. But, then, so is the alternative.

On Leaving Early

DEAR MISS MANNERS:

Please comment on etiquette for those attending the theater. I'd specifically like you to address the problem of rude audience members who leave a play during its final moments, presumably to avoid the delay of leaving along with everyone else after the curtain call. Such oafs disturb the enjoyment of patrons seated in their row, who must rise to let them out, as well as patrons seated in rows behind, who cannot see because so many are standing. If these offenders are seated near the stage, I am sure the actors' concentration may be broken in trying to guess which of their lines caused the commotion. Could you use your influence to the aid of playgoers?

GENTLE READER:

Miss Manners attends the theater often enough to wonder why no one seems to be worried about the rudeness of actors toward audiences. It is impolite to invite people to an evening of entertainment and then not entertain them, and forgivable if these people then wish to go home. She does agree, however, that this should be done with as little commotion as possible.

🌹 SPORTS

The Fox Hunt

It is strange that fox hunting should have the reputation of being a snobbish sport. Perhaps that is because the title role is played in an extravagant fur coat.

Actually, however, fox hunting conforms to Miss Manners' idea of the proper composition of an aristocracy in a democratic society. That is, participation is open to all who want it, provided they have the skill and the willingness to observe strictly the rules of behavior and the dress code. It was dear Anthony Trollope who first pointed out to Miss Manners that beyond these requirements, farmer and landowner become equals in the field, and ladies and gentlemen are ranked only by their ability and courage.

To participate in a hunt, one need only propose oneself to the Master of Foxhounds or the field secretary, and pay the ''capping'' (guest) fee. True, you should have a horse and be able to ride it, but Miss Manners does not consider this an outrageous requirement in a society where you are often expected to have an automobile in order to get or get to a job.

For individualistic dressing and improvised behavior, fox hunting is equivalent to, say, a nineteenth-century Russian ballet school. The rules include greeting the master and thanking him before departing. He is known by the title ''Master.''

Guests wear black Melton coats, or very dark gray or blue; light pants, black boots, and black hunting-derby hats. The scarlet coat, called pink for its original London tailor, Mr. Pink, and not for its color, with the hunt's individual colors on the collar, is worn by members of the hunt with the permission of the M.F.H. Only then do they wear boots with tan tops and high silk hats.

Ladies who ride sidesaddle may wear dark green informally, but their formal wear is black (with the hunt colors if permitted) with top hats and veils.

If there is to be a hunt breakfast afterward, it is considered polite not to presume upon everyone's enthusiasm for horse-related smells, but to bring a fresh tweed coat and a sponge to wipe from one's boots the sort of thing that tends to get on one's boots.

No one rides between the Master and the hounds; no one cuts off another rider or separates himself from the field; no one makes personal comments on another person's ability or horse unless it is to a close friend or about a spectacular and unusual feat (''Well ridden''); and no one having a jolly ride pretends not to notice that another rider is in trouble.

Children, who may be permitted to wear jodphurs, black or tweed jackets, and velvet hunting caps, ride to the rear and usefully close gates; guests should be allowed to ride in front, where they can observe the hound work.

A person present at his first kill may be dabbed on the forehead with blood from the pad of the fox, or may be given the mask to wear under his hat. It is considered polite to look honored.

As everyone knows from the comic strips, the cry of "Tally ho!" means that one has viewed the fox. The accompanying gesture is to point toward it with one's hat, taking care not to strangle oneself with braiding that ties the hat to the head.

Another useful expression to understand is that of the Master, when he declares it time to "draw towards the likker." Miss Manners is not sure of the meaning of that last word, but the phrase announces that the day's hunting has come to an end.

Rules for the Pool

Just as at Christmastime all well-bred people think of those less fortunate than themselves, summer is the time to think kindly about people who own swimming pools. One has to spread one's compassion around the calendar, anyway, and the muggy days could be devoted to these particular friends. Who knows what might happen if you cast bread upon their shining blue waters?

It is important to know that people who have swimming pools cherish the hope that they may be loved for themselves alone. Therefore it is a mistake to omit saying hello to them on your way from their front door to their patio. It is, in fact, rude to omit any of the social amenities, in the belief that these people don't need them because they are blessed with swimming pools. You should not drop in on them unannounced, with an expectant smile and your face and an inflatable sea horse tucked under your arm. Nor should you drop in on them announced. You must wait for them to invite you, and if you can't wait that long to see them, why, you just invite them over to your house. In other words, you treat them just as you would if they were high and dry.

If they do invite you, it might be a good idea to behave well so that they will invite you back. Start by bringing the proper equipment. This is tricky, because if you are not specifically invited over "to swim" you are supposed to pretend that you are coming in order to enjoy the hosts' company. But since they may mention swimming after you arrive, and you do not wish to put them to the burden of supplying you, what you do is to bring the gear along, but hide it. Leave it in the car or in an oversized handbag. This means a bathing suit, bathing cap, sandals, and whatever lifesaving devices or toys you may require when wet. Pool owners are reconciled to having to provide towels, but it is a nice touch to bring them, too. It is an even nicer touch to bring the wine or little edibles the hosts are probably also in the habit of having to provide. The caps and sandals are necessary to fulfill another obligation of the guest, which is not to leave the hosts' home, indoors or out, in a worse state than before your arrival. One puts on a cap in order not to clog the pool with hair, and one puts on sandals in order not to track up the floors.

There are also things to be omitted because they are bad for the water or the filtering system : suntan oil, insect repellent, Band-aids. You also have an obligation to keep yourself well on the premises, so that the host is not left feeling uncomfortable because you broke your neck doing fancy dives or drowned in his pool. For this reason, one does not show off in a friend's pool, endanger others, or learn to swim or dive there.

One does not engage in potentially offensive behavior there, such as merrily pushing others in the pool or stripping without the hosts' permission ; and one monitors the behavior of one's offensive dependents, keeping the dog from swimming at all, and the children from shouting or splashing. Especially, one does not stand still in the pool, with a vague, abstracted expression on one's face. One puts on those sandals and goes into the house for that.

Jogging

When ladies and gentlemen were in the habit of taking afternoon strolls, they did not bump into one another and shout rude remarks to warn others to get out of the way. Miss Manners realizes that the world has sped up considerably in the last few years, but expects people to maintain this civility even though they are now jogging.

Miss Manners does not herself jog. She would not know how to manage her parasol while out jogging in summer, nor her muff in winter. She is willing to allow the right of others to jog themselves silly, but only if they, in turn, respect the rights of those who choose other methods of mobility.

Recreational and utilitarian transportation in cities includes the automobile, the motorcycle, the horse, the bicycle, the roller skate, the jogging foot, and the walking foot. While there are specialized areas for these pursuits, such as streets, sidewalks, horse paths, and bicycle paths, many of these places must be shared, and none of them belongs exclusively to the jogger.

Two traffic rules should prevail. First, that the slower mover keep to the right and the faster pass on the left, and second, that the stronger should yield to the weaker. For example, a jogger pulls over to the right to let a bicyclist pass on the left. An automobile yields to a pedestrian, but so does a jogger, who should be stronger than the walker or else the jogger has poured out an awful lot of sweat for nothing. An exception is when the stronger method of transportation is likely to go out of control if startled. Miss Manners would not advise joggers to scare the horses on the horsepaths. Even though joggers are weaker than horses, they tend to be brighter. Nor is there a reason for joggers to do their jogging in places likely to frighten people. It is a poor idea to do one's jogging in crowded streets, and if one does so, one must remember to yield to pedestrians. Joggers who do not wish to break their activity must jog in place until pedestrians have been allowed to pass. If there should still be conflicts, the correct warning is, in a normal tone of voice, "Excuse me, please." Not "GET OUT OF MY WAY !"

The correct clothing for a jogger is a sports costume that clearly looks like a sports costume. No city can keep its self-respect if its streets are filled with citizens who appear to be running around in their underwear. The correct thing to do with this clothing is to jog it out of sight, putting it and oneself in the wash immediately after jogging. Nobody loves a stationary jogger.

DEAR MISS MANNERS:

If a gentleman walking along a narrow, cleared path through deep snow encounters a lady jogger coming around the bend at full tilt, who should yield and step into the deep snow?

GENTLE READER:

In all traffic situations, the first to yield should be the first who has realized that there is about to be a collision.

DEAR MISS MANNERS:

A friend of mine likes to go jogging with me, but he can't keep up with me. Do I have to slow down to his pace?

GENTLE READER:

Either that, or tell him before you start where you intend to finish and then go at your own pace, meeting him there. That hardly qualifies as going jogging with someone, but see if you can pass it off on him for that. If there are vegetable juice toddies at the end of the journey, it might work.

Tennis

The accident of two people being available at the same time, the physical stirrings that accompany pleasant weather, an attractive look, a well-turned remark —even, Miss Manners blushes to say, the fact that one person has a convenient place to go: These are the reasons for which people commit themselves. When they later discover each other's inadequacies, it is too late to dissolve the relationship without complications and hurt feelings. That is how people find themselves committed to playing tennis with partners who make them miserable.

Miss Manners is not, herself, a tennis player. Although warned by her dear mother, when she was a slip of a girl, that "all nice men play tennis," she soon figured out that it did not necessarily follow, therefore, that all nice men were seeking nice young ladies who played tennis. Nevertheless, Miss Manners is scrupulous about not limiting herself to giving advice in matters about which she happens to know something.

She does know that tennis players sometimes mistakenly feel that social rules prevail on the court when those of exercise or sports should apply. There is such a thing as purely social tennis, but this means, as in any other social activity such as conversation, that one person does not seek to demolish the other, but both endeavor to keep the ball going back and forth. It is best, in such cases, not to keep score if one person is markedly superior to another. Tennis for exercise is better if inequalities between the players are minimized; in tennis for sport, equality is essential. All social modesty and flattery should then be cast aside as people supply enough true information about their skills to enable them to find the right partners. If, as often happens in life, reality does not measure up to advance notice, the arrangements may be dissolved without hurt feelings, as never happens in life.

DEAR MISS MANNERS:

I am frankly a very good tennis player, and would enjoy meeting new partners I can play with. But I am always being asked to play by people who turn out to be much worse than I am, which makes the game no fun for me. When potential partners ask me how I play, I don't want to sound conceited, but I say, "OK" or "Not bad," and they say they are, too, and I end up wasting a lot of time, in addition, often, to court costs. How closely can I quiz people about their ability, and how frank should I be about mine?

GENTLE READER:

You may be quite blunt about both. In one-to-one sports, each person has an obligation to represent his degree of skill and experience as honestly as he can in order to avoid catastrophic mismatching. This rule does not apply to lovemaking.

Cards

DEAR MISS MANNERS:

I play in a weekly poker game with several of my neighbors and we are faced with a dilemma. One of the newer players has become a nuisance. He has a tendency to cheat on the amount he puts into the pot and feigns naïveté when caught. It has gotten to the point where we must watch him constantly to ensure that he does not shortchange the kitty, and this has turned a formerly enjoyable pastime into an ordeal. One week, we decided to move the game without telling him. He drove around the neighborhood until he found the spot where all our cars were parked, and had the nerve to come in and play. He is insensitive to any such insult or "subtle" hint that we would rather not share his company, but no one of us has the guts to confront him to say we are throwing him out of the game. What is the correct way to bar this unwanted player from future games?

GENTLE READER:

In a time of changing moral values, when sympathy is expected to be the proper response to unsocial behavior, cheating at cards is about the only clear-cut, unforgivable crime left. It is nice that you are trying to be subtle, but your hints are, as you have noticed, too subtle. Tell him, "We are sorry, but you are no longer in the game." This is sufficiently subtle if you compare it with the traditional American method of dealing with people who cheat at cards.

DEAR MISS MANNERS:

My brother is very rude. When I play solitaire, he either leans over me and says things like, "Why don't you put the red eight on the black nine, stupid?" or he just grabs the cards away and does it himself.

GENTLE READER:

Playing solitaire in front of another person is in itself an effrontery, if not legally what is termed an "attractive nuisance." Solitaire must be played in solitude. Brothers count as people.

Monopoly

DEAR MISS MANNERS:

My mother and my sister and I were playing Monopoly. My sister was going broke, and I offered to trade her a hundred dollars and the Water Works for Ventnor Avenue, which I needed to get a set, so I could start building. The rest of the property was bought up, so that nobody else had a set, except Mediterranean and Baltic, which don't charge much. Anyway, my sister was about to trade when my mother said to her, "Don't do it, he'll murder us both." Was that fair?

GENTLE READER:

As you play Monopoly, it should be unnecessary for Miss Manners to remind you that life is not fair. Is it fair for a person to bankrupt his dear mother and sister, just because they happen to find themselves staying in a hotel they can't afford? You will find, however, that it is in the selfish interest of the rich to keep the poor marginally alive, in order to have customers for their marketplace. Therefore, Miss Manners finds it advantageous to you, as well as fair, that your sister be taught basic survival.

Beauty Contests

DEAR MISS MANNERS:

Our daughter, Cynthia, has always been a good girl, and her father and I are very proud of her. But now she has thrown something at us that has me so upset I don't know what to do. My husband, who is a classics professor, refuses to get involved with it, and I don't know what to do.

Cynthia is a beautiful girl, and it's not just her mother who says so. Her boyfriends are all very nice young men. She has a B to B-plus average in nursing school, and has always wanted to work with children. She is also musical. She plays the cornet and the trombone and has recently started taking the flute. Now she thinks maybe she would like to have a career in music before going into nursing, or instead of, if it turned out to be a success.

The problem is that she thinks she can get started by entering a beauty pageant. Just the idea of my Cynthia parading around in a bathing suit before judges makes me sick. But she says that beauty isn't part of it anymore, it's personality and talent that is judged, and also that southern girls from the very best families enter these contests. I don't know about that. My New England forebears would be horrified at what Cynthia suggests, but she considers herself a southerner. I suppose I have no right to inflict other standards on her—as I said, she has always been a good girl—but she can't name me any other girl she knows who has competed in such a contest. Tell me, please—is she right? Are such things really considered proper behavior in the best southern families?

GENTLE READER:

Cynthia is right that southerners from all levels of society, like people elsewhere, relish competition. However, in the best families it is customary to show horses or dogs, rather than daughters. As for the object of such pageants, ask Cynthia whether she has ever observed a talented fat girl in one, or a girl who has a charming personality and a bad complexion.

Happily, however, the country is full of competitions for musicians, in which they need not submit their bust measurements, nor have their legs scrutinized. You might investigate these and steer her to auditioning for a music school, orchestra, or band. As for your husband, the classics professor, tell him that Miss Manners knows why he refuses to get involved. He knows that the ancient deities themselves once got into a beauty pageant, and while Cynthia, a.k.a. Artemis, didn't compete, Cytherea, a.k.a. Aphrodite, did, and won. You might remind him, however, that this caused nothing but trouble, a.k.a. the Trojan War. Also, if respectable people adopted the standards of the classical gods, there would be no decency left in the world.

CLUBS

Proposing Members

DEAR MISS MANNERS:

I belong to a very good club which is, although strictly a social club, not disadvantageous, shall we say, to the best businessmen in this city. I am a relatively new member, but am already thinking about proposing other members. In fact, I have been asked to put someone up, but it is someone I don't want to have in the club, although I don't want to alienate him permanently either. Can you tell me the appropriate way to (1) propose someone (2) propose someone without suggesting that I am putting my full influence behind his getting in.

GENTLE READER:

In the first, you write to the membership committee, "I would like to propose for membership Theobold Worthy, whom I know well and who I believe would be an addition to the club," followed by some information about his education, profession, and family. In the second, you introduce the same information by writing, "I am proposing for membership Earl Pushing, who seems anxious to join this club."

Resigning

DEAR MISS MANNERS:

Is there a correct form for resigning from a club?

GENTLE READER:

Yes, but it is only useful when one is resigning for some simple reason, such as moving out of town or realizing how much the one lunch a season one eats at the club is actually costing when the annual dues are figured into the bill. This letter of resignation, addressed to the club's secretary, expresses the member's regret at finding it necessary to resign and merely asks that this information be conveyed to the club's board. However, there is another reason for resigning from a club, which must be handled completely differently. Suppose you are resigning in high indignation because you have just discovered, as you are organizing your life in preparation for taking public office, that a club to which you have belonged for twenty years is not the affable community of like-minded spirits you had always assumed, but a hotbed of prejudice against blacks, Jews, Roman Catholics, women, and people with Hispanic surnames. You must then make your disillusionment known publicly, so that others will not be similarly deceived. It is wise to do so before the matter is brought to your attention— publicly by others.

A Thoughtless Reply

DEAR MISS MANNERS:

I have had many sleepless nights from a grave mistake on my part. I was a guest at my brother-in-law and sister's home in Los Angeles. He invited me, as I met him in the driveway of his house one morning, to be his guest at an exclusive club. He is a member of that club. Inadvertently, without thinking, I replied, "I will think it over."

As a result of this oversight on my part, he was insulted and spoke very little to me the rest of my two weeks' stay. I think the crime didn't fit the punishment. Please give me your opinion.

GENTLE READER:

Indeed, as the crime of blurting out misleading statements goes, yours is not serious. It would have been easy to rectify by your saying later, "Well, I did think about the honor you kindly offered me, and while I'm a little shy about it, truthfully I would love to go."

You didn't, though. Therefore, your crime, which is serious, is that you let that blurt grow malevolently in his mind, until he undoubtedly concluded that you thought his club not good enough for you.

Rather than criticizing his choice of punishment (for the sake of taking your own attention away from your own mistake) you should write him a letter now, explaining that you replied awkwardly to his invitation because you had been overwhelmed by it, but assuring him that you felt truly flattered to have been asked.

❦ ALCOHOL, TOBACCO, AND OTHER STIMULANTS

Why do people keep asking Miss Manners what to say, in a social situation, when they are offered drugs? What ever happened to "Yes, please," and "No, thank you"?

What happened was that the interesting combination of being both widespread and illegal has given the use of drugs an air that tends to cloud the social judgment of users and nonusers. The refusal of an offer is therefore often seized upon by the refuser, or by the refused, as an opportunity to belittle a person of different habits and beliefs, a motive that, however gratifying, is in direct conflict with the purpose of civilized society.

An offer to partake of any possibly pleasurable extra at a social event, whether it is a Campari and soda with lime, a third helping of peach pie, or a walk outside to see the stars, is only an offer, not a test and not a command. One accepts or refuses it simply, according to one's wishes, and one accepts a refusal as simply as an acceptance.

When the activity is one that is illegal (in addition to the disadvantages one might find in the above temptations), the person offering it has some special obligations. Everyone invited to a social event where there will be drugs should be notified of this in advance.

A host must never attempt to cut his entertainment expenses by offering any kind of refreshment to some guests and not to others. The cocaine party-within-a-party violates not only the law of the land, but the sacred laws of hospitality. The guest who chooses to participate has the normal obligations of curbing greediness and knowing his own limits, as well as one to remember that stimulants that make him more fascinating to himself do not have that effect on others. He should refrain as much as possible from describing his sensations. The one who chooses not to take drugs while others are doing so should try to refrain from supplementing his refusal with an excuse ("I work at the White House") or a boast ("I'm high on life").

No, No

DEAR MISS MANNERS:

While making new friends after moving to a large university town, I am faced with a curious problem of etiquette. When one goes visiting these days, one is rarely offered the customary ''something to drink'' or a box of bonbons, but rather the modern equivalent of the peace pipe—the joint.

It isn't the legal question which troubles me; the local laws are quite lenient. It's just that I simply don't like to smoke marijuana. In fact, I don't like to smoke anything at all. Besides, it reduces conversation to the vanishing point, even among champion talkers.

However, on those occasions when I have declined such generosity, my host—after suffering surprise—usually plies me with questions concerning my social, ethical, and yea, religious convictions. What seemed, ten years ago, like new freedoms have become today's new conventions, to be transgressed only at one's discomfort. Can Miss Manners help me frame a polite way to refuse the weed, which will brand me neither as an ingrate nor a fogey?

GENTLE READER:

It certainly is a curiosity of etiquette that you, upon whom a rudeness has been performed, should take the responsibility for the error committed. It is unfortunately customary for people who are offering what they consider to be a rare treat—marijuana, liquor, dessert, or a sexual encounter—to think it gracious to quiz, badger, and shame the object of their charity into accepting it. It is, in fact, extremely ungracious. One should always take ''no'' for an answer, no matter how delightful one considers the offering to be.

Since you ask what you should do if they violate this, the answer is to keep refusing politely until they go away. The first refusal consists merely of ''No, thank you.'' The subsequent ones should all be ''I really don't care to''; eventually, the generous one will get tired of hearing this repeated. Thus:

''Why not?''
''I really don't care to.''
''Oh, come on.''
''I really don't care to.''
''Is it against your principles?''
''I really don't care to.''
''Are you afraid of getting caught?''
''I really don't care to.''
''Do you think it's wrong?''
''I really don't care to.''

And so on. If you keep this up long enough, your friends will retire quietly in the corner to get high.

Smoking

DEAR MISS MANNERS:

Would you kindly discuss smoking etiquette, especially ladies' smoking etiquette? Some folks, in these advanced times, still rely on sensible and time-tested methods. Would you carry a lighter in your purse? Would you carry a cigarette case? Is it proper to allow men to light your smoke in these ''advanced'' days? Isn't it tacky to light your smoke with it dangling? Do you smoke on the street?

GENTLE READER:

We can discuss this only if everyone agrees that the subject is the etiquette of smoking, and not the health aspect. When Miss Manners tells you how to conduct a proper wedding, after all, she does not go into whether the person you are marrying is good for you.

A lady does not smoke on the street. That rule evolved in comparatively recent times (by Miss Manners' calendar), when it became proper for ladies to smoke at all. At that time, ladies were unfortunately not informed that they must also follow the existing rule about smoking, which Edwardian gentlemen already knew—namely, that one does not smoke in front of those who do not without first asking their permission. Certainly a lady who smokes should carry the proper equipment for doing so. Whether she puts her cigarettes into a jeweled case and carries a tiny enameled lighter is a matter of preference and budget. That way, she may graciously allow a gentleman to light her cigarette, but also not let her life pass while waiting for one to do so. Dangling one's cigarette is only proper for private detectives.

The Proper Place and Time

DEAR MISS MANNERS:

As a smoker, I am constantly having run-ins with nonsmokers who want to tell me when and where I can smoke. Are there any legitimate rules about this?

GENTLE READER:

Yes, and they never should have been abandoned, as they were when women began to smoke, which never should have happened, either. Smoking should be confined to certain parlors to which the smokers may retire from the sensible people and make their disgusting mess. One should not smoke at the same table where others are still eating. If you wish to smoke in the presence of clean people, you must ask their permission and be prepared to accept their refusal to grant it.

House Rules

DEAR MISS MANNERS:

I am almost at the point where I don't want to have people as friends if they smoke. It must be the most inconsiderate habit in the world, in terms of other people's health and convenience, and surely it is the ugliest. If I see people puffing away at parties, I steer clear of them. But sometimes the occasional smokers fool me. They're not smoking when I meet them, but when I invite them over—my husband and I enjoy doing a lot of entertaining, and like to mix in new people—they light up in my own house, which I hate. How can I stop this? I know it isn't nice to start giving guests orders, but, honestly, is there any reason to want to keep these people as friends?

GENTLE READER:

Actually, smokers make excellent friends at present-giving time, because they can always be given pretty lighters and ashtrays, and, if you are in love with one, although Miss Manners gathers you are not, an engraved silver cigarette case makes a marvelous present. However, that does not seem to cover your chief question. The answer to that is that when you invite them, you may say, "I hope you don't smoke, because we don't have smoking in the house," provided you laugh at your own inflexibility as you do so.

DEAR MISS MANNERS:

My beau and I have been asked to be weekend guests by his friends in another town. These friends do not smoke, nor does my beau. His friends do not permit smoking in their house. I am a smoker and have refused to go because of these circumstances. If the invitation had been for dinner only, I could oblige by not smoking, but a weekend is impossible. Do you think my behavior stubborn or justified?

GENTLE READER:

Both. An honest person cannot accept hospitality with the intention of disobeying the house rules, and yet you have been startlingly honest with your beau about what your greatest pleasure is. A little less honesty—whatever happened to sneaking out at night?—would have been more tactful.

In Public Places

DEAR MISS MANNERS:

How should a nonsmoker indicate his displeasure with those smoking in a public facility? I, of course, avoid such facilities when possible, preferring, for example, transport by private auto or airplane. Yet there are those times, in banks, stock companies, and doctors' waiting rooms, when one must deal at the common level. Does one address the smoker directly or does one address that person in charge of the office so that they may convey the request? Should it be phrased as a request, a mild complaint, or demand?

GENTLE READER:

All of the above. The request is addressed to the smoker. The mild complaint is addressed to the person in charge. And the demand is addressed to the assembly at large, or to God.

Not Drinking

DEAR MISS MANNERS:

I do have a problem: I do not care to drink. When I'm asked out to dinner, the first question is "What do you care to drink? What wine, etc.?" How can I properly say no to a predinner drink?

GENTLE READER:

The phrase is "No, thank you." Learn it. Otherwise, you will find yourself with drinks, second helpings, desserts, and heaven only knows what else that you do not want. Do not make any excuses, such as "I'm on a diet" or "I don't like the taste of liquor" or "I can't handle cocktails." This only leads to discussion of the matter. The only other proper answer to the query of "What do you want to drink" is "Water, please." For those who wish to dress up this reply, it is now possible in restaurants to order water that is just as expensive as liquor or wine.

The Day After

DEAR MISS MANNERS:

I went to a bar last night with a group of friends who are "social drinkers." (I don't drink.) Well, these social drinkers made complete fools of themselves last night. My question is, is it proper for me to remind them of their behavior (and subsequently) to laugh uproariously?

GENTLE READER:

No and yes. That is, have a good laugh, but do not share it with them. They had enough fun last night, and now it's your turn. It is, moreover, a bad precedent to tell people that they have made fools of themselves. Once that kind of honest criticism gets loose in the world, it is very difficult to control.

The Straw

DEAR MISS MANNERS:

While dining out, is it proper to use the small straw served with a mixed drink? This was brought to my attention and it was said that it was to be a stirrer. It was also mentioned that you get the full strength of the drink when using the straw. Is this true? I prefer using the straw and cannot see why this would not be permissible.

GENTLE READER:

There is no way you are going to win with one of those short thin bits of plastic that can't make up its mind what it is. Because it's not long enough for a straw, you are going to get your nose wet, and because it's not wide enough, you are going to get something stuck in it—a piece of pineapple, a mint leaf, or whatever other leftovers people toss into mixed drinks. However, you are most welcome to try. If a thing is going to take the shape of a straw, you cannot be blamed for attempting to use it as one.

Food in Drinks

DEAR MISS MANNERS:

When cocktails are served before dinner in a restaurant, those guests who order martinis find their olives neatly speared on a plastic skewer, so that they may snap their olives without seeming to anticipate dessert by using their drinks as finger bowls. But can you advise those of us who prefer old-fashioneds or whiskey sours, which provide both cherries and citrus slices but without a deft handle?

GENTLE READER:

In the case of nourishment served in a cocktail, you may, of course, finish the drink and then tip the glass toward you so that the wet orange slice falls smack onto your nose. Miss Manners suggests, however, using the nearest fork, plastic stirring gizmo, or spoon.

A Special Drink

DEAR MISS MANNERS:

My husband and I had a wonderful coffee-brandy drink in a restaurant recently. The rims of the glasses were frosted with sugar, which looked delicious. Would it have been proper for us to taste the sugar?

GENTLE READER:

Miss Manners can hardly imagine anything that would do more for an evening or a marriage than for a wife and husband to sit opposite, looking at each other, while silently licking the rims of fine glasses.

Wine

Wine can do evil things to people. Otherwise gentle and mannerly souls turn arrogant and belligerent. The most retiring types will not hesitate to make public spectacles of themselves. Those who are imbued with the graces of modesty and toleration are transformed into showoffs and bullies.

And that's before anyone has had a chance to drink the wine.

Miss Manners is the last person to question propriety and ritual. But she is getting tired of people treating the simple matter of selecting and approving a wine as if it were the Judgment of Paris. She is getting dangerously close to believing that anyone demonstrating an excessive interest in his automobile, sound-reproducing equipment, or wine is not a gentleman. (Horses and land are the traditional subjects on which gentlemen are permitted to lavish more care than on their families.)

The general rule is that the host selects the wine to complement the food, and the general beliefs are that chilled white wines are better with light food, such as fish, poultry, and veal; that full red wines are served at room temperature with game and heavy meat; that sweet wines are served with dessert; and that champagne goes with everything. Miss Manners holds to the last opinion very strongly.

But these rules are not engraved in stone or, shall we say, stained on white damask. A host who is sure of himself may try some more daring combination at home, or he may do so in a restaurant with the advice and consent of his guests.

There are so many expertoholics about these days, that it has become rather charming for a host to enlist help. Asking the lady to order the wine or entirely leaving the choice to a trusted sommelier or wine steward is, in Miss Manners' opinion, more gentlemanly than reeling off names and adjectives.

At one's own dinner table, the name of the wine may be made known upon request, but it is never written on the menu or otherwise used as a designer T-shirt to puff up the chest. The exception is a dinner among friends who are known to share a special interest in wine, and who may be especially invited to share a treat. (There is a similar rule about not discussing food at dinner parties, even to compliment it. Miss Manners bets you didn't know that. It has fallen into disuse because there seems to be no such person anymore as one who doesn't have a special interest in food.)

It is the job of the host to be sure that the wine is in good condition. This is the point at which many people become hysterical with the awesomeness of the duty.

One can occasionally be served a bad wine, just as one can occasionally be served food that has gone bad, and no one expects either to be consumed. It is, in fact, a favor to draw such a mistake to the attention of the responsible person.

But one does not enter suspiciously into a prolonged trial, any more than one generally employs a taster, these days, to sample the food and certify that one's friends, or, more likely, one's own household is attempting to poison one, unless it is proven otherwise.

The normal precautions are to smell the cork, checking to find if it has gone musty, and to pour a sip into one's own glass and sample it. This has the advantage of making the host, rather than the guests, choke on the bits of cork he has clumsily splintered into the bottle.

Please note that it does not include pushing the cork up the nose, lowering the face into the glass, swirling the wine about on the tongue, or discussing whether it has lived up to one's expectations.

The best rule is that if you cannot tell whether or not a wine has gone bad, you might just as well drink it.

(For more on wine in restaurants, please see pp. 651–652.)

Wine Tasting

DEAR MISS MANNERS:

I was clever enough to stock up on some very good wine years ago, and bottles I paid ten dollars for are now worth forty dollars and more. I would like to serve an occasional treat to friends, but I can't stand seeing unknowledgeable people pour it down their throats without realizing how valuable it is. I can't have a whole table full of nothing but wine experts, though. Is there any way, without bragging, that I can tell people what they're drinking?

GENTLE READER:

You might request a trusted friend to exclaim, "Good heavens, what is this?" at his first taste. Or you might apologetically ask your guests to let you know if the wine has turned because of its great age.

Champagne

DEAR MISS MANNERS:

Is it true that it's considered more elegant to open a bottle of champagne without getting the popping sound from the cork? I always associate that sound with special occasions, and think it's fun to let people know what's coming.

GENTLE READER:

It is not always fun for the person who finds out what is coming by getting a flying cork in the eye. Putting out champagne glasses is a more subtle announcement, and if that is too subtle, you can say in a hearty voice, "Well, let's have some champagne."

Rules for Toasting

DEAR MISS MANNERS:

When offering toasts, when do you clink glasses, and when do you smash glasses? I have heard of people throwing their glasses at the fireplace, but I'd hate to be the one to start it at a time when it turned out not to be the thing to do. Another question: my wife doesn't drink, and is always embarrassed during toasts, not knowing what to do. She says she doesn't want to insult anyone, but if it's a choice between insulting and drinking, she'll do the insulting. Now, I do drink, but I don't know how many people at a dinner table I'm supposed to clink glasses with before I can take a sip. What if someone drinks to my health?

GENTLE READER:

For some reason, there are a great many more legends and customs associated with drinking than with, for example, the taking of vitamins.

One story about the clinking of glasses is that the purpose is to spill each person's wine into the glass of the other, for assurance that nobody is being poisoned (or everyone is).

Another story is that the custom of clinking glasses originated in the Middle Ages when any alcoholic drink was thought to contain actual "spirits," such as the demons in "demon rum," who, when imbibed, inhabited the host's body, causing the imbiber to do things that he would not ordinarily do. Since bells and other sounds were thought to drive spirits away (à la, every church in America which to this day rings a bell to drive the "demons" away from the sanctuary before worship begins), the clinking of glasses was thought to drive the ''spirits'' out of the spirits and thus make it safe to drink.

Nowadays, it is better to touch the glasses of those next to you, and even better merely to raise your glass. Your wife should raise her glass, too, even if it is empty, and then put it down without drinking. One never, ever drinks to oneself, but babies being toasted at their christenings are among the few people to know this.

On the subject of smashing glasses in the fireplace, remember that until the late 1800s glassware for most people was a very high-priced luxury; the symbolism of smashing glasses in the fireplace meant either that the host (the host, while refraining from toasting himself, must always give his approval by tossing the first glass) wanted to show his true affluence, or that he considered the toast to be of such importance that the glasses would never be used for a less worthy drink. Do not toss glasses into a fireplace with a live fire in it, since it makes an awful mess when the glass melts and sticks to the brickwork, and is nearly impossible to remove; break the stems instead.

DEAR MISS MANNERS:

I can't always think of toasts to make when I'm having drinks with friends. Most of my friends think of something to say each time we raise a fresh glass, but I feel foolish just saying ''Here's to you,'' or ''Your health'' all the time, and I can't think of funny or complimentary remarks, the way they do. Can you suggest some that would fit any occasion? I'd like to keep up with my friends.

GENTLE READER:

You are making a terrible mistake. Your friends have a dangerous toasting habit, and you must make an effort to quit, before you find it impossible to control yourself from making silly remarks every time you take a drink. Miss Manners urges you to stop while you still can.

🌹 RESTAURANTS

It will astonish restaurant employees and patrons alike to hear this, but even the best restaurants are commercial establishments where people pay to be served meals, and not temples of social behavior where they submit themselves to be judged.

It astonishes Miss Manners to hear that many people who are confident of their behavior among their friends become terrified of embarrassing themselves before the imposing figures of maitre d's, as they call themselves, or other high officers in the restaurant service. One would think that if the people sitting at one's restaurant table are satisfied with one's manners, one would hardly care about the opinion of those standing behind it.

This odd state of affairs, a reversal of the usual customer–service person relationship—paralleled only among patients and the doctors they hire—seems to have come about by design of restaurant managers. Many of them believe that their patrons are sycophants who respect only those who look down upon them, and their success has proven them often correct.

The fact is that few restaurants, no matter how outrageously expensive, can provide formal service as it is known in social circumstances. It is rare, indeed, to dine in a restaurant where the service people do not interrupt the diners, where filled plates are never put before one, where trays, rather than hands are used to bring needed equipment. To those who believe that a fancy restaurant represents dining of a class higher than that to which they are accustomed, Miss Manners must explain that there is no necessity to feel inadequate. Good restaurant service may be pleasant and smooth, but it does not represent the equivalent of butlers and footmen.

As you are paying for your meal in a restaurant, it is perfectly proper to:

· Request a table in an area you prefer, say, near a window or away from musicians. For a customer to accept the employees' or owners' idea of ''good'' tables and ''bad'' tables and compete to be favored with their choices is childish.

· Sit next to whomever you want among those in your group. Unless one is giving a party in a restaurant, the social rules about seating do not apply. If couples want to sit next to each other, rather than across, or with the gentleman against the wall, rather than the lady, Miss Manners cannot see why they should not be permitted to do so.

· Know what is being offered, in the way of food and drink, and its price. If a list of ''specials of the day'' is recited, it is sensible to ask how much a dish will cost.

· Expect to be supplied with correct flatware, and resupplied, discreetly and tactfully, with replacements for dropped or misused implements.

· Talk only with those with whom one is dining. If strolling musicians, itinerant fashion models, or sociable waiters or other service people present themselves, they may be dismissed with a pleasant but abstracted nod.

· Remain ignorant of the personnel hierarchy of the restaurant. If a restaurant employs an army of captains, waiters, headwaiters, priests of wine, busboys, and hostesses, that is its privilege. But the customer should not be expected to recognize and treat according to rank the entire service. He may address any request to whoever presents himself with the expectation that that person, if not designated to perform the task, will find the person who is. Unless some special favor is given, the client should have to leave only one tip, to be divided by those involved according to their own standards.

· Enjoy his dinner, free of worries about the help critiquing his manners. Only Miss Manners is allowed to do that.

Ordering

DEAR MISS MANNERS:

When I first started dating, many, many years ago, my mother told me that when I went out to dinner with a boy, I should always order—not the cheapest thing on the menu, which would look obvious, but the second or third cheapest, for which I was supposed to show great enthusiasm. I never liked that system, especially when I would eat chicken à la king, while the man ordered himself a nice big steak, but it stuck with me, and I find that I still do it, now that I'm dating again. Isn't that ridiculous? Haven't times changed? Can you say something that will make me feel all right about ordering what I really want?

GENTLE READER:

Yes: These days a man could well eat his steak while you eat chicken à la king, and then offer to split the bill exactly in half with you.

If he is paying—especially if it is one of the surviving restaurants with "ladies' menus" (no prices)—you might ask him what he thinks might be good. He can then suggest either the lobster or the house salad served as a main course.

Restaurant Euphemisms

DEAR MISS MANNERS:

Recently some friends from out of town wrote and said they would be in town on a certain day, along with their two children, and wanted to take me, my husband, and our two children out to dinner. I wrote back accepting the invitation. We made reservations in three different restaurants so they could choose when they got here. All were in the mid-price range—five dollars to eight dollars a dinner. Should I have included a very reasonable restaurant in this list? The only good ones I know in the cheap category are ethnic, and my friends said their children don't like spicy food. I had everyone over after the dinner for dessert, but I still feel incorrect. I think they spent more than they wanted.

GENTLE READER:

Miss Manners absolves you of incorrectness, as you did so much work, in the way of telephoning and dessert making, in what was supposed to be the others' treat for you.

However, she would like to clarify the use of restaurant euphemisms for your future convenience. These are as imprecise as menu euphemisms ("fresh fish," "chopped sirloin," "home-baked pie"), but do not violate health regulations.

Look at the way you use the word "ethnic." Miss Manners knows a marvelous little ethnic restaurant where the spices are subtle and the prices are not. It is run by first-generation immigrants of French extraction. However, as you well know, the word "ethnic," in relation to restaurants, refers to only a few nationalities and is understood to translate as "spicy" and "cheap."

Allow Miss Manners to suggest another such euphemism: "Fun." If you had asked "Shall we go somewhere that's simple and fun, where the children will feel comfortable?" your friends would have known that you were offering to let them off cheap.

Splitting the Check

DEAR MISS MANNERS:
Recently, while visiting the city of Philadelphia, my companion and I had the occasion to join some friends for dinner. As we were unfamiliar with the local cuisine, we had asked our friends to choose a restaurant, assuming they would remember that we were on a tight budget. The prices on the menu were quite a bit higher than we had expected, but we carefully chose the less expensive entrées. Our friends selected more lavish main courses and added expensive à la carte salads and desserts. When the check arrived, one of our friends said, "I guess we can just split this four ways; I think that's how it's being done." We were, of course, shocked, but didn't want to create a scene over a few dollars, and so put in our twenty-five percent each.

Is this really the way it's "being done" in the City of Brotherly Love? Should we have objected at the time of payment? Must agreements be made in advance over the settlement of dinner checks? When I buy dinner for my friends, I would like to have some way of knowing in advance that I am about to do so.
GENTLE READER:
Brotherly love is, indeed, better served by making agreements in advance about who pays for what, and not only in Philadelphia, as Philadelphia is not the only place where prices are higher than one had expected. It is not necessary to voice objections to one's friends; one need only instruct the waiter, "Separate checks, please," at the time of ordering. Otherwise, there is the unpleasant task of asking "Who had the extra rum collins?" at the end of the meal, which is probably what your friends were trying to avoid, rather than the paying of their debts.

Separate Checks

DEAR MISS MANNERS:
What do you do if a waitress tells you it's not "restaurant policy" to issue separate checks to two couples dining together?
GENTLE READER:
Separate yourself from the restaurant before ordering dinner. If there are enough crumpled napkins left behind by people who depart from the restaurant when this is announced, there will be a change of policy.

A Reply

DEAR MISS MANNERS:

Refusal to give separate checks is not an attempt by the service people or a restaurant to be rude or unyielding. Rather, it is a policy to help ensure quality service and food for all of the patrons.

While most coffee shops and fast food establishments are able to handle separate checks, the finer dining establishments are not. In these restaurants, the policy is one check per table. To the restaurant, the dinner check is the primary source of control over their cash flow. It could be compared to a sales invoice. The order is taken, written on the check, with copies delivered to the various "departments" within the restaurant. One copy for the pantry person in charge of the hot food, and another copy for the pastry chef in charge of the dessert. There are often times additional checks written out for the bar and the food checker.

A request for separate checks immediately increases the number of copies going to the kitchen per table. The departments in the kitchen have been set up to prepare the order one check at a time; separate checks therefore make it difficult to control the preparation and delivery of the food. By increasing the paperwork for the waiter, you are actually preventing good service for yourself and affecting the service of the other patrons in the dining room. Extra time must be taken to add, figure the tax, total each ticket, and collect the payment. There is also the problem of who will be paying for the bottle of wine or an appetizer shared and consumed by four or more people.

Another consideration is the service person and the tip he or she receives. A request for separate checks will, in the majority of cases, result in a lower tip for the waiter. Separate checks relieves the responsibility of the tip from one specific person. The service personnel, as a result of past experience, will naturally give this table a lower priority, resulting in poorer service.

There are a number of ways this area can be handled on the part of the customer. First, bring cash. The waiter would be more than happy to get change or break a larger bill for you. The second method is to have one couple place the entire amount on their credit card and the other couple pay their share. If neither of these methods is acceptable, refrain from dining in the finer restaurants.

GENTLE READER:

Finer than what? Miss Manners fails to see how a restaurant taking the attitude that the customer must give way when his desires come into conflict with the convenience of the service people, and where it is called "natural" that the waiters will punish people whom they assume will not tip lavishly by giving them poor service, can call itself "finer" than anything.

Your writing paper shows you to be the head of a consultant firm for restaurants. Why are you not advising them to alter their methods to please their customers, rather than suggesting the reverse?

Miss Manners has no patience with the attitude that people must constantly adjust their behavior to fit the convenience of machinery or business methods. It is true enough that many expensive and pretentious restaurants, hotels, and other public facilities no longer pretend to care about the "whims" of customers. It is also true that many of them have employees who take no pride in doing their jobs well, and find satisfaction only in tips and not in good work.

Ladies Alone

DEAR MISS MANNERS:

I am a single woman who hates to cook and loves to eat. For years, I have coaxed people from the office to go to restaurants with me, bought carry-out food, treated people I didn't really like—all because I was embarrassed to eat in a restaurant alone. Now I've had enough of that. I've always been liberated enough to support myself—never had a good enough offer to do it for me—so I ought to be liberated enough to go out by myself. Do you have any hints on how a woman can manage by herself? Should I take a book, for instance? (I love to read almost as much as I love to eat, but I don't like to do the two together.) Someone suggested taking a briefcase, so I look like a traveling businesswoman, not a potential pickup. Do I have to stare out in space, pretending to see nothing? I would really prefer to look around—it is one of my hobbies to make up stories about the lives of people I glimpse in public—but I have heard that women alone are generally seated out of the way. What I need to know is how to be inconspicuous, so I can enjoy myself without being bothered.

GENTLE READER:

There is nothing so conspicuous as a woman struggling alone in a public place with the effort to appear inconspicuous. Such a performance positively inspires harassment of all kinds. A conspicuous woman, in contrast, inspires respect. Miss Manners is not talking about vulgar behavior, of course, but about the sort of aura that surrounds someone who not only has an obvious right to be there, but probably owns the corporation that owns the restaurant. Ask to be seated where you prefer, and behave as you normally do—good restaurant manners are no different for single women than for anyone else. The only prop Miss Manners uses for solo appearances is a head held high, although she has been known to render it more conspicuous by placing a hat on top of it.

Checking Coats

DEAR MISS MANNERS:

Does a woman have to check her coat at a restaurant? Some restaurants insist on it, and some won't even accept women's coats. If I keep it, what do I do with it—ask for another chair to put it on, or sit on it?

GENTLE READER:

Miss Manners wishes that restaurants would stop thinking of themselves as arbitrators of behavior and concentrate on getting the food to the table hot. It is true that the old-fashioned rule is that a lady does not check her coat. (An exception might be made for a nastily wet trench coat.) However, restaurants that do not accept women's coats are not thinking of correctness. They are thinking of their own skins or, as in the case of fur coats, their customers' skins. Safety and etiquette are thus making a rare appearance together. The coat is gently peeled back from the shoulders and hangs nonchalantly over the back of the chair. For this reason, a fur-lined raincoat is the ideal restaurant coat.

Chinese Restaurants

DEAR MISS MANNERS:

I don't expect you to be an expert on Chinese manners, but could you say a few words about Americans' manners when eating in Chinese restaurants in America? I like Chinese food but have had two difficult meals recently, because no one seemed to be able to agree on what the rules were.

The first was with eight other people from my office. The person who had recommended the restaurant to us took charge, did all the ordering, asked to have the forks cleared away and chopsticks brought, and generally ran the show. I found a dish that I enjoy very much on the lazy Susan when all the platters arrived, but I only got one helping of it and then everyone else demolished it. Also, I can't manage chopsticks, and felt like a fool. The second meal was a dinner date, just two of us. She kept telling me to try her dish, which I didn't like, but when I offered her some of mine, she didn't take it. What is the proper etiquette in these situations?

GENTLE READER:

You are correct in assuming that Chinese restaurant etiquette is a subspecialty of behavior only slightly related to native restaurant etiquette and hardly at all to Chinese etiquette. People who do not want to taste a wide variety of Chinese restaurant dishes should not go to Chinese restaurants with eight other people. One dish should be ordered for each person, but it is convenient to pick a leader to do this so that there is a balance of ingredients and exoticness. There is not much you can do if you do not agree with the leader the others have chosen, except to make mild requests or write his sins on a wall poster. You are, however, fully entitled to ask for a fork and knife, and also to ignore jokes, dares, and entreaties about chopsticks. The maximum number of people you may have at a table and not offer tastes is one. You were just lucky on that dinner date in having observed the formalities without having to share your goodies.

Dinner à Deux

DEAR MISS MANNERS:

Very often I have been in a restaurant when my dining partner and I decide to order two different dishes, so that we may each sample the diversity of the chef's culinary prowess. When the order arrives, we divide up its contents. On occasion, this practice has prompted derisive sneers or disdainfully raised eyebrows. I do not think this behavior should warrant a negative response. It is not as if we are masticating with open mouths or are chucking food across the table, soiling the table linens. I have heard that sharing is quite proper and even has a fancy French name.

Is my behavior proper and do you know the appellation for my actions?

GENTLE READER:

The word is *partager*. You are not going to ask Miss Manners to conjugate it, are you?

Sharing food in a restaurant is perfectly proper; what is raising eyebrows is your method of doing so. The only acceptable sharing one may arrange at the table is giving a beloved dinner partner one taste of one's food on one's fork, or a less intimate acquaintance a taste on his or her own fork.

If you plan to go halves, you must tell the waiter when you order, so the food may be served that way from the kitchen. That is why there is a word for it; get it?

If you say *"Nous voulons partager,"* you needn't conjugate the verb.

Seating the Ladies

DEAR MISS MANNERS:

If a gentleman and his wife, together with a friend of approximately the same age, eat at a restaurant where guests are shown their table but not seated by the hostess, should the gentleman seat his wife or the friend? The "friend" is a widow who dines out frequently (on her own as to paying her check) with the couple.

GENTLE READER:

The gentleman should first help the friend to her seat, and then his wife. The wife should not consider it a discourtesy to follow the ordinary procedure of deferring to a guest before a relative, other things being equal. The letter-writer should stop putting the word "friend" in quotation marks.

A Word of Advice

DEAR MISS MANNERS:
Where should I put my purse in a restaurant?
GENTLE READER:
Where you can keep an eye on it.

Wine in Restaurants

DEAR MISS MANNERS:
My dinner date and I were contemplating what size bottle of wine to order. He wanted to order a full bottle of wine and take home what was left in the bottle. I would be terribly embarrassed by this. Could you please tell me if taking leftover wine home in a doggie bag is poor etiquette?
GENTLE READER:
It is certainly poor nutrition for your dog. The only way to retain ownership of excess restaurant wine besides forcing it down your throat, is to compliment the restaurant manager lavishly and inform him that you will be back for another delicious meal and would like to have "your" bottle placed then on "your" table. This can only be done in very cheap pensions or in very expensive restaurants. If you go to ordinary restaurants, it would be best to adjust the size of your eyes to the size of your bladder, and order half bottles or house wine by the glass.

Wine Tasting

DEAR MISS MANNERS:
I was having lunch with a woman friend at a very good restaurant, and ordered a bottle of wine. The waiter poured some for me, as is proper, and I tasted it, nodded to him, and expected him to pour a full glass for her and then fill up my glass. Instead, to my surprise, he poured a small amount of wine in her glass and then just stood there, waiting for her to taste it and OK it also. I asked him if this were some kind of new women's lib routine, and he said that he always pours wine for everyone at the table, men and women, and lets them all approve it. I've never heard of such a thing; have you? I would think the restaurant would end up getting a lot of wine turned back because everyone couldn't agree on it, but he said that actually that never happens. If one person in a party of four doesn't like the wine, he said, the others will talk him (or her, I guess) into it. What do you think of such a thing? I still feel it sounds like women's rights gone berserk.

GENTLE READER:

This is a question of diner's rights, complicated, as politics always is, by the conflict between democracy and expediency. Everyone at the table should have a vote when the wine is chosen from the wine list. The taste, when it arrives, is not to decide whether the right choice has been made, but to determine that the wine is in a fit condition for drinking. If the traditional table representative, the man or woman who is going to pay the bill, cannot tell wine from vinegar, the entire table is in jeopardy. Your waiter is taking no chances on this when he returns for a popular vote.

A Second Opinion

DEAR MISS MANNERS:

When a waiter delivers a bottle of wine, he usually provides the gentleman with an opportunity to sample and approve of the selection before serving the lady. What does a gentleman do if he really doesn't like the taste of the wine? If I were sure the wine was bad, I wouldn't have the question. However, I'm not sure I could tell the difference between bad wine and bad-tasting wine. If the gentleman rejects the wine how does he handle the waiter who is only carrying out his instructions, or has long forgotten the purpose of sampling the wine? For that matter, most of the gentlemen are also just performing a ritual.

GENTLE READER:

In a rare combination of charm, ritual, and leadership, you seek a second opinion about the wine from the lady and a third—if she agrees that it may have gone bad—from the waiter himself or the wine steward. By this time, the waiter will not only feel flattered to have been consulted, but will realize that it is easier to recork this bottle and pass it off on the next customer, or use it in the salad, or split it with the busboy, than to argue.

(For more on rituals of wine, please see pp. 640–642.)

Pouring Beer

DEAR MISS MANNERS:

Should a gentleman pour his dinner partner's beer for her? My favorite companion and I often dine in exotic restaurants and she likes to drink beer with highly spiced food. The waiters usually pour out one glass and leave the bottle on the table near her. Am I responsible for refilling her glass myself, should I ask the waiter to do so, or is she on her own? I know that I am expected to see that her wine is refilled, by myself or, in more formal restaurants, by the waiter. Does this same rule apply to beer?

My own instinct is to refill her glass for her, but that may be less natural chivalry than an ingrained belief in Dorothy Parker's law of seduction: "Candy is dandy, but liquor is quicker." Please advise me.

GENTLE READER:

Miss Manners is under the impression that what beer does quickly is not what you have in mind. She is also under the impression that your Dorothy Parker quotation is a poem by Ogden Nash. You are probably under the impression that Miss Manners is never going to stop showing off and answer your question.

Pour the beer. You know perfectly well that the waiter is not going to get around to it, and women do not customarily pour from bottles at table, regardless of the symbolism.

Complaints

DEAR MISS MANNERS:

The other night, my date, another couple, and I went to a fairly pricey restaurant. When we got there, we were informed that our reservations were running late—we could spend the next forty-five minutes in the bar. We didn't feel like drinking, since we were holding out for a few bottles. When we were finally shown to our table, it was close to the kitchen door and we had a terrific view of the busboys, waiters, and kitchen help. To make matters worse, our waiter must've felt he was God's personal gift to food service. Yet the conversation was pleasant, and we ignored as best we could the problems. (Somebody had to sit near the kitchen; obviously we had sinned heavily in our previous lives.)

Until, that is, my broiled grouper was presented, dry and overcooked. When holier-than-thou returned, I requested that he send it back and ask the chef to try again. Please understand that there was no insulting or abusive language. No raised voices, just a simple: ''This isn't done properly—it is, in fact, overdone. Please, may I have another order?''

My date later told me that the other couple was horrified, or at least embarrassed, and that such an encounter may have ruined the evening for them. Heck! I felt I should have had a few words with the manager about the waiter, the lousy table, obnoxious service, and charcoal-treatment of the fish. Had I done this I'm sure my guests would have crawled under the table and died a slow death.

Query: How does Miss Manners handle such situations? How does Miss Manners toss a proper fit, complain of problems, and does she ever talk to the management (and if so, when)? I think many people accept shoddy service and near-inedible food because they do not know the proper etiquette of being forceful.

GENTLE READER:

Well, let's see. There was the time that Miss Manners asked a waiter, who had brought her nothing else in an hour, for a telephone to be brought to the table. She asked for the number of the kitchen, explaining politely that she wanted to call to inquire what was the matter. Failing that, she planned to ask for the number of a good carry-out restaurant in the neighborhood.

Then there was the time that her banana daiquiri came made with salt, instead of sugar. Would your friends have expected her to drink that, in the name of civility, put a weak smile on her face, and slide quietly under the table to a polite death?

That would certainly be wrong. Being polite does not mean that you have to eat salt.

But, no, Miss Manners does not toss fits in restaurants. There are acceptable ways of dealing with unacceptable service. A polite person does not jump to insult, as it were, assuming that he or she has been insulted, and answering in kind. Miss Manners always assumes that restaurants intend to serve her good food, well prepared, in an efficient and cheerful manner. She further assumes that if they have made an accidental lapse, they would want to know about it, so that they could correct it. A good chef would not be able to live with himself knowing that he had sent overcooked food out of the kitchen. It would be a kindness to tell him, so that he can erase this blot from his reputation and your fish. And if the waiter does not understand what you require in the way of service, it would be a kindness to enable the manager to explain it to him.

Enjoying (Others') Conversation

DEAR MISS MANNERS:

Is it polite to eavesdrop? I was at lunch at a famous restaurant where there were a lot of celebrities and was fascinated to hear what was going on, but my mother, who was with me, said it was very rude. Surely these people expected to be noticed, or they wouldn't eat there.

GENTLE READER:

Miss Manners deals in manners, rather than morals, and the answer is that it is highly impolite to be observed to eavesdrop. This is rude not only to the people whose conversation you are overhearing, but especially to your own companion, in this case your mother, whose conversation is thus pegged as being less interesting than that at other tables. As for listening to what is going on, that, of course, is what such restaurants are for. Until you learn to smile and nod at your mother while picking up gossip from three tables away, you do not deserve to be taken there.

Wrappings in Restaurants

DEAR MISS MANNERS:

What does one do with butter, cracker/breadstick, and sugar wrappers at the table?

At most private dinners, this is a rare problem, but at catered or restaurant affairs it is not uncommon. Does one place the wrapper in an ashtray, on the side of the bread plate, in a pocket?

GENTLE READER:

Ladies and gentlemen are only required to know how to respond to table service that, however complicated and artificial now, grew out of the natural causes.

Serving food in commercial packages is the invention of overzealous health departments or lazy restaurants. The recipient of such practices need not pocket the evidence. If packaged food is served at the table, one need only crumple up the trash and leave it on the table.

Lessening Diners' Din

DEAR MISS MANNERS:

A few weeks ago, my daughter and I stopped into a neighborhood Chinese restaurant for a quiet, simple dinner after a very hectic day. As we relaxed with our tea and gave our order for dinner, a very noisy foursome entered the small establishment and destroyed the atmosphere. As their loud talking and laughter continued, my daughter and I became more and more annoyed. A suggestion to our waitress that perhaps the noisy group would be requested to quiet down was ignored with a shy smile.

Being determined to salvage some peace and quiet to enjoy our own conversation, we finally decided to ask the table of loudmouths to lessen the din. I was afraid, however, that Miss Manners would consider this more ill-bred than the rudeness of inconsideration. As I pondered the situation, my daughter walked across the room and made a polite request that perhaps the volume of conversation be lowered, as we were not interested in sharing the information and humor being related at their table, and we were sitting as far away as the size of the dining room allowed. We hated to have to leave on their account, so could they please quiet down. It worked, but I hope our actions were not more gauche than the offenders. Please reassure or criticize.

GENTLE READER:

As we are talking about a Chinese restaurant, Miss Manners would like to offer you some of both. Reassurance: It was acceptable to ask the people politely to be quieter. Criticism: It was not necessary to critique their information and humor.

Fingers in Restaurants

DEAR MISS MANNERS:

I was wondering if it is polite to eat chicken with your fingers in a fancy restaurant.

GENTLE READER:

As you are no doubt aware, there are few treats better than crisp chicken, eaten with fingers. That this is incompatible with the treat of going to a fancy restaurant is one of life's paradoxes, which Miss Manners is afraid you must accept. As compensation, *coq au vin* was invented, so that patrons of fancy restaurants may eat chicken that falls right off the bones into the sauce if they so much as look at it. It is not much of a compensation, is it?

Removing Plates

DEAR MISS MANNERS:

Is it considered correct for a waiter to clear one person's plate away before another person in the same party has finished eating? I am forced to admire the efficient and courteous manner with which this service is performed in the better-class restaurants, but my conventional training still causes me to view this habit with some disdain.

GENTLE READER:

Both methods have been in fashion in social service at different times, and advocates have applied equal disdain to the barbarity of leaving dirty plates just because everyone hadn't finished, and seeming to rush the service by refusing to wait for everyone. Miss Manners now favors waiting until everyone is finished with a particular course before clearing the table for the next. People who order appetizers as main courses will just have to take their chances.

Checking the Bill

DEAR MISS MANNERS:

My husband has taken to using his pocket calculator for adding up the bills in restaurants. I don't mind his quietly checking the waiter's figures—he has caught mistakes many times, and never in our favor, either, but this seems a bit much. He says he does it because his arithmetic is bad, and this is the quickest, most accurate way of doing it. I hate the little clicking noises it makes. People always turn around and look.

GENTLE READER:

Isn't that preferable to their turning around to hear him say "four and carry the two, plus seven, is fourteen"?

Ladies' Room Questions

DEAR MISS MANNERS:

If I see a woman crying her heart out in the ladies' room of a restaurant, do I have to get involved? It happened to be someone I knew from college, but not well, and I was anxious to get back to my date and I guess I just looked at her and ran. It occurred to me afterward that she could have been in trouble and needed my help.

While we're on the subject of ladies' rooms, what is the proper tip for the woman who just sits there? I've run from them without doing anything, too.

GENTLE READER:

A good citizen offers help, even to strangers, when chancing upon the scene of an accident. However, this does not necessarily include emotional accidents—

it was not food poisoning that made this lady cry, Miss Manners trusts—because the assistance required could take years.

The offer of physical, but not psychological, help can be conveyed by asking, "May I get you a taxi?" It is safer than, "Is there anything I can do for you?"

As for tipping, no tip is fair for no service, but it requires some determination to carry out. If the attendant hands you a towel, twenty-five cents is sufficient, except in places where it is assumed that the customers are accustomed to overpaying, in which case you might make it fifty cents.

If the attendant performs real services, as defined above—if, for example, she sews up your dress and listens sympathetically to your story about how it got ripped—the tip should be at least five dollars.

Tipping

An aristocratic gentleman of Miss Manners' acquaintance is in the habit of showing his contempt for surly or inept service people by throwing money at them.

On a typical taxicab ride, he is rudely grilled by the driver to determine whether his destination is acceptable, he is then forced to listen to loud music from a speaker behind his right ear, he is addressed with bigoted remarks in which he is nudged to concur, and he is then left off a block from his destination because it would be too much trouble for the driver to maneuver closer. The gentleman's response is to thrust money scornfully at the driver and then stalk off haughtily, without waiting for change, confident that he has taught the fellow a lesson and left him withering with shame.

Miss Manners offers this strange story not only to illustrate the bizarre nature of her acquaintance, but to make the point that tipping, as a means of commentary on the quality of service, is open to misinterpretation. In theory, one can reward or insult a person by giving a tip, withholding it, giving more than is expected, or giving less than is expected. However, there is a missing ingredient in this formula, and that is the figure for What Is Expected. Nobody really knows any general rules about this, however authoritative he or she may sound. It seems simple to remember that fifteen percent of food bills at restaurants is a standard tip, but suppose you are having a forty-five-cent cup of coffee at the drugstore counter? Or suppose you eat at the world's most chic restaurant but, being chic yourself, never order more than one white asparagus spear?

Restaurants, mind you, are comparatively simple. How much, if anything, do you tip the shampoo girl at your dog's beauty salon if she did a bad job on the poodle but ran out and put change in your parking meter for you, and owns seventeen percent of the stock in the shop? If you tip her at all, are you insulting her? If you do not, are you depriving her of part of her expected income which, her employer has said, is the way in which the customer contributes to her salary? If you should give her too much, are you encouraging her to perform sloppy shampoos? If you give too little, will she take it out on your dog next time? Was the parking meter trip an extra service deserving of an extra tip? Does it matter that she put it in the wrong meter and you got a ticket?

Miss Manners dearly hopes that the day will come when the price of running such an establishment as a hotel, restaurant, or topless go-go palace will be figured with the full salaries of all the employees, and the customers will not be left to guess how much of it they must make up out of their pockets after they have paid the bills. This does not mean an extra ''service charge,'' as is often added abroad, but a clearly stated all-inclusive price, as overhead and salaries of clerks are included in the prices charged by shops. There will then be those who ask Miss Manners how they may deliver critiques of the performance of service people? With smiles, letters to employers, and the pressure with which you slam the taxicab door.

Inflation

DEAR MISS MANNERS:

I read recently that appropriate percentages for tipping are now running between fifteen and twenty percent. In the old days, ten percent was considered sufficient. Would you please tell me what is the rationale for this increase? It seems to me that if the basic price for a meal in a restaurant increases, as it has, then ten percent of the higher price still provides the waiter with the larger tip which is due him. But why fifteen to twenty percent?

GENTLE READER:

Ah, but the amount of service has not remained the same. There are so many things that a modern waiter must do, such as announcing ''Help yourself from the salad bar'' or arguing against giving out separate checks, that a waiter of the old days would never have dreamed of doing.

Free Lunch

DEAR MISS MANNERS:

The other day, at a restaurant, the waiter returned some time after I had ordered, saying they had found that their last supply of the food I had ordered was spoiled, and thus I could have another selection ''on the house.'' I chose a slightly higher priced meal. Now, assuming that the tip should be fifteen percent of something, should it be fifteen percent of zero, fifteen percent of the price of the meal I didn't have, or fifteen percent of the price of the meal I did have?

GENTLE READER:

Must you be so calculating? As you say, fifteen percent is now the standard tip. Standard procedure for restaurants, however, is for the waiter to figure that it's your tough luck that they ran out of what the menu promised. Fifteen percent of generosity is twenty-five percent of the value of what you ate, and a thank-you. You still come out ahead.

Buffet Service and Dinner Theaters

DEAR MISS MANNERS:

It's all very well to say that fifteen percent is a good standard tip for a restaurant meal, with up to twenty percent for a fancy restaurant, but life is no longer that simple. What about the newer type of buffet restaurant, where the customer does all the work of getting the food, and the waiter only brings the rolls and water? What about dinner theaters, where some of the bill is for the entertainment, not the food? And suppose the actors do the waiting on table before the show—do they still get tipped? How about all those captains and hostesses and people that restaurants have?

GENTLE READER:

Miss Manners would dearly love to help you save a buck, which is no doubt what you have in mind, but not by telling you that waiters and actors don't need the money. Tip those people as you would the help in an ordinary restaurant, although you can count only the value of the food in a dinner theater. If it is so much work for you to fill your dinner plate yourself, why do you go back and do it so often? Miss Manners saw you. However, you may save by not asking the captains or hostesses for favors, such as special tables. They should get bribes for such attentions—two dollars to five dollars, depending on the tone of the place and nature of the favor—but do not get ordinary tips.

The Owner

DEAR MISS MANNERS:

A friend has recently opened a very small restaurant in her home. She does all the shopping, cooking, and all the serving alone. I am planning on taking a few friends to dinner soon in her new establishment. My question: Is it proper to tip her, as proprietor, under the circumstances?

GENTLE READER:

Rule one: Friends are remunerated, in a business situation, to the same extent as are strangers who perform the same services. Rule two: The owner of a restaurant is not tipped. Rule three: It is gracious to express one's appreciation in words to the owner of a restaurant, if one has received her personal attention. Rule four: It is gracious to acknowledge a friendship with someone who is performing a business service to you. Conclusion: Introduce your friend to your guests, thank her, and save the tip.

Hailing Cabs

DEAR MISS MANNERS:

While it is certainly right to tip a hotel employee who summons a cab, I have read that a tip is not necessary if all the employee has to do is signal to a waiting line of cabs. Yet I have seen others pay a tip in such cases, and I hate to look cheap. What do you recommend?

GENTLE READER:

A good doorman cultivates a manner that is simultaneously decorative and threatening, a combination that alone inspires small tributes, such as quarters. Usually, however, he is expected to make something of an exertion for this, and raising one finger to a line of taxicabs is not considered sufficiently exhausting. If, however, you use his services often, including times when summoning taxicabs includes waving arms and legs in a rainy or snowy street, it might be wise to make a twenty-five-cent investment in his welfare on those occasions.

Hairdressers

DEAR MISS MANNERS:

The owner of the hair salon where I go regularly cuts my hair, and I do know that you don't tip the owner of the shop. I do know that you do tip the shampoo girl. But what about the girl who blow-dries my hair with that little handblower? When she's finished, the owner comes by and puts the final touches on my hair. It's no good watching the other ladies to see if they tip the blow-dry girl, because they have their hair dried under the regular machines. How many outstretched palms do I have to fill?

GENTLE READER:

Miss Manners has never had her hair ''done,'' or even cut, for that matter, and if you think tipping is difficult and expensive, try buying tortoise hairpins. However, she does find it silly, if not degrading, to dole out lots of little bits of money to several people. You haven't mentioned a colorist or a manicurist. Miss Manners suggests that you add twenty percent to the bill and request that it be divided in appropriate proportions.

❦ TRAVEL

If you want to give advice to tourists, you have to catch one first. People traveling abroad, seeing the sights, and wearing clothes they washed themselves in hotel bathroom sinks, all turn out to be ''travelers'' whose motivation for travel is ''to avoid the tourists.''

They are rarely successful at this, because "the place has been overrun by tourists," but as everyone one approaches turns out also to be a traveler, and the tourists are only "those vulgar people you see everywhere," it is a geographical impossibility to find one. That is too bad, because Miss Manners doesn't want to berate tourists, only to defend and help them. There was nothing wrong, in Miss Manners' day, with touring. Our best young gentlemen were always sent abroad during their troublesome years to commit follies that were unacceptable in the homeland. (Oh. Miss Manners suddenly remembers how touring got a bad name.)

At any rate, present-day tourists are not likely to be guilty of the standard charges against them, such as thinking the dollar is almighty and throwing American money around contemptuously. Americans are very careful now not to hurt the feelings of, say, Parisians, by implying that we find their standard of living pitiful. Another accusation is that American tourists dress funny. That would be dreadful. One should never be disrespectful of a host country by dressing for the beach or country in its big cities, but learn what is appropriate from the native dress. By this, one deduces that the proper form of city dress for the major cities of the world is a T-shirt with an American college name on it, and a foreign copy of a pair of blue jeans. Nor is it polite for Americans to expect to eat abroad the same food to which they are accustomed at home. This means that they should not crowd the local McDonald's franchise in a foreign city, but let the local people enjoy it.

Miss Manners does not defend tourists from the charge of being irritable and demanding, but notes that this is the natural state of people who live at the mercy of airlines, hotels, and taxi drivers anywhere in the world. However, she has some advice to relieve this unpleasantness. One suggestion is to accept the quaint and backward ways of the travel industry, and the other is to learn the rational ways of the society one is visiting.

If one thinks of travel services as being too primitive to be capable of efficiency, one is more tolerant of the inevitable mistakes. If you schedule no more than an hour of purposeful sightseeing, and an hour of aimless looking about in one day, this will leave plenty of time to deal in a relaxed fashion with food, accommodations, and transportation.

This will also relieve the tourist from overwork at national monuments, a major source of his peevishness. It is a proven fact that no one at home will ever know how many sights you missed, as one's friends always tune out or wander away three and a half minutes after saying, "Tell me about your trip."

In viewing foreign societies, one should assume that there is an orderly system for doing things, but that it may require translation. More important than learning the rate of currency exchange is finding out what is meant by such words as "You must come and stay with us," "That is a very fine antique and we won't accept anything less than one hundred dollars for it," and "Meet me at ten sharp."

The American Abroad

You may remember the Ugly American. Actually, he was the hero of the book by that name, who respected other people in their own countries, even if they happened to be foreigners.

The phrase came to be associated with rudeness abroad, and frightened lots of well-meaning Americans into going native in other countries which, in turn, frightened the natives of those countries. There has to be some mode of behavior other than irritating or imitating that we can practice as Americans in other lands.

Miss Manners proposes the Awkward American, a version of the Aw-shucks character who has proved so endearing around the world through the American cinema. This involves practicing basic American good manners, with an occasional adjustment to local conditions. The key is to maintain a bashful smile while performing such unnatural acts as walking about indoors with no shoes on or drinking clear but vicious liquids at one gulp.

The time is past, Miss Manners dearly hopes, when Americans who wished to be thought sophisticated adopted English or French manners. The excuse for using European table manners, for example, is always that they are ''more efficient''— as if we weren't getting our fast food fast enough. Nonsense. What they are is more European.

This is silly snobbery, and Miss Manners, as a practiced snob, finds it much more effective to insist on her own nationality. She does not dress up funny when traveling, or join in the conversations about how dreadful Americans are. She understands that it is the American burden to provide humor in other lands, but tries to confine it to speaking the local language as best she can. However, there are times when practicing American manners would involve committing rudenesses to foreigners. One must eat other people's disgusting delicacies as they do, and observe their proprieties. This is when the Awkward American can be most charming. The imitation foreigner will, for example, abandon in Japan the perfectly agreeable and internationally understood custom of handshaking and begin bowing to everyone. Not understanding that the timing and angle of bowing are complicated matters, he or she will bob about, offending everyone who is forced to keep smooth on the outside while convulsed with inner laughter.

The Awkward American, when bowed at, will incline the body slightly and ask shyly, ''Is this right?'' It will not be, of course, but nothing is more ingratiating than asking a foreigner for instruction in his code of manners. Why, Miss Manners herself is not immune to the charm of being asked what is proper to do.

"I'm Not a Tourist, I Live Here"

Abroad has become a good place for Americans to stay out of. We are a simple folk, and it is far too rich for our currency.

It was not always thus. Miss Manners remembers when Americans of comparatively modest means could venture forth as moneyed tourists. Many did not appreciate the pleasure of playing the crass and filthy-rich foreigner, for whom the cultured but impoverished local barely disguised his contempt in a flood of obsequiousness. These Americans longed to be recognized as people of fine feelings to whom money meant nothing.

Now we have our wish. It is time for us to learn how to play the quaint native for materialistic foreigners visiting our shores from more technologically advanced societies. The switch is sometimes difficult to make, even in cities where people are supposed to be used to entertaining foreigners. Miss Manners once saw a party of Japanese transportation experts bursting with the effort to control their hilarity at being asked to admire our train system. And she remembers the puzzlement of a State Department official whom Giovanni Leone, then president of Italy, had asked to take him to "a typical American restaurant." Someone suggested Mama Leone's.

With increased tourism, everyone will get the chance to do as well. Here are Miss Manners' suggestions for impressing loaded foreign guests with the cultural richness of America.

Basically, all one has to do is to remember what we really wanted to experience when we were the visitors. We weren't after the pathetic signs of progress people tried to show us—as if it would ever compare with our own. We wanted to see the colorful native costumes, the exotic local food, the anachronistic handicrafts, and the simple culture that was a true expression of a people's spirit. Well, we have those things, too. The ability to make cars, cameras, and television sets that work isn't everything. The native costume of the American of either sex and all classes consists of blue jeans, T-shirts with clever phrases on them, and sweat shirts with college or corporation logos. A foreigner will be delighted if you enable him to find the real article, as opposed to the imitations he can get at home, and advise him of the degree of obscenity on the T-shirt.

It is difficult to say, when foods have been borrowed and adapted all over the world, what is truly indigenous. But the typical American food of the moment, the staple of our diet, is yogurt. Many foreigners are not aware that this is produced in many forms and such flavors as bourbon and peanut butter, but they should be encouraged to overcome their reluctance so that they can tell their friends back home, and some of us, what this is like.

We are fortunate to have a great diversity of craftspeople, making everything from hammered earrings to hammered necklaces, but the chief American craft is scented candles. Your foreign visitor will want to see them in their proper setting, the shopping mall scented-candle boutique.

Of course, he will want to see American culture other than our fine music or dance performances at which the program reveals that the artist studied in his country. Fortunately, we have the best joggers in the world. We are also a naturally gracious people, and if we learn to be hospitable enough, perhaps one day the tables will turn.

Ships

People who go cruising on ships worry a great deal about the niceties of etiquette. Actually, it is the people who do their cruising in shopping mall parking lots who should be worrying about their manners, in Miss Manners' opinion. Shipboard behavior is comparatively simple.

The principal activities in which passengers engage on cruise ships are eating, dressing, tipping, and complaining. You will notice a similarity to pastimes in which many people engage on dry land. The difference is that on shipboard, you do a great deal more of each. There are also other options, such as seasickness and buying baskets in port (or port in baskets), but these are not bound by strict laws of the sea and tend to operate on an every-person-for-himself basis.

Miss Manners will assume that you have mastered the basics of each main activity at home, and will explain only the differences you may encounter at sea.

You have been taught to be friendly to whatever companions you find at the dinner table, to eat everything you are offered, and to keep all foods confined to plates, the bowls or prongs of eating utensils, or the mouth. None of these rules quite applies on a ship.

Ships serve the following meals: breakfast, elevenses, luncheon, tea, dinner, and midnight supper. Most people attempt to eat them all, including all the many courses of each, on the logical grounds that they have paid for this access to unlimited amounts of food. This is a mistake. Many people find out just how bad a mistake it is, the hard way. Take Miss Manners' word for it.

When you consider how time consuming it is to consume even some of this food, you will realize the importance of having compatible table companions. This is why the first thing you do aboard a ship is to get a table reservation—alone, with the people with whom you are traveling, or at a table to be arranged at the judgment of the dining room steward. If you choose the last, the second thing you do aboard ship is ask to be moved. This type of discreet snubbing may be applied to anyone on the ship except its captain. If you have the tremendous honor of being asked to sit at his table and can't quite bear his conversation, it is necessary to plead seasickness and to reassign yourself a table in your own cabin.

Spilling food is permissible aboard ship, if accompanied by a dark look over one's shoulder, to implicate the stabilizers and the ocean itself in this transgression.

Dressing on cruise ships has become Standard Tourist, which is to say sports clothes during the day and restaurant clothes at night. Miss Manners deeply regrets the general passing of wearing black tie to dinner, and applauds those few who steadfastly stick to the custom. Of course, one does not so dress the first night out, the last night out, the night before getting into port, nights when the ship is in port, or nights the ship is leaving port. On most cruises, this accounts for every night there is, but Miss Manners would still like to see evidence of the intention, such as a steamer trunk full of evening clothes in case the ship is unexpectedly stranded at sea.

Tipping, which most people fear, is actually easy, as all ship personnel are willing to tell you what is expected, and then some. Five percent of one's fare, which is what they recommend, is generous. Envelopes once a week, with five dollars to the waiter and a dollar or two less for cabin attendants, is a minimum. Wine stewards get fifteen percent of the wine bill, and bartenders fifteen percent of the bar bill. Others who perform special services are tipped as they would be in hotels.

As for complaining, it is the general cost of cruising that inspires many people who are otherwise meek and patient with whatever life gives them to become highly critical of everything the ship has to offer.

As cruising should be vacation time, Miss Manners recommends this constant harping only to those who find it relaxing. Personally, she prefers to sit in a deck chair and read *Moby-Dick*.

Airplane Maneuvers

DEAR MISS MANNERS:

I often take short business flights, and find that airplanes can be terrific places to meet people. Or they can be awful, if you know what I mean. I have just one etiquette problem about this; the rest I can handle myself. My wife drops me off early at the airport because she has to drive the children to school, and I have breakfast there and am the first person on the plane. This gives me the chance to take a seat in the middle, where I can look people over as they get on, and I find that if I smile at someone when she boards, she will often come and sit down next to me. Not always, but often. Sometimes I help it along by saying, "There's a seat here, Miss." My question is, what can I say if someone undesirable, if you know what I mean, tries to plop down next to me even before the plane begins to fill up when there are plenty of other seats?

GENTLE READER:

Yes, Miss Manners knows what you mean. There are days when Miss Manners has to say to herself, "Just answer the questions—you don't have to like them." You know what she means?

The answer to yours is that you should do your stalking in the small lounge area near the gate where you will be boarding. That is the place to go early, so that you can maneuver to get in line behind your intended victim. Then it is a simple matter to seat yourself next to her on the airplane, instead of taking a chance on who will sit next to you.

DEAR MISS MANNERS:

My job requires me to travel a lot, and I have often had pleasant experiences in getting to know businessmen who sit next to me in airplanes. They usually sit in the window and aisle seats, so I find two likely-looking candidates and plop myself down between them. If one doesn't turn out to be single and interested, the other usually does. My question concerns the occasions when I am on a plane before it's filling up, and there are seats next to me. This doesn't give me as much choice, of course, but I can still catch the eye of a nice man when he is looking for a seat, and he'll be pretty certain to sit down next to me. But what do I do if some other woman or some elderly man just dumps down next to me? I don't want to be nasty about it, but they don't realize it could spoil my whole trip. Often when I get to a new city, for instance, I'll have someone to have dinner with, if we've been chatting on the plane. Can you suggest something to say to keep the seat free for an appropriate man?

GENTLE READER:

Oh, dear, yes, Miss Manners can always suggest something to say. "I'm so sorry, I'm saving this for a friend," may be said in a quiet voice, without specifying that it's a friend you hope to make, and provided that there is ample seating elsewhere in the plane.

Now will you allow Miss Manners to say something? That is: She realizes that establishing sexual contact is now recognized as the most compelling reason we were put on earth, but may she suggest that people not immediately engaged in doing so may also have legitimate reasons to travel and should be given the same access to seats on public transportation?

Airline Brown Bags

DEAR MISS MANNERS:

My business has always required me to travel frequently, so I eat a lot of my meals on airplanes. Over the years, I have noticed that airplane food, never terrific, has gotten worse and worse. I have noticed other passengers refusing these repasts and taking out their own picnic lunches of delicious food. One man had strips of cold duck and a sauce he dipped them in, and an old woman had thick, delicatessen-type sandwiches. I could do something like that, either taking food from home, or buying good carry-out food. My worry is, though, whether it is rude to the airline, implying that their food is not good.

GENTLE READER:

You're not implying that, you're saying it outright. Miss Manners is not sure that an airline has feelings that can be hurt. But she is sure that the proper feeling for an airline to have is that survival is more important than anything else. Therefore, avoiding their food and bringing your own is perfectly acceptable. You need not share, as it is difficult to pack a basket that will feed a 747.

Presents

DEAR MISS MANNERS:

What's a good, fairly inexpensive, going away present for someone flying to Europe for the first time? I've looked at travel cases and electricity converters and such, but I'm not sure what he has, and I know he's planning to travel very light, so I don't want to add stuff he won't take with him.

GENTLE READER:

A bottle of wine and disposable cups. The same airline workers who can serve drinks, magazines, and dinner with seconds on coffee in a forty-nine-minute domestic flight take two hours to get organized enough on transatlantic flights to get anyone a drink, let alone dinner. During this period, your friend can make himself instantly popular by offering wine to his seat mates. If the flight is delayed, he can drink it all himself in the airport and not mind so much. In either case, he will be traveling light.

Freeing One's Feet

DEAR MISS MANNERS:

Is it proper to remove one's shoes in an airplane?

GENTLE READER:

Yes, but it is highly improper not to be able to get them on again when one has arrived at one's destination.

Pilfering

It is charming that people like to bring home small souvenirs to remind them of their holidays. Miss Manners would find it more charming, however, if they limited their mementos to items they bought or found on the beach, rather than little things they picked up while no one was looking.

It makes Miss Manners decidedly nervous to see, in someone's house, a towel, an ashtray, or a writing pad that bears the logo of a restaurant, hotel, or airline. Miss Manners tries her best to think charitably of such persons, in the style of a lady in a *Punch* drawing who, observing a towel marked "Victoria Hotel" in another lady's bathroom, suggested, "Perhaps it's her maiden name."

But Miss Manners does not succeed in distinguishing between stealing from individuals and stealing from corporations. Whenever she sees stolen goods in someone's house, she reminds herself not to invite them to come and be on terms of intimacy with her own monogrammed linens.

Miss Manners even feels this way about seeing items belonging to the user's employer. When Miss Manners visited the house of an acquaintance who worked at the White House and found the place stocked with White House stationery, memorandum pads, pens and pencils—he had apparently overlooked only the possibility of bringing home a rug with the presidential seal woven into it—she had unpleasant thoughts about her taxes.

But in that case there was, at least, the excuse that the employee needs such things because his work carries over to the home. Presumably, the president might call and not want his instruction copied on plain paper with the regular government-issue pen.

Travelers can make no such excuse. Towels, postal cards, forks, miniature bars of soap, and paper packets full of sugar are meant to be used by the customer on the premises only. They are not offered as compensation for high prices.

A person who has blown his travel budget on one such establishment and wishes to get his money's worth of status from it may honorably spend his entire vacation writing on the hotel stationery to everyone he knows in the world. What he may not do is to stash away the paper and use it for communications from humbler quarters, including his own.

DEAR MISS MANNERS:

Several years ago, we had a lovely stay at a hotel on the English Channel somewhere in Kent County, England. The ashtray had a gold coat-of-arms and as a romantic, I wanted to have it forever. My husband inquired at the desk about purchasing one and we were promptly presented a free, boxed ashtray. A similar vacation was spent in Acapulco, and I wanted several little handmade clay ashtrays. The hotel manager wrapped and boxed several for fifty cents. These little silly goodies provide a very special sweep of memories—so, if a memento of a special place is important, there is a proper way to obtain it.

GENTLE READER:

In a world where so many people will attempt to justify or conceal the use of petty dishonesty, Miss Manners is delighted to find someone who is using honest means to achieve the effect of pilfering.

Keeping a Secret

DEAR MISS MANNERS:

Whilst in Paris for my yearly sojourn, I happened upon an elegantly unpretentious hotel—on the Right Bank, *naturellement*. It was an unmitigated delight and one which I am not eager to share with others.

However, during tea, my acquaintances often ask the name of my latest hostelry discovery. This occasions agitation in my otherwise placid circumstance. How, Miss Manners, may I decline to reveal my little secret and still maintain my impeccable reputation for frankness and amiability?

GENTLE READER:

No one is expected to remember the exact name of a Parisian hotel. It is enough to show your willingness to share your discovery with your friends, as follows:

"You know the Métro stop with the interesting entrance? Oh yes, you do, it's very famous, the one with the carvings, you see its photograph everywhere. Well, you get out there, and then go across the street and you'll see the—oh, what's its name?—the boutique, the one with the frightfully expensive things? They have one in Nice, and I think London and Palm Beach, too, but I'm not sure. You'll recognize it. It has a silk scarf in the window, draped over a leather bag. Well, you go around the corner from that, and on the other side, about a block or two up, there's a *parfumerie,* and keep going and you'll come to a shop with rare books and prints, and that's where you turn left. Keep going until you get to the glove shop, and then it's right across the street. I think it's the Grand Something or the Petit Something, I'm not sure. You'll love it. And please remember me to Madame, who runs it. You'll be sure and remember that, won't you?"

Hotel Beds

DEAR MISS MANNERS:
My husband and I sleep in a double bed at home, and would like to do so when we travel. We always seem to be put in rooms that either have two single beds, or two double beds. The single beds are too small, and I get embarrassed to have the maid see that we use only one of the double beds, so I've even taken to messing the other one up to make it look slept in, which my husband says is silly. How can I get the kind of accommodations we want?

GENTLE READER:
By requesting them. If you find that this embarrasses the room clerk, you might introduce him to the hotel maid you think is also capable of embarrassment, and suggest that they both take up another line of work.

Registering

DEAR MISS MANNERS:
My girl friend and I are planning to do some traveling together, but we are arguing about how we should register at hotels. I don't see anything wrong with using both our names—we live together and are not ashamed of it at home. Also, even some married couples use separate names. But she says the hotel clerks would spot us and maybe not even rent us rooms unless we register as "Mr. and Mrs.," which I don't want to do because it's a lie.

GENTLE READER:
Hotel clerks tend to be amazingly less fascinated with the marital complications of transients than the couples themselves imagine. You may sign your own name only, with the notation that the room is requested for two, if you don't think that that would take all the fun out of it.

Vacations

There is no lack of advice being given out on how to meet interesting people on one's vacation. The lack, which Miss Manners proposes to fill, is of advice on how to avoid meeting interesting people on one's vacation.

People who take the first kind of advice are all over the place—on beaches, in airplanes, around swimming pools, on ships, in souvenir shops—with that bright opening remark on their tongues, and that eager look in their eyes, anticipating the friendship that will change and enrich their lives. Miss Manners hopes that they all meet one another and live happily ever after.

It's not that Miss Manners doesn't like to have friends. Some of Miss Manners' best friends are friends. But Miss Manners generally goes on vacation with the hope of getting reacquainted with Miss Manners, or whomever she has brought with her for the purpose. If that person happens to be Miss Jane Austen or Mr. Henry James, it does not mean that Miss Manners is therefore in need of meeting anyone noisier. However, people who carry books around with them as conversation starters often bear an uncanny resemblance to people who carry books around for the purpose of reading them. It is therefore necessary that we develop some sensitivity about conversing with strangers.

Many holiday settings come under the rule that says "the roof constitutes an introduction." This means, for one thing, that one cannot enter a friend's house without a willingness to attempt to reciprocate any friendship offered, however disastrous it may turn out to be. (Conversely, the sky does not necessarily constitute an introduction and a person who is, for example, stopped in an alley at night by a stranger and asked about his current finances is not rude if he resents it.)

Travel and resort situations usually permit people to open conversations with whomever they happen to find themselves near, but only provided that they await encouragement before launching full-scale into acquaintanceship. A person who addresses his airplane seatmate with a friendly but noncommittal remark, such as "I wonder if I might borrow the little bag from your seat pouch there—I don't think mine is going to be big enough," must be willing to allow that person the privilege of retreat.

Beauty and the Beach

People keep trying to enlist Miss Manners' help in clearing beaches of people whom they find aesthetically displeasing.

It can be the elderly, the fat, the skinny, the ugly, or the disabled. "Don't they realize how awful they look?" they ask. "Why do they parade themselves around in bathing suits where everybody can see them?"

This question puzzles Miss Manners. She would have thought it well known that the reason everybody wears bathing suits to the beach is that they are better suited for swimming and suntanning than ski clothes, for example. However, Miss Manners has never been one to be hostile to dumb questions. What irritates her about the letters is their assumption, which is by no means confined to the beach, that the world should belong to young, comely people.

Naturally, it is absurd to speak of beauty, or even youth, as if there were a national standard by which fitness may be recognized. But if there were, the idea would still be unbearably ugly. Beaches, like other public places and institutions, are for any members of the public who wish to use them properly. Ogling people one finds attractive is not the proper use of God's beaches. This does not mean that, as with so many improper functions, it may not be practiced and enjoyed if done discreetly. It does mean that the rights of people who properly use the beach to swim and sun take precedence.

Observing the human scene—now that is another activity, and the one for which God made sidewalk cafés. The difference between this and ogling, since you obviously intend to bring that up, is that a moving crowd on a sidewalk does not permit the observer to stare at any one person for a long time and thus force him or her into the game. The other difference is in sophistication. Those who can find beauty in human beings of many ages and shapes do not dispute the rights of others. But Miss Manners is hanged if she will try to clear the beaches for those who specialize in watching only certain types of people, and probably only certain parts of the bodies of those.

Now you will have to excuse Miss Manners. She has gotten so hot and bothered over this that she is going to go and put on her bathing suit—the one with the billowing sleeves and sailor collar—and go and cool off.

Postcards

Just when you think you have succeeded in getting away from it all, free of all questions of form because you are on holiday and don't even have to put your shoes on, let alone your manners, you will have a panicky thought about Miss Manners. The thought will be ''Wish you were here.''

This will have nothing to do with sympathy for your poor Miss Manners, stuck toiling away in the hot city. It will mean that you are in trouble. Big etiquette trouble. This will happen just after you have begun to wind down and relax. You will stop somewhere on the street, during a leisurely stroll, and purchase postcards. Or perhaps you will pick them up free from your hotel, or perhaps you will pick them up free from the lobby of a hotel more expensive than the one you are staying in.

Still calm and confident, you will make yourself comfortable at the beach, or at some foreign café, and go cheerfully to work, selecting which card should go to which person on your list, stamping and addressing them.

Then you will stare hopelessly at a blank space, not three inches square, while you slowly realize that you have nothing intelligent to say on a postcard. That is when you will wish for Miss Manners to explain correct postcard style. All year long, Miss Manners is asked about the complexities of writing letters of business, gratitude, condolence, and congratulation, but the postcard, that staple of summer correspondence, is something people mistakenly assume they can manage for themselves. If you could just write ''Wish you were here,'' not to Miss Manners but to all your friends, the matter would be simple. Unfortunately, this convenient message has gone out of fashion on the irrelevant grounds of being insincere.

The only easy thing about postcards is that they need not use any closing, or any opening either. The rest is difficult. Miss Manners' first solution is to prune your list. Like Christmastime, summertime is an opportunity to send brief greetings to people one does not otherwise remember. Just as at Christmastime, one tends to greet people who do not remember one. This is a reason to identify oneself clearly at the end of the postcard and not assume that its informality means that nicknames or initials will do. Postcards do not even give the clue of where the sender lives, only where he vacations.

Now for the message. The important thing to remember about a postcard is the wide audience it will receive. Reading someone else's letter is a high crime; reading someone else's postcard is in a category with jaywalking—not a good idea, but everyone does it and the chances for getting away with it are good. It should therefore be discreet, or at least ambiguous. ''Lola and kids staying on—meet you Tuesday, Marshland Marriott'' is not a good postcard message. Neither is the temperature or population of a foreign city, which is not only dull but sounds smug to a person stuck at home. ''Prices here out of sight'' is preferable, but not terrific.

Humor is out of the question. It looks terrible, when you get back to the office, to see something that was funny when you were full of piña coladas pinned on the bulletin board. Anyway, most postcard humor is unintelligible to the recipient, who forgets to look at the postcard picture on which the joke is based. Taking into account all these pitfalls, Miss Manners proposes the perfect all-purpose postcard message that can be sent to anyone: ''Thinking of you.'' It can mean anything up to, and even including, ''Wish you were here.''

✎ HOLIDAYS

The etiquette question that troubles so many fastidious people New Year's Day is: How am I ever going to face those people again?

Miss Manners recognizes that even the most well-bred person may be subject to a fit of bad behaving at holiday parties. One may suffer from an overdose, not necessarily of alcohol, but of frankness, cuddliness, reminiscences, or other enemies of the social structure.

The simplest thing is merely to write a charming note of apology. ''I'm sorry I drank all your wassail bowl and told you it was a mistake for you to get a divorce.''

A common complication, however, is that one doesn't know exactly what one should be sorry for. The major discomfort in what is designed as "remorse" is not shame, but the blind scrambling around an addled brain in search of the answer to "My God, what did I do?"

If you were lucky enough to have been accompanied by an intimate to the disaster-fiesta, you may hear the answer to this question. Without even asking it. This is unlucky. Miss Manners believes that the secret of an unhappy marriage is communication. A truly loving person volunteers nothing and, if pressed with "How bad was I?" replies, "Why, I thought you were cute."

This information is not so vital as one seems to think at the time. Socially, it is not useful until months later, when the adventure can be charmingly recounted at a party and leave you basking in self-admiration. The worse you behave, the better the anecdote will then be.

In the meantime, one must resist the impulse to call up the hostess under the pretense of chatting, to measure in her tone of voice the size of the misdemeanor. She's too busy. She has to clean up the mess you left, and to think what to say to those people she asked especially to meet you. Instead, send her a small present. This does not incriminate you, as an apology would, and on the fat chance that she thought you were cute, too, can be seen simply as a gracious gesture. On the other hand, it might help compensate her for the lamp or lifelong friendship of hers you don't remember breaking.

New Year's Day

If the society were not in a state of Etiquette Emergency, Miss Manners would not attempt to meddle with the ritual of the New Year's Resolution. She finds it sweet to hear people annually resolve to lose ten pounds and clean their desks—the air of modest moral struggle this lends to the first three days of every January is charming.

Times of crisis call for sacrifice. The national rudeness level has reached dangerous proportions. Each citizen has to commit himself or herself to behaving himself or herself, or we will all soon have to be committed. The situation, as Miss Manners sees it, arose from just the spirit of improvement that leads people to the excellent resolves associated with the beginning of a fresh year. There is a mistaken notion abroad that if one does one's best, one may be intolerant of those who do less.

Say you have given up smoking. Naturally, you will take the occasion to be grumpy and irritable in the bosom of your family. If you have stored up some personal credit there, through years of cheerful smoking, they may accept this good-naturedly for a short while. If it ends there, Miss Manners has no objection. The successful nonsmoker will then go on to attack perfect strangers, or rather, imperfect strangers, who smoke. If this were done politely, Miss Manners would still have no objection. The confinement of smoky air to the immediate and private vicinity of smoke producers is a valid goal. But what Miss Manners sees is an atmosphere polluted with self-righteous insults. Nonsmokers, joggers, food purists, and other such improved products feel they have a license to chastise the world.

Worse are the people who have had general self-overhauls, rather than specific repair jobs. Those who have newly discovered their personal worth through therapy, assertiveness training, or other odd religious sects often become public menaces. Their friendly behavior is to point out that you are in bad shape, a fact only confirmed by your failure to realize this; watch out for their unfriendly behavior. From a society that must once have been, by its own testimony, depressed, frightened, and ridden with bad habits, we have evolved into a people who are healthy, confident, and impossible to live with. Commands are barked at strangers. A person who is offensive to someone else, whether on purpose or accidentally, is viciously reprimanded.

These attacks, in turn, inspire counterattacks. It is not unusual for a mere peccadillo—an accidental push in a crowded bus, some harmless hesitation on the part of an automobile driver—to result in the exchange of screamed obscenities. This is dreadful. People who do no wrong are making the world unbearable for normal people.

Miss Manners asks that each person make it a New Year's resolution to be responsible for his own behavior and worry less about that of others. If correcting is imperative, she asks that it be done with gentleness and humility. If everyone refuses to engage in verbal combat, hostilities will soon cease. "He started it!" will not be accepted as an excuse.

DEAR MISS MANNERS:

Last year, I gave up eating between meals, and the year before, I gave up smoking. Can you suggest a New Year's resolution for me, for this year? It might be hard, not only because, as you can see, I am nearly perfect, but because, as you can also see, life is bleak enough for me without giving up any of my few remaining pleasures.

GENTLE READER:

Try giving up expecting the mechanics of life to work smoothly. For example, give up expecting a store to get your order right, or the car ahead of you to start when the light changes, or the mail to be delivered within a reasonable time. If you succeed in this, you will be deprived of nothing you had before except frustrating rage, and you will be contributing to the welfare of the world—not by improving it, but by ceasing to contribute to it your own dissatisfaction.

Easter Etiquette

DEAR MISS MANNERS:

How about Easter? I suppose you have etiquette rules that apply to Easter Day?

GENTLE READER:

Certainly, and when the Day of Judgment comes, Miss Manners will have etiquette rules to apply to that, as well. The chief rule in regard to Easter is that everyone must eat every egg given to him or her, or colored by him or her and not unload it on someone else. This is because Easter eggs are delightful on Easter Sunday, fun to play with on Easter Monday, and revolting on Easter Tuesday. They should be eaten before that, with a grain of salt.

Egg Rolling

DEAR MISS MANNERS:

I am taking my grandchildren to the Easter Egg Rolling at the White House, but they have asked me what egg rolling involves, and I don't know the answer. Also, do we bring our own eggs?

GENTLE READER:

"Rolling" must be interpreted in its political, rather than gravitational, sense, as in "log rolling." In other words, you had better look out for your own interests and bring your own eggs to feed your own family.

Hallowe'en

What has happened to the pleasant ritual of Hallowe'en is frightening. O'er the years, the customs associated with that holiday have become mixed with other folk customs, such as the street mugging, and Miss Manners feels that one must go back to the traditional form if Hallowe'en is to retain its place in our culture.

One source of confusion is that children who have not been taught the proper methods of trick-or-treating naturally assume that they can improvise this activity from the familiar year-round ones which they are taught, such as vandalism and writing on bathroom walls. Adults have incorrectly assumed that the occasion is a free-form one in which they can express their ordinary feelings about children through such methods as poison.

Actually, the trick-or-treat is an exact ritual. It should be performed by small children in costume—a six-footer would be out of place, for example, even wearing a Bill Blass patterned sheet—followed at a respectful distance by adults with an interest in their welfare. The child must ring each doorbell himself, and must be encouraged to return to the doorway after he has fled in stagefright. He then announces the traditional threat: "Trick or treat!" At this point, the involuntary co-celebrant, who has just answered his door to find a bunch of tiny Darth Vaders, must express surprise and fright. "Why, Sally Lynn, don't you look adorable," is an inappropriate remark. The correct one is "Good God, what's that?" The host must then decide whether he prefers to treat the visitors or let them trick him. The current definition of a treat is something that will rot the teeth; traditionalists prefer an apple or an orange, but traditionalists are never young enough to be on the consuming end of this. The child who has been treated may then say "You gave her more than you gave me," followed by "Thank you."

If, however, the challenge of the trick has been accepted, it is within the right of the child to perform it. Here is where it is especially important to distinguish trick-or-treating from other childish behavior, such as destroying property. Tricks that will later involve law-enforcement or other city services, such as the trash or fire departments, are not in the Hallowe'en tradition. The traditional trick is soaping windows, which is just unpleasant enough to indicate that the threat was not idle, in the way that diplomatically thwarted nations indulge in mild annoyances without starting wars. Parental guidance is suggested in the vocabularly to be used on the window. Four-letter words, such as may be appropriate on public bathroom walls, are inappropriate here. The ideal word for this occasion, in Miss Manners' opinion, is "Phooey."

DEAR MISS MANNERS:

When the neighborhood children come around trick-or-treating on Hallowe'en, I know who most of them are because their parents are standing in the background, or because they have been over earlier in the day to show my kids their costumes, so I can greet them by name. But sometimes there's no clue, and I wonder whether it's polite to say "Who are you?" to some little thing under a sheet. It sounds so abrupt.

GENTLE READER:

On the contrary, it is a *faux pas* to admit to recognizing anyone in a Hallowe'en costume. The polite way to act toward a trick-or-treater is to behave as if he or she were mugging you: Look scared and hand over the goods.

Thanksgiving

DEAR MISS MANNERS:

Are there any special rules for the eating of Thanksgiving dinner, or is it like any other big lunch or dinner?

GENTLE READER:

Yes, and yes. Thanksgiving dinner is like any other big lunch or dinner, only worse. The special rules are that several ordinary rules can, in fact must, be violated. It is held at a dreadful hour in the early afternoon, because a turkey must be cooked for many hours (and doesn't taste like much even then), and also so that many of the guests will eventually leave the table to watch football on television, which would be a rudeness at any other occasion but is a relief at Thanksgiving and probably the only way to get those people to budge. Next, excessive quantities of food must not only be served, but be urged with great emotional arguments on guests who have long since become uncomfortably bloated. Polite behavior on the part of guests involves literally eating themselves sick. They are also expected to hang around long after the children have gotten cross and the hosts are ready for a nap. All this makes for an unspeakable day, but who are we to argue with the wisdom of the Pilgrims?

DEAR MISS MANNERS:

I have a Thanksgiving question. We have a large family in town, including my sister's family and my stepbrother's, plus we usually invite a few stray friends for Thanksgiving dinner with all the trimmings. The problem is that when I say "Who wants a drumstick?" I get six yeses. At least. My wife suggested that we buy a lot of turkey legs, so everyone can have one, but I find it a real satisfaction to carve up one of those huge birds, and I don't like the idea of a lot of extra legs hanging around the platter. What should we do?

GENTLE READER:

It's a pettish sort of thankfulness that specifies exactly what one will accept before being thankful. The only proper question for the carver to ask is "White meat or dark?" The drumsticks are then offered to the smallest children, on the theory that the little ones chew on the bones O. The extra drumstick idea would make your platter look like a 1940s Radio City Music Hall chorus line.

Christmas Season

As Christmas approaches, wouldn't you know that Miss Manners would have a little something special for nearly everyone?

Not presents, of course. Miss Manners wouldn't want to embarrass you by giving you mere gold. Advice. Isn't that a treat? You may open it and use it right now, and it will still be with you when your Christmas furs are molting.

For Children Planning to Come Home from College, at Great Social Sacrifice, to Visit Their Parents for the Christmas Holidays: Kisses first, dirty laundry later. The idea is to appear pleased to see the old couple that live there, rather than to rejoice exclusively in the creature comforts they have to offer.

For Primary-School Teachers: After you have set the Christmas pageant and cookie party for two fifteen on a Wednesday afternoon, do not inform your pupils that "Now, we want to make sure all the mommies come." This plants the dark thought in little minds that a mother who fails to show up to watch her own child in a nonspeaking shepherd rôle is a callous woman who has abandoned her flesh-and-blood for personal fulfillment and creative gratification at a factory all day.

For Temporary Help in Department Stores: Granted that you cannot be expected to know the stock, be able to fill out the charge forms, or cannot have known just how unpleasant a task it was to deal with the general public, try to be patient and pleasant. Considering your qualifications, why else are you getting that miserable salary?

For Generous Souls, Who Always Invite the Elderly, the Orphaned, and the Otherwise Abandoned to Christmas Dinner: When you get a refusal, suggest immediately one of the other three-hundred-and-sixty-four days of the year that this person could dine with you. It makes the motive for your Christmas invitation sound less like a penance.

For Multigenerational Families Who Gather for Christmas Reunions: Do not relax and be less than a thoughtful houseguest, or allow your immediate descendants to do so, on the grounds that these people are related to you. Blood is not necessarily thicker than water, and it generally helps at this time of year to have a little Scotch in both.

For Those Who Do Christmas Up Perfectly Every Year, Sending Cards and Presents to Those Who Least Expect Them: Let up, will you? You're only showing off to make everybody else look bad.

Mailing Cards

DEAR MISS MANNERS:

How late can you mail Christmas cards? Every year we have the problem of the people who send them to us when it's too late to pretend that we had them on our list already and aren't just mailing them after Christmas because we were going to drop them from the list unless we heard from them.

GENTLE READER:

The last day for mailing Christmas cards is December 25. However, December 26 is a fine day for mailing New Year's greetings.

Single Christmas

DEAR MISS MANNERS:

I hesitate to make a recommendation to so outstanding an authority, but experience compels me. Miss Manners might suggest, before Christmas, that unless a specific invitation is being extended, Generous Souls—and others—refrain from asking people who are alone:

(a) What are your plans for Christmas?
(b) Did you have a nice Christmas?
(c) What did you do for Christmas?

It saves painful embarrassment if the answer is

(a) none
(b) no
(c) nothing.

GENTLE READER:

Conventional conversation is full of such questions, and one has to learn that they are only the meaningless devices of light sociability and not attempts to probe for information. Otherwise, an unhappy person could suffer fresh pain every time someone said, "How have things been going?" or "I hope you have a pleasant weekend."

Miss Manners understands that the Christmas season's emphasis on family life may produce some melancholy in those who live alone. But she cannot go along with the suggestion of making other people censor their careless conversation so as to avoid adding to the pain, as one watches one's words in front of someone in the midst of an acute tragedy. This artificiality, prompted by pity, is helpful to avoid jarring the feelings of a person in crisis, but bad and patronizing in a long-term situation.

Questions a, b, and c can all be answered by "Oh, the usual—what about you?" or one can say one is planning or has spent Christmas "overeating."

Christmas Day

Christmas is an important day for everyone to practice hypocrisy. Does that offend you? Miss Manners is so excessively polite that she rarely has the wicked pleasure of offending people, and you must allow her to relish the sensation for a moment before she explains what she means and spoils the effect.

There now. Miss Manners feels quite herself again and is prepared to discuss Christmas behavior with appropriate sobriety. What she means is that Christmas is an excellent time for people to forgo the honest expression of their true feelings and adjust—not to say dissemble—their behavior in order to cater to the feelings of others.

Take the difficult matter of midafternoon on Christmas Day. Everyone always feels cross then. This is perfectly understandable. They have been up too early. They have had little rest the night before, either because they have had visions of sugar plums dancing in their heads, or because they were trying to put together a vision for someone else, which had some of the parts or the directions missing and should have been put together by the store, which refused to do so. Some people are cross because they did not get what they wanted, and some are cross because they did and are now tired of it or are feeling postpartum depression. Some people are stiff from sitting in church, and others are stiff from sitting on the floor with the electric trains, and some are both.

Those who have Christmas dinner at night are cross because they are starved, and those who have it at midday are cross because they are overstuffed, and all of them are beginning to wish they had not eaten the candy canes off the tree. Christmas hypocrisy requires that everyone conceal these feelings and behave kindly and patiently to others.

It is especially important on Christmas that children be reinforced in their hypocritical behavior. Children must be taught to express pleasure and surprise when they open presents, concealing their actual assessment of the acquisitions if this is inconsistent with the official emotions. They must be instructed to refrain from making such true statements as "I already have one." And they must be taught the unnatural act of reading the card before opening the package.

They must also be forced into another unnatural act, that of sitting down and writing letters of thanks immediately—letters that express enthusiasm and gratitude with the best artifice they can muster in order to make the emotion sound genuine. (This is, incidentally, an excellent midafternoon activity for calming down overexcited children. Their little eyelids will be drooping in boredom in no time, and there will be a merciful moment of quiet in the house.)

Even adults accustomed to faking verbal and written joy often need practice in Christmas hypocrisy. It is not easy to sound convincing when one is expressing a wish to "help." Everyone at a Christmas gathering should be falsely shining with the apparent desire to set the table, pick up the torn wrappings, go for a walk in the snow as far as the garbage can, and fix the children's malfunctioning toys.

If you do not like the term hypocrisy, Miss Manners will permit you to call it "doing unto others."

Christmas Traditions

DEAR MISS MANNERS:
It's all very well to say that Christmas is too commercialized—nobody will argue with that. But how do you avoid the materialistic atmosphere that gets into even the coziest family gathering, when the most important part of the day is obviously opening the presents? Every Christmas we go to my mother's, where we have a big meal with my sister's family, my aunt and uncle, and their children and grandchildren. We are all on good terms, and it ought to be a lovely warm occasion. But the conversation among the children is about nothing but "What did you get?" and the grown-ups, too polite to do that, talk instead about food—"Have some more" or "I ate too much." We are not very religious people, and maybe that's the trouble. In my husband's family, they went to church on Christmas, so at least there was some time of the day not focused on appetite (for food or toys).

It's not that I'm trying to convert my family to stricter churchgoing habits, but I wish there were a way to make this Christmas just a tiny bit more—can I say it?—spiritual, or at least slightly less base.

GENTLE READER:
What you need, in a hurry, is some family tradition.

Christmas Day was traditionally filled with events—not only going to church, but caroling, visiting, and annoying the poor. One no longer drops in on other people's celebrations uninvited, and the poor have rebelled against being used as supernumeraries in others' Christmas pageants.

However, you can still organize your own activities among your own family. Reading aloud from the Bible or some Christmas-related book such as Charles Dickens' "A Christmas Carol"; singing carols, making the children who take music lessons play Christmas selections for the family, asking each person to tell what Christmas means to him or her—almost anything will do.

You just have to ignore protests that the activity is corny, or that you've all done it before. It is the simplicity and the repetition that make a tradition, and the children who have to be pried from their electronic games to participate this year will look forward to it next year, and will remember it fondly all their adult lives.

Presents

DEAR MISS MANNERS:

We hold open house every Christmas, inviting some people in advance and bringing others back from church with us—just people we happen to see but hadn't thought of beforehand. It's just lots of eggnog and cookies, and people seem to enjoy it very much.

My question is about those who bring presents. They're not really supposed to, but a few people do. I'm always afraid of this embarrassing other guests, who might then think they were supposed to, and I also feel funny about accepting these presents because I'm not giving them anything (or I'd have to have something for everyone and the whole open house idea would be impossible).

Should I open the presents when they are given to me? Should I send those people presents afterwards? One other question: I invited some Jewish friends, and they said they couldn't come. Was it wrong to invite them—were they offended because they don't celebrate Christmas?

GENTLE READER:

Unless you can open the presents inconspicuously—and how can you, with other guests to greet?—it is better to put them aside and thank the people the next day, by note. You don't owe them presents; you gave them a lovely day. There is a whole range of reasons that your Jewish friends might have had for refusing your invitation—from not wanting to participate in a Christmas celebration to having another Christmas celebration to attend. But however differently Jews may regard Christmas—from a religious holiday that they do not celebrate, to a winter festival that they might—they are all aware that it exists, and it cannot be considered offensive to mention it.

On Happy New Year's Eves

It is some time now since Miss Manners noticed that New Year's Eve is a great deal more fun in theory than in practice. Miss Manners has nothing against dressing up, drinking champagne, dancing through the night, and indulging in a modest amount of free-lance kissing—provided she doesn't have to do all this too often. Once a fortnight would be about right.

However, this kind of luxurious leisure is not what New Year's Eve is about any longer. New Year's Eve has become the national quintessential Saturday night, set aside as a social occasion with built-in disappointments for everyone. There is nothing like an officially designated time of glamor and excitement for producing mass discontent and depression. This effect is best achieved by not having been asked to celebrate New Year's Eve with someone else, although you can also manage it if you have a date but no party to go to or a party but no date to go with or the wrong date or the right date in the wrong mood.

Even if you have a full set of invitations, you can still spoil the occasion by watching the people at your party depart for better parties from which you were excluded. New Year's Eve parties, being long and not carefully orchestrated—as, say, a dinner is—offer many opportunities for behaving badly, in ways one will suddenly remember with a sickening flash at breakfast the next afternoon. If you can't manage this yourself, you can always observe a loved one behaving badly.

Miss Manners' suggestion for coping with this mess is that everyone calm down and build a New Year's Eve suited to the actual purpose of the holiday. The reason we divide time into years is to give everyone a fresh start, not to mention a clean calendar. New Year's Eve, therefore, has two purposes: to practice the better, more graceful living one has promised oneself, and to pack in a last bit of wickedness before reforming forever. One celebrates in a way that is slightly more expensive, more fattening, or more naughty than one can ordinarily afford to be. None of these require the sort of franticness that ends in accidents, automobile or marital, and various numbers can play. The ideal New Year's Eve leaves one with the will to get through a New Year's Day.

The New Year's Kiss

DEAR MISS MANNERS:

I know that there is special license about kissing at New Year's Eve parties, but I have questions about who and how much. Are you obliged to kiss the person you brought to the party exactly at midnight? If so, can you then go around kissing anybody you want to? Can a woman refuse a kiss or make a scene about it? How long after midnight can the kissing go on?

GENTLE READER:

Miss Manners hopes that the New Year's Eve party you are planning to attend is a masked ball in a damp Venetian palace, so that, mysteriously disguised, you can slither about kissing whomever you choose until it is time for your charter flight back home. The ordinary New Year's Eve party does not permit quite such an exciting suspension of the rules. The custom is to seek out, just before midnight, the person with whom you came to the party, or at least the person with whom you plan to leave it. As midnight strikes, you may kiss or not as you choose, but if you plan to do some general kissing, this is the place to start. Oddly enough, the degree of passion one properly exhibits is in inverse proportion to that believed to be associated with the relationship. Thus, a long-married couple should kiss with tremendous enthusiasm, while a pair of crazed new lovers should barely touch lips or cheeks. Please don't ask Miss Manners to explain why; these are examples of good taste.

You may then turn to people nearby, but the type of kisses you offer must be of the chaste variety many people use as greetings. Don't tell Miss Manners that she is spoiling your fun. It is perfectly possible to press a thrill of meaning into a cheek kiss, if that is what you want, and you do not run the risk of beginning a fresh year in a melée. Miss Manners would consider twelve fifteen a good time to get back to the more decorous task of drinking champagne. After all, you have a whole year ahead of you.

Death

It's wonderful how death transforms the spirit, so that everyone who is deceased becomes a self-effacing promoter of the comfort of the living.

Or so one would assume from hearing surviving friends and relations saying things like "He would have wanted me to go out and enjoy myself on a day like this," "She would have preferred that I go to the football game instead of being glum at her funeral service," and "He would have told us to go ahead with our festival and not cancel it on his account."

Nonsense. Miss Manners' knowledge of human emotions tells her that he would have wanted you to be too overcome with grief to be capable of enjoying anything, and she would have wanted national mourning. Putting sentiments in the mouths of others is always offensive, but Miss Manners finds it particularly so in the case of those who are not around to speak for themselves.

When a person dies, those who cared about him or her have the obligations of attending the funeral service and family gathering afterward, and of offering assistance, writing letters, and paying condolence visits to the immediate family. The most graceful way of getting through all of these is to search one's mind until one has a supply of anecdotes about the dead person that are both favorable and believable. Foibles that can be told with admiration are particularly effective. These stories are crucial at a funeral in which eulogies are delivered by friends. Such services can be quite moving—and anything is better than a funeral at which the clergyman says, "I didn't have the privilege of knowing Jeff Perfect" (groans from friends because he was never nicknamed Jeff), "but I feel as if I did. He was someone who had a rare zest and love for life. . . ." They are also the proper conversation for wakes, postfuneral gatherings, and other condolence visits, all of which should be bittersweet events in which one reminisces about the dead while consuming his liquor supply. Additional presents of liquor, along with the traditional offering of cooked food to the bereaved, are a way of keeping such events going. This is important to the immediate family. While you may not assume that the deceased is preoccupied with the convenience of his friends and their social calendars, you must act on the idea that he would have been concerned with the emotional welfare of his family. The formalities connected with death are designed with this in mind.

Honest mourning, Miss Manners has observed, is a matter for both laughter and tears; gloom unrelieved by happy memories is suspicious. Because this mixture of sudden hilarity and equally sudden depression is peculiar and unpredictable, it is customary for the recently bereaved not to attend ordinary social events.

This does not mean that they do not need, perhaps acutely, the company of others; and the services, gatherings, visits, and letters serve this purpose, along with requiring much activity—arranging services, notifying people, accepting condolences, responding to letters—that helps distract the grief-stricken and postpones their dealing with the void left by the death. It is a mistake to think that the living are too grief-struck to notice who fulfills these obligations and who doesn't. So you must inconvenience yourself, if you wish to honor someone who has died. Believe Miss Manners—he would have wanted it that way.

What One Says

Is it true that we now live in a world where there is more joy than sorrow? Miss Manners doesn't know how else to account for everyone's knowing how to wish fortunate people happiness, while expressing sympathy is so strange and frightening that many people will choose the rudeness of silence rather than even attempt it.

Statistically, it turns out, as many people as get married, die. In fact, more people die than marry although, unlike marriage, they tend to do it once and for all. Yet no one ever refuses to go to a wedding, crying pitifully as an excuse, "I just wouldn't know what to say."

As you know, Miss Manners requires you, when someone you know has died, to write a letter of condolence to the family, attend the funeral or memorial service, and pay a formal visit on the family afterward. So she will tell you what to say.

Say, "I'm sorry." Or "I'm so sorry"—Miss Manners allows for individuality of expression. If you can't manage that much, simply press the person's hand, look meaningfully into the eyes (this is done by raising the eyebrows from the nose bridge) and arrange the lips in a weight-of-the-world smile (done by raising the central part of the closed mouth at the same time as the corners are slightly raised).

There is a great variety of interesting things not to say. There is practically no limit to what imaginative and ill-meaning people will think of to increase the suffering and impair the dignity of the bereaved.

For instance:

"It's all for the best."

"You mustn't carry on like this. She wouldn't have wanted you to grieve."

"Do you really think you ought to be going about like this—so soon after?"

"Oh, well, you'll soon have another child (marry again, meet someone else)."

"I'm surprised to see you've changed things about so. I should have thought you would have wanted to leave the house as it was when he was here."

"Of course you feel terrible. You must have all kinds of guilt feelings about what you could have said or done differently before it was too late. Would you like to talk to me about it?"

"I don't want to interfere, but I notice that you've let the children go back to their play group. Don't you think it's a little early?"

"You must feel just awful. I know you're being brave, but you can let it out with me. Go ahead, cry. It must be a terrible strain for you to act as matter-of-fact as you do."

"It's really much better his way. You wouldn't have wanted her to linger on and deteriorate, and this way you can remember her at the height of her youth."

"At least you had many years together. It's not like what happened to me."

"Of course, you can do what you want. But do you really feel it's respectful to the dead?"

"Oh, dear. *What can I say?*"

On Euphemisms

DEAR MISS MANNERS:

I work in the intensive care unit of a hospital. Though many patients survive, many are injured or sick beyond medical help, and die. When family and friends call asking the condition of a recently deceased patient, what is the proper verb to use?

My etiquette-conscious mother ingrained in me never to say "passed away." Now, I cannot remember more than grammatical reasons for avoidance of the term, but the look of disgust on her face whenever she heard the phrase remains with me.

"Died" is the word I was taught to use, but I sometimes wonder if a gentler euphemism would not be kinder, under the circumstances. The medical term is "expired." However, that word seems too esoteric. Please advise me.

GENTLE READER:

There are euphemisms and euphemisms. Miss Manners agrees with your mother about "passed away," which suggests to her the train she just missed as it pulls out of the station, but does not eschew delicate phrases entirely. Nobody wants a vivid description, complete with active verbs, of what a person leaving a dinner table is about to do.

Euphemisms are worst when they are so elaborate as to call attention to themselves. If you told a relative that the patient was "no longer with us," he might conclude that the victim had checked out—another silly euphemism, come to think of it; Miss Manners had meant checked out from the hospital. "We lost him" is even worse, suggesting, as it does, that the next step is to find him,

"Expired" is both impersonal and clear. If you find its tone a little *too* impersonal, but feel "He died" is too brusque, you might say, "I'm sorry to have to tell you that he died just a few minutes ago."

Funerals

As no one ever chooses to put on a funeral, you might think that leniency would be granted in passing judgment on its taste and effectiveness as a public event. Lack of planning time could also be pleaded, and an absence of the social spirit.

Nevertheless, it is probably the most harshly appraised type of gathering held, and there is not, as after a botched dinner party, the possibility of erasing the failure by doing it over again, right.

The only comforts Miss Manners can offer are that the simplest arrangements are in the best of taste, and that the responsibilities may be divided among the friends of the deceased and the bereaved, with the chief mourner charged only with policy and major decisions.

For example, it is good to designate a friend, rather than an immediate relative, to make arrangements with those whose professional services are required. People in the funeral business naturally equate respect and love with elaborate furnishings and expensive fittings, and even those who know that these things are not related may not have the heart to conduct a skirmish on the subject.

Other assignments that may be made are:

· Notifying people of the death. Calls are made to those who are thought likely to be affected, and public notification is made by supplying the facts of the person's life to the newspapers.

- Answering telephones and doorbells. Someone with the instincts of a good butler in being able to judge and convey with gentleness which calls are convenient to be taken when, should be on duty in the house. He or she may also drop hints about the bereaved's being tired, if the sympathetic callers stay too long.
- Supervising the kitchen. The tradition of callers' bringing food is a widespread one, and someone has to be in charge of putting things away and arranging them into meals for the family and lesser offerings to other callers.
- Acting as pallbearers. This is a position of great honor, offered only to those closest to the deceased, and cannot be refused unless one has a dire excuse, such as a plan to have one's own funeral in the near future.
- Speaking at the funeral. In these days when many people's formal religious ties are somewhat casual, a stranger sometimes gives the eulogy. One way to avoid this is to have selected people who did have the privilege say a few plausible but tasteful words at the funeral. This honor may be refused on the grounds that one is not a good speaker or is too overcome to get up and talk. (The excuse of not having anything good to say about the person is sufficient, but must be disguised.)

Friends who do not receive assignments are responsible for sending letters of condolence, paying condolence calls, attending the funeral, and sending flowers or making charitable contributions.

This leaves the chief mourner, who has designated the tasks, to set the basic style and budget of the funeral, acknowledge the services and expressions of sympathy, readjust to life, and inherit the worldly goods.

He or she may be confident that his or her bearing under such weights is closely and mercilessly scrutinized by all. Consolation may be taken in the fact that at least the person most concerned need not suffer under society's judgment.

The Nature of the Service

DEAR MISS MANNERS:

What is the difference between a funeral and a memorial service?

GENTLE READER:

Put bluntly, it is the presence or absence of the honored person. A funeral precedes a burial or cremation. A memorial service is held afterward, or instead, if there is no such event for mourners to attend.

Social Behavior

DEAR MISS MANNERS:

How somber are you supposed to look at a funeral? My wife and I recently attended the funeral of a woman who used to work in my company until about two years ago, when she became too sick to stay. I wanted to show my respects, even though I hardly knew her, because she had been there ever since I first came, as a young man. She left no close relatives, and people who saw her in recent months said she is better off, as she had been in a lot of pain. Anyway, there were a lot of people from the old days at the funeral, people I was really friendly with years ago, who had left or been transferred to another city. So we had quite a reunion. I actually enjoyed the funeral for this reason, and that's how the argument started. My wife said I was smiling and laughing and running around clapping people on the shoulder and acting like I was at a party. It wasn't that bad, but I was glad to see people and I could hardly act as if I didn't notice my old friends after all these years, could I? My wife says a funeral is not a social occasion, that it is a private event, and one should be concerned only with the person who has died.

GENTLE READER:

Actually, the private event is death, and the funeral is the event in which society deals with it. Not every social event is a party. Gatherings before and after funeral ceremonies—Miss Manners is assuming you were not calling out "Hi!" during the service—require social behavior, but in the tone of the occasion.

In other words, you can certainly greet your friends, provided you do not do so in the same way you would do at your college reunion. The usual form is to fix the person with a warm, soulful look in your eyes, but a sad little smile on the lips, as if the corners of the lips were responding to the pleasure of the reunion, but the center part of the lips could not quite manage to join the smile. Rather than clapping the person on the back, one administers a short shoulder hug. Should you find that you have automatically declared, "Good to see you!" you must then add, "I'm sorry it has to be on such a sad occasion."

Signing the Registry

DEAR MISS MANNERS:

How does one sign the registry book at a funeral home when one attends the funeral of one in the immediate family or a very close relative? Is it Mr. and Mrs. John Doe? Is it John and Polly Doe? Or is there another way? What is the most correct? Several people I have asked confess they do not know and I feel there are many who would like to.

GENTLE READER:

It is true that the usual form for funeral registry books has been "Mr. and Mrs. John Doe," but Miss Manners firmly believes it should be "John and Margaret Doe." Note that nicknames should never be used and last names should always be included: this serves the purpose of the "Mr. and Mrs." form in making it clear how the bereaved should address these people. Miss Manners has two reasons for wishing the change. One is that the formal title seems cold, particularly in the cases you describe. The other is that Miss Manners believes that no one should write his own title under any circumstances. (Even Miss Manners does not do so. "Miss" is her given name.)

Legacies

DEAR MISS MANNERS:

My father-in-law died recently. He was a lovable, happy man and his death was indeed a loss to all his family and friends.

However, I felt very left out during the period when he was so ill and during the funeral arrangements. My husband and I, at this point, were married sixteen years. But he and his sisters became again a united family, with their spouses and their children almost excluded. Even at the funeral Mass, we sat behind them with the children, and they all went together in the limousines to the cemetery. I know of no tradition warranting this behavior. Maybe I'm being petty, but I loved him and wanted to be included in their decisions.

GENTLE READER:

Yes, you are being petty. Grief often inspires other odd emotions, and pettiness —the jealous assertion of one's own claims as a mourner—is one of the commonest.

Another such auxiliary emotion is the one your husband and his sisters have, of trying to recreate the original family unit during the tragedy. You were not a part of it, no matter how much you loved your father-in-law. Even in the happiest of in-law relationships, the pretense that a parent-child bond acquired through marriage is the same as the blood bond is obviously phoney. Miss Manners has never met anyone yet who didn't feel awkward about addressing in-laws by the same parental title as parents.

Of course it would have been flattering if your husband had turned to you at this time, rather than to his sisters. But he didn't. Do you really think this is the time to hold a loyalty competition?

What One Wears

DEAR MISS MANNERS:

Does it matter what you wear to a funeral? I hardly ever see anyone wearing black anymore, except possibly the widow.

GENTLE READER:

Dark clothes should be worn to a funeral, although most people cherish the mistaken notion that the deceased would prefer them to be casual and comfortable, rather than to make a special effort on his behalf. However, there is such a thing as ostentatious mourning. A mysterious woman who shows up at a funeral more droopily festooned in black than the widow is making what is known as a "fashion statement."

Notifying People

DEAR MISS MANNERS:

It is now six weeks since my father died, and we are just beginning to have the house free of the sickening smell of too many flowers—our church only permits one family wreath, and redirected the others here—and of the unpleasant telephone calls from people who demanded to know why we ''didn't let them know'' of the death. He was a man who hated any kind of fuss, although he touched many people's lives with his quiet kindness, and we did everything as privately as possible, to keep it in his style. But it didn't work. What should we have done?

GENTLE READER:

You have been following two rules of good taste that unfortunately apply to everything except funerals. Other of life's milestones, such as births, graduations, and weddings, are commonly rendered vulgar by people who try to use them to seek personal publicity and to manipulate their gift-giving potential. When someone dies, however, it is appropriate to inform the local newspaper and supply biographical material, and it is acceptable to inform people that flowers should be omitted—usually suggesting another means of expressing sympathy, such as a charitable donation. This is acceptable because these things are not being done by the honoree.

Bereavement

The great art of etiquette was invented to translate the incoherent jumble of human feelings to which we are all subject into something more presentable. When we cast it aside and let our emotions run around naked and exposed to public comment, as we have done by abandoning the formal customs of mourning, everybody suffers. And that saddens Miss Manners.

When someone dies, the bereaved are either grieved or they are not. Yet both true grief and the absence of grief are, in their natural states, socially intolerable. What we expect is quiet dignity, a kind of steadfast, restrained semblance of sorrow. Either joyous relief, or the ricocheting between hysteria and hilarity that is the natural reaction to deeply felt loss, is mistakenly perceived as an unnatural reaction.

Miss Manners approves of the return of the widow's veil, or its jazzier equivalent, the pair of oversized sunglasses, for funerals. She would like to see a more extensive return to formal mourning, in however modified a modern way, to protect survivors from public scrutiny of their inner feelings.

Before mourning was abolished, the deep crêpe veil was worn off the face for a year of deep mourning; a widower wore a black band on hat or sleeve. Clothes for both ladies and gentlemen were black, with dull surfaces, rather than shiny— suede gloves, for example, rather than kid. No jewelry was permitted except for pearls, diamonds, and black onyx. One did not go into society, and one's letters were written on black-bordered paper.

Second mourning, a year or sometimes two after the death, consisted of lightening the all-black effect with touches of lavender, purple, gray, or white.

Miss Manners can just hear the cries of how morbid this all is, and how life must go on. Of course, life goes on. The strictest instructions about old-fashioned mourning always had to include the information that a widow should cease to wear mourning immediately upon selecting her second husband. Do you think the Victorians didn't understand the charm of woefulness, or how fetching many ladies look in black?

The value of mourning is not to remind people to be unhappy, but to relieve them from the necessity of acting out unhappiness for the benefit of others. The most deeply grieved people will have, even quite soon after a death, moments of merriment, sometimes based on memories of the deceased and some unrelated to the death. If these occur when the person is gaily dressed and out socially, they will be taken as indications of callousness. If, however, a person in those circumstances suddenly bursts into tears on no apparent provocation, which also can happen, the same critics will be annoyed at the lack of control and may go so far as to level a charge of hypocrisy.

If mourners stay away from other people's parties, they do not subject themselves to this criticism. They needn't isolate themselves, but simply conduct their social relations in their own homes, where they may choose companions who share or at least understand their behavior.

Wearing mourning—the modern version would be somber, conservative clothes, although not necessarily black—serves, like the black borders on letters, as a warning that this is a person taking a death seriously. Establishing that fact through symbols saves one the trouble of having to prove it.

You know, and Miss Manners knows, that whatever you may say about getting back to normal, there is nothing that the acquaintances of bereaved people enjoy more than being shocked at their behavior for seeming so—normal.

Numbers

DEAR MISS MANNERS:

What would you, with your nineteenth-century rules, call Mrs., Sr. when there is no longer a Mr., Sr. and everyone else has moved up in the male line by your rules—Mrs. Left-Over?

In today's world, there are innumerable legal documents made out in "Jr.," "III," etc., and there would be much effort and years of confusion in changing them, not to say anything about the daily mail. They include deeds, titles, licenses, bank accounts, bonds, telephone directories, wills, and so on. Mail sometimes comes to this house addressed to "William Leavitt Sullivan," and I never know whether to mark it "deceased," "never lived here," "return to sender"; open it—which would be illegal if not intended for me; or refer it to my son—

who would open it illegally if not intended for him. Thus, the "Jr.," "III," etc., play both a legal and continuing role, in spite of Miss Manners.

Your comments about the cards of "Mrs., Sr." prove that you are way off base, and ought to stop misleading people.

GENTLE READER:

There are two ways of asking etiquette questions. One is "What is correct?" and the other is "Do you think it's all right to do what suits me best anyway?" Correctness refers to whenever a complete set of arbitrary rules about civilized behavior was last codified. In the case of Anglo-American society, nineteenth century is about right. Aren't you lucky that we're not still using the rules from the Court at Urbino?

By this strict usage, the oldest living male of a name does not use "Sr." or any other suffix; "Mrs., Sr." is used by a widow to distinguish herself from the wife of the man who is now the oldest person of the name. "Jr." is not part of your name, sir. There are also legal documents with such titles as "Mrs." or "Dr." used as if they were a part of names, but they aren't. If legal and correct usage were identical, lawyers would be the best behaved people on earth.

However, while Miss Manners has a head full of these nasty little strict rules, which she is delighted to supply on request, she sees no reason that people who do not wish to follow them should have to do so. If a lawyer is not to be confused with an arbitrator of etiquette, the latter should not be confused with a traffic policeman.

The Wedding Ring

DEAR MISS MANNERS:

My husband passed away two years ago. I am still wearing my wedding ring. I cannot get myself to take it off. Is it proper to keep on wearing it? I am fifty-nine years old and had been married for thirty-six years.

GENTLE READER:

If there were a standard of propriety forbidding you to, Miss Manners could think of no motivation for it except cruelty. Perhaps that is why there is no such rule, nor any other reason why you should not continue to wear your wedding ring. The ring is worn as long as the survivor feels like remaining a part of the marriage, and taken off if that person becomes again susceptible to romance. Unfortunately, there is no way of symbolizing the natural desire to do both.

A Widow's Ring(s)

DEAR MISS MANNERS:

I am a lady (I hope), of what is called a certain age. How certain, I don't care to say. I am also certain that I'm not going to marry again. The reason I'm certain is that my fiancé just died, two months ago, of old age. I lost two husbands to the same affliction (even when I was younger, I liked older men, and my second husband, whom I lost not to old age but to middle-aged crisis, was my only big mistake) and now it's enough. I plan to lead a nice, quiet, peaceful life being an old lady.

My question is about rings. My lifelong habit has been to wear a gold band whenever I was married, and to remove it in widowhood only when I had plans for another marriage. Thus I have been running around with a bare finger for a while, as I was engaged.

The peculiar thing is, though, that I have just gotten my first engagement ring. My first husband didn't have the money to buy me one, and no one else ever even thought of it until my last, late fiancé. He had been having a beautiful, large diamond set for me at the jewelers' (I'm sure it was his late wife's ring that was being sized for me, but a diamond is a diamond, and I wasn't going to question it), and they called me to come and pick it up.

I can't just wear a diamond engagement ring now, can I? I'll look like the world's oldest perpetual bride. I have a drawer full of wedding rings, but whose ring should I wear, when none of them is related to the diamond donor? I'm not really used to not wearing any ring, either, as if I were a spinster. All the other widows around here wear engagement and wedding sets, but they've all led simpler lives than I seem to have.

What do you suggest? I may sound flip, which is the way I'm endeavoring to look at life (what choice do I have?), but the truth is that I am proud of having been loved by three good men (husbands one and three and the last fiancé, God bless him), and don't feel I'm exactly living alone when I'm living with such nice memories. Also, the diamond is gorgeous.

GENTLE READER:

As you have noticed during your adventurous travels through life, wedding and engagement rings have two values: sentimental or symbolic, and aesthetic or, well, shall we say recognizable by one's insurance company. Let us spread out your collection of jewelry, and arrange it suitably for symbolic and pleasing effect.

Your situation is different from that of a widow whose memories are focused on one man. Miss Manners' suggestion is that you put on, first, the wedding ring of husband number one; then the diamond engagement ring; and then the wedding ring of husband number three.

The fact that Miss Manners thinks that a large diamond looks pretty when it is modestly nestling in a stack of plain bands has—well, only something to do with it.

Christmas Mourning

DEAR MISS MANNERS:

I am an eighty-year-old widow whose husband died last April, and I should like to know what is correct regarding my sending out Christmas cards this year.

Usually, I send out about forty cards to close relatives and friends, and in about three-quarters of them, I enclose letters and notes. Would it be correct to follow my usual custom this year, even though Christmas will be rather sad for me, or should I just send the letters and notes without the gay cards that I usually send?

Gentle Reader:

You would never know it from all the complicated rituals of partying and present giving associated with this time of the year, but Christmas is actually a religious holiday. Therefore the notion that only merrymakers may participate is rather ridiculous, although many people seem to hold it.

Of course, you should write to your friends—surely now, more than ever, it should be a comfort to be in touch with those you care about. And Miss Manners feels sure that those who suppose it ''tasteful'' not to send cards to you this year because you are presumably not in a festive mood are not going to impress you with their sensitivity.

The only difference is that one does not expect a bereaved person to overflow with merriment. A sense of gaiety you do not feel would be inappropriate on your cards, and those sent to people in mourning should not display this either. But it seems to Miss Manners that it is possible to discover a spirit of Christmas besides that symbolized by little hiccuping Santa Clauses brandishing cocktail glasses.

Beginning Again

Dear Miss Manners:

I would welcome instruction in the etiquette of bereavement, particularly in how the remaining member of a couple resumes relationships with couples who were friends before the mate's death. It is now three months since my wife passed away, and there are at least four couples with whom we had been friendly, couples who were solicitous during my wife's illness and who attended her funeral service, but who have made no effort since to get in touch with me.

I hesitate to get in touch with them. Indeed, I am under the impression that it is their social obligation to resume the relationship under the altered circumstances. Shouldn't they at least call to see how I am getting on, and perhaps invite me to come by for dinner or drinks or something sociable? I admit I am hurt and at a loss to understand their silence. I remember Danny Kaye's response when asked how he liked the Himalayas (''Loved her, hated him''), and entertain the terrible thought that these people were friendly because they only liked my wife. But rather than sulk and feel sorry for myself, I would like to bring my feelings in the situation under control. Is my experience an unusual one? Should I call them and see how they are getting on? (But doesn't that look as if I am angling for an invitation?) Shall I invite them to come visit me? (But I hate cooking or preparing for guests. My wife did that.) I welcome your comments and suggestions.

GENTLE READER:

Miss Manners' comment is that your situation is a very usual one, and her suggestion is that someone—in your case, you—had better do something about it.

Miss Manners has an explanation more likely (but less amusing) than that of the Himalayas. It is that, with the refusal of the society to recognize forms for bereavement after the funeral, people simply do not know what to do. As there is no official mourning period agreed upon, they are afraid of intruding into yours with festive invitations.

Another possibility is that these people have not discovered that it is impossible in modern society, for many reasons, to adhere to the once prevalent but always silly custom of entertaining only pairs and not individuals. Widows are more likely to be victims of this ridiculous notion than widowers, because women tend to live longer than men.

In either case, the social burden is put on the bereaved person, which is unfair because such a person is already in an emotionally weakened state. But shouldering it is, as you realize, better than the alternative, which is sulking.

In your normal state, you do not invent trouble for yourself by considering whether your friends will interpret your kindness in inquiring after them as angling for an invitation. Please cease that whole line of thinking. You can only flatter them by saying outright, "I am ready to see people again, and I've missed you."

You must also stop thinking that you cannot entertain people at home simply because you now have to do the work, instead of your wife. Hating to cook is an extremely poor idea for people who live alone. Your entertaining need not be as elaborate as was hers, but you can surely provide some sort of food and drinks to your friends. And if you can't, you can take them out.

Miss Manners hopes that these problems will be considered when people start parroting the idea that formal customs of mourning—including a general recognition of when mourning ends—are barbarous.

Addressing a Widow

DEAR MISS MANNERS:

In addressing mail to a widow, isn't it correct to address "Mrs. John Smith" (husband's name) instead of "Mrs. Mary Smith" (wife's name)? I'm a recent widow, and to be addressed in the mail by my name bugs me.

GENTLE READER:

What bugs Miss Manners, if Miss Manners can ever be said to be "bugged," is the prevalence of the belief, which is often as painful as it is incorrect, that a woman's mode of address changes when her husband dies. It is simply not true by any standards. We use many forms of addressing married and unmarried women these days, but there is not now, and never has been in the history of etiquette, a distinction between a wife and a widow. A woman who was "Mrs. John Smith" when her husband was alive still is, no matter how many of her friends attempt to harshen her bereavement by assuring her that "correctness" requires her to change her name.

Condolence Letters and Calls

Condolence Calls

DEAR MISS MANNERS:

Don't you think that nowadays, in modern life, the old-fashioned custom of the condolence call is out of date?

GENTLE READER:

Why is that? Is it because people don't die anymore, or is it because the bereaved no longer need the comfort of their friends? Miss Manners is always interested in hearing about how life has been improved by modern thinking or technology.

Sympathy Cards

DEAR MISS MANNERS:

What kind of sympathy card do you consider dignified? Does the sender need to do anything more than sign it? In that case, what is the proper response from the person who has received it? Also, would you give me the correct wording for a card for the family to send out acknowledging cards, flowers, visits, and gifts of food?

GENTLE READER:

Miss Manners is going to have to be very stern with you, in spite of her presumption that you are already feeling burdened, as well as grieved.

A death is one of the times when human contact among those who care is most important. No sympathy cards are proper. No acknowledgment cards are proper. Letters of condolence should be written by hand, as should the letters of thanks from the bereaved; two sentences will do. Writing these out by hand does not take a minute more than signing a card, but it makes the difference between a cold, canned sentiment and a fresh, warm one.

To Whom to Send Condolences

DEAR MISS MANNERS:

I am friends with a woman at work. Recently, her mother-in-law died, so my husband and I sent her husband a condolence note. Yesterday, my friend told me that she was highly insulted because we did not include her name on the note. (I had expressed our sympathy to her personally, at work.) She said that we had made her feel like a ''second-class'' relative. I don't know what to say to her, other than that I thought we had made the appropriate gesture. I explained to her that in my family, I was always told that ''formal'' expressions of sympathy are sent only to the deceased's spouse and blood relatives, and that to include the names of in-laws and friends is disrespectful to those who share the considerably greater loss. In this particular case, my friend was not close to her mother-in-law, while my friend's husband was his mother's only child.

Have I committed a social error? Or is my friend being unreasonably sensitive (and perhaps guilty)? I know this situation is going to arise again with other friends, and frankly, I'm going to hesitate to send any more condolences, even though I know that they are usually appreciated.

GENTLE READER:

Miss Manners hates to see death used as the occasion for claiming insult from people who mean well, when everyone knows that the proper occasion for such feuding is a wedding. It is never a social error to be kind.

However, Miss Manners is not familiar with your rule, or with the concept of ''formal'' sympathy, except as it involves signing registers at the embassies of dead heads of state. Allow Miss Manners to suggest an easier rule for personal life. In writing about a friend who has died, but whose family you do not know, you write to the closest relative. If your friend is the bereaved, rather than the deceased, you write to him or her.

Difficult Condolences

DEAR MISS MANNERS:

About a month ago, I had a prolonged, public argument with a friend within earshot of his wife. I've just heard that he has since died. Although we weren't on speaking terms recently, we'd been good friends in our time, so I feel I must express my sympathy. Writing letters of condolence is always awkward, but in this case, I'm finding it well nigh impossible. Should I apologize to the wife for the fight, or avoid the subject in favor of the usual banalities?

GENTLE READER:

Your friend has taken unfair advantage of you by putting himself beyond reach of settling the argument, but Miss Manners agrees that you ought not to hold it against him. She also agrees that conventional condolences will be received with irony. You need not go so far as to apologize for your position in the argument, unless you now believe it to have been in error, but it would be nice if you could bring yourself to say that you respected him in spite of your differences, and regretted the breach in your friendship, the former delights of which you can then stress.

An Unusual Condolence

DEAR MISS MANNERS:

The husband of a friend of mine died, and I asked a caterer to send a cooked turkey over to her house, it being the custom to have some food sent over for mourners who drop by after the funeral. I won't bother to explain why I couldn't cook one myself, or bring it over, but I couldn't, so I called around until I got a caterer. The problem came when I asked him to put in a card. Naturally, I wanted my friend to know where the turkey came from. But the caterer said, "Look, lady, this isn't a box of flowers. Where am I supposed to put a card?"

GENTLE READER:

Under the wing, of course. His or the turkey's.

Condolences for a Miscarriage

DEAR MISS MANNERS:

My sister-in-law recently had a miscarriage, one of several she has had over the years. They have one child. Do I mention the miscarriage when writing to her and my brother, and if so, what do I say about it?

GENTLE READER:

A miscarriage requires a particularly tricky kind of condolence letter, as it concerns the mother's health as well as the loss of the baby. Miss Manners suggests you do it very simply, staying entirely away from the medical aspects of the situation. The jolly assurance that "you will have other children" not only does not compensate for the loss of this one, but may not be true for reasons your sister-in-law does not wish to discuss with you. It is also offensive to announce that it was "probably better" that a child who could have had problems not be born. Excessive family talk is inappropriate, too, as it usually comes out sounding as if your side thought that if your brother had married the sturdy woman they fixed him up with, instead of getting carried away with this one, the line would have been better continued.

Mourning Paper

DEAR MISS MANNERS:
I know that mourning customs have almost disappeared, but I have seen black-bordered stationery in a store, and I wonder if I should get it for my mother to answer our condolence notes. (My father recently died.) She has put off writing them at all, saying she doesn't feel up to it, but it seems to me unkind to people, many of whom wrote very nice letters about my father, just to leave their condolences unacknowledged or answered by an impersonal card. What would you advise? My mother says she is too depressed, but would probably do what I insisted on.

GENTLE READER:
Miss Manners urges you to insist on the proprieties, not for Miss Manners' sake, but for your mother's. Funeral rituals are associated with all civilizations because they serve the purpose of forcing the bereaved to participate, in a dignified way, in the land of the living. Your mother has obligations to those who have shown, through their letters, that they, too, were to some extent bereaved by your father's death. The widow is in a unique position to assure people that they were esteemed by her husband. She should not grudge that comfort to anyone affected by his death. As for the writing paper, Miss Manners thinks a narrow black border an excellent way of signaling that this is not frivolous correspondence.

Acknowledgments

DEAR MISS MANNERS:
My dear husband passed away last week, and I am concerned about doing the correct acknowledgments. Do I send acknowledgments to everyone who attended the funeral service? Do I acknowledge sympathy cards purchased in a card shop? Anyone who brought food to my house? Contributions? People who wrote me beautiful letters? I received about two hundred condolences—where do I draw the line?

GENTLE READER:
After you have written a letter to each person who wrote you or sent a contribution in your husband's name, however long that takes, you may draw the line. (Of course, you thanked donors of food as they brought it.)

The charitable contributions, of whatever size, were made on behalf of your husband and you must represent him in expressing gratitude. And any person who cares enough about him or you or both to write a letter should be appreciated, and answered in kind. "Thank you for your kindness. It means a great deal to me" will do, if it is in your own hand.

STB

Dear Mrs. Perfect,

I was so sorry to read your sad news. In the few times that I was privileged to meet Mr. Perfect, he came to represent. for me, the ideal of a gentleman whom I hope some day to emulate. Please accept my deepest sympathy.

Sincerely yours,

Sean Botchitt

A letter of condolence. A man's private writing paper, marked with his initials.

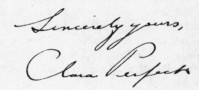

Dear Sean,

Thank you very much for your kind letter. It means a great deal to me that you admired my husband, and I am grateful for your sympathy.

Sincerely yours,

Clara Perfect

Letter of reply to letter of condolence. This is necessarily brief, because Mrs. Perfect has hundreds of them to write.

Miss Manners will then defend you from people who believe that funeral appearances or sympathy cards should be acknowledged—and some of these will attack, simply because people love to torture the bereaved on any excuse—on the grounds that attending the funeral is simply a mark of respect to your husband and an outlet for their own sorrow at his death, and that greeting cards are an impersonal and minimal form of communication.

Aid with Acknowledgments

DEAR MISS MANNERS:

I want to call your attention to this business of answering letters of condolence. The rule book is sometimes a burden. A friend of mine lived for many years with aged parents and an aged aunt. We always said they would go together, and they almost did. First the aunt, and my friend and her mother labored faithfully to answer the letters with handwritten notes. Then the father died and they went through the same thing within months. In another three months, the mother died suddenly. They told me that my friend had handwritten a hundred and fifty notes before her mother died. When you realize that most people these days only go to the ten-cent store and pick up a card, sign their name, and stamp the envelope, and the conscientious among us have to handwrite a reply, I think it is time to have some new rules. In some cases, friends have taken on the letter writing on behalf of a survivor. In many cases where there is a great burden of details on already ailing and aged survivors, that seems a solution if notes have to be written. In other words, Miss Manners, in this day of longevity, we have to use some sense.

GENTLE READER:

Miss Manners has no objection to using sense, provided it does not interfere with courtesy and compassion. She agrees that letters may be written on behalf of those who have difficulty doing them themselves, and further absolves people of writing letters in response to those unfortunate ''sympathy cards'' you describe. What Miss Manners considers important is that a personal expression of feelings about a death be acknowledged in an equally personal fashion, by, or on behalf of, the closest survivors. This may be done over a period of many months, but for anyone to send out form letters about a death—which is what printed sympathy cards or acknowledgments are—is callous.

Answers to Questions
Nobody Asked

Every so often, Miss Manners goes balmy and starts answering questions that nobody asked. She asks your indulgence and your compassion. Those who know what it is to have a head full of information that never comes up in the conversation—old baseball statistics, the histories of minor characters in minor operas, the world's records for undistinguished feats—will understand.

Here are some samples of what is clogging up poor Miss Manners' brain:

The correct form of address by the Holy Roman Emperor when speaking of himself to others, or when addressing himself, for that matter, is *"Ma Majesté."*

When giving a private ball in one's house, one must provide an awning and a red carpet from one's front door to the street.

Sable is the correct fur to wear when one is in mourning.

A gentleman may express his passion for a married woman in a letter, but the letter must not suggest that his love has been looked upon with favor in any way that would be intelligible to a jury of their peers.

When paying a formal call on someone one does not care to visit, a lady may have her chauffeur leave her card, but there must be a woman in the car, although it needn't be the lady whose card is being left.

It is permissible to dress one's chambermaids and parlormaids in the color theme of one's house in the morning, provided they change to their black uniforms with afternoon aprons, collars, and cuffs for luncheon.

If a gentleman does not have a silk house suit to wear to dinner at home alone or with his family, he may make do with wearing an old dinner jacket.

If one has chartered a train for the convenience of one's wedding guests, one should enclose an engraved card, four and a quarter inches by three and a half inches, giving the times of arrival and departure of the "special train" and serving, when presented to the conductor, as the ticket.

The only circumstances in which a host and hostess may sit next to each other at their own dinner party is when they have a horseshoe-shaped table and sit at the outside center of its curve.

There is no known correct way to eat pistachio nuts. Nevertheless, they are delicious. The pistachio nut must therefore be Nature's way of teaching us self-control. If so, it doesn't work.

It is wrong to wear diamonds before dusk, except on one's marriage rings. Before, after, and during breakfast, luncheon, and dinner, it is vulgar to wear a mixture of colored precious stones. It is always a comfort to know that so many things one can't afford to do anyway are vulgar.

"The numbers at a dinner should not be less than the Graces, nor more than the Muses," stated the Roman formula, when guests lay three to a couch. If the Graces are busy, you could try the Fates, who are not asked out as often.

"Your good friend" is the letter closing used not only by sweet, old-fashioned children but by kings and queens when they write to presidents.

An official speech made in front of the queen of England should begin, "May it please Your Majesty," but one should not expect reassurance at the end that it has.

Restaurants are not exempt from the rule that one never puts a filled plate in front of anyone, with the exception of the soup plate, but offers platters from which the person can serve himself. However, few restaurants in the United States realize this.

The only circumstances under which a lady can properly call upon a gentleman are if he is old and ill and has requested the visit. Whether he is also rich is irrelevant, but it never hurts.

If you habitually travel with a valet or maid, it is necessary to ascertain beforehand that your hosts will be able to accommodate extra servants.

A lady and gentleman who pay a call and find no one at home leave three cards—one of hers and two of his. Hers is for the lady of the house and one of his is for the lady and one for the gentleman. If this seems excessive, they can just go away and deny having ever been there.

An introduction made at a ball, for the purpose of forming couples to dance, does not count later. While other formal rules are going out of use, this one is actually being expanded. There are many instances nowadays of people who have been briefly in each other's arms but do not afterward recognize each other socially.

The title by which a sovereign is addressed is called his *petit titre,* but he may also have a *grand titre* and a *titre moyen.* The *grand titre* may include "the names of the fictitious as well as of the real dominions" he claims, which is to say that he can slip in all the places he used to have or thinks he is entitled to have. The *moyen titre* may be fairly long, but it is expected to be truthful.

The wide-tined fork is considered a more correct implement for eating ice cream than is the spoon, although the spoon is not actually incorrect. This leeway is permitted because any fool can see that ice cream will drip through the fork tines, however wide.

There now. Miss Manners feels better for having gotten all that out. Thank you for your kind patience.

Index

Acknowledgments

Miss Manners wishes to thank many kind people for the lovely book, which they helped to make just what she always wanted: David Hendin, vice president of United Feature Syndicate; Thomas A. Stewart, editor-in-chief of Atheneum Publishers; Diana L. Drake, assistant managing editor of United Feature Syndicate; Jennifer C. Georgia, Miss Manners' assistant; and all the Gentle Readers whose work appears in this book.

There is simply not enough blue-black ink in the world for Miss Manners to write all the thank you letters she owes to Wolf Von Eckardt.

Miss Manners, whose column by the same name is internationally syndicated by the United Features Syndicate, is a perfect lady.

Judith Martin, on the other hand, is the author of a collection of essays on White House and diplomatic social life in Washington, The Name on the White House Floor, *and of a forthcoming novel,* Gilbert, *a comedy of manners. Mrs. Martin is a graduate of Wellesley College, where she majored in Gracious Living.*